# MORTON & EDEN LTD

in association with Sotheby's

## Regular London Auctions of Coins, Medals and Banknotes

Visit us at our new offices at
**Nash House, St George Street, London W1S 2FQ**

or contact us for advice or
a free preliminary auction appraisal

www.mortonandeden.com +44 (0)20 7493 5344 info@mortonandeden.com

# A SELECTION OF COINS FROM STOCK

Many more gold, silver and copper coins on main list from £1 upwards.

### 2012 COINS AVAILABLE

**UNITES**
Jms I Unite Nice GVF+ S2620 P.O.A.
Jms I Unite GVF S2620........ P.O.A.

**ANGELS**
Edw IV Angel GVF+ Nice .... P.O.A.
Edw IV Angel S2091 GVF ... P.O.A.
H VII 1/2 Angel GVF+ S2192 P.O.A.
H VII Angel VF S2183 ......... P.O.A.
H VII Angel EF S2187 .......... P.O.A.
H VIII Angel VF+ S2265 ...... P.O.A.
H VIII Angel GVF S2265 ...... P.O.A.

**£2 PIECES**
1986 Pr FDC R.Mint Box ..........595
1989 Pr. GEM FDC £2 ............625
1989 £2 pr. FDC RM Box ........650
1997 Pr FDC R.Mint Box .........595
2001 Proof Sup BU .................595

**£5 PIECES**
1887 ABU/BU ..................... P.O.A.
1887 BU GEM ..................... P.O.A.
1893 ABU ........................... P.O.A.
1893 £5 EF Rare ................. P.O.A.
1893 £5 Nice BU Pr. Like Rare P.O.A.

**GUINEAS**
1673 EF ABU ....................... P.O.A.
1683 CHS II NVF Rare.......... P.O.A.
1726 CHS II VF ................... P.O.A.
1753 VF ................................875
1759 VF+ ..............................950
1778 GEO III GF Ex Rare ......975
1784 UNC/BU ..................... P.O.A.
1784 Nice BU Ex. Rare ........ P.O.A.
1788 GVF ..............................425
1791 GEO III EF .....................595
1795 ABT BU .........................750

**SOVEREIGNS**
**George IV**
1825 Bare Hd NVF ..................550
1825 EF Laur. Hd Ex. Rare ... P.O.A.
1825 Bare Hd. VF+...................675
1827 EF Rare .........................995
1829 Nice ABU/BU ............... P.O.A.
1830 EF .................................995

**Will IV**
1832 GF .................................695
1832 BU GEM ..................... P.O.A.
1832 VF 1st Bust.................. P.O.A.
1837 NVF................................650

**Victoria 1837 – 1887**
**Young Head Shield Rev.**
1838 Sov Ext. Rare NEF ....... P.O.A.
1838 VF Nice ...................... P.O.A.
1838 Nice VF+..................... P.O.A.
1839 GVF Ex. Rare .............. P.O.A.
1843 VF .................................350
1843 GVF+ Rare ....................475
1843 Nice ABU Rare ..............975

1846 GF ................................295
1846 EF .................................595
1847 F ...................................295
1847 EF .................................420
1847 GVF+ ............................375
1848 BU Rare .........................995
1848 EF Rare ..........................495
1849 GF Rare ..........................325
1849 GVF Rare ........................375
1850 Nice EF Rare...................550
1850 VF+ Rare ........................375
1851 EF/ABU ..........................450
1851 ABU Rare........................550
1852 ABU ...............................400
1852 GVF ...............................325
1853 GVF+ .............................325
1855 Sydney Australia ABU . P.O.A.
1856 EF Rare ..........................450
1857 GVF+ .............................350
1857 BU Rare .........................750
1858 NEF/EF Rare ..................420
1860 ABT BU Pr. Like...............595
**1861-2012 .........................ON LIST**

**CROWNS**
1658 Cromwell AUNC ........ P.O.A.
1667 F/GF Rare.......................250
1670 NVF Rare ........................250
1672 GVF+ .............................750
1673 ABT Fine ........................140
1676 NVF ...............................225
1676 UNC Lt. Tone Ex. Rare. P.O.A.
1677 ABT Fine ........................140
1679 Nice NVF ........................250
1679 EF Nice Vic. Primo .... P.O.A.
1680 CHS II EF .................... P.O.A.
1687 Jms II Nice BU............. P.O.A.
1687 Jms II BU Ex. Rare ..... P.O.A.
1688 Nice VF ..........................850
1688/7 GF ..............................375
1691 W+Mary VF+ .............. P.O.A.
1696 GF .................................150
1696 VF Octavo ......................295
1697 Fine Ex. Rare ............. P.O.A.
1723 Geo I SSC EF Ext. Rare P.O.A.
1732 GVF Lt. Tone ..................850
1732 EF Nice Tone Ex. Rare . P.O.A.
1739 GEO II A/UNC Nice Tone P.O.A.
1741 Nice GVF........................950
1743 Sup. Vir. UNC Lov. Tone P.O.A.
1751 ABT UNC ..................... P.O.A.
1780 Mar. Ther BU ...................28
1790 C-Mark Doll Oval ..............
    AUNC/UNC ......................850
1793 CM Doll Oval UNC ..... P.O.A.
1804 BE Doll EF Nice ..............395
1804 BE DON GVF..................240
1804 BE Doll Nice ABU/BU......475
1804 BE Doll VF+ ....................195
1804 BE Doll BU GEM .............675
1818 LIX GVF+........................150
1819 LIX G Fine ......................195
1820 LX A/UNC Rare ..............375

1820 GEM UNC ......................850
1820 AUNC Lt. Tone ................350
1820 VF+ ................................125
**1821-1960 ........................ON LIST**

**HALF CROWNS**
1551 EDW VI Nice GVF ...... P.O.A.
Jms I GF S2666 MM Lis Rare ....395
1623/4 JMS I VF+ S266 MM Lis 995
1658 Cromwell GVF+ Rare .. P.O.A.
1663 VF Rare ..........................395
1663 VF No Stops OBV. Rare ...595
1668/4 F/GF Rare ....................250
1670 GF .................................195
1673 Nice VF+ ........................495
1676 VF .................................375
1676 NEF/EF Nice Tone...........850
1685 Nice Vir. EF Rare............ P.O.A.
1685 JMS II GEM Vir. UNC .........
    Nice Tone Ex. Rare ....... P.O.A.
1685 Nice NVF ........................395
1686 VF ......................∴..........575
1686 Jms II NVF Rare .............395
1686 Jms II EF/AUNC ...............
    Nice Tone ...................... P.O.A.
1687 NEF Rare .......................995
1687 Jms II ABT VF .................575
1687 GVF 1st Bust Ex. Rare......950
1688 Fine Rare ........................395
1689 VF .................................250
1689 VF+ ...............................350
1689 NVF................................175
1689 G.Money VF Sept ...........150
1689 2/6 W+Mary Supb. UNC Lov.
    Col.................................. P.O.A.
1690 G.Money EF/UNC May .....275
1690 NEF Ex. Rare ............... P.O.A.
1692 Qvinto Nice VF................975
1693 W+Mary GVF+ S.3435 ....575
1693 Nice GVF ........................495
1693 GVF ...............................550
1698 UNC Nice Tone................950
1698 Nice UNC Lov. Col ..........995
1708 A/UNC Nice Plain Rev . P.O.A.
1709 EF ............................... P.O.A.
1712 ABT UNC Nice Lov. ColP.O.A.
1713 A/UNC Plain Rev Rare ...P.O.A
1720 GVF ...............................375
1723 SSC GVF ........................995
1731 Vir. EF ............................650
1734 Nice VF ..........................595
1739 UNC Nice Tone............. P.O.A.
1741 A/UNC Nice .....................950
1743 Superb Mint, Pr. like .... P.O.A.
1745 Lima GEM ABT .................
    UNC Lov. Col ....................750
1750 Sup. UNC. Lov. Col ..... P.O.A.
1751 GEM UNC Lov. Col ..... P.O.A.
1794 CM 1/2 Doll GVF+ ..........495
1817 Bull Hd. EF/ABU..............175
1817 Small Hd A/UNC .............175
1817 Sm. Hd. GVF+ ..................85
1818 Supb. UNC Supb. Tone......495

1818 UNC/BU .........................295
1819 BU .................................350
1820 Laur. Hd. Supb. UNC L.T. 575
1820 Supb. BU Supb. Strike Sm. Hd.
    Rare ................................650
1820 Sm. Hd NVF .....................55
1821 GVF+/NVF ......................150
1821 Supb. UNC Lov. Col .........595
1824 Nice BU ..........................995
1824 EF Nice Tone Rare ..........275
1825 Proof UNC Nice Tone... P.O.A.
1825 GVF+ .............................125
1826 VF ...................................85
1826 GVF ...............................100
1826 Nice GVF + .....................125
1828 Vir. EF Rare ....................395
1828 UNC Ex. Rare ............... P.O.A.
1829 GVF Rare .......................125
1829 GEM UNC Ex. Rare ..... P.O.A.
1829 NVF/VF ............................85
1834 BU GEM .........................575
1834 GEM BU Lt. Tone ............575
1836 GEM UNC Nice Tone .......650
**1841-1967 ........................ON LIST**

**MAUNDY SETS**
1682 UNC Nice Tone...............650
1686 NEF ...............................475
1732 Nice UNC Nice Tone .......575
1737 EF/AUNC ........................375
1818 UNC Nice Tone................375
1820 UNC Nice Tone................395
1822 GEM UNC Rare ..............375
1830 BU GEM .........................395
1834 UNC Nice Tone Ex. Rare ...595
1842 4d, 2d, 1d UNC ...............150
1845 Nice BU ..........................395
1850 GEM UNC ......................375
1856 Supb. BU ........................350
1859 UNC ...............................350
1860 GVF+ .............................150
1866 GVF ...............................120
1871 BU .................................295
1871 BU GEM .........................350
1872 BU GEM .........................350
1875 GEM UNC Lov. Col. .........350
1875 UNC Nice Tone................275
1877 BU GEM .........................350
1878 BU GEM .........................350
1879 Nice BU ..........................350
1880 Nice BU ..........................325
1880 BU ..................................225
1883 BU .................................195
1884 BU GEM .........................295
1886 BU .................................250
1889 BU GEM .........................175

2/-, 1/-, 6D, 4D, SIL.
3D, BRASS 3D, MNDY
SETS, 1D/BRONZE
COINS...............ON LIST

# "THE I.A.P.N. dealer, your guide to the world of numismatics"

"More than one hundred of the world's most respected coin dealers are members of the I.A.P.N. (International Association of Professional Numismatists). I.A.P.N. members offer the collector an exceptional selection of quality material, expert cataloguing, outstanding service, and realistic pricing. The I.A.P.N. also maintain the International Bureau for the Suppression of Counterfeit Coins (I.B.S.C.C.) which, for a fee can provide expert opinions on the authenticity of coin submitted to it. A booklet listing the name, address and specialities of all I.A.P.N. members is available without charge by writing to the I.A.P.N. Secretariat". Jean-Luc Van der Schueren, 14, Rue de la Bourse, B-1000, Bruxelles.
Tel: +32–2–513 3400   Fax: +32–2–512 2528   E-mail: iapnsecret@compuserve.com   Web site: http://www.iapn-coins.org

## AUSTRALIA
DOWNIES COINS Pty Ltd, PO Box 888, Abbotsford, VIC. 3067
NOBLE NUMISMATICS Pty Ltd, 169 Macquarie Street, SYDNEY NSW 2000

## AUSTRIA
HERINEK, Gerhard, Josefstädterstrasse 27, A-1082 WIEN

## BELGIUM
FRANCESCHI & Fils, B, 10, Rue Croix-de-Fer, B-1000 BRUXELLES
VAN DER SCHUEREN, Jean-Luc, 14, Rue de la Bourse, B-1000 BRUXELLES

## CANADA
WEIR LTD., Randy, PO Box 64577, UNIONVILLE, Ontario, L3R 0M9

## EGYPT
BAJOCCHI JEWELLERS, 45 Abdel Khalek Sarwat Street, 11511 CAIRO

## FRANCE
BOURGEY, Sabine, 7, Rue Drouot, F-75009 PARIS
BURGAN NUMISMATIQUE—Maison Florange, 8, Rue du 4 Septembre, F-75002, PARIS
GUILLARD, Patrick, Eurl, B. P. 41, F-75261 Paris Cedex 06
LA PARPAIOLLE, 10 rue Bernex – B. P. 30006, F–13191, Cedex 20, MARSEILLE
MAISON PLATT SA, 49, Rue de Richelieu, F–75001, PARIS
NUMISMATIQUE et CHANGE DE PARIS, 3, Rue de la Bourse, F–75002 PARIS
O.G.N., 64, Rue de Richelieu, F–75002 PARIS
POINSIGNON-NUMISMATIQUE, 4, Rue des Francs Bourgeois, F–67000 STRASBOURG
SAIVE NUMISMATIQUE, 18, rue Dupont des Loges, F–57000, METZ
VINCHON-NUMISMATIQUE, 77, Rue de Richelieu, F–75002 PARIS

## GERMANY
DILLER, Johannes, Postfach 70 04 29, D-81304 MÜNCHEN
FRITZ RUDOLF KÜNKER GmbH & Co. KG, Gutenbergstrasse 23, D–49076 OSNABRÜCK
GORNY & MOSCH, GIESSENER MÜNZHANDLUNG GmbH, Maximiliansplatz 20, D–80333 MÜNCHEN
GERHARD HIRSCH Nachfolger, Promenadeplatz 10/II, D–80333 MÜNCHEN
JACQUIER, Paul-Francis, Honsellstrasse 8, D–77694 KEHL am RHEIN
KAISER MÜNZFACHGESCHAFT, Mittelweg 54, D–60318 FRANKFURT
KRICHELDORF Nachf., H. H. Günter-stalstrasse 16, D–79100 FREIBURG i.Br.
KURPFÄLZISCHE MÜNZENHANDLUNG—KPM, Augusta-Anlage 52, D–68165 MANNHEIM
LEIPZIGER Münzhandlung und Auktion, Nikolaistrasse 25, D–04109, LEIPZIG
MANFRED OLDING MÜNZEN-HANDLUNG, Goldbreede 14, D–49078, OSNABRÜCK
MEISTER MÜNZENHANDLUNG, Moltkestrasse 6, D–71634 LUDWIGSBURG
MÜNZEN-UND MEDAILLEN-HANDLUG STUTTGART, Charlottenstrasse 4, D–70182 STUTTGART
NEUMANN GmbH, Ernst, Watteplatz 6, D–89312, GÜNZBURG
NUMISMATIK LANZ, Luitpoldblock-Maximiliansplatz 10, D–80333 MÜNCHEN
PEUS NACHF., Dr. Busso Bornwiesenweg 34, D–60322 FRANKFURT/M,
Münzhandlung RITTER GmbH Postfach 24 01 26, D–40090 DÜSSELDORF
TIETJEN + CO, Spitalerstrasse 30, D–20095 HAMBURG
WESTFÄLISCHE AUKTIONSGESELLSCHAFT oHG, Nordring 22, D–59821, ARNSBERG

## HUNGARY
NUMISMATICA EREMBOLT, Vörösmarty Tèr 6, HG–1051, BUDAPEST

## ITALY
BARANOWSKY s.a.s, Via del Corso 184, I–00187, ROMA
CRIPPA NUMISTMATIQUE s.a.s., Via Cavalieri del S. Sepolcro 10, I–20121 MILANO
DE FALCO, Corso Umberto 24, I–80138 NAPOLI
FALLANI, Via del Babuino 58a, I–00187, ROMA
GIULIO BERNARDI, Casella Postale 560, I–34 121 TRIESTE
PAOLUCCI NUMISMATICA s.a.s., Via San Francesco 154, I–35121 PADOVA
RANIERI Numismatica srl, Sign. Marco Ranieri, I–BOLOGNA
RINALDI & Figlio, O., Via Cappello 23 (Casa di Giulietta), I–37121 VERONA
VARESI Numismatica s.a.s., Alberto Varesi, Viale Montegrappa 3, 27100 PAVIA

## IRELAND
I.C.E. Ltd, Charter House, 5 Pembroke Row, DUBLIN 2

## JAPAN
DARUMA INTERNATIONAL GALLERIES, 2–16-32-701, Takanawa, Minato-ku, JP-TOKYO 108
WORLD COINS, 1-15-5, Hamamatsu-cho, Minato-Ku, TOKYO 105-0013

## MONACO
EDITIONS VICTOR GADOURY, 57 rue Grimaldi, "Le Panorama", MC–98000

## THE NETHERLANDS
MEVIUS NUMISBOOKS Int. BV Oosteinde 97, NL 7671 VRIEZENVEEN
SCHULMAN BV, PO Box 346, NL–1400 AH BUSSUM
VERSCHOOR MUNTHANDEL, Postbus 5803, 3291 AC STRIJEN
WESTERHOF, Trekpad 38–40, NL–8742 KP, Burgwerd

## NORWAY
OSLO MYNTHANDEL AS, Postboks 2745, Solli, N–0204, OSLO

## POLAND
ANTYKWARIAT NUMIZMATYCZNY, ul. Zelazna 67, pawilon 22, 00-871 WARSZAWA

## PORTUGAL
NUMISPORTO LDA, Av. Combatentes Grande Guerra 610 LJ6, P–4200-186 PORTO

## SPAIN
AUREO & CALICO, Plaza del Angel 2, E-08002 BARCELONA
CAYON, JANO S.L., Calle Orfila 10, E–28010 MADRID
SEGARRA, Plaza Mayor 26, E–28012, MADRID
Jesús VICO S.A., Jorge Juan n-83, Duplicado, E - 28009 MADRID

## SWEDEN
NORDLINDS MYNTHANDEL AB, ULF, Karlavagen 46, PO Box 5132, S–102 43 STOCKHOLM

## SWITZERLAND
ADOLPH HESS A. G Postfach 7070, CH-8023, ZÜRICH
HESS—DIVO AG, Postfach 7070, CH-8023, ZÜRICH
NOMOS AG, Zähringerstrasse 27, 8001 ZÜRICH
NUMISMATICA ARS CLASSICA AG, Postfach 2655, CH–8022 ZÜRICH
NUMISMATICA GENEVENSIS SA, 1 Rond-point de Plainpalais, CH–1205 GENEVE

## THAILAND
HOUSE OF THE GOLDEN COIN, 193/119 Moo 10, South Pattaya Road, Nongprue Banglamung, CHONBURI 20230

## UNITED KINGDOM
BALDWIN & SONS LTD., A.H., 11 Adelphi Terrace, LONDON WC2N 6BJ
PAUL DAVIES LTD, PO Box 17, ILKLEY, West Yorkshire LS29 8TZ
DIX NOONAN WEBB, 16 Bolton Street, Piccadilly, LONDON W1J 8BQ
CHRISTOPHER EIMER, PO Box 352, LONDON NW1 7RF
FORMAT OF BIRMINGHAM LTD Burlington Court, 18 Lower Temple Street, BIRMINGHAM B2 4JD
KNIGHTSBRIDGE COINS, 43 Duke Street. St. James's, LONDON SW1Y 6DD
RASMUSSEN Mark, PO Box 42, BETCHWORTH RH3 7YR
RUDD, Chris, PO Box 222, Aylsham, NORFOLK NR11 6TY
SAVILLE, Douglas, Chiltern Thameside, 37c St Peters Avenue, Caversham, READING RG4 7DH
SPINK & SON LTD, 69, Southampton Row, Bloomsbury, LONDON WC1B 4ET
WILKES, Tim, PO Box 150, Battle, TN33 0HA

## UNITED STATES OF AMERICA
BERK, LTD., 31 North Clark Street, CHICAGO, IL. 60602
BULLOWA, C.E. COINHUNTER, Suite 2112, 1616 Walnut Street, PHILADELPHIA, PA 19103
CEDERLIND Tom, P. O. BOX 1963, PORTLAND, OR 97207
CLASSICAL NUMISMATIC GROUP INC, PO Box 479, LANCASTER, PA 17608
COIN AND CURRENCY INSTITUTE INC, PO Box 1057, CLIFTON, NJ 07014
DAVISSON'S LTD, COLD SPRING, MN 56320–1050
DUNIGAN, Mike, 5332 Birchman, Fort Worth, TX 76107
FREEMAN & SEAR, PO Box 641352, LOS ANGELES, CA 90064–6352
FROSETH INC., K.M., PO Box 23116, MINNEAPOLIS, MN 55423
GILLIO INC. - GOLDMÜNZEN INTERNATIONAL 8 West Figueroa Street, SANTA BARBARA, CA. 93101
HARVEY, Stephen, PO Box 3778, BEVERLEY HILLS, CA 90212
JENCEK, John, 205 De Anza Blvd. No. 119, SAN MATEO, CA 94402
KERN, Jonathan K. Co., 441, S. Ashland Avenue, LEXINGTON, KY 40502–2114
KOLBE & FANNING Numismatic Booksellers LLC, 141 W. Johnstown Road, GAHANNA, OH. 43230-2700
MARGOLIS, Richard, PO Box 2054, TEANECK, NJ 07666
DMITRY MARKOV COINS & MEDALS, PO Box 950, NEW YORK, NY 10272
MEXICAN COIN Company LLC, P. O. Box 5270, CAREFREE, AZ.85377
MILCAREK, Dr. Ron, PO Box 1028, GREENFIELD, MA 01302
PEGASI Numismatics, PO. Box 131040 ANN ARBOR, MI. 48113
PONTERIO & ASSOCIATES, a division of Bowers & Merena, 18061 Fitch, IRVINE, CA. 92614-6018
RARCOA INC, 6262 South Route 83, WILLOWBROOK, IL 60514
WILLIAM M. ROSENBLUM RARE COINS, PO Box 785, LITTLETON, CO. 80160–0785
SEDWICK, Daniel Frank, LLC, 2180 North Park Avenue, Suite 200, Winter Park, FL. 32789
HLS STACKS Rare Coins, 18 Arlington Lane, BAYVILLE, N.Y.11709
STEPHEN ALBUM RARE COINS, P.O. Box 7386, Santa Rosa, CA. 95407
STEPHENS Inc., Karl, PO Box 3038, FALLBROOK, CA 92088
SUBAK Inc., 79 West Monroe Street, Room 1008, CHICAGO, IL 60603
TELLER NUMISMATIC ENTERPRISES, 16055 Ventura Blvd., Suite 635, ENCINO, CA 91436
WADDELL, Ltd., Edward J., PO Box 3759, FREDERICK, MD 21705–3759
WORLD-WIDE COINS OF CALIFORNIA, PO Box 3684, SANTA ROSA, CA 95402

## VENEZUELA
NUMISMATICA GLOBUS, Apartado de Correos 50418, CARACAS 1050–A

## ~ Visit our website at www.iapn-coins.org ~

8

THE
# COIN
## Yearbook
## 2013

Edited by
John W. Mussell, FRGS
and the Editorial Team of COIN NEWS

ISBN 978 1 908 828 02 6

Published by
TOKEN PUBLISHING LIMITED
Orchard House, Duchy Road, Heathpark, Honiton, EX14 1YD
Telephone: 01404 46972    Fax: 01404 44788
e-mail: info@tokenpublishing.com. Website: http://www.tokenpublishing.com

Printed in Great Britain by Polestar, Exeter

# CONTENTS

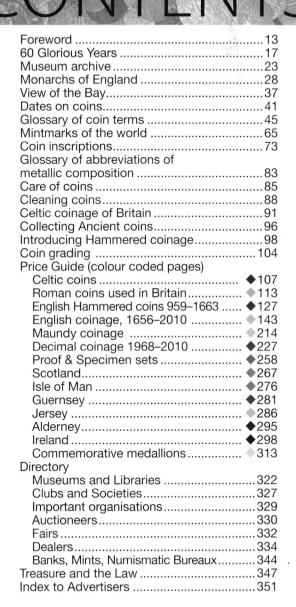

# FOREWORD

THE last three COIN YEARBOOK Forewords have been full of the doom and gloom of recession, the Eurozone crisis and other such troublesome tales ad nauseam. This year I am going to avoid such a start to this foreword, after all I am sure you are as bored as I am with the whole thing by now—Yes it's important, yes it affects us all but, let's face it there doesn't seem to be much you or I can do about it, so time to discuss other things! The most obvious thing to discuss, as the sun sets on 2012, is the Olympics and, of course, the coin programmes that the event gave rise to. I do not want to wax too lyrical about the Olympics themselves, I enjoyed watching them both on television and, as I was lucky enough to get tickets, at the Stadium itself; everyone I have spoken to with regard to the Games also seemed to enjoy them and I think we can say that "London did good". But of course the games are over now, the Paralympics are just finishing (as I write this in early September) and whilst the East End of London may experience an "Olympic Legacy, " for the rest of us things may seem a little flat. We have our memories of gold and records, our T-shirts and our flags, our photos and the fake Olympic torch we bought on eBay for £20,000(!) but perhaps little else. Except the coins…Slowly but surely over the past few months the Olympics 50p series has been getting into circulation and, judging by sales of the "Sports 50p Album" that we stock, there are hundreds of you out there who are collecting them. This is how it should be, people checking their change to find that elusive missing coin, people swapping the "Off-Side Rule" coin for the "Cycling" one, people eager to fill up their albums and, hopefully then moving on to the wider world of coin collecting. I cannot pretend that I wasn't disappointed in the way the Olympics 50p programme was delivered—originally we believed it was going to be similar to the States Quarters programme, with individual coins being released on a regular basis (there were 29 coins and we thought they were being released one a month in the 2+ years leading up to the Games) so collectors would know what to look out for—instead all the coins were sent out to banks at once and only some made it out to the general public when they should have. It wasn't what we'd hoped for and certainly was nothing like the US programme so initially we were disappointed, now though the coins are arriving in peoples' pockets, they are being collected and hopefully this will lead on to more "proper" collectors joining the numismatic world. Whether coin collecting benefits from its own Olympic Legacy remains to be seen. 2012 didn't just see the Olympic 50 pences though, there was the Olympic Countdown series launched in 2009 in silver and gold, the "Official" £5 coins for both the Olympics and Paralympics, the Handover to Rio coin the British Icons series and, it seems many more—and that's just from the Royal Mint, other Mints and issuing bureaux of the world had their own ideas and, as ever in an Olympic year, there is a plethora of coins, both circulating and commemorative to choose from. And it wasn't just the Olympics to celebrate in 2012, the Queen's Diamond Jubilee also saw a plethora of new issues from the Royal Mint and abroad both in circulating and precious metal varieties; these new issues, coupled with the various hoards unearthed, records broken at auction and new varieties coming to light in 2012 has meant that all in all it has been a pretty good year for coins! So what about 2013? What does that have in store for the numismatic world? Well I am afraid to answer that we probably have to go back to the world's economic crisis—with no Olympics or World Cup, no long-reigning monarch celebrating a Jubilee and no major world event to commemorate (just wait until 2014 and the centenary of World War I). 2013 may seem, on the surface, to be fairly barren in terms of numismatic opportunities and so it may prove but that doesn't mean we won't be living in interesting times. Should the economic woe continue then we can pretty much guarantee things will not remain as stable as they (relatively speaking) are at the moment. Gold has stopped its inexorable rise (although it's still high) and the silver price has stabilised but should the Eurozone collapse as many are predicting, how long will that situation be maintained? And what of the Eurozone? If Greece does become the first member to leave what does that mean for the single currency? Will "PIIGS" follow suit? Will the Euro collapse? Will there be a two tier system? Will countries resort to their own currencies? Nobody knows, but whatever happens there is vast potential for us collectors—Euro collecting hasn't really taken off in the UK as much as Europe (for obvious reasons) but I predict that should the single currency's demise seem imminent there will suddenly be a lot more people wanting to add to their collecting themes! What odds do I get on a "Last Euro/First New Drachma" set being produced by someone? As for British coins, well the precious metal market may well prove volatile and affect things in ways we cannot predict but what we can perhaps predict is that in general the hobby will continue to grow in strength as it has done in the past few years. We aren't recession proof of course, cannot sit back and pretend the outside world doesn't bother us, but if you stop and look at the hobby you will realise that actually we are doing OK—prices continue to rise (as reflected in this YEARBOOK), the fairs are still well attended and interest continues to grow. We may not be in a huge boom right now, disposable incomes being squeezed mean that new collectors aren't rushing into the hobby as we would maybe like, (although the investors are always willing to bring in new money!) but we certainly aren't in a bust and long may that continue! The fact that we are neither in huge boom nor dramatic bust does mean that prices are reasonably steady at the moment, no bad thing if you're a collector—although investors may be looking for a quick return us collectors prefer stability! That said there are changes, some quite considerable and as ever we have reflected that within these pages, in order to ensure the prices quoted in this book are accurate (and remember we do not buy or sell coins, we have no vested interest in doing anything other than reflect the market) we take averages from dealers' lists and websites as well as from auction results. Grading is very much a subjective issue that will always affect individual prices but we like to think that as a rule what is printed here is pretty much what you would pay for that coin anywhere in the UK. We haven't just relied on "averages" though—we have had a number of acknowledged experts in their field check and double check the Yearbook and as ever we are indebted to them. In particular we would like to thank Patrick Mackenzie and David Fletcher for their work on the decimals, Roy Norbury of West Essex Coins for checking the Milled section, Elizabeth Cottam and Chris Rudd for their input and help with the Celtic Section, Mike Vosper for his work on the Roman Section, Stephen Mitchell of Studio Coins for the Hammered coinage, Charles Riley for working on the medals section and Nick Swabey for his help with the Maundy sets and oddments. In addition we are indebted to a number of individuals, dealers and auction houses for help with the illustrations, in particular Baldwins, Del Parker (Irish) and David Stuart (Scottish).

# BALDWIN'S

*The Name for Numismatics*
*Established 1872*

## AUCTIONS AROUND THE WORLD

Sell your collection in the best place possible
and achieve the highest prices

New York ~ London ~ Hong Kong

### AUCTION ADVANCES

upto 50% pre-auction payment to you
for your coins and medals.
no need to wait for six months

### LOWEST CHARGES

we can charge less
than all other UK coin auctioneers
no hidden fees for photography,
insurance or unsold lots

For more information:
contact Seth Freeman, seth@baldwin.co.uk
or Matthew Curtis, matthew@baldwin.co.uk
or call our London showroom on +44 (0)207 930 9808
to make an appointment with our specialists.

## *Baldwin's Celebrating 140 Years*

*For a free guide to coin collecting email CY2011@baldwin.co.uk and quote this advertisement*

**11 Adelphi Terrace, London, WC2N 6BJ**
**tel: +44 (0)20 7930 9808   fax: +44 (0)20 7930 9450**
www.baldwin.co.uk
A Noble Investments (UK) PLC Company

For regular updates follow us on twitter @BaldwinsCoins

1911 G.BRITAIN 5SOV
**PF 65 CAMEO**
1998261-001

NGC

*The World coins you can trust.*

# GUARANTEED

Every NGC World coin is fully guaranteed, so you can buy and sell with confidence.
That's why we've graded more World coins than any other grading company, and how
we've become the largest grading company in the world.
NGC — the name you can trust. Guaranteed. NGCcoin.com

NGCcoin.com | 800-NGC-COIN

North America | Europe | Asia

# SIXTY *Glorious Years*

**Following the recent sixtieth anniversary of the Queen's accession to the throne and the events celebrating her Diamond Jubilee, RODERICK FAREY takes a quick look at the coinage struck during the long reign of Her Majesty Queen Elizabeth II**

The proclamation approving the designs for the new coinage was issued on November 25, 1952 with the first bust of the new Queen to appear on coins being the work of Mary Gillick. The special Coronation crown piece, however, features an innovative equestrian portrait by Gilbert Ledward, the first time such an image had been used for coins of the realm since Charles I. The reverse of the Coronation crown consists of four shields arranged in the form of a saltire with emblems of a rose, a thistle, a sprig of shamrock and a leek in the angles and a crown in the centre. The edge has the incuse inscription "FAITH AND TRUTH I WILL BEAR UNTO YOU". The halfcrown has a single crowned shield with E on one side and R on the other, recalling the term popular at the time that the reign was the start of a "New Elizabethan" age. The reverse of the florin portrays a ring of five thistles, four shamrocks and three leeks around a double rose. The practice, started in 1937, of having two versions of the shilling continued: that for England has a crowned shield with three lions while the Scottish shilling has a single lion rampant on the crowned shield. The sixpence has a reverse with a

*1953 Proof Crown.*

garland of interlaced rose, thistle, shamrock and leek while the duo-decagonal nickel brass threepence has a reverse with a chained portcullis surmounted by a coronet. The penny, halfpenny and farthing retained the Britannia, Golden Hind and wren, respectively, used on the reverses for the coins of George VI. The reverses for the crown, halfcrown, florin and sixpence were designed by Edgar Fuller and modelled by Cecil Thomas, while those for the shillings and threepence were designed and modelled by William Gardner. The proof set of ten coins from crown to farthing dated 1953 was issued in a maroon covered metal case and an unprecedented 40,000 were released. A set of uncirculated coins from the halfcrown to the farthing, encapsulated in plastic was also issued in the same year.

In 1954, BRITT OMN, standing for "of all the Britains" was deleted from the legend and the effigy, which was found to be too shallow to prevent premature wear of the design, was recut by Cecil Thomas and no farthing was struck for circulation after 1956.

Gold sovereigns were struck from 1957, in order to discourage the activities of foreign counterfeiters.

*1953 Proof Florin obverse by Mary Gillick.*

*1977 silver Jubilee Crown.*

The opportunity was also taken to produce a retrospective gold set from five pounds to half sovereign dated 1953 in order to complete national collections: such sets are extremely rare.

The New York Exhibition in 1960 was taken as a reason to issue a crown using polished blanks featuring the Mary Gillick bust, although a limited number using ordinary blanks were available from UK banks. The death of Sir Winston Churchill in January 1965 was commemorated by the issue of another crown with a bust of Churchill on the reverse, the first time a commoner had been portrayed since Oliver Cromwell. The last coins for the sterling coinage struck for circulation were dated 1967, although a 1970 proof set was issued as a souvenir of the system which was replaced on February 15, 1971.

Maundy coins present a unique continuity between the coinages with Mary Gillick's bust being used right up to the present day. This annual service which the Queen has attended almost every year since 1952, with the venue being changed regularly to visit different cathedrals, is a ceremony which maintains an ancient tradition. The 1953 set is the key date in the series and the tiny silver coins with the crowned value in a wreath on the reverses changed in value from old pence to new with decimalisation.

As a precursor to decimalisation, ten pence and five pence pieces were issued from 1968 and fifty pence pieces from 1969. The obverse designed by Arnold Machin, featuring a head and shoulders bust of the Queen wearing a tiara of festoons, scrolls and collet-spikes, which had been given to the Queen by Queen Mary as a wedding present in 1947, was used until 1984. The reverse of the ten pence piece has a crowned lion passant guardant, which was used from 1968 to 1992 and with a reduced size from 1992 to 2008. The five pence piece has a crowned thistle reverse and was used from 1968 to 1990 when the size was reduced and then through to 2008. The fifty pence piece which replaced the ten shilling note featured the familiar figure of Britannia and lasted until 2008 with a reduction in size in 1997. The three

bronze coins of twopence, penny and the halfpenny have reverse designs by Christopher Ironside, who also designed the reverses for the five, ten and fifty pence pieces. The two pence has the badge of the Prince of Wales consisting of three ostrich feathers, a coronet and the motto "ICH DIEN". The penny has a crowned portcullis with chains each side and the tiny half penny, which was discontinued after 1984, has a crowned ½. In 1982 the word "NEW" was dropped from the coinage and since 1992 copper plated steel has been used in place of bronze.

The decimal equivalent of the double florin, so unpopular when issued in Victoria's Jubilee Head coinage, was introduced as the denomination of twenty pence and featured a raised rim and incuse lettering reminiscent of the 1797 cartwheel pennies and two pences of Matthew Boulton. The shape was an equilateral curved heptagon matching the fifty pence piece and the reverse by William Gardner has a crowned double rose. A silver proof piedfort was issued for collectors, a novelty for the Royal Mint.

In 1983 a nickel brass pound coin was introduced with a reverse featuring the Royal Arms and an edge inscription "DECUS ET TUTAMEN", which first appeared on the edge of the 1662 crowns of Charles II. The Royal Mint released 10,000 silver proof piedforts, an issue which was heavily oversubscribed. The author remembers his disappointment at not being a successful applicant and having to be satisfied with the normal silver proof, of which 50,000 were issued. In subsequent years the reverse design and edge inscription changed annually. It is a sad fact that this denomination has in recent years been counterfeited extensively with varying degrees of competence.

*1983 silver Proof Pound obverse by Arnold Machin.*

On August 8, 1984 the Queen approved two new effigies with a couped version for circulating coins and a larger uncouped version for commemorative pieces. So in 1985 the obverse was changed and features the third effigy of the Queen to appear on the coinage. There is a more distinct truncation to the bust and the Royal Diadem, worn by the Queen for the State Opening of Parliament, replaces the previous tiara. The designer's initials RDM for Raphael David Maklouf appear on the truncation. The larger effigy was used on the non proof gold five pound pieces issued in 1987 and 1988 with a special U, for uncirculated, in a circle in the exergue of the St George and the Dragon reverse.

A nickel brass two pound piece was introduced in 1986 and was issued spasmodically until 1996 with reverses commemorating various events or anniversaries. Following discussion of replacing the coin with either a thinner version or a bi-metallic piece, a bimetallic coin was introduced in 1997 with a cupro-nickel inner and a surrounding ring of nickel brass. The reverse, designed by Bernard Rushin, a Norfolk art teacher, represents industrial progress from the Iron Age scrolls in the centre; cogs, wheels and gears representing the Industrial Revolution in the first ring; a design of silicon chips stands for computers in the second ring and the third ring has symbols joined to indicate the internet. The edge legend "STANDING ON THE SHOULDERS OF GIANTS" is attributed to Sir Isaac Newton, who had been Warden, then Master of the Royal Mint from 1696 to 1727. In 1997 the Royal Mint the made unusual step of issuing a trial piece dated 1994 for collectors, explaining how the bi-metallic coin was produced. In 1999 the Royal Mint issued a proof piedfort in silver with a coloured hologram for the rugby world cup; a real break with tradition !

The Royal Mint started issuing proof gold sovereigns in 1979 and in 1980 released the first full set from five pounds to half sovereign for the decimal coinage. In 1989 a set commemorating the 500th anniversary of the first sovereign was issued with a completely new design by Bernard Sindall, based on the Silver Jubilee medallion. The obverse has an image of the Queen at her coronation, seated in King Edward's Chair, holding Rod and Sceptre and the reverse has a crowned shield of arms superimposed on a double rose. The legends are unusual in featuring a font reminiscent of mediaeval script. This spectacular set is now highly sought after by collectors. The Royal Mint has issued sets with different reverses to the usual St George and the Dragon by Benedetto Pistrucci, dating back to 1817: in 2002 for the Golden Jubilee with a crowned shield within a wreath, similar to the Victoria Young Head crowns; in 2005 with a stylised St George and the Dragon also by Timothy Noads; and another representation of St George and the Dragon for the 2012 Diamond Jubilee, the work of Paul Day.

Proof sets which had previously been available to collectors in somewhat limited numbers were issued dated from 1970 onwards, initially through the Numismatic Bureau in Edinburgh. The sets for 1972 to 1976 were issued together in 1976 when it was decided that proof sets should be issued every year.

*1988 silver Proof Pound obverse by Raphael Maklouf.*

Complete sets of coins were included and coins were included even when none of that denomination was struck for currency in a particular year. In 1982 sets of uncirculated coins were added to the Royal Mint's portfolio of products and even special packs were produced for commercial concerns such as Heinz and Martini. A special set struck in silver marked the 25th anniversary of the introduction of decimal currency and the set marking the millennium, by special permission of the Queen, contained the Maundy coins, the first time these had been available to the general public since the proof sets of 1937. To mark the Golden Jubilee in 2002 sets of coins struck in gold were issued and again contained the Maundy coins.

Following the success of the South African Krugerrand series, the Royal Mint enlarged its customer appeal in 1987 by adding an annual series of bullion and proof gold issues featuring a standing figure of Britannia on the reverse. The pieces have nominal values of £10, £25, £50 and £100 and contain a tenth, quarter, half and a full ounce of fine gold alloyed initially with copper and then with silver from 1990. From 1997 a corresponding series of silver pieces have been issued with nominal values of twenty pence, fifty pence, one pound and two pounds representing respectively a tenth, quarter, half and one ounce of fine silver struck at the Britannia standard of 958 fine rather than the 925 fine of sterling silver. Different reverse designs based on the Britannia theme have appeared intermittently. Catering for collectors of specimens in precious metals, the Royal Mint has struck proofs of some coins in a metal other than that for currency, for example, five pound pieces, usually stuck in cupro-nickel, have been struck in silver, gold or, occasionally, platinum.

Following approval on October 22, 1997, the fourth head of the Queen was introduced from 1998, with the tiara replacing the Royal Diadem and the initials IRB, for Ian Rank-Broadley, below the truncation. A plethora of commemorative coins has been issued during the reign and a guide to these

*2001 50 pence silver Britannia.*

pieces can be found in the accompanying table which covers the crown, five pound, two pound and fifty pence pieces. A particularly interesting coin is the five pound piece struck at the Royal Mint stand in the Millennium Dome (now the O2 Arena). This has a tiny representation of the dome at the 3 o'clock position on the reverse and is the first time a provincial mintmark has been included on coins since the pennies of 1919 struck in Birmingham with H and KN for Heatons Mint Ltd and the Kings Norton Metal Co respectively.

In a new approach by the Royal Mint, a set of silver pattern pieces for the "Bridge" series of pound coins was issued to collectors in 2003 and a year later there was in issue of another pattern set of four silver pound coins featuring heraldic beasts on the reverses, which were not adopted for currency.

In 2008, marking the 40th anniversary of the introduction of the first decimal coins for circulation, the reverse designs for coins from the penny to the pound piece were changed with the coins up to the fifty pence piece representing just parts of the Royal Arms and the pound showing the complete design. This innovative feature, the work of Matthew Dent, is certainly a break with tradition and perhaps does not use the circular aspect of the flan in the same way as, for example, the reverse of the florin, or, for coins

other than the five pence and fifty pence pieces, display the individual symmetry seen, for example, in the previous two and one penny pieces. In 2009 the Royal Mint introduced a gold quarter sovereign, only available previously as extremely rare Victorian patterns or as George V concoctions, manufactured in Cyprus.

From 2008 onwards, preparations for the 2012 London Olympics and Paralympics have been celebrated numismatically with the issue of a multiplicity of commemorative pieces in cupro-nickel, silver and gold (all the different issues are listed in the appropriate pages of this Yearbook). However, probably the most innovative move was the issue of 29 different reverses of the circulating fifty pence pieces, which has gone a long way to revive interest in our coinage among the general public, many of whom continue to spend many happy hours checking their change.

*2012 Diamond Jubilee five pound piece.*

A fifth obverse design, used on the five pound pieces for the 2002 Golden Jubilee has a three quarter head and shoulders image of the Queen wearing the Royal Diadem and the reverse has a fine equestrian reverse which has elements of the 1953 coronation crown. The 2012 Diamond Jubilee crown piece has yet another head and shoulders bust but this time wearing the tiara with the reverse design including the Mary Gillick laureate head first used in 1953, reminiscent of the design of the Diamond Jubilee medallion for Queen Victoria which portrays both the Young Head and the Old Head.

It is hoped that this short account of the coinage of Queen Elizabeth II, while constrained by the limits of space, forms a guide to the comprehensive range and diversity of material available to collectors of coins covering the longest reign since Queen Victoria.

*This article first appeared in the June 2012 edition of COIN NEWS.*

*2002 Golden Jubilee five pound piece.*

# Chard

—— SINCE 1964 ——

Coins - Bullion - Gold

# MUSEUM *archive*

## Pattern New Zealand Threepence

The introduction of the New Zealand coinage in the 1930s is a tortuous story highlighting the age-old tussle in which politicians, government officials and artists have often engaged when confronted with how a nation should be represented on its coinage.

The rare and beautiful pattern threepence of 1933 stands as an unassuming symbol of the struggle to ensure the designs on New Zealand's first separate coinage appropriately represented the rich history and iconography of the country. The heraldic artist George Kruger Gray had prepared designs of the hei-tiki but use of the device was objected to on the grounds of its supposing to represent a human foetus and its being worn as a native fertility charm. The hei-tiki design was a casualty of the dialogue over the coinage changes in the 1930s but, looked at now from a distance of almost 80 years, it would have made a charming piece, fitting the size and proportions of such a small coin beautifully. A few years later, in 1940, the hei-tiki found its way onto the reverse of New Zealand halfpennies designed by Leonard Mitchell, suggesting a softening of views on the use of the well-known symbol.

# Edward VII trial shilling

Containing as it does many trial and experimental pieces, the contents of the Royal Mint Museum cannot always be taken for granted. Coins that appear the same may have slightly different compositions and there will invariably be a story behind the difference. The Edward VII trial shilling, dated 1905, shown here is a slightly more obvious imposter, made as it is from a copper-based alloy, being much thicker and heavier than a standard shilling and having a plain edge. To these rather obvious points of difference can be added the S shapes sunk into the dies that struck the coin and appearing as raised features on the obverse and reverse.

The question, then, is why the coin was made. There is no contemporary Museum accessions register to help us and the Royal Mint's Annual Report is silent on the matter. Rather helpfully, however, a ticket associated with the coin from the time has survived and indicates that its existence relates to experiments being conducted into wear. The technically less than perfect nature of De Saulles' portrait of Edward VII may provide us with a further clue but there, unfortunately, the trail runs cold—at least for the time being.

# Advertising on coins

Beyond the chief purpose of coins as money, there have been many ways in which they have been used and also many ways in which they have been abused. There are plenty of examples of coins being defaced to convey a political message and also, as in this instance, as a means through which to advertise. The piece illustrated is an 1861 Bun Penny bearing a sticker promoting the services of Henry Edwards, a grocer of Winchester Street, Andover. We know from census returns that he was active in business towards the end of the nineteenth century and sticker is therefore one of the earliest examples of its type in the Royal Mint Museum collection.

Making use of the coinage in this way is not something the Royal Mint would in any way encourage or condone but it does happen and, as such, it is wholly appropriate to have specimens in the collection as an illustration of the life coins can lead once they are let loose in circulation.

# Trial pieces for
# Victoria Coronation medals

A medal or a coin struck in high relief can be very attractive. It provides the artist with more freedom to explore the form of a portrait or can offer a more satisfying solution to a figurative composition. When working in high relief, however, certain technical problems arise, one of the most important being how much metal there is to play with across the obverse and reverse. As was evident on coins of George V, if a piece is too thin for the extent of the relief, metal can be drawn up and result in a hollowed out effect, or ghosting, on one side.

The trial pieces illustrated here, for a commemorative medal by Benedetto Pistrucci to mark the coronation of Victoria, appear to be the result of an experiment into how thick the medal would have to be in order to avoid ghosting. Several blanks of metal were placed in the press and struck together to gauge the point at which a sufficient amount of metal would be available to make the medal. The pieces are a recent acquisition to the Royal Mint Museum collection because of the interesting technical questions they raise about the consequences of high-relief designs.

# Diamond Jubilee Medal of Queen Victoria

The Diamond Jubilee year is now upon us and thoughts will inevitably turn to the only other instance in British history when the nation has celebrated such a remarkable occasion, the Diamond Jubilee of Queen Victoria. While no coins were issued, medals certainly were and the contribution of the Royal Mint was to produce a handsome medal, made available in more than one size and more than one metal. Indeed, to arrive at an appearance, or patination, judged to be of a suitable standard a series of experiments was carried out on the bronze medals in particular.

The Museum collection contains a tray of bronze Diamond Jubilee medals ranging from a deep chocolate colour to a shinier brassy treatment, and many hues and subtle variations in between. What is also interesting about the group is the presence on one specimen of an inked-on reference to its having received six blows from the dies. The care and attention to detail were not lost on collectors and the medal—undoubtedly worthy of such a momentous occasion—proved to be extremely popular.

# Victoria's Golden Jubilee coinage

The coinage issued on the occasion of the Golden Jubilee of Queen Victoria in 1887 was never conceived as any kind of commemorative coinage. Preparations for a new portrait and new reverse designs had begun many years before and eventually took so long to resolve that the release of the coins just happened to coincide with the year of the Jubilee. After such a long run-in, for the Royal Mint to be faced with near-panic on the eve of June 21, designated Jubilee Day, when the coinage had to be ready is somewhat ironic. Easter and Whitsun holidays for workers were cancelled, temporary staff were drafted in to help meet the workload and, rather than having royal approvals well in hand, the Deputy Master Charles Fremantle was only consulting the Queen about the new designs in March 1887.

As a further indication of how pressured it all became, when Victoria was shown samples of the coins they had to be presented as uniface pieces because the obverse tooling was not yet available. The sixpence illustrated here is from the limited production connected with those presented to the Queen for approval. As coins to mark her Jubilee it is not perhaps surprising for her to have commented on the lack of reference to the occasion of her half century on the throne. But while such a major change of inscription was not made, this piece differs in some respects from those actually issued, again testimony to how close a call it really was.

# Portraits of the Queen by Sir Charles Wheeler

SIR Charles Wheeler was part of a group of Royal Academicians, which also included Edward Bawden and Arnold Machin, who prepared portraits of the Queen in connection with the introduction of the decimal coinage. Wheeler had some limited involvement in modelling prospective coinage designs in 1936 during the reign of Edward VIII and was an accomplished sculptor in low relief but he was by no means a practised hand when it came to designing the nation's coinage. The three drawings shown here reveal his interest in design and are not dissimilar in style to his marble bust of the Queen at the Royal Academy.

Given the number of prominent public commissions he secured, including the figures around the fountains of Trafalgar Square and the stone carved figures above the entrance to the Bank of England, his involvement with public art in the shape of the coinage should not perhaps be surprising. His decimal coinage portraits of the Queen were not, however, selected but they can be seen at a new exhibition at the Royal Academy, alongside work by his fellow Academicians, Machin and Bawden, which has been staged to coincide with the Queen's Diamond Jubilee.

# MONARCHS
## of England

Here we list the Kings and Queens from Anglo-Saxon times to the present, with the dates of their rule. Before Eadgar became the King of all England the country had been divided up into small kingdoms, each with their own ruler.

## ANGLO-SAXON KINGS

The Anglo-Saxon monarchs ruled over the various kingdoms which existed in England following the withdrawal of the Romans in the 5th century AD. The most prominent kingdoms in the land were Kent, Sussex, Wessex, Mercia and Northumbria. Each kingdom produced its own coinage but in 973 Eadgar introduced a new coinage that became the standard for the whole of the country.

Eadgar (959–975)
Edward the Martyr (975–978)
Aethelred II (978–1016)
Cnut (1016–1035)
Harold I (1035–1040)
Harthacanut (1035–1042)
Edward the Confessor (1042–1066)
Harold II (1066)

## NORMAN KINGS

The Normans came to Britain from their native France following the establishment of a kingdom in Sicily and southern Italy. An expedition led by the powerful Duke William of Normandy culminated in the battle of Hastings in 1066 where he defeated Harold II and was proclaimed King of All England. Their influence spread from these new centres to the Crusader States in the Near East and to Scotland and Wales in Great Britain, and to Ireland. Today their influence can be seen in their typical Romanesque style of architecture.

William I (1066–1087)
William II (1087–1100)
Henry I (1100–1135)
Stephen (1135–1154)

## PLANTAGENETS

The Plantagenet kings of England were descended from the first House of Anjou who were established as rulers of England through the Treaty of Wallingford, which passed over the claims of Eustace and William, Stephen of Blois's sons, in favour of Henry of Anjou, son of the Empress Matilda and Geoffrey V, Count of Anjou.

Henry II (1154–1189)
Richard I (1189–1199)
John (1199–1216)
Henry III (1216–1272)
Edward I (1272–1307)
Edward II (1307–1327)
Edward III (1327–1377)
Richard II (1377–1399)

## HOUSE OF LANCASTER

The House of Lancaster, a branch of the English royal House of Plantagenet, was one of the opposing factions involved in the Wars of the Roses, the civil war which dominated England and Wales during the 15th century. Lancaster provided England with three Kings

Henry IV (1399–1413)
Henry V (1413–1422)
Henry VI (1422–1461) and again 1470

## HOUSE OF YORK

The House of York was the other branch of the House of Plantagenet involved in the disastrous Wars of the Roses. Edward IV was descended from Edmund of Langley, 1st Duke of York, the fourth surviving son of Edward III.

Edward IV (1461–1483 and again 1471–83)
Richard III (1483–1485)

## TUDORS

The House of Tudor was an English royal dynasty that lasted 118 years, from 1485 to 1603. The family descended from the Welsh courtier Owen Tudor (Tewdwr). Following the defeat of Richard III at Bosworth, the battle that ended the Wars of the Roses, Henry Tudor, 2nd Earl of Richmond, took the throne as Henry VII.

Henry VII (1485–1509)
Henry VIII (1509–1547)
Edward VI (1547–1553)
Mary (1553–1558)
Philip & Mary (1554–1558)
Elizabeth I (1558–1603)

## STUARTS

The House of Stuart ruled Scotland for 336 years, between 1371 and 1707. Elizabeth I of England's closest heir was James VI of Scotland via her grandfather Henry VII of England, who was founder of the Tudor dynasty. On Elizabeth's death, James Stuart ascended the thrones of England and Ireland and inherited the English claims to the French throne. The Stuarts styled themselves "Kings and Queens of Great Britain", although there was no parliamentary union until the reign of Queen Anne, the last monarch of the House of Stuart.

James I (1603–1625)
Charles I (1625–1649)
The Commonwealth (1653–1658)
Charles II (1660–1685)
James II (1685–1688)
William III & Mary (1688–1694)
William III (1694–1702)
Anne (1702–1714)

## HOUSE OF HANOVER

The House of Hanover was a Germanic royal dynasty which ruled the Duchy of Brunswick-Lüneburg and the Kingdom of Hanover. George Ludwig ascended to the throne of the Kingdom of Great Britain and Ireland through the female line from Princess Elizabeth, sister of Charles I.

George I (1714–1727)
George II (1727–1760)
George III (1760–1820)
George IV (1820–1830)
William IV (1830–1837)
Victoria (1837–1901)

## HOUSES OF SAXE-COBURG-GOTHA AND WINDSOR

The name Saxe-Coburg-Gotha was inherited by Edward VII from his father Prince Albert, the second son of the Duke of Saxe-Coburg-Gotha and husband of Victoria. During World War I the name was changed to Windsor to avoid the Germanic connotatiion.

Edward VII (1901–1910)
George V (1910–1936)
Edward VIII (1936)
George VI (1936–1952)
Elizabeth II (1952– )

# Leading the way in Numismatics

# VIEW of the Bay

**WILLIAM McCREATH offers some advice when it comes to the internet**

In the years that I've been registered on eBay the number of numismatic items listed has grown enormously as has the variety of items on offer, from the very common to the very rare and everything in-between, they will all appear at some time or another. eBay is a very rich hunting ground for those who are interested in items that are off the beaten track, countermarked coins, tokens, error coins and notes, old contemporary counterfeits, etc.—the variety on offer simply can't be found in any other one place. Buying these types of items holds few dangers for bidders as they are often in low grade but still desirable so it's difficult to go wrong, with a little caution. Very rare countermarked coins can be found where the seller is unaware of how rare they are, which can give the informed collector the chance to bag a real bargain, for example Spanish American dollars counterstamped by Scottish merchants that can be worth over £1,000 can turn up unrecognised by the seller.

Bidding on mainstream items is entirely a different matter however and extreme caution has to be exercised along with doing some homework before bidding. If a seller regularly lists nothing but "high grade" coins or notes, a collector should be asking themselves, where does the seller get their stock from, especially if they seem to be happy to frequently sell at "bargain" prices. It's astounding that this question does not even cross the mind of many collectors as they merrily bid away, snapping up what they see as bargain after bargain from the same seller. A few other sellers have now jumped on this bandwagon as they see this seller doing very well: one bad apple . . . etc.

A large percentage of coins listed are overgraded, no surprise perhaps. Coins in no better than fine condition can be found listed as being EF, or commonly a somewhat vague "high grade", which should be a red flag for prospective bidders. So many bidders seem happy to buy grossly overgraded coins that a dishonest seller could make handsome profits by buying accurately graded VF coins from leading dealers to be sold on eBay as EF.

A silver coin that appears to have original lustre may have been "dipped", which can sometimes give them a matt appearance, so watch out for this—especially if the majority of a seller's silver coins have this look. Coins that to an experienced collector look to have been cleaned or even harshly polished can still find inexperienced happy buyers.

I would recommend completely ignoring the stated grade, including coins that have been "slabbed", and grade from the photographs supplied: if they are of poor quality then do not bid as the seller is possibly trying to hide something. Good quality digital cameras are not expensive so there is no excuse for dark or fuzzy pictures. If a seller has the items that they have sold hidden as "private" in their feedbacks, thus making it impossible to find out what the item was, they may have a good reason for hiding this information so they should perhaps be avoided. Unfortunately a 100% positive feedback record for a seller no longer counts for as much as it once did, as inexperienced buyers now appear to be in the majority so they give positives to bad sellers when they should be giving strong negatives. One buyer gave positive feedback even when the coin they bought had been described as "EF" although it could at best be described as VF., A negative would have acting as a warning to other collectors.

Recommending to never to bid on a coin from a seller in China might be considered extreme, and perhaps unfair to honest sellers in that country, but there are huge numbers of fake coins being made in China for sale to collectors and some are very convincing. They range from rare crowns and thalers to more common USA trade dollars and modern coins. Some sell for suitably low prices but some sell for £100s of pounds to soon-to-be-disappointed buyers. As they are being made on an industrial scale the fakes will by now outnumber the genuine population of some rare coins, so buy from sellers in China only if the item is cheap and the postage charges not extortionate and you enjoy a gamble with long odds. A "Northumberland" shilling being offered by a seller in China will not be genuine—the fact that so many are for sale is a bit of a giveaway, but they still receive bids.

It's not all depressing news when it comes to the mainstream numismatic items listed on eBay, but good news can be thin on the ground. It may be possible to find a few sellers who do accurately grade the coins they list for sale and if that few are found use should be made of eBay's "saved sellers" feature. The chance of a bargain can be had when a seller offers a rare variety that they don't recognise. Just hope that you are one of just a few that have spotted it and bid at the last possible moment, but not more than you are prepared to pay. Placing a very high last minute "must have" bid is a very risky business because if another bidder does likewise the winning bid could be close to your maximum. Very rare notes or first or last serial number notes can sometimes be found where the seller is unaware of their status. However, there are many active banknote collectors on eBay so there may be some competition but a last minute bid may win the day.

"Buy the book before the coin, and read it" is advice that's often given to beginners, and very sound advice it is. Collectors may not consider eBay as a source of reference material but they should. In addition to the usual well known standard references very often auction catalogues can be

found, and with a bit of luck, complete with prices realised. For a specialist collector an auction catalogue containing their speciality can be a mine of information that's not available in any other single publication. There is a subsection for publications in the coins section but a search in the general "books" category for your chosen subject may reveal additional items. Numismatic ephemera is worth searching for as a gem or two might be found: Decimal Currency Board booklets and leaflets from the 1960s and 70s, old dealers list, old magazines, old banking letters perhaps signed by a high ranking bank official whose printed signature appeared on notes—there are many possibilities.

There is always a large variety of cheques listed on eBay, or "checks" if the seller is in North America, so if searching for your home town search for it with "cheque" and "check". Cheque collectors will be spoilt for choice and items can be found in the region of £50 for a single old cheque down to a few pounds or less. Old savings banks can be of interest to both coin and banknote collectors and the sturdy metal "home safe" types turn up regularly, sometimes unused in the original cardboard box of issue. Finding one with a key could be useful as most that contain a few coins have no key, which was retained by the bank, and there could be a rare date penny in there!

In the not too distant future it may become virtually impossible to find accurately graded coins and notes on eBay as more and more good sellers give up selling there. They find it frustrating to get a low price for their accurately graded coins, achieving just Fine prices for VF coins, while bad sellers find it easy to get high prices for their overgraded coins, achieving EF prices for VF coins. Some long term eBay coin sellers who used to offer accurately graded coins that sold for fair prices are now offering overgraded coins, a case of, "if you can't beat them, join them". It's getting closer to the stage where the only people buying "high grade" coins and notes off eBay are those who have no idea of how an accurately graded coin or note should look. A knowledgeable collector has little chance of bidding success if many are willing to pay EF money for VF coins or notes. I often wonder if the buyers of these overgraded coins and notes have had a shock when they try to sell them at a coin fair to dealers who recognise their true grade.

**ASK!**

**ASK YOURSELF AT LEAST SOME OF THESE QUESTIONS BEFORE BIDDING ON A NUMISMATIC ITEM ON EBAY . . .**

How can a seller have an-unending supply of old notes or coins that are claimed to be high grade?

How can a seller afford to frequently sell at below a likely dealer's buying price if the coins they offer are accurately graded?

Why does a seller keep some information private?

Do really I want to buy from a seller who describes every item they list as "rare" even if it's very common?

Why are this seller's coin photographs always dark or fuzzy or too small?

Do I really want that "rare" coin from a seller in China?

If you are considering placing a large bid spend some time on-line looking at photographs of similar coins in dealers' lists and in auction catalogues, as this can give a very good idea if the coins on eBay are overgraded or not—they probably will be. Some dealers have an archive on their web site of coins sold or auctioned over many years, which is a useful resource.

First time eBay bidders should perhaps start off by bidding on low cost items. Place low bids and just the get the "feel" of it, but beware, it will probably lead to eBay addiction with bids getting ever higher and when that elusive item that has been searched for for decades comes along, and it will eventually, costly bidding fever may strike.

The fact that there are now non gold British coins regularly fetching over £1,000 is an indication that more and more sellers now consider eBay to be a serious alternative to the long established traditional auction houses. The large buyer and seller premiums that are added by them, sometimes over 40% in total, may drive sellers to eBay in ever increasing numbers. One seller is listing his entire banknote collection on e~Bay over a period of time. It will be interesting to watch how well he does—if he does as well as he hopes this should be of concern to the auction houses. Will there come a time when only exceptionally rare items are consigned to the large auction houses and their currently thick auction catalogues will begin to slim down? Their very high commission charges may kill the goose that has been laying golden eggs for many years. As the popularity of selling rare and expensive coins on eBay increases, the profits of the traditional numismatic auction houses will decrease. Will they be forced to reduce the commonly applied very high buyer's premium of sometimes as much as 20%, which in effect reduces the amount of money received by sellers as bidders allow for this extra 20% when deciding on their maximum bid, in an attempt to tempt sellers back from eBay?

# DATES *on coins*

The vast majority of modern coins bear the date prominently on one side. In most cases dates are expressed in modified Arabic numerals according to the Christian calendar and present no problem in identification. There have been a few notable exceptions to this general rule, however. Morocco, for example, has used European numerals to express dates according to the Moslem calendar, so that a coin dated 1321 actually signifies 1903. Dates are almost invariably written from left to right—even in Arabic script which writes words from right to left. An exception, however, occurred in the Philippines quarto of 1822 where the date appeared as 2281, and the "2"s back to front for good measure.

| | ARABIC-TURKISH | CHINESE, JAPANESE KOREAN, ANNAMESE (ORDINARY) | CHINESE, JAPANESE KOREAN, ANNAMESE (OFFICIAL) | INDIAN | SIAMESE | BURMESE |
|---|---|---|---|---|---|---|
| 1 | ١ | 一 | 壹 | ٩ | ๑ | ၁ |
| 2 | ٢ | 二 | 貳 | ٢ | ๒ | ၂ |
| 3 | ٣ | 三 | 叁 | ٣ | ๓ | ၃ |
| 4 | ٤ | 四 | 肆 | ٨ | ๔ | ၄ |
| 5 | ٥ | 五 | 伍 | ٤ | ๕ | ၅ |
| 6 | ٦ | 六 | 陸 | ٤ | ๖ | ၆ |
| 7 | ٧ | 七 | 柒 | ٧ | ๗ | ၇ |
| 8 | ٨ | 八 | 捌 | ٢ | ๘ | ၈ |
| 9 | ٩ | 九 | 玖 | ٩ | ๙ | ၉ |
| 0 | ٠ | | | ٥ | ๐ | ၀ |
| 10 | ١٠ | 十 | 拾 | | ๑๐ | |
| 100 | ١٠٠ | 百 | | | ๑๐๐ | |
| 1000 | ١٠٠٠ | 千 | | | | |

Dates in Roman numerals have been used since 1234 when this practice was adopted by the Danish town of Roskilde. Such Roman numerals were used sporadically throughout the Middle Ages and in later centuries and survive fitfully to this day. This was the system used in England for the first dated coins, the gold half-sovereigns of Edward VI struck at Durham House in 1548 (MDXLVIII). This continued till 1550 (MDL) but thereafter Arabic numerals were used, beginning with the half-crown of 1551. Notable exceptions of more recent times include the Gothic coinage of Queen Victoria (1847–87).

The first coin with the date in European numerals was a plappart of St Gallen, Switzerland dated 1424, but this was an isolated case. In 1477 Maria of Burgundy issued a guldiner which bore a date on the reverse, in the form of two pairs of digits flanking the crown at the top. The numerals in this instance were true Gothic, an interesting transition between true Arabic numerals and the modified Arabic figures now used in Europe. The Tyrolese guldengroschen of 1484–6 were the first coins to be regularly dated in European numerals and thereafter this custom spread rapidly.

For the numismatist, the problem arises when coins bear a date in the numerals of a different alphabet or computed according to a different era. Opposite is a table showing the basic numerals used in different scripts. The various eras which may be found in coin dates are as listed and explained opposite.

## Hijra

The era used on Moslem coins dates from the flight of Mohammed from Mecca to Medina on July 15, 622 and is often expressed as digits followed by AH (Anno Hegirae). Moslems employ a lunar calendar of twelve months comprising 354 11/30 days. Tipu Sultan of Mysore in 1201 AH (the fifth year of his reign) introduced a new era dating from the birth of Mohammed in AD 570 and using a luni-solar system. Tipu also adopted the Hindu cycle of sixty years (the Tamil Brihaspate Cycle), but changed this two or three years later, from Hijra to Muludi.

Afghan coins used the lunar calendar until 1920 and during 1929–31, but at other times have used the solar calendar. Thus the Democratic Republic began issuing its coins in SH 1358 (1979).

To convert an AH date to the Christian calendar you must translate the Arabic into European numerals. Taking an Arabic coin dated 1320, for example, first deduct 3% (to convert from the Moslem lunar year to our solar year). This gives 39.6 which, rounded up to the nearest whole number, is 40. Deduct 40 from 1320 (1280), then add 622. The answer is 1902.

There have been a few notable exceptions. Thus the Khanian era of Ilkhan Ghazan Mahmud began on 1st Rajab 701 AH (1301). This era used a solar calendar, but was shortlived, being confined to coins of Mahmud and his nephew Abu Said down to year 34 (1333).

The era of Tarikh Ilahi was adopted by the Mughal emperor Akbar in the thirteenth year of his reign (922 AH). This era dated from his accession on 5th Rabi al-Sani 963 AH ( February 19, 1556). The calendar had solar months and days but no weeks, so each day of the month had a different name. This system was used by Akbar, Jahangir and Shah Jahan, often with a Hijra date as well.

## Saphar

The era of the Caesars began on January 1, 38 BC and dated from the conquest of Spain by Augustus. Its use on coinage, however, seems to have been confined to the marabotins of Alfonso VIII of Castile and was expressed in both Latin and Arabic.

## Samvat

The era of Vikramaditya began in 57 BC and was a luni-solar system used in some Indian states. Coins may be found with both Samvat and Hijra dates. Conversion to the Christian date is simple; merely subtract 57 from the Samvat to arrive at the AD date.

## Saka

This originated in the southwestern district of Northern India and began in AD 78. As it used the luni-solar system it converts easily by adding 78 to the Saka date.

## Nepal

Nepalese coins have used four different date systems. All coins of the Malla kings were dated in Nepal Samvat (NS) era, year 1 beginning in 881. This system was also used briefly by the state of Cooch Behar. Until 1888 all coins of the Gurkha dynasty were dated in the Saka era (SE) which began in AD 78. After 1888 most copper coins were dated in the Vikram Samvat (VS) era from 57 BC. With the exception of some gold coins struck in 1890 and 1892, silver and gold coins only changed to the VS era in 1911, but now this system is used for all coins struck in Nepal. Finally, dates in the Christian era have appeared on some commemorative coins of recent years.

## Ethiopian

This era dates from August AD 7, so that EE 1885 is AD 1892. Ethiopian dates are expressed in five digits using Amharic numerals. The first two are the digits of the centuries, the third is the character for 100, while the fourth and fifth are the digits representing the decade and year. On modern coins dates are rendered in Amharic numerals using the Christian era.

## Thailand

Thai coins mainly use the Buddhist era (BE) which dates from 543 BC, but some coins have used dates from the Chula-Sakarat calendar (CS) which began in AD 638, while others use a Ratanakosind Sok (RS) date from the foundation of the Chakri dynasty in AD 1781.

## Hebrew

The coins of Israel use the Jewish calendar dating from the beginning of the world (Adam and Eve in the Garden of Eden) in 3760 BC. Thus the year 1993 is rendered as 5753. The five millennia are assumed in dates, so that only the last three digits are expressed. 735 therefore equates with AD 1975. Dates are written in Hebrew letters, reading from right to left. The first two characters signify 400 and 300 respectively, totalling 700. The third letter denotes the decades (lamedh = 30) and the fourth letter, following the separation mark (") represents the final digit (heh = 5). The Jewish year runs from September or October in the Christian calendar.

## Dates from the creation of the world

This system was also used in Russia under Ivan IV. The dating system Anno Mundi (AM) was established by the Council of Constantinople in AD 680 which determined that the birth of Christ had occurred in 5508 AM. Ivan's coins expressed the date as 7055 (1447).

## Dynastic dates

The system of dating coinage according to regnal years is a feature of Chinese and Japanese coins. Chinese coins normally have an inscription stating that they are coins of such and such a reign period (not the emperor's name), and during the Southern Sung dynasty this was joined by the numeral of the year of the reign. This system was continued under the republic and survives in Taiwan to this day, although the coins of the Chinese Peoples Republic are dated in western numerals using the Christian calendar.

Early Japanese coins bore a reference to the era (the title assumed by each emperor on his accession) but, like Chinese coins, could not be dated accurately. From the beginning of the Meiji era (1867), however, coins have included a regnal number. The Showa era, beginning in 1926 with the accession of Hirohito, eventually ran to sixty-three (expressed in western numerals on some denominations, in Japanese ideograms on others) to denote 1988, although the rest of the inscription was in Japanese characters.

Dynastic dates were used on Korean milled coins introduced in 1888. These bore two characters at the top Kae Kuk (founding of the dynasty) followed by quantitative numerals. The system dated from the founding of the Yi dynasty in 1392. Curiously enough, some Korean banknotes have borne dates from the foundation of the first dynasty in 2333 BC.

Iran adopted a similar system in 1975, celebrating the 15th anniversary of the Pahlavi regime by harking back to the glories of Darius. The new calendar dated from the foundation of the Persian Empire 2535 years earlier, but was abolished only three years later when the Shah was overthrown.

## Political eras

France adopted a republican calendar in 1793 when the monarchy was abolished. Coins were then inscribed L'AN (the year) followed by Roman numerals, but later Arabic numerals were substituted. This continued to the year 14 (1806) but in that year the Emperor Napoleon restored the Christian calendar. The French system was emulated by Haiti whose coins dated from the revolution of 1803. The date appeared as AN followed by a number until AN 31 (1834) on some coins; others had both the evolutionary year and the Christian date from 1828 until 1850 (AN 47). Coins with a date in the Christian calendar appeared only in 1807–9 and then from 1850 onwards.

Mussolini introduced the Fascist calendar to Italy, dating from the seizure of power in October 1922. This system was widely employed on documents and memorials, but was first used on silver 20 lire coins of 1927 and then only in addition to the Christian date and appearing discreetly as Roman numerals. Subsequently it was extended to gold 50 lire and 100 lire coins in 1931 and the subsidiary coinage in 1936, being last used in the year XXI (1943).

# COIN TERMS *glossary*

**In this section we list all the terms commonly encountered in numismatics or in the production of coins.**

**Abbey Coins**  Medieval coins struck in the abbeys, convents and other great religious houses which were granted coinage rights. These coins were often used also by pilgrims journeying from one monastery to another.

**Abschlag**  (German for "discount") A *restrike* from an original die.

**Accolated**  Synonym for *conjoined* or *jugate* and signifying two or more profiles overlapping.

**Acmonital**  Acronym from *Aciaio Monetario Italiano*, a stainless steel alloy used for Italian coins since 1939.

**Adjustment**  Reduction of metal in a *flan* or *blank* to the specified weight prior to striking, accomplished by filing down the face. Such file marks often survived the coining process and are occasionally met with in coins, especially of the 18th century.

**Ae**  Abbreviation for the Latin *Aes* (bronze), used for coins made of brass, bronze or other copper alloys.

**Aes Grave**  (Latin for heavy bronze) Heavy circular coins first minted at Rome in 269 BC.

**Aes Rude**  (Latin for rough bronze) Irregular lumps of bronze which gradually developed into ingots of uniform shape and were the precursors of coins in Rome.

**Aes Signatum**  (Latin for signed bronze) Bronze ingots of regular size and weight, bearing marks of authority to guarantee their weight (289–269 BC).

**Agonistic**  (Greek) Term for coins issued to commemorate, or pertaining to, sporting events.

**Alliance**  Coinage struck by two or more states acting together and having common features of design or inscription.

*Aes Signatum— Roman Republic bronze ingot*

**Alloy**  Coinage metal composed of two or more metallic elements.

**Altered**  Deliberately changed, usually unofficially, with the aim of increasing the numismatic value of a coin, medal or note. This applies particularly to dates, where a common date may be altered to a rare date by filing or re-engraving one of the digits.

**Aluminium**  (American *Aluminum*)  Silvery lightweight metal, developed commercially in the late 19th century for commemorative medals, but used for tokens and emergency money during the First World War and since 1940 widely used in subsidiary coinage.

**Aluminium-bronze**  Alloy of aluminium and copper.  Hard-wearing and gold-coloured, it is now widely used in tokens and subsidiary coinage.

**Amulet**  Coin or medal believed to have talismanic qualities, such as warding off disease and bad luck.  Many Chinese and Korean pieces come into this category.  See also *Touchpiece*.

**Androcephalous**  Heraldic term for creatures with a human head.

45

**Anepigraphic**  Coins or medals without a legend.

**Annealing**  Process of heating and cooling applied to metal to relieve stresses and prepare it for striking into coins.

**Annulet**  Small circle often used as an ornament or spacing device in coin inscriptions.

**Antimony**  Brittle white metal, chemical symbol *Sb*, virtually impractical as a coinage metal but used for the Chinese 10 cents of Kweichow, 1931. Alloyed with tin, copper or lead, it produces the white metal popular as a medallic medium.

**Antoniniani**  Silver coins minted in Imperial Rome. The name derives from the Emperor Caracalla (Marcus Aurelius Antoninus) in whose reign they were first struck. The silver content was progressively reduced and by the last issue (AD 295) they were reduced to *billon*.

**Ar**  Abbreviation for Latin *Argentum* (silver), used for coins struck in this metal.

**Assay Mark**  Mark applied to a medal struck in precious metal by an assayer or assay office as a guarantee of the fineness of the metal.

**Assignat**  Type of paper money used in France 1789–96, representing the land assigned to the holders.

**Attribution**  Identification of a coin by characteristics such as issuing authority, date or reign, mint, denomination, metal, and by a standard reference.

**Au**  Abbreviation for *aurum* (Latin for gold), denoting coins of this metal.

**AU**  Abbreviation for "About Uncirculated", often found in catalogues and dealers' lists to describe the condition of a numismatic piece.

**Autodollar**  Name given to the silver yuan issued by Kweichow, 1928, and having a contemporary motor car as the obverse motif.

**Auxiliary Payment Certificate**  Form of paper money intended for use by American military personnel stationed in overseas countries. See also *Baf* and *Scrip*.

**Babel Note**  Nickname given to the paper money of the Russian Socialist Federated Soviet Republic (1919) because it bore the slogan "workers of the world unite" in seven languages, a reference to the biblical tower of Babel.

**Baf**  Acronym from British Armed Forces, the popular name for the vouchers which could only be exchanged for goods in service canteens from 1945 onwards.

**Bag Mark**  Minor scratch or abrasion on an otherwise uncirculated coin, caused by coins in mint bags knocking together.

**Banknote**  Form of paper money issued by banks and usually promising to pay the bearer on demand in coin of the realm.

**Barbarous**  Imitation of Greek or Roman coins by the Celtic and Germanic tribes who lived beyond the frontiers of the civilised world.

**Base**  Non-precious metals or alloys.

**Bath Metal**  Inferior bronze alloy, named after the English city where it was used for casting cannon. Used by William Wood of Bristol for Irish and American tokens and by Amos Topping for Manx coins of 1733/4.

**Beading**  Ornamental border found on the raised rim of a coin.

**Behalfszahlungsmittel**  German term for auxiliary payment certificates used in occupied Europe from 1939 to 1945.

**Bell Metal**  Alloy of copper and tin normally used for casting bells, but employed for the subsidiary coinage of the French Revolutionary period.

**Billon**  Silver alloy containing less than 50 per cent fine silver, usually mixed with copper. In Spain this alloy was known as *vellon*.

**Bi-metallic**  Coins struck in two separate metals or alloys. Patterns for such coins exist from the 19th century but actual coins with a centre of one metal surrounded by a ring of another did not appear till 1982 (Italy, San Marino and Vatican). Canada introduced coins with a tiny plaque inset in a second metal (1990). See also *Clad, Plugged* and *Sandwich*.

**Bi-metallism**  Monetary system in which two metals are in simultaneous use and equally available as legal tender, implying a definite ratio between the two. A double standard of gold and silver, with a ratio of 16:1, existed till the mid-19th century.

**Bingle**  American term for a trade token, more specifically the US government issue of tokens for the Matacuska, Alaska colonization project, 1935.

**Birthday Coins**  Coins celebrating the birthday of a ruler originated in Roman Imperial times, notably the reigns of Maximianus (286–305) and Constantinus I (307–37). Birthday talers were issued by many German states, and among recent examples may be cited coins marking the 70th, 80th and 90th birthdays of Gustaf Adolf VI of Sweden, 80th and 90th birthday coins from the British Commonwealth for the Queen Mother, and coins honouring Queen Elizabeth, the Duke of Edinburgh and the Prince of Wales.

*2012 Alderney coin commemorating Prince William's 30th birthday*

**Bit** Term denoting fragments of large silver coins, cut up and circulating as fractional values. Spanish dollars were frequently broken up for circulation in the American colonies and the West indies. Long bits and short bits circulated at 15 and 10 cents respectively, but the term came to be equated with the Spanish real or eighth peso, hence the American colloquialism "two-bit" signifying a quarter dollar.

**Black Money** English term for the debased silver deniers minted in France which circulated freely in England until they were banned by government decree in 1351.

**Blank** Piece of metal, cut or punched out of a roller bar or strip, and prepared for striking to produce coins. Alternate terms are *flan* and *planchet*.

**Blundered Inscription** Legend in which the lettering is jumbled or meaningless, indicating the illiteracy of the tribes who copied Greek and Roman coins.

**Bonnet Piece** Scottish gold coin, minted in 1539–40. The name is derived from the obverse portraying King James V in a large, flat bonnet.

*1539 Scottish James V bonnet coin*

**Bon Pour** French for "good for", inscribed on Chamber of Commerce brass tokens issued in 1920–7 during a shortage of legal tender coinage.

**Bouquet Sou** Canadian copper token halfpenny of 1837 deriving its name from the nosegay of heraldic flowers on the obverse.

**Box Coin** Small container formed by *obverse* and *reverse* of two coins, hollowed out and screwed together.

**Bracteate** (Latin *bractea*, a thin piece of metal) Coins struck on blanks so thin that the image applied to one side appears in reverse on the other. First minted in Erfurt and Thuringia in the 12th century, and later produced elsewhere in Germany, Switzerland and Poland till the 14th century.

**Brass** Alloy of copper and zinc, widely used for subsidiary coinage. The term was also formerly used for bronze Roman coins, known numismatically as first, second or third brass.

**Breeches Money** Derisive term given by the Royalists to the coinage of the Commonwealth, 1651, the conjoined elongated oval shields on the reverse resembling a pair of breeches.

**Brockage** Mis-struck coin with only one design, normal on one side and *incuse* on the other. This occurs when a coin previously struck adheres to the die and strikes the next blank to pass through the press.

**Broken Bank-note** Note issued by a bank which has failed, but this is often applied more generally to banknotes which have actually been demonetised.

**Bronze** Alloy of copper and tin, first used as a coinage metal by the Chinese c. 1000 BC. Often used synonymously with copper, though it should be noted that bronze only superseded copper as the constituent of the base metal British coins in 1860.

**Bull Neck** Popular term for the coins of King George III, 1816–17.

**Bullet Money** Pieces of silver, *globular* in shape, bearing various *countermarks* and used as coins in Siam (Thailand) in the 18th and 19th centuries.

**Bullion** Precious metal in bars, ingots, strip or scrap (i.e. broken jewellery mounts, watch-cases and plate), its weight reckoned solely by weight and fineness, before being converted into coin.

**Bullion Coin** A coin struck in platinum, gold or silver, whose value is determined solely by the prevailing market price for the metal as a commodity. Such coins do not generally have a nominal face value, but include in their inscriptions their weight and fineness. Good examples of recent times include the Krugerrand (South Africa), the Britannia (UK), the Maple Leaf (Canada), Libertad (Mexico), the Nugget (Australia) and the Eagle (USA).

**Bun Coinage** British coins of 1860–94 showing Queen Victoria with her hair in a bun.

**Bungtown Coppers** Derisive term (from Anglo-American slang *bung*, to swindle or bribe) for halfpence of English or Irish origin, often counterfeit, which circulated in North America towards the end of the colonial period.

**Carat** (American *Karat*) Originally a unit of weight for precious stones, based on carob seeds (ceratia), it also denotes the fineness or purity of gold, being 1/24th part of the whole. Thus 9 carat gold is .375 fine and 22 carat, the English sovereign standard, is .916 fine. Abbreviated as ct or kt.

**Cartwheel** Popular term for the large and cumbersome penny and twopenny pieces of 1797 weighing one and two ounces, struck by Matthew Boulton at the Soho Mint, Birmingham.

**Cased Set** Set of coins in mint condition, housed in the official case issued by the mint. Formerly leather cases with blue plush or velvet lining were used, but nowadays many sets are encapsulated in plastic to facilitate handling.

**Cash** (from Portuguese *caixa*, Hindi *kasu*). Round piece of bronze or brass with a square hole in the centre, used as subsidiary coinage in China for almost 2000 years, till the early 12th century. In Chinese these pieces were known as *Ch'ien* or *Li* and strung together in groups of 1000 were equivalent to a silver tael.

**Cast Coins** Coins cast from molten metals in moulds. This technique, widespread in the case of early commemorative medals, has been used infrequently in coins, the vast majority of which are struck from *dies*. Examples include the Chinese cash and the Manx coins of 1709.

**Check** A form of *token* given as a means of identification, or issued for small amounts of money or for services of a specific nature.

**Cheque** (American *Check*) A written order directing a bank to pay money.

**Chop** (Hindi, to seal). Countermark, usually consisting of a single character, applied by Chinese merchants to precious metal coins and ingots as a guarantee of their weight and fineness. Coins may be found with a wide variety of chop marks and the presence of several different marks on the same coin considerably enhances its interest and value. See also *Shroff mark*.

**Christmas** Coins issued as Christmas gifts date from the Middle Ages when the Venetian Doges struck *Osselle* as presents for their courtiers. In modern times, however, the custom has developed only since the late 1970s and several countries having issued them since then.

**Cistophori** (Greek for chest bearing) a generic term for the coins of Pergamum with an obverse motif of a chest showing a serpent crawling out of the half-opened lid. Cistophori became very popular all over Asia Minor in the 3rd and 2nd centuries BC and were struck also at mints in Ionia, Phrygia, Lydia and Mysia.

**Clad Coins** Coins with a core of one alloy, covered with a layer or coating of another. US half dollars from 1965 to 1970, for example, had a core of 21 per cent silver and 79 per cent copper, bonded to outer layers of 80 per cent silver and 20 per cent copper. More recently, however, coins usually have a body in a cheap alloy, with only a thin cladding of a more expensive material, such as the British 1p and 2p coins of stainless steel with a copper cladding, introduced late in 1992.

**Clash Marks** Mirror image traces found on a coin which has been struck from a pair of dies, themselves damaged by having been struck together without a blank between.

**Clipped Coins** Precious metal coins from which small amounts have been removed by clipping the edges. It was to prevent this that *graining* and *edge inscriptions* were adopted.

**Cob** Crude, irregularly shaped silver piece, often with little more than a vestige of die impressions, produced in the Spanish American mints in the 16th–18th centuries.

**Coin** Piece of metal, marked with a device, issued by government authority and intended for use as money.

**Collar** Retaining ring within which the *dies* for the *obverse* and *reverse* operate. When the *blank* is struck under high pressure between the dies the metal flows sideways and is formed by the collar, taking up the impression of *reeding* or *edge inscription* from it.

**Commemorative** Coin, medal, token or paper note issued to celebrate a current event or the anniversary of a historic event or personality.

*2012 Canadian $20 coin commemorating HM Queen Elizabeth's Diamond Jubilee*

**Communion Token** Token, cast in lead, but later struck in pewter, brass, bronze or white metal, issued to members of a congregation to permit them to partake of the annual communion service in the Calvinist and Presbyterian churches. John Calvin himself is said to have invented the communion token in 1561 but they were actually referred to in the minutes of the Scottish General Assembly in 1560. Later they were adopted by the Reformed churches in many parts of Europe. They survived in Scotland till the early years of this century. Each parish had its own tokens, often bearing the names or initials of individual ministers, with dates, symbols and biblical texts.

**Conjoined** Term denoting overlapped profiles of two or more rulers (e.g. William and Mary).

**Contorniate** (from Italian *contorno*, edge). Late 4th and 5th century Roman bronze piece whose name alludes to the characteristic grooving on the edges.

**Contribution Coins** Coins struck by Bamberg, Eichstatt, Fulda and other German cities in the 1790s during the First Coalition War against the French Republic. The name alludes to the fact that the bullion used to produce the coins necessary to pay troops was raised by contribution from the Church and the public.

**Convention Money** Any system of coinage agreed by neighbouring countries for mutual acceptance and interchange. Examples include the Amphictyonic coins of ancient Greece, and the Austrian and Bavarian talers and gulden of 1753–1857 which were copied by other south German states and paved the way for the German Monetary union.

**Copper** Metallic element, chemical symbol *Cu*, widely used as a coinage medium for 2,500 years. Pure or almost pure copper was used for subsidiary coinage in many countries till the mid-19th century, but has since been superseded by copper alloys which are cheaper and more durable: *bronze* (copper and tin), *brass* (copper and zinc), *Bath metal* or *bell metal* (low-grade copper and tin), *aluminium-bronze* (copper and aluminium), *potin* (copper, tin, lead and silver) or *cupro-nickel* (copper and nickel). Copper is also alloyed with gold to give it its reddish hue, and is normally alloyed with silver in coinage metals. When the copper exceeds the silver content the alloy is known as *billon*.

**Copperhead** Popular term for a copper *token* about the size and weight of an American cent which circulated in the USA during the Civil War (1861–65) during a shortage of subsidiary coinage. Many different types were produced, often of a political or patriotic nature.

**Coppernose** Popular name for the debased silver shillings of Henry VIII. Many of them were struck in copper with little more than a silver wash which tended to wear off at the highest point of the obverse, the nose on the full-face portrait of the king.

**Counter** A piece resembling a coin but intended for use on a medieval accountancy board or in gambling. See also *jeton*.

**Counterfeit** Imitation of a coin, token or banknote intended for circulation to deceive the public and defraud the state.

**Countermark** Punch mark applied to a coin some time after its original issue, either to alter its nominal value, or to authorise its circulation in some other country.

**Cowrie** Small shell (*Cypraea moneta*) circulating as a form of primitive currency from 1000 BC (China) to the present century (East and West Africa) and also used in the islands of the Indian and Pacific Oceans.

**Crockard** Debased silver imitation of English pennies produced in the Netherlands and imported into England in the late 13th century. Edward I tried to prevent their import then, in 1299, allowed them to pass current as halfpennies. As they contained more than

a halfpennyworth of silver this encouraged their trading in to be melted down and they disappeared from circulation within a year. Sometimes known as *pollards*. See also *Lushbourne*.

**Crown Gold** Gold of 22 carat (.916) fineness, so called on account of its adoption in 1526 for the English gold crown. It has remained the British standard gold fineness ever since.

**Cumberland Jack** Popular name for a counter or medalet of sovereign size, struck unofficially in 1837 in brass. The figure of St George was replaced with the Duke of Cumberland on horseback with the inscription "To Hanover" a reference to the unpopular Duke of Cumberland, uncle of Queen Victoria, who succeeded to the Hanoverian throne since Victoria, as a female, was debarred by Salic law from inheritance.

**Cupellation** (Latin *cupella*, a little cup). Process by which gold and silver were separated from lead and other impurities in their ores. A cupel is a shallow cup of bone-ash or other absorbent material which, when hot, absorbs any molten material that wets its surface. Lead melts and oxidises with impurities into the cupel, whereas gold and silver remain on the cupel. Cupellation is also used in assaying the fineness of these precious metals.

**Cupro-nickel** Coinage alloy of 75 per cent copper and 25 per cent nickel, now widely used as a base metal substitute for silver. A small amount of zinc is added to the alloy in modern Russian coins.

**Currency** Coins, tokens, paper notes and other articles intended to pass current in general circulation as money.

**Current** Coins and paper money still in circulation.

**Cut Money** Coins cut into smaller pieces to provide correspondingly smaller denominations. The cross on many medieval coins assisted the division of silver pennies into halfpence and farthings. Spanish dollars were frequently divided into *bits* which themselves became units of currency in America and the West Indies.

**Darlehnskassen** (German for "state loan notes"). Paper money issued during the First World War in an abortive bid to fill the shortage of coinage in circulation. These low-denomination notes failed to meet demand and were superseded by local issues of small *Notgeld* in 1916.

**Debasement** The reduction in the precious metal content of the coinage, widely practised since time immemorial by governments for economic reasons. British coins, for example, were debased from sterling (.925 fine) silver to .500 in 1920 and from silver to cupro-nickel in 1947.

**Decimalisation** A currency system in which the principal unit is subdivided into ten, a hundred, or a thousand fractions. Russia was the first country to decimalise, in 1534 when the rouble of 100 kopeks was introduced, but it was not till 1792 that France adopted the franc of 100 centimes and 1793 when the USA introduced the dollar of 100 cents. Most European countries decimalised their currency in the 19th century. Britain toyed with the idea, introducing the florin or tenth of a pound in 1849 as the first step, but did not complete the process till 1971. The last countries to decimalise were Malta and Nigeria, in 1972 and 1973 respectively.

**Demidiated** Heraldic term to describe the junction of two armorial devices, in which only half of each is shown.

**Demonetisation** The withdrawal of coins or paper money from circulation and declaring them to be worthless.

**Device** Heraldic term for the pattern or emblem on coins or paper notes.

**Die** Hardened piece of metal bearing a mirror image of the device to be struck on one side of a coin or medal.

**Die Proof** An impression, usually pulled on soft carton or India paper, of an *intaglio* engraving of a banknote, usually taken during the progress of the engraving to check the detail. Banknote proofs of this nature usually consist of the portrait or some detail of the design, such as the border, rather than the complete motif.

**Dodecagonal** Twelve-sided, a term applied to the nickel-brass threepence of Great Britain, 1937–67.

*Edward VIII dodecagonal threepence*

**Dump** Any primitive coin struck on a very thick *flan*, but more specifically applied to the circular pieces cut from the centre of Spanish dollars, countermarked with the name of the colony, a crown and the value, and circulated in New South Wales at 15 pence in 1813. See *Holey Dollar*.

**Duodecimal** Currency system based on units of twelve, i.e. medieval money of account (12 denarii = 1 soldo) which survived in Britain as 12 pence to the shilling as late as 1971.

**Ecclesiastical Coins** Coins struck by a religious authority, such as an archbishop, bishop, abbot, prior or the canons of a religious order. Such coins were common in medieval times but survived as late as the early 19th century, the bishops of Breslau (1817) and Gurk (1823) being the last prelates to exercise coinage rights. Coins were always struck by authority of the Pope at Rome till 1870 but since 1929 coinage has been struck at the Italian state mint on behalf of the Vatican.

**Edge Inscription** Lettering on the edge of a coin or medal to prevent clipping. Alluding to this, the Latin motto *Decus et Tutamen* (an ornament and a safeguard) was applied to the edge of English milled coins in the reign of Charles II.

**Edge Ornament** An elaboration of the *graining* found on many milled coins to prevent clipping, taking the form of tiny leaves, florets, interlocking rings, pellets and zigzag patterns. In some cases the ornament appears between layers of more conventional reeding.

**EF** Abbreviation for Extremely Fine.

**Effigy** An image or representation of a person, normally the head of state, a historical personage, or an allegorical figure, usually on the *obverse* or "heads" side of a coin or medal.

**Electrotype** A reproduction of a coin or medal made by an electrolytic process.

**Electrum** Alloy of gold and silver, sometimes called white gold, used for minting the staters of Lydia, 7th century BC, and other early European coins.

**Elongated Coin** An oval *medalet* created by passing a coin, such as an American cent, between rollers under pressure with the effect of squeezing it out and impressing on it a souvenir or commemorative motif.

**Emergency Money** Any form of money used in times of economic and political upheaval, when traditional kinds of currency are not available. Examples include the comparatively crude silver coins issued by the Royalists during the *Civil War* (1642–49), *obsidional* money, issued in time of siege, from Tyre (1122) to Mafeking (1900), the *Notgeld* issued by many German towns (1916–23), *encased money*, *fractional currency*, *guerrilla notes*, *invasion*, *liberation* and *occupation money* from the two World Wars and minor campaigns. Among the more recent examples may be cited the use of sweets and cheques in Italy (1976–77) and the issue of coupons and vouchers in many of the countries of the former Soviet Union pending the introduction of their own distinctive coins and notes.

**Enamelled Coins** Coins decorated by enamelling the obverse and reverse motifs in contrasting colours was an art practised by many jewellers in Birmingham and Paris in the 19th century, and revived in Europe and America in the 1970s.

**Encased Money** Postage and revenue stamps enclosed in small metal and mica-faced discs, circulated as small change in times of emergency. The practice was invented by John Gault, a Boston sewing-machine salesman, during the American Civil War (1862). The face of the stamp was visible through the transparent window, while the back of the disc was embossed with firms' advertisements. This practice was revived during and after the First World War when there was again a shortage of small coins. Encased stamps have also been recorded from France, Austria, Norway, Germany and Monaco. See also under *Stamp Money*.

**Engrailing** Technical term for the close serrations or vertical bars round the edge of a coin, applied as a security device.

**Engraving** The art of cutting lines or grooves in plates, blocks or dies. Numismatically this takes the form of engraving images into the face of the dies used in striking coins, a process which has now been almost completely superseded by *hubbing* and the use of *reducing machinery*. In the production of paper money, *intaglio* engraving is still commonly practised. In this process the engraver cuts the design into a steel die and the printing ink lies in the grooves. The paper is forced under great pressure into the grooves and picks up the ink, and this gives banknotes their characteristic ridged feeling to the touch. Nowadays many banknotes combine traditional intaglio engraving with multicolour lithography or photogravure to defeat the would-be counterfeiter.

**Epigraphy** The study of inscriptions, involving the classification and interpretation of coin legends, an invaluable adjunct to the study of a coin series, particularly the classical and medieval coins which, in the absence of dates and mintmarks, would otherwise be difficult to arrange in chronological sequence.

**Erasion** The removal of the title or effigy of a ruler from the coinage issued after his or her death. This process was practised in imperial Rome, and applied to the coins of Caligula, Nero and Geta, as part of the more general practice of *damnatio memoriae* (damnation of the memory) ordered by the Senate.

**Error** Mistakes on coins and paper money may be either caused at the design or engraving stage, or as a result of a fault in the production processes.

In the first category come mis-spellings in legends causing, in extreme cases, *blundered inscriptions*, or anachronisms or inaccuracies in details of the design. In the second, the most glaring error is the mule caused by marrying the wrong dies. Faulty alignment of dies can cause obverse and reverse to be out of true. Although many coins are issued with obverse and reverse upside down in relation to each other, this can also occur as an error in coins where both sides should normally be facing the same way up. Other errors caused at the production stage include striking coins in the wrong metal or with the wrong *collar* thus creating a different edge from the normal.

**Essay** (From the French *essai*, a trial piece). The term is applied to any piece struck for the purposes of examination, by parliamentary or financial bodies, prior to the authorisation of an issue of coins or paper money. The official nature of these items distinguishes them from *patterns*, which denote trial pieces often produced by mints or even private individuals bidding for coinage contracts.

**Evasion** Close copy or imitation of a coin, with sufficient deliberate differences in the design or inscription to avoid infringing counterfeit legislation. A good example is the imitation of Sumatran coins by European merchants, inscribed SULTANA instead of SUMATRA.

**Exergue** Lower segment of a coin or medal, usually divided from the rest of the *field* by a horizontal line, and often containing the date, value, ornament or identification symbols.

**Exonumia** Generic term for numismatic items not authorised by a government, e.g. *patterns*, *tokens*, *medalets* or *model coins*.

**F** Fine

**Face** The surface of a coin, medal or token, referred to as the *obverse* or the *reverse*. The corresponding faces of a paper note are more correctly termed *verso* and *recto*, but the coin terms are often used instead.

**Facing** Term for the portrait, usually on the obverse, which faces to the front instead of to the side (profile).

**Fantasy** Piece of metal purporting to be the coinage of a country which does not exist. Recent examples include the money of Atlantis and the Hutt River Province which declared its independence of Western Australia.

**FDC** Abbreviation for *Fleur de Coin*, a term denoting the finest possible condition of a coin.

**Fiat Money** Paper notes issued by a government but not redeemable in coin or bullion.

**Field** Flat part of the surface of a coin or medal, between the *legend*, the *effigy* and other raised parts of the design.

**Fillet** Heraldic term for the ribbon or headband on the effigy of a ruler or allegorical figure.

**Find** Term applied to an archaeological discovery of one or more coins. A large quantity of such material is described as a *hoard*.

**Flan** Alternative name for *blank* or *planchet*, the piece of metal struck between dies to produce a coin or medal.

**Forgery** An unauthorised copy or imitation, made with the intention of deceiving collectors. Forgeries intended to pass current for real coins or notes are more properly called *counterfeits*.

**Fractional Currency** Emergency issue of small-denomonation notes by the USA in 1863–5, following a shortage of coins caused by the Civil War. This issue superseded the *Postage Currency* notes, but bore the inscription "Receivable for all US stamps", alluding to the most popular medium of small change at that time. Denominations ranged from 3c to 50c.

**Franklinium** Cupro-nickel alloy developed by the Franklin Mint of Philadelphia and used for coins, medals and gaming tokens since 1967.

**Freak** An *error* or *variety* of a non-recurring type, usually caused accidentally during production.

**Frosting** Matt surface used for the high relief areas of many proof coins and medals, for greater contrast with the mirrored surface of the field.

**Funeral Money** Imitations of banknotes, used in China and Latin America in funeral ceremonies.

**Geat** (Git) Channel through which molten metal is ducted to the mould. Cast coins often show tiny protrusions known as geat marks.

**Ghost** Faint image of the design on one side of a coin visible on the other. Good examples were the British penny and halfpenny of George V, 1911–27, the ghosting being eliminated by the introduction of a smaller effigy in 1928.

**Globular** Coins struck on very thick *dumps* with convex faces. Examples include some Byzantine coins, and the *bullet money* of Siam (Thailand).

**Godless** (or *Graceless*) Epithet applied to any coin which omits the traditional reference to the deity, e.g. the British florin of 1849 which omitted D.G. (*Dei Gratia*, "by the Grace of God").

*1849 Victoria Godless florin*

**Gold** Precious metal, chemical symbol and numismatic abbreviation *Au*, from the *Latin Aurum*, used as a coinage medium from the 7th century BC till the present day. The purity of gold is reckoned in *carats* or a decimal system. Thus British gold sovereigns are 22 carat or .916 fine. Medieval coins were 23.5 carat or .995 fine, and some modern bullion coins are virtually pure gold, denoted by the inscription .999. Canadian maple leaves are now struck in "four nines" gold and bear the inscription .9999.

**Goodfor** Popular name for token coins and *emergency money* made of paper or card, from the inscription "Good for" or its equivalent in other languages (e.g. French *Bon pour* or Dutch *Goed voor*) followed by a monetary value. They have been recorded from Europe, Africa and America during times of economic crises or shortage of more traditional coinage.

**Gothic Crown** Popular name for the silver crown issued by the United Kingdom (1847–53), so-called on account of its script (more properly Old English, rather than Gothic).

**Grain** The weight of a single grain of wheat was taken as the smallest unit of weight in England. The troy grain was 1/5760 of a pound, while the avoirdupois grain was 1/7000 pound, the former being used in the weighing of precious metals and thus employed by numismatists in weighing coins. A grain is 1/480 troy ounce or 0.066 gram in the metric system.

**Graining** Term sometimes used as a synonym for the *reeding* on the edge of milled coins.

**Gripped Edge** Pattern of indentations found on the majority of American cents of 1797, caused by the milling process. Coins of the same date with a plain edge are rather scarcer.

**Guerrilla Money** Money issued in areas under the control of guerrillas and partisans during wartime range from the *veld ponds* of the Boers (1900–2) to the notes issued by the Garibaldi Brigade in Italy and the anti-fascist notes of Tito's forces in Yugoslavia. The most prolific issues were those produced in Luzon, Mindanao and Negros Occidental by the Filipino resistance during the Japanese occupation (1942–5).

**Guilloche** French term signifying the intricate pattern of curved lines produced by the rose engine and used as a security feature in the production of banknote, cheques, stocks and share certificates.

**Gun Money** Emergency coinage of Ireland (1689 –91) minted from gunmetal, a type of bronze used in the casting of cannon. All denominations of James II, from the sixpence to the crown, normally struck in silver, were produced in this base metal.

**Gutschein** German word for voucher or coupon, denoting the paper money used aboard ships of the Imperial Navy during the First World War. The last issue was made at Scapa Flow, 1918–19, during the internment of the High Seas Fleet.

**Hammered** Term denoting coins produce by the traditional method of striking a *flan* laid on an anvil with a hammer. A characteristic of hammered coins is their uneven shape which tended to encourage *clipping*. This abuse was gradually eliminated by the introduction of the screw press in the 15th century and the mechanisation of coining processes in the course of the 16th and 17th centuries.

**Hard Times Token** Copper piece the size of the large cent, issued in the USA, 1834–44, during a shortage of coins caused by the collapse of the Bank of the United States, the panic of 1837 and the economic crisis of 1839, the landmarks in the period known as the Hard Times. Banks suspended *specie* payments and the shortage of coinage was filled by tradesmen's tokens. Many of these were more in the nature of satirical *medalets* than circulating pieces.

**Hat Piece** Alternative name for the *bonnet piece* of James VI of Scotland, 1591.

**Hell Notes** Imitation paper money used in Chinese funeral ceremonies and buried with the dead to pay for services in the next world.

**Hoard** Accumulation of coins concealed in times of economic or political upheaval and discovered, often centuries later. Under English common law, such hoards are subject to th law of *treasure trove* if they contain precious metal.

**Hog Money** Popular name for the early coinage of Bermuda, issued about 1616. The coins were minted in brass with a silver wash and circulated at various values from twopence to a shilling. They derived their name from the hog depicted on the obverse, an allusion to the pigs introduced to the island in 1515 by Juan Bermudez.

**Holed** Term denoting two different categories: (a) coins which have been pierced for suspension as a form of jewellery or talisman, and (b) coins which have a hole as part of their design. In the latter category come the Chinese *cash* with a square hole, and numerous issues of the 19th and 20th centuries from many countries, with the object of reducing weight and metal without sacrificing overall diameter.

**Holey Dollar** Spanish silver peso of 8 reales with the centre removed. The resultant ring was counter-marked "New South Wales" and dated 1813, with "Five Shillings" on the reverse, and placed into circulation during a shortage of British coin. The centre, known as a *dump*, was circulated at 15 pence.

**Hub** Heavy circular piece of steel on which the *die* for a coin or medal is engraved. The process of cutting the die and transferring the master die, by means of intermediary *punches*, to the die from which the coins will be struck, is known as hubbing. Soft steel is used in the preliminary process, and after the design has been transferred, the hub is hardened by chemical action.

**Hybrid** Alternative name for a *mule*.

**Imitation Money** Also known as play money or toy money, it consists of coins and notes produced for games of chance (like Monopoly), children's toy shops and post offices, as tourist souvenirs, or for political satire (e.g. the shrinking pound or dollar). See also *funeral money*, *hell notes*, *model coins* and *skit notes*.

**Imprint** Inscription on a paper note giving the name of the printer.

**Incuse** Impression which cuts into the surface of a coin or medal, as opposed to the more usual raised relief. Many of the earliest coins, especially those with a device on one side only, bear an incuse impression often in a geometric pattern. An incuse impression appears on one side of the coins, reflecting the image on the other side. Few modern coins have had an incuse design, notable examples being the American half and quarter eagle gold coins of 1908–29 designed by Bela Pratt. Incuse inscriptions on a raised rim, however, are more common, and include the British *Cartwheel* coins of 1797 and the 20p coins since 1982.

**Inflation Money** Coins produced as a result of inflation date back to Roman times when bronze *minimi*, little bigger than a pinhead, circulated as *denarii*. Nearer the present day inflation has had devastating effects on the coinge and banknotes of Germany (1921–3), Austria (1923), Poland (1923), Hungary (1945–6), Greece (1946) and many Latin American countries since the 1980s. Hungary holds the record for the highest value of any note ever issued — one thousand million adopengos, which is written as 20,00 0,000,000,000,000,000,000,000,000 pengos.

**Ingot** Piece of precious metal, usually cast in a mould, and stamped with the weight and fineness. A convenient method of storing bullion, ingots have been used as currency in many countries, notably Russia and Japan.

**Inlay** Insertion into the surface of a coin or medal of another substance for decorative effect. e.g. Poland Amber Trade Routes 20zl (amber), Isle of Man Queen Mother centenery (pearl) and various coins incorporating rubies or diamonds.

**Intaglio** Form of *engraving* in which lines are cut into a steel die for the recess-printing of banknotes.

**Intrinsic**   The net metallic value of a coin, as distinguished from the nominal or face value.

**Iron**   Metal, chemical symbol *Fe* (from Latin *Ferrum*), used as a primitive form of currency from classical times onwards.   Iron spits (obeliskoi) preceded the obol as the lowest unit of Greek coinage, a handful of six spits being worth a drachma (from *drassomai*, "I grasp").   Cast iron coins were issued in China as a substitute for copper *cash*. Many of the emergency token issues of Germany during the First World War were struck in iron.   Iron coins were issued by Bulgaria in 1943. See also *Steel*.

**Ithyphallic**   (Greek for "erect penis"). Term descriptive of coins of classical Greece showing a satyr.

**Janiform**   Double profiles back to back, after the Roman god Janus.

**Jeton**   (From French *jeter*, to throw). Alternative term for *counter*, and used originally on the chequerboard employed by medieval accountants.   Nuremberg was the most important centre for the production of medieval jetons, often issued in lengthy portrait series. In modern parlance the term is often synonymous with *token*, though more specifically confined to pieces used in vending equipment, parking meters, laundromats, telephones and urban transport systems in many European countries. Apart from security, removing the temptation of vandals to break into the receptacles, the main advantage of such pieces is that they can be retariffed as charges increase, without any alteration in their design or composition, a method that is far cheaper than altering costly equipment to take larger coins.

**Jubilee Head**   The effigy of Queen Victoria by Joseph Boehm adopted for British coinage after the 1887 Golden Jubilee.

*William and Mary jugate heads on 1691 guinea*

**Jugate**   (From Latin *jugum*, a yoke). Alternative to *accolated* or *conjoined* to denote overlapping profiles of rulers.

**Key Date**   Term describing the rarest in a long-running series of coins with the dates changed at annual intervals.

**Kipperzeit**   German term meaning the time of clipped money, denoting the period during and after the Thirty Years War (1618–48) in which debased and clipped money was in circulation.

**Klippe**   Rectangular or square pieces of metal bearing the impression of a coin. Coins of this type were first struck in Sweden in the 16th century and were subsequently produced in many of the German states. The idea has been revived in recent years as a medium for striking commemorative pieces.

**Knife Money**   Cast bronze pieces, with an elongated blade and a ring at one end to facilitate stringing together in bunches, were used as currency in China from the 9th century BC until the 19th century.

**Kreditivsedlar**   (Swedish for "credit notes"). The name given to the first issue of paper money made in the western world. Paper money of this type was the brainchild of Johan Palmstruch at Riga in 1652, but nine years elapsed before it was implemented by the Stockholm Bank. The notes were redeemable in copper *platmynt*.

**Laureate**   Heraldic term for a laurel wreath, often framing a state emblem or shown, in the Roman fashion, as a crown on the ruler's forehead.

**Leather Money**   Pieces of leather embossed with an official device have been used as money on various occasions, including the sieges of Faenza and Leiden and in the Isle of Man in the 15th and 16th centuries. Several towns in Austria and Germany produced leather tokens during and after the First World War.

**Legal Tender**   Coins or paper money which are declared by law to be current money and which tradesmen and shopkeers are obliged to accept in payment for goods or services. (See *Money and the Law*).

**Legend**   The inscription on a coin or medal.

**Liberation Money**   Paper money prepared for use in parts of Europe and Asia, formerly under Axis occupation. Liberation notes were used in France, Belgium and the Netherlands in 1944–5, while various different Japanese and Chinese notes were overprinted for use in Hong Kong when it was liberated in 1945.   Indian notes overprinted for use in Burma were issued in 1945–6 when that country was freed from Japanese occupation.

**Ligature**   (From Latin *ligatus*, bound together). Term denoting the linking of two letters in a *legend*, e.g. Æ and Œ.

**Long Cross Coinage** Type of coinage introduced by King Henry III in 1247, deriving its name from the reverse which bore a cross whose arms extended right to the edge to help safeguard the coins against *clipping*. This remained the style of the silver penny, its fractions and multiples, till the reign of Henry VII, and vestiges of the long cross theme is seen in the silver coins throughout the remaining years of the Tudor period.

*Henry III groat showing the
Long Cross on the reverse*

**Love Token** A coin which has been altered by smoothing one or both surfaces and engraving initials, dates, scenes, symbols of affection and messages thereon.

**Lushbourne** English word for base pennies made of inferior silver, said to have emanated from Luxembourg, from which the name derived. These coins were first minted under John the Blind who adopted the curious spelling of his name EIWANES in the hope that illiterate English merchants might confuse it with EDWARDVS and thus be accepted as coin issued in the name of Edward III. Lushbournes were also minted by Robert of Bethune, William I of Namur and the bishops of Toul during the mid-14th century.

**Lustre** The sheen or bloom on the surface of an uncirculated coin resulting from the centrifugal flow of metal caused by striking.

**Magnimat** Trade name used by VDM (*Verein Deutscher Metallwerke*) for a high-security alloy containing copper, nickel and magnetised steel. First used for the 5 deutschemark coin of 1975, it has since been adopted for other high-value coins in Germany and other countries.

**Manilla** Copper, bronze or brass rings, sometimes shaped like horseshoes and sometimes open, with flattened terminals, used as currency in West Africa until recent years.

**Matrix** Secondary die for a coin or medal, produced from the master die by means of an intermediate punch. In this way dies can be duplicated from the original cut on the reducing machine.

**Matt or Matte** Finely granulated surface or overall satin finish to proof coins, a style which was briefly fashionable at the turn of the century. The Edward VII proof set of 1902 is a notable example. In more recent years many issues produced by the Franklin Mint have been issued with this finish.

**Maundy Money** Set of small silver coins, in denominations of 1, 2, 3 and 4 pence, distributed by the reigning British monarch to the poor and needy on Maundy Thursday. The custom dates back to the Middle Ages, but in its present form, of distributing pence to as many men and women as the years in the monarch's age, it dates from 1666. At first ordinary silver pennies and multiples were used but after they went out of everyday use distinctive silver coins were produced specifically for the purpose from the reign of George II (1727–60) onwards. For centuries the ceremony took place in Westminster Abbey but since 1955 other venues have been used in alternate years.

**Medal** (French *medaille*, Italian *medaglia*, from Latin *metallum*). A piece of metal bearing devices and legends commemorating an event or person, or given as an award. Military medals date from the 16th and 17th centuries, but were not generally awarded to all ranks till the 19th century. Commemora-tive medals can be traced back to Roman times, but in their present form they date from the Italian Renaissance when there was a fashion for large cast portrait medals.

**Medalet** A small medal, generally 25mm or less in diameter.

**Medallion** Synonym for medal, but usually confined to those with a diameter of 50mm or more.

**Milling** Process denoting the mechanical production of coins, as opposed to the handmade technique implied in *hammering*. It alludes to the use of watermills to drive the machinery of the screw presses and blank rollers developed in the 16th century. As the even thickness and diameter of milled coins permitted a security edge, the term milling is popularly, though erroneously, used as a synonym for *graining* or *reeding*.

**Mint** The place in which coins and medals are produced. Mint condition is a term sometimes used to denote pieces in an uncirculated state.

**Mint Set** A set of coins or medals in the package or case issued by the mint. See also *year set*.

**Mintmark** A device appearing on a coin to denote the place of minting. Athenian coins of classical times have been recorded with up to 40 different marks, denoting individual workshops. In the

4th century AD the Romans adopted this system to identify coins struck in provincial mints. This system was widely used in the Middle Ages and survives in France and Germany to this day. Initials and symbols are also used to identify mints, especially where the production of a coin is shared between several different mints. From 1351 onwards symbols were adopted in England to denote periods between trials of the *Pyx*, and thus assist the proper chronological sequence of coins, in an era prior to the adoption of dating. These mintmarks continued into the 17th century, but gradually died out as the use of dates became more widespread. See also *countermark* and *privy mark*.

**Mionnet Scale**  Scale of nineteen diameters covering all sizes of coins belonging to the classical period, devised by the French numismatist, Theodore-Edme Mionnet (1770–1842) during the compilation of his fifteen-volume catalogue of the numismatic collection in the Bibliotheque Nationale in Paris.

**Mirror Finish**  The highly polished surface of proof coins.

**Misstrike**  A coin or medal on which the impression has been struck off-centre.

**Model Coin**  Tiny pieces of metal, either reproducing the designs of existing coins (used as play money by children) or, more specifically, denoting patterns produced by Joseph Moore and Hyam Hyams in their attempts to promote an improved subsidiary coinage in 19th century Britain. These small coins were struck in bronze with a brass or silver centre and were designed to reduce the size of the existing cumbersome range of pence, halfpence and farthings.

**Modified Effigy**  Any coin in which the profile on the obverse has been subtly altered. Examples include minor changes in the Victorian Young Head and Old Head effigies and the George V profile by Sir Bertram Mackennal.

**Money Order**  Certificate for a specified amount of money, which may be transmitted by post and encashed at a money order office or post office. This system was pioneered by Britain and the United States in the early 19th century and is now virtually worldwide. The term is now confined to certificates above a certain value, the terms *postal order* and *postal note* being used for similar certificates covering small amounts.

**Mule**  Coin whose obverse is not matched with its official or regular reverse. Mules include the erroneous combination of dies from different reigns, but in recent years such hybrids have arisen in mints where coins for several countries are struck. Examples include the Coronation Anniversary crowns combining Ascension and Isle of Man dies and the 2 cent coins with Bahamas and New Zealand dies. *Restrikes* of rare American coins have been detected in which the dated die has been paired with the wrong reverse die, e.g. the 1860 restrike of the rare 1804 large cent.

**Mute**  An *anepigraphic* coin, identifiable only by the devices struck on it.

**Nail Mark**  Small indentation on ancient coins. The earliest coins of Asia Minor developed from the electrum *dumps* which merchants marked with a broken nail as their personal guarantee of value, the ancient counterpart of the *chop* marks used in China and Japan.

**NCLT Coins**  Abbreviation for "Non Circulating Legal Tender", a term devised by modern coin catalogues to denote coins which, though declared *legal tender*, are not intended for general circulation on account of their precious metal content or superior finish.

**Nicked Coin**  Coin bearing a tiny cut or nick in its edge. Silver coins were tested by this method, especially in the reign of Henry I (1100–35) when so many base silver pennies were in circulation. Eventually people refused to accept these nicked coins a problem which was only overcome when the state decreed that all coins should have a nick in them.

**Nickel**  Metallic element, chemical symbol *Ni*, a hard white metal relatively resistant to tarnish, and extensively used as a cheap substitute for silver. It was first used for the American 5 cent coin in 1866, hence its popular name which has stuck ever since, although nowadays the higher denominations are minted in an alloy of copper and nickel. Although best known as a silver substitute, nickel was widely used in Jamaica (1869–1969) for halfpence and pennies and in British West Africa for the tiny 1/10th pennies (1908–57). Pure nickel was used for French francs and German marks, but usually it is alloyed with copper or zinc to produce *cupro-nickel* or nickel brass.

**Notaphily**  Hybrid word from Latin *nota* (note) and Greek philos (love), coined about 1970 to denote the branch of numismatics devoted to the study of paper money.

**Notgeld**  German word meaning emergency money, applied to the *tokens*, in metals, wood, leather and even ceramic materials, issued during the First World War when coinage disappeared from circulation. These tokens were soon superseded by low-denomination paper money issued by shops and businessmen in denominations from 10 to 50 pfennige and known as *kleine Notgeld* (small emergency money). These notes were prohibited in

September 1922 but by that time some 50,000 varieties are thought to have been issued. Inflation raced out of control and the government permitted a second issue of local notes, known as *large Notgeld*, as the denomi-nations were in thousands, and latterly millions, of marks. Some 3,600 types appeared in 1922 and over 60,000 in 1923 alone. These mementoes of the German hyperinflation ceased to circulate in 1924 when the currency was reformed.

**Numismatics** The study of coins, medals and other related fields, a term derived from the Latin *numisma* and Greek *nomisma* (money).

**Obsidional Currency** (From Latin *obsidium*, a siege). Term for *emergency money* produced by the defenders of besieged towns and cities. These usually took the form of pieces of silver plate, commandeered for the purpose, crudely marked with an official device and the value. Instances of such seige coinage have been recorded from the 12th to the 19th centuries.

**Obverse** The "heads" side of a coin or medal, generally bearing the effigy of the head of state or an allegorical figure.

**Off Metal** Term denoting a piece struck in a metal other than the officially authorisied or issued alloy. This originally applied to *patterns* which were often struck in lead or copper instead of gold and silver as trial pieces or to test the dies; but in recent years it has applied to collectors' versions, e.g. proofs in platinum, gold or silver of coins normally issued in bronze or cupro-nickel.

**Overdate** One or more digits in a date altered by superimposing another figure. Alterations of this kind, by means of small hand punches, were made to dated dies so that they could be used in years other than that of the original manufacture. Coins with overdates invariably show traces of the original digit.

**Overstrike** Coin, token or medal produced by using a previously struck pieces as a flan. The Bank of England dollar of 1804 was overstruck on Spanish pieces of eight, and examples showing traces of the original coins are worth a good premium.

**Paduan** Name given to imitations of medals and bogus coins produced in Italy in the 16th century, and deriving from the city of Padua where forgeries of bronze sculpture were produced for the antique market.

**Patina** Oxidation forming on the surface of metallic objects. So far as coins and medals are concerned, this applies mainly to silver, brass, bronze and copper pieces which may acquire oxidation from the atmosphere, or spectacular patination from salts in the ground in which they have been buried. In extreme forms patina leads to verdigris and other forms of rust which corrode the surface, but in uncirculated coins it may be little more than a mellowing of the original *lustre*. Coins preserved in blue velvet presentation cases often acquire a subtle toning from the dyes in the material.

**Pattern** Piece resembling a coin or medal, prepared by the mint to the specifications or on the authorisation of the coin-issuing authority, but also applied to pieces produced by mints when tendering for coinage or medal contracts. Patterns may differ from the final coins as issued in the type of alloy used (*off metal*) but more often they differ in details of the design.

**Pellet** Raised circular ornament used as a spacing device between words and abbreviations in the *legend* of coins and medals. Groups of pellets were also used as ornaments in the angles of the cross on the reverse of English silver pennies.

**Piece de Plaisir** (French for "fancy piece"). Term given to coins struck in a superior precious metal, or to a superior finish, or on a much thicker flan than usual. See *off metal*, *piedfort* and *proof*.

**Piedfort (Piefort)** Piece struck with coinage dies on a *flan* of much more than normal thickness. This practice originated in France in the late 16th century and continues to the present day. In recent years it has been adopted by mints in Britain and other countries as a medium for collectors' pieces.

**Pile** Lower die incorporating the obverse motif, used in striking coins and medals. See also *trussel*.

**Planchet** French term used as an alternative for *blank* or *flan*.

**Plaque** or **Plaquette** Terms sometimes used for medals struck on a square or rectangular flan.

**Plaster** Cast taken from the original model for a coin or medal sculpted by an artist, and used in modern reducing machines in the manufacture of the master *die*.

**Plated Coins** Coins stuck in base metal but given a wash of silver or some other precious metal. This expedient was adopted in inflationary times, from the Roman Republic (91 BC) till the Tudor period. American cents of 1943 were struck in steel with a zinc coating, and more recently *clad* coins have produced similar results.

**Platinum** The noblest of all precious metals, platinum has a higher specific gravity than gold and a harder, brighter surface than silver. Until an industrial application was discovered in the mid-19th century, it was regarded as of little value, and was popular with counterfeiters as a cheap substitute for gold in their forgeries which, with a light gold wash, could be passed off as genuine. It was first used for circulating coins in Russia (the chief source of the metal since 1819) and 3, 6 and 12 rouble coins were mined at various times between 1828 and 1845. In recent years platinum has been a popular metal for limited-edition proof coins.

**Platmynt** (Swedish for "plate money"). Large copper plates bearing royal cyphers and values from half to ten dalers produced in Sweden between 1643 and 1768. They represented laudable attempts by a country rich in copper to produce a coinage in terms of its silver value, but the net result was far too cumbersome to be practical. The weight of the daler plate, for example, ranged from 766 grams to 1.1kg, and special carts had to be devised to transport them!

**Plugged Coins** Coins struck predominantly in one metal, but containing a small plug of another. This curious practice may be found in the farthings of Charles II (1684–85) and the halfpence or farthings of James II (1685–87), which were struck in tin, with a copper plug, to defeat forgers.

**Porcelain Money** Tokens made of porcelain circulated in Thailand from the late 18th century till 1868. The Meissen pottery struck tokens in 1920–22 as a form of small *Notgeld*, using reddish-brown Bottger stoneware and white *bisque* porcelain. These ceramic tokens circulated in various towns of Saxony.

**Postage Currency** Small paper notes in denominations of 5, 10, 25 and 50 cents, issued by the US federal government in 1862–63, were thus inscribed and had reproductions of postage stamps engraved on them — five 5c stamps on the 25c and five 10c stamps on the 50c notes. The earliest issue even had perforations in the manner of stamps, but this unnecessary device was soon done away with. See also *stamp money*.

**Postal Notes or Orders** Low-value notes intended for transmission by post and encashable at post offices. Introduced by Britain in 1883, they were an extension of the earlier *money order* system, and are now issued by virtually every country.

**Potin** (French for pewter). Alloy of copper, tin, lead and silver used as a coinage metal by the Celtic tribes of eastern Gaul at the beginning of the Christian era.

**Privy Mark** Secret mark incorporated in the design of a coin or medal to identify the minter, or even the particular die used. The term is also used more loosely to denote any small symbol or initials appearing on a coin other than a *mint mark*, and is sometimes applied to the symbols associated with the trial of the *Pyx* found on English coins.

**Prize Coins** Coins of large size and value struck primarily as prizes in sporting contests. this

principle dates from the late 5th century BC when Syracuse minted decadrachms as prizes in the Demareteian Games. The most notable example in modern times is the lengthy series of talers and five-franc coins issued by the Swiss cantons since 1842 as prizes in the annual shooting festivals, the last of which honoured the Lucerne contest of 1939.

**Profile** A side view of the human face, widely used as a coinage effigy.

**Proof** Originally a trial strike testing the *dies*, but now denoting a special collectors' version struck with dies that have been specially polished on *flans* with a mirror finish. Presses operating at a very slow speed, or multi-striking processes, are also used.

**Propaganda Notes** Paper money containing a political slogan or a didactic element. During the Second World War forgeries of German and Japanese notes were produced by the Allies and additionally inscribed or overprinted with slogans such as "Co-Prosperity Sphere— What is it worth?" (a reference to the Japanese occupied areas of SE Asia). Forged dollars with anti-American propaganda were airdropped over Sicily by the Germans in 1943 and counterfeit pounds with Arabic propaganda over Egypt in 1942–43. Various anti-communist organisations liberated propaganda forgeries of paper money by balloon over Eastern Europe during the Cold War period.

**Provenance Mark** Form of *privy mark* denoting the source of the metal used in coins. Examples include the plumes or roses on English coins denoting silver from Welsh or West of England mines, and the elephant or elephant and castle on gold coins denoting bullion imported by the African Company. Coins inscribed VIGO (1702–03) or LIMA (1745–46) denote bullion seized from the Spaniards by Anglo-Dutch privateers and Admiral Anson respectively. Other provenance marks on English coins include the letters EIC and SSC, denoting bullion imported by the East India Company or the South Sea Company.

**Pseudo Coins** Derisory term coined in recent years to signify pieces of precious metal, often struck in *proof* versions only, aimed at the international investment market. Many of these pieces, though bearing a nominal face value, are not *legal tender* in the countries purporting to issue them and in many cases they go straight from the overseas mint where they are produced to coin dealers in America and western Europe, without ever appearing in the so-called country of origin. See also *NCLT coins*.

**Punch or Puncheon** Intermediate *die* whereby working dies can be duplicated from the master die, prior to the striking of coins and medals.

**Pyx** Box in which a specimen from every 15 pounds troy weight of gold and every 60 pounds of silver minted in England is kept for annual trial by weight and assay. Many of the *mintmarks* on English coins of the 14th–17th centuries were in use from one trial to the next and still exist today and can therefore be used to date them.

**Reducing Machinery** Equipment designed on the pantographic principle for transferring the image from a *plaster* to a *hub* and reducing it to the size of the actual coin or medal. The image is transferred by means of a stylus operating rather like a gramophone needle, but working from the centre to the outer edge.

**Reeding** Security edging on coins, consisting of close vertical ridges. As a rule, this appears all round the edge but some coins, e.g. New Zealand's 50c (1967) and the Isle of Man's £1 (1978) have segments of reeding alternating with a plain edge, to help blind and partially sighted persons to identify these coins.

**Re-issue** A coin or note issued again after an extended lapse of time.

**Relief** Raised parts of the *obverse* and *reverse* of coins and medals, the opposite of *incuse*.

**Remainder** A note from a bank or issuing authority which has never been circulated, due to inflation, political changes or bank failure. Such notes, some-times in partial or unfinished state (e.g. missing serial numbers or signatures), are generally unloaded on to the numismatic market at a nominal sum and provide a good source of inexpensive material for the beginner.

**Restrike** Coin, medal or token produced from *dies* subsequent to the original use. Usually restrikes are made long after the original and can often be identified by marks caused by damage, pitting or corrosion of the dies after they were taken out of service.

**Retrograde** Term describing inscriptions running from right to left, or with the letters in a mirror image, thought to arise from unskilled die-cutters failing to realise that inscriptions have to be engraved in negative form to achieve a positive impression. Retrograde inscriptions are common on ancient Greek coins, but also found on Roman and Byzantine coins.

**Reverse** The side of a coin or medal regarded as of lesser importance; in colloquial parlance, the "tails" side.

**Saltire** Heraldic term for a cross in the shape of an X.

**Sandwich** Coin *blank* consisting of thin outer layers in one alloy bonded to a core in another. See *clad coins.*

**Sceat** (Anglo-Saxon for "treasure", or German *Schatz*). Money of account in Kent early in the 7th century as the twelfth part of a shilling or Merovingian gold tremissis. As a silver coin, it dates from about AD 680–700 and weighed about 20 grains, putting it on par with the Merovingian denier or penny. Sceats spread to other parts of England in the 8th century but tended to decline in weight and value, but from about 760 it was gradually superseded by the silver penny minted under Offa and his successors.

**Scissel** The clippings of metal left after a *blank* has been cut. Occasionally one of these clippings accidentally adheres to the blank during the striking process, producing characteristic crescent-shaped flaws which are present on on the finished coin.

**Scrip** Paper money of restricted validity or circulation, e.g.*Bafs* and other military scrip used in canteens and post exchanges.

**Scyphate** (Greek *scypha*, a skiff or small boat). Byzantine coin with a concave *flan*.

**Sede Vacante** (Latin for "Vacant See"). Coins struck at *ecclesiastical mints* between the death of a prelate and the election of his successor are often thus inscribed. This practice originated at Rome in the 13th century.

**Seignorage or Seigneurage** Royalty or percentage paid by persons bringing *bullion* to a mint for conversion into coin, but nowadays synonymous with the royalty paid by mints in respect of the precious metal versions of coins sold direct to collectors. It arises from the medieval right of the king to a small portion of the proceeds of a mint, and amounted to a tax on moneying. It has also been applied to the money accruing to the state when the coinage is re-issued in an alloy of lesser fineness, as, for example, the debased sovereigns of Henry VIII in 20 instead of 23 carat gold, the king's treasury collecting the difference.

**Series** Term applied to sets of medals of a thematic character, which first became fashionable in the early 18th century. Jean Dassier pioneered the medallic series in the 1720s with his set of 72 medals portraying the rulers of France till Louis XV. The idea was developed by J. Kirk, Sir Edward Thomason, J. Mudie and A. J. Stothard in Britain, and by Moritz Fuerst and Amedee Durand in Europe. The fashion died out in the 19th century, but has been revived in America and Europe since 1964.

**Serrated** Having a notched or toothed edge, rather like a cogwheel. Coins of this type, struck in *electrum,* an alloy of silver and gold, are known from Carthage in the 2nd century BC, and some silver denarii of Rome in the 2nd century AD also come into this category.

**Sexagesimal System**   Monetary system in which the principal unit is divided into 60 parts. The oldest system in the Western world was based on the gold talent of 60 minae and the mina of 60 shekels. In medieval Europe 60 groschen were worth a fine mark; in England from 1551, the silver coinage was based on the crown of 60 pence, and in the south German states till 1873 the gulden was worth 60 kreuzers.

**Shin Plasters**   Derisory term originally applied to the Continental currency notes issued during the American War of Independence, the fractional currency of the Civil War period and also the low-denomination notes of Canada between 1870 and 1935, but often applied indiscriminately to any other low-denomination, small-format notes.

**Short Cross Coinage**   Term for the silver coinage introduced by Henry II in 1180 and minted till 1247 at which time it was replaced by the *Long Cross* type. The termination of the arms of the cross on the reverse well within the circumference encouraged the dishonest practice of *clipping*.

*Henry II penny showing the
Short Cross on the reverse*

**Shroff Mark**   A *countermark* applied by Indian bankers or merchants to attest the full weight and purity of coins. See also *chop*.

**Siege Money**   See *Obsidional Currency*

**Silver**   Precious metal, chemical symbol *Ag*, numismatic abbreviation *Ar*, from Latin *Argentum*, widely used as a coinage metal from the 6th century BC to the present day.

**Sterling silver**   denotes an alloy of .925 fine silver with .075 copper. Fine silver alloys used over the past 2,500 years have ranged from .880 to .960 fine, but base silver has also been all too common. British coins from 1920 to 1946 were struck in .500 fine silver, while alloys of lesser fineness are known as *billon* or *vellon*. Silver alloyed with gold produces a metal called *electrum*, used for the earliest coinage of the western world, the staters of Lydia in the 7th century BC. Since 1970 silver as a medium for circulating coinage has almost virtually disappeared, yet the volume of silver coins for sale to collectors has risen considerably in recent years.

**Skit Note**   Piece of paper masquerading as a banknote. It differs from a *counterfeit* in that its design parodies that of a genuine note, often for political, satirical or advertising reasons. Others were produced as April Fools' Day jokes or a form of Valentine (e.g. the Bank of Lovers). In recent years they have been produced as advertising gimmicks, or as coupons permitting a discount off the list price of goods.

**Slug**   Popular name for the $50 gold pieces produced by private mints in California in the mid-19th century. The term is also applied nowadays to *tokens* intended for use in gaming machines.

**Spade Guinea**   Name given to the guineas of George III issued between 1787 and 1799 because the shield on the reverse design resembled the shape of a spade. In Victorian times the spade guinea was extensively copied in brass for gaming counters.

**Spade Money**   Cast bronze pieces resembling miniature spades and other agricultural implements, used as money and derived from the actual implements which had previously been used in barter. Often referred to as *Pu* or *Boo* money.

**Specie**   Financial term denoting money in the form of precious metals (silver and gold), usually struck as coin, as opposed to money in the form of paper notes and bills of exchange. It occurs in the name of some European coins (e.g. *speciedaler*, *speciestaler* and *speciesducat*) to denote the use of fine silver or gold.

**Specimen**   Generally used to denote a single piece, but more specifically applying to a coin in a special finish, less than *proof* in quality but superior to the general circulating version. It also denotes paper notes intended for circulation between banks or for press publicity and distinguished from the generally issued version by zero serial numbers, punch holes or a security endorsement.

**Spintriae**   Metal tokens produced in Roman imperial times, with erotic motifs, thought to have been tickets of admission to brothels.

**Spit**   Copper or iron rod used as a primitive form of currency in the Mediterranean area. The Greek word *belos* meant a spit, dart or bolt, and from this came the word *obolos* used for a coin worth a 6th of a drachma.

**Stamp Money**   Both postage and revenue (fiscal) stamps have circulated as money during shortages of coins, from the American Civil War onwards. *Encased postage stamps* were used in the USA, 1861–62, before they were superseded by *Postage Currency* notes, but the same expedient was adopted by many countries during and immediately after the First World War. Stamps affixed to special cards have circulated as money in Rhodesia (now Zimbabwe) in 1900, the French colonies and Turkey during the First World War, in Spain during the Civil War (1936–39) and the Philippines during the Second World War. Stamps printed on thick card, with an inscription on the reverse signifying their parity with silver coins, were issued in Russia (1917–18) and also in Armenia, the Crimea and the Ukraine (1918–20). During the Second World War Ceylon (now Sri Lanka) and several Indian states issued small money cards with contemporary stamps printed on them.

**Steel**   Refined and tempered from *iron*, and used in chromed or stainless versions as a coinage metal in the 20th century. Zinc-coated steel cents were issued by the USA (1943) but in the form known as *acmonital* (nickel steel) it has been extensively used by Italy since 1939. Other alloys of nickel and steel have been used for coins of the Philippines (1944–45) and Roumania since 1963. Chrome steel was used by France for 5 centime coins in 1961–64. Copper-clad steel is now extensively used for subsidiary coins formerly struck in bronze.

**Sterling**   Word of uncertain origin denoting money of a standard weight and fineness, and hence the more general meaning of recognised worth. The traditionally accepted derivation from the Easterlings, north German merchants who settled in London in the 13th century and produced silver pennies of uniform fineness, is unlikely as the term has been found in documents a century earlier. A more plausible explanation is from Old English *steorling* ("little coin with a star"), alluding to Viking pennies with this device, or even as a diminutive of *stater*. Sterling silver denotes silver of .925 fineness.

**Stone Money**   Primitive currency in the form of large stone discs, used in West Africa in the pre-colonial period, and in the Pacific island of Yap (now Micronesia) as recently as 1940.

**Striation**   A pattern of alternate light and dark parallel marks or minute grooves on the surface of a coin or medal. In the latter case it is sometimes done for textural effect, but in coins it may result from faulty *annealing*. Deliberate ridging of the surface, however, was a distinctive feature of Japanese *koban* and *goryoban* coins of 1736–1862.

**Styca**   Name given to the debased silver *sceats* of Northumbria in the 8th century.

**Tael**   Chinese unit of weight corresponding to the European ounce and sometimes referred to as a liang. It was a measure of silver varying between 32 and 39 grams. In the 19th century it served as *money of account*, 100 British or Mexican trade dollars being worth 72 tael. The term has also been loosely applied to the Chinese silver yuan, although this was worth only .72 tael, or 7 mace and 2 candareens (10 candareens = 1 mace; 10 mace = 1 tael).

**Thrymsa**   Early Anglo-Saxon gold coin based on the Merovingian tremissis or third-solidus, current in Kent, London and York around AD 63–75.

**Tical**   Unit of weight in Thailand, first appearing as coins in the form of crudely shaped *bullet money* current from the 14th till the late 19th centuries. When European-style coins were introduced in 1860 the word was retained as a denomination (32 solot = 16 atts = 8 peinung or sio = 4 songpy or sik = 2 fuang= 1 salung or quarter-tical. The currency was decimalised in 1909 (100 satangs = 1 tical), and the tical was superseded by the baht about 1950.

**Tin**   Metallic element, chemical symbol *Sn* (from Latin *Stannum*). Because of its unstable nature and tendency to oxidise badly when exposed to the atmosphere, it is unsatisfactory as a coinage metal, but has been used on several occasions, notably in Malaya, Thailand and the East Indies. In was also used for British halfpence and farthings, 1672–92.

**Token**   Any piece of money whose nominal value is greater than its intrinsic value is, strictly speaking, a token or promise. Thus most of the coins issued since 1964 can be regarded in this light, but numismatists reserve the term for a piece of limited validity and circulation, produced by tradesmen, chambers of commerce and other organisations during times of a shortage of government coinage. The term is also loosely applied to metal tickets of admission, such as *communion tokens*, or *jetons* and *counters* intended for games of chance. Tokens with a nominal value may be produced for security reasons to lessen the possibility of theft from milk bottles, vending machines, telephones, parking meters and transport facilities. Tokens exchangeable for goods have been issued by co-operative societies and used in prisons and internment camps in wartime. In addition to the traditional coinage alloys, tokens have been produced in ceramics, plastics, wood, stout card, leather and even rubber, in circular, square or polygonal shapes.

**Tombac**   Type of brass alloy with a high copper content, used in coinage requiring a rich golden colour. It is, in fact, a modern version of the *aurichalcum* used by the Romans. It was used for the Canadian 5-cent coins of 1942–43, while 5- and 10-pfennig coins of Germany have a tombac cladding on a steel core.

**Touchpiece** Coin kept as a lucky charm, but more specifically the medieval gold angel of England which was worn round the neck as an antidote to scrofula, otherwise known as king's evil, from the belief that the reigning monarch possessed the power of healing by touch. The ceremony of touching for king's evil involved the suspension of an angel round the victim's neck, hence the prevalence of these coins pierced for suspension.

**Trade Coins** Coins widely used as a medium of international trade, often far beyond the boundaries of the country issuing them. The earliest examples were the Aiginetan turtles and Athenian tetrdrachms of the classical period. In the Middle Ages the English *sterling* was widely prized on account of its silver purity. Arab dinars and Italian florins were popular as gold coins in late-medieval times, while the British gold sovereign has been the preferred gold coin of modern times. The Maria Theresa silver thaler of Austria, with its date frozen at 1782, has been minted widely down to the present time for circulation in the Near and Middle East as a trade coin. Trade dollars were minted by Britain, the USA, the Netherlands and Japan to compete with the Spanish, and later the Mexican, peso or 8-reales coins as a trading medium in the Far East.

**Transport Tokens** Coin-like pieces of metal, plastic or card, issued by companies and corporations to employees and exchangeable for rides on municipal transport systems, date from the mid-19th century. In more recent times similar tokens have been used in many countries to activate turnstiles in buses, trams and rapid-transit railway systems.

**Treasury Note** Paper money worth 10 shillings or one pound, issued by the British Treasury on the outbreak of the First World War when *specie* payments were suspended, and continuing till 1928 when the Bank of England took over responsibility for note-issuing.

**Treasure Trove** Articles of precious metal concealed in times of economic or political upheaval and discovered years (often centuries) later are deemed by law to be treasure trove (from the French word *trouve*, found). For further details see *Money and the Law*.

**Trial Plate** Plate of the same metal as the current coinage against which the fineness and quality of the coins produced are compared and tested.

**Troy Weight** System of weights derived from the French town of Troyes whose standard pound was adopted in England in 1526. It continued in Britain till 1879 when it was abolished, with the exception of the troy ounce and its decimal parts and multiples, which were retained for gold, silver, platinum and precious stones. The troy ounce of 480 grains is used for weighing coins.

**Truncation** Stylised cut at the base of a coinage effigy, sometimes containing a die number, engraver's initials or *mintmark*.

**Trussel** Reverse die in *hammered* coinage, the opposite of the *pile*.

**Type** Principal motif on a coin or medal, enabling numismatists to identify the issue.

**Type Set** A set of coins comprising one of each coin in a particular series, regardless of the actual date of issue.

**Uncirculated** Term used in grading coins to denote specimens in perfect condition, with original mint lustre. In recent years the term "Brilliant Uncirculated" has been adopted (abbreviated as BUnc or BU) both to indicate the condition of a coin, and, by The Royal Mint, to indicate the standard to which some coins are minted, being a standard between Circulation and Proof.

**Uniface** Coin with a device on one side only.

**Vecture** Term (mainly used in the US) for a *transport token*.

**Veiled Head** The effigy of Queen Victoria by Thomas Brock adopted for British coinage after 1893 — often referred to as the "Old Head" coinage.

**Veld Pond** (Dutch for "field pound"). Gold coin struck by the Boer guerrillas at Pilgrims Rest in 1902, in imitation of the British sovereign.

**VF** Abbreviation for Very Fine, used to describe the state of a coin or medal.

**VG** Abbreviation for Very Good, used to describe the state of a coin or medal.

**Vignette** Strictly speaking the pictorial element of a paper note shading off into the surrounding unprinted paper rather than having a clearly defined border or frame; but nowadays applied generally to the picture portion of a banknote, as opposed to portrait, armorial or numeral elements.

**Vis-à-Vis** (French for "face to face"). Term describing coins with double portraits of rulers, their profiles or busts facing each other. A good example is the English coinage of Philip and Mary, 1554–58.

**Wampum** Barter currency of the North American Indians, composed of shells of *Venus mercenaria* strung together to form belts or "fathoms" worth 5 shillings. Wampum were tariffed variously from three to six to the English penny in the American colonies till 1704.

**Wire Money** Primitive currency of the Maldive Islands in the form of lengths of silver wire known as lari, from which the modern currency unit *laree* is derived. The term was also applied to English coins of the 18th century in which the numerals of value were exceptionally thin, resembling wire.

**Wooden Coins** Thin pieces of wood used as tokens are known from many parts of China and Africa, and as small *Notgeld* from Austria and Germany during World War I. Wooden nickels is the name given to tokens of a commemorative nature, widely popular in the USA since 1930.

**Young Head** Profile of Queen Victoria sculpted by William Wyon for the Guildhall Medal of 1837 and subsequently utilised for British coins struck from 1837 to 1860 (copper) and 1887 (silver and gold).

**Zinc** Metallic element, chemical symbol *Zn*, widely used, with copper, as a constituent of brass. Alloyed with copper to form *tombac*, it was used for Canadian 5-cent coins (1942–43) and, coated on steel, it was used for American cents (1943). Zinc was used for *emergency coinage* in Austria, Belgium, Luxembourg and Germany (1915–18) and in Germany and German-occupied countries during World War II. Since then alloys of copper, nickel and zinc have been used for coinage in Eastern Europe.

*Victoria young head penny*

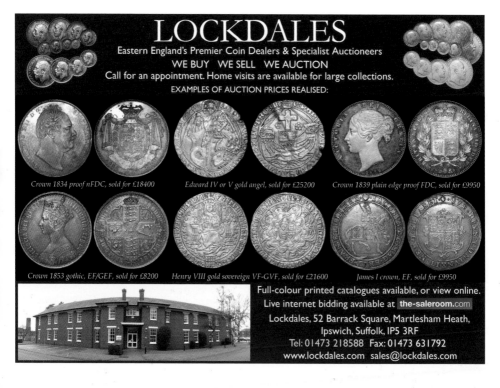

# KANGAROO
## AT SUNSET

## $1 FINE SILVER PROOF COIN

**Size 21.69 mm | Mintage 5000**

The contemporary design of the limited edition Kangaroo at Sunset coin has made it one of the most sought-after collector pieces from the Royal Australian Mint.

Reproduced on this fine silver $1 coin, the lone kangaroo bounding across the desert plains against a setting sun is a truly iconic Australian image.

Now available
through the Royal Australian Mint

**Australian Government**
Royal Australian Mint

# MINTMARKS
## of the world

**The following is a list of the initials and symbols denoting mints. In many cases, notably the Royal Mint, no mintmark was used on either British coins or those struck on behalf of other countries. Conversely many countries have only used one mintmark, that of one or other of the leading private mints.**

It should be noted that the mintmarks of the main private mints have been recorded on the coins of the following countries:

**H (Heaton, later the Birmingham Mint):**
Australia, Bolivia, British Honduras, British North Borneo, British West Africa, Bulgaria, Canada, Ceylon, Chile, Colombia, Costa Rica, Cyprus, Dominican Republic, East Africa, Ecuador, Egypt, El Salvador, Finland, French Indochina, Great Britain, Greece, Guatemala, Guernsey, Haiti, Hong Kong, Iran, Israel, Italy, Jamaica, Jersey, Liberia, Malaya and British Borneo, Mauritius, Mombasa, Mozambique, Newfoundland, Nicaragua, Poland, Roumania, Sarawak, Serbia, Siam, Straits Settlements, Uruguay and Venezuela.

**FM (Franklin Mint, Philadelphia):** Bahamas, Belize, British Virgin Islands, Cayman Islands, Cook Islands, Guyana, Jamaica, Liberia, Malaysia, Malta, Panama, Papua New Guinea, Philippines, Solomon Islands, Trinidad and Tobago.

**PM (Pobjoy Mint, Sutton, Surrey):** Ascension, Bosnia, Cook Islands, Gibraltar, Isle of Man, Liberia, Macau, Niue, Philippines, St Helena, Senegal, Seychelles, Tonga and Tristan da Cunha.

## ALBANIA
| | |
|---|---|
| L | London |
| R | Rome |
| V | Valona |

## ARGENTINA
| | |
|---|---|
| BA | Buenos Aires |
| Bs | Buenos Aires |
| B.AS | Buenos Aires |
| JPP | Jose Policarpo Patino |
| M | Mendoza |
| PNP | Pedro Nolasco Pizarro |
| PP | Pedro Nolasco Pizarro |
| PTS | Potosi |
| R | Rioja |
| RA | Rioja |
| SE | Santiago del Estero |
| SoEo | Santiago del Estero |
| TN | Tucuman |

## AUSTRALIA
| | |
|---|---|
| A | Perth |
| D | Denver |
| H | Heaton (1912–16) |
| I | Bombay (1942–43) |
| I | Calcutta (1916–18) |
| M | Melbourne |
| P | Perth |
| PL | Royal Mint, London |
| S | Sydney |
| S | San Francisco (1942–43) |
| *Dot before and after PENNY and I on obverse* | Bombay (1942–43) |
| *Dot before and after HALFPENNY and I on obverse* | Bombay (1942–43) |
| *Dot before and after PENNY* | Bombay (1942–43) |
| *Dot after HALFPENNY* | Perth |
| *Dot before SHILLING* | Perth (1946) |
| *Dot above scroll on reverse* | Sydney (1920) |
| *Dot below scroll on reverse* | Melbourne (1919–20) |
| *Dot between designer's initials KG* | Perth (1940–41) |
| *Dot after AUSTRALIA* | Perth (1952–53) |

## AUSTRIA

| | |
|---|---|
| A | Vienna (1765–1872) |
| AH–AG | Carlsburg, Transylvania (1765–76) |
| AH–GS | Carlsburg (1776–80) |
| A–S | Hall, Tyrol (1765–74) |
| AS–IE | Vienna (1745) |
| AW | Vienna (1764, 1768) |
| B | Kremnitz (1765–1857) |
| B–L | Nagybanya (1765–71) |
| B–V | Nagybanya (1772–80) |
| C | Carlsburg (1762–64) |
| C | Prague (1766–1855) |
| C–A | Carlsburg (1746–66) |
| C–A | Vienna (1774–80) |
| CG–AK | Graz (1767–72) |
| CG–AR | Graz (1767) |
| C–K | Vienna (1765–73) |
| CM | Kremnitz (1779) |
| CVG–AK | Graz (1767–72) |
| CVG–AR | Graz (1767) |
| D | Graz (1765–72), Salzburg (1800–09) |
| E | Carlsburg (1765–1867) |
| EC–SK | Vienna (1766) |
| EvM–D | Kremnitz (1765–74) |
| EvS–AS | Prague (1765–73) |
| EvS–IK | Prague (1774–80) |
| F | Hall (1765–1807) |
| FH | Hall |
| G | Graz (1761–63) |
| G | Gunzburg (1764–79) |
| G | Nagybanya (1766–1851) |
| G–K | Graz (1767–72) |
| G–R | Graz (1746–67) |
| GTK | Vienna (1761) |
| H | Hall (1760–80) |
| H | Gunzburg (1765–1805) |
| H–A | Hall (1746–65) |
| H–G | Carlsburg (1765–77) |
| H–S | Carlsburg (1777–80) |
| IB–FL | Nagybanya (1765–71) |
| IB–IV | Nagybanya (1772–80) |
| IC–FA | Vienna (1774–80) |
| IC–IA | Vienna (1780) |
| IC–SK | Vienna (1765–73) |
| I–K | Graz (1765–67) |
| I–K | Vienna (1767) |
| IZV | Vienna (1763–65) |
| K | Kremnitz (1760–63) |
| K–B | Kremnitz (1619–1765) |
| K–D | Kremnitz (1765) |
| K–M | Kremnitz (1763–65) |
| M | Milan (1780–1859) |
| N | Nagybanya (1780) |
| N–B | Nagybanya (1630–1777, 1849) |
| O | Oravicza (1783–1816) |
| P | Prague (1760–63) |
| P–R | Prague (1746–67) |
| PS–IK | Prague (1774–80) |
| S | Hall (1765–80), Schmollnitz (1763–1816) |

| | |
|---|---|
| S–C | Gunzburg (1765–74) |
| SC–G | Gunzburg (1765) |
| S–F | Gunzburg (1775–80) |
| S–G | Gunzburg (1764–65) |
| S–IE | Vienna (1745) |
| SK–PD | Kremnitz (1774–80) |
| TS | Gunzburg (1762–88) |
| V | Venice (1805–66) |
| VC–S | Hall (1774–80) |
| VS–K | Prague (1774–80) |
| VS–S | Prague (1765–73) |
| W | Vienna (1748–63) |
| W–I | Vienna (1746–71) |

## BAHAMAS

| | |
|---|---|
| FM | Franklin Mint |
| JP | John Pinches |

## BELGIUM

| | |
|---|---|
| A | Vienna |
| B | Kremnitz |
| C | Prague |
| E | Carlsburg |
| F | Hall |
| G | Nagybanya |
| H | Gunzburg |
| *hand* | Antwerp |
| *lion* | Bruges |

## BELIZE (British Honduras)

| | |
|---|---|
| FM | Franklin Mint |
| H | Heaton (1912–16) |

## BOLIVIA

| | |
|---|---|
| H | Heaton (1892–1953) |
| P, PTR, PTS | Potosi |

## BRAZIL

| | |
|---|---|
| A | Berlin (1913) |
| B | Bahia (1714–1831) |
| C | Cuiaba (1823–33) |
| G | Goias (1823–33) |
| M | Minas Gerais (1823–28) |
| P | Pernambuco |
| R | Rio de Janeiro (1703–1834) |
| RS | Rio de Janeiro (1869) |
| SP | Sao Paulo (1825–32) |

## BRITISH NORTH BORNEO (Sabah)

| | |
|---|---|
| H | Heaton (1882–1941) |

## BRITISH WEST AFRICA

| | |
|---|---|
| G | JR Gaunt, Birmingham |
| H | Heaton, Birmingham (1911–57) |
| K | King's Norton |
| KN | King's Norton |
| SA | Pretoria |

**BULGARIA**

| | |
|---|---|
| A | Berlin |
| BP | Budapest |
| Heaton | Heaton, Birmingham (1881–1923) |
| KB | Kormoczbanya |
| *cornucopia* | Paris |
| *thunderbolt* | Poissy |

**CANADA**

| | |
|---|---|
| C | Ottawa |
| H | Heaton (1871–1907) |
| *maple leaf* | Ottawa (on coins struck after the year inscribed on them) |

**CENTRAL AMERICAN REPUBLIC**

| | |
|---|---|
| CR | San Jose (Costa Rica) |
| G | Guatemala |
| NG | Guatemala |
| T | Tegucigalpa (Honduras) |

**CEYLON**

| | |
|---|---|
| H | Heaton (1912) |

**CHILE**

| | |
|---|---|
| A | Agustin de Infante y Prado (1768–72) |
| AJ | The above and Jose Maria de Bobadilla (1800–01) |
| D | Domingo Eizaguirre |
| DA | Domingo Eizaguirre and Agustin de Infante (1772–99) |
| BFF | Francisco Rodriguez Brochero |
| FJJF | Brochero and Jose Maria de Bobadilla (1803–17) |
| H | Heaton (1851) |
| J | Jose Larraneta (1749–67) |
| So | Santiago |
| VA | Val Distra |

**COLOMBIA**

| | |
|---|---|
| A | Paris |
| B | Bogota |
| BA | Bogota |
| B.B | Bogota |
| H | Heaton (1912) |
| M | Medellin |
| NR | Nuevo Reino |
| NoRo | Nuevo Reino |
| P | Popayan |
| PN, Pn | Popayan |
| SM | Santa Marta |

**COSTA RICA**

| | |
|---|---|
| CR | San Jose (1825–1947) |
| HBM | Heaton (1889–93) |
| S | San Domingo |
| SD | San Domingo |

**COURLAND**

| | |
|---|---|
| ICS | Justin Carl Schroder |

| | |
|---|---|
| IFS | Johan Friedrich Schmickert |

**CYPRUS**

| | |
|---|---|
| H | Heaton (1881–2) |

**DENMARK**

| | |
|---|---|
| FF | Altona |
| KM | Copenhagen Altona (1842) |
| *crown* | Copenhagen |
| *heart* | Copenhagen |
| *orb* | Altona (1839–48) |

Other letters are the initials of mintmasters and moneyers

**DOMINICAN REPUBLIC**

| | |
|---|---|
| HH | Heaton (1888–1919) |

**EAST AFRICA**

| | |
|---|---|
| A | Ackroyd & Best, Morley |
| H | Heaton (1910–64) |
| I | Bombay |
| K | Kynoch (IMI) |
| KN | King's Norton |
| SA | Pretoria |

**ECUADOR**

| | |
|---|---|
| BIRM$^M$H | Heaton (1915) |
| BIRMING-HAM | Heaton (1899–1900, 1928) |
| D | Denver |
| H | Heaton (1890, 1909, 1924–5) |
| HEATON BIRMING-HAM | Heaton (1872–95) |
| HF | Le Locle |
| LIMA | Lima |
| Mo | Mexico |
| PHILA | Philadelphia |
| QUITO | Quito |
| SANTIAGO | Santiago de Chile |

**EGYPT**

| | |
|---|---|
| H | Heaton (1904–37) |

**EL SALVADOR**

| | |
|---|---|
| CAM | Central American Mint, San Salvador |
| H | Heaton (1889–1913) |
| Mo | Mexico |
| S | San Francisco |

**FIJI**

| | |
|---|---|
| S | San Francisco |

**FINLAND**

| | |
|---|---|
| H | Heaton (1921) |
| *heart* | Copenhagen (1922). Since then coins have been struck at Helsinki without a mintmark. |

Initials of mintmasters:

| | |
|---|---|
| S | August Soldan (1864–85) |
| L | Johan Lihr (1885–1912) |
| S | Isaac Sundell (1915–47) |
| L | V. U. Liuhto (1948) |
| H | Uolevi Helle (1948–58) |
| S | Allan Soiniemi (1958–75) |
| SH | Soiniemi & Heikki Halvaoja (1967–71) |
| K | Timo Koivuranta (1977, 1979) |
| KN | Koivuranta and Antti Neuvonen (1978) |
| KT | Koivuranta and Erja Tielinen (1982) |
| KM | Koivuranta and Pertti Makinen (1983) |
| N | Reino Nevalainen (1983) |

**FRANCE**

| | |
|---|---|
| A | Paris (1768) |
| AA | Metz (1775–98) |
| B | Rouen (1786–1857) |
| B | Beaumont le Roger (1943–58) |
| BB | Strasbourg (1743–1870) |
| C | Castelsarrasin (1914, 1942–46) |
| CC | Genoa (1805) |
| CL | Genoa (1813–14) |
| D | Lyons (1771–1857) |
| G | Geneva (1796–1805) |
| H | La Rochelle (1770–1837) |
| L | Limoges (1766–1837) |
| K | Bordeaux (1759–1878) |
| L | Bayonne (1761–1837) |
| M | Toulouse (1766–1837) |
| MA | Marseilles (1787–1857) |
| N | Montpellier (1766–93) |
| O | Riom |
| P | Dijon |
| Q | Perpignan (1777–1837) |
| R | Royal Mint, London (1815) |
| R | Orleans (1780–92) |
| T | Nantes (1739–1835) |
| U | Turin (1814) |
| V | Troyes |
| W | Lille (1759–1857) |
| X | Amiens (1740) |
| & | Aix en Provence (1775) |
| 9 | Rennes |
| *cow* | Pau (1746–93) |
| *flag* | Utrecht (1811–14) |
| *crowned R* | Rome (1811–14) |
| *thunderbolt* | Poissy (1922-24) |
| *star* | Madrid (1916) |

In addition, French coins include symbols denoting the privy marks of Engravers General (Chief Engravers since 1880) and Mint Directors.

**GERMANY**

The first name gives the location of the mint, and the second the name of the country or state issuing the coins.

| | |
|---|---|
| A | Amberg, Bavaria (1763–94) |
| A | Berlin (1850) |
| A | Clausthal, Hannover (1832–49) |
| AE | Breslau, Silesia (1743–51) |
| AGP | Cleve, Rhineland (1742–43) |
| AK | Dusseldorf, Julich-Berg (1749–66) |
| ALS | Berlin (1749) |
| B | Bayreuth, Franconia (1796–1804) |
| B | Breslau, Silesia (1750–1826) |
| B | Brunswick, Brunswick (1850–60) |
| B | Brunswick, Westphalia (1809–13) |
| B | Dresden, Saxony (1861–72) |
| B | Hannover, Brunswick (1860–71) |
| B | Hannover, East Friesland (1823–25) |
| B | Hannover, Hannover (1821–66) |
| B | Hannover, Germany (1866-78) |
| B | Regensburg, Regensburg (1809) |
| B | Vienna, Germany (1938–45) |
| BH | Frankfurt (1808) |
| B–H | Regensburg, Rhenish Confederation (1802–12) |
| C | Cassel, Westphalia (1810–13) |
| C | Clausthal, Brunswick |
| C | Clausthal, Westphalia (1810–11) |
| C | Dresden, Saxony (1779–1804) |
| C | Frankfurt, Germany (1866–79) |
| CHI | Berlin (1749–63) |
| CLS | Dusseldorf, Julich-Berg (1767–70) |
| D | Aurich, East Friesland (1750–1806) |
| D | Dusseldorf, Rhineland (1816–48) |
| D | Munich, Germany (1872) |
| E | Dresden, Germany (1872–87) |
| E | Koenigberg, East Prussia (1750–98) |
| E | Muldenhutte, Germany (1887–1953) |
| EC | Leipzig, Saxony (1753–63) |
| EGN | Berlin (1725–49) |
| F | Dresden, Saxony (1845–58) |
| F | Magdeburg, Lower Saxony (1740–1806) |
| F | Cassel, Hesse-Cassel (1803–07) |
| F | Stuttgart, Germany (1872) |
| FW | Dresden, Saxony (1734–63) |
| G | Dresden, Saxony (1833–44, 1850–54) |
| G | Glatz, Silesia (1807–09) |
| G | Karlsruhe, Germany (1872) |
| G | Stettin, Pomerania (1750–1806) |
| GK | Cleve (1740–55) |
| GN | Bamberg, Bamberg |
| H | Darmstadt, Germany (1872–82) |
| H | Dresden, Saxony (1804–12) |
| HK | Rostock, Rostock (1862–64) |
| I | Hamburg, Germany (1872) |
| IDB | Dresden, Prussian occupation (1756–59) |
| IEC | Dresden, Saxony (1779–1804) |
| IF | Leipzig, Saxony (1763–65) |
| IGG | Leipzig, Saxony (1716–34, 1813–32) |
| J | Hamburg, Germany (1873) |
| J | Paris, Westphalia (1808–09) |
| L | Leipzig, Saxony (1761–62) |
| MC | Brunswick, Brunswick (1813–14, 1820) |
| PM | Dusseldorf, Julich-Berg (1771–83) |
| PR | Dusseldorf, Julich-Berg (1783–1804) |

| | |
|---|---|
| S | Dresden, Saxony (1813–32) |
| S | Hannover, Hannover (1839–44) |
| S | Schwabach, Franconia (1792–94) |
| SGH | Dresden, Saxony (1804–12) |
| ST | Strickling, Blomberg (1820–40) |

## GREAT BRITAIN

| | |
|---|---|
| A | Ashby (1645) |
| B | Nicolas Briot (1631–39) |
| B | Bridgnorth (1646) |
| B | Bristol (1696) |
| Br | Bristol (1643–45) |
| C | Chester (1696) |
| CARL | Carlisle (1644–45) |
| CC | Corfe Castle (1644) |
| CHST | Chester (1644) |
| CR | Chester (1644) |
| E | Southwark (1547–49) |
| E | Exeter (1696) |
| E | Edinburgh (1707–13) |
| E* | Edinburgh (1707–09) |
| H | Heaton, Birmingham (1874–1919) |
| HC | Hartlebury Castle (1646) |
| K | London (1547–49) |
| KN | King's Norton |
| N | Norwich (1696) |
| OX | Oxford (1644–45) |
| OXON | Oxford (1644) |
| PC | Pontefract (1648–49) |
| SC | Scarborough (1644–45) |
| SOHO | Birmingham (1797–1806) |
| T | Canterbury (1549) |
| TC | Bristol (1549) |
| WS | Bristol (1547–49) |
| Y | Southwark (1551) |
| boar | Shrewsbury (1643–44) |
| book | Aberystwyth (1638–42) |
| bow | Durham House (1548–49) |
| castle | Exeter (1644–45) |
| crown | Aberystwyth Furnace (1648–49) |
| plume | Shrewsbury (1642) |
| plume | Oxford (1642–46) |
| plume | Bristol (1643–46) |

Other symbols and marks on the hammered coins of Great Britain are usually referred to as Initial Marks. Complete listings of these marks appear in a number of specialist publications.

## GREECE

| | |
|---|---|
| A | Paris |
| B | Vienna |
| BB | Strasbourg |
| H | Heaton (1921) |
| K | Bordeaux |
| KN | King's Norton |
| owl | Aegina (1828–32) |
| owl | Athens (1838-55) |
| thunderbolt | Poissy |

## GUATEMALA

| | |
|---|---|
| CG | Guatemala City (1733-76) |
| G | Guatemala City (1776) |
| H | Heaton (1894–1901) |
| NG | Nueva Guatemala (1777) |

## GUERNSEY

| | |
|---|---|
| H | Heaton (1855–1949) |

## HAITI

| | |
|---|---|
| A | Paris |
| HEATON | Heaton (1863) |

## HONDURAS

| | |
|---|---|
| A | Paris (1869–71) |
| T | Tegucigalpa (1825–62) |

## HONG KONG

| | |
|---|---|
| H | Heaton (1872–1971) |
| KN | King's Norton |

## HUNGARY

| | |
|---|---|
| A | Vienna |
| B | Kremnitz |
| BP | Budapest |
| CA | Vienna |
| G | Nagybanya |
| GN | Nagybanya |
| GYF | Carlsburg |
| HA | Hall |
| K | Kremnitz |
| KB | Kremnitz |
| NB | Nagybanya |
| S | Schmollnitz |
| WI | Vienna |

## INDIA

| | |
|---|---|
| B | Bombay (1835-1947) |
| C | Calcutta (1835-1947) |
| I | Bombay (1918) |
| L | Lahore (1943-45) |
| M | Madras (1869) |
| P | Pretoria (1943-44) |
| diamond | Bombay |
| dot in diamond | Hyderabad |
| split diamond | Hyderabad |
| star | Hyderabad |

## IRAN

| | |
|---|---|
| H | Heaton (1928–29) |

## IRAQ

| | |
|---|---|
| I | Bombay |

## ISRAEL

| | |
|---|---|
| H | Heaton (1951–52) |
| star of David | Jerusalem |

## ITALY AND STATES

| | |
|---|---|
| B | Bologna |

| | |
|---|---|
| B/I | Birmingham (1893–4) |
| FIRENZE | Florence |
| H | Heaton (1866–67) |
| KB | Berlin |
| M | Milan |
| N | Naples |
| OM | Strasbourg |
| R | Rome |
| T | Turin |
| V | Venice |
| ZV | Venice |
| *anchor* | Genoa |
| *eagle head* | Turin |

## JAMAICA
| | |
|---|---|
| C | Ottawa |
| FM | Franklin Mint |
| H | Heaton (1882–1916) |

## JERSEY
| | |
|---|---|
| H | Heaton (1877) |

## KENYA
| | |
|---|---|
| C/M | Calcutta |
| H | Heaton (1911–64) |

## LIBERIA
| | |
|---|---|
| B | Berne |
| FM | Franklin Mint |
| H | Heaton (1896–1906) |
| PM | Pobjoy Mint |

## LIECHTENSTEIN
| | |
|---|---|
| A | Vienna |
| B | Berne |
| M | Munich |

## LUXEMBOURG
| | |
|---|---|
| A | Paris |
| H | Gunzburg |
| *anchor* | Paris |
| *angel* | Brussels |
| *caduceus* | Utrecht |
| *double eagle* | Brussels |
| *sword* | Utrecht |

## MALAYSIA
| | |
|---|---|
| B | Bombay |
| FM | Franklin Mint |
| H | Heaton (1955–61) |
| I | Calcutta (1941) |
| I | Bombay (1945) |
| KN | King's Norton |
| W | James Watt, Birmingham |

## MAURITIUS
| | |
|---|---|
| H | Heaton (1877–90) |
| SA | Pretoria |

## MEXICO
| | |
|---|---|
| A, As | Alamos |
| C, CN | Culiacan |
| CA, CH | Chihuahua |
| Ce | Real del Catorce |
| D, Do | Durango |
| Eo | Tlalpam |
| GA | Guadalajara |
| GC | Guadelupe y Calvo |
| Go | Guanajuato |
| Ho | Hermosillo |
| M, Mo | Mexico City |
| Mo | Morelos |
| MX | Mexico City |
| O, OA, OKA | Oaxaca |
| Pi | San Luis Potosi |
| SLPi | San Luis Potosi |
| TC | Tierra Caliente |
| Z, Zs | Zacatecas |

## MONACO
| | |
|---|---|
| A | Paris |
| M | Monte Carlo |
| *clasped hands* | Cabanis |
| *thunderbolt* | Poissy |

## MOZAMBIQUE
| | |
|---|---|
| H | Heaton (1894) |
| R | Rio |

## NETHERLANDS AND COLONIES
### Austrian Netherlands (1700-93)
| | |
|---|---|
| H | Amsterdam |
| S | Utrecht |
| W | Vienna |
| *hand* | Antwerp |
| *head* | Brussels |
| *lion* | Bruges |

### Kingdom of the Netherlands
| | |
|---|---|
| B | Brussels (1821–30) |
| D | Denver (1943–45) |
| P | Philadelphia (1941–45) |
| S | Utrecht (1816–36) |
| S | San Francisco (1944–45) |
| Sa | Surabaya |
| *caduceus* | Utrecht |

## NICARAGUA
| | |
|---|---|
| H | Heaton (1880–1916) |
| NR | Leon de Nicaragua |

## NORWAY
| | |
|---|---|
| *hammers* | Kongsberg |

## PANAMA
| | |
|---|---|
| CHI | Valcambi |
| FM | Franklin Mint |

## PERU

| | |
|---|---|
| AREQ, AREQUIPA | Arequipa |
| AYACUCHO | Ayacucho |
| CUZCO, Co | Cuzco |
| L, LM, LR | Lima |
| LIMAE | Lima |
| PASCO | Pasco |
| Paz, Po | Pasco |
| P | Lima (1568-70) |
| P | Philadelphia |
| S | San Francisco |

## PHILIPPINES

| | |
|---|---|
| BSP | Bangko Sentral Pilipinas |
| D | Denver (1944–45) |
| FM | Franklin Mint |
| M, MA | Manila |
| PM | Pobjoy Mint |
| S | San Francisco (1903–47) |
| *5 point star* | Manila |

## POLAND

| | |
|---|---|
| AP | Warsaw (1772–74) |
| CI | Cracow (1765–68) |
| EB | Warsaw (1774–92) |
| EC | Leipzig (1758–63) |
| FF | Stuttgart (1916–17) |
| FH | Warsaw (1815–27) |
| FS | Warsaw (1765–68) |
| FWoF | Dresden (1734–64) |
| G | Cracow (1765–72) |
| H | Heaton (1924) |
| IB | Warsaw (1811–27) |
| IGS | Dresden (1716–34) |
| IP | Warsaw (1834–43) |
| IS | Warsaw (1768–74) |
| JGG | Leipzig (1750–53) |
| JS | Warsaw (1810–11) |
| KG | Warsaw (1829–34) |
| MV, MW | Warsaw |
| *arrow* | Warsaw (1925–39) |
| *Dot after date* | Royal Mint (1925) |
| *8 torches* | Paris (1924) |

## ROUMANIA

| | |
|---|---|
| B | Bucharest (1879–85) |
| C | Bucharest (1886) |
| H | Heaton (1867–1930) |
| HUGUENIN | Le Locle |
| J | Hamburg |
| KN | King's Norton |
| V | Vienna |
| W | Watt, Birmingham |
| *thunderbolt* | Poissy |

## RUSSIA

| | |
|---|---|
| AM | Annensk (1762–96) |
| BM | Warsaw (1825–55) |
| bM | St Petersburg (1796) |
| C–M | Sestroretsk (1762–96) |
| CM | Souzan (1825–55) |
| E–M | Ekaterinburg (1762–1810) |
| KM | Kolpina (1810) |
| K–M | Kolyvan (1762–1810) |
| MM, M–M | Moscow (1730–96) |
| MMD | Moscow (1730–96) |
| MW | Warsaw (1842–54) |
| NM | Izhorsk (1811–21) |
| SP | St Petersburg (1798–1800) |
| SPB | St Petersburg (1724–1915) |
| SPM | St Petersburg (1825–55) |
| T–M | Feodosia (1762–96) |

## SAN MARINO

| | |
|---|---|
| M | Milan |
| R | Rome |
| SIAM (Thailand) | H Heaton (1898) |

## SOUTH AFRICA

| | |
|---|---|
| SA | Pretoria |

## SPAIN

| | |
|---|---|
| B | Burgos |
| B, BA | Barcelona |
| Bo | Bilbao |
| C | Catalonia |
| C | Cuenca |
| C | Reus |
| CA | Zaragoza |
| G | Granada |
| GNA | Gerona |
| LD | Lerida |
| J, JA | Jubia |
| M, MD | Madrid |
| P | Palma de Majorca |
| PpP, PL, PA | Pamplona |
| S, S/L | Seville |
| Sr | Santander |
| T, To, Tole | Toledo |
| TOR:SA | Tortosa |
| V, VA, VAL | Valencia |
| *crowned C* | Cadiz |
| *crowned M* | Madrid |
| *aqueduct* | Segovia |
| *crowned shield* | Tarragona |
| *pomegranate* | Granada |
| *quartered shield* | Palma |
| *scallop* | Coruna |
| *stars:* | |
| *3 points* | Segovia |
| *4 points* | Jubia |
| *5 points* | Manila |
| *6 points* | Madrid |
| *7 points* | Seville (1833) |
| *8 points* | Barcelona (1838) |
| *wavy lines* | Valladolid |

## SURINAM

| | |
|---|---|
| P | Philadelphia |
| S | Sydney |
| *caduceus* | Utrecht |

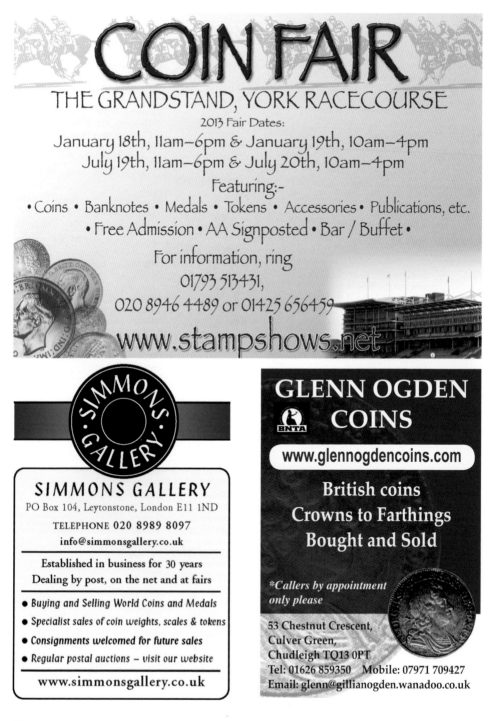

# COIN *inscriptions*

This alphabetical listing is confined to inscriptions found on coins, mainly in the form of mottoes or of a commemorative nature. Names of rulers are, for the most part, excluded. Where the inscription is in a language other than English a translation is given, followed by the name of the issuing country or authority in parentheses.

**A Deo et Caesare** From God and the Emperor (Frankfurt).

**A Domino Factum est Istud et est Mirabile in Oculis Nostris** This is the Lord's doing and it is marvellous in our eyes (England, Mary).

**A Solo Iehova Sapientia** From God alone comes true wisdom (Wittgenstein).

**Ab Inimicis Meis Libera Me Deus** Free me from enemies (Burgundy).

**Ad Legem Conventionis** According to the law of the Convention (Furstenberg).

**Ad Normam Conventionis** According to the standard of the Convention (Prussia).

**Ad Palmam Pressa Laeturo Resurgo** Pressed to the palm I rise more joyfully (Wittgenstein).

**Ad Usam Luxemburgi CC Vallati** For the use of the besieged Luxembourgers (Luxembourg siege coins).

**Adiuva Nos Deus Salutaris Noster** Help us, O God, our Saviour (Lorraine).

**Adventus Optimi Principis** The coming of the noblest prince (Papacy).

**Aes Usibus Aptius Auro** Bronze in its uses is more suitable than gold (Brazil).

**Aeternum Meditans Decus** An ornament intended for all time (Alencon).

**Aliis Inserviendo Consumor** I spend my life devoted to others (Brunswick-Wolfenbuttel).

**Alles Mit Bedacht** All with reflection (Brunswick).

**Amor Populi Praesidium Regis** The love of the people is the king's protection (England, Charles I).

**Ang Fra Dom Hib & Aquit** (King) of England and France, Lord of Ireland and Aquitaine (England, Edward III).

**Anno Regni Primo** In the first year of the reign (Britain, edge inscription on crowns).

**Apres les Tenebres la Lumiere** After the shadows, the light (Geneva).

**Archangelus Michael** Archangel Michael (Italy, Grimoald IV).

**Ardua ad Gloriam Via** Struggles are the way to glory (Waldeck).

**Arte Mea Bis Iustus Moneta Lud Iust** By my art I am twice the just coin of King Louis (France, 1641).

**Aspera Oblectant** Wild places delight (Nassau-Weilburg).

**Aspice Pisas Sup Omnes Specio** Behold the coin of Pisa, superior to all (Pisa).

**Audiatur Altera Pars** Let the other part be heard (Stavelot).

**Auf Gott Trawe Ich** In God I trust (Brunswick).

**Ausen Gefaesen der Kirchen und Burger** From the vessels of the Church and citizens (Frankfurt siege, 1796).

**Auspicio Regis et Senatus Angliae** By authority of the king and parliament of England (East India Company).

**Auxilio fortissimo Dei** With the strongest help of God (Mecklenburg).

**Auxilium de Sanctio** Aid from the sanctuary (Papacy).

**Auxilium Meum a Dno Qui Fecit Celum e Terram** My help comes from God who made heaven and earth (Portugal).

**Beata Tranquillatis** Blessed tranquillity (Rome, Licinius II).

**Beatus Qui Speravit in dom** Blessed is he who has hoped in the Lord (Mansfeld).

**Benedic Haereditati Tuae** Blessings on your inheritance (Savoy).

**Benedicta Sit Sancta Trinitas** Blessed be the Holy Trinity (Albon).

**Benedictio Domini Divites Facit** The blessing of the Lord makes the rich (Teschen).

**Benedictus Qui Venit in Nomine Domini** Blessed is he who comes in the name of the Lord (Flanders).

**Beschaw das Ziel Sage Nicht Viel** Consider the matter but say little (Quedlinburg).

**Besser Land und Lud Verloren als ein Falscher Aid Geschworn**   Better to lose land and wealth than swear a false oath (Hesse).

**Bey Gott ist Rath und That**   With God is counsel and deed (Mansfeld).

**Britanniarum Regina**   Queen of the Britains (Britain, Victoria).

**Britt Omn Rex**   King of all the Britains (i.e. Britain and the overseas dominions) (Britain, 1902–52).

**Cal et Car Com de Fugger in Zin et Norn Sen & Adm Fam**   Cajetan and Carl, Counts of Fugger in Zinnenberg and Nordendorf, Lords and Administrators of the Family (Empire, Fugger).

**Candide et Constanter**   Sincerely and steadfastly (Hesse-Cassel).

**Candide sed Provide**   Clearly but cautiously (Osterwitz).

**Candore et Amore**   With sincerity and love (Fulda).

**Candore et Constantia**   With sincerity and constancy (Bavaria).

**Capit Cath Ecclesia Monasteriensis**   Chapter of the Cathedral Church of Munster (Munster).

**Capit Eccle Metropolit Colon**   Chapter of the Metropolitan Church of Cologne (Cologne).

**Capitulum Regnans Sede Vacante**   Chapter governing, the See being vacant (Eichstadt).

**Carola Magna Ducissa Feliciter Regnante**   Grand Duchess Charlotte, happily reigning (Luxembourg).

**Carolus a Carolo**   Charles (I) to Charles (II) (England).

**Cedunt Prementi Fata**   The fates yield to him who presses (Ploen, Hese-Cassel).

**Charitate et Candore**   With charity and sincerity (East Frisia).

**Charta Magna Bavariae**   The Great Charter of Bavaria (Bavaria).

**Christo Auspice Regno**   I reign under the auspices of Christ (England, Charles I).

**Christus Spes Una Salutis**   Christ is our one hope of salvation (Cleve).

**Chur Mainz**   Electoral Principality of Mainz (Mainz).

**Circumeundo Servat et Ornat**   It serves and decorates by going around (Sweden).

**Civibus Quorum Pietas Coniuratione Die III Mai MDCCXCI Obrutam et Deletam Libertate Polona Tueri Conabatur Respublica Resurgens**   To the citizens whose piety the resurgent commonwealth tried to protect Poland overturned and deprived of liberty by the conspiracy of the third day of May 1791 (Poland).

**Civitas Lucemborgiensis Millesimum Ovans Expletannum**   Completing the celebration of a thousand years of the city of Luxembourg (Luxembourg).

**Civium Industria Floret Civitas**   By the industry of its people the state flourishes (Festival of Britain crown, 1951).

**Cluniaco Cenobio Petrus et Paulus**   Peter and Paul from the Abbey of Cluny (Cluny).

**Comes Provincie Fili Regis Francie**   Court of Provence and son of the King of France (Provence).

**Communitas et Senatus Bonon**   City and senate of Bologna (Bologna).

**Concordia Fratrum**   The harmony of the brothers (Iever).

**Concordia Patriae Nutrix**   Peace, the nurse of the fatherland (Waldeck).

**Concordia Res Parvae Crescunt**   Little things increase through harmony (Batavian Republic).

**Concordia Res Parvae Crescunt, Discordia Dilabuntur**   By harmony little things increase, by discord they fall apart (Lowenstein-Wertheim-Virneburg).

**Concordia Stabili**   With lasting peace (Hildesheim).

**Confidens Dno Non Movetur**   He who trusts in God is unmoved (Spanish Netherlands).

**Confidentia in Deo et Vigilantia**   Trust in God and vigilance (Prussian Asiatic Company).

**Confoederato Helvetica**   Swiss Confederation (Switzerland)

**Conjuncto Felix**   Fortunate in his connections (Solms).

**Conservator Urbis Suae**   Saviour of his city (Rome, 4th century).

**Consilio et Aequitate**   With deliberation and justice (Fulda).

**Consilio et Virtutis**   With deliberation and valour (Hesse-Cassel).

**Constanter et Sincere**   Steadfastly and sincerely (Lautern).

**Crescite et Multiplicamini**   Increase and multiply (Maryland).

**Cristiana Religio**   Christian religion (Germany, 11th century).

**Crux Benedicat**   May the cross bless you (Oldenburg).

**Cuius Cruore Sanati Sumus**   By His sacrifice are we healed (Reggio).

**Cultores Sui Deus Protegit**   God protects His followers (England, Charles I).

**Cum Deo et Die (Jure)**   With God and the day (Wurttemberg).

**Cum Deo et Jure**   With God and the law (Wurttemberg).

**Cum Deo et Labore**   With God and work (Wittgenstein).

**Cum His Qui Orderant Pacem Eram Pacificus**   With those who order peace I was peaceful (Zug).

**Curie Bonthon to so Doulo**   Protect his servant, o Lord (Byzantine Empire).

**Custos Regni Deus**   God is the guardian of the kingdom (Naples and Sicily).

**Da Gloriam Deo et Eius Genitrici Marie**   Give glory to God and His mother Mary (Wurttemberg).

**Da Mihi Virtutem Contra Hostes Tuos**   Give me valour against mine enemies (Netherlands, Charles V).

**Dat Wort is Fleis Gworden**   The word is made flesh (Muster).

**Date Caesaris Caesari et Quae Sunt Dei Deo**   Render unto Caesar the things that are Caesar's and unto God the things that are God's (Stralsund).

**De Oficina . . .**   From the mint of . . . (France, medieval).

**Decreto Reipublicae Nexu Confoederationis Iunctae Die V Xbris MDCCXCII Stanislao Augusto Regnante**   By decree of the state in conjunction with the joint federation on the fifth day of December 1792, Stanislaus Augustus ruling (Poland).

**Decus et Tutamen**   An ornament and a safeguard (Britain, pound).

**Deducet Nos Mirabiliter Dextera Tua**   Thy right hand will guide us miraculously (Savoy).

**Denarium Terrae Mariae**   Penny of Maryland (Maryland).

**Deo Conservatori Pacis**   To God, preserver of peace (Brandenburg-Ansbach).

**Deo OM Auspice Suaviter et Fortiter sed Luste nec Sibi sed Suis**   Under the auspices of God, greatest and best, pleasantly and bravely but justly, not for himself but for his people (Speyer).

**Deo Patriae et Subditio**   For God, fatherland and neighbourhood (Mainz).

**Der Recht Glaubt In Ewig Lebt**   Who believes in right will live in eternity (Linange-Westerburg).

**Der Rhein ist Deutschlands Strom Nicht Deutschlands Grenze**   The Rhine is Germany's River not Germany's Frontier.

**Deum Solum Adorabis**   You will venerate God alone (Hesse).

**Deus Constituit Regna**   God establishes kingdoms (Ni jmegen).

**Deus Dat Qui Vult**   God gives to him who wishes (Hanau-Munzenberg).

**Deus et Dominus**   God and Lord (Rome, 3rd century).

**Deus in Adiutorium Meum Intende**   God stretch out in my assistance (France).

**Deus Providebit**   God will provide (Lowenstein-Wertheim-Virnehoe).

**Deus Refugium Meum**   God is my refuge (Cleve).

**Deus Solatium Meum**   God is my comfort (Sweden).

**Dextera Domini Exaltavit Me**   The right hand of God has raised me up (Modena, Spain).

**Dextra Dei Exalta Me**   The right hand of God exalts me (Denmark).

**Dieu et Mon Droit**   God and my right (Britain, George IV).

**Dilexit Dns Andream**   The Lord delights in St Andrew (Holstein).

**Dilexit Dominus Decorem Iustitiae**   The Lord is pleased with the beauty of justice (Unterwalden).

**Dirige Deus Gressus Meos**   O God, direct my steps (Tuscany, Britain, Una £5).

**Discerne Causam Meam**   Distinguish my cause (Savoy).

**Divina Benedictiae et Caesarea Iustitia**   Sacrifice of blessings and imperial justice (Coblenz).

**Dn Ihs Chs Rex Regnantium**   Lord Jesus Christ, King of Kings (Rome, Justinian II).

**Dns Ptetor Ms Z Lib'ator Ms**   The Lord is my protector and liberator (Scotland, David II).

**Dominabitur Gentium et Ipse**   He himself will also be lord of the nations (Austrian Netherlands).

**Domine Conserva Nos in Pace**   O Lord preserve us in peace (Basle, Mulhausen).

**Domine Elegisti Lilium Tibi**   O Lord Thou hast chosen the lily for Thyself (France, Louis XIV).

**Domine ne in Furore Tuo Arguas Me**   O Lord rebuke me not in Thine anger (England, Edward III).

**Domine Probasti Me et Congnovisti Me**   O Lord Thou hast tested me and recognised me (Mantua).

**Domini est Regnum**   The Kingdom is the Lord's (Austrian Netherlands).

**Dominus Deus Omnipotens Rex**   Lord God, almighty King (Viking coins).

**Dominus Mihi Adiutor**   The Lord is my helper (Spanish Netherlands).

**Dominus Providebit**   The Lord will provide (Berne).

**Dominus Spes Populi Sui**   The Lord is the hope of his people (Lucerne).

**Donum Dei ex Fodinis Vilmariens**   A gift of God from the Vilmar mines (Coblenz).

**Duce Deo Fide et Justicia**   By faith and justice lead us to God (Ragusa).

**Dum Praemor Amplior**   I increase while I die prematurely (Savoy).

**Dum Spiro Spero**   While I live, I hope (Pontefract siege coins).

**Dum Totum Compleat Orbem**   Until it fills the world (France, Henri II).

**Dura Pati Virtus**   Valour endures hardships (Saxe-Lauenburg).

**Durae Necessitatis**   Through force of necessity (Bommel siege, 1599).

**Durum Telum Necessitas**   Hardship is a weapon of necessity (Minden).

**Dux et Gubernatores Reip Genu**   Duke and governors of the republic of Genoa (Genoa).

**E Pluribus Unum**   One out of more (USA).

**Eccl S. Barbarae Patronae Fodin Kuttenbergensium Duo Flor Arg Puri**   The church of St Barbara, patron of the Kuttensberg mines, two florins of pure silver (Hungary).

**Een en Ondelbaer Sterk**   One and indivisible (Batavian Republic).

**Eendracht Mag Macht**   Unity makes strength (Belgium, South African Republic).

**Einigkeit Recht und Freiheit**   Union, right and freedom (Germany).

**Electorus Saxoniae Administrator**   Elector and administrator of Saxony (Saxony).

**Elimosina**   Alms (France, Pepin).

**Ep Fris & Ratisb Ad Prum Pp Coad Aug**   Bishop of Freising and Regensburg, administrator of Pruem, prince-provost, co-adjutant bishop of Augsburg (Trier).

**Equa Libertas Deo Gratia Frat Pax in Virtute Tua et in Domino Confido**   I believe in equal liberty by the grace of God, brotherly love in Thy valour and in the Lord (Burgundy).

**Equitas Iudicia Tua Dom**   Equity and Thy judgments O Lord (Gelderland).

**Espoir Me Conforte**   Hope comforts me (Mansfeld).

**Espreuve Faicto Par Lexpres Commandement du Roy**   Proof made by the express commandment of the King (France, piedforts).

**Et in Minimis Integer**   Faithful even in the smallest things (Olmutz).

**Ex Auro Argentes Resurgit**   From gold it arises, silver again (Sicily).

**Ex Auro Sinico**   From Chinese gold (Denmark).

**Ex Flammis Orior**   I arise from the flames (Hohenlohe-Neuenstein-Ohringen).

**Ex Fodinis Bipontio Seelbergensibus**   From the Seelberg mines of Zweibrucken (Pfalz-Birkenfeld).

**Ex Metallo Novo**   From new metal (Spain).

**Ex Uno Omnis Nostra Salus**   From one is all our salvation (Eichstadt, Mulhouse).

**Ex Vasis Argent Cleri Mogunt Pro Aris et Focis**   From the silver vessels of the clergy of Mainz for altars and for hearths (Mainz).

**Ex Visceribus Fodinse Bieber**   From the bowels of the Bieber mine (Hanau-Munzenberg).

**Exaltabitur in Gloria**   He shall be exalted in glory (England, quarter nobles).

**Exemplum Probati Numismatis**   An example of a proof coin (France, Louis XIII piedforts).

**Exemtae Eccle Passau Episc et SRI Princ**   Prince Bishop of the freed church of Passau, prince of the Holy Roman Empire (Passau).

**Expectate Veni**   Come, o expected one (Roman Britain, Carausius).

**Extremum Subidium Campen**   Kampen under extreme siege (Kampen, 1578).

**Exurgat Deus et Dissipentur Inimici Eius**   Let God arise and let His enemies be scattered (England, James I).

**Faciam Eos in Gentem Unam**   I will make them one nation (England, unites and laurels).

**Faith and Truth I will Bear unto You**   (UK £5, 1993).

**Fata Consiliis Potiora**   The fates are more powerful than councils (Hesse-Cassel).

**Fata Viam Invenient**   The fates will find a way (Gelderland).

**Fecit Potentiam in Brachio Suo**   He put power in your forearm (Lorraine).

**Fecunditas**   Fertility (Naples and Sicily).

**Fel Temp Reparatio**   The restoration of lucky times (Rome, AD 348).

**Felicitas Perpetua**   Everlasting good fortune (Rome, Constantius II).

**Felix coniunctio**   Happy Union (Brandenburg-Ansbach).

**Fiat Misericordia Tua Dne**   Let Thy mercy be O Lord (Gelderland).

**Fiat Voluntas Domini Perpetuo**   Let the goodwill of the Lord last for ever (Fulda).

**Fidei Defensor**   Defender of the Faith (Britain).

**Fidelitate et Fortitudine**   With fidelity and fortitude (Batthanyi).

**Fideliter et Constanter**   Faithfully and steadfastly (Saxe-Coburg-Gotha).

**Fidem Servando Patriam Tuendo**   By keeping faith and protecting the fatherland (Savoy).

**Filius Augustorum**   Son of emperors (Rome, 4th century).

**Fisci Iudaici Calumnia Sublata**   The false accusation of the Jewish tax lifted (Rome, Nerva).

**Florent Concordia Regna**   Through harmony kingdoms flourish (England, Charles I and II).

**Fortitudo et Laus Mea Dominu**   Fortitude and my praise in the Lord (Sardinia).

**Free Trade to Africa by Act of Parliment** (*Sic*) (Gold Coast).

**Friedt Ernehrt Unfriedt Verzehrt**   Peace nourishes, unrest wastes (Brunswick).

**Fulgent Sic Littora Rheni**   Thus shine the banks of the Rhine (Mannheim).

**Fundator Pacis**   Founder of peace (Rome, Severus).

**Gaudium Populi Romani**   The joy of the Roman people (Rome, 4th century).

**Gen C Mar VI Dim Col USC & RAMAI Cons & S Conf M**   General field marshal, colonel of the only dragoon regiment, present privy councillor of both their sacred imperial and royal apostolic majesties, and state conference minister (Batthanyi).

**Gerecht und Beharrlich**   Just and steadfast (Bavaria).

**Germ Hun Boh Rex AAD Loth Ven Sal**   King of Germany, Hungary and Bohemia, Archduke of Austria, Duke of Lorraine, Venice and Salzburg (Austria).

**Germ Jero Rex Loth Bar Mag Het Dux**   King of Germany, Jerusalem, Lorraine and Bar, Grand Duke of Tuscany (Austrian Netherlands).

**Germania Voti Compos**   Germany sharing the vows (Brandenburg-Ansbach).

**Gloria ex Amore Patriae**   Glory from love of country (Denmark).

**Gloria in Excelsis Deo**   Glory to God in the highest (France, Sweden).

**Gloria Novi Saeculi**   The glory of a new century (Rome, Gratian).

**God With Us**   (England, Commonwealth).

**Godt Met Ons**   God with us (Oudewater).

**Gottes Freundt der Pfaffen Feindt**   God's friend, the Pope's enemy (Brunswick, Christian).

**Gratia Dei Sum Id Quod Sum**   By the grace of God, I am what I am (Navarre).
**Gratia Di Rex**   By the grace of God, king (France, 8th century).
**Gratitudo Concivibus Exemplum Posteritati**   Gratitude to fellow Citizens, an example to posterity (Poland).
**Gud och Folket**   God and the people (Sweden).
**Hac Nitimur Hanc Tuemur**   With this we strive, this we shall defend (Batavian Republic).
**Hac Sub Tutela**   Under this protection (Eichstadt).
**Haec Sunt Munera Minerae S Antony Eremitae**   These are the rewards of the mine of St Antony the hermit (Hildesheim).
**Hanc Deus Dedit**   God has given this (Pontefract siege coins).
**Hanc Tuemur Hac Nitimur**   This we defend, by this we strive (Batavian Republic).
**Has Nisi Periturus Mihi Adimat Nemo**   Let no one remove these (Letters) from me under penalty of death (Commonwealth, edge inscription).
**Henricus Rosas Regna Jacobus**   Henry (united) the roses, James the kingdoms (England and Scotland, James VI and I).
**Herculeo Vincta Nodo**   Bound by a Herculean fetter (Savoy).
**Herr Nach Deinem Willen**   O Lord Thy will be done (Palatinate, Erbach).
**Herre Gott Verleich Uns Gnade**   Lord God grant us grace (Brunswick).
**Hic Est Qui Multum Orat Pro Populo**   Here is he who prays a lot for the people (Paderborn).
**Hir Steid te Biscop**   Here is represented the bishop (Gittelde).
**His Ventis Vela Levantur**   By these winds the sails are raised up (Hesse-Cassel).
**Hispaniarum Infans**   Infante of Spain and its dominions (Spain).
**Hispaniarum et Ind Rex**   King of Spain and the Indies.
**Hispaniarum Rex**   King of Spain (Spain).
**Hoc Signo Victor Eris**   With this sign you will be victor (Rome, Vetranio).
**Honeste et Decenter**   Honestly and decently (Nassau-Idstein).
**Honi Soit Qui Mal y Pense**   Evil to him who evil thinks (Britain, George III).
**Honni Soit Qui Mal y Pense**   (Hesse-Cassel).
**Hospitalis et S Sepul Hierusal**   Hospital and Holy Sepulchre of Jerusalem (Malta).
**Hun Boh Gal Rex AA Lo Wi et in Fr Dux**   King of Hungary, Bohemia and Galicia, Archduke of Austria, Dalmatia, Lodomeria, Wurzburg and Duke in Franconia (Austria).
**Hung Boh Lomb et Ven Gal Lod III Rex Aa**   King of Hungary, Bohemia, Lombardo-Venezia, Galicia, Lodomeria and Illyria, Archduke of Austria (Austria).
**Ich Dien**   I serve (Aberystwyth 2d, UK 2p).
**Ich Getrawe Got in Aller Noth**   I trust in God in all my needs (Hesse-Marburg).
**Ich Habe Nur Ein Vaterland und das Heisst Deutschland**   I have only one fatherland and that is called Germany (Germany).
**Ielithes Penniae**   Penny of Gittelde (Gittelde, 11th century).
**Iesus Autem Transiens Per Medium Illorum Ibat**   But Jesus, passing through the midst of them, went His way (England, Scotland, Anglo-Gallic).
**Iesus Rex Noster et Deus Noster**   Jesus is our king and our God (Florence).
**Ihs Xs Rex Regnantium**   Jesus Christ, King of Kings (Byzantine Empire).
**Ihsus Xristus Basileu Baslie**   Jesus Christ, King of Kings (Byzantine Empire).
**Imago Sanch Regis Illustris Castelle Legionis e Toleto**   The image of Sancho the illustrious king of Castile, Leon and Toledo.
**In Casus Per Vigil Omnes**   In all seasons through vigil (Wertheim).
**In Deo Meo Transgrediar Murum**   In my God I shall pass through walls (Teschen).
**In Deo Spes Mea**   In God is my hope (Gelderland).
**In Domino Fiducia Nostra**   In the Lord is our trust (Iever).
**In Equitate Tua Vivificasti Me**   In thy equity Thou hast vivified me (Gelderland).
**In God We Trust**   (USA).
**In Hoc Signo Vinces**   In this sign shalt thou conquer (Portugal).
**In Honore Sci Mavrici Marti**   In honour of the martyr St Maurice (St Maurice, 8th century).
**In Manibus Domini sortes Meae**   In the hands of the Lord are my fates (Mainz siege, 1688–9).
**In Memor Vindicatae Libere ac Relig**   In memory of the establishment of freedom and religion (Sweden).
**In Memoriam Conjunctionis Utriusque Burgraviatus Norice**   In memory of the union of both burgraviates in peace (Brandenburg-Ansbach).
**In Memorian Connub Feliciaes Inter Princ Her Frider Carol et Dub Sax August Louis Frider Rodas D 28 Nov 1780 Celebrati**   In memory of the most happy marriage between the hereditary prince Friedrich Karl and the Duchess of Saxony Augusta Louisa Frederika, celebrated on 28 Nov 1780 (Schwarzburg-Rudolstadt).
**In Memorian Felicisssimi Matrimonii**   In memory of the most happy marriage (Wied).
**In Memoriam Pacis Teschinensis**   Commemorating the Treaty of Teschen (Brandenburg-Ansbach).
**In Nomine Domini Amen**   In the name of the Lord amen (Zaltbommel).
**In Omnem Terram Sonus Eorum**   In to all the land their shall go sound (Chateau Renault, Papal States).
**In Silencio et Spe Fortitudo Mea**   In silence and hope is my fortitude (Brandenburg-Kustrin).

**In Spe et Silentio Fortitudo Mea**   In hope and silence is my fortitude (Vianen).

**In Te Domine Confido**   In you O Lord I place my trust (Hesse).

**In Te Domine Speravi**   In You, O Lord, I have hoped (Gurk).

**In Terra Pax**   Peace in the land (Papacy).

**In Via Virtuti Nulla Via**   There is no way for virtue on the way. (Veldenz).

**Ind Imp, Indiae Imperator, Imperatrix**   Emperor (Empress) of India (Britain).

**India Tibi Cessit**   India has yielded to thee (Portuguese India).

**Infestus Infestis**   Hostile to the troublesome (Savoy).

**Inimicos Eius Induam Confusione**   As for his enemies, I shall clothe them in shame (Sardinia, England, Edward VI).

**Insignia Capituli Brixensis**   The badge of the chapter of Brixen (Brixen).

**Isti Sunt Patres Tui Verique Pastores**   These are your fathers and true shepherds (Papacy).

**Iudicium Melius Posteritatis Erit**   Posterity's judgment will be better (Paderborn).

**Iure et Tempore**   By right and time (Groningen).

**Iusques a Sa Plenitude**   As far as your plenitude (France, Henri II).

**Iuste et Constanter**   Justly and constantly (Paderborn).

**Iustirt**   Adjusted (Hesse-Cassel).

**Iustitia et Concordia**   Justice and harmony (Zurich).

**Iustitia et Mansuetudine**   By justice and mildness (Bavaria, Cologne).

**Iustitia Regnorum Fundamentum**   Justice is the foundation of kingdoms (Austria).

**Iustitia Thronum Firmat**   Justice strengthens the throne (England, Charles I).

**Iustus Non Derelinquitur**   The just person is not deserted (Brandenburg-Calenberg).

**Iustus Ut Palma Florebit**   The just will flourish like the palm (Portugal).

**L Mun Planco Rauracorum Illustratori Vetustissimo**   To L Municius Plancus the most ancient and celebrated of the Rauraci (Basle).

**Landgr in Cleggov Com in Sulz Dux Crum**   Landgrave of Klettgau, count of Sulz, duke of Krumlau (Schwarzburg-Sonderhausen).

**Latina Emeri Munita**   Latin money of Merida (Suevi).

**Lege et Fide**   By law and faith (Austria).

**Lex Tua Veritas**   Thy law is the truth (Tuscany).

**Liberta Eguaglianza**   Freedom and equality (Venice)

**Libertad en la Ley**   Freedom within the law (Mexico).

**Libertas Carior Auro**   Freedom is dearer than gold (St Gall).

**Libertas Vita Carior**   Freedom is dearer than life (Kulenberg).

**Libertas Xpo Firmata**   Freedom strengthened by Christ (Genoa).

**Liberte, Egalite, Fraternite**   Liberty, equality, fraternity (France).

**Lucerna Pedibus Meis Verbum Est**   Thy word is a lamp unto mine feet (England, Edward VI).

**Lumen ad Revelationem Gentium**   Light to enlighten the nations (Papacy).

**L'Union Fait la Force**   The union makes strength (Belgium)

**Macula Non Est in Te**   There is no sin in Thee (Essen).

**Magnus ab Integro Saeculorum Nascitur Ordo**   The great order of the centuries is born anew (Bavaria).

**Mandavit Dominus Palatie hanc Monetam Fiert**   The lord of the Palatine ordained this coin to be made (Balath).

**Manibus Ne Laedar Avaris**   Lest I be injured by greedy hands (Sweden).

**Mar Bran Sac Rom Imp Arcam et Elec Sup Dux Siles**   Margrave of Brandenburg, archchamberlain of the Holy Roman Empire and elector, senior duke of Silesia (Prussia).

**Maria Mater Domini Xpi**   Mary mother of Christ the Lord (Teutonic Knights).

**Maria Unxit Pedes Xpisti**   Mary washes the feet of Christ (France, Rene d'Anjou).

**Mater Castrorum**   Mother of fortresses (Rome, Marcus Aurelius).

**Matrimonio Conjuncti**   Joined in wedlock (Austria).

**Me Coniunctio Servat Dum Scinditur Frangor**   The relationship serves me while I am being torn to pieces (Lowenstein-Wertheim).

**Mediolani Dux**   Duke of Milan (Milan).

**Mediolani et Man**   Duke of Mantua and Milan (Milan).

**Memor Ero Tui Iustina Virgo**   I shall remember you, o maiden Justina (Venice).

**Merces Laborum**   Wages of work (Wurzburg).

**Mirabilia Fecit**   He wrought marvels (Viking coinage).

**Misericordia Di Rex**   King by the mercy of God (France, Louis II).

**Mo Arg Ord Foe Belg D Gel & CZ**   Silver coin of the order of the Belgian Federation, duchy of Guelder-land, county of Zutphen (Guelderland).

**Moneta Abbatis**   Coin of the abbey (German ecclesiastical coins, 13th–14th centuries).

**Moneta Argentiae Ord Foed Belgii Holl**   Silver coin of the federated union of Belgium and Holland (Batavian Republic).

**Mo No Arg Con Foe Belg Pro Hol**   New silver coin of the Belgian Federation, province of Holland (Holland).

**Mo No Arg Pro Confoe Belg Trai Holl**   New silver coin of the confederated Belgian provinces, Utrecht and Holland (Batavian Republic).

**Mon Lib Reip Bremens**   Coin of the free state of Bremen (Bremen).

**Mon Nova Arg Duc Curl Ad Norma Tal Alb**   New silver coin of the duchy of Courland, according to the standard of the Albert thaler (Courland).

**Mon Nov Castri Imp**   New coin of the Imperial free city of . . . (Friedberg).

**Moneta Bipont**   Coin of Zweibrucken (Pfalz-Birkenfeld-Zweibrucken).

**Monet Capit Cathedr Fuld Sede Vacante**   Coin of the cathedral chapter of Fulda, the see being vacant (Fulda).

**Moneta in Obsidione Tornacensi Cusa**   Coin struck during the siege of Tournai (Tournai, 1709).

**Moneta Livosesthonica**   Coin of Livonia (Estonia).

**Moneta Nov Arg Regis Daniae**   New silver coin of the king of Denmark (Denmark).

**Moneta Nova Ad Norman Conventionis**   New coin according to the Convention standard (Orsini-Rosenberg).

**Moneta Nova Domini Imperatoris**   New coin of the lord emperor (Brunswick, 13th century).

**Moneta Nova Lubecensis**   New coin of Lubeck.

**Moneta Nova Reipublicae Halae Suevicae**   New coin of the republic of Hall in Swabia.

**Moneta Reipublicae Ratisbonensis**   Coin of the republic of Regensburg.

**Nach Alt Reichs Schrot und Korn**   According to the old empire's grits and grain (Hesse).

**Nach dem Conventions Fusse**   According to the Convention's basis (German Conventionsthalers).

**Nach dem Frankf Schlus**   According to the Frankfurt standard (Solms).

**Nach dem Schlus der V Staend**   According to the standard of the union (Hesse).

**Navigare Necesse Est**   It is necessary to navigate (Germany).

**Nec Aspera Terrent**   Nor do difficulties terrify (Brunswick).

**Nec Cito Nec Temere**   Neither hastily nor rashlly (Cambrai).

**Nec Numina Desunt**   Nor is the divine will absent (Savoy).

**Nec Temere Nec Timide**   Neither rashly nor timidly (Danzig, Lippe).

**Necessitas Legem Non Habet**   Necessity has no law (Magdeburg).

**Nemo Me Impune Lacessit**   No one touches me with impunity (UK, Scottish pound edge inscription).

**Nihil Restat Reliqui**   No relic remains (Ypres).

**Nil Ultra Aras**   Nothing beyond the rocks (Franque-mont).

**No Nobis Dne Sed Noi Tuo Da Gloriam**   Not to us, o Lord but to Thy name be glory given (France, Francis I).

**Nobilissimum Dom Ac Com in Lipp & St**   Most noble lord and count in Lippe and Sternberg (Schaumburg-Lippe).

**Nomen Domini Turris Fortissima**   The name of the Lord is the strongest tower (Frankfurt).

**Non Aes Sed Fides**   Not bronze but trust (Malta).

**Non Est Mortale Quod Opto**   What I desire is not mortal. (Mecklenburg).

**Non Mihi Sed Populo**   Not to me but to the people (Bavaria).

**Non Relinquam Vos Orphanos**   I shall not leave you as orphans (Papacy).

**Non Surrexit Major**   None greater has arisen (Genoa, Malta).

**Nullum Simulatum Diuturnum Tandem**   Nothing that is feigned lasts long (Wittgenstein).

**Nummorum Famulus**   The servant of the coinage (England, tin halfpence and farthings).

**Nunquam Retrorsum**   Never backwards (Brunswick-Wolfenbuttel).

**O Crux Ave Spes Unica**   Hail, o Cross, our only hope (England half-angels, France, Rene d'Anjou).

**O Maria Ora Pro Me**   O Mary pray for me (Bavaria).

**Ob Cives Servatos**   On account of the rescued citizens (Rome, Augustus).

**Oculi Domini Super Iustos**   The eyes of the Lord look down on the just (Neuchatel).

**Omnia Auxiliante Maria**   Mary helping everything (Schwyz).

**Omnia Cum Deo**   Everything with God (Reuss-Greiz).

**Omnia cum Deo et Nihil Sine Eo**   Everthing with God and nothing without Him (Erbach).

**Omnis Potestas a Deo Est**   All power comes from God (Sweden).

**Opp & Carn Dux Comm Rittb SCM Cons Int & Compi Mareschal**   Duke of Troppau and Carniola, count of Rietberg, privy councillor of his sacred imperial majesty, field marshal (Liechtenstein).

**Opp & Carn . . . Aur Velleris Eques**   Duke of Troppau . . . knight of the Golden Fleece (Liechtenstein).

**Opportune**   Conveniently (Savoy).

**Optimus Princeps**   Best prince (Rome, Trajan).

**Opulentia Salerno**   Wealthy Salerno (Siculo-Norman kingdom).

**Pace et Iustitia**   With peace and justice (Spanish Netherlands).

**Pacator Orbis**   Pacifier of the world (Rome, Aurelian).

**Palma Sub Pondere Crescit**   The palm grows under its weight (Waldeck).

**Pater Noster**   Our Father (Flanders, 14th century).

**Pater Patriae**   Farther of his country (Rome, Caligula).

**Patria Si Dreptul Meu**   The country and my right (Roumania).

**Patrimon Henr Frid Sorte Divisum**   The heritage of Heinrich Friedrich divided by lot (Hohenlohe-Langenberg).

**Patrimonia Beati Petri**   The inheritance of the blessed Peter (Papacy).

**Patrona Franconiae**   Patron of Franconia (Wurzburg).

**Pax Aeterna**   Eternal peace (Rome, Marcus Aurelius).

**Pax et Abundantia**   Peace and plenty (Burgundy, Gelderland).

**Pax Missa Per Orbem**   Peace sent throughout the world (England, Anne).

**Pax Petrus**   Peace Peter (Trier, 10th century).

**Pax Praevalet Armis**   May peace prevail by force of arms (Mainz).

**Pax Quaeritur Bello**   Peace is sought by war (Commonwealth, Cromwell).

**Pecunia Totum Circumit Orbem**   Money goes round the whole world (Brazil).

**Per Aspera Ad Astra**   Through difficulties to the stars (Mecklenburg-Schwerin).

**Per Angusta ad Augusta**   Through precarious times to the majestic (Solms-Roedelheim, a pun on the name of the ruler Johan August).

**Per Crucem Tuam Salva Nos Christe Redemptor**   By Thy cross save us, O Christ our Redeemer (England, angels).

**Per Crucem Tuam Salva Nos Xpe Redemt**   By Thy cross save us, O Christ our Redeemer (Portugal, 15th century).

**Perdam Babillonis Nomen**   May the name of Babylon perish (Naples).

**Perennitati Iustissimi Regis**   For the duration of the most just king (France, Louis XIII).

**Perennitati Principis Galliae Restitutionis**   For the duration of the restoration of the prince of the Gauls (France, Henri IV).

**Perfer et Obdura Bruxella**   Carry on and stick it out, Brussels (Brussels siege, 1579–80).

**Perpetuus in Nemet Vivar**   Hereditary count in Nemt-Ujvar (Batthyani).

**Pietate et Constantia**   By piety and constancy (Fulda).

**Pietate et Iustitia**   By piety and justice (Denmark).

**Plebei Urbanae Frumento Constituto**   Free distribu-tion of grain to the urban working-class established (Rome, Nerva).

**Pleidio Wyf Im Gwlad**   True am I to my country (UK, Welsh pound edge inscription).

**Plus Ultra**   Beyond (the Pillars of Hercules) (Spanish America).

**Point du Couronne sans Peine**   Point of the crown without penalty (Coburg).

**Pons Civit Castellana**   The bridge of the town of Castellana (Papacy).

**Populus et Senatus Bonon**   The people and senate of Bologna (Bologna).

**Post Mortem Patris Pro Filio**   For the son after his father's death (Pontefract siege coins).

**Post Tenebras Lux**   After darkness light (Geneva).

**Post Tenebras Spero Lucem**   After darkness I hope for light (Geneva).

**Posui Deum Adiutorem Meum**   I have made God my helper (England, Ireland, 1351–1603).

**Praesidium et Decus**   Protection and ornament (Bologna).

**Prima Sedes Galliarum**   First see of the Gauls (Lyon).

**Primitiae Fodin Kuttenb ab Aerari Iterum Susceptarum**   First results dug from the Kuttenberg mines in a renewed undertaking (Austria).

**Princps Iuventutis**   Prince of youth (Roman Empire).

**Pro Defensione Urbis et Patriae**   For the defence of city and country (France, Louis XIV).

**Pro Deo et Patria**   For God and the fatherland (Fulda).

**Pro Deo et Populo**   For God and the people (Bavaria).

**Pro Ecclesia et Pro Patria**   For the church and the fatherland (Constance).

**Pro Fausio PP Reitur VS**   For happy returns of the princes of the Two Sicilies (Naples and Sicily).

**Pro Lege et Grege**   For law and the flock (Fulda).

**Pro maximo Dei Gloria et Bono Publico**   For the greatest glory of God and the good of the people (Wurttemberg).

**Pro Patria**   For the fatherland (Wurzburg).

**Propitio Deo Secura Ago**   With God's favour I lead a secure life. (Saxe-Lauenburg).

**Protector Literis Literae Nummis Corona et Salus**   A protection to the letters (on the face of the coin), the letters (on the edge) are a garland and a safeguard to the coinage (Commonwealth, Cromwell broad).

**Protege Virgo Pisas**   Protect Pisa, O Virgin (Pisa).

**Provide et Constanter**   Wisely and firmly (Wurttem-berg).

**Providentia et Pactis**   Through foresight and pacts (Brandenburg-Ansbach).

**Providentia Optimi Principis**   With the foresight of the best prince (Naples and Sicily).

**Proxima Fisica Finis**   Nearest to natural end (Orciano).

**Proxima Soli**   Nearest to the sun (Modena).

**Pulcra Virtutis Imago**   The beautiful image of virtue (Genoa).

**Pupillum et Viduam Suscipiat**   May he support the orphan and the widow (Savoy).

**Quae Deus Conjunxit Nemo Separet**   What God hath joined let no man put asunder (England, James I).

**Quem Quadragesies et Semel Patriae Natum Esse Gratulamur**   Whom we congratulate for the forty-first time for being born for the fatherland (Lippe-Detmold).

**Qui Dat Pauperi Non Indigebit**   Who gives to the poor will never be in need (Munster).

**Quid Non Cogit Necessitas**   To what does Necessity not drive. (Ypres).

**Quin Matrimonii Lustrum Celebrant**   They celebrate their silver wedding (Austria, 1879).

**Quocunque Gesseris (Jeceris) Stabit**   Whichever way you throw it it will stand (Isle of Man).

**Quod Deus Vult Hoc Semper Fit**   What God wishes always occurs. (Saxe-Weimar).

**Reconduntur non Retonduntur**   They are laid up in store, not thundered back (Savoy).

**Recta Tueri**   Defend the right (Austria).

**Recte Constanter et Fortiter**   Rightly, constantly and bravely (Bavaria).

**Recte Faciendo Neminem Timeas**   May you fear no one in doing right. (Solms-Laubach).

**Rector Orbis**   Ruler of the world (Rome, Didius Julianus).

**Rectus et Immotus**   Right and immovable (Hesse).

**Redde Cuique Quod Suum Est**   Render to each that which is his own (England, Henry VIII).

**Redeunt antiqui Gaudia Moris**   There return the joys of ancient custom (Regensburg).

**Reg Pr Pol et Lith Saxon Dux**   Royal prince of Poland and Lithuania and duke of Saxony (Trier).

**Regia Boruss Societas Asiat Embdae**   Royal Prussian Asiatic Society of Emden (Prussia).

**Regier Mich Her Nach Deinen Wort**   Govern me here according to Thy word (Palatinate).

**Regnans Capitulum Ecclesiae Cathedralis Ratisbonensis Sede Vacante**   Administering the chapter of the cathedral church at Regensburg, the see being vacant (Regensburg).

**Regni Utr Sic et Hier**   Of the kingdom of the Two Sicilies and of Jerusalem (Naples and Sicily).

**Religio Protestantium Leges Angliae Libertas Parliamenti**   The religion of the Protestants, the laws of England and the freedom of Parliament (England, Royalists, 1642).

**Relinquo Vos Liberos ab Utroque Homine**   I leave you as children of each man (San Marino).

**Restauracao da Independencia**   Restoration of inde-pendence (Portugal, 1990).

**Restitutor Exercitus**   Restorer of the army (Rome, Aurelian).

**Restitutor Galliarum**   Restorer of the Gauls (Rome, Gallienus).

**Restitutor Generis Humani**   Restorer of mankind (Rome, Valerian).

**Restitutor Libertatis**   Restorer of freedom (Rome, Constantine).

**Restitutor Orbis**   Restorer of the world (Rome, Valerian).

**Restitutor Orientis**   Restorer of the east (Rome, Valerian).

**Restitutor Saeculi**   Restorer of the century (Rome, Valerian).

**Restitutor Urbis**   Restorer of the city (Rome, Severus).

**Rosa Americana Utile Dulci**   The American rose, useful and sweet (American colonies).

**Rosa Sine Spina**   A rose without a thorn (England, Tudor coins).

**Rutilans Rosa Sine Spina**   A dazzling rose without a thorn (England, Tudor gold coins).

**S Annae Fundgruben Ausb Tha in N Oe**   Mining thaler of the St Anne mine in Lower Austria (Austria).

**S Ap S Leg Nat Germ Primas**   Legate of the Holy Apostolic See, born Primate of Germany (Salzburg).

**S Carolus Magnus Fundator**   Charlemagne founder (Munster).

**S. Gertrudis Virgo Prudens Niviella**   St Gertrude the wise virgin of Nivelles (Nivelles).

**Sl Aul Reg Her & P Ge H Post Mag**   General hereditary postmaster, supreme of the imperial court of the hereditary kingdom and provinces (Paar).

**S. Ian Bapt F. Zachari**   St John the Baptist, son of Zachary (Florence).

**S. Kilianus Cum Sociis Francorum Apostoli**   St Kilian and his companions, apostles to the Franks (Wurzburg).

**S. Lambertus Patronus Leodiensis**   St Lambert, patron of Liege (Liege).

**Sac Nupt Celeb Berol**   For the holy matrimony celebrated at Berlin (Brandenburg-Ansbach).

**Sac Rom Imp**   Holy Roman Empire (German states).

**Sac Rom Imp Provisor Iterum**   Administrator of the Holy Roman Empire for the second time (Saxony).

**Salus Generis Humani**   Safety of mankind (Rome, Vindex).

**Salus Patriae**   Safety of the fatherland (Italy).

**Salus Populi**   The safety of the people (Spain).

**Salus Provinciarum**   Safety of the provinces (Rome, Postumus).

**Salus Publica Salus Mea**   Public safety is my safety (Sweden).

**Salus Reipublicae**   The safety of the republic (Rome, Theodosius II).

**Salus Reipublicae Suprema Lex**   The safety of the republic is the supreme law (Poland).

**Salvam Fac Rempublicam Tuam**   Make your state safe (San Marino).

**Sanctus Iohannes Innoce**   St John the harmless (Gandersheim).

**Sans Changer**   Without changing (Isle of Man).

**Sans Eclat**   Without pomp (Bouchain siege, 1711).

**Sapiente Diffidentia**   Wise distrust (Teschen).

**Scutum Fidei Proteget Eum / Eam**   The shield of faith shall protect him / her (England, Edward VI and Elizabeth I).

**Secundum Voluntatem Tuam Domine**   Your favourable will o Lord (Hesse).

**Securitati Publicae**   For the public safety (Brandenburg-Ansbach).

**Sede Vacante**   The see being vacant (Papal states, Vatican and ecclesiastical coinage).

**Sena Vetus Alpha et W Principum et Finis**   Old Siena alpha and omega, the beginning and the end (Siena).

**Senatus Populus QR**   Senate and people of Rome (Rome, 1188).

**Si Deus Nobiscum Quis Contra Nos**   If God is with us who can oppose us (Hesse).

**Si Deus Pro Nobis Quis Contra Nos**  If God is for us who can oppose us (Roemhild).

**Sieh Deine Seeligkeit Steht Fest Ins Vaters Liebe**  Behold thy salvation stands surely in thy Father's love (Gotha).

**Signis Receptis**  When the standards had been recovered (Rome, Augustus).

**Signum Crucis**  The sign of the cross (Groningen).

**Sincere et Constanter**  Truthfully and steadfastly (Hesse-Darmstadt).

**Sit Nomen Domini Benedictum**  Blessed be the name of the Lord (Burgundy, Strasbourg).

**St T X Adiuto Reg Iste Domba**  Let it be to you, o Christ, the assistant to the king of Dombes (Dombes).

**Sit Tibi Xpe Dat q'tu Regis Iste Ducat**  May this duchy which Thou rulest be given to Thee, O Christ (Venice, ducat).

**Sit Unio Haec Perennis**  May this union last for ever (Hohenlohe-Langenberg).

**Sola Bona Quae Honesta**  The only good things are those which are honest (Brunswick).

**Sola Facta Deum Sequor**  Through deeds alone I strive to follow God (Milan).

**Soli Deo Honor et Gloria**  To God alone be honour and glory (Nassau).

**Soli Reduci**  To him, the only one restored (Naples and Sicily).

**Solius Virtutis Flos Perpetuus**  The flower of Virtue alone is perpetual (Strasbourg).

**Spes Confisa Deo Nunquam Confusa Recedit**  Hope entrusted in God never retreats in a disorderly fashion (Lippe).

**Spes Nr Deus**  God is our hope (Oudenarde siege, 1582).

**Spes Rei Publicae**  The hope of the republic (Rome, Valens).

**Strena ex Argyrocopeo Vallis S Christoph**  A New Year's gift from the silver-bearing valley of St Christopher (Wurttemberg, 1625).

**Sub His Secura Spes Clupeus Omnibus in Te Sperantibus**  Under these hope is safe, a shield for all who reside hope in Thee (Bavaria).

**Sub Pondere**  Under weight (Fulda).

**Sub Protectione Caesarea**  Under imperial protection (Soragna).

**Sub Tuum Praesidium Confug**  We flee to Thy protection (Salzburg).

**Sub Umbra Alarum Tuarum**  Under the shadow of Thy wings (Iever, Scotland, James V).

**Subditorum Salus Felicitas Summa**  The safety of the subjects is the highest happiness (Lubeck).

**Sufficit Mihi Gratia Tua Domine**  Sufficient to me is Thy grace, o Lord (Ploen).

**Supra Firmam Petram**  Upon a firm rock (Papacy).

**Susceptor Noster Deus**  God is our defence (Tuscany).

**Sydera Favent Industriae**  The stars favour industry (Furstenberg).

**Sylvarum Culturae Praemium**  Prize for the culture of the forest (Brandenburg-Ansbach).

**Tali Dicata Signo Mens Fluctuari Nequit**  Consecrated by such a sign the mind cannot waver (England, Henry VIII George noble).

**Tandem Bona Caus Triumphat**  A good cause eventually triumphs (Dillenburg).

**Tandem Fortuna Obstetrice**  With good luck ultimately as the midwife (Wittgenstein).

**Te Stante Virebo**  With you at my side I shall be strong (Moravia).

**Tene Mensuram et Respice Finem**  Hold the measure and look to the end (Burgundy).

**Tert Ducat Secular**  Tercentenary of the duchy (Wurttemberg).

**Thu Recht Schev Niemand**  Go with right and fear no one (Saxe-Lauenburg).

**Tibi Laus et Gloria**  To Thee be praise and glory (Venice).

**Timor Domini Fons Vitae**  The fear of the Lord is a fountain of life (England, Edward VI shillings).

**Tout Avec Dieu**  Everything with God (Brunswick, 1626).

**Traiectum ad Mosam**  The crossing of the Maas (Maastricht).

**Transvolat Nubila Virtus**  Marriageable virtue soon flies past (Grueyeres).

**Travail, Famille, Patrie**  Work, family, country (Vichy France).

**Triumphator Gent Barb**  Victor over the barbarian people (Byzantine Empire, Arcadius).

**Tueatur Unita Deus**  May God guard these united (Kingdoms) (England, James I; Britain, 1847).

**Turck Blegert Wien**  Vienna besieged by the Turks (Vienna, 1531).

**Tut Mar Gab Pr Vid de Lobk Nat Pr Sab Car et Aug Pr de Lobk**  Regency of Maria Gabriela, widow of the prince of Lobkowitz, born princess of Savoy-Carignan, and August prince of Lobkowitz (Lobkowitz).

**Tutela Italiae**  The guardianship of Italy (Rome, Nerva).

**Ubi Vult Spirat**  He breathes where he will (Papacy).

**Ubique Pax**  Peace everywhere (Rome, Gallienus).

**Union et Force**  Union and strength (France).

**Urbe Obsessa**  The city under siege (Maastricht).

**Urbem Virgo Tuam Serva**  Protects thy city o virgin (Mary) (Strasbourg).

**USC & RAM Cons Int Gen C Mar & Nob Praet H Turmae Capit**  Privy councillor of both their holy imperial and royal apostolic majesties, general field marshal and captain of the noble praetorian Hungarian squadrons (Eszterhazy).

**Veni Luumen Cordium**  Come light of hearts (Vatican).

**Veni Sancte Spiritus**  Come Holy Ghost (Vatican).

**Verbum Domini Manet in Aeternum**  The word of the Lord abides forever (Hesse-Darmstadt, Veldenz).

**Veritas Lex Tua**   The truth is your law (Salzburg).

**Veritas Temporis Filia**   Truth is the daughter of time (England and Ireland, Mary Tudor).

**Veritate et Labore**   By truth and work (Wittgenstein).

**Veritate et Iustitia**   By truth and justice (German states).

**Victoria Principum**   The victory of princes (Ostrogoths).

**Videant Pauperes et Laetentur**   Let the poor see and rejoice (Tuscany).

**Virgo Maria Protege Civitatem Savonae**   Virgin Mary Protect the city of Savona (Savona).

**Viribus Unitis**   With united strength (Austria).

**Virtute et Fidelitate**   By virtue and faithfulness (Hesse-Cassel).

**Virtute et Prudentia**   With virtue and prudence (Auersperg).

**Virtute Viam Dimetiar**   I shall mark the way with valour (Waldeck).

**Virtutis Gloria Merces**   Glory is the reward of valour (Holstein-Gottorp).

**Vis Unita Concordia Fratrum Fortior**   United power is the stronger harmony of brothers (Mansfeld).

**Visitavit Nos Oriens ex Alto**   He has visited us arising on high (Luneburg).

**Vivit Post Funera**   He lives after death (Bremen).

**Vota Optata Romae Fel**   Vows taken for the luck of Rome (Rome, Maxentius).

**Vox de Throno**   A voice from the throne (Papacy).

**Was Got Beschert Bleibet Unerwert**   What God hath endowed leave undisturbed

**Wider macht und List Mein Fels Gott Ist**   Against might and trickery God is my rock (Hesse-Cassel).

**Xpc Vincit Xpc Regnat**   Christ conquers, Christ reigns (Scotland, Spain).

**Xpc Vivet Xpc Regnat Xpc Impat**   Christ lives, Christ reigns, Christ commands (Cambrai).

**Xpe Resurescit**   Christ lives again (Venice).

**Xpistiana Religio**   Christian religion (Carolingian Empire).

**Xps Ihs Elegit me Regem Populo**   Jesus Christ chose me as king to the people (Norway).

**Zelator Fidei Usque ad Montem**   An upholder of the faith through and through (Portugal).

**Zum Besten des Vaterlands**   To the best of the fatherland (Bamberg).

| ABBREVIATIONS COMMONLY USED TO DENOTE METALLIC COMPOSITION | |
| --- | --- |
| Cu | Copper |
| Cu/Steel | Copper plated Steel |
| Ag/Cu | Silver plated copper |
| Ae | Bronze |
| Cu-Ni | Cupro-Nickel |
| Ni-Ag | Nickel Silver (note-does not contain silver) |
| Brass/Cu-Ni | Brass outer, Cupro-Nickel inner |
| Ni-Brass | Nickel-Brass |
| Ag | Silver |
| Au/Ag | Gold plated silver |
| Au | Gold |
| Pl | Platinum |

# CARE *of coins*

There is no point in going to a great deal of trouble and expense in selecting the best coins you can afford, only to let them deteriorate in value by neglect and mishandling. Unless you give some thought to the proper care of your coins, your collection is unlikely to make a profit for you if and when you come to sell it. Housing your coins is the biggest problem of all, so it is important to give a lot of attention to this.

## Storage

The ideal, but admittedly the most expensive, method is the coin cabinet, constructed of air-dried mahogany, walnut or rosewood (*never* oak, cedar or any highly resinous timber likely to cause chemical tarnish). These cabinets have banks of shallow drawers containing trays made of the same wood, with half-drilled holes of various sizes to accommodate the different denominations of coins. Such cabinets are handsome pieces of furniture but, being largely handmade, tend to be rather expensive. Occasionally good specimens can be picked up in secondhand furniture shops, or at the dispersal of house contents by auction, but the best bet is still to purchase a new cabinet, tailored to your own requirements. These collectors cabinets are hand-made using certified solid mahogany, as

specified by leading museums, as mahogany does not contain any chemicals or resins that could result in the discolouration of the collection inside the cabinet. The polish used on the outside of the cabinets is based on natural oils and hand applied then finished with bees wax. The trays are left as untreated mahogany so as not to introduce any harmful contaminants. The coin trays are available as single thickness or double thickness for holding thicker coins, capsules or artifacts.

Peter Nichols Cabinets (telephone 0115 9224149, www.coincabinets.com) was established in 1967. In October 2010 Peter retired and passed the cabinet making business on to Geoff Skinner, Shirley Watts and Ben Skinner-Watts. Now based in Nottingham, the family run business continues to provide specialist and bespoke display and storage

*Above: The Mascle Classic—the ideal "entry-level" coin cabinet for collectors. Left: The Martlet—a four-tray cabinet suitable for the specialist collection.*

systems to suit every need from the seven-tray Pheon all the way up to the massive 40-tray specials supplied to the British Museum. All cabinets are fitted with double doors. Prices start at around £80 and go up to about £350 for the thirty-tray Coronet. They are not cheap, but you have the satisfaction of acquiring exquisite examples of the cabinet maker's craft.

An excellent storage option is provided by a number of firms who manufacture coin trays in durable, felt-lined materials with shallow compartments to suit the various sizes of coins. Most of these trays interlock so that they build up into a cabinet of the desired size, and there are also versions designed as carrying cases, which are ideal for transporting coins.

The popular and extensive Lighthouse range is available from The Duncannon Partnership, 4 Beaufort Road, Reigate, RH2 9DJ (telephone 01737 244222, www.duncannon.co.uk) or Token Publishing Ltd (telephone 01404 44167, www.tokenpublishing.com). This range includes a wide variety of cases and albums for the general collector in basic or de luxe styles as required, as well as printed albums for the specialist. Their cases, including the popular aluminium range, are manufactured to the highest standards, lined with blue plush which displays any coin to its best advantage. The red-lined single trays come in deep or standard size and make an ideal cabinet when stacked together or housed in their attractive aluminium case, which is available separately. The trays themselves come with a variety of compartments for every size of coin. Their complete range can be viewed on-line.

Adding on to the stacking Lindner range is easy.

The extensive Lindner range is supplied in the UK by Prinze Publications of 3A Hayle Industrial Park, Hayle, Cornwall TR27 5JR (telephone 01736 751914, www.prinz.co.uk or from Token Publishing Ltd telephone 01404 44167, www.tokenpublishing.com). Well-known for their wide range of philatelic and numismatic accessories, but these include a full array of coin boxes, capsules, carrying cases and trays . The basic Lindner coin box is, in fact,

Safe's cabinet combines elegance with security.

a shallow tray available in a standard version or a smoked glass version. These trays have a crystal clear frame, red felt inserts and holes for various diameters of coins and medals. A novel feature of these trays is the rounded insert which facilitates the removal of coins from their spaces with the minimum of handling. These boxes are designed in such a manner that they interlock and can be built up into banks of trays, each fitted with a draw-handle and sliding in and out easily. Various types of chemically inert plastic capsules and envelopes have been designed for use in combination with plain shallow trays, without holes drilled. Lindner also manufacture a range of luxury cases lined in velvet and Atlas silk with padded covers and gold embossing on the spines, producing a most tasteful and elegant appearance.

Safe Albums of 16 Falcon Business Park, 38 Ivanhoe Road, Finchampstead, Berkshire RG40 4QQ (telephone 0118 932 8976, www.safealbums.co.uk) are the UK agents for the German Stapel-Element, a drawer-stacking system with clear plasticiser-free trays that fit into standard bookshelves. The sliding coin compartments, lined with blue velvet, can be angled for display to best advantage. Stackable drawers can be built up to any height desired. A wide range of drawer sizes is available, with compartments suitable for the smallest coins right up to four-compartment trays designed for very large artefacts such as card-cases or cigarette cases. The Mobel-Element cabinet is a superb specialised cabinet constructed of the finest timber with a steel frame and steel grip bars which can be securely locked. It thus combines elegance with security and is the ideal medium for the most valuable coins and medals.

There are also various storage systems, such as Coindex, which operate on the principle of narrow drawers in which the coins are stored in envelopes of chemically-inert plastic. A strip across the top holds a little slip giving a brief description, catalogue number and the price of each coin.

The Sydney Museum in Australia, for example, keeps its coins in manila envelopes stored in plastic lunch-boxes which seemed to do the job pretty well!

### Coin Albums

When coin collecting became a popular hobby in the 1960s, several firms marketed ranges of coin albums. They had clear plastic sleeves divided into tiny compartments of various sizes and had the merit of being cheap and taking up little room on a bookshelf.

They had several drawbacks, however, not the least being the tendency of the pages to sag with the weight of the coins, or even, in extreme cases, to pull away from the pegs or rings holding them on to the spine. They required very careful handling as the coins could easily fall out of the top row as the pages were turned. The more expensive albums had little flaps that folded over the top of the coin to overcome this problem.

Arguably the worst aspect of these albums was the use of polyvinyl chloride (PVC) in the construction of the sleeves. Collectors soon discovered to their horror that this reacted chemically with their coins, especially those made of silver, causing a rather disgusting yellow slime to adhere to the coins' surface. I shudder to think how many fine collections were ruined as a result, or of the countless coins that required highly expert treatment in a bid to restore them to as near the original condition as possible.

Fortunately the lesson has been learned and the coin albums now on the market are quite safe. Lighthouse and Lindner offer a wide range of albums designed to house coins, medals or banknotes.

*The Lighthouse range includes a wide selection of de luxe and printed albums.*

The old problem about sagging pages is overcome by the use of a multi-ring binding welded to a very stout spine, while the sleeves contain neither Styrol nor PVC and will not affect any metals at all. In addition to pages with pockets of uniform size, the Karat range of albums operates on a slide principle which enables the user to insert vertical strips of different sizes on the same page, so that the coins of one country or series, or perhaps a thematic display of coins from different countries, can be displayed side by side.

Safe Albums offer a wide range of albums in the Coinholder System and Coin-Combi ranges. These, too, offer the choice of fixed pages with uniform-sized pockets, or interchangeable sliding inserts for different sizes side by side.

Token Publishing Ltd stock a varied range of coin accessories from magnifying glasses to coin albums. To find out more, simply log onto www.tokenpublishing.com or call 01404 44167 for an up-to-date illustrated, colour catalogue.

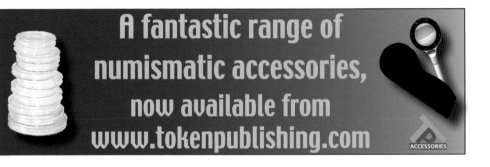

# CLEANING *coins*

This is like matrimony—it should not be embarked on lightly. Indeed, the advice given by the magazine *Punch* in regard to marriage is equally sound in this case—don't do it! It is far better to have a dirty coin than an irretrievably damaged one. Every dealer has horror stories of handling coins that previous owners have cleaned, to their detriment. The worst example I ever saw was a display of coins found by a metal detectorist who "improved" his finds by abrading them in the kind of rotary drum used by lapidarists to polish gemstones. If you really must remove the dirt and grease from coins, it is advisable to practise on coins of little value.

Warm water containing a mild household detergent or washing-up liquid will work wonders in removing surface dirt and grease from most coins, but silver is best washed in a weak solution of ammonia and warm water—one part ammonia to ten parts water. Gold coins can be cleaned with diluted citric acid, such as lemon juice. Copper or bronze coins present more of a problem, but patches of verdigris can usually be removed by careful washing in a 20 per cent solution of sodium sesquicarbonate. Wartime coins made of tin, zinc,

iron or steel can be cleaned in a 5 per cent solution of caustic soda containing some aluminium or zinc foil or filings, but they must be rinsed afterwards in clean water and carefully dried. Cotton buds are ideal for gently prising dirt out of coin legends and crevices in the designs. Soft brushes (with animal bristles—*never* nylon or other artificial bristles) designed for cleaning silver are most suitable for gently cleaning coins.

Coins recovered from the soil or the sea bed present special problems, due to chemical reaction between the metals and the salts in the earth or sea water. In such cases, the best advice is to take them to the nearest museum and let the professional experts decide on what can or should be done.

Both Lindner and Safe Albums offer a range of coin-cleaning kits and materials suitable for gold, silver, copper and other base alloys respectively. Safe (living up to their name) also provide a stern warning that rubber gloves should be worn and care taken to avoid breathing fumes or getting splashes of liquid in your eyes or on your skin. Obviously, the whole business of cleaning is a matter that should not be entered into without the utmost care and forethought.

## POLISHING: A WARNING

If cleaning should only be approached with the greatest trepidation, polishing is definitely *out!* Beginners sometimes fall into the appalling error of thinking that a smart rub with metal polish might improve the appearance of their coins. Short of actually punching a hole through it, there can hardly be a more destructive act. Polishing a coin may improve its superficial appearance for a few days, but such abrasive action will destroy the patina and reduce the fineness of the high points of the surface.

Even if a coin is only polished once, it will never be quite the same again, and an expert can tell this a mile off.

# CELTIC coinage of Britain

**Pritanic coins were the first coins made in Britain. They were issued for a century and a half before the Roman invasion, and possibly a little later in some areas. They were minted by the rulers of thirteen tribal groups or administrative authorities situated on the southeast of a line from the Humber to the Severn. In this short article Pritanic specialist CHRIS RUDD introduces this increasingly popular series.**

Most folk call them British Celtic or Celtic coins of Britain. But I'll begin by letting you into a little known secret: most folk may be wrong. You see, there is no ancient textual evidence—none whatsoever—that anyone in iron age Britain called themselves a Celt. Neither is there a hint—not a whisper—that anyone else in the ancient world ever referred to the Brits as Celts. The Greeks didn't, the Gauls didn't, the Romans didn't. The correct name for iron age Britons is Pritani—well formed people or people of the forms. How do we know? Because a sailor from Marseilles said so.

## The first coins made in Britain were made like this

Molten tin-rich bronze was poured into clay moulds.

Coin designs were scribed onto clay strip-moulds with a stylus prior to firing. Tentative reconstruction.

## and look like this

Cast bronze
c.120-100 BC

Cast potin
c.80-50 BC

*Many Gaulish coins were imported to Britain, like this silver stater of the Coriosolites (ABC 70), typical of many in the huge Jersey hoard found in June 2012, containing an estimated 50,000 coins.*

Around 330 BC an explorer, Pytheas of Marseilles, sailed to Britain in search of tin. His visit indicates early trade links with southern Gaul and that the Britons were called Pritani. Marseilles inspired Britain's first homemade coinage: potin coins cast in clay strip-moulds, with Apollo on one side and a bull on the other, plus MA for Massalia (Marseilles). Made in Kent c. 120–100 BC, these cast potins circulated alongside gold coins imported from Gaul. During the Gallic Wars (58–51 BC) many other Gaulish coins—gold, silver and bronze—came to Britain, some brought by refugees, others by British mercenaries, others by trade.

The most famous Gallic migrant was Commios "friend", a former ally of Caesar, who became king of the Regini and Atrebates in the south of England c. 50–25 BC. Commios was the first British ruler to place his name on coins. His three sons—Tincomarus (great in peace), Eppillus (little horse) and Verica (the high one), made the Commian dynasty one of the wealthiest and most powerful in Britain. Most of their coins adopted Roman imagery and archaeology indicates that they imported Roman luxury goods, especially Italian wine. Many coins of Verica show grapes, vine leaves and wine cups.

The main rivals of the Regini and Atrebates were the Catuvellauni of Hertfordshire. Their first known ruler was probably Cassivellaunos "bronze commander", leader of the British coalition against Caesar in 54 BC. Many of Britain's earliest gold coins were probably struck to fund resistance to Caesar and then to pay tribute to him. Cassivellaunos may have organised this war money. Addedomaros "great in chariots" (c. 45–25 BC) was the first ruler north of the Thames to inscribe his coins, perhaps copying Commios.

*Thirteen possible tribal groups which were producing coins by c.50-40 BC (Cantiaci much earlier). By c.30 BC the Belgae, East Wiltshire and Berkshire group had apparently stopped minting independently.*

*Gold stater of Commios (ABC 1022) the first British king to place his name on coins. There are two hidden faces on the obverse.*

*Verica silver minim with wine cup (ABC 1331) and Verica gold stater with vine leaf (ABC 1193)—evidence of Britain's thirst for fine Italian wine and Roman silverware.*

Catuvellaunian expansion continued under Tasciovanos "killer of badgers" whose coins became increasingly Roman in style. His son Cunobelinus "hound of Belenus"—Shakespeare's *Cymbeline*) was the most potent tribal king in Atlantic Europe. Suetonius called him "king of the Britons". During his thirty-year reign (c. AD 8–41) Cunobelinus may have minted well over a million gold staters, most of them displaying a corn ear and CAMV— short for *Camulodunon* (Colchester). When his brother Epaticcus "leader of horsemen" and his son Caratacus "the beloved"—both clad as Hercules on their silver coins—crossed the Thames and attacked the Atrebates, Verica fled to Claudius who invaded Britain in AD 43. The minting of tribal coins ceased shortly afterwards.

Other tribes that issued coins included the Cantiaci of Kent, the Belgae of Hampshire, the Durotriges of Dorset, the Dobunni of the West Midlands, the Trinovantes of Essex, the Iceni of East Anglia and the Corieltavi of Lincolnshire. However, only a minority of people in the British Isles used coins regularly—the moneyed minority in southeast England. Cornwall, Devon, Wales, northern England, Scotland and Ireland remained coinless. Which is why ancient British coins are relatively rare. For example, whereas Greek coins were minted for about 600 years, Roman for about 800 years and Gaulish for about 250 years, ancient British coins were produced for little more than 150 years, and often in much smaller runs.

| 700 | 600 | 500 | 400 | 300 | 200 | 100 | BC-AD | 100 | 200 | 300 | 400 | 500 | 600 |
|-----|-----|-----|-----|-----|-----|-----|-------|-----|-----|-----|-----|-----|-----|

**GREEK**

**ROMAN**

**GAULISH**

**BRITISH**

*Ancient British coins weren't minted for as long as Greek, Roman or Gaulish coins were. That's one of the reasons they are so scarce.*

This century and a half of Pritanic (not Celtic) coin production generated a remarkable flowering of insular creativity and insular technology, unmatched by any other northern European nation of the period. Though initially influenced by Gallic minting techniques and Gallic iconography, ancient British coinage rapidly developed its own denominational systems, its own gold standards and its own highly distinctive coin designs—often inspired by Roman prototypes, but invariably modified to suit local needs. Between c. 110 BC and c. AD 45 around a thousand different coin types were minted in Britain. Many if not most of these thousand types displayed what might loosely be described as "religious" imagery. Not surprising, really, when one recalls that Caesar says that Druidism originated in Britain. Moreover, Tasciovanos struck coins in no fewer than five different denominations, whereas most Gaulish rulers issued no more than two or three.

The history of late iron age Britain, particularly the century prior to the Claudian conquest, has largely been rewritten with the help of ancient British coins. Most of the recent advances in our knowledge of this period have been due to amateur metal detecting. As a direct result of coin finds made by metal detectorists since the 1970s four new coin-issuing groups and maybe ten new rulers, previously unknown or unrecognised, have been identified. Not bad for barely forty years of

*Unlike Gaul, most of the British Isles was virtually coinless throughout the late iron age (and later). Coin production was confined to south-east Britain. That's why, overall, ancient British coins are much rarer than Gaulish coins.*

unfunded, unofficial fieldwork.

What is it about ancient British coins that is making them increasingly popular with collectors all over the world? Having been involved with them for many years (I excavated my first in 1952) I'll tell you why they appeal to me.

I love the *primal antiquity* of Pritanic coins. They were the first coins made in Britain over two thousand years ago. When you see the flamboyant freedom of their designs you realise that they are the most boisterously British coins ever minted, unlike the unsmiling Roman, Anglo-Saxon and Norman series that marched soberly in their dancing footsteps.

I love the *anarchic regality* of Pritanic coins. Like the rumbustious tribal kings that issued them, their personality is wild, strong and highly irregular. These coins were made by the first British rulers known by name to us—unruly, quarrelsome, beer-swilling, tribal warlords such as Cassivellaunos who fought Julius Caesar in 54 BC and Caratacus, the British resistance leader who opposed Claudius in AD 43.

I love the *imaginative imagery* you find on Pritanic coins: all the different gods and goddesses, armed warriors, chariot wheels, hidden faces, decapitated heads, suns, moons, stars, thunderbolts, floral motifs, magic signs and phallic symbols. Plus an amazing menagerie of wild animals, birds and mythical beasts.

I love the *myths, mystery and mysticism* behind Pritanic coins. Look closely at this late iron

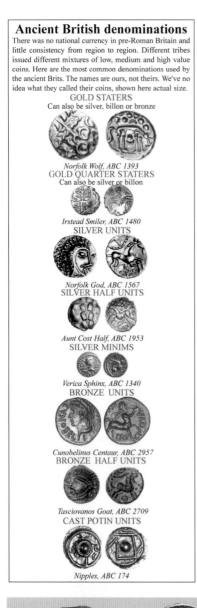

## Ancient British denominations

There was no national currency in pre-Roman Britain and little consistency from region to region. Different tribes issued different mixtures of low, medium and high value coins. Here are the most common denominations used by the ancient Brits. The names are ours, not theirs. We've no idea what they called their coins, shown here actual size.

GOLD STATERS
Can also be silver, billon or bronze

*Norfolk Wolf, ABC 1393*
GOLD QUARTER STATERS
Can also be silver or billon

*Irstead Smiler, ABC 1480*
SILVER UNITS

*Norfolk God, ABC 1567*
SILVER HALF UNITS

*Aunt Cost Half, ABC 1953*
SILVER MINIMS

*Verica Sphinx, ABC 1340*
BRONZE UNITS

*Cunobelinus Centaur, ABC 2957*
BRONZE HALF UNITS

*Tasciovanos Goat, ABC 2709*
CAST POTIN UNITS

*Nipples, ABC 174*

age money of Albion and you'll catch glimpses of long-lost legends and ancient pagan rituals such as head-hunting, bull sacrificing and shape-shifting. You'll marvel at the plethora of occult signs and arcane symbols and you may even feel the secret power of the Druids.

I love the *palpitating unpredictability* of Pritanic coins. Even after sixty years of heart-racing intimacy they are constantly and delightfully surprising me. Attributions, names and dates are always being revised. Not long ago the Coritani were renamed Corieltavi and Tincommios was rechristened Tincomarus. Almost every month exciting new types and new variants keep leaping out of the ground, thanks to metal detectorists.

*Bronze units of Cunobelinus, son of Tasciovanos, showing a bull being sacrificed (ABC 2972) and a man—perhaps a Druid priest?—carrying a severed human head (ABC 2987).*

For example, on September 4, 2010 the late Danny Baldock discovered the first recorded coin of Anarevitos, a Kentish ruler previously unknown to history.

I love the *uncommon scarcity* of Pritanic coins. Ask any metdet how many so-called Celtic coins he or she has found and you'll immediately realise that they are rarer than Roman coins—at least a thousand times rarer on average—for the reasons stated above.

Finally I love the *galloping good value* of this horsey money (some Pritanic horses have three tails, some breathe fire, others have a human

*Silver unit of freedom-fighter Caratacus (ABC 1376) who defied the Roman invaders for eight years until he was betrayed by Cartimandua, queen of the Brigantes.*

torso). Their greater rarity doesn't mean they are costlier than other ancient coins. In fact, they are often cheaper because demand determines price and because there are far fewer collectors of ancient British coins than there are, say, of Greek or Roman coins. For example, a very fine British gold stater typically costs less than half the price—sometimes even a third the price of a Roman aureus or English gold noble of comparable quality and rarity. But the disparity is gradually diminishing as more and more canny collectors are appreciating the untamed beauty and undervalued scarcity of Pritanic coins.

*Coin Yearbook* provides a great guide to current prices of commoner Pritanic types, but because new types keep turning up and because big hoards are sometimes found (causing values to fluctuate temporarily) you'd be well advised to also keep an eye on dealers' catalogues and prices realised at auction. If you're buying in Britain, buy from people who are members of the BNTA (British Numismatic Trade Association). If

you're buying overseas, check that your suppliers belong to the IAPN (International Association of Professional Numismatists). And, if you're a beginner, beware of dodgy traders on the internet, or you could end up with a fistful of fakes and no refund.

I'd also counsel you to spend a day at the British Museum. Its collection of almost 7,000 ancient British coins is the most comprehensive, publicly accessible collection of its kind in the world. As their curator, Ian Leins, says: "They're public coins . . . your coins, and they're here for you to see. So come and see them. We'll be pleased to show them to you". Access to the collection is free for everyone. But you'll need to make an appointment before you go, and take some photo ID and proof of address. Email: coins@thebritishmuseum.ac.uk or telephone: 020 7323 8607.

Before you buy coins—any coins of any period—it always pays to read about them first. As an old adman I'm not shy about blowing my own trumpet. The best little introduction to Pritanic coins is *Britain's First Coins* by Chris Rudd (expected late 2012) and the most comprehensive catalogue of the series is *Ancient British Coins* also by Chris Rudd (2010), known in the trade as ABC. If you have even half the fun I've had with ancient British coins (and am still having)—I can promise you that you'll be a very happy person indeed. Never bored, and never with a complete collection.

*A unique gold stater of Anarevitos, a previously unknown ruler of the Cantiaci, probably a son of Eppillus, king of Calleva (Silchester). Sold by Elizabeth Cottam of Chris Rudd for £21,000, a record price for an ancient British coin (Coin News, December 2010).*

*Chris Rudd started studying ancient British coins sixty years ago and has written a hundred articles about them, many published by COIN NEWS. "I've still got a lot to learn" he says.*

# COLLECTING
## *ancient coins*

Ancient coins differ from most other series which are collected in Britain in that every piece has spent the major part of the last two thousand years in the ground. As **JOHN CUMMINGS**, dealer in ancient coins and antiquities explains here, the effect that burial has had on the surface of the coin determines more than anything else the value of a particular piece. With more modern coins, the only things which affect price are rarity and grade. There may be a premium for coins exhibiting particularly fine tone, or with outstanding pedigrees, but an 1887 crown in "extremely fine" condition has virtually the same value as every other piece with the same grade and of the same date. With ancient coins the story is very different.

A large number of different criteria affect the price of an ancient coin. Factors affecting prices can be broken down into several categories:

### Condition

The most important factor by far in determining price. Ancient coins were struck by hand and can exhibit striking faults. Value suffers if the coin is struck with the designs off-centre, is weakly struck, or if the flan is irregular in shape. Many of the Celtic tribes issued coins of varying fineness and those made from low quality gold or silver are worth less than similar specimens where the metal quality is better. Conversely, coins on exceptional flans, particularly well struck, or with fine patinas command a premium.

Many ancient coins have suffered during their stay in the ground. It must be borne in mind that the prices given in the price guide are for uncorroded, undamaged examples. A Roman denarius should be graded using the same criteria as those used for grading modern coins. The surfaces must be good, and the coin intact. The fact that the coin is 2,000 years old is irrelevant as far as grading is concerned. Coins which are not perfectly preserved are certainly not without value, however, the value for a given grade decreases with the degree of fault.

### Rarity

As with all other series, rare coins usually command higher prices than common ones. A unique variety of a small fourth century Roman bronze coin, even in perfect condition, can be worth much less than a more worn and common piece from an earlier part of the empire. In the Celtic series, there is an almost infinite variety of minor types and a unique variety of an uninscribed type will rarely outbid an inscribed issue of a known king.

### Historical and local significance

Types which have historical or local interest can command a price far above their scarcity value. Denarii of the emperor Tiberius are believed to have been referred to in the New Testament and command a far higher price than a less interesting piece of similar rarity. Similarly, pieces which have British reverse types such as the "VICT BRIT" reverse of the third century AD are more expensive than their scarcity would indicate. The 12 Caesars remain ever popular especially in the American market and this affects prices throughout the world. In the Celtic series, coins of Cunobelin or Boudicca are far more popular than pieces which have no historical interest but which may be far scarcer.

## Reverse types

All Roman emperors who survived for a reasonable time issued coins with many different reverse types. The most common of these usually show various Roman gods. When a coin has an unusual reverse it always enhances the value. Particularly popular are architectural scenes, animals, references to Judaism, and legionary types.

## Artistic merit

The Roman coinage is blessed with a large number of bust varieties and these can have a startling effect on price. For example, a common coin with the bust facing left instead of right can be worth several times the price of a normal specimen. Like many of the emperors, the coinage of Hadrian has a large number of bust varieties, some of which are extremely artistic and these, too, can command a premium.

**The coinage used in Britain from the time of the invasion in AD 43 was the same as that introduced throughout the Empire by the emperor Augustus around 20 BC. The simple divisions of 2 asses equal to one dupondius, 2 dupondii equal to 1 sestertius, 4 sestertii equal to one denarius and 25 denarii equal to one aureus continued in use until the reformation of the coinage by Caracalla in AD 214.**

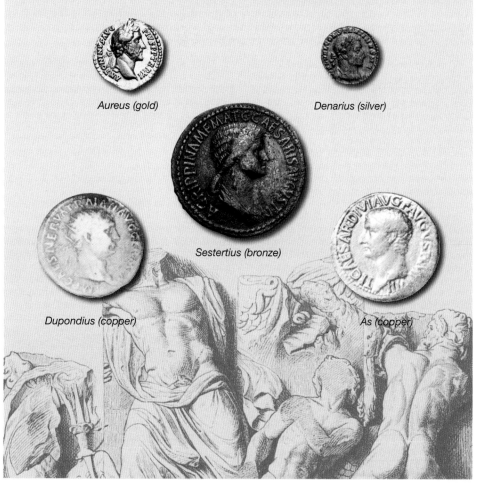

*Aureus (gold)*

*Denarius (silver)*

*Sestertius (bronze)*

*Dupondius (copper)*

*As (copper)*

# introducing
# HAMMERED
## coinage

**The hammered currency of medieval Britain is among some of the most interesting coinage in the world. The turbulent history of these islands is reflected in the fascinating changes in size, design, fineness and workmanship, culminating in the many strange examples that emanated from the strife of the Civil War.**

The Norman Conquest of England in 1066 and succeeding years had far-reaching effects on all aspects of life. Surprisingly, however, it had little impact on the coinage. William the Conqueror was anxious to emphasise the continuity of his reign, so far as the ordinary people were concerned, and therefore he retained the fabric, size and general design pattern of the silver penny. Almost 70 mints were in operation during this reign, but by the middle of the 12th century the number was reduced to 55 and under Henry II (1154–89) it fell to 30 and latterly to only eleven. By the early 14th century the production of coins had been centralised on London and Canterbury, together with the ecclesiastical mints at York and Canterbury. The silver penny was the principal denomination throughout the Norman period, pieces cut along the lines of the cross on the reverse continuing to serve as halfpence and farthings.

Eight types of penny were struck under William I and five under his son William Rufus, both profiles (left and right) and facing portraits being used in both reigns allied to crosses of various types. Fifteen types were minted under Henry I (1100–35), portraiture having now degenerated to crude caricature, the lines engraved on the coinage dies being built up by means of various punches. Halfpence modelled on the same pattern were also struck, but very sparingly and are very rare.

On Henry's death the succession was contested by his daughter Matilda and his nephew Stephen of Blois. Civil war broke out in 1138 and continued till 1153. Stephen controlled London and its mint, but Matilda and her supporters occupied the West Country and struck their own coins at Bristol. Several of the powerful barons struck their own coins, and there were distinct regional variants of the regal coinage. Of particular interest are the coins

*Silver pennies of, from left to right, William I, William Rufus, Henry I and Stephen.*

struck from obverse dies with Stephen's portrait erased or defaced, believed to date from 1148 when the usurper was under papal interdict.

Peace was restored in 1153 when it was agreed that Matilda's son Henry should succeed Stephen. On the latter's death the following year, Henry II ascended the throne. Coins of Stephen's last type continued to be minted till 1158, but Henry then took the opportunity to overhaul the coinage which had become irregular and sub-standard during the civil war. The new "Cross Crosslet" coins, usually known as the Tealby coinage (from the hoard of over 5,000 pennies found at Tealby, Lincolnshire in 1807), were produced at 30 mints, but when the recoinage was completed this number was reduced to a dozen. The design of Henry's coins remained virtually the same throughout more than two decades, apart from minor variants. Then, in 1180, a new type, known as the Short Cross coinage, was introduced. This was a vast improvement over the poorly struck Cross Crosslet coins and continued without alteration, not only to the end of the reign of Henry II in 1189, but throughout the reigns of his sons Richard (1189–99) and John (1199–1216) and the first half of the reign of his grandson Henry III (1216–46). Throughout that 66 year period, however, there were minor variations in portraits and lettering which enable numismatists to attribute the HENRICUS coins to specific reigns and periods.

*"Tealby" type penny (top), and "Short Cross" penny of Henry II.*

The style and workmanship of the Short Cross coinage deteriorated in the reign of Henry III. By the 1220s coin production was confined to the regal mints at London and Canterbury, the sole exception being the ecclesiastical mint maintained by the Abbot of Bury St Edmunds.

Halfpence and farthings were briefly struck in 1221–30, though halfpence are now extremely rare and so far only a solitary farthing has been discovered.

By the middle of this reign the coinage was in a deplorable state, being poorly struck, badly worn and often ruthlessly clipped. In 1247 Henry ordered a new coinage and in this the arms of the cross on the reverse were extended to the rim as a safeguard against clipping. This established a pattern of facing portrait and long cross on obverse and reverse respectively that was to continue till the beginning of the 16th century. Several provincial mints were re-activated to assist with the recoinage but they were all closed down again by 1250, only the regal mints at London and Canterbury and the ecclesiastical mints at Durham and Bury St Edmunds remaining active.

*"Long Cross" pennies of Henry III (top), and Edward I.*

In 1257 Henry tentatively introduced a gold penny (worth 20 silver pence and twice the weight of a silver penny). The coin was undervalued and soon disappeared from circulation.

The Long Cross coinage of Henry III continued under Edward I till 1279 when the king introduced a new coinage in his own name. The penny continued the style of its predecessors, though much better designed and executed; but new denominations were now added. Henceforward halfpence and farthings became a regular issue and, at the same time, a fourpenny coin known as the groat (from French *gros*) was briefly introduced (minting ceased in 1282 and was not revived till 1351). Due to the centralisation of coin production the name of the moneyer was now generally dropped, although it lingered on a few years at Bury St Edmunds. The provincial mints were again revived in 1299–1302 to recoin the lightweight foreign imitations of pennies which had flooded in from the Continent.

The coinage of Edward II (1307–27) differed only in minor respects from that of his father, and a similar pattern prevailed in the first years of Edward III. In 1335 halfpence and farthings below the sterling fineness were struck. More importantly, further attempts were made to introduce gold coins. In 1344 the florin or double

*Pre-Treaty Noble of Edward III which contained reference to France in the legend.*

leopard of six shillings was introduced, along with its half and quarter. This coinage was not successful and was soon replaced by a heavier series based on the noble of 80 pence (6s. 8d.), half a mark or one third of a pound. The noble originally weighed 138.5 grains but it was successively reduced to 120 grains, at which weight it continued from 1351. During this reign the protracted conflict with France known as the Hundred Years' War erupted. Edward III, through his mother, claimed the French throne and inscribed this title on his coins. By the Treaty of Bretigny (1361) Edward temporarily gave up his claim and the reference to France

*Noble of Edward IV, issued before he was forced to abandon the throne of England.*

was dropped from the coins, but when war was renewed in 1369 the title was resumed, and remained on many English coins until the end of the 18th century. The silver coinage followed the pattern of the previous reign, but in 1351 the groat was re-introduced and with it came the twopence or half-groat. Another innovation was the use of mintmarks at the beginning of the inscriptions. Seven types of cross and one crown were employed from 1334 onwards and their sequence enables numismatists to date coins fairly accurately.

The full range of gold (noble, half-noble and quarter-noble) and silver (groat, half-groat, penny, halfpenny and farthing) continued under Richard II (1377–99). Little attempt was made to alter the facing portrait on the silver coins, by now little more than a stylised caricature anyway.

*Noble of Henry IV which was reduced in weight due to the shortage of gold.*

Under Henry IV (1399–1413) the pattern of previous reigns prevailed, but in 1412 the weights of the coinage were reduced due to a shortage of bullion. The noble was reduced to 108 grains and its sub-divisions lightened proportionately. The penny was reduced by 3 grains, and its multiples and sub-divisions correspondingly reduced. One interesting change was the reduction of the fleur de lis of France from four to three in the heraldic shield on the reverse of the noble; this change corresponded with the alteration in the arms used in France itself. The Calais mint, opened by Edward III in 1363, was closed in 1411. There was no change in the designs used for the coins of Henry V (1413–22) but greater use was now made of mintmarks to distinguish the various periods of production. Coins were by now produced mainly at London, although the episcopal mints at Durham and York were permitted to strike pennies.

The supply of gold dwindled early in the reign of Henry VI and few nobles were struck after 1426. The Calais mint was re-opened in 1424 and struck a large amount of gold before closing finally in 1440. A regal mint briefly operated at York in 1423–24. Mintmarks were now much more widely used and tended to correspond more closely to the annual trials of the Pyx. The series of civil upheavals known as the Wars of the Roses erupted in this period.

In 1461 Henry VI was deposed by the Yorkist Earl of March after he defeated the Lancastrians at Mortimer's Cross. The Yorkists advanced on London where the victor was crowned Edward IV. At first he continued the gold series of his predecessor, issuing nobles and quarter-nobles, but in 1464 the weight of the penny was reduced to 12 grains and the value of the noble was raised to 100 pence (8s. 4d.). The ryal or rose-

*Groat of Richard III (1483–85).*

noble of 120 grains, together with its half and quarter, was introduced in 1465 and tariffed at ten shillings or half a pound. The need for a coin worth a third of a pound, however, led to the issue of the angel of 80 grains, worth 6s. 8d., but this was initially unsucessful and very few examples are now extant. The angel derived its name from the figure of the Archangel Michael on the obverse; a cross surmounting a shield appeared on the reverse.

In 1470 Edward was forced to flee to Holland and Henry VI was briefly restored. During this brief period (to April 1471) the ryal was discontinued but a substantial issue of angels and half-angels was made both at London and Bristol. Silver coins were struck at York as well as London and Bristol, the issues of the provincial mints being identified by the initials B or E (Eboracum, Latin for York). Edward defeated the Lancastrians at Tewkesbury and deposed the luckless Henry once more. In his

second reign Edward struck only angels and half-angels as well as silver from the groat to halfpenny. In addition to the three existing mints, silver coins were struck at Canterbury, Durham and the archiepiscopal mint at York. Mintmarks were now much more frequent and varied. Coins with a mark of a halved sun and rose are usually assigned to the reign of Edward IV, but they were probably also struck in the nominal reign of Edward V, the twelve-year-old prince held in the Tower of London under the protection of his uncle Richard, Duke of Gloucester. Coins with this mark on the reverse had an obverse mark of a boar's head, Richard's personal emblem. The brief reign of Richard III (1483–5) came to an end with his defeat at Bosworth and the relatively scarce coins of this period followed the pattern of the previous reigns, distinguished by the sequence of mint marks and the inscription RICAD or RICARD.

In the early years of Henry VII's reign the coinage likewise followed the previous patterns, but in 1489 the first of several radical changes was effected, with the introduction of the gold sovereign of 20 shillings showing a full-length portrait of the monarch seated on an elaborate throne. For reverse, this coin depicted a Tudor rose surmounted by a heraldic shield. A similar reverse appeared on the ryal of 10 shillings, but the angel and angelet retained previous motifs. The silver coins at first adhered to the medieval pattern, with the stylised facing portrait and long cross, but at the beginning of the 16th century a large silver coin, the testoon or shilling of 12 pence, was introduced and adopted a realistic profile of the king, allied to a reverse showing a cross surmounted by the royal arms. The same design was also used for the later issue of groat and half groat.

*First coinage Angel of Henry VIII which retained the traditional 23.5 carat fineness.*

This established a pattern which was to continue till the reign of Charles I. In the reign of Henry VIII, however, the coinage was subject to considerable debasement. This led to the eventual introduction of 22 carat (.916 fine) gold for the crown while the traditional 23 1/2 carat gold was retained for the angel and ryal. This dual system continued until the angel was discontinued at the outset of the Civil War in 1642; latterly it had been associated with the ceremony of touching for "King's Evil" or scrofula, a ritual used by the early Stuart monarchs to bolster their belief in the divine right of kings.

Under the Tudors and Stuarts the range and complexity of the gold coinage increased, but it was not until the reign of Edward VI that the silver series was expanded. In 1551 he introduced the silver crown of five shillings, the first English coin to bear a clear date on the obverse. Under Mary dates were extended to the shilling and sixpence.

The mixture of dated and undated coins continued under Elizabeth I, a reign remarkable for the range of denominations — nine gold and

*The magnificent second coinage Rose-Ryal of James I (1603–25).*

eight silver. The latter included the sixpence, threepence, threehalfpence and threefarthings, distinguished by the rose which appeared behind the Queen's head.

The coinage of James I was even more complex, reflecting the king's attempts to unite his dominions. The first issue bore the legend ANG: SCO (England and Scotland), but from 1604 this was altered to MAG: BRIT (Great Britain). This period witnessed new denominations, such as the rose-ryal and spur-ryal, the unite, the Britain crown and the thistle crown, and finally the laurel of 20 shillings and its sub-divisions.

In the reign of Elizabeth experiments began with milled coinage under Eloi Mestrell. These continued sporadically in the 17th century, culminating in the beautiful coins struck by Nicholas Briot (1631–39). A branch mint was established at Aberystwyth in 1637 to refine and coin silver from the Welsh mines. Relations between King and Parliament deteriorated in the reign of Charles I and led to the Civil War (1642). Parliament controlled London but continued to strike coins in the King's name. The Royalists struck coins, both in pre-war and new types, at Shrewsbury, Oxford, Bristol, Worcester, Exeter, Chester, Hereford and other Royalist strongholds, while curious siege pieces were pressed into service at Newark, Pontefract and Scarborough.

After the execution of Charles I in 1649 the Commonwealth was proclaimed and gold and silver coins were now inscribed in English instead of Latin. Patterns portraying Cromwell and a crowned shield restored Latin in 1656. Plans for milled coinage were already being considered before the Restoration of the monarchy in 1660. Hammered coinage appeared initially, resuming the style of coins under Charles I, but in 1662 the hand-hammering of coins was abandoned in favour of coins struck on the mill and screw press. The hammered coins of 1660–62 were undated and bore a crown mintmark, the last vestiges of medievalism in British coinage.

# COIN *grading*

Condition is the secret to the value of virtually anything, whether it be antiques, jewellery, horses or second-hand cars—and coins are certainly no exception. When collecting coins it is vital to understand the recognised standard British system of grading, i.e. accurately assessing a coin's condition or state of wear. Grading is an art which can only be learned by experience and so often it remains one person's opinion against another's, therefore it is important for the beginner or inexperienced collector to seek assistance from a reputable dealer or knowledgeable numismatist when making major purchases.

| The standard grades as used in the Price Guide are as follows: | |
|---|---|
| **UNC** | **Uncirculated**<br>A coin that has never been in circulation, although it may show signs of contact with other coins during the minting process. |
| **EF** | **Extremely Fine**<br>A coin in this grade may appear uncirculated to the naked eye but on closer examination will show signs of minor friction on the highest surface. |
| **VF** | **Very Fine**<br>A coin that has had very little use, but shows signs of wear on the high surfaces. |
| **F** | **Fine**<br>A coin that has been in circulation and shows general signs of wear, but with all legends and date clearly visible. |
| Other grades used in the normal grading system are: | |
| **BU** | **Brilliant Uncirculated**<br>As the name implies, a coin retaining its mint lustre. |
| **Fair** | A coin extensively worn but still quite recognisable and legends readable. |
| **Poor** | A coin very worn and only just recognisable. |
| Other abbreviations used in the Price Guide are: | |
| **Obv** | **Obverse** |
| **Rev** | **Reverse** |
| Other abbreviations, mintmarks, etc. can be identified under the appropriate section of this Yearbook. | |

A SIMPLIFIED PRICE GUIDE TO

# ANCIENT COINS
# USED IN BRITAIN

**PART I**

*Celtic*

The prices given in this section are those that you would expect to pay from a reputable dealer and not the prices at which you could expect to sell coins.

The list below, which has been generously provided by Celtic coin dealer Elizabeth Cottam, contains most of the commonly available types: a full comprehensive guide is beyond the scope of this book. Prices are for coins with good surfaces which are not weakly struck or struck from worn dies. Examples which are struck from worn or damaged dies can be worth considerably less. Particularly attractive examples of bronze Celtic coins command a very high premium. Where a price is given for an issue of which there are many varieties, the price is for the most common type. The illustrations are representative examples only and are not shown actual size.

|  | F | VF | EF |
|---|---|---|---|
| **UNINSCRIBED COINAGE** | | | |
| **GOLD STATERS** | | | |
| Broad Flan | £700 | £1750 | £5500 |
| Gallic War Uniface | £200 | £300 | £600 |
| Remic types | £250 | £400 | £750 |
| Wonersh types | £250 | £450 | £1750 |
| Chute | £200 | £300 | £600 |
| Cheriton | £250 | £450 | £850 |
| Iceni (various types) | £300 | £500 | £1250 |
| Norfolk "wolf" type | | | |
| fine gold | £250 | £450 | £1250 |
| brassy gold | £150 | £300 | £650 |
| very debased | £100 | £200 | £400 |
| Corieltavi (various types) | £200 | £400 | £850 |
| Dobunni | £250 | £500 | £1250 |
| Whaddon Chase types | £250 | £450 | £1250 |
| **GOLD QUARTER STATERS** | | | |
| Gallic Imported Types | £75 | £150 | £350 |
| Kent types | £200 | £300 | £500 |
| Southern types | £125 | £200 | £350 |
| Iceni | £150 | £250 | £400 |
| Corieltavi | £125 | £200 | £450 |
| Dobunni | £175 | £300 | £550 |
| East Wiltshire | £300 | £500 | £850 |
| Durotriges | £100 | £200 | £350 |
| North Thames types | £200 | £300 | £500 |
| **SILVER COINAGE** | | | |
| Armorican billion statrs | £75 | £150 | £400 |
| Kent Types | £150 | £300 | £650 |
| South Thames types | £100 | £175 | £325 |

*Cheriton Smiler gold stater*

*Cranborne Chase silver stater*

|  | F | VF | EF |
|---|---|---|---|
| Iceni ('crescent' types)......................... | £30 | £75 | £150 |
| Iceni ('Norfolk God' types).................. | £50 | £100 | £250 |
| Corieltavi............................................. | £45 | £100 | £200 |
| Dobunni............................................... | £75 | £125 | £275 |
| Durotriges full stater |  |  |  |
| fine silver......................................... | £75 | £175 | £300 |
| base silver....................................... | £25 | £55 | £150 |
| Durotriges quarter silver....................... | £20 | £35 | £75 |

(Note—most examples are for base coins as better quality items are appreciably higher)

|  | F | VF | EF |
|---|---|---|---|
| North Thames types............................ | £100 | £175 | £325 |

### POTIN COINAGE

|  | F | VF | EF |
|---|---|---|---|
| Kent..................................................... | £20 | £50 | £120 |

### BRONZE COINAGE

|  | F | VF | EF |
|---|---|---|---|
| Durotriges debased stater................... | £25 | £55 | £100 |
| Durotriges cast bronze........................ | £60 | £120 | £200 |
| North Thames types. Various issues from: | £40 | £100 | £400 |

*Hengistbury cast bronze*

## INSCRIBED CELTIC COINAGE

### CANTIACI
**Dubnovellaunos**

|  | F | VF | EF |
|---|---|---|---|
| stater............................................... | £300 | £575 | £1250 |
| silver unit........................................ | £130 | £210 | £500 |
| bronze unit...................................... | £55 | £150 | £350 |
| **Vosenos** |  |  |  |
| stater............................................... | £1000 | £2500 | £5000 |
| quarter stater.................................. | £275 | £585 | £1200 |
| silver unit........................................ | £135 | £285 | £650 |
| **Sam** |  |  |  |
| silver unit........................................ | £175 | £350 | £750 |
| bronze unit...................................... | £100 | £250 | £500 |
| **Eppillus** |  |  |  |
| stater............................................... | £1000 | £2000 | £4250 |
| quarter stater.................................. | £145 | £255 | £500 |
| silver unit........................................ | £65 | £145 | £350 |
| bronze unit...................................... | £55 | £125 | £450 |
| bronze minim................................... | £85 | £150 | £275 |
| **Anarevitos** |  |  |  |
| stater (unique)................................. | — |  |  |
| **Touto** |  |  |  |
| silver unit........................................ | £200 | £450 | £850 |
| **Verica** |  |  |  |
| silver unit........................................ | £200 | £350 | £650 |
| bronze unit...................................... | £150 | £300 | £600 |
| **Sego** |  |  |  |
| stater............................................... | £500 | £1000 | £3000 |
| quarter stater.................................. | £200 | £500 | £1000 |
| silver unit........................................ | £150 | £350 | £600 |
| silver minim.................................... | £75 | £200 | £400 |
| bronze unit...................................... | £75 | £150 | £450 |
| **Amminus** |  |  |  |
| silver unit........................................ | £155 | £320 | £650 |
| silver minim.................................... | £110 | £215 | £450 |
| bronze unit...................................... | £80 | £155 | £500 |
| **Solidus** |  |  |  |
| silver unit........................................ | £500 | £1000 | £2250 |
| silver minim.................................... | £500 | £1000 | £1500 |

*Vosenos gold quarter stater*

*Verica gold stater*

|  | F | VF | EF |
|---|---|---|---|
| **REGNI & ATREBATES** | | | |
| Commios | | | |
| stater | £550 | £1500 | £2850 |
| silver unit | £75 | £150 | £300 |
| silver minim | £60 | £120 | £250 |
| Tincomarus | | | |
| stater | £450 | £850 | £2000 |
| quarter stater | £150 | £250 | £450 |
| silver unit | £75 | £140 | £275 |
| silver minim | £60 | £120 | £175 |
| Eppillus | | | |
| quarter stater | £150 | £235 | £500 |
| silver unit | £75 | £145 | £300 |
| Verica | | | |
| stater | £275 | £550 | £1250 |
| quarter stater | £155 | £275 | £425 |
| silver unit | £55 | £150 | £250 |
| silver minim | £50 | £120 | £225 |
| Epaticcus | | | |
| stater | £1000 | £2000 | £4000 |
| silver unit | £50 | £100 | £265 |
| silver minim | £55 | £110 | £275 |
| Caratacos | | | |
| silver unit | £165 | £320 | £465 |
| silver minim | £110 | £220 | £325 |
| | | | |
| **VECTUARII** | | | |
| Crab | | | |
| silver unit | £155 | £320 | £650 |
| silver minim | £100 | £250 | £400 |
| | | | |
| **ICENI** | | | |
| Cani Duro | | | |
| silver unit | £110 | £265 | £550 |
| Antedios | | | |
| stater | £425 | £1000 | £2500 |
| silver unit | £35 | £65 | £185 |
| silver half unit | £45 | £95 | £150 |
| Ecen | | | |
| stater | £425 | £1000 | £2500 |
| silver unit | £40 | £75 | £185 |
| silver half unit | £45 | £95 | £150 |
| Saenu | | | |
| silver unit | £65 | £125 | £285 |
| Aesu | | | |
| silver unit | £65 | £125 | £285 |
| Ale Scavo | | | |
| silver unit | £250 | £500 | £1000 |
| Esuprasto | | | |
| silver unit | £420 | £1000 | £1850 |
| | | | |
| **CORIELTAVI** | | | |
| Cat | | | |
| silver unit | £400 | £1000 | £2000 |
| silver half unit (unique) | | | — |
| VEPO | | | |
| stater | £450 | £1000 | £2500 |
| silver unit | £75 | £150 | £300 |
| Esuprasu | | | |
| stater | £350 | £675 | £1250 |
| silver unit | £155 | £310 | £550 |

*Tincomarus gold stater*

*Ale Scavo silver unit*

*Vep CorF gold stater*

|  | F | VF | EF |
|---|---|---|---|
| **Aunt Cost** | | | |
| stater | £275 | £575 | £1000 |
| silver unit | £85 | £185 | £315 |
| silver half unit | £85 | £160 | £300 |
| **Lat Ison** | | | |
| stater | £1000 | £2000 | £4000 |
| silver unit | £155 | £420 | £1150 |
| silver half unit | £150 | £300 | £500 |
| **Dumnocoveros Tigirseno** | | | |
| stater | £800 | £2000 | £3500 |
| silver unit | £100 | £185 | £500 |
| silver half unit | £100 | £200 | £600 |
| **Volisios Dumnocoveros** | | | |
| stater | £350 | £675 | £1250 |
| silver unit | £100 | £185 | £475 |
| silver half unit | £100 | £185 | £450 |
| **Volisios Cartivellaunos** | | | |
| stater | £1000 | £2000 | £4000 |
| silver half unit | £300 | £650 | £1150 |
| **Volisios Dumnovellaunos** | | | |
| stater | £310 | £725 | £1550 |
| silver half unit | £150 | £325 | £650 |

*Catti gold stater*

## DOBUNNI
| | F | VF | EF |
|---|---|---|---|
| **Bodvoc** | | | |
| stater | £1000 | £2250 | £3000 |
| quarter stater (unique) | | | — |
| silver unit | £200 | £500 | £850 |
| **Corio** | | | |
| stater | £275 | £550 | £1500 |
| quarter stater | £200 | £350 | £650 |
| **Comux** | | | |
| stater | £275 | £550 | £1500 |
| **Catti** | | | |
| stater | £275 | £550 | £1500 |
| **Inamn** | | | |
| plated stater (unique) | | | — |
| silver unit (unique) | | | — |
| **Anted** | | | |
| stater | £350 | £700 | £1500 |
| silver unit | £55 | £120 | £300 |
| **Eisu** | | | |
| stater | £450 | £750 | £1500 |
| silver unit | £65 | £125 | £325 |

*Dumno Tigir Seno gold stater*

## TRINOVANTES
| | F | VF | EF |
|---|---|---|---|
| **Dubnovellaunos** | | | |
| stater | £275 | £475 | £1250 |
| quarter stater | £175 | £350 | £600 |
| silver unit | £75 | £150 | £350 |
| silver half unit | £100 | £200 | £450 |
| bronze unit | £55 | £130 | £250 |

## CATUVELLAUNI
| | F | VF | EF |
|---|---|---|---|
| **Addedomaros** | | | |
| stater | £300 | £450 | £1250 |
| quarter stater | £300 | £550 | £1250 |
| silver unit | £100 | £200 | £400 |
| silver half unit | £100 | £200 | £450 |
| bronze unit | £30 | £65 | £250 |

*Addedomaros gold stater*

|  | F | VF | EF |
|---|---|---|---|
| Tasciovanos |  |  |  |
| stater | £250 | £450 | £1500 |
| quarter stater | £150 | £250 | £475 |
| silver unit | £80 | £165 | £375 |
| bronze unit | £55 | £135 | £250 |
| bronze half unit | £55 | £135 | £275 |
| Andeco |  |  |  |
| stater | £350 | £550 | £1500 |
| quarter stater | £200 | £420 | £750 |
| silver unit | £155 | £400 | £750 |
| bronze unit | £85 | £220 | £350 |
| Dias |  |  |  |
| silver unit | £100 | £200 | £400 |
| bronze unit | £50 | £150 | £400 |
| Rues |  |  |  |
| bronze unit | £50 | £150 | £400 |
| Cat |  |  |  |
| plated silver unit (unique) |  |  | — |

*Tasciovanos gold stater*

## CATUVELLAUNI & TRINOVANTES

| | F | VF | EF |
|---|---|---|---|
| Cunobelinus |  |  |  |
| stater | £250 | £450 | £1500 |
| quarter stater | £150 | £250 | £475 |
| silver unit | £80 | £165 | £475 |
| bronze unit | £55 | £135 | £350 |
| bronze half | £55 | £135 | £275 |
| Trocc |  |  |  |
| bronze unit | £50 | £150 | £500 |
| Agr |  |  |  |
| quarter stater | £120 | £250 | £850 |
| silver unit | £100 | £200 | £500 |
| bronze unit (only two) |  | (too rare to price) |  |
| Dubn |  |  |  |
| quarter stater (only three) |  | (too rare to price) |  |

*Cunobelinus gold stater*

*Illustrations by courtesy of*
*Chris Rudd*

# A SIMPLIFIED PRICE GUIDE TO
# ANCIENT COINS USED IN BRITAIN

**PART II**

*Roman Britain*

The list below has been generously provided by coin dealer Mike Vosper. These prices are for the most common types unless otherwise noted. In most cases, especially with large bronze coins, the price for coins in extremely fine condition will be <u>much</u> higher than the price for the same coin in very fine condition as early bronze coins are seldom found in hoards and perfect, undamaged examples are rarely available.

The illustrations provided are a representative guide to assist with identification only.

## REPUBLICAN COINAGE 280–41 BC

| | FROM F | VF | EF |
|---|---|---|---|
| **Republican** | | | |
| Quadrigatus (or Didrachm) (Janus/Quadriga) | £120 | £425 | £1350 |
| Victoriatus (Jupiter/Victory) | £35 | £95 | £375 |
| +Denarius (Roma/Biga) | £20 | £75 | £350 |
| +Denarius (other types) | £30 | £85 | £350 |
| Denarius (Gallic warrior—L.Hostilius Saserna) | £375 | £1050 | £4500 |
| Quinarius | £25 | £80 | £350 |
| Cast Aes Grave, As | £185 | £600 | — |
| Struck As/Semis/Litra | £60 | £200 | — |
| Struck Triens/Quadrands | £50 | £150 | — |

*Gnaeus Pompey Junior*

## IMPERATORIAL COINAGE 49–27 BC

| | FROM F | VF | EF |
|---|---|---|---|
| **Pompey the Great** | | | |
| Denarius (Hd. of Pompilius/Prow) | £145 | £400 | £2,000 |
| **Scipio** | | | |
| Denarius (Jupiter/Elephant | £70 | £225 | £900 |
| **Cato Uticensis** | | | |
| Quinarius (Bacchus/Victory) | £45 | £125 | £500 |
| **Gnaeus Pompey Junior** | | | |
| Denarius (Roma/Hispania) | £110 | £325 | £1,100 |
| **Sextus Pompey** | | | |
| Denarius (his bust) | £275 | £750 | £3,000 |
| Denarius (other types) | £180 | £550 | £2,500 |
| As | £160 | £550 | — |
| **Julius Caesar** | | | |
| Aureus | £1,100 | £3,000 | £78500 |
| Denarius ("elephant" type) | £140 | £450 | £1500 |
| Denarius (Ceasar portrait) | £350 | £1250 | £5000 |
| Denarius (heads of godesses) | £115 | £350 | £1450 |

*Julius Caesar*

| | FROM F | VF | EF |
|---|---|---|---|
| **Brutus** | | | |
| Denarius (his portrait/EID MAR)........ | £20000 | £60000 | £230000 |
| Denarius (others)............................... | £140 | £425 | £1725 |
| **Cassius** | | | |
| Denarius..................... | £120 | £350 | £1300 |
| **Ahenobarbus** | | | |
| Denarius ..................... | £400 | £1400 | £5700 |
| **Mark Antony** | | | |
| Denarius ("Galley" type) .................. | £75 | £250 | £1500 |
| Denarius (with portrait) ..................... | £100 | £360 | £1800 |
| Denarius (other types) ..................... | £70 | £285 | £1650 |
| **Mark Antony & Lepidus** | | | |
| AR quinarius ..................................... | £65 | £185 | £950 |
| **Mark Antony & Octavian** | | | |
| AR denarius ..................................... | £175 | £600 | £2400 |
| Quninarius ....................................... | £55 | £165 | £800 |
| **Mark Antony & Lucius Antony** | | | |
| AR denarius ..................................... | £335 | £800 | £3500 |
| **Mark Antony & Octavia** | | | |
| AR Cistophorus ................................ | £225 | £650 | £3000 |
| **Cleopatra VII & Mark Antony** | | | |
| AR denarius ..................................... | £1000 | £3000 | £19000 |
| **Fulvia** | | | |
| AR quinarius ..................................... | £125 | £350 | £1700 |
| **Octavian (later known as Augustus)** | | | |
| Gold Aureus ..................................... | £1100 | £3500 | £14500 |
| Denarius ........................................... | £125 | £350 | £2000 |
| Quinarius (ASIA RECEPTA) ............ | £45 | £120 | £650 |
| **Octavian & Divos Julius Caesar** | | | |
| AE sestertius ................................... | £275 | £1500 | — |

*Brutus*

*Mark Antony & Octavian*

## IMPERIAL COINAGE—Julio-Claudian Dynasty 27BC–AD 69

| | | | |
|---|---|---|---|
| **Augustus** | | | |
| Gold Aureus (Caius & Lucius Caesar) | £1200 | £3000 | £13000 |
| AR Cistophorus............................... | £200 | £650 | £2750 |
| Denarius (Caius & Lucius Caesar) .... | £60 | £175 | £700 |
| Denarius (other types) ..................... | £65 | £215 | £1000 |
| AR quinarius ..................................... | £60 | £160 | £750 |
| Sestertius (large SC) ....................... | £135 | £395 | £1850 |
| Dupondius or as (large SC).............. | £60 | £170 | £700 |
| Quadrans ......................................... | £18 | £50 | £220 |
| **Divus Augustus (struck under Tiberius)** | | | |
| As ..................................................... | £70 | £195 | £1000 |
| **Augustus & Agrippa** | | | |
| Dupondius (Crocodile rev) .............. | £70 | £195 | £1000 |
| **Livia** | | | |
| Sestertius or Dupondius .................. | £195 | £595 | £3500 |
| **Gaius Caesar** | | | |
| AR denarius ..................................... | £350 | £1500 | £3450 |
| **Tiberius** | | | |
| Aureus (Tribute penny) ..................... | £1000 | £2750 | £7000 |
| Denarius (Tribute penny) ................. | £70 | £225 | £800 |
| Sestertius ......................................... | £195 | £595 | £3000 |
| Dupondius ........................................ | £160 | £550 | £2500 |
| As ..................................................... | £70 | £200 | £850 |
| **Drusus** | | | |
| Sestertius.......................................... | £275 | £900 | £4250 |
| As (Large S C).................................. | £75 | £200 | £900 |
| **Caligula** | | | |
| Denarius (rev. portrait) ..................... | £450 | £1300 | £5500 |
| Sestertius (PIETAS & Temple) .......... | £300 | £1750 | £7500 |
| As (VESTA)....................................... | £90 | £300 | £1200 |

*Augustus*

*Tiberius*

| | FROM F | VF | EF |
|---|---|---|---|
| **Agrippa (struck under Caligula)** | | | |
| As..................................................... | £60 | £170 | £800 |
| **Germanicus (struck under Caligula or Claudius)** | | | |
| As (Large S C) ................................ | £70 | £190 | £900 |
| **Agrippina Senior (struck under Caligula)** | | | |
| Sestertius (Carpentum).................... | £500 | £1450 | £7000 |
| **Nero & Drusus (struck under Caligula)** | | | |
| Dupondius (On horseback, galloping) | £180 | £600 | £3000 |
| **Claudius** | | | |
| Aureus ("DE BRITANN" type) ........... | £1350 | £4500 | £18000 |
| Denarius as above ......................... | £450 | £1500 | £6250 |
| Didrachm as above ........................ | £350 | £1000 | £5000 |
| Denarius other types ...................... | £350 | £950 | £4500 |
| Sestertius ....................................... | £175 | £550 | £3000 |
| Dupondius ..................................... | £60 | £200 | £1250 |
| As .................................................. | £55 | £150 | £900 |
| Quadrans ....................................... | £20 | £55 | £265 |
| Irregular British Sestertius............... | £30 | £85 | £450 |
| Irregular British As ......................... | £22 | £60 | £285 |
| **Claudius & Agrippina Junior or Nero** | | | |
| Denarius ......................................... | £450 | £1350 | £6500 |
| **Nero Cludius Drusus (struck under Claudius)** | | | |
| Sestertius ....................................... | £250 | £850 | £5000 |
| **Antonia (struck under Claudius)** | | | |
| Dupondius ...................................... | £130 | £450 | £2250 |
| **Britannicus** | | | |
| Sestertius ....................................... | £6500 | £28000 | — |
| **Nero** | | | |
| Aureus ............................................ | £1000 | £3200 | £12000 |
| Denarius ......................................... | £95 | £260 | £1500 |
| Sestertius ....................................... | £135 | £550 | £3300 |
| Sestertius (Port of Ostia) ................. | £1800 | £6000 | £39000 |
| Dupondius ...................................... | £85 | £250 | £1250 |
| As .................................................. | £50 | £155 | £850 |
| Semis ............................................. | £42 | £115 | £545 |
| Quadrans ....................................... | £22 | £55 | £275 |
| **Civil War** | | | |
| Denarius ......................................... | £180 | £550 | £2500 |
| **Galba** | | | |
| Denarius ......................................... | £100 | £340 | £1800 |
| Sestertius ....................................... | £160 | £475 | £2300 |
| Dupondius ...................................... | £175 | £500 | £2300 |
| As .................................................. | £110 | £325 | £1750 |
| **Otho** | | | |
| Denarius ......................................... | £190 | £575 | £3000 |
| **Vitellius** | | | |
| Denarius ......................................... | £95 | £280 | £1400 |
| Sestertius ....................................... | £1000 | £2800 | £15000 |
| Dupondius ...................................... | £350 | £900 | £5175 |
| As .................................................. | £1965 | £500 | £2750 |

## IMPERIAL COINAGE—Flavian Dynasty AD 69–96

| | | | |
|---|---|---|---|
| **Vespasian** | | | |
| Aureus ............................................ | £850 | £2400 | £11000 |
| Denarius ......................................... | £30 | £80 | £400 |
| Denarius (IVDAEA) ............................ | £86 | £200 | £1000 |
| Sestertius ....................................... | £190 | £595 | £4000 |
| Dupondius ...................................... | £70 | £210 | £1200 |
| As .................................................. | £55 | £180 | £1100 |
| **Titus** | | | |
| Aureus ............................................ | £850 | £2500 | £11500 |
| Denarius as Caesar ......................... | £40 | £110 | £625 |
| Denarius as Augustus ..................... | £45 | £125 | £700 |

*Caligula*

*Agrippina Senior*

*Claudius*

*Nero*

*Galba*

115

|  | FROM F | VF | EF |
|---|---|---|---|
| Sestertius | £135 | £450 | £3000 |
| Dupondius | £55 | £175 | £1150 |
| As | £50 | £160 | £1150 |
| As (IVDAEA CAPTA) | £160 | £500 | £2500 |

**Julia Titi**

| Denarious | £190 | £565 | £2500 |
|---|---|---|---|

**Domitian**

| Aureus | £850 | £2400 | £11000 |
|---|---|---|---|
| Cistophorus | £115 | £375 | £1600 |
| Denarius as Caesar | £35 | £85 | £400 |
| Denarius as Augustus | £25 | £70 | £300 |
| Sestertius | £95 | £340 | £1100 |
| Dupondius | £35 | £120 | £1300 |
| As | £45 | £110 | £600 |
| Ae Semis | £35 | £90 | £425 |
| Ae Quadrands | £25 | £70 | £295 |

**Domitia**

| Cistophorus | £235 | £695 | £2500 |
|---|---|---|---|

*Titus*

*Domitian*

## IMPERIAL COINAGE—Adoptive Emperors AD 96–138

**Nerva**

| Aureus | £1850 | £5500 | £24000 |
|---|---|---|---|
| Denarius | £60 | £125 | £650 |
| Sestertius | £155 | £500 | £2750 |
| Sestertius (Palm-tree) | £500 | £1600 | £9000 |
| Dupondius | £70 | £215 | £1100 |
| As | £55 | £165 | £900 |

**Trajan**

| Aureus | £800 | £2200 | £9500 |
|---|---|---|---|
| Denarius | £25 | £55 | £300 |
| Denarius (Trajan's Column) | £45 | £130 | £675 |
| Sestertius | £65 | £215 | £1200 |
| Sestertius (Dacian rev.) | £70 | £250 | £1400 |
| Dupondius or as | £35 | £95 | £495 |
| Ae Quadrands | £25 | £65 | £300 |

**Plotina, Marciana or Matidia**

| Denarius | £425 | £1400 | £4750 |
|---|---|---|---|

**Hadrian**

| Aureus | £850 | £2600 | £11500 |
|---|---|---|---|
| Cistophourus | £100 | £450 | £1500 |
| Denarius (Provinces) | £45 | £135 | £700 |
| Denarius other types | £25 | £75 | £400 |
| Sestertius | £80 | £235 | £1300 |
| Sestertius (RETITVTORI province types) | £135 | £420 | £2300 |
| Sestertius (Britannia std) | £3000 | £10000 | — |
| Dupondius or As | £35 | £120 | £600 |
| As (Britannia std) | £190 | £600 | — |
| Ae Semiis or Quadrands | £30 | £90 | £425 |
| Eygpt, Alexandrian Billon Tetradrachm | £30 | £85 | £475 |

**Sabina**

| Denarius | £35 | £85 | £450 |
|---|---|---|---|
| Sestertius | £115 | £350 | £1900 |
| As or Dupondius | £75 | £195 | £950 |

**Aelius Ceasar**

| Denarius | £70 | £200 | £1000 |
|---|---|---|---|
| Sestertius | £145 | £450 | £2250 |
| As or Dupondius | £68 | £190 | £950 |

*Nerva*

*Trajan*

*Hadrian*

| | FROM F | VF | EF |
|---|---|---|---|

## IMPERIAL COINAGE—The Antonines AD 138–193

**Antoninus Pius**

| | FROM F | VF | EF |
|---|---|---|---|
| Aureus ........................................... | £650 | £2000 | £8500 |
| Denarius ....................................... | £18 | £45 | £225 |
| Sestertius Britannia seated ............ | £475 | £1400 | £8500 |
| Sestertius other types ................... | £45 | £145 | £750 |
| As - Britannia rev. .......................... | £65 | £195 | £1100 |
| Dupondius or As other types ......... | £30 | £70 | £350 |

**Antoninus Pius & Marcus Aurelius**

| | | | |
|---|---|---|---|
| Denarius (bust each side) .............. | £30 | £90 | £450 |

**Diva Faustina Senior**

| | | | |
|---|---|---|---|
| Denarius ....................................... | £18 | £45 | £235 |
| Sestertius ...................................... | £38 | £145 | £750 |
| As or Dupondius ........................... | £25 | £75 | £375 |

**Marcus Aurelius**

| | | | |
|---|---|---|---|
| Aureus........................................... | £725 | £2200 | £9500 |
| Denarius as Caesar ....................... | £18 | £55 | £285 |
| Denarius as Augustus ................... | £17 | £50 | £255 |
| Sestertius ..................................... | £45 | £160 | £850 |
| As or Dupondius ........................... | £25 | £75 | £375 |

**Faustina Junior**

| | | | |
|---|---|---|---|
| Denarius ....................................... | £18 | £50 | £265 |
| Sestertius ..................................... | £40 | £175 | £850 |
| As or Dupondius ........................... | £28 | £85 | £400 |

**Lucius Verus**

| | | | |
|---|---|---|---|
| Denarius ....................................... | £20 | £70 | £375 |
| Sestertius ..................................... | £55 | £190 | £1000 |
| As or Dupondius ........................... | £30 | £85 | £425 |

**Lucilla**

| | | | |
|---|---|---|---|
| Denarius ....................................... | £20 | £65 | £325 |
| Sestertius ..................................... | £55 | £175 | £900 |
| As or Dupondius ........................... | £30 | £95 | £425 |

**Commodus**

| | | | |
|---|---|---|---|
| Aureus .......................................... | £900 | £2700 | £12000 |
| Denarius as Caesar ....................... | £28 | £75 | £325 |
| Denarius as Augustus ................... | £18 | £50 | £275 |
| Sestertius ..................................... | £45 | £145 | £900 |
| Sestertius (VICT BRIT) ................... | £125 | £450 | £2500 |
| As or Dupondius ........................... | £22 | £85 | £450 |

**Crispina**

| | | | |
|---|---|---|---|
| Denarius ....................................... | £22 | £75 | £350 |
| Sestertius ..................................... | £68 | £225 | £1100 |
| As or Dupondius ........................... | £32 | £110 | £525 |

*Antoninus Pius*

*Marcus Aurelius*

*Faustina Junior*

## IMPERIAL COINAGE—The Severan Dynasty AD 193–235

**Pertinax**

| | | | |
|---|---|---|---|
| Denarius......................................... | £225 | £645 | £2875 |
| Sestertius ...................................... | £550 | £1750 | £10500 |

**Didius Julianus**

| | | | |
|---|---|---|---|
| Denarius......................................... | £395 | £1250 | £7000 |
| Sestertius or Dupondius ............... | £325 | £1000 | £7,50 |

**Manlia Scantilla or Didia Clara**

| | | | |
|---|---|---|---|
| Denarius ....................................... | £395 | £1250 | £8000 |

**Pescennius Niger**

| | | | |
|---|---|---|---|
| Denarius ....................................... | £295 | £800 | £4500 |

**Clodius Albinus**

| | | | |
|---|---|---|---|
| Denarius as Caesar ....................... | £45 | £140 | £600 |
| Denarius as Augustus ................... | £85 | £255 | £1100 |
| Sestertius ...................................... | £275 | £800 | £3300 |
| As .................................................. | £80 | £250 | £1100 |

*Lucius Verus*

*Commodus*

| | FROM F | VF | EF |
|---|---|---|---|
| **Septimius Severus** | | | |
| Aureus ............................................ | £850 | £2500 | £12000 |
| Aureus (VICT BRIT) ......................... | £1150 | £3500 | £16000 |
| +Denarius (Mint of Rome) ............... | £15 | £40 | £170 |
| +Denarius (Mints of Emesa & Laodicea) | £15 | £45 | £195 |
| Denarius (LEG XIIII) ........................ | £25 | £85 | £400 |
| Denarius (VICT BRIT) ..................... | £25 | £90 | £400 |
| Sestertius other types.................... | £75 | £240 | £1400 |
| Sestertius (VICT BRIT)..................... | £350 | £1100 | £6000 |
| Dupondius or as ............................ | £50 | £160 | £850 |
| Dupondius or As (VICT BRIT) .......... | £125 | £365 | £1900 |
| **Julia Domna** | | | |
| Denarius ........................................ | £15 | £40 | £175 |
| Sestertius ...................................... | £75 | £230 | £1300 |
| As or Dupondius ........................... | £50 | £160 | £800 |
| **Caracalla** | | | |
| Aureus (VICT BRIT) ........................ | £1250 | £3700 | £17500 |
| Denarius as Caesar ........................ | £14 | £45 | £200 |
| Denarius as Augustus ..................... | £14 | £40 | £185 |
| Denarius (VICT BRIT) ..................... | £30 | £95 | £395 |
| Antoninianus ................................. | £30 | £75 | £350 |
| Sestertius ...................................... | £90 | £295 | £1500 |
| Sestertius (VICT BRIT)..................... | £300 | £860 | £5000 |
| Dupondius or As ............................ | £50 | £165 | £700 |
| Dupondius or As (VICT BRIT) .......... | £100 | £300 | £1450 |
| **Plautilla** | | | |
| Denarius ........................................ | £25 | £75 | £400 |
| **Geta** | | | |
| Denarius as Caesar ........................ | £18 | £45 | £200 |
| Denarius as Augustus ..................... | £20 | £70 | £300 |
| Denarius (VICT BRIT) ..................... | £30 | £95 | £425 |
| Sestertius ...................................... | £125 | £350 | £1750 |
| Sestertius (VICT BRIT)..................... | £230 | £770 | £4000 |
| Dupondius or as ............................ | £75 | £230 | £1100 |
| As (VICT BRIT) ............................... | £120 | £340 | £1700 |
| **Macrinus** | | | |
| Antoninianus ................................. | £90 | £275 | £1200 |
| Denarius ........................................ | £30 | £120 | £495 |
| Sestertius ...................................... | £175 | £400 | £3000 |
| **Diadumenian** | | | |
| Denarius ........................................ | £65 | £195 | £700 |
| Dupondius or As ............................ | £125 | £395 | £2200 |
| Aureus .......................................... | £1000 | £3200 | £14000 |
| Antoninianus ................................. | £20 | £65 | £275 |
| Denarius ........................................ | £15 | £35 | £175 |
| Sestertius ...................................... | £100 | £320 | £1400 |
| Dupondius or As ............................ | £60 | £175 | £775 |
| **Elagabalus** | | | |
| Aureus .......................................... | £1150 | £3500 | £14000 |
| Antoninianus ................................. | £20 | £65 | £375 |
| Denarius ........................................ | £15 | £35 | £175 |
| Sestertius ...................................... | £100 | £320 | £1600 |
| Dupondius or As ............................ | £60 | £175 | £900 |
| **Julia Paula** | | | |
| Denarius ........................................ | £30 | £100 | £450 |
| **Aquilla Severa** | | | |
| Denarius ........................................ | £55 | £175 | £800 |
| **Julia Soaemias** | | | |
| Denarius ........................................ | £28 | £75 | £300 |
| Dupondius or As ............................ | £65 | £225 | £1200 |
| **Julia Maesa** | | | |
| Denarius ........................................ | £15 | £45 | £225 |
| Sestertius ...................................... | £85 | £240 | £1600 |

Septimus Severus

Julia Domna

Geta

Macrinus

Elagabalus

Julia Maesa

| | FROM F | VF | EF |
|---|---|---|---|
| **Severus Alexander** | | | |
| Aureus ............................................. | £675 | £2000 | £82500 |
| Denarius as Caesar ........................ | £65 | £200 | £950 |
| Denarius as Augustus ..................... | £12 | £35 | £160 |
| Sestertius ....................................... | £35 | £100 | £500 |
| Dupondius or As ............................. | £25 | £90 | £425 |
| **Orbiana** | | | |
| Denarius ......................................... | £58 | £185 | £800 |
| As ................................................... | £90 | £325 | £1500 |
| **Julia Mamaea** | | | |
| Denarius ......................................... | £14 | £40 | £175 |
| Sestertius ....................................... | £35 | £110 | £500 |

*Orbiana*

## IMPERIAL COINAGE—Military Anarchy AD 235–270

| | FROM F | VF | EF |
|---|---|---|---|
| **Maximinus I** | | | |
| Denarius ......................................... | £12 | £45 | £175 |
| Sestertius, Dupondius or As ........... | £30 | £125 | £500 |
| **Diva Paula** | | | |
| Denarius ......................................... | £140 | £450 | £1500 |
| **Maximus Caesar** | | | |
| Denarius ......................................... | £70 | £200 | £850 |
| Sestertius ....................................... | £55 | £165 | £950 |
| **Gordian I & II, Africanus** | | | |
| Denarius ......................................... | £450 | £1500 | £4500 |
| Sestertius ....................................... | £500 | £1650 | £6000 |
| **Balbinus & Pupienus** | | | |
| Antoninianus .................................. | £70 | £210 | £875 |
| Denarius ......................................... | £70 | £210 | £875 |
| **Gordian III** | | | |
| Antoninianus ................................... | £5 | £22 | £95 |
| Denarius .......................................... | £9 | £35 | £130 |
| Sestertius or As .............................. | £22 | £85 | £360 |
| **Tranquillina** | | | |
| Common Colonial ........................... | £30 | £110 | £450 |
| **Philip I** | | | |
| Antoninianus "Animal" | | | |
| Lion, stag, antelope, wolf & twins ... | £14 | £50 | £200 |
| Other Antoninianus ........................ | £5 | £20 | £95 |
| Sestertius, Dupondius or As ........... | £25 | £80 | £395 |
| **Otacilla Severa** | | | |
| Antoninianus .................................. | £8 | £25 | £100 |
| Antoninianus "Hipo" ........................ | £20 | £65 | £250 |
| Sestertius ....................................... | £25 | £85 | £395 |
| **Philip II** | | | |
| Antoninianus .................................. | £7 | £22 | £100 |
| Antoninianus "Goat" ....................... | £16 | £65 | £250 |
| Sestertius, Dupondius or As ........... | £27 | £85 | £395 |
| **Pacatian** | | | |
| Antoninianus .................................. | £1500 | £4500 | — |
| **Trajan Decius** | | | |
| Antoninianus .................................. | £6 | £22 | £100 |
| Antoninianus (DIVI series Augustus, Trajan etc) | £30 | £100 | £395 |
| Double Sestertius ........................... | £260 | £800 | £3200 |
| Sestertius, Dupondius or As ........... | £27 | £85 | £395 |
| **Herennius Etruscilla** | | | |
| Antoninianus .................................. | £7 | £27 | £115 |
| Sestertius, Dupondius or As ............ | £30 | £100 | £425 |
| **Herennius Etruscus** | | | |
| Antoninianus .................................. | £16 | £55 | £175 |
| Sestertius, Dupondius or As ............ | £55 | £185 | £775 |
| **Hostilian** | | | |
| Antoninianus as Caesar ................. | £28 | £100 | £425 |
| Antoninianus as Augustus .............. | £70 | £220 | £395 |

*Julia Mamaea*

*Diva Paula*

*Gordian III*

*Trajan Decius*

*Hostilian*

| | FROM F | VF | EF |
|---|---|---|---|
| **Trebonianus Gallus** | | | |
| Antoninianus..................................... | £7 | £26 | £110 |
| Sestertius or As .............................. | £25 | £95 | £400 |
| **Volusian** | | | |
| Antoninianus..................................... | £9 | £35 | £120 |
| Sestertius......................................... | £28 | £95 | £400 |
| **Aemilian** | | | |
| Antoninianus ..................................... | £45 | £135 | £575 |
| **Valerian I** | | | |
| Antoninianus ..................................... | £6 | £25 | £100 |
| Sestertius & As................................. | £45 | £150 | £630 |
| **Diva Mariniana** | | | |
| Antoninianus ..................................... | £35 | £125 | £500 |
| **Gallienus** | | | |
| Silver Antoninianus ........................... | £8 | £25 | £100 |
| AE Antoninianus................................ | £4 | £20 | £80 |
| Ae Antoninianus (Military bust) ......... | £8 | £25 | £100 |
| AE Antoninianus (Legionary) ........... | £60 | £220 | — |
| Ae Sestertius ................................... | £40 | £140 | £595 |
| Ae Denarius ..................................... | £45 | £125 | £500 |
| **Saloninus** | | | |
| Ae Antoninianus .............................. | £6 | £20 | £90 |
| **Valerian II** | | | |
| Billon Antoninianus .......................... | £10 | £35 | £150 |
| **Saloninus** | | | |
| Antoninianus ................................... | £12 | £45 | £180 |
| **Macrianus & Quietus** | | | |
| Billon Antoninianus .......................... | £35 | £110 | £500 |
| **Regalianus or Dryantilla** | | | |
| Billon Antoninianus .......................... | £1750 | £6500 | — |
| **Postumus** | | | |
| Silver Antoninianus ........................... | £7 | £25 | £100 |
| Ae Antoninianus ............................... | £5 | £25 | £90 |
| Radiated sestertius............................ | £45 | £175 | £1000 |
| **Laelianus** | | | |
| Ae Antoninianus .............................. | £200 | £650 | £2675 |
| **Marius** | | | |
| Ae Antoninianus ............................... | £35 | £110 | £450 |
| **Victorinus** | | | |
| Ae Antoninianus .............................. | £5 | £20 | £80 |
| **Tetricus I & II** | | | |
| Ae Antoninianus .............................. | £5 | £20 | £90 |
| **Claudius II Gothicus** | | | |
| Ae Antoninianus ............................... | £4 | £22 | £90 |
| Egypt, Alexandrian Billon tetradrachm | £5 | £25 | £100 |
| DIVO Ae Antoninianus ..................... | £5 | £25 | £100 |
| **Quintillus** | | | |
| Ae Antoninianus ............................... | £13 | £40 | £175 |

*Postumus*

*Aurelian*

*Severina*

## IMPERIAL COINAGE—The Illyrian Emperors—AD 270–285

| | | | |
|---|---|---|---|
| **Aurelian** | | | |
| Ae Antoninianus ............................... | £6 | £25 | £95 |
| Ae Denarius ..................................... | £18 | £65 | £260 |
| **Vabalathus & Aurelian** | | | |
| Ae Antoninianus (bust both sides) ... | £23 | £65 | £260 |
| **Vabalathus** | | | |
| Ae Antoninianus ............................... | £300 | £850 | — |
| **Severina** | | | |
| Ae Antoninianus ............................... | £12 | £45 | £185 |
| Ae As............................................... | £35 | £100 | £450 |
| **Zenobia** | | | |
| Eygpt, Alexandrian Billon Tetradrachm | £700 | £2200 | — |

*Tacitus*

*Florian*

| | FROM F | VF | EF |
|---|---|---|---|
| **Tacitus** | | | |
| Ae Antoninianus ............................... | £15 | £35 | £150 |
| **Florian** | | | |
| Ae Antoninianus .............................. | £35 | £85 | £400 |
| **Probus** | | | |
| Gold Aureus ...................................... | £1000 | £2800 | £10000 |
| Ae Antoninianus .............................. | £6 | £22 | £100 |
| Antoninianus (military or imp. Busts RIC G or H) | £9 | £32 | £150 |
| Antoninianus | | | |
| (Other military or imp NOT BUSTS G or H) | £15 | £55 | £250 |
| Antoninianus (VICTOR GERM rev.) .. | £11 | £35 | £140 |
| Egypt, Alexandrian Billon tetradrachm | £2 | £15 | £65 |
| **Carus** | | | |
| Ae Antoninianus .............................. | £13 | £40 | £180 |
| **Numerian** | | | |
| Ae Antoninianus .............................. | £12 | £38 | £170 |
| **Carinus** | | | |
| Ae Antoninianus .............................. | £11 | £35 | £155 |
| **Magna Urbica** | | | |
| Ae Antoninianus .............................. | £80 | £250 | £1000 |
| **Julian of Pannonia** | | | |
| Ae Antoninianus .............................. | £500 | £2000 | - |

*Diocletian*

*Maximianus*

## IMPERIAL COINAGE—The Tetrarchy AD 285–307

| | FROM F | VF | EF |
|---|---|---|---|
| **Diocletian** | | | |
| Gold Aureus ...................................... | £900 | £2750 | £11000 |
| AR Argenteus .................................. | £90 | £275 | £800 |
| Ae Antoninianus & Radiates ........... | £7 | £25 | £95 |
| Ae Follis (London Mint) .................... | £12 | £45 | £170 |
| As above with LON mint mark ........ | £100 | £295 | £1100 |
| Ae Follis (other mints) ..................... | £10 | £30 | £110 |
| Ae Follis (Imperial bust).................... | £23 | £75 | £300 |
| **Maximianus** | | | |
| AR Argenteus .................................. | £85 | £250 | £750 |
| Ae Follis (London mint) ................... | £12 | £40 | £170 |
| Ae Follis (other mints) ..................... | £8 | £27 | £100 |
| Ae Follis (MONETA rev.) ................... | £10 | £32 | £140 |
| **Carausius** | | | |
| Aureus ............................................. | £7300 | £22000 | — |
| Denarius .......................................... | £400 | £1200 | £4500 |
| Ae Antoninianus (PAX)..................... | £22 | £80 | £400 |
| As above but full silvering .............. | £30 | £110 | £550 |
| Legionary Antoninianus ................... | £70 | £200 | £1110 |
| Expectate Veni Antoninianus .......... | £95 | £295 | — |
| In the name of Diocletian or Maximian | £30 | £100 | £500 |
| **Allectus** | | | |
| Aureus............................................. | £10000 | £30000 | — |
| Ae Antoninianus .............................. | £25 | £90 | £450 |
| As above but full silvering .............. | £40 | £135 | £675 |
| Quinarius ......................................... | £25 | £90 | £450 |
| **Constantius I** | | | |
| AR Argenteus .................................. | £90 | £285 | £825 |
| Ae Follis (London Mint) .................... | £12 | £45 | £170 |
| Ae Follis (other mints) ..................... | £8 | £30 | £100 |
| Ae Follis (SALVS rev.) ..................... | £11 | £40 | £150 |
| Ae 4 (Lion or Eagle) ........................ | £9 | £30 | £120 |
| **Galerius** | | | |
| Ae Follis (London mint) .................... | £12 | £35 | £140 |
| Ae Follis (other mints) ..................... | £7 | £25 | £100 |
| **Galeria Valeria** | | | |
| Ae Follis ........................................... | £28 | £80 | £325 |
| **Severus II** | | | |
| Ae Follis (London mint) ................. | £33 | £100 | £450 |
| Ae Follis (other mints) .................... | £27 | £85 | £325 |

*Carausius*

*Severus II*

*Maximinus II*

| | FROM F | VF | EF |
|---|---|---|---|
| Ae Radiate .................................... | £15 | £50 | £165 |
| Ae Denarius ................................. | £25 | £85 | £300 |
| **Maximinus II** | | | |
| Ae Follis (London mint) ................ | £12 | £40 | £155 |
| Ae Follis (other mints) ................... | £5 | £18 | £80 |
| Ae Radiate ................................... | £8 | £28 | £110 |
| **Maxentius** | | | |
| Ae Follis ....................................... | £8 | £27 | £125 |
| **Romulus** | | | |
| Ae Follis ....................................... | £40 | £130 | £1200 |
| **Licinius I** | | | |
| Billon Argenteus ........................... | £45 | £140 | £575 |
| Ae Follis (London mint) ................ | £7 | £25 | £100 |
| Ae Follis (other mints) ................. | £6 | £18 | £70 |
| AE3 .............................................. | £5 | £18 | £70 |
| **Licinius II** | | | |
| AE3 .............................................. | £7 | £20 | £65 |
| **Alexander or Martinian** | | | |
| AE ............................................... | £1500 | £4000 | — |

*Licinius II*

## IMPERIAL COINAGE—Family of Constantine AD 307–350

**Constantine I**

*Constantine I*

| | | | |
|---|---|---|---|
| Billon Argenteus ........................... | £50 | £150 | £625 |
| Ae Follis (London mint) ................ | £8 | £25 | £100 |
| As above—helmeted bust ............ | £13 | £42 | £150 |
| Ae Follis (other mints) as Caesar ... | £12 | £50 | £185 |
| Ae Follis (other mints) as Augustus | £4 | £15 | £65 |
| AE3 .............................................. | £4 | £15 | £65 |
| AE3 (London mint) ........................ | £7 | £25 | £100 |
| AE3 (SARMATIA rev) ..................... | £10 | £35 | £150 |
| Urbs Roma / Wolf & twins AE3/4......... | £4 | £18 | £70 |
| Constantinopolis AE3/4 ................. | £3 | £15 | £60 |
| **Fausta & Helena** | | | |
| AE3 (London mint) ........................ | £50 | £150 | £600 |
| AE3 (other mints) ........................... | £14 | £45 | £170 |
| **Theodora** | | | |
| AE4 .............................................. | £7 | £25 | £100 |
| **Crispus** | | | |
| AE3 (London mint) ........................ | £8 | £30 | £115 |
| AE3 .............................................. | £7 | £20 | £80 |
| **Delmatius** | | | |
| AE3/4 ........................................... | £12 | £40 | £150 |
| **Hanniballianus Rex** | | | |
| AE4 .............................................. | £80 | £250 | £1000 |
| **Constantine II** | | | |
| AE3 (London mint) ........................ | £8 | £25 | £85 |
| AE3 .............................................. | £5 | £18 | £60 |
| AE3/4 ........................................... | £2 | £10 | £40 |
| **Constans** | | | |
| AE2 (centenionalis) ...................... | £9 | £28 | £90 |
| AE3 (half centenionalis) ................ | £5 | £20 | £65 |
| AE4 .............................................. | £2 | £10 | £40 |
| **Constantius II** | | | |
| Gold Solidus ................................ | £250 | £700 | £2850 |
| Siliqua ......................................... | £23 | £80 | £250 |
| AE2 (or centenionalis) ................... | £7 | £25 | £100 |
| AE3 (or half centenionalis) ............. | £4 | £15 | £60 |
| AE3 (London mint).......................... | £16 | £50 | £200 |
| AE3................................................ | £2 | £8 | £35 |

*Constantine II*

*Magnentius*

## IMPERIAL COINAGE—Late period to the collapse of the Empire AD 350 to end

**Magnentius**

| | | | |
|---|---|---|---|
| Gold Solidus.................................. | £700 | £2200 | £8000 |
| Silver Siliqua ................................ | £200 | £790 | £2875 |
| Double centenionalis ..................... | £45 | £185 | £950 |

*Vetranio*

| | FROM F | VF | EF |
|---|---|---|---|
| Centenionalis ................................. | £12 | £50 | £250 |
| **Decentius** | | | |
| Double centenionalis...................... | £65 | £225 | £1175 |
| Centenionalis ................................. | £17 | £60 | £300 |
| **Vetranio** | | | |
| AE2 (centenionalis) ........................ | £35 | £115 | £500 |
| AE3 (half centenionalis) ................. | £30 | £100 | £425 |
| **Nepotian** | | | |
| AE2 (centenionalis) ........................ | £1950 | £6300 | — |
| **Constantius Gallus** | | | |
| AE2 (centenionalis) ........................ | £11 | £32 | £145 |
| AE3 (half centenionalis) ................. | £5 | £17 | £75 |
| **Julian II** | | | |
| Siliqua ........................................... | £25 | £75 | £295 |
| AE1 ................................................ | £40 | £125 | £550 |
| AE3 (helmeted bust) ...................... | £8 | £28 | £110 |
| Anonymous, Serapis + Jupiter AE3 | £195 | £550 | — |
| **Jovian** | | | |
| AE1 ................................................ | £65 | £210 | £750 |
| AE3 ................................................ | £12 | £40 | £150 |
| **Valentinian I** | | | |
| Sold Solidus .................................. | £200 | £510 | £1600 |
| Silver Milliarense............................ | £165 | £550 | £1800 |
| Siliqua ........................................... | £25 | £85 | £300 |
| AE3 ................................................ | £5 | £18 | £65 |
| **Valens** | | | |
| Gold Solidus ................................. | £200 | £500 | £1500 |
| Silver Milliarense............................ | £190 | £600 | £2000 |
| Siliqua ........................................... | £22 | £80 | £295 |
| AE3 ................................................ | £5 | £18 | £65 |
| **Procopius** | | | |
| AE3 ................................................ | £45 | £140 | £600 |
| **Gratian** | | | |
| Silver Milliarense............................ | £165 | £520 | £1600 |
| Siliqua ........................................... | £24 | £75 | £235 |
| AE3 ................................................ | £4 | £18 | £65 |
| AE4 ................................................ | £3 | £14 | £50 |
| **Valentinian II** | | | |
| Solidus .......................................... | £220 | £550 | £1650 |
| Siliqua ........................................... | £25 | £80 | £295 |
| AE2 ................................................ | £10 | £30 | £115 |
| AE4 ................................................ | £2 | £10 | £45 |
| **Theodosius I** | | | |
| Solidus .......................................... | £225 | £550 | £1700 |
| Siliqua ........................................... | £28 | £95 | £350 |
| AE2 ................................................ | £10 | £35 | £130 |
| AE3 ................................................ | £8 | £30 | £110 |
| **Aelia Flaccilla** | | | |
| AE2 ................................................ | £30 | £100 | £375 |
| AE4................................................ | £15 | £45 | £175 |
| **Magnus Maximus** | | | |
| Solidus (AVGOB) ........................... | £4800 | £12500 | — |
| Solidus .......................................... | £700 | £2300 | £10000 |
| Siliqua ........................................... | £30 | £100 | £400 |
| Siliqua (AVGPS) ............................ | £700 | £2000 | — |
| AE2 ................................................ | £18 | £65 | £250 |
| **Flavius Victor** | | | |
| Silver Sliqua .................................. | £140 | £450 | £1400 |
| AE4 ................................................ | £30 | £95 | £350 |
| **Eugenius** | | | |
| Silver Siliqua .................................. | £150 | £475 | £1500 |

*Julian II*

*Jovian*

*Valentinian I*

*Valens*

*Theodosius I*

*Arcadius*

| | FROM F | VF | EF |
|---|---|---|---|
| **Arcadius** | | | |
| Gold Solidus.................................. | £200 | £500 | £1500 |
| Silver Siliqua.................................. | £25 | £85 | £300 |
| Silver Half-siliqua .......................... | £130 | £450 | £1500 |
| AE2 ............................................... | £10 | £30 | £110 |
| AE4 ............................................... | £2 | £12 | £50 |
| **Eudoxia** | | | |
| AE3 ............................................... | £25 | £70 | £295 |
| **Honorius** | | | |
| Gold Solidus ................................. | £200 | £425 | £1300 |
| Silver Siliqua ................................ | £30 | £90 | £350 |
| AE4 ............................................... | £5 | £20 | £75 |
| **Constantine III** | | | |
| Silver Siliqua ................................ | £130 | £450 | £1600 |
| **Theodosius II** | | | |
| Gold Solidus ................................. | £200 | £425 | £1300 |
| **Johannes** | | | |
| AE4 ............................................... | £110 | £435 | — |
| **Valentinian III** | | | |
| Gold Soldius.................................. | £200 | £450 | £1400 |
| AE4 ............................................... | £25 | £90 | £350 |

*Honorius*

*Theodosius II*

Ae = bronze; AE 1, 2, 3, 4 = bronze coins in descending order of size.

*Illustrations by courtesy of Classical Numismatic Group/Seaby Coins.*

A SIMPLIFIED PRICE GUIDE TO

# ENGLISH
# HAMMERED COINS

**PART I**

959–1485

## INTRODUCTION

We have taken our starting point for hammered coin prices back to the Anglo-Saxon reign of Edgar; who could reasonably claim to be the first king of All England. Also it is from this time onwards that we start to get regular "portraits" as well as moneyers and mints on most issues. This gives a total of eight rulers to the list of kings prior to the Norman Conquest and most of these have coin issues that can be purchased quite reasonably. It is also worth pointing out here that of course coins had previously been struck in England for approximately 1000 years prior to our listings by Celtic, Roman and earlier Saxon rulers, details of which can be found in more specific publications.

## PRICING

The prices given in the following pages are intended to be used as a "Pocket book guide" to the values of the *most common* coins within any denomination of any one reign. The price quoted is what a collector may expect to pay for such a piece in the condition indicated. For more detailed information we recommend the reader to one of the many specialist publications.

## GRADING

The prices quoted are for three different grades of condition: Fine (F), Very Fine (VF) and Extremely Fine (EF). A "Fine" coin is assumed to be a fairly worn, circulated, piece but with all or most of the main features and lettering still clear. "Very Fine" is a middle grade with a small amount of wear and most details fairly clear. For this edition we have included the prices for coins in Extremely Fine condition where appropriate, although very few hammered coins actually turn up in this grade (i.e. nearly mint state with hardly any wear). In some instances the prices quoted are theoretically based and are only included to provide a guide. It is important to note that on all hammered coins the very nature of striking, i.e. individually, by hand, means hammered coinage is rarely a straight grade and when listed by a dealer the overall condition will often be qualified by terms such as: *weak in parts, struck off-centre, cracked or chipped flan, double struck,* etc. When applicable the price should be adjusted accordingly.

## HISTORY

Below the heading for each monarch we have given a few historical notes as and when they apply to significant changes in the coinage.

# EDGAR (First King of All England) (959–975)

| | F | VF | EF |
|---|---|---|---|
| Edgar Penny, non portrait (2 line inscription) | £275 | £600 | — |

# EDWARD THE MARTYR (975–978)

| | F | VF | EF |
|---|---|---|---|
| Edward, Penny, Portrait | £1350 | £4000 | — |

# AETHELRED II (978–1016)

| | F | VF | EF |
|---|---|---|---|
| Aethelred II, Penny, last small cross type ( First hand type illustrated) | £165 | £300 | £650 |

# CNUT (1016–1035)

| | F | VF | EF |
|---|---|---|---|
| Cnut, Penny (short cross type) (*Quatrefoil type illustrated*) | £145 | £275 | £525 |

# HAROLD I
## (1035–40)

|  | F | VF | EF |
|---|---|---|---|
| Harold I, Penny | £400 | £925 | — |

# HARTHACANUTE
## (1035–42)

|  | F | VF | EF |
|---|---|---|---|
| Harthacanute, Penny, English Mint (in his own name) | £1000 | £3250 | — |
| Harthacanute, Penny, Danish type | £300 | £700 | — |

*Danish type*

# EDWARD THE CONFESSOR
## (1042–66)

|  | F | VF | EF |
|---|---|---|---|
| Edward the Confessor, Penny | £160 | £325 | — |

# HAROLD II
## (1066)

|  | F | VF | EF |
|---|---|---|---|
| Harold II, Penny | £1000 | £2250 | — |

# WILLIAM I
# (1066–87)

The Norman Conquest had very little immediate effect on the coinage of England. The Anglo-Saxon standard of minting silver pennies was very high and the practice of the moneyer putting his name and mint town on the reverse continued as before, except with William's portrait of course. It is worth noting here that non-realistic, stylised portraits were used until the reign of Henry VII.

There are eight major types of pennies of which the last, the PAXS type, is by far the commonest.

|  | F | VF | EF |
|---|---|---|---|
| William I, Penny | £300 | £525 | £1000 |

# WILLIAM II
# (1087–1100)

Very little change from his father's reign except that five new types were issued, most of which were much more crudely designed than previous, all are scarce.

|  | F | VF | EF |
|---|---|---|---|
| William II, Penny | £800 | £2000 | — |

# HENRY I
# (1100–35)

There are fifteen different types of penny for this reign of which the last two are the most common. Most issues are of a very poor standard both in workmanship and metal, the prices reflect a poor quality of issue.

|  | F | VF | EF |
|---|---|---|---|
| Henry I, Penny | £175 | £475 | — |
| Halfpenny | £1500 | — | — |

# STEPHEN
## (1135–54)

This is historically a very complicated time for the coinage, mainly due to civil war and a consequential lack of central control in the country which resulted in very poor quality and deliberately damaged pieces. Coins were struck not only in the name of Stephen and his main rival claimant Matilda but also by their supporters. The commonest issue is the "Watford" type; so named, as are many issues, after the area in which a hoard was found.

|  | F | VF | EF |
|---|---|---|---|
| Stephen, Penny | £300 | £700 | — |

# HENRY II
## (1154–89)

There were two distinct issues struck during this reign. The first, Cross and Crosslets or "Tealby" coinage (named after Tealby in Lincolnshire), continued to be very poorly made and lasted 20 years. However, in 1180 the new and superior "Short Cross" issue commenced, being issued from only twelve major towns.

|  | F | VF | EF |
|---|---|---|---|
| Henry II, Penny, Tealby | £110 | £300 | — |

|  | F | VF | EF |
|---|---|---|---|
| Henry II, Penny, Short Cross | £65 | £170 | — |

# RICHARD I
## (1189–1199)

There were no major changes during this reign, in fact pennies continued to be struck with his father Henry's name throughout the reign. The coins struck under Richard tend to be rather crude in style.

|  | F | VF | EF |
|---|---|---|---|
| Richard I, Penny | £90 | £265 | — |

# JOHN
## (1199–1216)

As with his brother before him, there were no major changes during the reign of King John, and pennies with his father's name were struck throughout the reign, although they tended to be somewhat neater in style than those struck during the reign of Richard I.

| | F | VF | EF |
|---|---|---|---|
| John, Penny..................................... | £60 | £140 | £300 |

# HENRY III
## (1216–72)

The coinage during Henry III's reign continued as before with the short cross issue. However, in 1247 a new long cross design was introduced to prevent clipping. This design was to last in one form or another for many centuries. A gold penny is known with a throned monarch on the obverse.

| | F | VF | EF |
|---|---|---|---|
| Henry III, Penny, Short Cross .................. | £35 | £100 | £250 |
| Henry III, Penny, Long Cross................... | £30 | £65 | £160 |

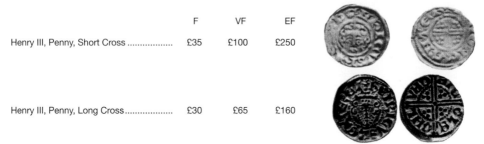

# EDWARD I
## (1272–1307)

After a few years of issuing similar pieces to his father, in 1279 Edward I ordered a major re-coinage. This consisted of well-made pennies, halfpennies and farthings in relatively large quantities, and for a brief period a groat (four pence) was produced. The pennies are amongst the most common of all hammered coins.

| | F | VF | EF |
|---|---|---|---|
| Edward I (and Edward II) | | | |
| Groat (often damaged)..................... | £3500 | £8000 | — |
| Penny.................................................. | £25 | £55 | £190 |
| Halfpenny........................................... | £25 | £75 | £230 |
| Farthing.............................................. | £20 | £70 | £220 |

*Edward I penny*

# EDWARD II
## (1307–1327)

The coinage of Edward II differs in only a very few minor details from that of Edward I and are of similar value for the common types.

# EDWARD III
## (1327–77)

This was a long reign which saw major changes in the coinage, the most significant being the introduction of a gold coinage (based on the Noble, valued at 6s 8d, and its fractions) and a regular issue of a large silver groat (and half groat). The mints were limited to a few episcopal cities but coins of English type were also struck in the newly-acquired Calais.

| | F | VF | EF |
|---|---|---|---|
| Gold | | | |
| Noble | £800 | £1900 | £3500 |
| Half Noble | £500 | £1350 | £2500 |
| Quarter Noble | £300 | £600 | £1100 |
| | | | |
| Silver | | | |
| Groat | £50 | £175 | £750 |
| Half Groat | £30 | £115 | £350 |
| Penny | £30 | £90 | £260 |
| Half Penny | £25 | £75 | £200 |
| Farthing | £30 | £110 | £250 |

*Gold Noble*

# RICHARD II
## (1377–1399)

The denominations continued during this reign much as before. However, coins are quite rare mainly due to the lack of bullion gold and silver going into the mints, mainly because of an inbalance with European weights and fineness.

| | F | VF | EF |
|---|---|---|---|
| Gold | | | |
| Noble | £1000 | £2750 | — |
| Half Noble | £1050 | £3500 | — |
| Quarter Noble | £455 | £1000 | — |
| | | | |
| Silver | | | |
| Groat | £475 | £1650 | — |
| Half Groat | £275 | £800 | — |
| Penny | £70 | £250 | — |
| Half Penny | £45 | £150 | — |
| Farthing | £130 | £425 | — |

*Gold Noble*

# HENRY IV
# (1399–1413)

Because of the continuing problems with the scarcity of gold and silver the coinage was reduced in weight in 1412, towards the end of the reign. All coins of this reign are quite scarce.

|  | F | VF |
|---|---|---|
| **Gold** | | |
| Noble | £1750 | £5000 |
| Half Noble | £2100 | £6750 |
| Quarter Noble | £775 | £1750 |
| **Silver** | | |
| Groat | £2750 | £7000 |
| Half Groat | £825 | £2250 |
| Penny | £450 | £1200 |
| Half Penny | £325 | £750 |
| Farthing | £750 | £2250 |

*Noble*

# HENRY V
# (1413–22)

Monetary reform introduced towards the end of his father's reign in 1412 improved the supply of bullion and hence coins of Henry V are far more common. All of the main denominations continued as before.

|  | F | VF | EF |
|---|---|---|---|
| **Gold** | | | |
| Noble | £900 | £2400 | £4500 |
| Half Noble | £775 | £2250 | — |
| Quarter Noble | £375 | £775 | £1450 |
| **Silver** | | | |
| Groat | £190 | £565 | — |
| Half Groat | £150 | £425 | — |
| Penny | £45 | £150 | — |
| Half Penny | £35 | £115 | — |
| Farthing | £375 | £900 | — |

*Groat*

# HENRY VI
# (1422–61 and again 1470–71)

Although there were no new denominations during these reigns (see Edward IV below), Henry's first reign saw eleven different issues, each for a few years and distinguished by privy marks, i.e. crosses, pellets, annulets, etc.

## HENRY VI *continued*

| | F | VF | EF |
|---|---|---|---|
| **Gold** | | | |
| *First reign—* | | | |
| Noble .................................£825 | £2400 | £4250 |
| Half Noble..........................£650 | £1750 | £3000 |
| Quarter Noble ....................£320 | £675 | £1200 |
| *2nd reign—* | | | |
| Angel.................................£1750 | £4250 | — |
| Half Angel .........................£3750 | £10000 | — |
| | | | |
| **Silver** | | | |
| Groat....................................£60 | £140 | £300 |
| Half Groat ............................£35 | £110 | £265 |
| Penny...................................£35 | £120 | £275 |
| Half Penny ...........................£30 | £85 | £175 |
| Farthing..............................£110 | £325 | — |

*Noble*

---

# EDWARD IV
## (1461–70 and again 1471–83)

The significant changes during these reigns were the replacement of the noble by the rose ryal (and revalued at 10 shillings) and the introduction of the angel at the old noble value. We also start to see mint-marks or initial marks appearing, usually at the top of the coin, they were used to denote the period of issue for dating purposes and often lasted for two to three years.

| | F | VF | EF |
|---|---|---|---|
| **Gold** | | | |
| Ryal.....................................£800 | £1875 | £3500 |
| Half Ryal ............................£700 | £1750 | £2850 |
| Quarter Ryal.......................£425 | £1000 | £1750 |
| Angel..................................£725 | £1850 | £3250 |
| Half Angel ..........................£625 | £1600 | — |
| | | | |
| **Silver** | | | |
| Groat....................................£60 | £160 | £425 |
| Half Groat ............................£55 | £170 | £400 |
| Penny...................................£35 | £130 | £325 |
| Half Penny ...........................£30 | £115 | — |
| Farthing..............................£300 | £900 | — |

*Angel*

---

# RICHARD III
## (1483–85)

The close of the Yorkist Plantagenet and Medieval period come together at this time. There are no new significant numismatic changes but most coins of Richard whilst not really rare, continue to be very popular and priced quite high.

| | F | VF | EF |
|---|---|---|---|
| **Gold** | | | |
| Angel.................................£4000 | £11000 | — |
| Half Angel .........................£6500 | £17500 | — |
| | | | |
| **Silver** | | | |
| Groat...................................£850 | £1900 | — |
| Half Groat .........................£1250 | £3500 | — |
| Penny.................................£425 | £1150 | — |
| Half Penny ........................£350 | £900 | — |
| Farthing.............................£1400 | £4000 | — |

*Groat*

# PART II
# 1485–1663

Among the more significant features of the post-Renaissance period as it affected coinage is the introduction of realistic portraiture during the reign of Henry VII. We also have a much wider and varied number of new and revised denominations, for example eleven different gold denominations of Henry VIII and the same number of silver for Elizabeth I. Here we only mention the introduction or changes in the main denominations, giving a value for all of them, once again listing the commonest type.

## HENRY VII
## (1485–1509)

The gold sovereign of 20 shillings makes its first appearance in 1489 as does the testoon (later shilling) in about 1500. The silver penny was re-designed to a rather crude likeness of the sovereign.

| | F | VF | EF |
|---|---|---|---|
| **Gold** | | | |
| Sovereign | £25000 | £250000 | — |
| Ryal | £30000 | £85000 | — |
| Angel | £1700 | £1800 | — |
| Half Angel | £650 | £1650 | — |
| **Silver** | | | |
| Testoon 1/- | £15000 | £30,000 | — |
| Groat | £75 | £200 | £550 |
| Half Groat | £40 | £125 | £350 |
| Penny | £40 | £110 | £275 |
| Half Penny | £30 | £85 | — |
| Farthing | £375 | £1100 | — |

*Profile Groat*

## HENRY VIII
## (1509–47)

After a long initial period of very little change in the coinage, in 1526 there were many, with an attempt to bring the gold/silver ratio in line with the continental currencies. Some gold coins only lasted a short time and are very rare. The crown (in gold) makes its first appearance. Towards the end of the reign we see large issues of debased silver coins (with a high copper content) bearing the well-known facing portrait of the ageing King. These tend to turn up in poor condition.

| **Gold** | | | |
|---|---|---|---|
| Sovereign | £5000 | £17,500 | — |
| Half Sovereign | £900 | £2850 | — |
| Angel | £725 | £1850 | £3000 |
| Half Angel | £675 | £1700 | £2400 |
| Quarter Angel | £700 | £1850 | — |
| George Noble | £9000 | £27,500 | — |
| Half George Noble | £8000 | — | — |
| Crown of the rose | £6500 | — | — |
| Crown of the double rose | £675 | £1850 | £2400 |
| Half Crown of the double rose | £550 | £1200 | — |
| **Silver** | | | |
| Testoon 1/- | £850 | £3750 | — |
| Groat | £125 | £300 | £900 |
| Half Groat | £50 | £150 | £500 |
| Penny | £50 | £150 | £325 |
| Half Penny | £35 | £125 | — |
| Farthing | £275 | £725 | — |

*Gold Sovereign*

# EDWARD VI
## (1547–53)

Some of the coins struck in the first few years of this short reign could really be called Henry VIII posthumous issues as there is continuity in both name and style from his father's last issue. However, overlapping this period are portrait issues of the boy King, particularly shillings (usually poor quality coins). This period also sees the first dated English coin (shown in Roman numerals). In 1551 however, a new coinage was introduced with a restored silver quality from the Crown (dated 1551) down to the new sixpence and threepence.

| | F | VF | EF |
|---|---|---|---|
| **Gold** | | | |
| Sovereign (30s) | £5500 | £18500 | — |
| Half Sovereign | £1600 | £4750 | — |
| Crown | £1800 | £5750 | — |
| Half Crown | £1400 | £4250 | — |
| Angel | £9500 | £30000 | — |
| Half Angel | — | — | — |
| Sovereign (20s) | £4000 | £13000 | — |
| **Silver** | | | |
| Crown | £1000 | £2600 | — |
| Half Crown | £700 | £1850 | — |
| Shilling | £135 | £425 | £1700 |
| Sixpence | £130 | £500 | — |
| Groat | £825 | £3000 | — |
| Threepence | £200 | £850 | — |
| Half Groat | £475 | £1300 | — |
| Penny | £70 | £250 | — |
| Half Penny | £175 | £700 | — |
| Farthing | £1150 | £3250 | — |

*Crowned bust half sovereign*

# MARY
## (1553–54)

The early coins of Mary's sole reign are limited and continue to use the same denominations as Edward, except that the gold ryal was reintroduced.

| | F | VF |
|---|---|---|
| **Gold** | | |
| Sovereign (30s) | £5500 | £17500 |
| Ryal | £30000 | — |
| Angel | £2200 | £5000 |
| Half Angel | £4000 | £11500 |
| **Silver** | | |
| Groat | £160 | £525 |
| Half Groat | £700 | £2000 |
| Penny | £600 | £1900 |

*Groat*

# PHILIP & MARY
## (1554–58)

After a very short reign alone, Mary married Philip of Spain and they technically ruled jointly (although not for very long in practise) until her death. After her marriage we see both her and Philip on the shillings and sixpences.

| | F | VF |
|---|---|---|
| **Gold** | | |
| Angel | £5000 | £16000 |
| Half Angel | £10000 | — |
| **Silver** | | |
| Shilling | £500 | £1850 |
| Sixpence | £500 | £1750 |
| Groat | £175 | £575 |
| Half Groat | £500 | £1600 |
| Penny | £90 | £265 |

*Shilling*

# ELIZABETH I
## (1558–1603)

As might be expected with a long reign there are a number of significant changes in the coinage which include several new denominations—so many in silver that every value from the shilling downwards was marked and dated to distinguish them. Early on we have old base Edward VI shillings countermarked to a new reduced value (not priced here). Also due to a lack of small change and the expense of making a miniscule farthing we have a new threehalfpence and threefarthings. Finally we see the beginnings of a milled (machine produced) coinage for a brief period from 1561–71.

| | F | VF | EF |
|---|---|---|---|
| **Gold** | | | |
| Sovereign (30s) | £5000 | £14500 | — |
| Ryal (15s) | £15000 | £40000 | — |
| Angel | £1000 | £2750 | — |
| Half Angel | £925 | £2500 | — |
| Quarter Angel | £875 | £2450 | — |
| Pound (20s) | £2650 | £7250 | — |
| Half Pound | £1375 | £4100 | — |
| Crown | £950 | £3200 | — |
| Half Crown | £900 | £2850 | — |
| **Silver** | | | |
| Crown | £1450 | £4000 | — |
| Half Crown | £1200 | £2650 | — |
| Shilling | £120 | £400 | £1250 |
| Sixpence | £60 | £200 | £750 |
| Groat | £90 | £265 | £725 |
| Threepence | £40 | £150 | £400 |
| Half Groat | £35 | £100 | £275 |
| Threehalfpence | £50 | £175 | — |
| Penny | £35 | £110 | £235 |
| Threefarthings | £90 | £235 | — |
| Half Penny | £40 | £100 | £175 |

*Shilling*

# JAMES I
# (1603–25)

Although the size of the gold coinage remains much the same as Elizabeth's reign, the name and weight or value of the denominations have several changes, i.e. Pound = Sovereign = Unite = Laurel. A new four shilling gold coin (thistle crown) was introduced. A number of the silver coins now have their value in Roman numerals on the coin. Relatively few angels were made from this period onwards and they are usually found pierced.

|  | F | VF | EF |
|---|---|---|---|
| **Gold** | | | |
| Sovereign (20s) | £2250 | £8000 | — |
| Unite | £650 | £1600 | £2750 |
| Double crown/half unite | £425 | £1000 | £2250 |
| Crown | £300 | £675 | £1750 |
| Thistle Crown | £325 | £725 | £1600 |
| Half Crown | £235 | £525 | — |
| Rose Ryal (30s) | £2850 | £8000 | — |
| Spur Ryal (15s) | £6000 | £20000 | — |
| Angel (pierced) | £900 | £2250 | — |
| Half Angel (Unpierced) | £2250 | £6500 | — |
| Laurel | £625 | £1575 | £2850 |
| Half Laurel | £500 | £1150 | £2250 |
| Quarter Laurel | £275 | £625 | £1500 |
| | | | |
| **Silver** | | | |
| Crown | £750 | £1850 | — |
| Half Crown | £325 | £775 | — |
| Shilling | £75 | £265 | — |
| Sixpence | £60 | £225 | — |
| Half Groat | £25 | £65 | £120 |
| Penny | £20 | £60 | £110 |
| Half Penny | £20 | £50 | £85 |

*Halfcrown*

# CHARLES I
# (1625–49)

This reign is probably the most difficult to simplify as there are so many different issues and whole books have been produced on this period alone. From the beginning of the King's reign and throughout the Civil War, a number of mints operated for varying lengths of time, producing both regular and irregular issues. The Tower mint was taken over by Parliament in 1642 but before this a small quantity of milled coinage was produced alongside the regular hammered issues. The Court then moved to Oxford from where, for the next three years, large quantities of gold and silver were struck (including rare triple unites and large silver pounds). The most prolific of the provincial mints were those situated at Aberystwyth, York, Oxford, Shrewsbury, Bristol, Exeter, Truro, Chester and Worcester as well as some smaller mints mainly situated in the West Country. Among the more interesting coins of the period are the pieces struck on unusually-shaped flans at Newark and Pontefract whilst those towns were under siege. As many of the coins struck during the Civil War were crudely struck on hastily gathered bullion and plate, they provide a fascinating area of study. The prices indicated below are the minimum for the commonest examples of each denomination irrespective of town of origin.

|  | F | VF | EF |
|---|---|---|---|
| **Gold** | | | |
| Triple Unite (£3) | £15000 | £45000 | — |
| Unite | £700 | £1700 | — |
| Double crown/Half unite | £475 | £1250 | — |
| Crown | £275 | £600 | — |
| Angel (pierced) | £850 | £2400 | — |
| Angel (unpierced) | £2450 | £8000 | — |
| **Silver** | | | |
| Pound (20 shillings—Oxford) | £2700 | £7500 | — |
| Half Pound (Shrewsbury) | £1500 | £3350 | — |
| Crown (Truro, Exeter) | £500 | £1100 | — |
| Half Crown | £70 | £225 | — |
| Shilling | £55 | £175 | £800 |
| Sixpence | £55 | £185 | £700 |
| Groat | £75 | £200 | £500 |
| Threepence | £70 | £175 | £450 |
| Half Groat | £25 | £75 | £185 |
| Penny | £20 | £70 | £175 |
| Half Penny | £15 | £30 | £65 |

Triple unite

Oxford Halfcrown

Above: Newark siege shilling.

# THE COMMONWEALTH
# (1649–60)

After the execution of Charles I, Parliament changed the design of the coinage. They are simple non- portrait pieces with an English legend.

|  | F | VF | EF |
|---|---|---|---|
| **Gold** | | | |
| Unite | £2000 | £5000 | — |
| Double crown/Half unite | £1000 | £3000 | — |
| Crown | £1000 | £2750 | — |
| **Silver** | | | |
| Crown | £850 | £2000 | £6000 |
| Half Crown | £300 | £725 | £3250 |
| Shilling | £220 | £550 | £1850 |
| Sixpence | £200 | £500 | £1600 |
| Half Groat | £45 | £140 | £300 |
| Penny | £45 | £150 | £325 |
| Halfpenny | £35 | £100 | £185 |

*Crown*

# CHARLES II
# (1660–85)

Although milled coins had been produced for Oliver Cromwell in 1656–58, after the Restoration of the monarchy hammered coins continued to be produced until 1663, when the machinery was ready to manufacture large quantities of good milled pieces.

|  | F | VF | EF |
|---|---|---|---|
| **Gold** | | | |
| Unite | £1550 | £4500 | — |
| Double crown/Half unite | £1000 | £3500 | — |
| Crown | £1450 | £5000 | — |
| **Silver** | | | |
| Half Crown | £300 | £850 | — |
| Shilling | £175 | £585 | — |
| Sixpence | £150 | £500 | — |
| Fourpence | £40 | £125 | £200 |
| Threepence | £35 | £110 | £185 |
| Twopence | £25 | £65 | £125 |
| Penny | £35 | £90 | £150 |

*Halfcrown*

A COMPREHENSIVE PRICE GUIDE
TO THE COINS OF

# THE
# UNITED KINGDOM
# 1656–2011
including

*England, Scotland,
Isle Of Man,
Guernsey, Jersey, Alderney,
also Ireland*

When referring to this price guide one must bear a number of important points in mind. The points listed here have been taken into consideration during the preparation of this guide and we hope that the prices given will provide a true reflection of the market at the time of going to press. Nevertheless, the publishers can accept no liability for the accuracy of the prices quoted.

1. "As struck" examples with flaws will be worth less than the indicated price.
2. Any coin which is particularly outstanding, with an attractive natural toning or in superb state will command a much *higher* price than that shown.
3. These prices refer strictly to the British market, and do not reflect outside opinions.
4. Some prices given for coins not seen in recent years are estimates based on a knowledge of the market.
5. In the case of coins of high rarity, prices are not generally given.
6. In the listing, "—" indicates, where applicable, one of the following:
    a. Metal or bullion value only
    b. Not usually found in this grade
    c. Not collected in this condition
7. Proof coins are listed in FDC under the UNC column.
8. All prices are quoted in £ sterling, exclusive of VAT (where applicable).

# FIVE GUINEAS

|  | F | VF | EF |
|---|---|---|---|
| **CHARLES II (1660–85)** | | | |
| 1668 First bust | £3000 | £6000 | £18000 |
| 1668 — Elephant below bust | £2500 | £5500 | £18000 |
| 1669 — | £2500 | £6000 | — |
| 1669 — Elephant | £3000 | £6500 | — |
| 1670 — | £2750 | £6000 | £18000 |
| 1670 Proof | — | — | £120000 |
| 1671 — | £3000 | £6500 | £18000 |
| 1672 — | £2750 | £6000 | £18000 |
| 1673 — | £2750 | £6000 | £18000 |
| 1674 — | £3000 | £6750 | £20000 |
| 1675 — | £3000 | £6500 | £19000 |
| 1675 — Elephant | £3200 | £6750 | — |
| 1675 — Elephant & Castle below bust... | £3500 | £7000 | £25000 |
| 1676 — | £3000 | £6000 | £20000 |
| 1676 — Elephant & Castle | £3000 | £6500 | £20000 |
| 1677 — | £2500 | £6000 | £18000 |
| 1677/5 — Elephant | £3000 | £7500 | £25000 |
| 1677 — Elephant & Castle | £3000 | £6500 | £22000 |
| 1678/7 — 8 over 7 | £2500 | £6000 | £18000 |
| 1678/7 — Elephant & Castle | £3250 | £7000 | £22000 |
| 1678/7 Second Bust | £2800 | £6000 | £18000 |
| 1679 — | £2400 | £6000 | £18000 |
| 1680 — | £2700 | £6000 | £18000 |
| 1680 — Elephant & Castle | £3000 | £7000 | £22000 |
| 1681 — | £3000 | £6500 | £20000 |
| 1681 — Elephant & Castle | £3000 | £6500 | £20000 |
| 1682 — | £2500 | £6000 | £18000 |
| 1682 — Elephant & Castle | £2500 | £6000 | £18000 |
| 1683 — | £2400 | £6000 | £18000 |
| 1683 — Elephant & Castle | £3000 | £6500 | £20000 |
| 1684 — | £2500 | £6500 | £17500 |
| 1684 — Elephant & Castle | £2500 | £6000 | £18000 |

Charles II

|  | F | VF | EF |
|---|---|---|---|
| **JAMES II (1685–88)** | | | |
| 1686 | £3500 | £7000 | £24000 |
| 1687 | £3250 | £7000 | £20000 |
| 1687 Elephant & Castle | £3300 | £7000 | £20000 |
| 1688 | £3300 | £7500 | £20000 |
| 1688 Elephant & Castle | £3500 | £8000 | £23000 |

|  | F | VF | EF |
|---|---|---|---|
| **WILLIAM AND MARY (1688–94)** | | | |
| 1691 | £2600 | £5500 | £18000 |
| 1691 Elephant & Castle | £2700 | £5700 | £18000 |
| 1692 | £2750 | £6000 | £17500 |
| 1692 Elephant & Castle | £3000 | £6000 | £18000 |
| 1693 | £2700 | £5800 | £18000 |
| 1693 Elephant & Castle | £2600 | £6000 | £18000 |
| 1694 | £2600 | £6000 | £18000 |
| 1694 Elephant & Castle | £2600 | £6000 | £18000 |

|  | F | VF | EF |
|---|---|---|---|
| **WILLIAM III (1694–1702)** | | | |
| 1699 First bust | £2800 | £6250 | £20000 |
| 1699 — Elephant & Castle | £3000 | £7000 | £22000 |
| 1700 — | £3000 | £6500 | £20000 |
| 1701 Second bust "fine work" | £2750 | £6500 | £18000 |
| *(1701 "fine work"—beware recent forgeries)* | | | |

William & Mary

|  | F | VF | EF |
|---|---|---|---|
| **ANNE (1702–14)** | | | |
| *Pre-Union with Scotland* | | | |
| 1703 VIGO below bust | £35000 | £75000 | £220000 |
| 1705 | £4000 | £10000 | £35000 |
| 1706 | £3800 | £9000 | £32000 |
| *Post-Union (different shields)* | | | |
| 1706 | £3000 | £6000 | £18000 |
| 1709 Narrow shields | £3000 | £6500 | £20000 |
| 1711 Broader shields | £3200 | £6500 | £20000 |
| 1713 — | £3200 | £6500 | £20000 |
| 1714 — | £3200 | £6500 | £20000 |
| 1714/3 | £3200 | £6500 | £20000 |
| **GEORGE I (1714–27)** | | | |
| 1716 | £4000 | £8000 | £25000 |
| 1717 | £4000 | £8500 | £27500 |
| 1720 | £3800 | £8500 | £27500 |
| 1726 | £3250 | £6750 | £24000 |
| **GEORGE II (1727–60)** | | | |
| 1729 Young head | £2600 | £5000 | £16000 |
| 1729 — E.I.C. below head | £2500 | £5000 | £15000 |
| 1731 — | £3250 | £6000 | £22000 |
| 1735 — | £2500 | £5000 | £22000 |
| 1738 — | £2500 | £5500 | £18000 |
| 1741 | £2500 | £5000 | £16000 |
| 1741/38 41 over 38 | £2500 | £5000 | £16000 |
| 1746 Old head, LIMA | £2650 | £5000 | £15000 |
| 1748 — | £2750 | £5000 | £15000 |
| 1753 — | £2750 | £5000 | £16000 |
| **GEORGE III (1760–1820)** | | | |
| 1770 Patterns | — | — | £165000 |
| 1773 | — | — | £165000 |
| 1777 | — | — | £150000 |

*Anne*

# TWO GUINEAS

|  | F | VF | EF |
|---|---|---|---|

## CHARLES II (1660–85)

| | F | VF | EF |
|---|---|---|---|
| 1664 First bust | £1400 | £3250 | £8000 |
| 1664 — Elephant | £1250 | £3000 | £7000 |
| 1665 — | | Extremely rare | |
| 1669 — | | Extremely rare | |
| 1671 — | £1600 | £4500 | £12000 |
| 1675 Second bust | £1500 | £3850 | £8000 |
| 1676 — | £1500 | £3850 | £8000 |
| 1676 — Elephant & Castle | £1600 | £3750 | £8000 |
| 1677 — | £1500 | £3600 | £7000 |
| 1677 — Elephant & Castle | | Extremely rare | |
| 1678/7 — | £1300 | £3000 | £7000 |
| 1678 — Elephant | £1500 | £3500 | £8000 |
| 1678 — Elephant & Castle | £1500 | £3500 | £8000 |
| 1679 — | £1500 | £3800 | £8500 |
| 1680 — | £1700 | £4500 | £10000 |
| 1681 — | £1400 | £3250 | £7000 |
| 1682 — Elephant & Castle | £1400 | £3250 | £7500 |
| 1683 — | £1250 | £3200 | £7000 |
| 1683 — Elephant & Castle | £1700 | £4250 | £10000 |
| 1684 — | £1400 | £3500 | £7000 |
| 1684 — Elephant & Castle | £1500 | £4000 | £9000 |

*Charles II*

## JAMES II (1685–88)

| | F | VF | EF |
|---|---|---|---|
| 1687 | £2000 | £4000 | £11500 |
| 1688/7 | £2000 | £4250 | £12000 |

## WILLIAM AND MARY (1688–94)

| | F | VF | EF |
|---|---|---|---|
| 1691 Elephant & Castle | | Extremely rare | |
| 1693 | £1600 | £3750 | £9000 |
| 1693 Elephant & Castle | £1800 | £4000 | £11500 |
| 1694 — 4 over 3 | £1500 | £3500 | £9000 |
| 1694/3 Elephant & Castle | £1500 | £4000 | £10000 |

*James II*

## WILLIAM III (1694–1702)

| | F | VF | EF |
|---|---|---|---|
| 1701 "fine work" | £1800 | £4000 | £9000 |

## ANNE (1702–14)

| | F | VF | EF |
|---|---|---|---|
| 1709 | £1250 | £3000 | £8000 |
| 1711 | £1100 | £3000 | £7000 |
| 1713 | £1100 | £3000 | £7000 |
| 1714/3 | £1400 | £3500 | £8000 |

## GEORGE I (1714–27)

| | F | VF | EF |
|---|---|---|---|
| 1717 | £1100 | £2500 | £6000 |
| 1720 | £1100 | £2500 | £6250 |
| 1720/17 | £1250 | £2600 | £6750 |
| 1726 | £1100 | £2200 | £6000 |

*Anne*

|  | F | VF | EF |
|---|---|---|---|

## GEORGE II (1727–60)

| | F | VF | EF |
|---|---|---|---|
| 1733 Proof only FDC | | Extremely Rare | |
| 1734 Young head 4 over 3 | £1250 | £3000 | — |
| 1735 — | £1000 | £2000 | £5000 |
| 1738 — | £850 | £1600 | £2750 |
| 1739 — | £850 | £1600 | £2750 |
| 1739 Intermediate head | £850 | £1600 | £2750 |
| 1740 — | £850 | £1600 | £2800 |
| 1748 Old head | £800 | £1500 | £3500 |
| 1753 — | £800 | £1750 | £4500 |

## GEORGE III (1760–1820)

| | F | VF | EF |
|---|---|---|---|
| 1768 Patterns only | — | Extremely Rare | |
| 1773 Patterns only | — | Extremely Rare | |
| 1777 Patterns only | — | Extremely Rare | |

*George II*

# GUINEAS

|  | F | VF | EF |
|---|---|---|---|

## CHARLES II (1660–85)

| | F | VF | EF |
|---|---|---|---|
| 1663 First bust | £3000 | £8000 | £30000 |
| 1663 — Elephant below | £2500 | £7500 | — |
| 1664 Second bust | £2000 | £6000 | — |
| 1664 — Elephant | £3500 | £10000 | £35000 |
| 1664 Third bust | £900 | £3000 | £9000 |
| 1664 — Elephant | £1400 | £4000 | £12500 |
| 1665 — | £800 | £2500 | £9000 |
| 1665 — Elephant | £1500 | £4000 | £15000 |
| 1666 — | £800 | £2500 | £9000 |
| 1667 — | £800 | £2500 | £9000 |
| 1668 — | £800 | £2400 | £8750 |
| 1668 — Elephant | | Extremely rare | |
| 1669 — | £800 | £2750 | £9000 |
| 1670 — | £800 | £2500 | £8500 |
| 1671 — | £800 | £2400 | £9000 |
| 1672 — | £750 | £2800 | £9000 |
| 1672 Fourth bust | £650 | £2000 | £5000 |
| 1673 Third bust | £900 | £3000 | £10000 |
| 1673 Fourth bust | £700 | £2000 | £6000 |
| 1674 — | £700 | £2000 | £6000 |
| 1674 — Elephant & Castle | | Extremely rare | |
| 1675 — | £700 | £2200 | £6000 |
| 1675 — CRAOLVS Error | | Extremely rare | |
| 1675 — Elephant & Castle | £800 | £2500 | £9000 |
| 1676 — | £700 | £2200 | £5500 |
| 1676 — Elephant & Castle | £800 | £2500 | £8500 |
| 1677 — | £600 | £1800 | £6000 |
| 1677/5 — Elephant 7 over 5 | | Extremely rare | |
| 1677 — Elephant & Castle | £600 | £2000 | £8000 |
| 1678 — | £500 | £1600 | £5500 |
| 1678 — Elephant | | Extremely rare | |
| 1678 — Elephant & Castle | £800 | £2500 | £10000 |

*Charles II, third bust*

*Charles II, fourth bust, elephant & castle below*

|  | F | VF | EF |
|---|---|---|---|
| 1679 — | £550 | £1750 | £6000 |
| 1679 — Elephant & Castle | £800 | £2500 | £9000 |
| 1680 — | £600 | £1800 | £6000 |
| 1680 — Elephant & Castle | £800 | £2500 | £9000 |
| 1681 — | £700 | £2000 | £6000 |
| 1681 — Elephant & Castle | £750 | £2500 | £9000 |
| 1682 — | £650 | £2000 | £6000 |
| 1682 — Elephant & Castle | £800 | £2600 | £9000 |
| 1683 — | £550 | £1700 | £6000 |
| 1683 — Elephant & Castle | £800 | £2500 | £9000 |
| 1684 — | £650 | £2000 | £6000 |
| 1684 — Elephant & Castle | £800 | £2500 | £9000 |

*James II, first bust, elephant & castle below*

## JAMES II (1685–1688)

|  | F | VF | EF |
|---|---|---|---|
| 1685 First bust | £650 | £2200 | £7000 |
| 1685 — Elephant & Castle | £800 | £2600 | £9000 |
| 1686 — | £800 | £2600 | £9000 |
| 1686 — Elephant & Castle | | Extremely rare | |
| 1686 Second bust | £600 | £1900 | £6250 |
| 1686 — Elephant & Castle | £800 | £2500 | £8000 |
| 1687 — | £700 | £2000 | £6000 |
| 1687 —Elephant & Castle | £750 | £2500 | £8000 |
| 1688 — | £600 | £2000 | £6000 |
| 1688 — Elephant & Castle | £700 | £2500 | £8000 |

*James II, second bust*

## WILLIAM AND MARY (1688–94)

|  | F | VF | EF |
|---|---|---|---|
| 1689 | £600 | £1800 | £6000 |
| 1689 Elephant & Castle | £600 | £2000 | £6000 |
| 1690 | £600 | £2200 | £7000 |
| 1690 GVLIFLMVS | £700 | £2200 | £8000 |
| 1690 Elephant & Castle | £800 | £2400 | £8000 |
| 1691 | £575 | £2200 | £6500 |
| 1691 Elephant & Castle | £600 | £2200 | £7000 |
| 1692 | £600 | £2000 | £7000 |
| 1692 Elephant | £900 | £3000 | £8500 |
| 1692 Elephant & Castle | £650 | £2400 | £7000 |
| 1693 | £550 | £2000 | £7000 |
| 1693 Elephant | | Extremely rare | |
| 1693 Elephant & Castle | | Extremely rare | |
| 1694 | £600 | £2000 | £6000 |
| 1694/3 | £600 | £2000 | £6000 |
| 1694 Elephant & Castle | £625 | £2200 | £6250 |
| 1694/3 Elephant & Castle | £625 | £2200 | £6250 |

## WILLIAM III (1694–1702)

|  | F | VF | EF |
|---|---|---|---|
| 1695 First bust | £600 | £1800 | £5800 |
| 1695 — Elephant & Castle | £1000 | £2800 | £10000 |
| 1696 — | £550 | £2000 | £6500 |
| 1696 — Elephant & Castle | | Extremely rare | |
| 1697 — | £600 | £1800 | £6000 |
| 1697 Second bust | £500 | £1800 | £6000 |
| 1697 — Elephant & Castle | £1250 | £4000 | — |
| 1698 — | £500 | £1800 | £5500 |
| 1698 — Elephant & Castle | £500 | £1900 | £5500 |
| 1699 — | £550 | £1750 | £6000 |
| 1699 — Elephant & Castle | | Extremely rare | |
| 1700 — | £500 | £1750 | £5500 |
| 1700 — Elephant & Castle | £1050 | £3750 | — |
| 1701 — | £500 | £1650 | £5000 |
| 1701 — Elephant & Castle | | Extremely rare | |
| 1701 Third bust "fine work" | £850 | £2750 | £9000 |

*William III, second bust*

|  | F | VF | EF |
|---|---|---|---|

## ANNE (1702–1714)

| | F | VF | EF |
|---|---|---|---|
| 1702 (Pre-Union) First bust | £900 | £3000 | £9000 |
| 1703 — VIGO below | £11000 | £30000 | £70000 |
| 1705 — | £900 | £3000 | £10000 |
| 1706 — | £900 | £3000 | £10000 |
| 1707 — | £900 | £3000 | £10000 |
| 1707 — (Post-Union) | £600 | £2500 | £8000 |
| 1707 — Elephant & Castle | £750 | £3000 | £10000 |
| 1707 Second bust | £550 | £2000 | £7000 |
| 1708 First bust | £650 | £2500 | £8000 |
| 1708 Second bust | £500 | £1800 | £6000 |
| 1708 — Elephant & Castle | £800 | £3000 | £9000 |
| 1709 — | £450 | £1800 | £6000 |
| 1709 — Elephant & Castle | £800 | £2800 | £7500 |
| 1710 Third bust | £600 | £1400 | £4000 |
| 1711 — | £600 | £1400 | £4250 |
| 1712 — | £600 | £1400 | £4250 |
| 1713 — | £500 | £1200 | £3750 |
| 1714 — | £550 | £1300 | £4000 |
| 1714 GRΛTIΛ | £700 | £1650 | £4000 |

*Anne, second bust*

## GEORGE I (1714–27)

| | F | VF | EF |
|---|---|---|---|
| 1714 First bust (Prince Elector) | £1200 | £3000 | £8000 |
| 1715 Second bust | £600 | £1500 | £3500 |
| 1715 Third bust | £500 | £1500 | £4000 |
| 1716 — | £500 | £1500 | £3500 |
| 1716 Fourth bust | £450 | £1300 | £3500 |
| 1717 — | £450 | £1300 | £3500 |
| 1718 — | | Extremely rare | |
| 1719 — | £500 | £1400 | £3650 |
| 1720 — | £500 | £1400 | £3750 |
| 1721 — | £500 | £1400 | £3750 |
| 1721 — Elephant & Castle | | Extremely rare | |
| 1722 — | £500 | £1300 | £3600 |
| 1722 — Elephant & Castle | | Extremely rare | |
| 1723 — | £525 | £1400 | £3700 |
| 1723 Fifth bust | £525 | £1400 | £3700 |
| 1724 — | £525 | £1300 | £3650 |
| 1725 — | £525 | £1300 | £3750 |
| 1726 — | £500 | £1250 | £3500 |
| 1726 — Elephant & Castle | £1750 | £4000 | £15000 |
| 1727 — | £600 | £1800 | £5000 |

*George I, third bust*

## GEORGE II (1727–60)

| | F | VF | EF |
|---|---|---|---|
| 1727 First young head, early large shield | £800 | £2500 | £8000 |
| 1727 — Larger lettering, early small shield | £800 | £2500 | £8000 |
| 1728 — — | £900 | £2750 | £8500 |
| 1729 2nd young head E.I.C. below | £1000 | £3000 | £9000 |
| 1729 — Proof | | Very Rare | |
| 1730 — | £600 | £1500 | £5000 |
| 1731 — | £500 | £1500 | £4250 |
| 1731 — E.I.C. below | £840 | £2750 | £8000 |
| 1732 — | £700 | £2500 | £7000 |
| 1732 — E.I.C. below | £800 | £2500 | £8000 |
| 1732 — Larger lettering obverse | £550 | £1500 | £4500 |
| 1732 — — E.I.C. below | £900 | £1800 | £8000 |
| 1733 — — | £500 | £1250 | £3000 |
| 1734 — — | £500 | £1250 | £3000 |
| 1735 — — | £500 | £1250 | £3000 |
| 1736 — — | £500 | £1500 | £3250 |
| 1737 — — | £500 | £1500 | £3250 |

*George II, 1759, old head, larger lettering*

| | F | VF | EF |
|---|---|---|---|
| 1738 — — | £500 | £1400 | £3500 |
| 1739 Intermediate head | £500 | £1100 | £2800 |
| 1739 — E.I.C. below | £1100 | £2800 | £8000 |
| 1740 — | £500 | £1400 | £5000 |
| 1741/39 — | £800 | £2400 | £6250 |
| 1743 — | £800 | £2400 | £6250 |
| 1745 — Larger lettering obv. Older bust | £500 | £1200 | £4000 |
| 1745 — LIMA below | £1100 | £3250 | £9000 |
| 1746 — (GEORGIVS) Larger lettering obv. | £500 | £1500 | £3750 |
| 1747 Old head, large lettering | £400 | £1000 | £3000 |
| 1748 — | £400 | £1000 | £3000 |
| 1749 — | £400 | £1000 | £3000 |
| 1750 — | £400 | £1000 | £3000 |
| 1751 — small lettering | £400 | £1000 | £3000 |
| 1753 — | £400 | £1000 | £3000 |
| 1755 — | £400 | £1000 | £3000 |
| 1756 — | £400 | £1000 | £3000 |
| 1758 — | £400 | £1000 | £3000 |
| 1759 — | £400 | £1000 | £3000 |
| 1760 — | £400 | £1000 | £2250 |

*George III first head*

# GEORGE III (1760–1820)

| | F | VF | EF |
|---|---|---|---|
| 1761 First head | £1500 | £4000 | £7250 |
| 1763 Second head | £1200 | £3500 | £6750 |
| 1764 — | £1000 | £3000 | £6500 |
| 1765 Third head | £350 | £600 | £1500 |
| 1766 — | £350 | £600 | £1400 |
| 1767 — | £500 | £800 | £2000 |
| 1768 — | £400 | £700 | £1600 |
| 1769 — | £400 | £700 | £1800 |
| 1770 — | £800 | £1800 | £3250 |
| 1771 — | £400 | £500 | £1250 |
| 1772 — | £400 | £500 | £1250 |
| 1773 — | £400 | £550 | £1400 |
| 1774 Fourth head | £350 | £550 | £900 |
| 1775 — | £350 | £550 | £900 |
| 1776 — | £350 | £550 | £900 |
| 1777 — | £350 | £550 | £900 |
| 1778 — | £450 | £800 | £2000 |
| 1779 — | £400 | £700 | £1250 |
| 1781 — | £350 | £550 | £1100 |
| 1782 — | £350 | £550 | £1100 |
| 1783 — | £350 | £550 | £1100 |
| 1784 — | £350 | £600 | £1150 |
| 1785 — | £350 | £600 | £1100 |
| 1786 — | £400 | £650 | £1150 |
| 1787 Fifth head, "Spade" reverse | £325 | £500 | £850 |
| 1788 — | £325 | £500 | £850 |
| 1789 — | £325 | £500 | £850 |
| 1790 — | £325 | £500 | £850 |
| 1791 — | £325 | £500 | £850 |
| 1792 — | £325 | £500 | £850 |
| 1793 — | £325 | £500 | £850 |
| 1794 — | £325 | £500 | £850 |
| 1795 — | £325 | £500 | £850 |
| 1796 — | £325 | £500 | £850 |
| 1797 — | £325 | £500 | £850 |
| 1798 — | £325 | £500 | £850 |
| 1799 — | £325 | £500 | £1100 |
| 1813 Sixth head, "Military" reverse | £800 | £1800 | £3750 |

*Fourth head*

*Fifth head, Spade reverse*

*Sixth "Military" head*

*(Beware of counterfeits of this series—many dangerous copies exist)*

# HALF GUINEAS

|  | F | VF | EF |
|---|---|---|---|
| **CHARLES II (1660–85)** | | | |
| 1669 First bust | £350 | £1000 | £3750 |
| 1670 — | £350 | £1000 | £3250 |
| 1671 — | £450 | £1300 | £4750 |
| 1672 — | £400 | £1100 | £4000 |
| 1672 Second bust | £375 | £950 | £3500 |
| 1673 — | £450 | £1300 | £4000 |
| 1674 — | £500 | £1600 | £4000 |
| 1675 — | £500 | £1600 | £4000 |
| 1676 — | £350 | £1000 | £3250 |
| 1676 — Elephant & Castle | £675 | £2400 | — |
| 1677 — | £350 | £1000 | £3250 |
| 1677 — Elephant & Castle | £600 | £1750 | — |
| 1678 — | £400 | £1100 | £3500 |
| 1678 — Elephant & Castle | £500 | £1500 | £5000 |
| 1679 — | £400 | £1100 | £3250 |
| 1680 — | £400 | £1750 | — |
| 1680 — Elephant & Castle | £600 | £1750 | £5500 |
| 1681 — | £400 | £1500 | — |
| 1682 — | £400 | £1300 | £3500 |
| 1682 — Elephant & Castle | £600 | £1700 | — |
| 1683 — | £375 | £1000 | £3500 |
| 1683 — Elephant & Castle | | Extremely rare | |
| 1684 — | £350 | £900 | £3500 |
| 1684 — Elephant & Castle | £600 | £1500 | £5500 |

*Charles II, first bust*

| | F | VF | EF |
|---|---|---|---|
| **JAMES II (1685–88)** | | | |
| 1686 | £400 | £1100 | £3500 |
| 1686 Elephant & Castle | £800 | £3750 | £7000 |
| 1687 | £400 | £1300 | £4000 |
| 1688 | £400 | £1300 | £3800 |

| | F | VF | EF |
|---|---|---|---|
| **WILLIAM AND MARY (1688–94)** | | | |
| 1689 First busts | £500 | £1800 | £4000 |
| 1690 Second busts | £500 | £1850 | £4200 |
| 1691 — | £500 | £1800 | £4000 |
| 1691 — Elephant & Castle | £500 | £1700 | £4000 |
| 1692 — | £450 | £1500 | £3500 |
| 1692 — Elephant | | Extremely rare | |
| 1692 — Elephant & Castle | £450 | £1600 | £4000 |
| 1693 — | | Extremely rare | |
| 1694 — | £450 | £1600 | £3750 |

*Williuam & Mary, first busts*

| | F | VF | EF |
|---|---|---|---|
| **WILLIAM III (1694–1702)** | | | |
| 1695 | £350 | £800 | £3000 |
| 1695 Elephant & Castle | £600 | £1500 | £4500 |
| 1696 — | £400 | £1000 | £3250 |
| 1697 Larger Harp rev. | £500 | £1400 | £4500 |
| 1698 | £500 | £1200 | £4000 |
| 1698 Elephant & Castle | £600 | £1500 | £3250 |
| 1699 | | Extremely rare | |
| 1700 | £300 | £800 | £3000 |
| 1701 | £300 | £800 | £3000 |

*William III, elephant & castle below bust*

| | F | VF | EF |
|---|---|---|---|

## ANNE (1702–14)

| | | | |
|---|---|---|---|
| 1702 (Pre-Union) | £700 | £2200 | £6500 |
| 1703 VIGO below bust | £5000 | £12000 | £28000 |
| 1705 | £600 | £2000 | £6000 |
| 1707 (Post-Union) | £300 | £900 | £2500 |
| 1708 | £325 | £900 | £2500 |
| 1709 | £350 | £900 | £2500 |
| 1710 | £300 | £750 | £2200 |
| 1711 | £275 | £750 | £2200 |
| 1712 | £300 | £800 | £2500 |
| 1713 | £300 | £750 | £2200 |
| 1714 | £300 | £750 | £2200 |

*Anne*

## GEORGE I (1714–27)

| | | | |
|---|---|---|---|
| 1715 First bust | £600 | £120 | £4000 |
| 1717 — | £300 | £700 | £2500 |
| 1718 — | £300 | £700 | £2500 |
| 1719 — | £300 | £700 | £2500 |
| 1720 — | £325 | £700 | £2750 |
| 1721 — | | | Extremely rare |
| 1721 — Elephant & Castle | | | Extremely rare |
| 1722 — | £300 | £700 | £2500 |
| 1723 — | £400 | £800 | £3000 |
| 1724 — | £325 | £800 | £2650 |
| 1725 Second bust | £300 | £575 | £2250 |
| 1726 — | £300 | £575 | £2400 |
| 1727 — | £300 | £575 | £2750 |

*George I, second bust*

## GEORGE II (1727–60)

| | | | |
|---|---|---|---|
| 1728 Young head | £500 | £1250 | £3750 |
| 1729 — | £500 | £1250 | £3500 |
| 1729 — E.I.C. | £600 | £1500 | £4500 |
| 1730 — | £700 | £2000 | — |
| 1730 — E.I.C. | £675 | £2000 | — |
| 1731 — | £300 | £950 | £3000 |
| 1731 — E.I.C. | | | Extremely rare |
| 1732 — | £300 | £900 | £3000 |
| 1732 — E.I.C. | | | Extremely rare |
| 1733 — | | | Unknown |
| 1734 — | £300 | £800 | £2500 |
| 1735 — | | | Extremely rare |
| 1736 — | £300 | £800 | £3000 |
| 1737 — | £400 | £800 | £3000 |
| 1738 — | £300 | £750 | £2500 |
| 1739 — | £300 | £750 | £2500 |
| 1739 — E.I.C. | | | Extremely rare |
| 1740 Intermediate head | £375 | £1000 | £3000 |
| 1743 — | | | Extremely rare |
| 1745 — | £300 | £900 | £3000 |
| 1745 — LIMA | £1100 | £3500 | £6000 |
| 1746 — | £275 | £700 | £2200 |
| 1747 Old head | £300 | £700 | £2200 |
| 1748 — | £275 | £800 | £2200 |
| 1749 — | £300 | £650 | £2000 |
| 1750 — | £300 | £650 | £1850 |
| 1751 — | £275 | £600 | £1800 |
| 1752 — | £275 | £600 | £1800 |
| 1753 — | £275 | £600 | £1800 |
| 1755 — | £275 | £600 | £1800 |
| 1756 — | £260 | £800 | £2000 |
| 1758 — | £300 | £700 | £2000 |

*George II, young head*

*George II, old head*

|  | F | VF | EF |
|---|---|---|---|
| 1759 — | £260 | £650 | £1800 |
| 1760 — | £260 | £650 | £1800 |

# GEORGE III (1760–1820)

|  | F | VF | EF |
|---|---|---|---|
| 1762 First head | £600 | £1750 | £4000 |
| 1763 — | £700 | £2000 | £3750 |
| 1764 Second head | £250 | £500 | £1100 |
| 1765 — | £500 | £1200 | £3000 |
| 1766 — | £250 | £500 | £1300 |
| 1768 — | £250 | £550 | £1300 |
| 1769 — | £225 | £550 | £1400 |
| 1772 — | | Extremely rare | |
| 1773 — | £300 | £600 | £1400 |
| 1774 — | £350 | £700 | £1800 |
| 1774 Third head | | Extremely rare | |
| 1775 — | £1000 | £2500 | £5000 |
| 1775 Fourth head | £200 | £275 | £550 |
| 1775 — Proof | | Extremely rare | |
| 1776 — | £200 | £400 | £1000 |
| 1777 — | £200 | £400 | £800 |
| 1778 — | £200 | £400 | £800 |
| 1779 — | £200 | £400 | £900 |
| 1781 — | £200 | £400 | £950 |
| 1783 — | £500 | £1500 | — |
| 1784 — | £220 | £375 | £800 |
| 1785 — | £220 | £375 | £700 |
| 1786 — | £220 | £375 | £700 |
| 1787 Fifth head, "Spade" rev. | £220 | £375 | £675 |
| 1788 — | £220 | £375 | £675 |
| 1789 — | £220 | £375 | £750 |
| 1790 — | £220 | £375 | £600 |
| 1791 — | £220 | £375 | £600 |
| 1792 — | £800 | £2400 | — |
| 1793 — | £200 | £400 | £700 |
| 1794 — | £200 | £400 | £700 |
| 1795 — | £200 | £500 | £800 |
| 1796 — | £200 | £400 | £700 |
| 1797 — | £200 | £400 | £700 |
| 1798 — | £200 | £400 | £700 |
| 1800 — | £300 | £800 | £1800 |
| 1801 Sixth head, Shield in Garter rev. | £200 | £300 | £550 |
| 1802 — | £200 | £300 | £550 |
| 1803 — | £200 | £300 | £550 |
| 1804 Seventh head | £200 | £300 | £550 |
| 1805 | | Extremely rare | |
| 1806 — | £200 | £300 | £600 |
| 1808 — | £200 | £300 | £600 |
| 1899 — | £200 | £300 | £600 |
| 1810 — | £200 | £300 | £625 |
| 1811 — | £300 | £550 | £900 |
| 1813 — | £300 | £550 | £800 |

*George III, second head*

*George III, fifth head, "spade" reverse*

# THIRD GUINEAS

|  | F | VF | EF |
|---|---|---|---|

## GEORGE III (1760–1820)

| | F | VF | EF |
|---|---|---|---|
| 1797 First head, date in legend | £125 | £220 | £475 |
| 1798 — — | £125 | £220 | £475 |
| 1799 — — | £125 | £260 | £500 |
| 1800 — — | £125 | £220 | £500 |
| 1801 Date under crown | £125 | £220 | £500 |
| 1802 — | £125 | £220 | £500 |
| 1803 — | £125 | £220 | £500 |
| 1804 Second head | £85 | £140 | £450 |
| 1806 — | £95 | £240 | £475 |
| 1808 — | £125 | £300 | £500 |
| 1809 — | £125 | £300 | £500 |
| 1810 — | £125 | £300 | £500 |
| 1811 — | £400 | £1000 | £2000 |
| 1813 — | £250 | £450 | £700 |

George III, date in legend

George III, date under crown

# QUARTER GUINEAS

## GEORGE I (1714–27)

| | F | VF | EF |
|---|---|---|---|
| 1718 | £150 | £270 | £550 |

## GEORGE III (1760–1820)

| | F | VF | EF |
|---|---|---|---|
| 1762 | £200 | £400 | £675 |

George I

# FIVE POUNDS

| DATE | Mintage | F | VF | EF | UNC |
|---|---|---|---|---|---|

## GEORGE III (1760–1820)

| | Mintage | F | VF | EF | UNC |
|---|---|---|---|---|---|
| 1820 (pattern only) | — | | | Extremely rare | |

## GEORGE IV (1820–30)

| | Mintage | F | VF | EF | UNC |
|---|---|---|---|---|---|
| 1826 proof only | — | — | — | — | £25,000 |

## VICTORIA (1837–1901)

| | Mintage | F | VF | EF | UNC |
|---|---|---|---|---|---|
| 1839 Proof Only (Una & The Lion) Many Varieties FDC £35,000 upwards | | | | | |
| 1887 | 53,844 | £1200 | £1400 | £1800 | £2750 |
| 1887 Proof | 797 | — | — | — | £4250 |
| 1887 S on ground on rev. (Sydney Mint) | | | | Excessively rare | |
| 1893 | 20,405 | £1400 | £2000 | £2500 | £4000 |
| 1893 Proof | 773 | — | — | — | £5500 |

## EDWARD VII (1902–10)

| | Mintage | F | VF | EF | UNC |
|---|---|---|---|---|---|
| 1902 | 34,910 | £1250 | £1600 | £2200 | £2750 |
| 1902 Matt proof | 8,066 | — | — | — | £2500 |

| DATE | MINTAGE | F | VF | EF | UNC |
|---|---|---|---|---|---|

### GEORGE V (1911–36)
1911 Proof only ................ 2,812 — — — £3000

### GEORGE VI (1937–52)
1937 Proof only ................ 5,501 — — — £1800

*Later issues are listed in the Decimal section.*

# TWO POUNDS

### GEORGE III (1760–1820)
1820 (pattern only)............ — — — Extremely rare

### GEORGE IV (1820–30)
1823 St George reverse..... — £750 £1000 £1600 £2500
1826 Proof only, shield reverse — — — — £7500

### WILLIAM IV (1830–37)
1831 Proof only ................ 225 — — — £6000

### VICTORIA (1837–1901)
1887.................................. 91,345 £450 £550 £600 £725
1887 Proof........................ 797 — — — £1275
1887 S on ground of rev. (Sydney Mint) Excessively rare
1893.................................. 52,212 £450 £575 £800 £1400
1893 Proof........................ 773 — — — £1800

### EDWARD VII (1902–10)
1902.................................. 45,807 £400 £500 £575 £775
1902 Matt proof................ 8,066 — — — £700

### GEORGE V (1911–36)
1911 Proof only ................ 2,812 — — — £1000

### GEORGE VI (1937–52)
1937 Proof only ................ 5,501 — — — £825
*Later issues are listed in the Decimal section.*

# SOVEREIGNS

| DATE | MINTAGE | F | VF | EF | UNC |
|------|---------|---|----|----|-----|

## GEORGE III (1760–1820)

| DATE | MINTAGE | F | VF | EF | UNC |
|------|---------|---|----|----|-----|
| 1817 | 3,235,239 | £500 | £800 | £1800 | £2850 |
| 1818 | 2,347,230 | £500 | £800 | £1800 | £3000 |
| 1819 | 3,574 | | Exceedingly rare | | |
| 1820 | 931,994 | £475 | £775 | £1750 | £2750 |

George III

## GEORGE IV (1820–30)

| DATE | MINTAGE | F | VF | EF | UNC |
|------|---------|---|----|----|-----|
| 1821 First bust, St George reverse | 9,405,114 | £400 | £675 | £1500 | £2250 |
| 1821 — Proof | incl. above | — | — | — | £5500 |
| 1822 — | 5,356,787 | £400 | £675 | £1500 | £2500 |
| 1823 — | 616,770 | £1000 | £2750 | £6000 | — |
| 1824 — | 3,767,904 | £500 | £900 | £2000 | £2850 |
| 1825 — | 4,200,343 | £700 | £2000 | £5000 | £8000 |
| 1825 Second bust, shield reverse | incl. above | £400 | £700 | £1200 | £2200 |
| 1826 — | 5,724,046 | £400 | £700 | £1200 | £2200 |
| 1826 — Proof | — | — | — | — | £4000 |
| 1827 — | 2,266,629 | £450 | £750 | £1500 | £2500 |
| 1828 — | 386,182 | £5000 | £10000 | £25000 | — |
| 1829 — | 2,444,652 | £450 | £750 | £1800 | £2750 |
| 1830 — | 2,387,881 | £450 | £750 | £1800 | £2750 |

George IV, shield reverse

## WILLIAM IV (1830–37)

| DATE | MINTAGE | F | VF | EF | UNC |
|------|---------|---|----|----|-----|
| 1831 | 598,547 | £600 | £1000 | £2200 | £3500 |
| 1831 Proof, plain edge | — | — | — | — | £4750 |
| 1832 | 3,737,065 | £475 | £900 | £2000 | £3250 |
| 1833 | 1,225,269 | £475 | £900 | £2000 | £3250 |
| 1835 | 723,441 | £475 | £900 | £2000 | £3500 |
| 1836 | 1,714,349 | £475 | £900 | £2000 | £3250 |
| 1837 | 1,172,984 | £500 | £700 | £2000 | £3250 |

William IV

*Note—from the Victoria reign onwards, the prices of coins in lower grade will be subject to the bullion price of gold.*

## VICTORIA (1837–1901)

*Many of the gold coins struck at the colonial mints found their way into circulation in Britain, for the sake of completeness these coins are listed here. These can easily be identified by a tiny initial letter for the appropriate mint which can be found below the base of the reverse shield or, in the case of the St George reverse, below the bust on the obverse of the Young Head issues, or on the "ground" below the horse's hoof on the later issues.*

### YOUNG HEAD ISSUES

#### Shield reverse
*(Note—Shield back sovereigns in Fine/VF condition, common dates, are normally traded as bullion + a percentage)*

| DATE | MINTAGE | F | VF | EF | UNC |
|------|---------|---|----|----|-----|
| 1838 | 2,718,694 | £700 | £1200 | £2500 | £4400 |
| 1839 | 503,695 | £800 | £2500 | £4500 | £6000 |
| 1839 Proof, plain edge | — | — | — | — | £5000 |
| 1841 | 124,054 | £3250 | £8000 | £18000 | — |
| 1841 Roman I in date | — | £700 | 1400 | — | — |
| 1842 | 4,865,375 | £265 | £275 | £375 | £800 |
| 1843 | 5,981,968 | £265 | £275 | £375 | £800 |
| 1843 "Narrow shield" variety | incl. above | £4000 | £8000 | | |
| 1844 | 3,000,445 | £265 | £275 | £375 | £800 |
| 1845 | 3,800,845 | £265 | £275 | £375 | £800 |
| 1846 | 3,802,947 | £265 | £275 | £375 | £800 |

| DATE | MINTAGE | F | VF | EF | UNC |
|---|---|---|---|---|---|
| 1847 | 4,667,126 | £265 | £275 | £375 | £800 |
| 1848 | 2,246,701 | £265 | £275 | £300 | £800 |
| 1849 | 1,755,399 | £265 | £275 | £300 | £800 |
| 1850 | 1,402,039 | £265 | £275 | £300 | £800 |
| 1851 | 4,013,624 | £265 | £275 | £300 | £800 |
| 1852 | 8,053,435 | £265 | £275 | £300 | £800 |
| 1853 | 10,597,993 | £265 | £275 | £300 | £800 |
| 1853 Proof | — | — | — | —£12000 | |
| 1854 Incuse WW | 3,589,611 | £265 | £275 | £300 | £800 |
| 1854 Surface raised WW | 3,589,611 | £265 | £275 | £750 | £1500 |
| 1855 | 4,806,160 | £265 | £275 | £300 | £750 |
| 1856 | 8,448,482 | £265 | £275 | £350 | £750 |
| 1857 | 4,495,748 | £265 | £275 | £300 | £750 |
| 1858 | 803,234 | £265 | £275 | £300 | £750 |
| 1859 | 1,547,603 | £265 | £275 | £300 | £750 |
| 1859 "Ansell" (additional line on lower part of hair ribbon) | — | £700 | £1600 | £6000 | — |
| 1860 | 2,555,958 | £265 | £275 | £285 | £725 |
| 1861 | 7,624,736 | £265 | £275 | £285 | £725 |
| 1862 | 7,836,413 | £265 | £275 | £285 | £725 |
| 1863 | 5,921,669 | £265 | £275 | £285 | £725 |
| 1863 Die No 827 on Truncation | | | | Extremely rare | |
| 1863 with Die number below shield | incl. above | £265 | £275 | £285 | £725 |
| 1864 — | 8,656,352 | £265 | £275 | £285 | £725 |
| 1865 — | 1,450,238 | £265 | £275 | £285 | £725 |
| 1866 — | 4,047,288 | £265 | £275 | £285 | £725 |
| 1868 — | 1,653,384 | £265 | £275 | £285 | £725 |
| 1869 — | 6,441,322 | £265 | £275 | £285 | £725 |
| 1870 — | 2,189,960 | £265 | £275 | £285 | £725 |
| 1871 — | 8,767,250 | £265 | £275 | £285 | £725 |
| 1872 — | 8,767,250 | £265 | £275 | £285 | £725 |
| 1872 no Die number | incl. above | £265 | £275 | £285 | £725 |
| 1873 with Die number | 2,368,215 | £265 | £275 | £285 | £725 |
| 1874 — | 520,713 | £1700 | £4000 | £7500 | — |

*M below reverse shield (Melbourne Mint)*

| | | | | | |
|---|---|---|---|---|---|
| 1872 | 748,180 | £275 | £285 | £300 | £800 |
| 1873 | — | | | Extremely rare | |
| 1874 | 1,373,298 | £275 | £285 | £300 | £900 |
| 1879 | | | | Extremely rare | |
| 1880 | 3,053,454 | £600 | £1500 | £3500 | £8500 |
| 1881 | 2,325,303 | £265 | £275 | £300 | £1500 |
| 1882 | 2,465,781 | £265 | £275 | £285 | £1000 |
| 1883 | 2,050,450 | £265 | £300 | £700 | — |
| 1884 | 2,942,630 | £265 | £275 | £285 | £800 |
| 1885 | 2,967,143 | £265 | £275 | £285 | £800 |
| 1886 | 2,902,131 | £1800 | £4000 | £6000 | £17500 |
| 1887 | 1,916,424 | £550 | £1350 | £4000 | £10000 |

*S below reverse shield (Sydney Mint)*

| | | | | | |
|---|---|---|---|---|---|
| 1871 | 2,814,000 | £265 | £275 | £300 | £1200 |
| 1872 | 1,815,000 | £265 | £275 | £300 | £1400 |
| 1873 | 1,478,000 | £265 | £275 | £300 | £1200 |
| 1875 | 2,122,000 | £265 | £275 | £300 | £1200 |
| 1877 | 1,590,000 | £265 | £275 | £300 | £1200 |
| 1878 | 1,259,000 | £265 | £275 | £300 | £1200 |
| 1879 | 1,366,000 | £265 | £275 | £300 | £1200 |
| 1880 | 1,459,000 | £265 | £275 | £300 | £1600 |
| 1881 | 1,360,000 | £265 | £275 | £300 | £1500 |
| 1882 | 1,298,000 | £265 | £275 | £300 | £1300 |
| 1883 | 1,108,000 | £265 | £275 | £300 | £1000 |
| 1884 | 1,595,000 | £265 | £275 | £300 | £1000 |
| 1885 | 1,486,000 | £265 | £275 | £300 | £1000 |
| 1886 | 1,667,000 | £265 | £275 | £300 | £1000 |
| 1887 | 1,000,000 | £265 | £275 | £300 | £1000 |

*The mint initial appears below the shield, i.e. "S" indicates that the coin was struck at the Sydney Mint*

| DATE | MINTAGE | F | VF | EF | UNC |
|---|---|---|---|---|---|
| **St George & Dragon reverse** | | | | | |
| 1871 | incl. above | £265 | £275 | £285 | £450 |
| 1872 | incl. above | £265 | £275 | £285 | £450 |
| 1873 | incl. above | £265 | £275 | £285 | £450 |
| 1874 | incl. above | £265 | £275 | £285 | £450 |
| 1876 | 3,318,866 | £265 | £275 | £285 | £450 |
| 1878 | 1,091,275 | £265 | £275 | £285 | £450 |
| 1879 | 20,013 | £500 | £1100 | £4000 | — |
| 1880 | 3,650,080 | £265 | £275 | £285 | £450 |
| 1884 | 1,769,635 | £265 | £275 | £285 | £450 |
| 1885 | 717,723 | £265 | £275 | £285 | £450 |
| *M below bust on obverse (Melbourne Mint)* | | | | | |
| 1872 | incl. above | £300 | £500 | £1100 | £4000 |
| 1873 | 752,199 | £265 | £275 | £285 | £500 |
| 1874 | incl. above | £265 | £275 | £285 | £500 |
| 1875 | incl. above | £265 | £275 | £285 | £500 |
| 1876 | 2,124,445 | £265 | £275 | £285 | £500 |
| 1877 | 1,487,316 | £265 | £275 | £285 | £500 |
| 1878 | 2,171,457 | £265 | £275 | £285 | £500 |
| 1879 | 2,740,594 | £265 | £275 | £285 | £500 |
| 1880 | incl. above | £265 | £275 | £285 | £500 |
| 1881 | incl. above | £265 | £275 | £285 | £500 |
| 1882 | incl. above | £265 | £275 | £285 | £500 |
| 1883 | incl. above | £265 | £275 | £285 | £500 |
| 1884 | incl. above | £265 | £275 | £285 | £500 |
| 1885 | incl. above | £265 | £275 | £285 | £500 |
| 1886 | incl. above | £265 | £275 | £285 | £500 |
| 1887 | incl. above | £265 | £275 | £285 | £500 |
| *S below bust on obverse (Sydney Mint)* | | | | | |
| 1871 | 2,814,000 | £265 | £275 | £285 | £500 |
| 1872 | incl. above | £265 | £275 | £285 | £600 |
| 1873 | incl. above | £265 | £275 | £285 | £500 |
| 1874 | 1,899,000 | £265 | £275 | £285 | £500 |
| 1875 | inc above | £265 | £275 | £285 | £500 |
| 1876 | 1,613,000 | £265 | £275 | £285 | £500 |
| 1877 | — | | | Unknown | |
| 1879 | incl. above | £265 | £275 | £285 | £500 |
| 1880 | incl. above | £265 | £275 | £285 | £500 |
| 1881 | incl. above | £265 | £275 | £285 | £500 |
| 1882 | incl. above | £265 | £275 | £285 | £550 |
| 1883 | incl. above | £265 | £275 | £285 | £500 |
| 1884 | incl. above | £265 | £275 | £285 | £500 |
| 1885 | incl. above | £265 | £275 | £285 | £500 |
| 1886 | incl. above | £265 | £275 | £285 | £500 |
| 1887 | incl. above | £265 | £275 | £285 | £500 |
| **JUBILEE HEAD ISSUES** | | | | | |
| 1887 | 1,111,280 | £265 | £275 | £285 | £350 |
| 1887 Proof | 797 | — | — | — | £1600 |
| 1888 | 2,717,424 | £265 | £275 | £285 | £350 |
| 1889 | 7,257,455 | £265 | £275 | £285 | £350 |
| 1890 | 6,529.887 | £265 | £275 | £285 | £350 |
| 1891 | 6,329,476 | £265 | £275 | £285 | £350 |
| 1892 | 7,104,720 | £265 | £275 | £285 | £350 |
| *M on ground on reverse (Melbourne Mint)* | | | | | |
| 1887 | 940,000 | £265 | £275 | £285 | £350 |
| 1888 | 2,830,612 | £265 | £275 | £300 | £350 |
| 1889 | 2,732,590 | £265 | £275 | £285 | £350 |
| 1890 | 2,473,537 | £265 | £275 | £285 | £350 |
| 1891 | 2,749,592 | £265 | £275 | £285 | £350 |
| 1892 | 3,488,750 | £265 | £275 | £285 | £350 |
| 1893 | 1,649,352 | £265 | £275 | £285 | £350 |

*"M" below the horse's hoof above the date indicates that the coin was struck at the Melbourne Mint*

*Jubilee head type*

| DATE | MINTAGE | F | VF | EF | UNC |
|---|---|---|---|---|---|
| **S on ground on reverse** *(Sydney Mint)* | | | | | |
| 1887 | 1,002,000 | £265 | £400 | £1000 | £2500 |
| 1888 | 2,187,000 | £265 | £275 | £285 | £300 |
| 1889 | 3,262,000 | £265 | £275 | £285 | £300 |
| 1890 | 2,808,000 | £265 | £275 | £285 | £300 |
| 1891 | 2,596,000 | £265 | £275 | £285 | £300 |
| 1892 | 2,837,000 | £265 | £275 | £285 | £300 |
| 1893 | 1,498,000 | £265 | £275 | £285 | £300 |
| **OLD HEAD ISSUES** | | | | | |
| 1893 | 6,898,260 | £265 | £275 | £285 | £300 |
| 1893 Proof | 773 | — | — | — | £1800 |
| 1894 | 3,782,611 | £265 | £275 | £285 | £300 |
| 1895 | 2,285,317 | £265 | £275 | £285 | £300 |
| 1896 | 3,334,065 | £265 | £275 | £285 | £300 |
| 1898 | 4,361,347 | £265 | £275 | £285 | £300 |
| 1899 | 7,515,978 | £265 | £275 | £285 | £300 |
| 1900 | 10,846,741 | £265 | £275 | £285 | £300 |
| 1901 | 1,578,948 | £265 | £275 | £285 | £300 |
| **M on ground on reverse** *(Melbourne Mint)* | | | | | |
| 1893 | 1,914,000 | £265 | £275 | £285 | £300 |
| 1894 | 4,166,874 | £265 | £275 | £285 | £300 |
| 1895 | 4,165,869 | £265 | £275 | £285 | £300 |
| 1896 | 4,456,932 | £265 | £275 | £285 | £300 |
| 1897 | 5,130,565 | £265 | £275 | £285 | £300 |
| 1898 | 5,509,138 | £265 | £275 | £285 | £300 |
| 1899 | 5,579,157 | £265 | £275 | £285 | £300 |
| 1900 | 4,305,904 | £265 | £275 | £285 | £300 |
| 1901 | 3,987,701 | £265 | £275 | £285 | £300 |
| **P on ground on reverse** *(Perth Mint)* | | | | | |
| 1899 | 690,992 | £265 | £275 | £350 | £1250 |
| 1900 | 1,886,089 | £265 | £275 | £285 | £300 |
| 1901 | 2,889,333 | £265 | £275 | £285 | £300 |
| **S on ground on reverse** *(Sydney Mint)* | | | | | |
| 1893 | 1,346,000 | £265 | £300 | £500 | £1000 |
| 1894 | 3,067,000 | £265 | £275 | £285 | £300 |
| 1895 | 2,758,000 | £265 | £275 | £285 | £300 |
| 1896 | 2,544,000 | £265 | £275 | £285 | £300 |
| 1897 | 2,532,000 | £265 | £275 | £285 | £300 |
| 1898 | 2,548,000 | £265 | £275 | £285 | £300 |
| 1899 | 3,259,000 | £265 | £275 | £285 | £300 |
| 1900 | 3,586,000 | £265 | £275 | £285 | £300 |
| 1901 | 3,012,000 | £265 | £275 | £285 | £300 |

*Old head type*

# EDWARD VII (1902–10)

| | MINTAGE | F | VF | EF | UNC |
|---|---|---|---|---|---|
| 1902 | 4,737,796 | £265 | £275 | £285 | £300 |
| 1902 Matt proof | 15,123 | — | — | — | £400 |
| 1903 | 8,888,627 | £265 | £275 | £285 | £300 |
| 1904 | 10,041,369 | £265 | £275 | £285 | £300 |
| 1905 | 5,910,403 | £265 | £275 | £285 | £300 |
| 1906 | 10,466,981 | £265 | £275 | £285 | £300 |
| 1907 | 18,458,663 | £265 | £275 | £285 | £300 |
| 1908 | 11,729,006 | £265 | £275 | £285 | £300 |
| 1909 | 12,157,099 | £265 | £275 | £285 | £300 |
| 1910 | 22,379,624 | £265 | £275 | £285 | £300 |
| **C on ground on reverse** *(Ottawa Mint)* | | | | | |
| 1908 Satin finish Proof only | 633 | | | Extremely rare | |
| 1909 | 16,300 | £265 | £275 | £325 | £500 |
| 1910 | 28,020 | £265 | £275 | £325 | £500 |

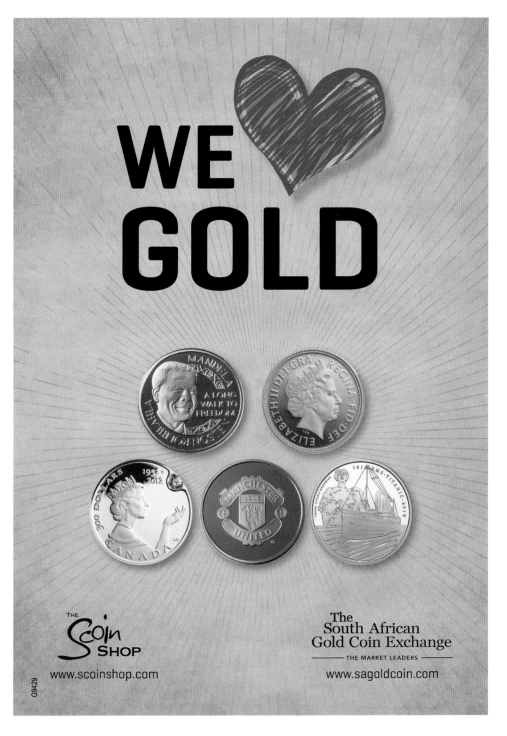

161

| DATE | MINTAGE | F | VF | EF | UNC |
|------|--------:|---|----|----|-----|
| *M on ground on reverse (Melbourne Mint)* | | | | | |
| 1902 | 4,267,157 | £265 | £275 | £285 | £300 |
| 1903 | 3,521,780 | £265 | £275 | £285 | £300 |
| 1904 | 3,743,897 | £265 | £275 | £285 | £300 |
| 1905 | 3,633,838 | £265 | £275 | £285 | £300 |
| 1906 | 3,657,853 | £265 | £275 | £285 | £300 |
| 1907 | 3,332,691 | £265 | £275 | £285 | £300 |
| 1908 | 3,080,148 | £265 | £275 | £285 | £300 |
| 1909 | 3,029,538 | £265 | £275 | £285 | £300 |
| 1910 | 3,054,547 | £265 | £275 | £285 | £300 |
| *P on ground on reverse (Perth Mint)* | | | | | |
| 1902 | 3,289,122 | £265 | £275 | £285 | £300 |
| 1903 | 4,674,783 | £256 | £275 | £285 | £300 |
| 1904 | 4,506,756 | £265 | £275 | £285 | £300 |
| 1905 | 4,876,193 | £265 | £275 | £285 | £300 |
| 1906 | 4,829,817 | £265 | £275 | £285 | £300 |
| 1907 | 4,972,289 | £265 | £275 | £285 | £300 |
| 1908 | 4,875,617 | £265 | £275 | £285 | £300 |
| 1909 | 4,524,241 | £265 | £275 | £285 | £300 |
| 1910 | 4,690,625 | £265 | £275 | £285 | £300 |
| *S on ground on reverse (Sydney Mint)* | | | | | |
| 1902 | 2,813,000 | £265 | £275 | £285 | £280 |
| 1902 Proof | incl. above | | | Extremely rare | |
| 1903 | 2,806,000 | £265 | £275 | £285 | £300 |
| 1904 | 2,986,000 | £265 | £275 | £285 | £300 |
| 1905 | 2,778,000 | £265 | £275 | £285 | £300 |
| 1906 | 2,792,000 | £265 | £275 | £285 | £300 |
| 1907 | 2,539,000 | £265 | £275 | £285 | £300 |
| 1908 | 2,017,000 | £265 | £275 | £285 | £300 |
| 1909 | 2,057,000 | £265 | £275 | £285 | £300 |
| 1910 | 2,135,000 | £265 | £275 | £285 | £300 |

> **IMPORTANT NOTE:**
> The prices quoted in this guide are set at August 2012 with the price of gold at £920 per ounce and silver £16 per ounce — market fluctuations can have a marked effect on the values of modern precious metal coins.

# GEORGE V (1911–36)

*(Extra care should be exercised when purchasing as good quality forgeries exist of virtually all dates and mintmarks)*

| DATE | MINTAGE | F | VF | EF | UNC |
|------|--------:|---|----|----|-----|
| 1911 | 30,044,105 | £265 | £275 | £285 | £300 |
| 1911 Proof | 3,764 | — | — | — | £700 |
| 1912 | 30,317,921 | £265 | £275 | £285 | £300 |
| 1913 | 24,539,672 | £265 | £275 | £285 | £300 |
| 1914 | 11,501,117 | £265 | £275 | £285 | £300 |
| 1915 | 20,295,280 | £265 | £275 | £285 | £300 |
| 1916 | 1,554,120 | £265 | £275 | £285 | £300 |
| 1917 | 1,014,714 | £1500 | £3000 | £8000 | — |
| 1925 | 4,406,431 | £265 | £275 | £285 | £300 |
| *C on ground on reverse (Ottawa Mint)* | | | | | |
| 1911 | 256,946 | £265 | £275 | £285 | £350 |
| 1913 | 3,715 | £275 | £300 | £1200 | — |
| 1914 | 14,891 | £265 | £275 | £600 | — |
| 1916 | 6,111 | | | Extremely rare | |
| 1917 | 58,845 | £265 | £275 | £285 | £350 |
| 1918 | 106,516 | £265 | £275 | £285 | £350 |
| 1919 | 135,889 | £265 | £275 | £285 | £375 |
| *I on ground on reverse (Bombay Mint)* | | | | | |
| 1918 | 1,295,372 | £265 | £265 | £275 | — |
| *M on ground on reverse (Melbourne Mint)* | | | | | |
| 1911 | 2,851,451 | £265 | £275 | £285 | £300 |
| 1912 | 2,469,257 | £265 | £275 | £285 | £300 |
| 1913 | 2,323,180 | £265 | £275 | £285 | £300 |
| 1914 | 2,012,029 | £265 | £275 | £285 | £300 |
| 1915 | 1,637,839 | £265 | £275 | £285 | £300 |
| 1916 | 1,273,643 | £265 | £275 | £285 | £300 |
| 1917 | 934,469 | £265 | £275 | £285 | £300 |
| 1918 | 4,969,493 | £265 | £275 | £285 | £300 |

| DATE | MINTAGE | F | VF | EF | UNC |
|---|---|---|---|---|---|
| 1919 | 514,257 | £265 | £275 | £300 | £425 |
| 1920 | 530,266 | £1200 | £2000 | £4000 | £6500 |
| 1921 | 240,121 | £3000 | £6000 | £10000 | £20000 |
| 1922 | 608,306 | £3700 | £5500 | £9000 | £15000 |
| 1923 | 510,870 | £265 | £275 | £285 | £300 |
| 1924 | 278,140 | £265 | £275 | £285 | £300 |
| 1925 | 3,311,622 | £265 | £275 | £285 | £300 |
| 1926 | 211,107 | £265 | £275 | £285 | £300 |
| 1928 | 413,208 | £500 | £900 | £1500 | £3000 |
| 1929 | 436,719 | £900 | £1500 | £2500 | £4750 |
| 1930 | 77,547 | £265 | £275 | £285 | £300 |
| 1931 | 57,779 | £265 | £275 | £400 | £700 |

*P on ground on reverse (Perth Mint)*

| | | | | | |
|---|---|---|---|---|---|
| 1911 | 4,373,165 | £265 | £275 | £285 | £300 |
| 1912 | 4,278,144 | £265 | £275 | £285 | £300 |
| 1913 | 4,635,287 | £265 | £275 | £285 | £300 |
| 1914 | 4,815,996 | £265 | £275 | £285 | £300 |
| 1915 | 4,373,596 | £265 | £275 | £285 | £300 |
| 1916 | 4,096,771 | £265 | £275 | £285 | £300 |
| 1917 | 4,110,286 | £265 | £275 | £285 | £300 |
| 1918 | 3,812,884 | £265 | £275 | £285 | £300 |
| 1919 | 2,995,216 | £265 | £275 | £285 | £300 |
| 1920 | 2,421,196 | £265 | £275 | £285 | £300 |
| 1921 | 2,134,360 | £265 | £275 | £285 | £300 |
| 1922 | 2,298,884 | £265 | £275 | £285 | £300 |
| 1923 | 2,124,154 | £265 | £275 | £285 | £300 |
| 1924 | 1,464,416 | £265 | £275 | £285 | £300 |
| 1925 | 1,837,901 | £265 | £275 | £400 | £600 |
| 1926 | 1,313,578 | £400 | £750 | £1500 | £3000 |
| 1927 | 1,383,544 | £265 | £275 | £285 | £500 |
| 1928 | 1,333,417 | £265 | £275 | £285 | £375 |
| 1929 | 1,606,625 | £265 | £275 | £285 | £375 |
| 1930 | 1,915,352 | £265 | £275 | £285 | £375 |
| 1931 | 1,173,568 | £265 | £275 | £285 | £375 |

*S on ground on reverse (Sydney Mint)*

| | | | | | |
|---|---|---|---|---|---|
| 1911 | 2,519,000 | £265 | £275 | £285 | £300 |
| 1912 | 2,227,000 | £265 | £275 | £285 | £300 |
| 1913 | 2,249,000 | £265 | £275 | £285 | £300 |
| 1914 | 1,774,000 | £265 | £275 | £285 | £300 |
| 1915 | 1,346,000 | £265 | £275 | £285 | £300 |
| 1916 | 1,242,000 | £265 | £275 | £285 | £300 |
| 1917 | 1,666,000 | £265 | £275 | £285 | £300 |
| 1918 | 3,716,000 | £265 | £275 | £285 | £300 |
| 1919 | 1,835,000 | £265 | £275 | £285 | £300 |

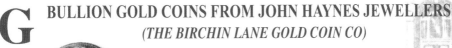

| DATE | MINTAGE | F | VF | EF | UNC |
|------|---------|---|----|----|-----|
| 1920............................................ | — | | | Excessively rare* | |
| 1921............................................ | 839,000 | £500 | £750 | £1800 | £2600 |
| 1922............................................ | 578,000 | | | Extremely rare | |
| 1923............................................ | 416,000 | | | Extremely rare | |
| 1924............................................ | 394,000 | £500 | £800 | £1500 | £2500 |
| 1925............................................ | 5,632,000 | £265 | £275 | £285 | £300 |
| 1926............................................ | 1,031,050 | | | Extremely rare | |

*SA on ground on reverse (Pretoria Mint)*

| | | | | | |
|------|---------|---|----|----|-----|
| 1923 ............................................ | 719 | £800 | £1800 | £4000 | £7000 |
| 1923 Proof.................................... | 655 | | | Extremely rare | |
| 1924............................................ | 3,184 | — | £1750 | £3750 | — |
| 1925............................................ | 6,086,264 | £265 | £275 | £285 | £300 |
| 1926............................................ | 11,107,611 | £265 | £275 | £285 | £300 |
| 1927............................................ | 16,379,704 | £265 | £275 | £285 | £300 |
| 1928............................................ | 18,235,057 | £265 | £275 | £285 | £300 |
| 1929............................................ | 12,024,107 | £265 | £275 | £285 | £300 |
| 1930............................................ | 10,027,756 | £265 | £275 | £285 | £300 |
| 1931............................................ | 8,511,792 | £265 | £275 | £285 | £300 |
| 1932............................................ | 1,066,680 | £265 | £275 | £285 | £300 |

## GEORGE VI (1937–52)

| | | | | | |
|------|---------|---|----|----|-----|
| 1937 Proof only .......................... | 5,501 | — | — | £1000 | £1750 |

## ELIZABETH II (1952–    )

**Pre Decimal Issues**

| | | | | | |
|------|---------|---|----|----|-----|
| 1957............................................ | 2,072,000 | £265 | £275 | £285 | £300 |
| 1958............................................ | 8,700,140 | £265 | £275 | £285 | £300 |
| 1959............................................ | 1,358,228 | £265 | £275 | £285 | £300 |
| 1962............................................ | 3,000,000 | £265 | £275 | £285 | £300 |
| 1963............................................ | 7,400,000 | £265 | £275 | £285 | £300 |
| 1964............................................ | 3,000,000 | £265 | £275 | £285 | £300 |
| 1965............................................ | 3,800,000 | £265 | £275 | £285 | £300 |
| 1966............................................ | 7,050,000 | £265 | £275 | £285 | £300 |
| 1967............................................ | 5,000,000 | £265 | £275 | £285 | £300 |
| 1968............................................ | 4,203,000 | £265 | £275 | £285 | £300 |

*Later issues are included in the Decimal section. *In 2009 one sold for £415,000.*

# HALF SOVEREIGNS

## GEORGE III (1760–1820)

| | | | | | |
|------|---------|---|----|----|-----|
| 1817............................................ | 2,080,197 | £175 | £300 | £500 | £900 |
| 1818............................................ | 1,030,286 | £180 | £300 | £600 | £950 |
| 1820............................................ | 35,043 | £180 | £300 | £550 | £950 |

## GEORGE IV (1820–30)

| | | | | | |
|------|---------|---|----|----|-----|
| 1821 First bust,<br>    ornate shield reverse ............. | 231,288 | £600 | £1500 | £3000 | £4500 |
| 1821 — Proof ............................. | unrecorded | — | — | — | £5000 |
| 1823 First bust, Plain<br>    shield rev................................ | 224,280 | £170 | £275 | £550 | £1000 |
| 1824 — ...................................... | 591,538 | £170 | £275 | £550 | £1000 |
| 1825 — ...................................... | 761,150 | £170 | £275 | £550 | £1000 |
| 1826 bare head, shield<br>    with full legend reverse ........... | 344,830 | £170 | £275 | £550 | £950 |
| 1826 — Proof ............................. | unrecorded | — | — | — | £1850 |
| 1827 — ...................................... | 492,014 | £170 | £275 | £550 | £900 |
| 1828 — ...................................... | 1,224,754 | £170 | £275 | £550 | £1050 |

| DATE | MINTAGE | F | VF | EF | UNC |
|---|---|---|---|---|---|

## WILLIAM IV (1830–37)

| DATE | MINTAGE | F | VF | EF | UNC |
|---|---|---|---|---|---|
| 1831 Proof only | unrecorded | — | — | — | £2800 |
| 1834 | 133,899 | £225 | £500 | £800 | £1750 |
| 1835 | 772,554 | £225 | £550 | £750 | £1500 |
| 1836 | 146,865 | £200 | £400 | £700 | £1500 |
| 1836 obverse from 6d die | incl. above | £1200 | £3000 | £6000 | — |
| 1837 | 160,207 | £200 | £450 | £600 | £1450 |

## VICTORIA (1837–1901)

**YOUNG HEAD ISSUES**
*Shield reverse*

| DATE | MINTAGE | F | VF | EF | UNC |
|---|---|---|---|---|---|
| 1838 | 273,341 | £140 | £160 | £350 | £1250 |
| 1839 Proof only | 1,230 | — | — | — | £2750 |
| 1841 | 508,835 | £140 | £160 | £350 | £1200 |
| 1842 | 2,223,352 | £140 | £160 | £350 | £750 |
| 1843 | 1,251,762 | £140 | £160 | £350 | £850 |
| 1844 | 1,127,007 | £140 | £160 | £350 | £700 |
| 1845 | 887,526 | £250 | £600 | £1800 | £3500 |
| 1846 | 1,063,928 | £140 | £160 | £300 | £750 |
| 1847 | 982,636 | £140 | £160 | £300 | £750 |
| 1848 | 410,595 | £140 | £160 | £300 | £750 |
| 1849 | 845,112 | £140 | £160 | £300 | £700 |
| 1850 | 179,595 | £140 | £400 | £800 | £2000 |
| 1851 | 773,573 | £140 | £160 | £300 | £700 |
| 1852 | 1,377,671 | £140 | £160 | £300 | £700 |
| 1853 | 2,708,796 | £140 | £160 | £300 | £700 |
| 1853 Proof | unrecorded | £140 | — | — | £7000 |
| 1854 | 1,125,144 | | Extremely rare | | |
| 1855 | 1,120,362 | £140 | £160 | £300 | £600 |
| 1856 | 2,391,909 | £140 | £160 | £300 | £600 |
| 1857 | 728,223 | £140 | £160 | £300 | £600 |
| 1858 | 855,578 | £140 | £160 | £300 | £600 |
| 1859 | 2,203,813 | £140 | £160 | £300 | £600 |
| 1860 | 1,131,500 | £140 | £160 | £300 | £600 |
| 1861 | 1,130,867 | £140 | £160 | £300 | £600 |
| 1862 | unrecorded | £700 | £1800 | £7000 | — |
| 1863 | 1,571,574 | £140 | £160 | £300 | £500 |
| 1863 with Die number | incl. above | £140 | £160 | £300 | £500 |
| 1864 — | 1,758,490 | £140 | £160 | £300 | £500 |
| 1865 — | 1,834,750 | £140 | £160 | £300 | £500 |
| 1866 — | 2,058,776 | £140 | £160 | £300 | £500 |
| 1867 — | 992,795 | £140 | £160 | £300 | £470 |
| 1869 — | 1,861,764 | £140 | £160 | £300 | £470 |
| 1870 — | 1,159,544 | £140 | £160 | £300 | £380 |
| 1871 — | 2,062,970 | £140 | £160 | £300 | £380 |
| 1872 — | 3,248,627 | £140 | £160 | £300 | £380 |
| 1873 — | 1,927,050 | £140 | £160 | £300 | £380 |
| 1874 — | 1,884,432 | £140 | £160 | £300 | £380 |
| 1875 — | 516,240 | £140 | £160 | £300 | £380 |
| 1876 — | 2,785,187 | £140 | £160 | £300 | £380 |
| 1877 — | 2,197,482 | £140 | £160 | £300 | £380 |
| 1878 — | 2,081,941 | £140 | £160 | £300 | £380 |
| 1879 — | 35,201 | £140 | £160 | £300 | £380 |
| 1880 — | 1,009,049 | £140 | £160 | £300 | £380 |
| 1880 no Die number | incl. above | £140 | £160 | £300 | £380 |
| 1883 — | 2,870,457 | £140 | £160 | £300 | £325 |
| 1884 — | 1,113,756 | £140 | £160 | £300 | £325 |
| 1885 — | 4,468,871 | £140 | £160 | £300 | £325 |

*M below shield (Melbourne Mint)*

| DATE | MINTAGE | F | VF | EF | UNC |
|---|---|---|---|---|---|
| 1873 | 165,034 | £140 | £160 | £700 | — |
| 1877 | 80,016 | £140 | £160 | £600 | — |
| 1881 | 42,009 | £140 | £240 | £750 | — |
| 1882 | 107,522 | £140 | £160 | £700 | — |
| 1884 | 48,009 | £140 | £160 | £700 | — |

| Date | Mintage | F | VF | EF | UNC |
|---|---|---|---|---|---|
| 1885 | 11,003 | £140 | £300 | £1500 | — |
| 1886 | 38,008 | £140 | £160 | £1500 | — |
| 1887 | 64,013 | £175 | £400 | £1500 | £4500 |

*S below shield (Sydney Mint)*

| | | | | | |
|---|---|---|---|---|---|
| 1871 | 180,000 (?) | £140 | £160 | £700 | — |
| 1872 | 356,000 | £140 | £160 | £700 | — |
| 1875 | unrecorded | £140 | £160 | £700 | — |
| 1879 | 94,000 | £140 | £160 | £1000 | — |
| 1880 | 80,000 | £140 | £400 | £1000 | — |
| 1881 | 62,000 | £140 | £160 | £1000 | — |
| 1882 | 52,000 | | | Extremely rare | |
| 1883 | 220,000 | £140 | £160 | £900 | — |
| 1886 | 82,000 | £140 | £160 | £900 | — |
| 1887 | 134,000 | £140 | £160 | £1100 | £3750 |

**JUBILEE HEAD ISSUES**

| | | | | | |
|---|---|---|---|---|---|
| 1887 | 871,770 | £130 | £135 | £140 | £175 |
| 1887 Proof | 797 | £130 | £135 | — | £800 |
| 1890 | 2.266,023 | £130 | £135 | £140 | £175 |
| 1891 | 1,079,286 | £130 | £135 | £140 | £175 |
| 1892 | 13,680,486 | £130 | £136 | £140 | £175 |
| 1893 | 4,426,625 | £130 | £136 | £140 | £175 |

*M below shield (Melbourne Mint)*

| | | | | | |
|---|---|---|---|---|---|
| 1887 | incl. above | £130 | £140 | £300 | £600 |
| 1893 | 110,024 | £130 | £140 | £550 | — |

*S below shield (Sydney Mint)*

| | | | | | |
|---|---|---|---|---|---|
| 1887 | incl. above | £130 | £140 | £280 | £500 |
| 1889 | 64,000 | £130 | £140 | £280 | — |
| 1891 | 154,000 | £130 | £140 | £280 | — |

**OLD HEAD ISSUES**

| | | | | | |
|---|---|---|---|---|---|
| 1893 | incl. above | £130 | £135 | £140 | £175 |
| 1893 Proof | 773 | — | — | — | £800 |
| 1894 | 3,794,591 | £130 | £135 | £140 | £175 |
| 1895 | 2,869,183 | £130 | £135 | £140 | £175 |
| 1896 | 2,946,605 | £130 | £135 | £140 | £175 |
| 1897 | 3,568,156 | £130 | £135 | £140 | £175 |
| 1898 | 2,868,527 | £130 | £135 | £140 | £175 |
| 1899 | 3,361,881 | £130 | £135 | £140 | £175 |
| 1900 | 4,307,372 | £130 | £135 | £140 | £175 |
| 1901 | 2,037,664 | £130 | £135 | £140 | £175 |

*M on ground on reverse (Melbourne Mint)*

| | | | | | |
|---|---|---|---|---|---|
| 1893 | unrecorded | | | Extremely rare | |
| 1896 | 218,946 | £130 | £135 | £450 | — |
| 1899 | 97,221 | £130 | £135 | £450 | — |
| 1900 | 112,920 | £130 | £135 | £450 | — |

*P on ground on reverse (Perth Mint)*

| | | | | | |
|---|---|---|---|---|---|
| 1899 | | | | Proof Unique | |
| 1900 | 119,376 | £130 | £300 | £550 | — |

*S on ground on reverse (Sydney Mint)*

| | | | | | |
|---|---|---|---|---|---|
| 1893 | 250,000 | £130 | £135 | £375 | — |
| 1897 | unrecorded | £130 | £135 | £350 | — |
| 1900 | 260,00 | £130 | £135 | £350 | — |

# EDWARD VII (1902–10)

| | | | | | |
|---|---|---|---|---|---|
| 1902 | 4,244,457 | £130 | £135 | £140 | £150 |
| 1902 Matt proof | 15,123 | — | — | — | £275 |
| 1903 | 2,522,057 | £130 | £135 | £140 | £150 |
| 1904 | 1,717,440 | £130 | £135 | £140 | £150 |
| 1905 | 3,023,993 | £130 | £135 | £140 | £150 |
| 1906 | 4,245,437 | £130 | £135 | £140 | £150 |
| 1907 | 4,233,421 | £130 | £135 | £140 | £150 |
| 1908 | 3,996,992 | £130 | £135 | £140 | £150 |
| 1909 | 4,010,715 | £130 | £135 | £140 | £150 |
| 1910 | 5,023,881 | £130 | £135 | £140 | £150 |

| DATE | | F | VF | EF | UNC |
|---|---|---|---|---|---|
| *M on ground on reverse (Melbourne Mint)* | | | | | |
| 1906 | 82,042 | £120 | £130 | £150 | £350 |
| 1907 | 405,034 | £120 | £130 | £150 | £325 |
| 1908 | incl. above | £120 | £130 | £150 | £350 |
| 1909 | 186,094 | £120 | £130 | £150 | £325 |
| *P on ground on reverse (Perth Mint)* | | | | | |
| 1904 | 60,030 | £120 | £130 | £500 | — |
| 1908 | 24,668 | £120 | £130 | £500 | — |
| 1909 | 44,022 | £120 | £130 | £500 | — |
| *S on ground on reverse (Sydney Mint)* | | | | | |
| 1902 | 84,000 | £120 | £130 | £140 | £325 |
| 1902 Proof | | | Extremely rare | | |
| 1903 | 231,000 | | | | £275 |
| 1906 | 308,00 | £120 | £130 | £140 | £300 |
| 1908 | 538,000 | £120 | £130 | £140 | £300 |
| 1910 | 474,000 | £120 | £130 | £140 | £300 |

## GEORGE V (1911–36)

| | | F | VF | EF | UNC |
|---|---|---|---|---|---|
| 1911 | 6,104,106 | £120 | £130 | £140 | £150 |
| 1911 Proof | 3,764 | — | — | — | £400 |
| 1912 | 6,224,316 | £120 | £130 | £140 | £150 |
| 1913 | 6,094,290 | £120 | £130 | £140 | £150 |
| 1914 | 7,251,124 | £120 | £130 | £140 | £150 |
| 1915 | 2,042,747 | £120 | £130 | £140 | £150 |
| *M on ground on reverse (Melbourne Mint)* | | | | | |
| 1915 | 125,664 | £120 | £130 | £140 | £150 |
| *P on ground on reverse (Perth Mint)* | | | | | |
| 1911 | 130,373 | £120 | £130 | £140 | £225 |
| 1915 | 136,219 | £120 | £130 | £140 | £225 |
| 1918 | unrecorded | £175 | £500 | £1000 | £2000 |
| *S on ground on reverse (Sydney Mint)* | | | | | |
| 1911 | 252,000 | £120 | £130 | £140 | £150 |
| 1912 | 278,000 | £120 | £130 | £140 | £150 |
| 1914 | 322,000 | £120 | £130 | £140 | £150 |
| 1915 | 892,000 | £120 | £130 | £140 | £150 |
| 1916 | 448,000 | £120 | £130 | £140 | £150 |
| *SA on ground on reverse (Pretoria Mint)* | | | | | |
| 1923 Proof only | 655 | — | — | — | £750 |
| 1925 | 946,615 | £120 | £130 | £140 | £150 |
| 1926 | 806,540 | £120 | £130 | £140 | £150 |

## GEORGE VI (1937–52)

| | | F | VF | EF | UNC |
|---|---|---|---|---|---|
| 1937 Proof only | 5,501 | — | — | — | £550 |

*Later issues are included in the Decimal section.*

![Coincraft storefront — COINCRAFT, COINS, ANCIENT COINS, ANTIQUITIES, BANKNOTES signs above windows labelled ANTIQUITIES, ROMAN, GREEK, COINS, BANKNOTES]

# Coincraft

# *In These Troubled Times, When You Sell Your Collection, How Can You be Sure You Will get Paid?*

By dealing with one of Britain's oldest, largest, friendliest and most financially secure coin dealers, Coincraft.

Coincraft has been helping collectors for the past 54 years. We own the freehold of our building, just across the street from the British Museum and have been here for the past 33 years. Our company balance sheet is extremely strong, as we have always reinvested our profits into the company.

At Coincraft we will buy everything that you have for sale, not just the cream. Unlike auction houses, you will not have to wait months for your material to come up for sale and then have any unsold lots returned to you. Over 90% of the offers we make, are accepted.

When we agree a price, we pay you on the spot, no waiting for an auction, no giving your material on approval. You want to sell, we want to buy and we pay you immediately. In these troubled times, isn't it nice to know that you are dealing with friendly people who are also financially strong enough to pay you instantly?

**Call in person** at either of our two shops at 44 & 45 Great Russell Street, just across from the British Museum. Open Monday to Friday 9.30 to 5.00 and Saturday from 10.00 till 2.30.

Friendly, personal service and an interesting display of coins, banknotes, medallions, ancient coins and antiquities, to tempt and delight you.

**We always need to buy** Coincraft needs to buy: single items to entire collections, dealers inventories, hoards, accumulations, you name it and we will make you an offer. Over 90% of our offers are accepted. Sell where the dealers sell.

*Find out why collectors say; Coincraft, nice people to do business with.*

**Buy by post** through Britain's only coin newspaper, The Phoenix, published every three weeks. It contains 24 tabloid sized pages of special offers and rare items, many not available anywhere else.

You can't buy a subscription, but you can get a complimentary copy free, just for the asking.

**On the Internet** Our website, www.coincraft.com is available 24 hours a day. There are many interesting features including a comprehensive numismatic glossary. Keep looking, more is being added every day.

# Coincraft
**FRIENDLY PROFESSIONAL SERVICE SINCE 1955**

44 & 45 Great Russell Street, London WC1B 3JL
(opposite the British Museum)

Tel 020 7636 1188 and 020 7637 8785
Fax 020 7323 2860 and 020 7637 7635
Web www.coincraft.com  Email info@coincraft.co

# CROWNS

| DATE | F | VF | EF | UNC |
|------|---|----|----|-----|

## OLIVER CROMWELL

| | | | | |
|------|---|----|----|-----|
| 1658 8 over 7 (always) | £1800 | £3500 | £6000 | — |
| 1658 Dutch Copy | | Extremely rare | | |
| 1658 Patterns. In Various Metals | | Extremely rare | | |

## CHARLES II (1660–85)

| | | | | |
|------|---|----|----|-----|
| 1662 First bust, rose (2 varieties) | £250 | £800 | £4500 | — |
| 1662 — no rose (2 varieties) | £250 | £800 | £4500 | — |
| 1663 — | £250 | £800 | £4000 | — |
| 1664 Second bust | £200 | £800 | £4000 | — |
| 1665 — | £1350 | £4000 | — | — |
| 1666 — | £250 | £900 | £4500 | — |
| 1666 — error RE.X for REX | | Extremely rare | | |
| 1666 — Elephant below bust | £600 | £2000 | £15000 | — |
| 1667 — | £160 | £500 | £3000 | — |
| 1668/7 — 8 over 7 | £170 | £550 | — | — |
| 1668 — | £170 | £550 | £3500 | — |
| 1669/8 — 9 over 8 | £350 | £800 | — | — |
| 1669 — | £300 | £1000 | £4500 | — |
| 1670/69 — 70 over 69 | £175 | £1000 | — | — |
| 1670 — | £170 | £600 | £3500 | — |
| 1671 | £160 | £600 | £3000 | — |
| 1671 Third bust | £160 | £600 | £3000 | — |
| 1672 — | £160 | £500 | £3000 | — |
| 1673 — | £160 | £500 | £3000 | — |
| 1674 — | | Extremely rare | | |
| 1675 — | £700 | £2000 | — | — |
| 1675/3 — | £700 | £2200 | — | — |
| 1676 — | £160 | £550 | £3000 | — |
| 1677 — | £150 | £550 | £3000 | — |
| 1677/6 — 7 over 6 | £175 | £900 | — | — |
| 1678/7 — | £175 | £900 | — | — |
| 1678/7 — 8 over 7 | £260 | £800 | — | — |
| 1679 — | £160 | £600 | £3000 | — |
| 1679 Fourth bust | £160 | £600 | £3000 | — |
| 1680 Third bust | £160 | £800 | £3500 | — |
| 1680/79 — 80 over 79 | £180 | £800 | — | — |
| 1680 Fourth bust | £170 | £700 | £4000 | — |
| 1680/79 — 80 over 79 | £190 | £1000 | — | — |
| 1681 — | £160 | £600 | £3500 | — |
| 1681 — Elephant & Castle below bust | £3000 | £8000 | — | — |
| 1682/1 — | £170 | £650 | £3250 | — |
| 1682 — edge error QVRRTO for QVARTO | £400 | — | — | — |
| 1683 — | £400 | £1000 | £4000 | — |
| 1684 — | £400 | £1300 | — | — |

## JAMES II (1685–88)

| | | | | |
|------|---|----|----|-----|
| 1686 First bust | £300 | £900 | £4250 | — |
| 1686 — No stops on obv | £400 | £1400 | — | — |
| 1687 Second bust | £275 | £700 | £3500 | — |
| 1688/7 — 8 over 7 | £280 | £800 | — | — |
| 1688 — | £275 | £800 | £3500 | — |

## WILLIAM AND MARY (1688–94)

| | | | | |
|------|---|----|----|-----|
| 1691 | £525 | £1500 | £4500 | — |
| 1692 | £525 | £1500 | £4500 | — |
| 1692 2 over upside down 2 | £525 | £1500 | £4500 | — |

| DATE | F | VF | EF | UNC |
|---|---|---|---|---|

## WILLIAM III (1694–1702)

| | F | VF | EF | UNC |
|---|---|---|---|---|
| 1695 First bust | £100 | £300 | £1800 | — |
| 1696 — | £90 | £275 | £1600 | — |
| 1696 — no stops on obv. | £225 | £400 | — | — |
| 1996 — no stops obv./rev. | £250 | £400 | — | — |
| 1696 — GEI for DEI | £700 | £1600 | — | — |
| 1696 Second bust | | | | Unique |
| 1696 Third bust | £90 | £275 | £1600 | — |
| 1697 — | £1200 | £4000 | £7500 | — |
| 1700 Third bust variety edge year DUODECIMO | £140 | £550 | £1750 | — |
| 1700 — edge year DUODECIMO TERTIO.. | £140 | £550 | £1750 | — |

## ANNE (1702–14)

| | F | VF | EF | UNC |
|---|---|---|---|---|
| 1703 First bust, VIGO | £350 | £1000 | £4000 | — |
| 1705 — Plumes in angles on rev. | £500 | £1500 | £5500 | — |
| 1706 — Roses & Plumes in angles on rev... | £160 | £600 | £2200 | — |
| 1707 — — | £160 | £600 | £2200 | — |
| 1707 Second bust, E below | £160 | £500 | £2000 | — |
| 1707 — Plain | £160 | £500 | £2000 | — |
| 1708 — E below | £160 | £500 | £2000 | — |
| 1708/7 — 8 over 7 | £160 | £800 | — | — |
| 1708 — Plain | £160 | £600 | £2000 | — |
| 1708 — — error BR for BRI | | | Extremely rare | |
| 1708 — Plumes in angles on rev. | £180 | £700 | £2500 | — |
| 1713 Third bust, Roses & Plumes in angles on rev. | £180 | £700 | £2300 | — |

## GEORGE I (1714–27)

| | F | VF | EF | UNC |
|---|---|---|---|---|
| 1716 | £525 | £1500 | £6000 | — |
| 1718 8 over 6 | £525 | £1500 | £5000 | — |
| 1720 20 over 18 | £525 | £1500 | £5000 | — |
| 1723 SSC in angles on rev. (South Sea Co.) | £525 | £1500 | £5000 | — |
| 1726 | £525 | £1500 | £5250 | — |

## GEORGE II (1727–60)

| | F | VF | EF | UNC |
|---|---|---|---|---|
| 1732 Young head, Plain, Proof | — | — | £10000 | |
| 1732 — Roses & Plumes in angles on rev .. | £250 | £700 | £2500 | — |
| 1734 — — | £250 | £700 | £2500 | — |
| 1735 — — | £250 | £700 | £2500 | — |
| 1736 — — | £260 | £700 | £2500 | — |
| 1739 — Roses in angles on rev | £240 | £600 | £2500 | — |
| 1741 — — | £240 | £600 | £2500 | — |
| 1743 Old head, Roses in angles on rev | £225 | £600 | £2250 | — |
| 1746 — — LIMA below bust | £225 | £600 | £2250 | — |
| 1746 — Plain, Proof | — | — | £6000 | — |
| 1750 — — | £400 | £1100 | £3500 | — |
| 1751 — — | £500 | £1400 | £3600 | — |

## GEORGE III (1760–1820)

| | F | VF | EF | UNC |
|---|---|---|---|---|
| Dollar with oval counterstamp | £125 | £400 | £750 | — |
| Dollar with octagonal counterstamp | £175 | £500 | £800 | — |
| 1804 Bank of England Dollar, Britannia rev. | £100 | £225 | £500 | — |
| 1818 LVIII | £40 | £100 | £250 | £800 |
| 1818 LIX | £40 | £100 | £250 | £800 |
| 1819 LIX | £40 | £100 | £250 | £800 |
| 1819 LIX 9 over 8 | £45 | £150 | £400 | — |
| 1819 LIX no stops on edge | £60 | £150 | £400 | £1000 |
| 1819 LX | £40 | £100 | £325 | £900 |
| 1820 LX | £35 | £100 | £300 | £800 |
| 1820 LX 20 over 19 | £35 | £200 | £500 | — |

| DATE | MINTAGE | F | VF | EF | UNC |
|---|---|---|---|---|---|

## GEORGE IV (1820–30)

1821 First bust, St George rev.

| | | | | | |
|---|---|---|---|---|---|
| SECUNDO on edge .................... | 437,976 | £40 | £180 | £700 | £1500 |
| 1821 — — Proof........................Incl. above | | £40 | £180 | — | £4250 |
| 1821 — — Proof TERTIO (error edge)Incl above | | £40 | £180 | — | £4000 |
| 1822 — — SECUNDO................... | 124,929 | £40 | £180 | £700 | £1500 |
| 1822 — — TERTIO......................Incl above | | £40 | £180 | £700 | £1500 |
| 1823 — — Proof only ................................. | | | | Extremely rare | |
| 1826 Second bust, shield rev, SEPTIMO | | | | | |
| Proof only................................................. | | — | — | £2000 | £7000 |

## WILLIAM IV (1830–37)

| | | | | UNC |
|---|---|---|---|---|
| 1831 Proof only W.W. on truncation............ | — | — | £12500 |
| 1831 Proof only W. WYON on truncation.... | — | — | £15000 |
| 1834 Proof only ............................................ | — | — | —£30000 |

## VICTORIA (1837–1901)

**YOUNG HEAD ISSUES**

| | | | | | |
|---|---|---|---|---|---|
| 1839 Proof only ........................... | — | — | — | — | £9000 |
| 1844 Star stops on edge............. | 94,248 | £50 | £260 | £1200 | £3000 |
| 1844 Cinquefoil stops on edge ... | incl. above | £50 | £260 | £1200 | £3000 |
| 1845 Star stops on edge............. | 159,192 | £50 | £260 | £1200 | £3000 |
| 1845 Cinquefoil stops on edge ... | incl. above | £50 | £260 | £1200 | £3000 |
| 1847........................................... | 140,976 | £60 | £275 | £1300 | £3500 |

**GOTHIC HEAD ISSUES (Proof only)**

| | | | | | |
|---|---|---|---|---|---|
| 1847 mdcccxlvii UNDECIMO on edge | 8,000 | £500 | £900 | £1750 | £3000 |
| 1847 — Plain edge...................... | — | — | — | — | £3500 |
| 1853 mdcccliii SEPTIMO on edge | 460 | — | — | — | £8000 |
| 1853 — Plain edge...................... | — | — | — | —£15000 | |

**JUBILEE HEAD ISSUES**

| | | | | | |
|---|---|---|---|---|---|
| 1887 ...................................... | 173,581 | £20 | £30 | £60 | £150 |
| 1887 Proof................................... | 1,084 | — | — | — | £950 |
| 1888 Narrow date........................ | 131,899 | £20 | £35 | £90 | £240 |
| 1888 Wide date .......................... | incl above | £25 | £60 | £300 | — |
| 1889........................................... | 1,807,224 | £20 | £30 | £60 | £150 |
| 1890........................................... | 997,862 | £20 | £30 | £70 | £225 |
| 1891........................................... | 556,394 | £20 | £30 | £70 | £225 |
| 1892........................................... | 451,334 | £20 | £30 | £80 | £250 |

**OLD HEAD ISSUES** (Regnal date on edge in Roman numerals)

| | | | | | |
|---|---|---|---|---|---|
| 1893 LVI..................................... | 497,845 | £20 | £45 | £150 | £375 |
| 1893 LVII.................................... | incl. above | £20 | £45 | £200 | £425 |
| 1893 Proof................................... | 1,312 | — | — | — | £1000 |
| 1894 LVII.................................... | 144,906 | £20 | £45 | £175 | £400 |
| 1894 LVIII................................... | incl. above | £20 | £45 | £175 | £400 |
| 1895 LVIII ................................... | 252,862 | £20 | £45 | £175 | £400 |
| 1895 LIX ..................................... | incl. above | £20 | £45 | £175 | £400 |
| 1896 LIX ..................................... | 317,599 | £20 | £45 | £175 | £450 |
| 1896 LX ...................................... | incl. above | £20 | £45 | £175 | £400 |
| 1897 LX ...................................... | 262,118 | £20 | £45 | £175 | £400 |
| 1897 LXI ..................................... | incl. above | £20 | £45 | £175 | £450 |
| 1898 LXI ..................................... | 166,150 | £20 | £45 | £175 | £500 |
| 1898 LXII .................................... | incl. above | £20 | £45 | £175 | £400 |
| 1899 LXII .................................... | 166,300 | £20 | £45 | £175 | £400 |
| 1899 LXIII................................... | incl. above | £20 | £45 | £175 | £400 |
| 1900 LXIII................................... | 353,356 | £20 | £45 | £175 | £400 |
| 1900 LXIV ................................... | incl. above | £20 | £45 | £175 | £400 |

*Victoria, Jubilee head*

| DATE | MINTAGE | F | VF | EF | UNC |
|---|---|---|---|---|---|
| **EDWARD VII (1901–10)** | | | | | |
| 1902 | 256,020 | £60 | £120 | £185 | £275 |
| 1902 "Matt Proof" | 15,123 | — | — | — | £250 |
| **GEORGE V (1910–36)** | | | | | |
| 1927 Proof only | 15,030 | — | £100 | £170 | £275 |
| 1928 | 9,034 | £110 | £160 | £300 | £500 |
| 1929 | 4,994 | £110 | £160 | £300 | £500 |
| 1930 | 4,847 | £110 | £160 | £300 | £525 |
| 1931 | 4,056 | £110 | £160 | £300 | £500 |
| 1932 | 2,395 | £200 | £400 | £800 | £1250 |
| 1933 | 7,132 | £110 | £160 | £300 | £525 |
| 1934 | 932 | £800 | £1600 | £3500 | £5000 |
| 1935 Jubilee issue. Incuse edge inscription | 714,769 | £15 | £20 | £30 | £45 |
| 1935 — — error edge inscription | incl. above | — | — | — | £1500 |
| 1935 — Specimen in box | incl. above | — | — | — | £60 |
| 1935 — Proof | incl. above | — | — | — | £200 |
| 1935 — Proof. Raised edge inscription | 2,500 | — | — | £175 | £300 |
| 1935 — — fine lettering | incl. above | — | — | — | £1000 |
| 1935 — — error edge inscription | incl. above | — | — | — | £1500 |
| 1935 — Gold proof | 30 | — | — | Extremely rare | |
| 1936 | 2,473 | £170 | £340 | £600 | £1000 |
| **GEORGE VI (1936–52)** | | | | | |
| 1937 Coronation | 418,699 | £18 | £24 | £38 | £55 |
| 1937 Proof | 26,402 | — | — | — | £60 |
| 1951 Festival of Britain, Proof-like | 1,983,540 | — | — | £4 | £7 |
| **ELIZABETH II (1952–  )** | | | | | |
| Pre-Decimal issues (Five Shillings) | | | | | |
| 1953 | 5,962,621 | — | — | £3 | £6 |
| 1953 Proof | 40,000 | — | — | — | £20 |
| 1960 | 1,024,038 | — | — | £3 | £6 |
| 1960 Polished dies | 70,000 | — | — | — | £9 |
| 1965 Churchill | 19,640,000 | — | — | — | £1 |

*Later issues are listed in the Decimal section.*

# DOUBLE FLORINS

## VICTORIA (1837–1901)

| | MINTAGE | F | VF | EF | UNC |
|---|---|---|---|---|---|
| 1887 Roman I | 483,347 | £15 | £30 | £50 | £110 |
| 1887 Roman I Proof | incl. above | — | — | — | £500 |
| 1887 Arabic 1 | incl. above | £15 | £30 | £50 | £110 |
| 1887 Arabic 1 Proof | incl. above | — | — | — | £500 |
| 1888 | 243,340 | £15 | £40 | £80 | £130 |
| 1888 Second I in VICTORIA an inverted 1 | incl. above | £22 | £45 | £90 | £350 |
| 1889 | 1,185,111 | £18 | £30 | £45 | £130 |
| 1889 inverted 1 | incl. above | £25 | £45 | £90 | £350 |
| 1890 | 782,146 | £15 | £40 | £60 | £130 |

*Patterns were also produced in 1911, 1914 and 1950 and are all extremely rare.*

# HALFCROWNS

| DATE | MINTAGE | F | VF | EF | UNC |
|------|---------|---|----|----|----|

## OLIVER CROMWELL

| | | | | | |
|------|---------|---|----|----|----|
| 1656 | | | | Extremely rare | |
| 1658 | | £1000 | £1800 | £3750 | — |
| 1658 Proof in Gold | | | | Extremely rare | |

## CHARLES II (1660–1685)

| | | | | | |
|------|---------|---|----|----|----|
| 1663 First bust | | £150 | £600 | £3500 | — |
| 1663 — no stops on obv. | | £200 | £800 | — | — |
| 1664 Second bust | | £250 | £1200 | £5000 | — |
| 1666 Third bust | | £900 | — | — | — |
| 1666 — Elephant | | £800 | £3000 | — | — |
| 1667/4 — 7 over 4 | | | | Extremely rare | |
| 1668/4 — 8 over 4 | | £300 | £1500 | — | — |
| 1669 — | | £400 | £1600 | — | — |
| 1669/4 — 9 over 4 | | £250 | £900 | — | — |
| 1670 — | | £125 | £500 | £2500 | — |
| 1670 — MRG for MAG | | £300 | £1000 | — | — |
| 1671 — | | £125 | £450 | £2500 | — |
| 1671/0 — 1 over 0 | | £150 | £600 | £2750 | — |
| 1672 — Third bust | | | | Extremely rare | |
| 1672 Fourth bust | | £125 | £500 | £2750 | — |
| 1673 — | | £125 | £500 | £2500 | — |
| 1673 — Plumes both sides | | | | Extremely rare | |
| 1673 — Plume below bust | | £6000 | £16000 | — | — |
| 1674 — | | £140 | £650 | — | — |
| 1675 — | | £125 | £400 | £2000 | — |
| 1676 — | | £125 | £400 | £1900 | — |
| 1676 — inverted 1 in date | | £125 | £400 | £2000 | — |
| 1677 — | | £125 | £400 | £1750 | — |
| 1678 — | | £200 | £800 | — | — |
| 1679 — GRATTA error | | | | Extremely rare | |
| 1679 — | | £120 | £400 | £1800 | — |
| 1680 — | | £160 | £725 | — | — |
| 1681/0 — 1 over 0 | | £250 | — | — | — |
| 1681 — | | £125 | £450 | £2000 | — |
| 1681 — Elephant & Castle | | £3500 | £10000 | — | — |
| 1682 — | | £120 | £450 | £2750 | — |
| 1683 — | | £120 | £500 | £2400 | — |
| 1683 — Plume below bust | | | | Extremely rare | |
| 1684/3 — 4 over 3 | | £275 | £850 | £4000 | — |

## JAMES II (1685–1688)

| | | | | | |
|------|---------|---|----|----|----|
| 1685 First bust | | £220 | £600 | £3000 | — |
| 1686 — | | £220 | £600 | £3000 | — |
| 1686/5 — 6 over 5 | | £220 | £700 | — | — |
| 1686 — V over S | | £225 | £750 | — | — |
| 1687 — | | £220 | £650 | £3000 | — |
| 1687/6 — 7 over 6 | | £300 | £850 | — | — |
| 1687 Second bust | | £200 | £600 | £3000 | — |
| 1688 — | | £200 | £600 | £2750 | — |

## WILLIAM AND MARY (1688–1694)

| | | | | | |
|------|---------|---|----|----|----|
| 1689 First busts; first shield | | £100 | £350 | £1600 | — |
| 1689 — — no pearls in crown | | £100 | £350 | £1600 | — |
| 1689 — — FRA for FR | | £160 | £600 | £2000 | — |
| 1689 — — No stop on obv. | | £100 | £500 | £1850 | — |
| 1689 — Second shield | | £100 | £350 | £1500 | — |
| 1689 — — no pearls in crown | | £100 | £350 | £1600 | — |
| 1690 — — | | £160 | £700 | £2600 | — |
| 1690 — — error GRETIA for GRATIA | | £350 | £1500 | £4200 | — |
| 1691 Second busts | | £150 | £450 | £2100 | — |
| 1692 — | | £150 | £450 | £2100 | — |

| DATE | MINTAGE | F | VF | EF | UNC |
|---|---|---|---|---|---|
| 1693 — | | £160 | £450 | £2000 | — |
| 1693 — 3 over inverted 3 | | £170 | £625 | £2500 | — |

## WILLIAM III (1694–1702)

| | | F | VF | EF | UNC |
|---|---|---|---|---|---|
| 1696 First bust, large shields, early harp | | £70 | £240 | £900 | — |
| 1696 — — B (Bristol) below bust | | £70 | £240 | £1000 | — |
| 1696 — — — C (Chester) | | £80 | £325 | £1100 | — |
| 1696 — — — E (Exeter) | | £100 | £400 | £1300 | — |
| 1696 — — — N (Norwich) | | £90 | £400 | £1300 | — |
| 1696 — — — y (York) | | £80 | £350 | £1500 | — |
| 1696 — — — — Scottish arms at date | | | | Extremely rare | |
| 1696 — — ordinary harp | | £80 | £275 | £1350 | — |
| 1696 — — — C | | £110 | £500 | £1000 | — |
| 1696 — — — E | | £100 | £500 | £1000 | — |
| 1696 — — — N | | £150 | £600 | £2250 | — |
| 1696 — Small shields, ordinary harp | | £70 | £250 | £900 | — |
| 1696 — — — B | | £90 | £300 | £1000 | — |
| 1696 — — — C | | £90 | £300 | £1200 | — |
| 1696 — — — E | | £100 | £450 | £2000 | — |
| 1696 — — — N | | £110 | £450 | £1500 | — |
| 1696 — — — y | | £100 | £500 | £1600 | — |
| 1696 Second bust | | | | Only one known | |
| 1697 First bust, large shields, ordinary harp | | £75 | £300 | £1000 | — |
| 1697 — — — GRR for GRA | | | | Extremely rare | |
| 1697 — — — B | | £80 | £300 | £1000 | — |
| 1697 — — — C | | £80 | £350 | £1100 | — |
| 1697 — — — E | | £90 | £350 | £1100 | — |
| 1697 — — — N | | £100 | £350 | £1100 | — |
| 1697 — — — y | | £90 | £350 | £1200 | — |
| 1698 — — | | £100 | £350 | £1200 | — |
| 1698/7 — — 8 over 7 | | | | Extremely rare | |
| 1699 — — | | £130 | £425 | £1600 | — |
| 1699 — — Scottish arms at date | | | | Extremely rare | |
| 1700 — — | | £120 | £375 | £1500 | — |
| 1701 — — | | £125 | £400 | £1550 | — |
| 1701 — — No stops on rev | | £150 | £600 | — | — |
| 1701 — — Elephant & Castle below | Fair £2000 | | | | |
| 1701 — — Plumes in angles on rev. | | £230 | £625 | £2400 | — |

## ANNE (1702–1714)

| | | F | VF | EF | UNC |
|---|---|---|---|---|---|
| 1703 Plain (pre-Union) | | £500 | £2200 | — | — |
| 1703 VIGO below bust | | £100 | £340 | £1100 | — |
| 1704 Plumes in angles on rev. | | £150 | £500 | £1600 | — |
| 1705 — | | £120 | £500 | £1600 | — |
| 1706 Roses & Plumes in angles on rev. | | £90 | £350 | £1200 | — |
| 1707 — | | £80 | £300 | £1100 | — |
| 1707 Plain (post-Union) | | £80 | £200 | £900 | — |
| 1707 E below bust | | £80 | £200 | £900 | — |
| 1707 — SEPTIMO edge | | | | Extremely rare | |
| 1708 Plain | | £80 | £250 | £1000 | — |
| 1708 E below bust | | £80 | £250 | £1000 | — |
| 1708 Plumes in angles on rev. | | £90 | £275 | £1100 | — |
| 1709 Plain | | £75 | £270 | £900 | — |
| 1709 E below bust | | £220 | £900 | — | — |
| 1710 Roses & Plumes in angles on rev. | | £80 | £325 | £1000 | — |
| 1712 — | | £80 | £325 | £1000 | — |
| 1713 Plain | | £80 | £325 | £1000 | — |
| 1713 Roses & Plumes in angles on rev. | | £80 | £325 | £1000 | — |
| 1714 — | | £80 | £325 | £1000 | — |
| 1714/3 4 over 3 | | £125 | £500 | — | — |

## GEORGE I (1714–1727)

| | | F | VF | EF | UNC |
|---|---|---|---|---|---|
| 1715 Roses & Plumes in angles on rev. | | £450 | £900 | £3200 | — |
| 1715 Plain edge | | | | Extremely rare | |
| 1717 — | | £450 | £900 | £3200 | — |
| 1720 — | | £425 | £900 | £3200 | — |
| 1720/17 20 over 17 | | £400 | £800 | £3000 | — |
| 1723 SSC in angles on rev. | | £400 | £800 | £2750 | — |
| 1726 Small Roses & Plumes in angles on rev... | £3500 | £22000 | — | — |

| DATE | MINTAGE | F | VF | EF | UNC |
|------|---------|---|----|----|-----|

## GEORGE II (1727–1760)

| | | | | | |
|------|---------|---|----|----|-----|
| 1731 Young head, Plain, proof only.................. | — | — | £5000 | — | |
| 1731 — Roses & Plumes in angles on rev......... | £140 | £400 | £1350 | — | |
| 1732 — — ................................................. | £140 | £400 | £1350 | — | |
| 1734 — — ................................................. | £140 | £400 | £1450 | — | |
| 1735 — — ................................................. | £150 | £400 | £1500 | — | |
| 1736 — — ................................................. | £150 | £400 | £1500 | — | |
| 1739 — Roses in angles on rev. ...................... | £140 | £370 | £1200 | — | |
| 1741/39 — — 41 over 30 ............................. | £150 | £550 | — | — | |
| 1741 — — ................................................. | £140 | £400 | £1100 | — | |
| 1743 Old head, Roses in angles on rev. ........... | £85 | £225 | £1000 | — | |
| 1745 — — ................................................. | £85 | £225 | £1000 | — | |
| 1745 — LIMA below bust.............................. | £70 | £175 | £650 | — | |
| 1746 — — ................................................. | £70 | £175 | £650 | — | |
| 1746/5 — — 6 over 5 ................................... | £80 | £220 | £800 | — | |
| 1746 — Plain, Proof ..................................... | — | — | £2250 | — | |
| 1750 — — ................................................. | £200 | £500 | £1750 | — | |
| 1751 — — ................................................. | £240 | £700 | £2000 | — | |

## GEORGE III (1760–1820)

| | | | | | |
|------|---------|---|----|----|-----|
| 1816 "Bull head" .......................... | — | £25 | £80 | £250 | £500 |
| 1817 — .................................. | 8,092,656 | £25 | £80 | £250 | £500 |
| 1817 "Small head".................. | incl. above | £25 | £80 | £250 | £500 |
| 1818 — .................................. | 2,905,056 | £25 | £80 | £250 | £500 |
| 1819/8 — 9 over 8.................... | incl. above | | | Extremely rare | |
| 1819 — .................................. | 4,790,016 | £25 | £80 | £250 | £525 |
| 1820 — .................................. | 2,396,592 | £50 | £140 | £500 | £950 |

## GEORGE IV (1820–30)

| | | | | | |
|------|---------|---|----|----|-----|
| 1820 First bust, first reverse........ | incl. above | £30 | £80 | £280 | £600 |
| 1821 — — .................................. | 1,435,104 | £30 | £80 | £280 | £600 |
| 1821 — — Proof.......................... | incl. above | — | — | — | £2000 |
| 1823 — — .................................. | 2,003,760 | £900 | £2750 | — | — |
| 1823 — Second reverse.............. | incl. above | £30 | £80 | £275 | £600 |
| 1824 — — .................................. | 465,696 | £30 | £90 | £250 | £650 |
| 1824 Second bust, third reverse . | incl. above | | | Extremely rare | |
| 1825 — — .................................. | 2,258,784 | £30 | £80 | £200 | £450 |
| 1826 — — .................................. | 2,189,088 | £30 | £80 | £200 | £450 |
| 1826 — — Proof.......................... | incl. above | — | — | — | £1500 |
| 1828 — — .................................. | 49,890 | £80 | £200 | £600 | £1100 |
| 1829 — — .................................. | 508,464 | £60 | £150 | £450 | £900 |

## WILLIAM IV (1830–37)

| | | | | | |
|------|---------|---|----|----|-----|
| 1831............................................. | — | | | Extremely rare | |
| 1831 Proof (W.W. in script & block) | — | — | — | — | £2000 |
| 1834 W.W. in block...................... | 993,168 | £30 | £80 | £300 | £700 |
| 1834 W.W. in script...................... | incl. above | £30 | £80 | £300 | £700 |
| 1835............................................. | 281,952 | £35 | £90 | £300 | £725 |
| 1836............................................. | 1,588,752 | £30 | £70 | £250 | £650 |
| 1836/5 6 over 5 ............................ | incl. above | £60 | £125 | £600 | — |
| 1837............................................. | 150,526 | £45 | £160 | £550 | £1150 |

## VICTORIA (1837–1901)

**YOUNG HEAD ISSUES**

| | | | | | |
|------|---------|---|----|----|-----|
| 1839 (two varieties) .................... | — | £900 | £3000 | £6500 | — |
| 1839 Proof.................................... | — | — | — | — | £4000 |
| 1840............................................. | 386,496 | £60 | £200 | £700 | £1600 |
| 1841............................................. | 42,768 | £900 | £2000 | £4000 | £6750 |
| 1842............................................. | 486,288 | £55 | £150 | £700 | £1400 |
| 1843............................................. | 454,608 | £140 | £450 | £1100 | £2800 |
| 1844............................................. | 1,999,008 | £45 | £110 | £550 | £1200 |
| 1845............................................. | 2,231,856 | £45 | £110 | £550 | £1200 |
| 1846............................................. | 1,539,668 | £55 | £140 | £600 | £1300 |
| 1848 Plain 8................................. | 367,488 | £150 | £450 | £1400 | £3200 |
| 1848/6 ........................................ | incl. above | £110 | £300 | £800 | £2750 |
| 1849............................................. | 261,360 | £70 | £160 | £600 | £1400 |
| 1849 Small date .......................... | incl. above | £90 | £220 | £850 | £1600 |

| DATE | MINTAGE | F | VF | EF | UNC |
|------|---------|---|----|----|----|
| 1850........................... | 484,613 | £70 | £200 | £600 | £1800 |
| 1853 Proof only ......................... | — | — | — | — | £3500 |
| 1874........................... | 2,188,599 | £25 | £70 | £250 | £550 |
| 1875........................... | 1,113,483 | £25 | £70 | £250 | £475 |
| 1876 ......................... | 633,221 | £30 | £80 | £270 | £650 |
| 1876/5 6 over 5 ...................... | incl. above | £35 | £80 | £270 | £650 |
| 1877........................... | 447,059 | £25 | £70 | £250 | £475 |
| 1878........................... | 1,466,323 | £25 | £70 | £250 | £475 |
| 1879........................... | 901,356 | £35 | £80 | £280 | £600 |
| 1880........................... | 1,346,350 | £25 | £70 | £250 | £425 |
| 1881........................... | 2,301,495 | £25 | £70 | £250 | £400 |
| 1882........................... | 808,227 | £25 | £70 | £250 | £440 |
| 1883........................... | 2,982,779 | £25 | £70 | £250 | £400 |
| 1884........................... | 1,569,175 | £25 | £70 | £250 | £400 |
| 1885........................... | 1,628,438 | £25 | £70 | £250 | £400 |
| 1886........................... | 891,767 | £25 | £70 | £250 | £410 |
| 1887 ......................... | 1,438,046 | £22 | £60 | £225 | £400 |
| **JUBILEE HEAD ISSUES** | | | | | |
| 1887 ......................... | incl. above | £8 | £14 | £30 | £75 |
| 1887 Proof................................. | 1,084 | — | — | — | £300 |
| 1888........................... | 1,428,787 | £12 | £25 | £50 | £160 |
| 1889........................... | 4,811,954 | £10 | £20 | £50 | £130 |
| 1890........................... | 3,228,111 | £12 | £22 | £70 | £160 |
| 1891........................... | 2,284,632 | £12 | £22 | £70 | £160 |
| 1892........................... | 1,710,946 | £12 | £22 | £75 | £170 |
| **OLD HEAD ISSUES** | | | | | |
| 1893........................... | 1,792,600 | £12 | £24 | £60 | £100 |
| 1893 Proof................................. | 1,312 | — | — | — | £400 |
| 1894........................... | 1,524,960 | £15 | £35 | £90 | £225 |
| 1895 ......................... | 1,772,662 | £12 | £30 | £70 | £160 |
| 1896........................... | 2,148,505 | £12 | £22 | £65 | £180 |
| 1897........................... | 1,678,643 | £12 | £22 | £65 | £160 |
| 1898........................... | 1,870,055 | £12 | £22 | £65 | £160 |
| 1899........................... | 2,865,872 | £12 | £22 | £65 | £160 |
| 1900........................... | 4,479,128 | £12 | £22 | £65 | £160 |
| 1901........................... | 1,516,570 | £12 | £22 | £65 | £160 |

| DATE | MINTAGE | F | VF | EF | UNC |
|---|---|---|---|---|---|

## EDWARD VII (1901–10)

| DATE | MINTAGE | F | VF | EF | UNC |
|---|---|---|---|---|---|
| 1902 | 1,316,008 | £12 | £30 | £80 | £145 |
| 1902 "Matt Proof" | 15,123 | — | — | — | £180 |
| 1903 | 274,840 | £175 | £550 | £2200 | £4500 |
| 1904 | 709,652 | £60 | £225 | £500 | £1500 |
| 1905 | 166,008 | £500 | £1400 | £5000 | £9000 |
| 1906 | 2,886,206 | £12 | £50 | £200 | £800 |
| 1907 | 3,693,930 | £12 | £50 | £200 | £800 |
| 1908 | 1,758,889 | £20 | £80 | £400 | £1000 |
| 1909 | 3,051,592 | £12 | £60 | £340 | £700 |
| 1910 | 2,557,685 | £12 | £45 | £110 | £425 |

## GEORGE V (1910–36)

### First issue

| DATE | MINTAGE | F | VF | EF | UNC |
|---|---|---|---|---|---|
| 1911 | 2,914,573 | £12 | £30 | £70 | £160 |
| 1911 Proof | 6,007 | — | — | — | £220 |
| 1912 | 4,700,789 | £10 | £22 | £50 | £175 |
| 1913 | 4,090,169 | £10 | £24 | £75 | £185 |
| 1914 | 18,333,003 | £7 | £12 | £40 | £65 |
| 1915 | 32,433,066 | £7 | £12 | £35 | £60 |
| 1916 | 29,530,020 | £7 | £12 | £35 | £60 |
| 1917 | 11,172,052 | £8 | £15 | £45 | £95 |
| 1918 | 29,079,592 | £7 | £12 | £35 | £70 |
| 1919 | 10,266,737 | £7 | £15 | £45 | £95 |

### Second issue—debased silver

| | | | | | |
|---|---|---|---|---|---|
| 1920 | 17,982,077 | £4 | £8 | £22 | £70 |
| 1921 | 23,677,889 | £4 | £8 | £22 | £60 |
| 1922 | 16,396,724 | £5 | £9 | £24 | £70 |
| 1923 | 26,308,526 | £6 | £8 | £20 | £45 |
| 1924 | 5,866,294 | £15 | £35 | £90 | £175 |
| 1925 | 1,413,461 | £30 | £75 | £300 | £800 |
| 1926 | 4,473,516 | £9 | £22 | £45 | £160 |

### Third issue —Modified effigy

| | | | | | |
|---|---|---|---|---|---|
| 1926 | incl. above | £6 | £14 | £40 | £100 |
| 1927 | 6,837,872 | £6 | £12 | £35 | £70 |

### Fourth issue—New shield reverse

| | | | | | |
|---|---|---|---|---|---|
| 1927 Proof | 15,000 | — | — | — | £90 |
| 1928 | 18,762,727 | £5 | £8 | £18 | £35 |
| 1929 | 17,632,636 | £5 | £8 | £18 | £35 |
| 1930 | 809,051 | £15 | £60 | £300 | £800 |
| 1931 | 11,264,468 | £5 | £8 | £18 | £35 |
| 1932 | 4,793,643 | £6 | £10 | £25 | £90 |
| 1933 | 10,311,494 | £5 | £8 | £18 | £40 |
| 1934 | 2,422,399 | £7 | £12 | £65 | £175 |
| 1935 | 7,022,216 | £5 | £8 | £15 | £22 |
| 1936 | 7,039,423 | £5 | £8 | £15 | £20 |

*George V, fourth issue, new shield reverse*

## GEORGE VI (1936–52)

| | | | | | |
|---|---|---|---|---|---|
| 1937 | 9,106,440 | — | £6 | £9 | £14 |
| 1937 Proof | 26,402 | — | — | — | £20 |
| 1938 | 6,426,478 | £5 | £6 | £15 | £25 |
| 1939 | 15,478,635 | £5 | £6 | £9 | £10 |
| 1940 | 17,948,439 | £5 | £6 | £9 | £10 |
| 1941 | 15,773,984 | £5 | £6 | £9 | £10 |
| 1942 | 31,220,090 | £5 | £6 | £9 | £10 |
| 1943 | 15,462,875 | £5 | £6 | £9 | £10 |
| 1944 | 15,255,165 | £5 | £6 | £9 | £10 |
| 1945 | 19,849,242 | £5 | £6 | £9 | £10 |
| 1946 | 22,724,873 | £5 | £6 | £9 | £10 |

### Cupro-nickel

| | | | | | |
|---|---|---|---|---|---|
| 1947 | 21,911,484 | — | £1 | £2 | £4 |
| 1948 | 71,164,703 | — | £1 | £2 | £4 |
| 1949 | 28,272,512 | — | £1 | £2 | £6 |
| 1950 | 28,335,500 | — | £1 | £2 | £6 |
| 1950 Proof | 17,513 | — | £1 | £2 | £9 |
| 1951 | 9,003,520 | — | £1 | £2 | £6 |
| 1951 Proof | 20,000 | — | — | — | £9 |
| 1952 | | | Only one known | | |

| DATE | MINTAGE | F | VF | EF | UNC |
|---|---|---|---|---|---|

## ELIZABETH II (1952–  )

| DATE | MINTAGE | F | VF | EF | UNC |
|---|---|---|---|---|---|
| 1953 | 4,333,214 | — | — | £1 | £3 |
| 1953 Proof | 40,000 | — | — | — | £8 |
| 1954 | 11,614,953 | — | £1 | £6 | £30 |
| 1955 | 23,628,726 | — | — | £1 | £6 |
| 1956 | 33,934,909 | — | — | £1 | £6 |
| 1957 | 34,200,563 | — | — | £1 | £6 |
| 1958 | 15,745,668 | — | £1 | £6 | £25 |
| 1959 | 9,028,844 | — | £1 | £9 | £30 |
| 1960 | 19,929,191 | — | — | £1 | £2 |
| 1961 | 25,887,897 | — | — | — | £2 |
| 1961 Polished dies | incl. above | — | — | £1 | £2 |
| 1962 | 24,013,312 | — | — | — | £1 |
| 1963 | 17,625,200 | — | — | — | £1 |
| 1964 | 5,973,600 | — | — | — | £1 |
| 1965 | 9,778,440 | — | — | — | £1 |
| 1966 | 13,375,200 | — | — | — | £1 |
| 1967 | 33,058,400 | — | — | — | £1 |

# FLORINS

## VICTORIA (1837–1901)

### YOUNG (CROWNED) HEAD ISSUES

**"Godless" type (without D.G.— "Dei Gratia")**

| | MINTAGE | F | VF | EF | UNC |
|---|---|---|---|---|---|
| 1848 "Godless" Pattern only plain edge | — | | | Very rare | |
| 1848 "Godless" Pattern only milled edge | — | | | Extremely rare | |
| 1849 | 413,820 | £25 | £55 | £200 | £400 |

*(Beware of recent forgeries)*

**"Gothic" type i.e. date in Roman numerals in obverse legend**

*"brit." in legend. No die no.*

| | MINTAGE | F | VF | EF | UNC |
|---|---|---|---|---|---|
| 1851 mdcccli Proof | 1,540 | | | Extremely rare | |
| 1852 mdccclii | 1,014,552 | £22 | £60 | £200 | £500 |
| 1853 mdcccliii | 3,919,950 | £22 | £55 | £200 | £550 |
| 1853 — Proof | incl. above | — | — | — | £3000 |
| 1854 mdcccliv | 550,413 | £500 | £1400 | — | — |
| 1855 mdccclv | 831,017 | £25 | £70 | £225 | £550 |
| 1856 mdccclvi | 2,201,760 | £25 | £70 | £225 | £550 |
| 1857 mdccclvii | 1,671,120 | £25 | £55 | £225 | £550 |
| 1858 mdccclviii | 2,239,380 | £22 | £55 | £225 | £550 |
| 1859 mdccclix | 2,568,060 | £22 | £55 | £200 | £550 |
| 1860 mdccclx | 1,475,100 | £35 | £80 | £250 | £700 |
| 1862 mdccclxii | 594,000 | £200 | £500 | £1200 | £3000 |
| 1863 mdccclxiii | 938,520 | £700 | £1500 | £3000 | £6000 |

*"brit" in legend. Die no. below bust*

| | MINTAGE | F | VF | EF | UNC |
|---|---|---|---|---|---|
| 1864 mdccclxiv | 1,861,200 | £22 | £55 | £220 | £525 |
| 1864 Gothic Piedfort flan | incl. above | | | Extremely rare | |
| 1865 mdccclxv | 1,580,044 | £35 | £70 | £275 | £625 |
| 1866 mdccclxvi | 914,760 | £35 | £70 | £275 | £550 |
| 1867 mdccclxvii | 423,720 | £40 | £100 | £350 | £750 |
| 1867 — only 42 arcs in border | incl. above | | | Extremely rare | |

*"britt" in legend. Die no. below bust*

| | MINTAGE | F | VF | EF | UNC |
|---|---|---|---|---|---|
| 1868 mdccclxviii | 896,940 | £30 | £75 | £300 | £700 |
| 1869 mdccclxix | 297,000 | £30 | £75 | £300 | £725 |
| 1870 mdccclxx | 1,080,648 | £20 | £55 | £200 | £500 |
| 1871 mdccclxxi | 3,425,605 | £22 | £55 | £200 | £500 |
| 1872 mdccclxxii | 7,199,690 | £22 | £55 | £175 | £450 |
| 1873 mdccclxxiii | 5,921,839 | £22 | £55 | £200 | £450 |
| 1874 mdccclxxiv | 1,642,630 | £22 | £55 | £200 | £450 |
| 1874 — iv over iii in date | incl. above | £30 | £70 | £300 | £625 |
| 1875 mdccclxxv | 1,117,030 | £20 | £55 | £200 | £475 |
| 1876 mdccclxxvi | 580,034 | £40 | £110 | £400 | £800 |
| 1877 mdccclxxvii | 682,292 | £25 | £60 | £200 | £450 |
| 1877 — 48 arcs in border no W.W. | incl. above | £25 | £60 | £200 | £450 |
| 1877 — 42 arcs | incl. above | £25 | £60 | £200 | £450 |
| 1877 — — no die number | incl. above | | | Extremely rare | |
| 1878 mdccclxxviii with die number | 1,786,680 | £20 | £55 | £200 | £425 |

"Gothic" florin

| DATE | MINTAGE | F | VF | EF | UNC |
|------|---------|---|----|----|----|
| 1879 mdccclxxix no die no ........ | 1,512,247 | | | Extremely rare | |
| 1879 — 48 arcs in border ........... | incl. above | £25 | £60 | £220 | £450 |
| 1879 — no die number .............. | incl. above | | | Extremely rare | |
| 1879 — 38 arcs, no W.W.. ......... | incl. above | £20 | £55 | £200 | £450 |
| 1880 mdccclxxx Younger portrait | — | | | Extremely rare | |
| 1880 — 34 arcs, Older portrait ... | 2,167,170 | £25 | £60 | £200 | £425 |
| 1881 mdccclxxxi — — ............... | 2,570,337 | £20 | £55 | £200 | £525 |
| 1881 — xxГi broken puncheon... | incl. above | £30 | £70 | £200 | £450 |
| 1883 mdccclxxxiii — — ............. | 3,555,667 | £20 | £50 | £170 | £400 |
| 1884 mdccclxxxiv — — ............. | 1,447,379 | £20 | £50 | £170 | £400 |
| 1885 mdccclxxxv — — .............. | 1,758,210 | £20 | £50 | £170 | £400 |
| 1886 mdccclxxxvi — — ............. | 591,773 | £20 | £50 | £170 | £400 |
| 1887 mdccclxxxvii — — ............ | 1,776,903 | £50 | £120 | £300 | £650 |
| 1887 — 46 arcs.......................... | incl. above | £50 | £120 | £350 | £700 |

**JUBILEE HEAD ISSUES**

| | | | | | |
|------|---------|---|----|----|----|
| 1887 ...................................... | incl. above | £6 | £15 | £30 | £55 |
| 1887 Proof .............................. | 1,084 | — | — | — | £225 |
| 1888 ...................................... | 1,547,540 | £7 | £15 | £45 | £120 |
| 1889 ...................................... | 2,973,561 | £8 | £18 | £50 | £140 |
| 1890 ...................................... | 1,684,737 | £10 | £25 | £80 | £225 |
| 1891 ...................................... | 836,438 | £20 | £60 | £200 | £475 |
| 1892 ...................................... | 283,401 | £30 | £100 | £325 | £800 |

**VICTORIA — OLD HEAD ISSUES**

| | | | | | |
|------|---------|---|----|----|----|
| 1893 ...................................... | 1,666,103 | £7 | £16 | £40 | £85 |
| 1893 Proof .............................. | 1,312 | — | — | — | £250 |
| 1894 ...................................... | 1,952,842 | £10 | £18 | £70 | £220 |
| 1895 ...................................... | 2,182,968 | £9 | £25 | £70 | £200 |
| 1896 ...................................... | 2,944,416 | £7 | £20 | £55 | £150 |
| 1897 ...................................... | 1,699,921 | £7 | £20 | £55 | £140 |
| 1898 ...................................... | 3,061,343 | £7 | £20 | £55 | £140 |
| 1899 ...................................... | 3,966,953 | £7 | £20 | £55 | £140 |
| 1900 ...................................... | 5,528,630 | £7 | £20 | £55 | £140 |
| 1901 ...................................... | 2,648,870 | £7 | £20 | £55 | £140 |

# EDWARD VII (1901–10)

| | | | | | |
|------|---------|---|----|----|----|
| 1902 ...................................... | 2,189,575 | £10 | £22 | £60 | £100 |
| 1902 "Matt Proof" ...................... | 15,123 | — | — | — | £130 |
| 1903 ...................................... | 1,995,298 | £10 | £35 | £120 | £550 |
| 1904 ...................................... | 2,769,932 | £12 | £40 | £150 | £500 |
| 1905 ...................................... | 1,187,596 | £60 | £160 | £600 | £1600 |
| 1906 ...................................... | 6,910,128 | £10 | £35 | £130 | £500 |
| 1907 ...................................... | 5,947,895 | £11 | £35 | £130 | £500 |
| 1908 ...................................... | 3,280,010 | £18 | £55 | £350 | £900 |
| 1909 ...................................... | 3,482,829 | £15 | £50 | £240 | £700 |
| 1910 ...................................... | 5,650,713 | £14 | £35 | £100 | £300 |

# GEORGE V (1910–36)

*First issue*

| | | | | | |
|------|---------|---|----|----|----|
| 1911 ...................................... | 5,951,284 | £6 | £12 | £40 | £85 |
| 1911 Proof .............................. | 6,007 | — | — | — | £140 |
| 1912 ...................................... | 8,571,731 | £6 | £15 | £35 | £125 |
| 1913 ...................................... | 4,545,278 | £10 | £25 | £50 | £170 |
| 1914 ...................................... | 21,252,701 | £6 | £18 | £28 | £60 |
| 1915 ...................................... | 12,367,939 | £7 | £18 | £26 | £60 |
| 1916 ...................................... | 21,064,337 | £6 | £18 | £25 | £60 |
| 1917 ...................................... | 11,181,617 | £7 | £22 | £35 | £90 |
| 1918 ...................................... | 29,211,792 | £6 | £18 | £28 | £90 |
| 1919 ...................................... | 9,469,292 | £8 | £20 | £40 | £90 |

*Second issue* — *debased silver*

| | | | | | |
|------|---------|---|----|----|----|
| 1920 ...................................... | 15,387,833 | £4 | £12 | £40 | £85 |
| 1921 ...................................... | 34,863,895 | £4 | £12 | £40 | £65 |
| 1922 ...................................... | 23,861,044 | £4 | £12 | £40 | £65 |
| 1923 ...................................... | 21,546,533 | £4 | £10 | £30 | £60 |
| 1924 ...................................... | 4,582,372 | £12 | £35 | £95 | £240 |
| 1925 ...................................... | 1,404,136 | £30 | £75 | £300 | £800 |
| 1926 ...................................... | 5,125,410 | £7 | £22 | £50 | £145 |

*Fourth issue* — *new reverse*

| | | | | | |
|------|---------|---|----|----|----|
| 1927 Proof only.......................... | 101,497 | — | — | — | £100 |
| 1928 ...................................... | 11,087,186 | £4 | £7 | £15 | £40 |

| DATE | MINTAGE | F | VF | EF | UNC |
|---|---|---|---|---|---|
| 1929 | 16,397,279 | £4 | £7 | £16 | £35 |
| 1930 | 5,753,568 | £4 | £7 | £20 | £45 |
| 1931 | 6,556,331 | £4 | £7 | £18 | £35 |
| 1932 | 717,041 | £12 | £30 | £225 | £600 |
| 1933 | 8,685,303 | £4 | £7 | £18 | £40 |
| 1935 | 7,540,546 | £4 | £7 | £14 | £30 |
| 1936 | 9,897,448 | £4 | £7 | £14 | £30 |

## GEORGE VI (1936–52)

| DATE | MINTAGE | F | VF | EF | UNC |
|---|---|---|---|---|---|
| 1937 | 13,006,781 | £4 | £5 | £7 | £12 |
| 1937 Proof | 26,402 | — | — | — | £15 |
| 1938 | 7,909,388 | £6 | £8 | £15 | £30 |
| 1939 | 20,850,607 | £4 | £5 | £8 | £10 |
| 1940 | 18,700,338 | £4 | £5 | £7 | £12 |
| 1941 | 24,451,079 | £4 | £5 | £7 | £9 |
| 1942 | 39,895,243 | £4 | £5 | £7 | £9 |
| 1943 | 26,711,987 | £4 | £5 | £7 | £9 |
| 1944 | 27,560,005 | £4 | £5 | £7 | £9 |
| 1945 | 25,858,049 | £4 | £5 | £7 | £9 |
| 1946 | 22,300,254 | £4 | £5 | £7 | £9 |
| *Cupro-nickel* | | | | | |
| 1947 | 22,910,085 | — | — | £1 | £3 |
| 1948 | 67,553,636 | — | — | £1 | £3 |
| 1949 | 28,614,939 | — | — | £1 | £5 |
| 1950 | 24,357,490 | — | — | £2 | £7 |
| 1950 Proof | 17,513 | — | — | £1 | £9 |
| 1951 | 27,411,747 | — | — | £2 | £8 |
| 1951 Proof | 20,000 | — | — | — | £9 |

## ELIZABETH II (1952–  )

| DATE | MINTAGE | F | VF | EF | UNC |
|---|---|---|---|---|---|
| 1953 | 11,958,710 | — | — | — | £2 |
| 1953 Proof | 40,000 | — | — | — | £6 |
| 1954 | 13,085,422 | — | — | £6 | £30 |
| 1955 | 25,887,253 | — | — | £1 | £3 |
| 1956 | 47,824,500 | — | — | £1 | £3 |
| 1957 | 33,071,282 | — | — | £4 | £25 |
| 1958 | 9,564,580 | — | — | £3 | £25 |
| 1959 | 14,080,319 | — | — | £4 | £30 |
| 1960 | 13,831,782 | — | — | £1 | £4 |
| 1961 | 37,735,315 | — | — | £1 | £2 |
| 1962 | 35,147,903 | — | — | £1 | £2 |
| 1963 | 26,471,000 | — | — | £1 | £2 |
| 1964 | 16,539,000 | — | — | £1 | £2 |
| 1965 | 48,163,000 | — | — | — | £1.50 |
| 1966 | 83,999,000 | — | — | — | £1.50 |
| 1967 | 39,718,000 | — | — | — | £1.50 |

# SHILLINGS

## OLIVER CROMWELL

| | | | | |
|---|---|---|---|---|
| 1658 | £700 | £1400 | £3250 | — |
| 1658 Dutch Copy | | Extremely rare | | |

## CHARLES II (1660–85)

| | | | | |
|---|---|---|---|---|
| 1663 First bust | £110 | £450 | £1200 | — |
| 1663 — GARTIA error | | Extremely rare | | |
| 1663 — Irish & Scottish shields transposed | £225 | £800 | — | — |
| 1666 — Elephant below bust | £500 | £1500 | £6000 | — |
| 1666 "Guinea" head, elephant | £1800 | £4500 | — | — |
| 1666 Second bust | | Extremely rare | | |
| 1668 — | £110 | £325 | £1200 | — |
| 1668/7 — 8 over 7 | £150 | £500 | — | — |
| 1668 Second bust | £100 | £400 | £1200 | — |
| 1669/6 First bust variety | | Extremely rare | | |
| 1669 | | Extremely rare | | |
| 1669 Second bust | | Extremely rare | | |

| DATE | F | VF | EF | UNC |
|---|---|---|---|---|
| 1670 — ........................................................ | £140 | £500 | £1750 | — |
| 1671 — ........................................................ | £140 | £500 | £1750 | — |
| 1671 — Plume below, plume in centre rev. ....... | £400 | £1000 | £3500 | — |
| 1672 — ........................................................ | £140 | £550 | £1750 | — |
| 1673 — ........................................................ | £140 | £550 | £1750 | — |
| 1673 — Plume below, plume in centre rev. ....... | £400 | £1100 | £3750 | — |
| 1673/2 — 3 over 2........................................ | £175 | £600 | — | — |
| 1674/3 — 4 over 3........................................ | £150 | £550 | — | — |
| 1674 — ........................................................ | £150 | £500 | £2000 | — |
| 1674 — Plume below bust, plume in centre rev. | £350 | £1100 | £3500 | — |
| 1674 — Plume rev. only.................................. | £650 | £2000 | £4000 | — |
| 1674 Third bust ............................................ | £450 | £1600 | — | — |
| 1675 Second bust ......................................... | £200 | £800 | — | — |
| 1675/4 — 5 over 4........................................ | £220 | £850 | — | — |
| 1675 — Plume below bust, plume in centre rev. | £400 | £1100 | £4250 | — |
| 1675 Third bust ............................................ | £350 | £1250 | — | — |
| 1675/3 — 5 over 3........................................ | £300 | £1100 | — | — |
| 1676 Second bust......................................... | £125 | £450 | £1600 | — |
| 1676/5 — 6 over 5........................................ | £150 | £550 | — | — |
| 1676 — Plume below bust, plume in centre rev. | £400 | £1400 | £4500 | — |
| 1677 — ........................................................ | £120 | £500 | £1800 | — |
| 1677 — Plume below bust ............................. | £700 | £2200 | £6000 | — |
| 1678 — ........................................................ | £140 | £500 | £1600 | — |
| 1678/7 — 8 over 7........................................ | £160 | £700 | — | — |
| 1679 — ........................................................ | £140 | £500 | £1750 | — |
| 1679 — Plume below bust, plume in centre rev. | £400 | £1100 | £4250 | — |
| 1679 — Plume below bust ............................. | £700 | £2400 | £4500 | — |
| 1679 — 9 over 7........................................... | £160 | £600 | — | — |
| 1680 — ........................................................ | | | Extremely rare | |
| 1680 — Plume below bust, plume in centre rev. | £850 | £2500 | £5000 | — |
| 1680/79 — — 80 over 79 .............................. | £850 | £2500 | — | — |
| 1681 — ........................................................ | £300 | £850 | £3000 | — |
| 1681 — 1 over 0.......................................... | £320 | £900 | £3100 | — |
| 1681/0 Elephant & Castle below bust .............. | £2500 | £8000 | — | — |
| 1682/1 — 2 over 1........................................ | £900 | £2750 | — | — |
| 1683 — ........................................................ | | | Extremely rare | |
| 1683 Fourth (Larger) bust................................ | £220 | £700 | £2250 | — |
| 1684 — ........................................................ | £220 | £700 | £2250 | — |

## JAMES II (1685–88)

| | F | VF | EF | UNC |
|---|---|---|---|---|
| 1685............................................................ | £160 | £500 | £1600 | — |
| 1685 Plume in centre rev. rev ........................... | | | Extremely rare | |
| 1685 No stops on rev. .................................... | £220 | £650 | — | — |
| 1686............................................................ | £200 | £550 | £1850 | — |
| 1686/5 6 over 5 ............................................ | £225 | £600 | £1900 | — |
| 1687............................................................ | £200 | £600 | £1900 | — |
| 1687/6 7 over 6 ............................................ | £200 | £550 | £2000 | — |
| 1688............................................................ | £200 | £600 | £2000 | — |
| 1688/7 last 8 over 7....................................... | £200 | £500 | £1900 | — |

## WILLIAM & MARY (1688–94)

| | F | VF | EF | UNC |
|---|---|---|---|---|
| 1692 ........................................................... | £175 | £500 | £2100 | — |
| 1692 inverted 1.............................................. | £210 | £550 | £2200 | — |
| 1693............................................................ | £175 | £500 | £2100 | — |

## WILLIAM III (1694–1702)

*Provincially produced shillings carry privy marks or initials below the bust:*
*B: Bristol. C: Chester. E: Exeter. N: Norwich. Y or y: York.*

| | F | VF | EF | UNC |
|---|---|---|---|---|
| 1695 First bust ............................................. | £40 | £120 | £600 | — |
| 1696 — ........................................................ | £40 | £100 | £425 | — |
| 1696 — no stops on rev. ................................ | £60 | £140 | £750 | — |
| 1696 — MAB for MAG.................................... | | | Extremely rare | |
| 1696 — 1669 error ....................................... | | | Extremely rare | |
| 1696 — 1669 various GVLELMVS errors .......... | | | Extremely rare | |
| 1696 — B below bust ..................................... | £55 | £150 | £750 | — |
| 1696 — C .................................................... | £55 | £150 | £750 | — |
| 1696 — E..................................................... | £55 | £160 | £800 | — |
| 1696 — N..................................................... | £50 | £150 | £700 | — |

| DATE | F | VF | EF | UNC |
|---|---|---|---|---|
| 1696 — y | £55 | £130 | £650 | — |
| 1696 — Y | £50 | £130 | £650 | — |
| 1696 Second bust | | Only one known | | |
| 1696 Third bust C below | £160 | £400 | £1250 | — |
| 1696 — Y | | Extremely rare | | |
| 1697 First bust | £50 | £110 | £400 | — |
| 1697 — GRI for GRA error | | Extremely rare | | |
| 1697 — Scottish & Irish shields transposed | | Extremely rare | | |
| 1697 — Irish arms at date | | Extremely rare | | |
| 1697 — no stops on rev | £55 | £180 | £700 | — |
| 1697 — GVLELMVS error | | Extremely rare | | |
| 1697 — B | £55 | £150 | £750 | — |
| 1697 — C | £55 | £140 | £750 | — |
| 1697 — E | £55 | £140 | £750 | — |
| 1697 — N | £55 | £130 | £725 | — |
| 1697 — — no stops on obv | | Extremely rare | | |
| 1697 — y | £55 | £150 | £650 | — |
| 1697 — — arms of France & Ireland transposed | | Extremely rare | | |
| 1697 — Y | £50 | £140 | £600 | — |
| 1697 Third bust | £45 | £125 | £550 | — |
| 1697 — B | £55 | £140 | £600 | — |
| 1697 — C | £55 | £140 | £650 | — |
| 1697 — — Fr.a error | £150 | £450 | — | — |
| 1697 — — no stops on obv | £80 | £275 | — | — |
| 1697 — — arms of Scotland at date | | Extremely rare | | |
| 1697 — E | £55 | £140 | £700 | — |
| 1697 — N | £55 | £140 | £700 | — |
| 1697 — y | £55 | £140 | £675 | — |
| 1697 Third bust variety | £50 | £130 | £450 | — |
| 1697 — B | £55 | £150 | £700 | — |
| 1697 — C | £110 | £525 | — | — |
| 1698 — | £70 | £200 | £750 | — |
| 1698 — Plumes in angles of rev. | £200 | £500 | £1750 | — |
| 1698 Fourth bust "Flaming hair" | £140 | £475 | £1800 | — |
| 1699 — | £110 | £400 | £1250 | — |
| 1699 Fifth bust | £100 | £300 | £1000 | — |
| 1699 — Plumes in angles on rev. | £150 | £450 | £1800 | — |
| 1699 — Roses in angles on rev. | £160 | £500 | £1800 | — |
| 1700 — | £65 | £120 | £525 | — |
| 1700 — Small round oo in date | £65 | £120 | £525 | — |
| 1700 — no stop after DEI | | Extremely rare | | |
| 1700 — Plume below bust | £2000 | £8000 | — | — |
| 1701 — | £80 | £220 | £700 | — |
| 1701 — Plumes in angles on rev. | £150 | £550 | £1800 | — |

*William III First bust*

## ANNE (1702–14)

| DATE | F | VF | EF | UNC |
|---|---|---|---|---|
| 1702 First bust (pre-Union with Scotland) | £80 | £300 | £700 | — |
| 1702 — Plumes in angles on rev. | £90 | £275 | £800 | — |
| 1702 — VIGO below bust | £70 | £220 | £650 | — |
| 1702 — — colon before ANNA | | Extremely rare | | |
| 1703 Second bust, VIGO below | £65 | £180 | £600 | — |
| 1704 — Plain | £500 | £1800 | — | — |
| 1704 — Plumes in angles on rev. | £80 | £200 | £750 | — |
| 1705 — Plain | £75 | £200 | £650 | — |
| 1705 — Plumes in angles on rev. | £70 | £200 | £700 | — |
| 1705 — Roses & Plumes in angles on rev. | £70 | £200 | £650 | — |
| 1707 — — | £60 | £180 | £600 | — |
| 1707 Second bust (post-Union) E below bust | £50 | £125 | £500 | — |
| 1707 — E* below bust | £70 | £200 | £700 | — |
| 1707 Third bust, Plain | £35 | £100 | £400 | — |
| 1707 — Plumes in angles on rev. | £50 | £160 | £750 | — |
| 1707 — E below bust | £40 | £90 | £450 | — |
| 1707 "Edinburgh" bust, E* below | | Extremely rare | | |
| 1708 Second bust, E below | £50 | £100 | £450 | — |
| 1708 — E* below bust | £55 | £165 | £700 | — |
| 1708/7 — — 8 over 7 | | Extremely rare | | |
| 1708 — Roses & Plumes in angles on rev. | £80 | £275 | £650 | — |

*Anne, VIGO below bust*

| DATE | MINTAGE | F | VF | EF | UNC |
|---|---|---|---|---|---|
| 1708 Third bust, Plain | | £40 | £100 | £350 | — |
| 1708 — Plumes in angles on rev. | | £70 | £200 | £550 | — |
| 1708 Third bust, E below bust | | £60 | £175 | £600 | — |
| 1708/7 — — 8 over 7 | | £200 | £450 | — | — |
| 1708 — Roses & Plumes in angles on rev. | | £70 | £180 | £550 | — |
| 1708 "Edinburgh" bust, E* below | | £60 | £170 | £525 | — |
| 1709 Third bust, Plain | | £50 | £125 | £500 | — |
| 1709 "Edinburgh" bust, E* below | | £50 | £170 | £650 | — |
| 1709 — E no star (filled in die?) | | £70 | £160 | £550 | — |
| 1710 Third bust, Roses & Plumes in angles | | £60 | £140 | £600 | — |
| 1710 Fourth bust, Roses & Plumes in angles | | £60 | £150 | £600 | — |
| 1711 Third bust, Plain | | £70 | £160 | £425 | — |
| 1711 Fourth bust, Plain | | £30 | £75 | £220 | — |
| 1712 — Roses & Plumes in angles on rev. | | £60 | £120 | £400 | — |
| 1713 — — | | £60 | £120 | £375 | — |
| 1713/2 — 3 over 2 | | £60 | £200 | — | — |
| 1714 — — | | £60 | £100 | £325 | — |
| 1714/3 — | | | | Extremely rare | |

## GEORGE I (1714–27)

| DATE | MINTAGE | F | VF | EF | UNC |
|---|---|---|---|---|---|
| 1715 First bust, Roses & Plumes in angles on rev. | £80 | £200 | £850 | — |
| 1716 — — | | £150 | £500 | £1800 | — |
| 1717 — — | | £90 | £300 | £1250 | — |
| 1718 — — | | £70 | £225 | £750 | — |
| 1719 — — | | £120 | £400 | £1450 | — |
| 1720 — — | | £70 | £175 | £450 | — |
| 1720/18 — — | | £150 | £500 | £1400 | — |
| 1720 — Plain | | £40 | £100 | £450 | — |
| 1721 — Roses & Plumes in angles on rev. | | £100 | £350 | £1500 | — |
| 1721/0 — — 1 over 0 | | £70 | £220 | £850 | — |
| 1721 — Plain | | £120 | £450 | £1250 | — |
| 1721/19 — — 21 over 19 | | £125 | £350 | — | — |
| 1721/18 21 over 18 error, Plumes & Roses | | £500 | £1800 | — | — |
| 1722 — Roses & Plumes in angles on rev. | | £80 | £220 | £900 | — |
| 1723 — — | | £90 | £240 | £1000 | — |
| 1723 — SSC rev., Arms of France at date | | £100 | £275 | £750 | — |
| 1723 — SSC in angles on rev | | £35 | £110 | £240 | — |
| 1723 Second bust, SSC in angles on rev. | | £50 | £160 | £525 | — |
| 1723 — Roses & Plumes in angles | | £90 | £240 | £1000 | — |
| 1723 — WCC (Welsh Copper Co) below bust | | £550 | £1500 | £5000 | — |
| 1724 — Roses & Plumes in angles on rev. | | £80 | £200 | £750 | — |
| 1724 — WCC below bust | | £550 | £1500 | £5000 | — |
| 1725 — Roses & Plumes in angles on rev. | | £80 | £200 | £1000 | — |
| 1725 — — no stops on obv. | | £90 | £225 | £1100 | — |
| 1725 — WCC below bust | | £600 | £1600 | £5250 | — |
| 1726 — — Roses & Plumes | | £650 | £1750 | £6250 | — |
| 1726 — WCC below bust | | £550 | £1600 | £5500 | — |
| 1727 — — | | | | Extremely rare | |
| 1727 — — no stops on obv | | | | Extremely rare | |

## GEORGE II (1727–60)

*George II Young head*

| DATE | MINTAGE | F | VF | EF | UNC |
|---|---|---|---|---|---|
| 1727 Young head, Plumes in angles on rev. | | £75 | £300 | £950 | — |
| 1727 — Roses & Plumes in angles on rev. | | £60 | £180 | £650 | — |
| 1728 — — | | £65 | £180 | £650 | — |
| 1728 — Plain | | £75 | £220 | £700 | — |
| 1729 — Roses & Plumes in angles on rev. | | £60 | £200 | £700 | — |
| 1731 — — | | £70 | £200 | £700 | — |
| 1731 — Plumes in angles on rev. | | £100 | £400 | £1250 | — |
| 1732 — Roses & Plumes in angles on rev. | | £65 | £200 | £750 | — |
| 1734 — — | | £65 | £200 | £700 | — |
| 1735 — — | | £65 | £200 | £700 | — |
| 1736 — — | | £65 | £200 | £700 | — |
| 1736/5 — — 6 over 5 | | £70 | £200 | £800 | — |
| 1737 — — | | £65 | £200 | £650 | — |
| 1739 — Roses in angles on rev. | | £50 | £160 | £450 | — |
| 1739/7 — — 9 over 7 | | | | Extremely rare | |
| 1741 — — | | £50 | £160 | £450 | — |
| 1741/39 — — 41 over 39 | | | | Extremely rare | |
| 1743 Old head, Roses in angles on rev. | | £30 | £80 | £325 | — |
| 1745 — — | | £30 | £80 | £325 | — |

| DATE | MINTAGE | F | VF | EF | UNC |
|------|---------|---|----|----|-----|
| 1745 — — LIMA below bust | | £30 | £90 | £325 | — |
| 1745/3 — — — 5 over 3 | | £60 | £175 | £400 | — |
| 1746 — — — | | £50 | £175 | £650 | — |
| 1746/5 — — — 6 over 5 | | £100 | £300 | — | — |
| 1746 — Plain, Proof | — | — | £2000 | — | |
| 1747 — Roses in angles on rev. | | £45 | £100 | £375 | — |
| 1750 — Plain | | £40 | £130 | £375 | — |
| 1750/6 — — 0 over 6 | | £60 | £150 | £500 | — |
| 1751 — — | | £100 | £275 | £750 | — |
| 1758 — — | | £20 | £50 | £140 | — |

*George II
Old head*

## GEORGE III (1760–1820)

| | MINTAGE | F | VF | EF | UNC |
|--|---------|---|----|----|-----|
| 1763 "Northumberland" bust | | £450 | £800 | £1500 | — |
| 1787 rev. no semée of hearts in 4th shield | | £15 | £30 | £90 | — |
| 1787 — No stop over head | | £15 | £30 | £90 | — |
| 1787 — No stop at date | | £15 | £30 | £90 | — |
| 1787 — No stops on obv | | £18 | £35 | £95 | — |
| 1787 rev. with semée of hearts in shield | | £15 | £30 | £95 | — |
| 1798 "Dorrien Magens" bust | — | — | — | £18000 | |

**NEW COINAGE—shield in garter reverse**

| | MINTAGE | F | VF | EF | UNC |
|--|---------|---|----|----|-----|
| 1816 | — | £8 | £22 | £50 | £110 |
| 1817 | 3,031,360 | £8 | £22 | £50 | £110 |
| 1817 GEOE for GEOR | incl. above | £110 | £250 | £600 | — |
| 1818 | 1,342,440 | £9 | £25 | £90 | £160 |
| 1819 | 7,595,280 | £8 | £22 | £50 | £110 |
| 1819/8 9 over 8 | incl. above | £18 | £40 | £90 | — |
| 1820 | 7,975,440 | £8 | £22 | £50 | £110 |

## GEORGE IV (1820–30)

| | MINTAGE | F | VF | EF | UNC |
|--|---------|---|----|----|-----|
| 1821 First bust, first reverse | 2,463,120 | £10 | £40 | £150 | £400 |
| 1821 — — Proof | incl. above | — | — | — | £1100 |
| 1823 — Second reverse | 693,000 | £40 | £75 | £250 | £550 |
| 1824 — — | 4,158,000 | £10 | £40 | £150 | £375 |
| 1825 — — | 2,459,160 | £20 | £50 | £150 | £500 |
| 1825/3 — — 5 over 3 | incl. above | | | Extremely rare | |
| 1825 Second bust, third reverse . | incl. above | £6 | £20 | £60 | £200 |
| 1825 — — Roman I | incl. above | | | Extremely rare | |
| 1826 — — | 6,351,840 | £6 | £20 | £60 | £200 |
| 1826 — — Proof | incl. above | — | — | — | £500 |
| 1827 — — | 574,200 | £30 | £70 | £200 | £475 |
| 1829 — — | 879,120 | £20 | £60 | £175 | £425 |

## WILLIAM IV (1830–37)

| | MINTAGE | F | VF | EF | UNC |
|--|---------|---|----|----|-----|
| 1831 Proof only | — | — | — | — | £750 |
| 1834 | 3,223,440 | £15 | £35 | £170 | £400 |
| 1835 | 1,449,360 | £15 | £35 | £170 | £400 |
| 1836 | 3,567,960 | £15 | £35 | £170 | £400 |
| 1837 | 478,160 | £20 | £60 | £200 | £500 |

## VICTORIA (1837–1901)

**YOUNG HEAD ISSUES**
*First head*

| | MINTAGE | F | VF | EF | UNC |
|--|---------|---|----|----|-----|
| 1838 WW on truncation | 1,956,240 | £20 | £50 | £200 | £400 |
| 1839 — | 5,666,760 | £20 | £50 | £200 | £400 |

*Second head*

| | MINTAGE | F | VF | EF | UNC |
|--|---------|---|----|----|-----|
| 1839 WW on truncation, Proof only | incl. above | — | — | — | £750 |
| 1839 no WW | incl. above | £20 | £50 | £180 | £400 |
| 1840 | 1,639,440 | £20 | £50 | £180 | £400 |
| 1841 | 875,160 | £22 | £50 | £180 | £400 |
| 1842 | 2,094,840 | £20 | £45 | £170 | £400 |
| 1843 | 1,465,200 | £20 | £50 | £180 | £450 |
| 1844 | 4,466,880 | £15 | £40 | £150 | £340 |
| 1845 | 4,082,760 | £15 | £40 | £150 | £340 |
| 1846 | 4,031,280 | £15 | £40 | £150 | £340 |
| 1848 last 8 of date over 6 | 1,041,480 | £80 | £160 | £600 | £1000 |

| DATE | MINTAGE | F | VF | EF | UNC |
|---|---|---|---|---|---|
| 1849 | 845,480 | £25 | £60 | £200 | £600 |
| 1850 | 685,080 | £700 | £1400 | £3000 | £6000 |
| 1850/49 | incl. above | £700 | £1500 | £4000 | — |
| 1851 | 470,071 | £40 | £110 | £400 | £700 |
| 1852 | 1,306,574 | £15 | £35 | £125 | £350 |
| 1853 | 4,256,188 | £15 | £35 | £125 | £350 |
| 1853 Proof | incl. above | — | — | — | £1100 |
| 1854 | 552,414 | £200 | £450 | £1200 | £2750 |
| 1854/1 4 over 1 | incl. above | £200 | £800 | — | — |
| 1855 | 1,368,400 | £12 | £30 | £110 | £250 |
| 1856 | 3,168,000 | £12 | £30 | £110 | £250 |
| 1857 | 2,562,120 | £12 | £30 | £110 | £250 |
| 1857 error F:G with inverted G | incl. above | £150 | £500 | — | — |
| 1858 | 3,108,600 | £12 | £30 | £110 | £300 |
| 1859 | 4,561,920 | £12 | £30 | £110 | £275 |
| 1860 | 1,671,120 | £12 | £30 | £110 | £350 |
| 1861 | 1,382,040 | £14 | £40 | £150 | £450 |
| 1862 | 954,360 | £50 | £120 | £300 | £1000 |
| 1863 | 859,320 | £110 | £300 | £750 | £1600 |
| 1863/1 3 over 1 | | | | Extremely rare | |

*Victoria Jubilee head*

*Die no. added above date up to 1879*

| DATE | MINTAGE | F | VF | EF | UNC |
|---|---|---|---|---|---|
| 1864 | 4,518,360 | £10 | £30 | £110 | £225 |
| 1865 | 5,619,240 | £10 | £30 | £110 | £225 |
| 1866 | 4,984,600 | £10 | £30 | £110 | £225 |
| 1866 error BBITANNIAR | incl. above | £80 | £250 | £800 | — |
| 1867 | 2,166,120 | £10 | £35 | £110 | £260 |

**Third head**—with die no

| DATE | MINTAGE | F | VF | EF | UNC |
|---|---|---|---|---|---|
| 1867 | incl. above | £100 | £400 | — | — |
| 1868 | 3,330,360 | £10 | £40 | £110 | £250 |
| 1869 | 736,560 | £15 | £50 | £120 | £300 |
| 1870 | 1,467,471 | £10 | £40 | £100 | £250 |
| 1871 | 4,910,010 | £10 | £40 | £100 | £250 |
| 1872 | 8,897,781 | £10 | £40 | £100 | £250 |
| 1873 | 6,489,598 | £10 | £40 | £100 | £250 |
| 1874 | 5,503,747 | £10 | £40 | £100 | £250 |
| 1875 | 4,353,983 | £10 | £40 | £100 | £250 |
| 1876 | 1,057,487 | £10 | £40 | £100 | £300 |
| 1877 | 2,989,703 | £10 | £40 | £100 | £250 |
| 1878 | 3,127,131 | £10 | £40 | £100 | £250 |
| 1879 | 3,611,507 | £20 | £60 | £200 | £500 |

**Fourth head**—no die no

| DATE | MINTAGE | F | VF | EF | UNC |
|---|---|---|---|---|---|
| 1879 no Die no. | incl. above | £8 | £25 | £75 | £185 |
| 1880 | 4,842,786 | £8 | £25 | £75 | £185 |
| 1881 | 5,255,332 | £8 | £25 | £75 | £185 |
| 1882 | 1,611,786 | £20 | £65 | £200 | £425 |
| 1883 | 7,281,450 | £8 | £25 | £65 | £170 |
| 1884 | 3,923,993 | £8 | £25 | £65 | £170 |
| 1885 | 3,336,526 | £8 | £25 | £65 | £170 |
| 1886 | 2,086,819 | £8 | £25 | £65 | £170 |
| 1887 | 4,034,133 | £8 | £25 | £65 | £170 |

## JUBILEE HEAD ISSUES

| DATE | MINTAGE | F | VF | EF | UNC |
|---|---|---|---|---|---|
| 1887 | incl. above | £4 | £8 | £15 | £40 |
| 1887 Proof | 1,084 | — | — | — | £200 |
| 1888 | 4,526,856 | £6 | £10 | £25 | £60 |
| 1889 | 7,039,628 | £35 | £90 | £300 | — |
| 1889 Large bust (until 1892) | incl. above | £6 | £12 | £45 | £75 |
| 1890 | 8,794,042 | £6 | £12 | £45 | £75 |
| 1891 | 5,665,348 | £6 | £12 | £45 | £80 |
| 1892 | 4,591,622 | £6 | £12 | £45 | £100 |

*Victoria Old or Veiled head*

## OLD HEAD ISSUES

| DATE | MINTAGE | F | VF | EF | UNC |
|---|---|---|---|---|---|
| 1893 | 7,039,074 | £5 | £10 | £30 | £65 |
| 1893 small lettering | incl. above | £5 | £10 | £30 | £65 |
| 1893 Proof | 1,312 | — | — | — | £175 |
| 1894 | 5,953,152 | £9 | £25 | £60 | £140 |
| 1895 | 8,880,651 | £9 | £25 | £55 | £140 |
| 1896 | 9,264,551 | £7 | £15 | £40 | £80 |
| 1897 | 6,270,364 | £7 | £12 | £40 | £75 |
| 1898 | 9,768,703 | £7 | £12 | £40 | £70 |
| 1899 | 10,965,382 | £7 | £12 | £40 | £70 |
| 1900 | 10,937,590 | £7 | £12 | £40 | £75 |
| 1901 | 3,426,294 | £7 | £12 | £40 | £70 |

| DATE | MINTAGE | F | VF | EF | UNC |
|---|---|---|---|---|---|

## EDWARD VII (1901–10)

| DATE | MINTAGE | F | VF | EF | UNC |
|---|---|---|---|---|---|
| 1902 | 7,809,481 | £5 | £15 | £45 | £80 |
| 1902 Proof matt | 13,123 | – | – | – | £95 |
| 1903 | 2,061,823 | £10 | £35 | £140 | £475 |
| 1904 | 2,040,161 | £8 | £35 | £120 | £440 |
| 1905 | 488,390 | £100 | £300 | £1100 | £3500 |
| 1906 | 10,791,025 | £5 | £12 | £40 | £120 |
| 1907 | 14,083,418 | £5 | £12 | £40 | £125 |
| 1908 | 3,806,969 | £10 | £25 | £150 | £450 |
| 1909 | 5,664,982 | £9 | £22 | £110 | £350 |
| 1910 | 26,547,236 | £5 | £10 | £45 | £100 |

## GEORGE V (1910–36)

### First issue

| DATE | MINTAGE | F | VF | EF | UNC |
|---|---|---|---|---|---|
| 1911 | 20,065,901 | £4 | £8 | £20 | £55 |
| 1911 Proof | 6,007 | – | – | – | £90 |
| 1912 | 15,594,009 | £5 | £10 | £25 | £75 |
| 1913 | 9,011,509 | £7 | £20 | £50 | £140 |
| 1914 | 23,415,843 | £4 | £7 | £25 | £55 |
| 1915 | 39,279,024 | £4 | £7 | £25 | £55 |
| 1916 | 35,862,015 | £4 | £7 | £25 | £55 |
| 1917 | 22,202,608 | £4 | £7 | £25 | £60 |
| 1918 | 34,915,934 | £4 | £7 | £25 | £55 |
| 1919 | 10,823,824 | £5 | £8 | £30 | £65 |

### Second issue — debased silver

| DATE | MINTAGE | F | VF | EF | UNC |
|---|---|---|---|---|---|
| 1920 | 22,825,142 | £2 | £4 | £20 | £45 |
| 1921 | 22,648,763 | £2 | £4 | £20 | £45 |
| 1922 | 27,215,738 | £2 | £4 | £20 | £45 |
| 1923 | 14,575,243 | £2 | £4 | £20 | £45 |
| 1924 | 9,250,095 | £7 | £15 | £50 | £150 |
| 1925 | 5,418,764 | £6 | £10 | £40 | £110 |
| 1926 | 22,516,453 | £3 | £8 | £28 | £110 |

*George V First obverse*

### Third issue — Modified bust

| DATE | MINTAGE | F | VF | EF | UNC |
|---|---|---|---|---|---|
| 1926 | incl. above | £2 | £4 | £25 | £55 |
| 1927 — | 9,247,344 | £2 | £4 | £25 | £55 |

### Fourth issue — large lion and crown on rev., date in legend

| DATE | MINTAGE | F | VF | EF | UNC |
|---|---|---|---|---|---|
| 1927 | incl. above | £2 | £4 | £20 | £40 |
| 1927 Proof | 15,000 | – | – | – | £60 |
| 1928 | 18,136,778 | £2 | £4 | £15 | £40 |
| 1929 | 19,343,006 | £2 | £4 | £15 | £40 |
| 1930 | 3,172,092 | £2 | £4 | £18 | £50 |
| 1931 | 6,993,926 | £2 | £4 | £15 | £40 |
| 1932 | 12,168,101 | £2 | £4 | £15 | £45 |
| 1933 | 11,511,624 | £2 | £4 | £15 | £35 |
| 1934 | 6,138,463 | £2 | £4 | £18 | £50 |
| 1935 | 9,183,462 | – | £4 | £10 | £22 |
| 1936 | 11,910,613 | – | £4 | £9 | £20 |

## GEORGE VI (1936–52)

*George V Second obverse*

E = England rev. (lion standing on large crown). S = Scotland rev. (lion seated on small crown holding sword and mace)

| DATE | MINTAGE | F | VF | EF | UNC |
|---|---|---|---|---|---|
| 1937 E | 8,359,122 | – | £2 | £4 | £6 |
| 1937 E Proof | 26,402 | – | – | – | £18 |
| 1937 S | 6,748,875 | – | £2 | £4 | £6 |
| 1937 S Proof | 26,402 | – | – | – | £18 |
| 1938 E | 4,833,436 | – | £3 | £10 | £20 |
| 1938 S | 4,797,852 | – | £3 | £10 | £20 |
| 1939 E | 11,052,677 | – | £2 | £4 | £6 |
| 1939 S | 10,263,892 | – | £2 | £4 | £6 |
| 1940 E | 11,099,126 | – | – | £4 | £7 |
| 1940 S | 9,913,089 | – | – | £4 | £7 |

| DATE | MINTAGE | F | VF | EF | UNC |
|---|---|---|---|---|---|
| 1941 E | 11,391,883 | — | — | £4 | £6 |
| 1941 S | 8,086,030 | — | — | £4 | £5 |
| 1942 E | 17,453,643 | — | — | £4 | £5 |
| 1942 S | 13,676,759 | — | — | £4 | £5 |
| 1943 E | 11,404,213 | — | — | £4 | £6 |
| 1943 S | 9,824,214 | — | — | £4 | £5 |
| 1944 E | 11,586,751 | — | — | £4 | £5 |
| 1944 S | 10,990,167 | — | — | £4 | £5 |
| 1945 E | 15,143,404 | — | — | £4 | £6 |
| 1945 S | 15,106,270 | — | — | £4 | £5 |
| 1946 E | 16,663,797 | — | — | £4 | £5 |
| 1946 S | 16,381,501 | — | — | £4 | £5 |
| **Cupro-nickel** | | | | | |
| 1947 E | 12,120,611 | — | — | — | £2 |
| 1947 S | 12,283,223 | — | — | — | £2 |
| 1948 E | 45,576,923 | — | — | — | £2 |
| 1948 S | 45,351,937 | — | — | — | £2 |
| 1949 E | 19,328,405 | — | — | — | £5 |
| 1949 S | 21,243,074 | — | — | — | £5 |
| 1950 E | 19,243,872 | — | — | — | £5 |
| 1950 E Proof | 17,513 | — | — | — | £18 |
| 1950 S | 14,299,601 | — | — | — | £5 |
| 1950 S Proof | 17,513 | — | — | — | £18 |
| 1951 E | 9,956,930 | — | — | — | £5 |
| 1951 E Proof | 20,000 | — | — | — | £18 |
| 1951 S | 10,961,174 | — | — | — | £6 |
| 1951 S Proof | 20,000 | — | — | — | £18 |

*English reverse*

*Scottish reverse*

# ELIZABETH II (1952–   )

*E = England rev. (shield with three lions). S = Scotland rev. (shield with one lion).*

| | | | | | |
|---|---|---|---|---|---|
| 1953 E | 41,942,894 | — | — | — | £1 |
| 1953 E Proof | 40,000 | — | — | — | £4 |
| 1953 S | 20,663,528 | — | — | — | £1 |
| 1953 S Proof | 40,000 | — | — | — | £4 |
| 1954 E | 30,262,032 | — | — | — | £2 |
| 1954 S | 26,771,735 | — | — | — | £2 |
| 1955 E | 45,259,908 | — | — | — | £2 |
| 1955 S | 27,950,906 | — | — | — | £2 |
| 1956 E | 44,907,008 | — | — | — | £10 |
| 1956 S | 42,853,639 | — | — | — | £10 |
| 1957 E | 42,774,217 | — | — | — | £1 |
| 1957 S | 17,959,988 | — | — | — | £10 |
| 1958 E | 14,392,305 | — | — | — | £10 |
| 1958 S | 40,822,557 | — | — | — | £1 |
| 1959 E | 19,442,778 | — | — | — | £1 |
| 1959 S | 1,012,988 | £1 | £3 | £10 | £35 |
| 1960 E | 27,027,914 | — | — | — | £1 |
| 1960 S | 14,376,932 | — | — | — | £1 |
| 1961 E | 39,816,907 | — | — | — | £1 |
| 1961 S | 2,762,558 | — | — | — | £3 |
| 1962 E | 36,704,379 | — | — | — | £1 |
| 1962 S | 17,475,310 | — | — | — | £1 |
| 1963 E | 49,433,607 | — | — | — | £1 |
| 1963 S | 32,300,000 | — | — | — | £1 |
| 1964 E | 8,590,900 | — | — | — | £1 |
| 1964 S | 5,239,100 | — | — | — | £1 |
| 1965 E | 9,216,000 | — | — | — | £1 |
| 1965 S | 2,774,000 | — | — | — | £2 |
| 1966 E | 15,002,000 | — | — | — | £1 |
| 1966 S | 15,604,000 | — | — | — | £1 |

*English reverse*

*Scottish reverse*

# SIXPENCES

DATE                                    F      VF     EF    UNC

## OLIVER CROMWELL
1658 Patterns by Thos. Simon & Tanner
  Four varieties .................................................     Extremely rare

## CHARLES II (1660–85)

| Date | F | VF | EF | UNC |
|---|---|---|---|---|
| 1674 | £70 | £300 | £900 | — |
| 1675 | £70 | £300 | £900 | — |
| 1675/4 5 over 4 | £80 | £300 | £925 | — |
| 1676 | £80 | £300 | £900 | — |
| 1676/5 6 over 5 | £85 | £300 | £900 | — |
| 1677 | £70 | £300 | £900 | — |
| 1678/7 | £70 | £280 | £900 | — |
| 1679 | £75 | £300 | £900 | — |
| 1680 | £90 | £500 | £1000 | — |
| 1681 | £80 | £300 | £900 | — |
| 1682/1 | £80 | £300 | £1000 | — |
| 1682 | £95 | £320 | £950 | — |
| 1683 | £70 | £300 | £925 | — |
| 1684 | £75 | £300 | £900 | — |

## JAMES II (1685–88)

| Date | F | VF | EF | UNC |
|---|---|---|---|---|
| 1686 Early shields | £120 | £400 | £1000 | — |
| 1687/6 — 7 over 6 | £125 | £400 | £1000 | — |
| 1687 Late shields | £120 | £400 | £1000 | — |
| 1687/6 — 7 over 6 | £120 | £425 | £1100 | — |
| 1688 — | £110 | £425 | £1100 | — |

## WILLIAM & MARY (1688–94)

| Date | F | VF | EF | UNC |
|---|---|---|---|---|
| 1693 | £120 | £425 | £950 | — |
| 1693 error inverted 3 | £150 | £500 | £1050 | — |
| 1694 | £120 | £450 | £1050 | — |

## WILLIAM III (1694–1702)
*Provincially produced sixpences carry privy marks or initials below the bust:*
*B: Bristol. C: Chester. E: Exeter. N: Norwich. Y or y: York.*

| Date | F | VF | EF | UNC |
|---|---|---|---|---|
| 1695 First bust, early harp in 4th shield on rev. | £35 | £100 | £400 | — |
| 1696 — — | £35 | £100 | £325 | — |
| 1696 — — French arms at date | Extremely rare | | | |
| 1696 — — Scottish arms at date | Extremely rare | | | |
| 1696 — — DFI for DEI | Extremely rare | | | |
| 1696 — — No stops on obv. | £40 | £110 | £400 | — |
| 1696 — — B | £40 | £100 | £400 | — |
| 1696 — — — B over E | Extremely rare | | | |
| 1696 — — C | £35 | £100 | £425 | — |
| 1696 — — E | £50 | £110 | £425 | — |
| 1696 — — N | £40 | £100 | £425 | — |
| 1696 — — y | £40 | £110 | £475 | — |
| 1696 — — Y | £45 | £200 | £500 | — |
| 1696 — Later harp | £50 | £175 | £400 | — |
| 1696 — — B | £70 | £225 | £550 | — |
| 1696 — — — no stops on obv | £80 | £275 | £550 | — |
| 1696 — — C | £80 | £350 | £850 | — |
| 1696 — — N | £70 | £325 | — | — |
| 1696 Second bust | £300 | £800 | — | — |
| 1697 First bust, later harp | £30 | £75 | £300 | — |
| 1697 — — Arms of France & Ireland transposed | Extremely rare | | | |

| DATE | MINTAGE | F | VF | EF | UNC |
|---|---|---|---|---|---|
| 1697 — — B | | £50 | £110 | £425 | — |
| 1697 — — C | | £70 | £200 | £475 | — |
| 1697 — — — Irish shield at date | | | Extremely rare | | |
| 1697 — — E | | £70 | £200 | £450 | — |
| 1697 — — — error GVLIEMVS | | | Extremely rare | | |
| 1697 — — y | | £60 | £125 | £450 | — |
| 1697 — — — Irish shield at date | | | Extremely rare | | |
| 1697 Second bust | | £120 | £400 | £1200 | — |
| 1697 Third bust | | £25 | £70 | £275 | — |
| 1697 — error GVLIEIMVS | | | Extremely rare | | |
| 1697 — B | | £50 | £110 | £450 | — |
| 1697 — IRA for FRA | | | Extremely rare | | |
| 1697 — C | | £75 | £220 | £500 | — |
| 1697 — E | | £75 | £200 | £550 | — |
| 1697 — Y | | £60 | £200 | £500 | — |
| 1698 — | | £60 | £170 | £450 | — |
| 1698 — Plumes in angles on rev. | | £70 | £200 | £650 | — |
| 1699 — | | £80 | £250 | £750 | — |
| 1699 — Plumes in angles on rev. | | £70 | £250 | £700 | — |
| 1699 — Roses in angles on rev. | | £70 | £250 | £700 | — |
| 1699 — — error G  LIELMVS | | | Extremely rare | | |
| 1700 — | | £40 | £90 | £350 | — |
| 1700 — Plume below bust | | £2000 | — | — | — |
| 1701 — | | £55 | £120 | £425 | — |

## ANNE (1702–14)

| | | F | VF | EF | UNC |
|---|---|---|---|---|---|
| 1703 VIGO below bust Before Union with Scotland | £40 | £130 | £400 | — | |
| 1705 Plain | | £60 | £170 | £500 | — |
| 1705 Plumes in angles on rev. | | £45 | £150 | £450 | — |
| 1705 Roses & Plumes in angles on rev. | | £60 | £150 | £425 | — |
| 1707 Roses & Plumes in angles on rev. | | £50 | £150 | £400 | — |
| 1707 (Post-Union), Plain | | £40 | £80 | £275 | — |
| 1707 E (Edinburgh) below bust | | £40 | £80 | £300 | — |
| 1707 Plumes in angles on rev. | | £45 | £120 | £325 | — |
| 1708 Plain | | £45 | £100 | £400 | — |
| 1708 E below bust | | £50 | £100 | £350 | — |
| 1708 E* below bust | | £60 | £140 | £400 | — |
| 1708 "Edinburgh" bust E* below | | £50 | £140 | £400 | — |
| 1708 Plumes in angles on rev. | | £55 | £140 | £450 | — |
| 1710 Roses & Plumes in angles on rev. | | £35 | £110 | £450 | — |
| 1711 Plain | | £25 | £70 | £200 | — |

## GEORGE I (1714–27)

| | | F | VF | EF | UNC |
|---|---|---|---|---|---|
| 1717 Roses & Plumes in angles on rev. | | £90 | £250 | £700 | — |
| 1717 Plain edge | | | Extremely rare | | |
| 1720 — | | £80 | £220 | £600 | — |
| 1723 SSC in angles on rev. | | £30 | £70 | £200 | — |
| 1723 Larger lettering | | £30 | £70 | £200 | — |
| 1726 Small Roses & Plumes in angles on rev. .. | | £80 | £225 | £650 | — |

## GEORGE II (1727–60)

| | | F | VF | EF | UNC |
|---|---|---|---|---|---|
| 1728 Young head, Plain | | £70 | £240 | £525 | — |
| 1728 — Proof | | — | — | £3300 | — |
| 1728 — Plumes in angles on rev. | | £40 | £140 | £400 | — |
| 1728 — Roses & Plumes in angles on rev. | | £35 | £125 | £300 | — |
| 1731 — — | | £40 | £140 | £325 | — |
| 1732 — — | | £35 | £125 | £300 | — |
| 1734 — — | | £40 | £140 | £350 | — |
| 1735 — — | | £35 | £140 | £350 | — |
| 1735/4 5 over 4 | | £45 | £150 | £400 | — |
| 1736 — — | | £45 | £150 | £375 | — |
| 1739 — Roses in angles on rev. | | £30 | £100 | £275 | — |
| 1741 — | | £30 | £100 | £275 | — |
| 1743 Old head, Roses in angles on rev. | | £25 | £75 | £250 | — |

| DATE | MINTAGE | F | VF | EF | UNC |
|---|---|---|---|---|---|
| 1745 — — | | £25 | £75 | £250 | — |
| 1745 — — 5 over 3 | | £30 | £85 | £275 | — |
| 1745 — Plain, LIMA below bust | | £30 | £80 | £260 | — |
| 1746 — — | | £30 | £80 | £260 | — |
| 1746 — — Proof | | — | — | £1000 | — |
| 1750 — — | | £30 | £120 | £325 | — |
| 1751 — — | | £35 | £150 | £350 | — |
| 1757 — — | | £15 | £30 | £80 | — |
| 1758 — — | | £15 | £30 | £80 | — |

## GEORGE III (1760–1820)

| | | F | VF | EF | UNC |
|---|---|---|---|---|---|
| 1787 rev. no semée of hearts on 4th shield | | £15 | £35 | £80 | £110 |
| 1787 rev. with semée of hearts | | £15 | £35 | £80 | £110 |

**NEW COINAGE**

| | | F | VF | EF | UNC |
|---|---|---|---|---|---|
| 1816 | — | £6 | £15 | £40 | £95 |
| 1817 | 10,921,680 | £7 | £15 | £40 | £95 |
| 1818 | 4,284,720 | £10 | £25 | £80 | £175 |
| 1819 | 4,712,400 | £7 | £15 | £40 | £80 |
| 1819 very small 8 in date | incl. above | £7 | £15 | £40 | £100 |
| 1820 | 1,488,960 | £7 | £15 | £40 | £100 |

## GEORGE IV (1820–30)

| | | F | VF | EF | UNC |
|---|---|---|---|---|---|
| 1821 First bust, first reverse | 863,280 | £12 | £25 | £100 | £300 |
| 1821 error BBRITANNIAR | | £80 | £250 | £750 | — |
| 1821 — — Proof | incl. above | — | — | — | £700 |
| 1824 — Second (garter) reverse | 633,600 | £10 | £25 | £100 | £300 |
| 1825 — | 483,120 | £12 | £25 | £90 | £275 |
| 1826 — — | 689,040 | £30 | £80 | £200 | £475 |
| 1826 Second bust, third (lion on crown) reverse | incl. above | £10 | £25 | £90 | £200 |
| 1826 — — Proof | incl. above | — | — | — | £450 |
| 1827 — — | 166,320 | £25 | £80 | £240 | £450 |
| 1828 — — | 15,840 | £16 | £40 | £125 | £275 |
| 1829 — — | 403,290 | £12 | £40 | £110 | £300 |

## WILLIAM IV (1830–37)

| | | F | VF | EF | UNC |
|---|---|---|---|---|---|
| 1831 | 1,340,195 | £15 | £40 | £125 | £275 |
| 1831 Proof, milled edge | incl. above | — | — | — | £500 |
| 1834 | 5,892,480 | £15 | £40 | £125 | £275 |
| 1835 | 1,552,320 | £15 | £40 | £125 | £275 |
| 1836 | 1,987,920 | £15 | £45 | £250 | £325 |
| 1837 | 506,880 | £18 | £40 | £200 | £450 |

## VICTORIA (1837–1901)
**YOUNG HEAD ISSUES**
*First head*

| | | F | VF | EF | UNC |
|---|---|---|---|---|---|
| 1838 | 1,607,760 | £12 | £35 | £90 | £250 |
| 1839 | 3,310,560 | £12 | £35 | £80 | £250 |
| 1839 Proof | incl. above | — | — | — | £650 |
| 1840 | 2,098,800 | £12 | £35 | £85 | £250 |
| 1841 | 1,386,000 | £12 | £35 | £80 | £250 |
| 1842 | 601,920 | £12 | £35 | £80 | £250 |
| 1843 | 3,160,080 | £12 | £35 | £80 | £250 |
| 1844 | 3,975,840 | £12 | £30 | £60 | £250 |
| 1844 Large 44 in date | incl. above | £15 | £40 | £100 | £300 |
| 1845 | 3,714,480 | £12 | £30 | £70 | £250 |
| 1846 | 4,226,880 | £12 | £30 | £70 | £250 |
| 1848 | 586,080 | £50 | £90 | £275 | £800 |
| 1848/6 final 8 over 6 | incl. above | £40 | £90 | £300 | — |
| 1850 | 498,960 | £12 | £35 | £80 | £250 |
| 1850/3 0 over 3 | incl. above | £15 | £35 | £90 | £325 |
| 1851 | 2,288,107 | £10 | £30 | £80 | £250 |

| DATE | MINTAGE | F | VF | EF | UNC |
|---|---|---|---|---|---|
| 1852 | 904,586 | £10 | £30 | £100 | £250 |
| 1853 | 3,837,930 | £10 | £30 | £100 | £250 |
| 1853 Proof | incl above | — | — | — | £750 |
| 1854 | 840,116 | £150 | £350 | £800 | £1600 |
| 1855 | 1,129,684 | £10 | £30 | £70 | £175 |
| 1855/3 last 5 over 3 | incl. above | £12 | £40 | £80 | £225 |
| 1856 | 2,779,920 | £10 | £30 | £70 | £200 |
| 1857 | 2,233,440 | £10 | £30 | £70 | £200 |
| 1858 | 1,932,480 | £10 | £30 | £70 | £200 |
| 1859 | 4,688,640 | £10 | £30 | £75 | £200 |
| 1859/8 9 over 8 | incl. above | £12 | £35 | £90 | £275 |
| 1860 | 1,100,880 | £10 | £25 | £80 | £225 |
| 1862 | 990,000 | £70 | £170 | £500 | £1000 |
| 1863 | 491,040 | £70 | £140 | £400 | £900 |

*Die no. added above date from 1864 to 1879*

| | | | | | |
|---|---|---|---|---|---|
| 1864 | 4,253,040 | £8 | £25 | £80 | £200 |
| 1865 | 1,631,520 | £8 | £25 | £70 | £200 |
| 1866 | 4,140,080 | £8 | £25 | £70 | £200 |
| 1866 no Die no. | incl. above | | | Extremely Rare | |

**Second head**

| | | | | | |
|---|---|---|---|---|---|
| 1867 | 1,362,240 | £8 | £20 | £75 | £225 |
| 1868 | 1,069,200 | £8 | £20 | £70 | £175 |
| 1869 | 388,080 | £8 | £20 | £70 | £175 |
| 1870 | 479,613 | £8 | £20 | £70 | £175 |
| 1871 | 3,662,684 | £7 | £20 | £60 | £170 |
| 1871 no Die no. | incl. above | £7 | £20 | £60 | £170 |
| 1872 | 3,382,048 | £7 | £20 | £60 | £170 |
| 1873 | 4,594,733 | £7 | £20 | £60 | £170 |
| 1874 | 4,225,726 | £7 | £20 | £60 | £170 |
| 1875 | 3,256,545 | £7 | £20 | £60 | £170 |
| 1876 | 841,435 | £7 | £20 | £60 | £170 |
| 1877 | 4,066,486 | £7 | £20 | £60 | £170 |
| 1877 no Die no | incl. above | £7 | £20 | £60 | £170 |
| 1878 | 2,624,525 | £7 | £20 | £60 | £160 |
| 1878 Dritanniar Error | incl. above | £100 | £300 | — | — |
| 1879 | 3,326,313 | £7 | £18 | £60 | £150 |
| 1879 no Die no | incl. above | £6 | £18 | £60 | £150 |
| 1880 no Die no | 3,892,501 | £6 | £20 | £50 | £150 |

**Third head**

| | | | | | |
|---|---|---|---|---|---|
| 1880 | incl above | £7 | £20 | £50 | £120 |
| 1881 | 6,239,447 | £7 | £20 | £50 | £120 |
| 1882 | 759,809 | £12 | £40 | £125 | £340 |
| 1883 | 4,986,558 | £7 | £18 | £40 | £100 |
| 1884 | 3,422,565 | £7 | £18 | £40 | £100 |
| 1885 | 4,652,771 | £7 | £18 | £40 | £100 |
| 1886 | 2,728,249 | £7 | £18 | £40 | £90 |
| 1887 | 3,675,607 | £7 | £18 | £40 | £90 |

**JUBILEE HEAD ISSUES**

| | | | | | |
|---|---|---|---|---|---|
| 1887 Shield reverse | incl. above | £5 | £8 | £10 | £25 |
| 1887 — Proof | incl. above | — | — | — | £120 |
| 1887 Six Pence in wreath reverse | incl. above | £4 | £5 | £15 | £30 |
| 1888 — | 4,197,698 | £6 | £9 | £25 | £45 |
| 1889 — | 8,738,928 | £6 | £9 | £25 | £55 |
| 1890 — | 9,386,955 | £6 | £9 | £25 | £55 |
| 1891 — | 7,022,734 | £6 | £9 | £25 | £55 |
| 1892 — | 6,245,746 | £6 | £10 | £30 | £65 |
| 1893 — | 7,350,619 | £500 | £1000 | £3000 | — |

**OLD HEAD ISSUES**

| | | | | | |
|---|---|---|---|---|---|
| 1893 | incl. above | £5 | £10 | £20 | £45 |
| 1893 Proof | 1,312 | — | — | — | £95 |
| 1894 | 3,467,704 | £7 | £14 | £40 | £90 |
| 1895 | 7,024,631 | £6 | £14 | £35 | £80 |
| 1896 | 6,651,699 | £5 | £10 | £30 | £55 |
| 1897 | 5,031,498 | £5 | £10 | £30 | £55 |
| 1898 | 5,914,100 | £5 | £10 | £30 | £50 |
| 1899 | 7,996,80 | £5 | £10 | £30 | £50 |
| 1900 | 8,984,354 | £5 | £10 | £30 | £50 |
| 1901 | 5,108,757 | £5 | £10 | £30 | £50 |

*Jubilee head, shield reverse*

*Jubilee head, wreath reverse*

| DATE | MINTAGE | F | VF | EF | UNC |
|------|---------|---|----|----|----|

## EDWARD VII (1901–10)

| DATE | MINTAGE | F | VF | EF | UNC |
|------|---------|---|----|----|----|
| 1902 | 6,367,378 | £4 | £10 | £30 | £50 |
| 1902 "Matt Proof" | 15,123 | — | — | — | £80 |
| 1903 | 5,410,096 | £6 | £18 | £50 | £150 |
| 1904 | 4,487,098 | £12 | £45 | £160 | £400 |
| 1905 | 4,235,556 | £7 | £20 | £60 | £180 |
| 1906 | 7,641,146 | £5 | £10 | £35 | £95 |
| 1907 | 8,733,673 | £5 | £10 | £40 | £100 |
| 1908 | 6,739,491 | £8 | £25 | £80 | £300 |
| 1909 | 6,584,017 | £6 | £15 | £45 | £160 |
| 1910 | 12,490,724 | £4 | £6 | £22 | £45 |

*Edward VII*

## GEORGE V (1910–36)

**First issue**

| DATE | MINTAGE | F | VF | EF | UNC |
|------|---------|---|----|----|----|
| 1911 | 9,155,310 | £2 | £5 | £10 | £35 |
| 1911 Proof | 6,007 | — | — | — | £45 |
| 1912 | 10,984,129 | £2 | £5 | £20 | £50 |
| 1913 | 7,499,833 | £2 | £6 | £22 | £60 |
| 1914 | 22,714,602 | £2 | £5 | £10 | £30 |
| 1915 | 15,694,597 | £2 | £5 | £12 | £35 |
| 1916 | 22,207,178 | £2 | £5 | £10 | £25 |
| 1917 | 7,725,475 | £7 | £20 | £50 | £110 |
| 1918 | 27,553,743 | £2 | £5 | £12 | £25 |
| 1919 | 13,375,447 | £2 | £5 | £12 | £35 |
| 1920 | 14,136,287 | £2 | £5 | £10 | £25 |

**Second issue** — debased silver

| DATE | MINTAGE | F | VF | EF | UNC |
|------|---------|---|----|----|----|
| 1920 | incl. above | £1 | £3 | £10 | £30 |
| 1921 | 30,339,741 | £1 | £3 | £10 | £30 |
| 1922 | 16,878,890 | £1 | £3 | £10 | £30 |
| 1923 | 6,382,793 | £3 | £8 | £40 | £100 |
| 1924 | 17,444,218 | £1 | £5 | £10 | £30 |
| 1925 | 12,720,558 | £1 | £3 | £10 | £30 |
| 1925 Broad rim | incl. above | £1 | £3 | £10 | £30 |
| 1926 — | 21,809,621 | £1 | £3 | £10 | £30 |

**Third issue** — Modified bust

| DATE | MINTAGE | F | VF | EF | UNC |
|------|---------|---|----|----|----|
| 1926 | incl. above | £1 | £2 | £10 | £30 |
| 1927 | 8,924,873 | — | £2 | £10 | £30 |

**Fourth issue** — New design (oakleaves)

| DATE | MINTAGE | F | VF | EF | UNC |
|------|---------|---|----|----|----|
| 1927 Proof only | 15,000 | £1 | £2 | £10 | £35 |
| 1928 | 23,123,384 | £1 | £2 | £8 | £25 |
| 1929 | 28,319,326 | £1 | £2 | £8 | £25 |
| 1930 | 16,990,289 | £1 | £2 | £8 | £28 |
| 1931 | 16,873,268 | £1 | £2 | £8 | £25 |
| 1932 | 9,406,117 | £1 | £2 | £8 | £35 |
| 1933 | 22,185,083 | £1 | £2 | £8 | £24 |
| 1934 | 9,304,009 | £1 | £2 | £12 | £30 |
| 1935 | 13,995,621 | £1 | £2 | £6 | £12 |
| 1936 | 24,380,171 | £1 | £2 | £6 | £12 |

*George V,*
*first reverse*
*above and*
*second reverse*
*below*

## GEORGE VI (1936–52)

**First type**

| DATE | MINTAGE | F | VF | EF | UNC |
|------|---------|---|----|----|----|
| 1937 | 22,302,524 | — | — | £1 | £5 |
| 1937 Proof | 26,402 | — | — | — | £10 |
| 1938 | 13,402,701 | — | £2 | £5 | £18 |
| 1939 | 28,670,304 | — | — | £1 | £5 |
| 1940 | 20,875,196 | — | — | £1 | £5 |
| 1941 | 23,086,616 | — | — | £1 | £5 |
| 1942 | 44,942,785 | — | — | £1 | £4 |
| 1943 | 46,927,111 | — | — | £1 | £4 |
| 1944 | 36,952,600 | — | — | £1 | £4 |
| 1945 | 39,939,259 | — | — | £1 | £3 |
| 1946 | 43,466,407 | — | — | £1 | £3 |

*Cupro-nickel*

| DATE | MINTAGE | F | VF | EF | UNC |
|------|---------|---|----|----|----|
| 1947 | 29,993,263 | — | — | £1 | £3 |
| 1948 | 88,323,540 | — | — | £1 | £3 |

**Second type** — new cypher on rev.

| DATE | MINTAGE | F | VF | EF | UNC |
|------|---------|---|----|----|----|
| 1949 | 41,335,515 | — | — | £1 | £3 |

*George VI first reverse*

*George VI second reverse*

| DATE | MINTAGE | F | VF | EF | UNC |
|------|---------|---|----|----|----|
| 1950 | 32,741,955 | — | — | £1 | £3 |
| 1950 Proof | 17,513 | — | — | — | £7 |
| 1951 | 40,399,491 | — | — | £1 | £3 |
| 1951 Proof | 20,000 | — | — | — | £7 |
| 1952 | 1,013,477 | £5 | £18 | £45 | £100 |

## ELIZABETH II (1952–    )

| DATE | MINTAGE | F | VF | EF | UNC |
|------|---------|---|----|----|----|
| 1953 | 70,323,876 | — | — | — | £2 |
| 1953 Proof | 40,000 | — | — | — | £4 |
| 1954 | 105,241,150 | — | — | — | £3 |
| 1955 | 109,929,554 | — | — | — | £1 |
| 1956 | 109,841,555 | — | — | — | £1 |
| 1957 | 105,654,290 | — | — | — | £1 |
| 1958 | 123,518,527 | — | — | — | £3 |
| 1959 | 93,089,441 | — | — | — | £1 |
| 1960 | 103,283,346 | — | — | — | £3 |
| 1961 | 115,052,017 | — | — | — | £3 |
| 1962 | 166,483,637 | — | — | — | 25p |
| 1963 | 120,056,000 | — | — | — | 25p |
| 1964 | 152,336,000 | — | — | — | 25p |
| 1965 | 129,644,000 | — | — | — | 25p |
| 1966 | 175,676,000 | — | — | — | 25p |
| 1967 | 240,788,000 | — | — | — | 25p |

# GROATS OR FOURPENCES

| DATE | MINTAGE | F | VF | EF | UNC |
|------|---------|---|----|----|----|

*The earlier fourpences are included in the Maundy oddments section as they are generally considered to have been issued for the Maundy ceremony.*

## WILLIAM IV  (1831–37)

| | MINTAGE | F | VF | EF | UNC |
|------|---------|---|----|----|----|
| 1836 | — | £8 | £18 | £40 | £85 |
| 1837 | 962,280 | £8 | £18 | £40 | £90 |

## VICTORIA (1838–1901)

| | MINTAGE | F | VF | EF | UNC |
|------|---------|---|----|----|----|
| 1837 | Extremely Rare Proofs or Patterns only | | | | |
| 1838 | 2,150,280 | £7 | £15 | £30 | £80 |
| 1838 over last 8 on its side | | £10 | £20 | £55 | £110 |
| 1839 | 1,461,240 | £7 | £16 | £40 | £90 |
| 1839 Proof | incl. above | | | | Rare |
| 1840 | 1,496,880 | £7 | £15 | £40 | £85 |
| 1840 Small 0 in date | incl. above | £7 | £15 | £40 | £85 |
| 1841 | 344,520 | £7 | £15 | £40 | £85 |
| 1842/1 2 over 1 | incl. above | £7 | £15 | £40 | £85 |
| 1842 | 724,680 | £7 | £15 | £35 | £80 |
| 1843 | 1,817640 | £8 | £16 | £40 | £100 |
| 1843 4 over 5 | incl. above | £7 | £15 | £40 | £100 |
| 1844 | 855,360 | £7 | £15 | £40 | £90 |
| 1845 | 914,760 | £7 | £15 | £40 | £90 |
| 1846 | 1,366,200 | £7 | £15 | £40 | £90 |
| 1847 7 over 6 | 225,720 | £15 | £35 | £110 | — |
| 1848 | 712,800 | £7 | £15 | £40 | £80 |
| 1848/6  8 over 6 | incl. above | £30 | £110 | — | — |
| 1848/7  8 over 7 | incl. above | £8 | £20 | £50 | £100 |
| 1849 | 380,160 | £7 | £15 | £40 | £85 |
| 1849/8 9 over 8 | incl. above | £8 | £20 | £60 | £125 |
| 1851 | 594,000 | £30 | £80 | £200 | £375 |
| 1852 | 31,300 | £50 | £120 | £350 | — |
| 1853 | 11,880 | £40 | £100 | £375 | — |
| 1853 Proof Milled Rim | incl. above | — | — | — | £800 |
| 1853 Plain edge Proof | | | | Extremely rare | |
| 1854 | 1,096,613 | £7 | £15 | £40 | £85 |
| 1855 | 646,041 | £7 | £15 | £40 | £85 |
| 1857 Proofs only | | | | Extremely rare | |
| 1862 Proofs only | | | | Extremely rare | |
| 1888 Jubilee Head | — | £8 | £18 | £40 | £85 |

# THREEPENCES

| DATE | MINTAGE | F | VF | EF | UNC |
|------|---------|---|----|----|----|

*The earlier threepences are included in the Maundy oddments section.*

## WILLIAM IV (1830–37)
(issued for use in the West Indies)

| DATE | MINTAGE | F | VF | EF | UNC |
|------|---------|---|----|----|----|
| 1834 | | £7 | £15 | £60 | £150 |
| 1835 | | £7 | £15 | £60 | £150 |
| 1836 | | £7 | £15 | £60 | £150 |
| 1837 | | £7 | £20 | £85 | £170 |

## VICTORIA (1837–1901)
**YOUNG HEAD ISSUES**

| DATE | MINTAGE | F | VF | EF | UNC |
|------|---------|---|----|----|----|
| 1838 BRITANNIAB error | | | Extremely rare | | |
| 1838 | — | £8 | £20 | £70 | £140 |
| 1839 | — | £8 | £20 | £70 | £140 |
| 18t40 | — | £8 | £20 | £70 | £140 |
| 1841 | — | £8 | £20 | £60 | £160 |
| 1842 | — | £8 | £20 | £60 | £160 |
| 1843 | — | £8 | £20 | £50 | £135 |
| 1843/34 43 over 34 | — | £8 | £20 | £80 | £175 |
| 1844 | — | £10 | £20 | £70 | £160 |
| 1845 | 1,319,208 | £9 | £20 | £60 | £145 |
| 1846 | 52,008 | £9 | £25 | £80 | £200 |
| 1847 | 4,488 | | Extremely rare | | |
| 1848 | incl. above | | Extremely rare | | |
| 1849 | 131,208 | £10 | £24 | £70 | £170 |
| 1850 | 954,888 | £10 | £22 | £40 | £100 |
| 1851 | 479,065 | £10 | £24 | £50 | £130 |
| 1851 5 over 8 | incl. above | £20 | £40 | £120 | — |
| 1852 | 4,488 | | Extremely rare | | |
| 1853 | 36,168 | £25 | £60 | £110 | £300 |
| 1854 | 1,467,246 | £7 | £20 | £50 | £130 |
| 1855 | 383,350 | £7 | £20 | £50 | £140 |
| 1856 | 1,013,760 | £7 | £20 | £55 | £130 |
| 1857 | 1,758,240 | £7 | £20 | £60 | £150 |
| 1858 | 1,441,440 | £7 | £20 | £50 | £130 |
| 1858 BRITANNIAB error | incl. above | | Extremely rare | | |
| 1858/6 final 8 over 6 | incl. above | £10 | £30 | £100 | — |
| 1858/5 final 8 over 5 | incl. above | £10 | £30 | £100 | — |
| 1859 | 3,579,840 | £6 | £18 | £50 | £120 |
| 1860 | 3,405,600 | £7 | £20 | £50 | £130 |
| 1861 | 3,294,720 | £7 | £20 | £50 | £120 |
| 1862 | 1,156,320 | £7 | £20 | £50 | £120 |
| 1863 | 950,400 | £10 | £40 | £100 | £225 |
| 1864 | 1,330,560 | £6 | £20 | £50 | £120 |
| 1865 | 1,742,400 | £6 | £20 | £50 | £110 |
| 1866 | 1,900,800 | £6 | £20 | £50 | £110 |
| 1867 | 712,800 | £6 | £20 | £50 | £110 |
| 1868 | 1,457,280 | £6 | £20 | £50 | £110 |
| 1868 RRITANNIAR error | incl. above | | Extremely rare | | |
| 1869 | — | £35 | £70 | £175 | £350 |
| 1870 | 1,283,218 | £5 | £16 | £45 | £90 |
| 1871 | 999,633 | £5 | £16 | £40 | £90 |
| 1872 | 1,293,271 | £5 | £16 | £40 | £90 |
| 1873 | 4,055,550 | £5 | £16 | £40 | £90 |
| 1874 | 4,427,031 | £5 | £16 | £40 | £90 |
| 1875 | 3,306,500 | £5 | £16 | £40 | £90 |
| 1876 | 1,834,389 | £5 | £16 | £40 | £90 |
| 1877 | 2,622,393 | £5 | £16 | £40 | £90 |
| 1878 | 2,419,975 | £5 | £16 | £40 | £90 |
| 1879 | 3,140,265 | £5 | £16 | £40 | £90 |
| 1880 | 1,610,069 | £5 | £16 | £40 | £75 |
| 1881 | 3,248,265 | £5 | £16 | £40 | £75 |
| 1882 | 472,965 | £7 | £22 | £60 | £140 |
| 1883 | 4,369,971 | £5 | £10 | £30 | £60 |

Victoria first type

| DATE | MINTAGE | F | VF | EF | UNC |
|---|---|---|---|---|---|
| 1884 | 3,322,424 | £5 | £10 | £30 | £60 |
| 1885 | 5,183,653 | £5 | £10 | £30 | £60 |
| 1886 | 6,152,669 | £5 | £10 | £30 | £60 |
| 1887 | 2,780,761 | £5 | £10 | £30 | £60 |

**JUBILEE HEAD ISSUES**

| | | | | | |
|---|---|---|---|---|---|
| 1887 | incl. above | £2 | £4 | £10 | £22 |
| 1887 Proof | incl. above | — | — | — | £60 |
| 1888 | 518,199 | £2 | £5 | £20 | £40 |
| 1889 | 4,587,010 | £2 | £5 | £20 | £40 |
| 1890 | 4,465,834 | £2 | £5 | £20 | £40 |
| 1891 | 6,323,027 | £2 | £5 | £20 | £40 |
| 1892 | 2,578,226 | £2 | £5 | £20 | £40 |
| 1893 | 3,067,243 | £10 | £30 | £110 | £240 |

*Victoria
Jubilee head*

**OLD HEAD ISSUES**

| | | | | | |
|---|---|---|---|---|---|
| 1893 | incl. above | £1 | £4 | £15 | £30 |
| 1893 Proof | incl. above | — | — | — | £45 |
| 1894 | 1,608,603 | £2 | £6 | £24 | £50 |
| 1895 | 4,788,609 | £1 | £5 | £22 | £50 |
| 1896 | 4,598,442 | £1 | £5 | £18 | £35 |
| 1897 | 4,541,294 | £1 | £5 | £18 | £35 |
| 1898 | 4,567,177 | £1 | £5 | £18 | £35 |
| 1899 | 6,246,281 | £1 | £5 | £18 | £35 |
| 1900 | 10,644,480 | £1 | £5 | £18 | £35 |
| 1901 | 6,098,400 | £1 | £5 | £14 | £30 |

*Victoria
Old or Veiled
head*

# EDWARD VII (1901–10)

| | | | | | |
|---|---|---|---|---|---|
| 1902 | 8,268,480 | £1 | £2 | £7 | £15 |
| 1902 "Matt Proof" | incl. above | — | — | — | £20 |
| 1903 | 5,227,200 | £1 | £4 | £20 | £45 |
| 1904 | 3,627,360 | £3 | £10 | £45 | £90 |
| 1905 | 3,548,160 | £1 | £4 | £25 | £60 |
| 1906 | 3,152,160 | £1 | £5 | £22 | £55 |
| 1907 | 4,831,200 | £1 | £4 | £20 | £50 |
| 1908 | 8,157,600 | £1 | £3 | £20 | £50 |
| 1909 | 4,055,040 | £1 | £4 | £20 | £50 |
| 1910 | 4,563,380 | £1 | £4 | £18 | £35 |

# GEORGE V (1910–36)

**First issue**

| | | | | | |
|---|---|---|---|---|---|
| 1911 | 5,841,084 | — | — | £3 | £10 |
| 1911 Proof | incl. above | — | — | — | £40 |
| 1912 | 8,932,825 | — | — | £3 | £12 |
| 1913 | 7,143,242 | — | — | £3 | £12 |
| 1914 | 6,733,584 | — | — | £3 | £12 |
| 1915 | 5,450,617 | — | — | £3 | £15 |
| 1916 | 18,555,201 | — | — | £3 | £10 |
| 1917 | 21,662,490 | — | — | £3 | £10 |
| 1918 | 20,630,909 | — | — | £3 | £10 |
| 1919 | 16,845,687 | — | — | £3 | £10 |
| 1920 | 16,703,597 | — | — | £3 | £10 |

**Second issue**—debased silver

| | | | | | |
|---|---|---|---|---|---|
| 1920 | incl. above | — | — | £3 | £12 |
| 1921 | 8,749,301 | — | — | £3 | £12 |
| 1922 | 7,979,998 | — | — | £3 | £40 |
| 1925 | 3,731,859 | — | — | £5 | £25 |
| 1926 | 4,107,910 | — | — | £7 | £28 |

**Third issue**—Modified bust

| | | | | | |
|---|---|---|---|---|---|
| 1926 | incl. above | — | — | £8 | £22 |

**Fourth issue**—new design (oakleaves)

| | | | | | |
|---|---|---|---|---|---|
| 1927 Proof only | 15,022 | — | — | — | £80 |
| 1928 | 1,302,106 | £4 | £9 | £28 | £65 |
| 1930 | 1,319,412 | £2 | £4 | £10 | £40 |
| 1931 | 6,251,936 | — | — | £2 | £7 |
| 1932 | 5,887,325 | — | — | £2 | £7 |
| 1933 | 5,578,541 | — | — | £2 | £7 |
| 1934 | 7,405,954 | — | — | £2 | £7 |
| 1935 | 7,027,654 | — | — | £2 | £7 |
| 1936 | 3,328,670 | — | — | £2 | £7 |

*George V,
fourth issue
oak leaves
design reverse*

| DATE | MINTAGE | F | VF | EF | UNC |
|---|---|---|---|---|---|

## GEORGE VI (1936–52)

Silver

| DATE | MINTAGE | F | VF | EF | UNC |
|---|---|---|---|---|---|
| 1937 | 8,148,156 | — | — | £1 | £4 |
| 1937 Proof | 26,402 | — | — | — | £15 |
| 1938 | 6,402,473 | — | — | £1 | £4 |
| 1939 | 1,355,860 | — | — | £4 | £15 |
| 1940 | 7,914,401 | — | — | £1 | £3 |
| 1941 | 7,979,411 | — | — | £1 | £3 |
| 1942 | 4,144,051 | £2 | £5 | £12 | £35 |
| 1943 | 1,397,220 | £2 | £5 | £12 | £35 |
| 1944 | 2,005,553 | £5 | £12 | £35 | £80 |
| 1945 | Only one known | | | | |

Brass—larger size, 12 sided, "Thrift" design

| DATE | MINTAGE | F | VF | EF | UNC |
|---|---|---|---|---|---|
| 1937 | 45,707,957 | — | — | £1 | £4 |
| 1937 Proof | 26,402 | — | — | — | £10 |
| 1938 | 14,532,332 | — | — | £1 | £18 |
| 1939 | 5,603,021 | — | — | £3 | £40 |
| 1940 | 12,636,018 | — | — | £3 | £30 |
| 1941 | 60,239,489 | — | — | £1 | £8 |
| 1942 | 103,214,400 | — | — | £1 | £8 |
| 1943 | 101,702,400 | — | — | £1 | £8 |
| 1944 | 69,760,000 | — | — | £1 | £8 |
| 1945 | 33,942,466 | — | — | £3 | £20 |
| 1946 | 620,734 | £6 | £25 | £125 | £500 |
| 1948 | 4,230,400 | — | — | £5 | £45 |
| 1949 | 464,000 | £5 | £25 | £150 | £650 |
| 1950 | 1,600,000 | — | £2 | £20 | £110 |
| 1950 Proof | 17,513 | — | — | — | £15 |
| 1951 | 1,184,000 | — | £2 | £20 | £100 |
| 1951 Proof | 20,000 | — | — | — | £15 |
| 1952 | 25,494,400 | — | — | — | £10 |

*George VI "Thrift" design
of the brass 3d*

## ELIZABETH II (1952–    )

| DATE | MINTAGE | F | VF | EF | UNC |
|---|---|---|---|---|---|
| 1953 | 30,618,000 | — | — | — | £1 |
| 1953 Proof | 40,000 | — | — | — | £6 |
| 1954 | 41,720,000 | — | — | — | £5 |
| 1955 | 41,075,200 | — | — | — | £5 |
| 1956 | 36,801,600 | — | — | — | £6 |
| 1957 | 24,294,500 | — | — | — | £6 |
| 1958 | 20,504,000 | — | — | — | £9 |
| 1959 | 28,499,200 | — | — | — | £6 |
| 1960 | 83,078,400 | — | — | — | £2 |
| 1961 | 41,102,400 | — | — | — | £1 |
| 1962 | 51,545,600 | — | — | — | £1 |
| 1963 | 39,482,866 | — | — | — | £1 |
| 1964 | 44,867,200 | — | — | — | — |
| 1965 | 27,160,000 | — | — | — | — |
| 1966 | 53,160,000 | — | — | — | — |
| 1967 | 151,780,800 | — | — | — | — |

# TWO PENCES

It is generally accepted that earlier issues of the small silver twopences were
only produced for inclusion with the Maundy sets, q.v., except for those listed
below.

| | | F | VF | EF | UNC |
|---|---|---|---|---|---|
| 1797 "Cartwheel" | | £25 | £50 | £300 | £800 |
| 1797 Copper Proofs | Many varieties from £500+ | | | | |

## VICTORIA (1837–1901)

For use in the Colonies

| | | F | VF | EF | UNC |
|---|---|---|---|---|---|
| 1838 | | £4 | £10 | £18 | £35 |
| 1848 | | £4 | £12 | £20 | £40 |

# THREE-HALFPENCES

| DATE | | F | VF | EF | UNC |
|---|---|---|---|---|---|

### WILLIAM IV (1830–37)

*For use in the Colonies*

| | | F | VF | EF | UNC |
|---|---|---|---|---|---|
| 1834 | | £6 | £16 | £35 | £80 |
| 1835 | | £10 | £25 | £75 | £200 |
| 1835 over 4 | | £6 | £16 | £40 | £90 |
| 1836 | | £8 | £18 | £40 | £95 |
| 1837 | | £15 | £35 | £110 | £300 |

### VICTORIA (1837–1901)

*For use in the Colonies*

| | | F | VF | EF | UNC |
|---|---|---|---|---|---|
| 1838 | | £6 | £15 | £35 | £75 |
| 1839 | | £6 | £15 | £35 | £75 |
| 1840 | | £8 | £20 | £60 | £125 |
| 1841 | | £6 | £15 | £35 | £80 |
| 1842 | | £6 | £18 | £40 | £90 |
| 1843 | | £6 | £15 | £30 | £70 |
| 1860 | | £9 | £20 | £70 | £150 |
| 1862 | | £9 | £20 | £70 | £150 |

# PENNIES

| DATE | MINTAGE | F | VF | EF | UNC |
|---|---|---|---|---|---|

*The earlier small silver pennies are included in the Maundy oddments section.*

### GEORGE III (1760–1820)

| | MINTAGE | F | VF | EF | UNC |
|---|---|---|---|---|---|
| 1797 "Cartwheel", 10 laurel leaves | 8,601,600 | £25 | £60 | £300 | £900 |
| 1797 — 11 laurel leaves | incl. above | £25 | £60 | £300 | £900 |
| 1806 Third type | — | £7 | £18 | £70 | £250 |
| 1807 | — | £7 | £18 | £70 | £250 |
| 1808 | | | | | Unique |

### GEORGE IV (1820–30)

| | MINTAGE | F | VF | EF | UNC |
|---|---|---|---|---|---|
| 1825 | 1,075,200 | £12 | £40 | £240 | £550 |
| 1826 (varieties) | 5,913,600 | £12 | £40 | £240 | £550 |
| 1826 Proof | — | — | — | — | £550 |
| 1827 | 1,451,520 | £200 | £700 | £2500 | — |

### WILLIAM IV (1830–37)

| | MINTAGE | F | VF | EF | UNC |
|---|---|---|---|---|---|
| 1831 (varieties) | 806,400 | £20 | £70 | £400 | £950 |
| 1831 Proof | — | — | — | — | £650 |
| 1834 | 322,560 | £25 | £70 | £400 | £1100 |
| 1837 | 174,720 | £60 | £180 | £700 | £2000 |

### VICTORIA (1837–1901)

**YOUNG HEAD ISSUES**

*Copper*

| | MINTAGE | F | VF | EF | UNC |
|---|---|---|---|---|---|
| 1839 Proof | unrecorded | — | — | — | £1250 |
| 1841 | 913,920 | £7 | £20 | £140 | £600 |
| 1841 No colon after REG | incl. above | £8 | £20 | £140 | £550 |
| 1843 | 483,840 | £75 | £250 | £1500 | £3500 |
| 1844 | 215,040 | £12 | £25 | £110 | £350 |
| 1845 | 322,560 | £15 | £35 | £180 | £550 |
| 1846 | 483,840 | £15 | £25 | £170 | £500 |
| 1846 FID: DEF colon spaced | incl. above | £15 | £25 | £170 | £500 |
| 1846 FID:DEF colon close | incl. above | £16 | £25 | £170 | £500 |
| 1847 | 430,080 | £10 | £25 | £160 | £400 |

*"Cartwheel" penny*

| DATE | MINTAGE | F | VF | EF | UNC |
|---|---|---|---|---|---|
| 1848 | 161,280 | £8 | £25 | £130 | £400 |
| 1848/7 final 8 over 7 | incl. above | £7 | £20 | £130 | £350 |
| 1848/6 final 8 over 6 | incl. above | £20 | £100 | £450 | — |
| 1849 | 268,800 | £200 | £600 | £2000 | — |
| 1851 | 268,800 | £10 | £30 | £150 | £500 |
| 1853 | 1,021,440 | £7 | £15 | £80 | £140 |
| 1853 Proof | — | — | — | — | £1500 |
| 1854 | 6,720,000 | £8 | £18 | £80 | £140 |
| 1854/3 4 over 3 | incl. above | £12 | £40 | £150 | — |
| 1855 | 5,273,856 | £8 | £18 | £80 | £200 |
| 1856 | 1,212,288 | £100 | £250 | £700 | £2200 |
| 1857 Plain trident | 752,640 | £7 | £18 | £80 | £230 |
| 1857 Ornamental trident | incl. above | £6 | £18 | £70 | £220 |
| 1858/7 final 8 over 7 | incl. above | £7 | £18 | £75 | £250 |
| 1858/6 final 8 over 6 | — | £40 | £120 | £500 | — |
| 1858/3 final 8 over 3 | incl. above | £25 | £90 | £400 | — |
| 1858 | 1,599,040 | £7 | £16 | £80 | £220 |
| 1859 | 1,075,200 | £8 | £25 | £100 | £300 |
| 1860/59 | 32,256 | £500 | £1500 | £3750 | £6000 |

*Prices of bronze pennies of Victoria bun head are for the common type, there are many varieties.*

**Bronze**

| DATE | MINTAGE | F | VF | EF | UNC |
|---|---|---|---|---|---|
| 1860 Beaded border | 5,053,440 | £25 | £45 | £150 | £600 |
| 1860 Toothed border | incl. above | £6 | £16 | £55 | £250 |
| 1860 — Piedfort flan | — | Extremely rare | | | |
| 1861 | 36,449,280 | £5 | £12 | £50 | £220 |
| 1862 | 50,534,400 | £5 | £12 | £50 | £220 |
| 1862 8 over 6 | incl. above | Extremely rare | | | |
| 1863 | 28,062,720 | £5 | £12 | £45 | £200 |
| 1863 Die no below date | incl. above | Extremely rare | | | |
| 1864 Plain 4 | 3,440,640 | £25 | £140 | £500 | £2200 |
| 1864 Crosslet 4 | incl. above | £25 | £125 | £500 | £2500 |
| 1865 | 8,601,600 | £7 | £16 | £55 | £300 |
| 1865/3 5 over 3 | incl. above | £40 | £125 | £450 | — |
| 1866 | 9,999,360 | £6 | £18 | £70 | £350 |
| 1867 | 5,483,520 | £7 | £18 | £85 | £650 |
| 1868 | 1,182,720 | £15 | £70 | £200 | £700 |
| 1869 | 2,580,480 | £120 | £400 | £1250 | £4000 |
| 1870 | 5,695,022 | £9 | £35 | £125 | £500 |
| 1871 | 1,290,318 | £35 | £120 | £450 | £1750 |
| 1872 | 8,494,572 | £6 | £20 | £60 | £225 |
| 1873 | 8,494,200 | £6 | £20 | £60 | £225 |
| 1874 | 5,621,865 | £7 | £20 | £60 | £225 |
| 1874 H | 6,666,240 | £7 | £22 | £60 | £225 |
| 1874 Later (older) bust | incl. above | £12 | £30 | £85 | £350 |
| 1875 | 10,691,040 | £7 | £22 | £75 | £275 |
| 1875 H | 752,640 | £35 | £110 | £800 | £2500 |
| 1876 H | 11,074,560 | £5 | £12 | £60 | £220 |
| 1877 | 9,624,747 | £5 | £14 | £55 | £220 |
| 1878 | 2,764,470 | £5 | £14 | £55 | £220 |
| 1879 | 7,666,476 | £4 | £12 | £55 | £220 |
| 1880 | 3,000,831 | £4 | £12 | £55 | £220 |

*Victoria*
*copper penny*

*(N.B. Prices for Victoria Bun head coins will be considerably higher in mint with full lustre)*

| DATE | MINTAGE | F | VF | EF | UNC |
|---|---|---|---|---|---|
| 1881 | 2,302,362 | £5 | £12 | £55 | £220 |
| 1881 H | 3,763,200 | £5 | £12 | £55 | £200 |
| 1882 H | 7,526,400 | £5 | £12 | £55 | £200 |
| 1882 no H | — | | Extremely Rare | | |
| 1883 | 6,237,438 | £5 | £14 | £55 | £200 |
| 1884 | 11,702,802 | £5 | £14 | £55 | £190 |
| 1885 | 7,145,862 | £5 | £14 | £55 | £190 |
| 1886 | 6,087,759 | £5 | £14 | £55 | £190 |
| 1887 | 5,315,085 | £5 | £14 | £55 | £190 |
| 1888 | 5,125,020 | £5 | £14 | £55 | £190 |
| 1889 | 12,559,737 | £4 | £14 | £50 | £200 |
| 1890 | 15,330,840 | £4 | £14 | £50 | £180 |
| 1891 | 17,885,961 | £4 | £12 | £50 | £180 |
| 1892 | 10,501,671 | £5 | £14 | £70 | £200 |
| 1893 | 8,161,737 | £4 | £12 | £50 | £175 |
| 1894 | 3,883,452 | £8 | £30 | £110 | £325 |

**OLD HEAD ISSUES**

| | | | | | |
|---|---|---|---|---|---|
| 1895 Trident 2mm from P(ENNY) | 5,395,830 | £15 | £65 | £175 | £500 |
| 1895 Trident 1mm from P | incl. above | — | £2 | £18 | £75 |
| 1896 | 24,147,156 | — | £2 | £18 | £65 |
| 1897 | 20,756,620 | — | £2 | £15 | £60 |
| 1897 Raised dot after One (O·NE) | | £125 | £225 | £700 | — |
| 1898 | 14,296,836 | — | £3 | £18 | £60 |
| 1899 | 26,441,069 | — | £3 | £16 | £50 |
| 1900 | 31,778,109 | — | £3 | £16 | £40 |
| 1901 | 22,205,568 | — | £3 | £10 | £30 |

## EDWARD VII (1901–10)

| | | | | | |
|---|---|---|---|---|---|
| 1902 | 26,976,768 | — | £1 | £8 | £25 |
| 1902 "Low tide" to sea line | incl. above | £4 | £15 | £60 | £200 |
| 1903 | 21,415,296 | — | £3 | £15 | £80 |
| 1904 | 12,913,152 | — | £4 | £25 | £150 |
| 1905 | 17,783,808 | — | £3 | £15 | £80 |
| 1906 | 37,989,504 | — | £3 | £15 | £70 |
| 1907 | 47,322,240 | — | £3 | £15 | £70 |
| 1908 | 31,506,048 | — | £3 | £18 | £90 |
| 1909 | 19,617,024 | — | £3 | £20 | £140 |
| 1910 | 29,549,184 | — | £3 | £15 | £60 |

## GEORGE V (1910–36)

| | | | | | |
|---|---|---|---|---|---|
| 1911 | 23,079,168 | — | £3 | £12 | £50 |
| 1912 | 48,306,048 | — | £3 | £12 | £45 |
| 1912 H | 16,800,000 | — | £4 | £40 | £220 |
| 1913 | 65,497,812 | — | £3 | £15 | £70 |
| 1914 | 50,820,997 | — | £3 | £18 | £70 |
| 1915 | 47,310,807 | — | £3 | £20 | £80 |
| 1916 | 86,411,165 | — | £3 | £15 | £60 |
| 1917 | 107,905,436 | — | £3 | £15 | £50 |
| 1918 | 84,227,372 | — | £3 | £12 | £50 |
| 1918 H | 3,660,800 | £1 | £15 | £100 | £450 |
| 1918 KN | incl. above | £7 | £70 | £500 | £2000 |
| 1919 | 113,761,090 | — | £2 | £15 | £45 |
| 1919 H | 5,209,600 | £1 | £15 | £200 | £700 |
| 1919 KN | incl. above | £10 | £85 | £650 | £2500 |
| 1920 | 124,693,485 | — | £2 | £12 | £30 |
| 1921 | 129,717,693 | — | £2 | £12 | £30 |
| 1922 | 16,346,711 | — | £3 | £25 | £100 |
| 1922 with reverse of 1927 | | £1000 | £2500 | — | — |
| 1926 | 4,498,519 | — | £6 | £25 | £120 |
| 1926 Modified effigy | incl above | £25 | £150 | £800 | £2500 |
| 1927 | 60,989,561 | — | £2 | £10 | £35 |
| 1928 | 50,178,00 | — | £2 | £10 | £35 |
| 1929 | 49,132,800 | — | £2 | £10 | £35 |
| 1930 | 29,097,600 | — | £2 | £20 | £65 |
| 1931 | 19,843,200 | — | £2 | £10 | £45 |
| 1932 | 8,277,600 | — | £2 | £15 | £90 |
| 1933 | | | Only 7 examples known | | |

| DATE | MINTAGE | F | VF | EF | UNC |
|------|---------|---|----|----|-----|
| 1934 | 13,965,600 | — | £2 | £25 | £70 |
| 1935 | 56,070,000 | — | — | £2 | £10 |
| 1936 | 154,296,000 | — | — | £2 | £10 |

### GEORGE VI (1936–52)

| DATE | MINTAGE | F | VF | EF | UNC |
|------|---------|---|----|----|-----|
| 1937 | 88,896,000 | — | — | — | £4 |
| 1937 Proof | 26,402 | — | — | — | £14 |
| 1938 | 121,560,000 | — | — | — | £6 |
| 1939 | 55,560,000 | — | — | — | £15 |
| 1940 | 42,284,400 | — | — | £8 | £25 |
| 1944 Mint Dark | 42,600,000 | — | — | — | £8 |
| 1945 Mint Dark | 79,531,200 | — | — | — | £8 |
| 1946 Mint Dark | 66,855,600 | — | — | — | £8 |
| 1947 | 52,220,400 | — | — | — | £5 |
| 1948 | 63,961,200 | — | — | — | £5 |
| 1949 | 14,324,400 | — | — | — | £8 |
| 1950 | 240,000 | £7 | £15 | £30 | £50 |
| 1950 Proof | 17,513 | — | — | — | £25 |
| 1951 | 120,000 | £18 | £30 | £50 | £75 |
| 1951 Proof | 20,000 | — | — | — | £40 |

### ELIZABETH II (1952–   )

| DATE | MINTAGE | F | VF | EF | UNC |
|------|---------|---|----|----|-----|
| 1953 | 1,308,400 | — | — | £1 | £4 |
| 1953 Proof | 40,000 | — | — | — | £7 |
| 1954 | Only one known | | | | |
| 1961 | 48,313,400 | — | — | — | £2 |
| 1962 | 143,308,600 | — | — | — | 50p |
| 1963 | 125,235,600 | — | — | — | 50p |
| 1964 | 153,294,000 | — | — | — | 50p |
| 1965 | 121,310,400 | — | — | — | 50p |
| 1966 | 165,739,200 | — | — | — | 50p |
| 1967 | 654,564,000 | — | — | — | — |

*Later issues are included in the Decimal section.*

# HALFPENNIES

| DATE | F | VF | EF | UNC |
|------|---|----|----|-----|

### CHARLES II (1660–85)

| | F | VF | EF | UNC |
|---|---|----|----|-----|
| 1672 | £70 | £300 | £1200 | — |
| 1672 CRAOLVS error | | Extremely rare | | |
| 1673 | £70 | £300 | £1150 | — |
| 1673 CRAOLVS error | | Extremely rare | | |
| 1673 No rev. stop | £100 | £600 | — | — |
| 1673 No stops on obv. | | Extremely rare | | |
| 1675 | £60 | £500 | £1250 | — |
| 1675 No stops on obv. | £80 | £550 | — | — |
| 1675/3 5 over 3 | £175 | £600 | — | — |

### JAMES II (1685–88)

| | F | VF | EF | UNC |
|---|---|----|----|-----|
| 1685 (tin) | £225 | £700 | £3250 | — |
| 1686 (tin) | £250 | £700 | £3750 | — |
| 1687 (tin) | £300 | £750 | £3750 | — |

### WILLIAM & MARY (1688–94)

*Tin*

| | F | VF | EF | UNC |
|---|---|----|----|-----|
| 1689 Small draped busts, edge dated | | Extremely rare | | |
| 1690 Large cuirassed busts, edge dated | £175 | £700 | £3000 | — |
| 1691 — date on edge and in exergue | £160 | £650 | £2800 | — |
| 1692 — — | £160 | £650 | £2800 | — |

| DATE | F | VF | EF | UNC |
|------|---|----|----|-----|

*Copper*

| | F | VF | EF | UNC |
|------|---|----|----|-----|
| 1694 Large cuirassed busts, date in exergue .. | £75 | £300 | £1000 | — |
| 1694 — — GVLIEMVS error | | | Extremely rare | |
| 1694 — — MΛRIΛ error | | | Extremely rare | |
| 1694 — — No stops on rev. | | | Extremely rare | |

## WILLIAM III (1694–1702)

| | F | VF | EF | UNC |
|------|---|----|----|-----|
| 1695 First issue (date in exergue) | £45 | £175 | £1000 | — |
| 1695 — No stop after BRITANNIA on rev. | | | Extremely rare | |
| 1696 — | £35 | £160 | £900 | — |
| 1696 — TERTVS error | | | Extremely rare | |
| 1697 — | £35 | £150 | £850 | — |
| 1697 — No stop after TERTIVS on obv. | £50 | £275 | — | — |
| 1698 — | £45 | £200 | £1000 | — |
| 1698 Second issue (date in legend) | £45 | £180 | — | — |
| 1698 — No stop after date | £45 | £180 | — | — |
| 1699 — | £50 | £200 | £1000 | — |
| 1699 — No stop after date | £225 | — | — | — |
| 1699 Third issue (date in exergue) (Britannia with right hand on knee) | £40 | £160 | £850 | — |
| 1699 — No stop after date | | | Extremely rare | |
| 1699 — BRITΛNNIΛ error | £200 | — | — | — |
| 1699 — TERTVS error | | | Extremely rare | |
| 1699 — No stop on rev. | | | Extremely rare | |
| 1699 — No stops on obv. | £90 | £350 | — | — |
| 1700 — | £40 | £170 | £850 | — |
| 1700 — No stops on obv. | £100 | £350 | — | — |
| 1700 — No stops after GVLIELMUS | £100 | £350 | — | — |
| 1700 — BRITVANNIA error | | | Extremely rare | |
| 1700 — GVIELMS error | £100 | £350 | — | — |
| 1700 — GVLIEEMVS error | £100 | £350 | — | — |
| 1701 — | £40 | £175 | £850 | — |
| 1701 — BRITΛNNIΛ error | £70 | £275 | — | — |
| 1701 — No stops on obv. | | | Extremely rare | |
| 1701 — inverted As for Vs | £70 | £300 | — | — |

## GEORGE I (1714–27)

| | F | VF | EF | UNC |
|------|---|----|----|-----|
| 1717 "Dump" issue | £40 | £225 | £800 | |
| 1718 — | £35 | £200 | £700 | |
| 1719 "Dump" issue. Patterns | | | | Rare |
| 1719 Second issue | £40 | £180 | £800 | — |
| 1720 — | £30 | £160 | £575 | — |
| 1721 — | £30 | £140 | £550 | — |
| 1721 — Stop after date | £40 | £150 | — | — |
| 1722 — | £30 | £140 | £600 | — |
| 1722 — inverted A for V on obv. | | | Extremely rare | |
| 1723 — | £30 | £140 | £600 | — |
| 1723 — No stop on rev. | £100 | £375 | — | — |
| 1724 — | £30 | £140 | £600 | — |

## GEORGE II (1727–60)

| | F | VF | EF | UNC |
|------|---|----|----|-----|
| 1729 Young head | £25 | £80 | £400 | — |
| 1729 — No stop on rev. | £25 | £75 | £400 | — |
| 1730 — | £20 | £80 | £400 | — |
| 1730 — GEOGIVS error | £70 | £225 | £650 | — |
| 1730 — Stop after date | £25 | £110 | £400 | — |
| 1730 — No stop after REX on obv. | £30 | £140 | £450 | — |
| 1731 — | £20 | £100 | £400 | — |
| 1731 — No rev. stop | £25 | £125 | £425 | — |
| 1732 — | £20 | £100 | £375 | — |
| 1732 — No rev. stop | £25 | £125 | £450 | — |
| 1733 — | £20 | £80 | £375 | — |

| DATE | MINTAGE | F | VF | EF | UNC |
|------|--------:|---|----|----|-----|
| 1734/3 — 4 over 3 | | £35 | £200 | — | — |
| 1734 — No stop on obv. | | £35 | £200 | — | — |
| 1735 — | | £20 | £80 | £375 | — |
| 1736 — | | £20 | £80 | £375 | — |
| 1737 — | | £20 | £85 | £400 | — |
| 1738 — | | £20 | £80 | £340 | — |
| 1739 — | | £18 | £70 | £325 | — |
| 1740 Old head | | £15 | £70 | £300 | — |
| 1742 — | | £15 | £70 | £300 | — |
| 1742/0 — 2 over 0 | | £25 | £150 | £400 | — |
| 1743 — | | £15 | £70 | £300 | — |
| 1744 — | | £15 | £70 | £300 | — |
| 1745 — | | £15 | £70 | £300 | — |
| 1746 — | | £15 | £70 | £300 | — |
| 1747 — | | £15 | £70 | £300 | — |
| 1748 — | | £15 | £70 | £300 | — |
| 1749 — | | £15 | £70 | £300 | — |
| 1750 — | | £15 | £70 | £300 | — |
| 1751 — | | £15 | £70 | £300 | — |
| 1752 — | | £15 | £70 | £300 | — |
| 1753 — | | £15 | £70 | £300 | — |
| 1754 — | | £15 | £70 | £300 | — |

## GEORGE III (1760–1820)

*First type—Royal Mint*

| DATE | MINTAGE | F | VF | EF | UNC |
|------|--------:|---|----|----|-----|
| 1770 | | £18 | £50 | £250 | — |
| 1770 No stop on rev. | | £25 | £65 | £300 | — |
| 1771 | | £12 | £50 | £280 | — |
| 1771 No stop on rev. | | £20 | £65 | £300 | — |
| 1772 Error GEORIVS | | £60 | £200 | £650 | |
| 1772 | | £12 | £45 | £200 | — |
| 1772 No stop on rev | | £20 | £65 | £280 | — |
| 1773 | | £10 | £45 | £250 | — |
| 1773 No stop after REX | | £25 | £70 | £350 | — |
| 1773 No stop on rev. | | £20 | £65 | £280 | — |
| 1774 | | £12 | £40 | £220 | — |
| 1775 | | £12 | £40 | £220 | — |

*Second type—Soho Mint*

| | | | | | |
|------|--------:|---|----|----|-----|
| 1799 | | £5 | £12 | £55 | £120 |

*Third type*

| | | | | | |
|------|--------:|---|----|----|-----|
| 1806 | | £5 | £11 | £60 | £110 |
| 1807 | | £5 | £11 | £60 | £110 |

*George III second type*

## GEORGE IV (1820–30)

| DATE | MINTAGE | F | VF | EF | UNC |
|------|--------:|---|----|----|-----|
| 1825 | 215,040 | £12 | £45 | £160 | £300 |
| 1826 (varieties) | 9,031,630 | £12 | £45 | £160 | £300 |
| 1826 Proof | — | — | — | — | £450 |
| 1827 | 5,376,000 | £12 | £45 | £130 | £260 |

## WILLIAM IV (1830–37)

| DATE | MINTAGE | F | VF | EF | UNC |
|------|--------:|---|----|----|-----|
| 1831 | 806,400 | £12 | £30 | £110 | £300 |
| 1831 Proof | — | — | — | — | £400 |
| 1834 | 537,600 | £12 | £30 | £110 | £300 |
| 1837 | 349,440 | £12 | £30 | £110 | £300 |

## VICTORIA (1837–1901)

### YOUNG HEAD ISSUES

*Copper*

| DATE | MINTAGE | F | VF | EF | UNC |
|------|--------:|---|----|----|-----|
| 1838 | 456,960 | £7 | £18 | £80 | £250 |
| 1839 Proof | 268,800 | — | — | — | £400 |

| DATE | MINTAGE | F | VF | EF | UNC |
|---|---|---|---|---|---|
| 1841 | 1,075,200 | £5 | £16 | £60 | £175 |
| 1843 | 967,680 | £25 | £50 | £200 | £600 |
| 1844 | 1,075,200 | £6 | £18 | £60 | |
| £2001845 | 1,075,200 | £110 | £275 | £1250 | — |
| 1846 | 860,160 | £8 | £20 | £65 | £180 |
| 1847 | 725,640 | £8 | £18 | £65 | £175 |
| 1848 | 322,560 | £8 | £18 | £60 | £175 |
| 1848/7 final 8 OVER 7 | incl. above | £10 | £25 | £70 | £220 |
| 1851 | 215,040 | £5 | £15 | £60 | £175 |
| 1852 | 637,056 | £8 | £20 | £60 | £180 |
| 1853 | 1,559,040 | £4 | £8 | £35 | £100 |
| 1853/2 3 over 2 | incl. above | £15 | £30 | £60 | £200 |
| 1853 Proof | — | — | — | — | £550 |
| 1854 | 12,354,048 | £4 | £8 | £40 | £100 |
| 1855 | 1,455,837 | £4 | £8 | £40 | £100 |
| 1856 | 1,942,080 | £8 | £20 | £70 | £220 |
| 1857 | 1,820,720 | £5 | £15 | £50 | £100 |
| 1858 | 2,472,960 | £4 | £10 | £45 | £100 |
| 1858/7 final 8 over 7 | incl. above | £4 | £10 | £45 | £100 |
| 1858/6 final 8 over 6 | incl. above | £4 | £10 | £45 | £100 |
| 1859 | 1,290,240 | £7 | £20 | £60 | £180 |
| 1859/8 9 over 8 | incl. above | £8 | £25 | £70 | £220 |
| 1860 | unrecorded | £1200 | £3000 | £6500 | £10000 |

*Bronze*

| DATE | MINTAGE | F | VF | EF | UNC |
|---|---|---|---|---|---|
| 1860 Beaded border | 6,630,400 | £3 | £10 | £50 | £180 |
| 1860 Toothed border | | £4 | £12 | £60 | £250 |
| 1861 | 54,118,400 | £4 | £10 | £40 | £160 |
| 1862 Die letter A, B or C to left of lighthouse | | | | Extremely rare | |
| 1862 | 61,107,200 | £3 | £9 | £40 | £140 |
| 1863 | 15,948,800 | £3 | £9 | £75 | £140 |
| 1864 | 537,600 | £3 | £10 | £45 | £150 |
| 1865 | 8,064,000 | £4 | £18 | £75 | £250 |
| 1865/3 5 over 3 | incl. above | £40 | £100 | £400 | — |
| 1866 | 2,508,800 | £5 | £15 | £60 | £200 |
| 1867 | 2,508,800 | £5 | £15 | £50 | £180 |
| 1868 | 3,046,400 | £5 | £15 | £60 | £220 |
| 1869 | 3,225,600 | £20 | £80 | £225 | £900 |
| 1870 | 4,350,739 | £5 | £15 | £60 | £220 |
| 1871 | 1,075,280 | £75 | £100 | £400 | £1250 |
| 1872 | 4,659,410 | £4 | £10 | £50 | £170 |
| 1873 | 3,404,880 | £4 | £10 | £50 | £200 |
| 1874 | 1,347,655 | £5 | £25 | £110 | £300 |
| 1874 H | 5,017,600 | £3 | £10 | £60 | £210 |
| 1875 | 5,430,815 | £3 | £8 | £60 | £175 |
| 1875 H | 1,254,400 | £5 | £12 | £60 | £200 |
| 1876 H | 5,809,600 | £4 | £10 | £60 | £220 |
| 1877 | 5,209,505 | £3 | £10 | £60 | £175 |
| 1878 | 1,425,535 | £5 | £20 | £100 | £300 |
| 1878 Wide date | | £100 | £200 | £400 | — |
| 1879 | 3,582,545 | £3 | £10 | £40 | £175 |
| 1880 | 2,423,465 | £4 | £12 | £60 | £190 |
| 1881 | 2,007,515 | £4 | £12 | £50 | £160 |
| 1881 H | 1,792,000 | £3 | £10 | £50 | £175 |
| 1882 H | 4,480,000 | £3 | £10 | £50 | £180 |
| 1883 | 3,000,725 | £3 | £12 | £55 | £175 |
| 1884 | 6,989,580 | £3 | £10 | £45 | £140 |
| 1885 | 8,600,574 | £3 | £10 | £45 | £140 |
| 1886 | 8,586,155 | £3 | £10 | £45 | £140 |
| 1887 | 10,701,305 | £3 | £10 | £45 | £110 |
| 1888 | 6,814,670 | £3 | £10 | £45 | £140 |
| 1889 | 7,748,234 | £3 | £10 | £45 | £140 |
| 1889/8 9 over 8 | incl. above | £20 | £50 | £160 | — |

*Victoria copper halfpenny*

*Victoria bronze halfpenny*

| DATE | MINTAGE | F | VF | EF | UNC |
|------|---------|---|----|----|----|
| 1890 | 11,254,235 | £3 | £10 | £40 | £110 |
| 1891 | 13,192,260 | £3 | £10 | £35 | £110 |
| 1892 | 2,478,335 | £3 | £10 | £45 | £140 |
| 1893 | 7,229,344 | £3 | £10 | £35 | £110 |
| 1894 | 1,767,635 | £5 | £10 | £70 | £220 |

**OLD HEAD ISSUES**

| | | | | | |
|------|---------|---|----|----|----|
| 1895 | 3,032,154 | £2 | £6 | £18 | £60 |
| 1896 | 9,142,500 | £1 | £4 | £10 | £45 |
| 1897 | 8,690,315 | £1 | £4 | £10 | £45 |
| 1898 | 8,595,180 | £1 | £5 | £12 | £50 |
| 1899 | 12,108,001 | £1 | £4 | £10 | £45 |
| 1900 | 13,805,190 | £1 | £4 | £10 | £35 |
| 1901 | 11,127,360 | £1 | £2 | £8 | £22 |

## EDWARD VII (1901–10)

| | | | | | |
|------|---------|---|----|----|----|
| 1902 | 13,672,960 | £2 | £4 | £8 | £30 |
| 1902 "Low tide" | incl. above | £15 | £60 | £150 | £375 |
| 1903 | 11,450,880 | £2 | £5 | £20 | £50 |
| 1904 | 8,131,200 | £2 | £6 | £25 | £70 |
| 1905 | 10,124,800 | £2 | £5 | £20 | £45 |
| 1906 | 16,849,280 | £2 | £5 | £25 | £60 |
| 1907 | 16,849,280 | £2 | £5 | £20 | £60 |
| 1908 | 16,620,800 | £2 | £5 | £20 | £60 |
| 1909 | 8,279,040 | £2 | £5 | £20 | £60 |
| 1910 | 10,769,920 | £2 | £5 | £20 | £50 |

## GEORGE V (1910–36)

| | | | | | |
|------|---------|---|----|----|----|
| 1911 | 12,570,880 | £1 | £4 | £15 | £40 |
| 1912 | 21,185,920 | £1 | £3 | £15 | £35 |
| 1913 | 17,476,480 | £1 | £3 | £15 | £40 |
| 1914 | 20,289,111 | £1 | £3 | £15 | £40 |
| 1915 | 21,563,040 | £2 | £3 | £20 | £55 |
| 1916 | 39,386,143 | £1 | £2 | £15 | £40 |
| 1917 | 38,245,436 | £1 | £2 | £15 | £35 |
| 1918 | 22,321,072 | £1 | £2 | £15 | £35 |
| 1919 | 28,104,001 | £1 | £2 | £15 | £35 |
| 1920 | 35,146,793 | £1 | £2 | £15 | £40 |
| 1921 | 28,027,293 | £1 | £2 | £15 | £40 |
| 1922 | 10,734,964 | £1 | £3 | £20 | £45 |
| 1923 | 12,266,282 | £1 | £2 | £15 | £35 |
| 1924 | 13,971,038 | £1 | £2 | £15 | £30 |
| 1925 | 12,216,123 | — | £2 | £15 | £30 |
| 1925 Modified effigy | incl. above | £3 | £8 | £40 | £80 |
| 1926 | 6,172,306 | — | £2 | £10 | £40 |
| 1927 | 15,589,622 | — | £2 | £10 | £35 |
| 1928 | 20,935,200 | — | £2 | £8 | £30 |
| 1929 | 25,680,000 | — | £2 | £8 | £30 |
| 1930 | 12,532,800 | — | £2 | £8 | £30 |
| 1931 | 16,137,600 | — | £2 | £8 | £30 |
| 1932 | 14,448,000 | — | £2 | £8 | £30 |
| 1933 | 10,560,000 | — | £2 | £8 | £30 |
| 1934 | 7,704,000 | | £2 | £12 | £40 |
| 1935 | 12,180,000 | — | £1 | £6 | £18 |
| 1936 | 23,008,800 | — | £1 | £5 | £15 |

## GEORGE VI (1936–52)

| | | | | | |
|------|---------|---|----|----|----|
| 1937 | 24,504,000 | — | — | £1 | £5 |
| 1937 Proof | 26,402 | — | — | — | £12 |
| 1938 | 40,320,000 | — | — | £1 | £6 |
| 1939 | 28,924,800 | — | — | £1 | £5 |

| DATE | MINTAGE | F | VF | EF | UNC |
|---|---|---|---|---|---|
| 1940 | 32,162,400 | — | — | £2 | £10 |
| 1941 | 45,120,000 | — | — | £1 | £8 |
| 1942 | 71,908,800 | — | — | £1 | £5 |
| 1943 | 76,200,000 | — | — | £1 | £5 |
| 1944 | 81,840,000 | — | — | £1 | £5 |
| 1945 | 57,000,000 | — | — | £1 | £5 |
| 1946 | 22,725,600 | — | — | £1 | £6 |
| 1947 | 21,266,400 | — | — | £1 | £6 |
| 1948 | 26,947,200 | — | — | £1 | £4 |
| 1949 | 24,744,000 | — | — | £1 | £4 |
| 1950 | 24,153,600 | — | — | £1 | £5 |
| 1950 Proof | 17,513 | — | — | — | £12 |
| 1951 | 14,868,000 | — | — | £1 | £6 |
| 1951 Proof | 20,000 | — | — | — | £12 |
| 1952 | 33,78,400 | — | — | £1 | £4 |

## ELIZABETH II (1952–    )

| | | | | | |
|---|---|---|---|---|---|
| 1953 | 8,926,366 | — | — | — | £1 |
| 1953 Proof | 40,000 | — | — | — | £4 |
| 1954 | 19,375,000 | — | — | — | £3 |
| 1955 | 18,799,200 | — | — | — | £3 |
| 1956 | 21,799,200 | — | — | — | £3 |
| 1957 | 43,684,800 | — | — | — | £1 |
| 1957 Calm sea | incl. above8 | — | — | £10 | £30 |
| 1958 | 62,318,400 | — | — | — | £1 |
| 1959 | 79,176,000 | — | — | — | £1 |
| 1960 | 41,340,000 | — | — | — | £1 |
| 1962 | 41,779,200 | — | — | — | £1 |
| 1963 | 45,036,000 | — | — | — | 20p |
| 1964 | 78,583,200 | — | — | — | 20p |
| 1965 | 98,083,200 | — | — | — | 20p |
| 1966 | 95,289,600 | — | — | — | 20p |
| 1967 | 146,491,200 | — | — | — | 10p |

*Later issues are included in the Decimal section.*

# FARTHINGS

| DATE | | F | VF | EF | UNC |
|---|---|---|---|---|---|

## OLIVER CROMWELL

Undated (copper) Draped bust, shield rev. Variations  Extremely rare

## CHARLES II (1660–85)

*Copper*

| | F | VF | EF | |
|---|---|---|---|---|
| 1672 | £40 | £225 | £700 | — |
| 1673 | £45 | £240 | £725 | — |
| 1673 CAROLA for CAROLO error | £125 | £500 | — | — |
| 1673 No stops on obv. | | | Extremely rare | |
| 1673 No stop on rev. | | | Extremely rare | |
| 1674 | £45 | £250 | £750 | — |
| 1675 | £40 | £220 | £675 | — |
| 1675 No stop after CAROLVS | | | Extremely rare | |
| 1679 | £55 | £250 | £800 | — |
| 1679 No stop on rev. | £60 | £300 | — | — |
| *Tin* | | | | |
| 1684 with date on edge | £200 | £650 | — | — |
| 1685 — | | | Extremely rare | |

| DATE | F | VF | EF | UNC |
|---|---|---|---|---|

## JAMES II (1685–88)

| | F | VF | EF | UNC |
|---|---|---|---|---|
| 1684 (tin) Cuirassed bust...................................... | | Extremely rare | | |
| 1685 (tin) — ....................................................... | £170 | £600 | £2250 | — |
| 1686 (tin) — ....................................................... | £180 | £600 | £2250 | — |
| 1687 (tin) — ....................................................... | | Extremely rare | | |
| 1687 (tin) Draped bust...................................... | £220 | £800 | — | — |

## WILLIAM & MARY (1688–94)

| | F | VF | EF | UNC |
|---|---|---|---|---|
| 1689 (tin) Small draped busts............................ | £650 | — | — | — |
| 1689 (tin) — with edge date 1690 ..................... | | Extremely rare | | |
| 1690 (tin) Large cuirassed busts ...................... | £150 | £600 | £2750 | — |
| 1690 (tin) — with edge date 1689 ..................... | | Extremely rare | | |
| 1691 (tin) — ....................................................... | £160 | £600 | | |
| 1692 (tin) — ....................................................... | £175 | £650 | £2750 | — |
| 1694 (copper) — ............................................... | £70 | £240 | £850 | — |
| 1694 No stop after MARIΛ ................................ | | Extremely rare | | |
| 1694 No stop on obv. ....................................... | | Extremely rare | | |
| 1694 No stop on rev. ........................................ | | Extremely rare | | |
| 1694 Unbarred As in BRITANNIA ...................... | | Extremely rare | | |

## WILLIAM III (1694–1702)

| | F | VF | EF | UNC |
|---|---|---|---|---|
| 1695 First issue (date in exergue)...................... | £40 | £200 | £800 | — |
| 1695 — GVLIELMV error.................................... | | Extremely rare | | |
| 1696 — ............................................................. | £40 | £200 | £800 | — |
| 1697 — ............................................................. | £40 | £200 | £800 | — |
| 1697 — GVLIELMS error................................... | | Extremely rare | | |
| 1698 — ............................................................. | £200 | £700 | — | — |
| 1698 Second issue (date in legend) ................. | £50 | £250 | £800 | — |
| 1699 First issue ............................................... | £40 | £200 | £750 | — |
| 1699 Second issue ........................................... | £40 | £200 | £750 | — |
| 1699 — No stop after date.............................. | £50 | £275 | — | — |
| 1700 First issue ............................................... | £35 | £140 | £650 | — |
| 1700 — error RRITANNIA ................................. | | Extremely rare | | |

## ANNE (1702–14)

| | F | VF | EF | UNC |
|---|---|---|---|---|
| 1714.................................................................. | £350 | £600 | £1250 | — |

## GEORGE I (1714–27)

| | F | VF | EF | UNC |
|---|---|---|---|---|
| 1717 First small "Dump" issue .......................... | £200 | £575 | £1100 | — |
| 1718 1 Known .................................................. | | | | — |
| 1719 Second issue........................................... | £30 | £140 | £450 | — |
| 1719 — No stop on rev.................................... | £70 | £350 | — | — |
| 1719 — No stops on obv................................. | £70 | £300 | — | — |
| 1720 — ............................................................. | £30 | £140 | £475 | — |
| 1721 — ............................................................. | £25 | £140 | £475 | — |
| 1721/0 — Last 1 over 0 .................................. | £40 | £150 | — | — |
| 1722 — ............................................................. | £35 | £125 | £450 | — |
| 1723 — ............................................................. | £35 | £125 | £475 | — |
| 1723 — R over sideways R in REX .................. | | Extremely rare | | |
| 1724 — ............................................................. | £35 | £140 | £475 | — |

## GEORGE II (1727–60)

| | F | VF | EF | UNC |
|---|---|---|---|---|
| 1730 Young head ............................................. | £15 | £60 | £275 | — |
| 1731 — ............................................................. | £15 | £60 | £275 | — |
| 1732 — ............................................................. | £15 | £75 | £325 | — |
| 1733 — ............................................................. | £15 | £70 | £325 | — |
| 1734 — ............................................................. | £15 | £65 | £325 | — |
| 1734 — No stop on obv. .................................. | £30 | £110 | £375 | — |

*George I, first type*

*George I second type*

| DATE | MINTAGE | F | VF | EF | UNC |
|---|---|---|---|---|---|
| 1735 — | | £15 | £60 | £275 | — |
| 1735 — 3 over 5 | | £20 | £100 | £375 | — |
| 1736 — | | £12 | £60 | £275 | — |
| 1737 — | | £12 | £60 | £275 | — |
| 1739 — | | £12 | £60 | £275 | — |
| 1741 Old Head | | £12 | £50 | £270 | — |
| 1744 — | | £11 | £50 | £275 | — |
| 1746 — | | £11 | £50 | £275 | — |
| 1746 — V over LL in GEORGIVS | | | | Extremely rare | |
| 1749 — | | £15 | £60 | £250 | — |
| 1750 — | | £15 | £55 | £240 | — |
| 1754 — | | £9 | £30 | £175 | — |
| 1754 — 4 over 0 | | £25 | £100 | £300 | — |

## GEORGE III (1760–1820)

| DATE | MINTAGE | F | VF | EF | UNC |
|---|---|---|---|---|---|
| 1771 First (London) issue | | £20 | £60 | £250 | — |
| 1773 — | | £12 | £40 | £200 | — |
| 1773 — No stop on rev. | | £18 | £60 | £220 | — |
| 1773 — No stop after REX | | £25 | £75 | £250 | |
| 1774 — | | £10 | £40 | £180 | — |
| 1775 — | | £10 | £40 | £180 | — |
| 1797 Second (Soho Mint) issue | | | | Patterns only | |
| 1799 Third (Soho Mint) issue | | £2 | £8 | £40 | £100 |
| 1806 Fourth (Soho Mint) issue | | £2 | £8 | £40 | £100 |
| 1807 — | | £2 | £8 | £40 | £100 |

George III, third (Soho Mint) issue

## GEORGE IV (1820–30)

| DATE | MINTAGE | F | VF | EF | UNC |
|---|---|---|---|---|---|
| 1821 First bust (laureate, draped), first reverse (date in exergue) | 2,688,000 | £3 | £10 | £60 | £110 |
| 1822 — | 5,924,350 | £3 | £10 | £60 | £110 |
| 1823 — | 2,365,440 | £4 | £10 | £60 | £110 |
| 1823 I for 1 in date | incl. above | £20 | £70 | £250 | £110 |
| 1825 — | 4,300.800 | £4 | £10 | £60 | £130 |
| 1826 — | 6,666,240 | £4 | £10 | £60 | £110 |
| 1826 Second bust (couped, date below), second reverse (ornament in exergue) | incl. above | £4 | £10 | £60 | £110 |
| 1826 — Proof | — | — | — | — | £340 |
| 1827 — | 2,365,440 | £4 | £10 | £60 | £140 |
| 1828 — | 2,365,440 | £4 | £12 | £60 | £140 |
| 1829 — | 1,505,280 | £4 | £12 | £60 | £140 |
| 1830 — | 2,365,440 | £4 | £12 | £60 | £140 |

George III, fourth (Soho Mint) issue

## WILLIAM IV (1830–37)

| DATE | MINTAGE | F | VF | EF | UNC |
|---|---|---|---|---|---|
| 1831 | 2,688,000 | £5 | £12 | £45 | £120 |
| 1831 Proof | — | — | — | — | £340 |
| 1834 | 1,935,360 | £5 | £12 | £50 | £120 |
| 1835 | 1.720,320 | £5 | £12 | £50 | £120 |
| 1836 | 1,290.240 | £5 | £12 | £55 | £120 |
| 1837 | 3.010,560 | £5 | £12 | £55 | £135 |

## VICTORIA (1837–1901)

### FIRST YOUNG HEAD (COPPER) ISSUES

| DATE | MINTAGE | F | VF | EF | UNC |
|---|---|---|---|---|---|
| 1838 | 591,360 | £5 | £15 | £45 | £140 |
| 1839 | 4,300,800 | £5 | £15 | £45 | £140 |
| 1839 Proof | — | — | — | — | £350 |
| 1840 | 3,010,560 | £4 | £15 | £40 | £120 |
| 1841 | 1,720,320 | £4 | £15 | £40 | £140 |
| 1841 Proof | | | | Extremely rare | |
| 1842 | 1,290,240 | £10 | £35 | £100 | £300 |

| DATE | MINTAGE | F | VF | EF | UNC |
|---|---|---|---|---|---|
| 1843 | 4,085,760 | £5 | £12 | £40 | £140 |
| 1843 I for 1 in date | — | £80 | £400 | — | — |
| 1844 | 430,080 | £70 | £160 | £800 | £2000 |
| 1845 | 3,225,600 | £6 | £10 | £40 | £120 |
| 1846 | 2,580,480 | £7 | £20 | £55 | £170 |
| 1847 | 3,879,720 | £5 | £12 | £50 | £125 |
| 1848 | 1,290,240 | £5 | £12 | £50 | £125 |
| 1849 | 645,120 | £40 | £80 | £300 | £700 |
| 1850 | 430,080 | £5 | £10 | £40 | £110 |
| 1851 | 1,935,360 | £8 | £20 | £70 | £200 |
| 1851 D over sideways D in DEI | incl. above | £70 | £100 | £400 | — |
| 1852 | 822,528 | £10 | £20 | £70 | £200 |
| 1853 | 1,028,628 | £4 | £7 | £30 | £65 |
| 1853 Proof | — | — | — | — | £750 |
| 1854 | 6,504,960 | £4 | £10 | £35 | £60 |
| 1855 | 3,440,640 | £4 | £10 | £35 | £60 |
| 1856 | 1,771,392 | £8 | £20 | £65 | £200 |
| 1856 R over E in VICTORIA | incl. above | £20 | £50 | £200 | — |
| 1857 | 1,075,200 | £4 | £10 | £35 | £75 |
| 1858 | 1,720,320 | £4 | £10 | £35 | £75 |
| 1859 | 1,290,240 | £10 | £25 | £70 | £240 |
| 1860 | unrecorded | £1100 | £3000 | £6000 | — |

*Victoria Young Head first (copper) issue*

## SECOND YOUNG OR "BUN" HEAD (BRONZE) ISSUES

| DATE | MINTAGE | F | VF | EF | UNC |
|---|---|---|---|---|---|
| 1860 Toothed border | 2,867,200 | £2 | £5 | £40 | £100 |
| 1860 Beaded border | incl. above | £3 | £7 | £40 | £110 |
| 1860 Toothed/Beaded border mule | incl. above | | | Extremely rare | |
| 1861 | 8,601,600 | £2 | £5 | £35 | £100 |
| 1862 | 14,336,000 | £1 | £5 | £35 | £100 |
| 1862 Large 8 in date | incl. above | | | Extremely rare | |
| 1863 | 1,433,600 | £25 | £60 | £225 | £600 |
| 1864 | 2,508,800 | £1 | £5 | £30 | £100 |
| 1865 | 4,659,200 | £1 | £5 | £30 | £85 |
| 1865 5 over 2 | incl. above | £10 | £20 | £60 | — |
| 1866 | 3,584,000 | £1 | £5 | £25 | £85 |
| 1867 | 5,017,600 | £1 | £5 | £25 | £85 |
| 1868 | 4,851,210 | £1 | £5 | £25 | £85 |
| 1869 | 3,225,600 | £1 | £8 | £40 | £140 |
| 1872 | 2,150,400 | £1 | £5 | £25 | £70 |
| 1873 | 3,225,620 | £1 | £5 | £25 | £70 |
| 1874 H | 3,584,000 | £1 | £5 | £25 | £100 |
| 1874 H both Gs over sideways G | incl. above | £150 | £300 | £900 | — |
| 1875 | 712,760 | £4 | £12 | £40 | £125 |
| 1875 H | 6,092,800 | £1 | £5 | £20 | £70 |
| 1876 H | 1,175,200 | £3 | £12 | £50 | £140 |
| 1878 | 4,008,540 | £1 | £4 | £20 | £70 |
| 1879 | 3,977,180 | £1 | £4 | £20 | £70 |
| 1880 | 1,842,710 | £1 | £4 | £20 | £70 |
| 1881 | 3,494,670 | £1 | £4 | £20 | £70 |
| 1881 H | 1,792,000 | £1 | £4 | £20 | £70 |
| 1882 H | 1,792,000 | £1 | £5 | £20 | £70 |
| 1883 | 1,128,680 | £5 | £18 | £60 | £150 |
| 1884 | 5,782,000 | £1 | £4 | £20 | £40 |
| 1885 | 5,442,308 | £1 | £4 | £20 | £40 |
| 1886 | 7,707,790 | £1 | £4 | £20 | £40 |
| 1887 | 1,340,800 | £1 | £4 | £20 | £40 |
| 1888 | 1,887,250 | £1 | £4 | £20 | £40 |
| 1890 | 2,133,070 | £1 | £4 | £20 | £40 |
| 1891 | 4,959,690 | £1 | £4 | £20 | £40 |
| 1892 | 887,240 | £2 | £10 | £50 | £125 |
| 1893 | 3,904,320 | £1 | £4 | £20 | £40 |

*Victoria Young Head second (bronze) issue*

| DATE | MINTAGE | F | VF | EF | UNC |
|---|---|---|---|---|---|
| 1894 | 2,396,770 | £1 | £4 | £20 | £40 |
| 1895 | 2,852,852 | £10 | £25 | £80 | £220 |

**OLD HEAD ISSUES**

| | | | | | |
|---|---|---|---|---|---|
| 1895 Bright finish | incl. above | £1 | £2 | £16 | £35 |
| 1896 — | 3,668,610 | £1 | £2 | £16 | £25 |
| 1897 — | 4,579,800 | £1 | £2 | £16 | £25 |
| 1897 Dark finish | incl. above | £1 | £2 | £16 | £25 |
| 1898 — | 4,010,080 | £1 | £2 | £16 | £25 |
| 1899 — | 3,864,616 | £1 | £2 | £16 | £25 |
| 1900 — | 5,969,317 | £1 | £2 | £16 | £25 |
| 1901 — | 8,016,460 | £1 | £2 | £10 | £20 |

# EDWARD VII (1901–10)

| | | | | | |
|---|---|---|---|---|---|
| 1902 | 5,125,120 | 50p | £1 | £10 | £15 |
| 1903 | 5,331,200 | 50p | £1 | £12 | £20 |
| 1904 | 3,628,800 | £2 | £5 | £20 | £45 |
| 1905 | 4,076,800 | £1 | £2 | £12 | £30 |
| 1906 | 5,340,160 | 50p | £1 | £12 | £25 |
| 1907 | 4,399,360 | 50p | £1 | £10 | £20 |
| 1908 | 4,264,960 | 50p | £1 | £10 | £20 |
| 1909 | 8,852,480 | 50p | £1 | £10 | £20 |
| 1910 | 2,298,400 | £3 | £8 | £25 | £65 |

# GEORGE V (1910–36)

| | | | | | |
|---|---|---|---|---|---|
| 1911 | 5,196,800 | 25p | 50p | £5 | £12 |
| 1912 | 7,669,760 | 25p | 50p | £8 | £12 |
| 1913 | 4,184,320 | 25p | 50p | £5 | £12 |
| 1914 | 6,126,988 | 25p | 50p | £4 | £12 |
| 1915 | 7,129,255 | 25p | 50p | £4 | £14 |
| 1916 | 10,993,325 | 25p | 50p | £4 | £12 |
| 1917 | 21,434,844 | 25p | 50p | £4 | £10 |
| 1918 | 19,362,818 | 25p | 50p | £4 | £10 |
| 1919 | 15,089,425 | 25p | 50p | £4 | £10 |
| 1920 | 11,480,536 | 25p | 50p | £4 | £8 |
| 1921 | 9,469,097 | 25p | 50p | £4 | £8 |
| 1922 | 9,956,983 | 25p | 50p | £4 | £8 |
| 1923 | 8,034,457 | 25p | 50p | £4 | £8 |
| 1924 | 8,733,414 | 25p | 50p | £4 | £8 |
| 1925 | 12,634,697 | 25p | 50p | £4 | £8 |
| 1926 Modified effigy | 9,792,397 | 25p | 50p | £4 | £8 |
| 1927 | 7,868,355 | 25p | 50p | £4 | £8 |
| 1928 | 11,625,600 | 25p | 50p | £4 | £8 |
| 1929 | 8,419,200 | 25p | 50p | £4 | £8 |
| 1930 | 4,195,200 | 25p | 50p | £4 | £8 |
| 1931 | 6,595,200 | 25p | 50p | £4 | £8 |
| 1932 | 9,292,800 | 25p | 50p | £4 | £8 |
| 1933 | 4,560,000 | 25p | 50p | £4 | £8 |
| 1934 | 3,052,800 | 25p | 50p | £4 | £8 |
| 1935 | 2.227,200 | £1 | £3 | £10 | £25 |
| 1936 | 9,734,400 | 25p | 50p | £3 | £6 |

# GEORGE VI (1936–52)

| | | | | | |
|---|---|---|---|---|---|
| 1937 | 8,131,200 | — | — | 50p | £1 |
| 1937 Proof | 26,402 | — | — | — | £7 |
| 1938 | 7,449,600 | — | — | £1 | £6 |
| 1939 | 31,440,000 | — | — | 50p | £1 |
| 1940 | 18,360,000 | — | — | 50p | £1 |
| 1941 | 27,312,000 | — | — | 50p | £1 |
| 1942 | 28,857,600 | — | — | 50p | £1 |
| 1943 | 33,345,600 | — | — | 50p | £1 |

| DATE | MINTAGE | F | VF | EF | UNC |
|---|---|---|---|---|---|
| 1944 | 25,137,600 | — | — | 50p | £1 |
| 1945 | 23,736,000 | — | — | 50p | £1 |
| 1946 | 24,364,800 | — | — | 50p | £1 |
| 1947 | 14,745,600 | — | — | 50p | £1 |
| 1948 | 16,622,400 | — | — | 50p | £1 |
| 1949 | 8,424,000 | — | — | 50p | £1 |
| 1950 | 10,324,800 | — | — | 50p | £1 |
| 1950 Proof | 17,513 | — | — | 50p | £8 |
| 1951 | 14,016,000 | — | — | 50p | £1 |
| 1951 Proof | 20,000 | — | — | 50p | £8 |
| 1952 | 5,251,200 | — | — | 50p | £1 |

### ELIZABETH II (1952–  )

| | | | | | |
|---|---|---|---|---|---|
| 1953 | 6,131,037 | — | — | — | £1 |
| 1953 Proof | 40,000 | — | — | — | £7 |
| 1954 | 6,566,400 | — | — | — | £1 |
| 1955 | 5,779,200 | — | — | — | £1 |
| 1956 | 1,996,800 | — | £1 | £2 | £5 |

# HALF FARTHINGS

| DATE | MINTAGE | F | VF | EF | UNC |
|---|---|---|---|---|---|

### GEORGE IV (1820–30)

| | | | | | |
|---|---|---|---|---|---|
| 1828 (two different obverses) (issued for Ceylon) | 7,680,000 | £10 | £20 | £50 | £150 |
| 1830 (large or small date) (issued for Ceylon) | 8,766,320 | £10 | £20 | £50 | £140 |

### WILLIAM IV (1830–37)

| | | | | | |
|---|---|---|---|---|---|
| 1837 (issued for Ceylon) | 1,935,360 | £20 | £55 | £140 | £250 |

### VICTORIA (1837–1901)

| | | | | | |
|---|---|---|---|---|---|
| 1839 | 2,042,880 | £5 | £10 | £30 | £80 |
| 1842 | unrecorded | £4 | £8 | £25 | £80 |
| 1843 | 3,440,640 | £3 | £6 | £20 | £50 |
| 1844 | 6,451,200 | £3 | £6 | £15 | £50 |
| 1844 E over N in REGINA | incl. above | £10 | £45 | £100 | — |
| 1847 | 3,010,560 | £6 | £12 | £35 | £75 |
| 1851 | unrecorded | £5 | £12 | £35 | £100 |
| 1851 5 over 0 | unrecorded | £8 | £20 | £60 | £135 |
| 1852 | 989,184 | £5 | £12 | £40 | £100 |
| 1853 | 955,224 | £5 | £15 | £50 | £120 |
| 1853 Proof | incl. above | — | — | — | £400 |
| 1854 | 677,376 | £8 | £25 | £75 | £175 |
| 1856 | 913,920 | £8 | £25 | £75 | £175 |
| 1868 | unrecorded | — | — | — | Rare |
| 1868 | unrecorded | — | — | — | Rare |

# THIRD FARTHINGS

| DATE | MINTAGE | F | VF | EF | UNC |
|------|---------|---|----|----|----|

### GEORGE IV (1820–30)

| DATE | MINTAGE | F | VF | EF | UNC |
|------|---------|---|----|----|-----|
| 1827 (issued for Malta)............... | unrecorded | £8 | £18 | £50 | £125 |

### WILLIAM IV (1830–37)

| DATE | MINTAGE | F | VF | EF | UNC |
|------|---------|---|----|----|-----|
| 1835 (issued for Malta)............... | unrecorded | £8 | £18 | £50 | £140 |

### VICTORIA (1837–1901)

| DATE | MINTAGE | F | VF | EF | UNC |
|------|---------|---|----|----|-----|
| 1844 (issued for Malta)............... | 1,301,040 | £10 | £25 | £75 | £180 |
| 1844 RE for REG ........................ | incl. above | £30 | £60 | £250 | — |
| 1866............................................. | 576,000 | £6 | £15 | £35 | £70 |
| 1868............................................. | 144,000 | £6 | £15 | £35 | £65 |
| 1876............................................. | 162,000 | £6 | £15 | £35 | £80 |
| 1878............................................. | 288,000 | £6 | £15 | £35 | £70 |
| 1881............................................. | 144,000 | £6 | £15 | £35 | £75 |
| 1884............................................. | 144,000 | £6 | £15 | £35 | £75 |
| 1885............................................. | 288,000 | £6 | £15 | £35 | £75 |

### EDWARD VII (1902–10)

| DATE | MINTAGE | F | VF | EF | UNC |
|------|---------|---|----|----|-----|
| 1902 (issued for Malta)............... | 288,000 | £4 | £8 | £22 | £40 |

### GEORGE V (1911–36)

| DATE | MINTAGE | F | VF | EF | UNC |
|------|---------|---|----|----|-----|
| 1913 (issued for Malta)............... | 288,000 | £4 | £8 | £22 | £40 |

# QUARTER FARTHINGS

| DATE | MINTAGE | F | VF | EF | UNC |
|------|---------|---|----|----|----|

### VICTORIA (1837–1901)

| DATE | MINTAGE | F | VF | EF | UNC |
|------|---------|---|----|----|-----|
| 1839 (issued for Ceylon).............. | 3,840,000 | £30 | £50 | £90 | £200 |
| 1851 (issued for Ceylon).............. | 2,215,680 | £30 | £50 | £90 | £200 |
| 1852 (issued for Ceylon).............. | incl. above | £30 | £50 | £90 | £200 |
| 1853 (issued for Ceylon).............. | incl. above | £30 | £50 | £90 | £200 |
| 1853 Proof.................................... | — | — | — | — | £650 |

# EMERGENCY ISSUES

| DATE | F | VF | EF | UNC |
|------|---|-----|-----|------|

## GEORGE III (1760–1820)

*To alleviate the shortage of circulating coinage during the Napoleonic Wars the Bank of England firstly authorised the countermarking of other countries' coins, enabling them to pass as English currency. The coins, countermarked with punches depicting the head of George III, were mostly Spanish American 8 reales of Charles III. Although this had limited success it was later decided to completely overstrike the coins with a new English design on both sides— specimens that still show traces of the original host coin's date are avidly sought after by collectors. This overstriking continued for a number of years although all the known coins are dated 1804. Finally, in 1811 the Bank of England issued silver tokens which continued up to 1816 when a completely new regal coinage was introduced.*

### DOLLAR
*Oval countermark of George III*

| | F | VF | EF | UNC |
|---|---|-----|------|---|
| On "Pillar" type 8 reales .... | £175 | £650 | £1000 | — |
| *On "Portrait" type............. | £200 | £350 | £750 | — |

*Octagonal countermark of George III*

| | F | VF | EF | UNC |
|---|---|-----|------|---|
| On "Portrait" type ............. | £200 | £600 | £850 | — |

### HALF DOLLAR
*Oval countermark of George III*

| | F | VF | EF | UNC |
|---|---|-----|------|---|
| On "Portrait" type 4 reales | £200 | £400 | £900 | — |

### FIVE SHILLINGS OR ONE DOLLAR
*These coins were overstruck on Spanish-American coins*

| | F | VF | EF | UNC |
|---|---|-----|------|---|
| 1804................... | £110 | £275 | £550 | — |

— With details of original coin still visible add from 10%.

## BANK OF ENGLAND TOKENS

### THREE SHILLINGS

| | F | VF | EF | UNC |
|---|-----|------|-------|---|
| 1811 Draped bust............. | £35 | £60 | £200 | — |
| 1812 — ............................. | £35 | £60 | £220 | — |
| 1812 Laureate bust .......... | £35 | £60 | £150 | — |
| 1813 — ............................. | £35 | £60 | £150 | — |
| 1814 — ............................. | £35 | £60 | £150 | — |
| 1815 — ............................. | £35 | £60 | £150 | — |
| 1816 — ............................. | £200 | £400 | £1250 | — |

### ONE SHILLING AND SIXPENCE

| | F | VF | EF | UNC |
|---|-----|------|------|------|
| 1811 Draped bust............. | £20 | £45 | £100 | £175 |
| 1812 — ............................. | £20 | £45 | £100 | £175 |
| 1812 Laureate bust .......... | £20 | £45 | £100 | £175 |
| 1812 Proof in platinum ...... | | | | Unique |
| 1813 — ............................. | £20 | £40 | £75 | £175 |
| 1813 Proof in platinum ...... | | | | Unique |
| 1814 — ............................. | £20 | £35 | £75 | £160 |
| 1815 — ............................. | £20 | £35 | £75 | £160 |
| 1816 — ............................. | £20 | £35 | £75 | £160 |

### NINEPENCE

| | F | VF | EF | UNC |
|---|---|---|------|---|
| 1812 Pattern only ............. | — | — | Very Rare | |

# MAUNDY SETS

Sets in contemporary dated boxes are usually worth a higher premium. For example approximately £30 can be added to sets from Victoria to George VI in contemporary undated boxes and above £40 for dated boxes.

## CHARLES II (1660–85)

| DATE | F | VF | EF | UNC |
|---|---|---|---|---|
| Undated | £215 | £340 | £725 | — |
| 1670 | £195 | £330 | £700 | — |
| 1671 | £185 | £300 | £650 | — |
| 1672 | £185 | £300 | £670 | — |
| 1673 | £185 | £285 | £650 | — |
| 1674 | £190 | £290 | £670 | — |
| 1675 | £185 | £295 | £660 | — |
| 1676 | £200 | £325 | £680 | — |
| 1677 | £170 | £290 | £640 | — |
| 1678 | £240 | £435 | £800 | — |
| 1679 | £190 | £315 | £685 | — |
| 1680 | £185 | £300 | £650 | — |
| 1681 | £205 | £305 | £700 | — |
| 1682 | £190 | £310 | £650 | — |
| 1683 | £195 | £310 | £670 | — |
| 1684 | £215 | £385 | £715 | — |

## JAMES II (1685–88)

| DATE | F | VF | EF | UNC |
|---|---|---|---|---|
| 1686 | £205 | £330 | £685 | — |
| 1687 | £205 | £330 | £690 | — |
| 1688 | £210 | £360 | £700 | — |

## WILLIAM & MARY (1688–94)

| DATE | F | VF | EF | UNC |
|---|---|---|---|---|
| 1689 | £800 | £1100 | £1800 | — |
| 1691 | £675 | £800 | £1650 | — |
| 1692 | £650 | £875 | £1575 | — |
| 1693 | £450 | £725 | £1350 | — |
| 1694 | £425 | £675 | £1100 | — |

## WILLIAM III (1694–1702)

| DATE | F | VF | EF | UNC |
|---|---|---|---|---|
| 1698 | £220 | £425 | £825 | — |
| 1699 | £475 | £600 | £1400 | — |
| 1700 | £225 | £425 | £825 | — |
| 1701 | £215 | £400 | £795 | — |

## ANNE (1702–14)

| DATE | F | VF | EF | UNC |
|---|---|---|---|---|
| 1703 | £195 | £375 | £700 | — |
| 1705 | £185 | £340 | £675 | — |
| 1706 | £170 | £325 | £615 | — |
| 1708 | £515 | £800 | £1700 | — |
| 1709 | £220 | £400 | £775 | — |
| 1710 | £225 | £400 | £750 | — |
| 1713 | £190 | £375 | £675 | — |

## GEORGE I (1714–27)

| DATE | F | VF | EF | UNC |
|---|---|---|---|---|
| 1723 | £200 | £380 | £725 | — |
| 1727 | £195 | £375 | £705 | — |

## GEORGE II (1727–60)

| DATE | F | VF | EF | UNC |
|---|---|---|---|---|
| 1729 | £170 | £285 | £600 | — |
| 1731 | £170 | £290 | £600 | — |
| 1732 | £160 | £285 | £580 | — |
| 1735 | £155 | £275 | £580 | — |
| 1737 | £165 | £280 | £590 | — |
| 1739 | £155 | £275 | £550 | — |
| 1740 | £150 | £260 | £525 | — |
| 1743 | £240 | £375 | £800 | — |
| 1746 | £150 | £260 | £500 | — |
| 1760 | £165 | £270 | £540 | — |

## GEORGE III (1760–1820)

| DATE | F | VF | EF | UNC |
|---|---|---|---|---|
| 1763 | £145 | £260 | £440 | — |
| 1763 Proof | — | Extremely rare | | |
| 1766 | £160 | £255 | £465 | — |
| 1772 | £160 | £260 | £465 | — |
| 1780 | £150 | £270 | £480 | — |
| 1784 | £165 | £285 | £450 | — |
| 1786 | £160 | £260 | £450 | — |
| 1792 Wire | £215 | £370 | £575 | £725 |
| 1795 | £110 | £170 | £260 | £370 |
| 1800 | £110 | £160 | £250 | £350 |
| **New Coinage** | | | | |
| 1817 | £120 | £185 | £245 | £390 |
| 1818 | £115 | £175 | £240 | £385 |
| 1820 | £120 | £180 | £245 | £385 |

## GEORGE IV (1820–30)

| DATE | F | VF | EF | UNC |
|---|---|---|---|---|
| 1822 | — | £135 | £215 | £375 |
| 1823 | — | £130 | £225 | £350 |
| 1824 | — | £135 | £225 | £350 |
| 1825 | — | £125 | £220 | £350 |
| 1826 | — | £115 | £210 | £340 |
| 1827 | — | £115 | £220 | £345 |
| 1828 | — | £125 | £220 | £350 |
| 1828 Proof | — | — | — | £3250 |
| 1829 | — | £125 | £210 | £350 |
| 1830 | — | £125 | £215 | £350 |

## WILLIAM IV (1830–37)

| DATE | F | VF | EF | UNC |
|---|---|---|---|---|
| 1831 | — | £145 | £240 | £400 |
| 1831 Proof | — | — | — | £1200 |
| 1831 Proof Gold | — | — | | £32000 |
| 1832 | — | £145 | £235 | £385 |
| 1833 | — | £145 | £240 | £375 |
| 1834 | — | £145 | £245 | £375 |
| 1835 | — | £140 | £240 | £375 |
| 1836 | — | £150 | £235 | £395 |
| 1837 | — | £165 | £260 | £410 |

# VICTORIA (1837–1901)

**YOUNG HEAD ISSUES**

| DATE | MINTAGE | EF | UNC |
|---|---|---|---|
| 1838 | 4,158 | £185 | £350 |
| 1838 Proof | unrecorded | | £2400 |
| 1838 Proof Gold | | | £28000 |
| 1839 | 4,125 | £210 | £350 |
| 1839 Proof | unrecorded | £580 | £1050 |
| 1840 | 4,125 | £250 | £375 |
| 1841 | 2,574 | £280 | £475 |
| 1842 | 4,125 | £280 | £485 |
| 1843 | 4,158 | £215 | £350 |
| 1844 | 4,158 | £270 | £460 |
| 1845 | 4,158 | £190 | £315 |
| 1846 | 4,158 | £480 | £785 |
| 1847 | 4,158 | £470 | £750 |
| 1848 | 4,158 | £470 | £750 |
| 1849 | 4,158 | £290 | £450 |
| 1850 | 4,158 | £200 | £345 |
| 1851 | 4,158 | £205 | £345 |
| 1852 | 4,158 | £495 | £800 |
| 1853 | 4,158 | £480 | £800 |
| 1853 Proof | unrecorded | | £1400 |
| 1854 | 4,158 | £215 | £360 |
| 1855 | 4,158 | £225 | £375 |
| 1856 | 4,158 | £195 | £300 |
| 1857 | 4,158 | £215 | £350 |
| 1858 | 4,158 | £200 | £300 |
| 1859 | 4,158 | £185 | £285 |
| 1860 | 4,158 | £200 | £325 |
| 1861 | 4,158 | £175 | £310 |
| 1862 | 4,158 | £205 | £330 |
| 1863 | 4,158 | £225 | £370 |
| 1864 | 4,158 | £200 | £295 |
| 1865 | 4,158 | £205 | £305 |
| 1866 | 4,158 | £200 | £305 |
| 1867 | 4,158 | £190 | £310 |
| 1867 Proof | unrecorded | — | £2400 |
| 1868 | 4,158 | £180 | £270 |
| 1869 | 4,158 | £210 | £340 |
| 1870 | 4,458 | £165 | £250 |
| 1871 | 4,488 | £165 | £240 |
| 1871 Proof | unrecorded | — | £2100 |
| 1872 | 4,328 | £160 | £240 |
| 1873 | 4,162 | £160 | £230 |
| 1874 | 4,488 | £165 | £230 |
| 1875 | 4,154 | £160 | £230 |
| 1876 | 4,488 | £160 | £235 |
| 1877 | 4,488 | £160 | £205 |
| 1878 | 4,488 | £165 | £205 |
| 1878 Proof | unrecorded | — | £2100 |
| 1879 | 4,488 | £165 | £205 |
| 1879 Proof | unrecorded | — | £2500 |
| 1880 | 4,488 | £160 | £205 |
| 1881 | 4,488 | £160 | £210 |
| 1881 Proof | unrecorded | — | £1950 |
| 1882 | 4,146 | £175 | £240 |
| 1882 Proof | unrecorded | — | £2000 |
| 1883 | 4,488 | £135 | £195 |
| 1884 | 4,488 | £135 | £195 |
| 1885 | 4,488 | £135 | £195 |
| 1886 | 4,488 | £135 | £195 |
| 1887 | 4,488 | £160 | £225 |

**JUBILEE HEAD ISSUES**

| DATE | MINTAGE | EF | UNC |
|---|---|---|---|
| 1888 | 4,488 | £140 | £205 |
| 1888 Proof | unrecorded | — | £1850 |
| 1889 | 4,488 | £135 | £195 |
| 1890 | 4,488 | £140 | £200 |
| 1891 | 4,488 | £135 | £195 |
| 1892 | 4,488 | £145 | £205 |

**OLD HEAD ISSUES**

| DATE | MINTAGE | EF | UNC |
|---|---|---|---|
| 1893 | 8,976 | £90 | £150 |
| 1894 | 8,976 | £100 | £160 |
| 1895 | 8,976 | £90 | £150 |
| 1896 | 8,976 | £90 | £150 |
| 1897 | 8,976 | £90 | £150 |
| 1898 | 8,976 | £90 | £150 |
| 1899 | 8,976 | £90 | £150 |
| 1900 | 8,976 | £80 | £145 |
| 1901 | 8,976 | £80 | £145 |

# EDWARD VII (1902–110)

| DATE | MINTAGE | EF | UNC |
|---|---|---|---|
| 1902 | 8,976 | £75 | £135 |
| 1902 Matt proof | 15,123 | — | £150 |
| 1903 | 8,976 | £80 | £140 |
| 1904 | 8,976 | £95 | £150 |
| 1905 | 8,976 | £100 | £150 |
| 1906 | 8,800 | £90 | £145 |
| 1907 | 8,760 | £90 | £145 |
| 1908 | 8,769 | £85 | £140 |
| 1909 | 1,983 | £140 | £215 |
| 1910 | 1,440 | £165 | £245 |

# GEORGE V (1911–136)

| DATE | MINTAGE | EF | UNC |
|---|---|---|---|
| 1911 | 1,786 | £120 | £205 |
| 1911 Proof | 6,007 | — | £215 |
| 1912 | 1,246 | £130 | £205 |
| 1913 | 1,228 | £120 | £205 |
| 1914 | 982 | £140 | £225 |
| 1915 | 1,293 | £125 | £205 |
| 1916 | 1,128 | £125 | £205 |
| 1917 | 1,237 | £125 | £205 |
| 1918 | 1,375 | £125 | £205 |
| 1919 | 1,258 | £130 | £205 |
| 1920 | 1,399 | £130 | £210 |
| 1921 | 1,386 | £125 | £210 |
| 1922 | 1,373 | £125 | £215 |
| 1923 | 1,430 | £125 | £210 |
| 1924 | 1,515 | £130 | £210 |
| 1925 | 1,438 | £125 | £205 |
| 1926 | 1,504 | £125 | £205 |
| 1927 | 1,647 | £130 | £200 |
| 1928 | 1,642 | £130 | £215 |
| 1929 | 1,761 | £130 | £215 |
| 1930 | 1,724 | £120 | £200 |
| 1931 | 1,759 | £120 | £200 |
| 1932 | 1,835 | £120 | £200 |
| 1933 | 1,872 | £120 | £200 |
| 1934 | 1,887 | £120 | £200 |
| 1935 | 1,928 | £140 | £215 |
| 1936 | 1,323 | £150 | £240 |

# GEORGE VI (1936–52)

| DATE | MINTAGE | EF | UNC |
|---|---|---|---|
| 1937 | 1,325 | £130 | £200 |
| 1937 Proof | 20,900 | £130 | £200 |
| 1938 | 1,275 | £135 | £220 |
| 1939 | 1,234 | £135 | £220 |
| 1940 | 1,277 | £135 | £220 |
| 1941 | 1,253 | £145 | £230 |
| 1942 | 1,231 | £135 | £220 |
| 1943 | 1,239 | £135 | £220 |
| 1944 | 1,259 | £135 | £220 |

| DATE AND PLACE OF ISSUE | MINTAGE | UNC |
|---|---|---|
| 1945 | 1,355 | £135 £220 |
| 1946 | 1,365 | £135 £220 |
| 1947 | 1,375 | £145 £230 |
| 1948 | 1,385 | £145 £235 |
| 1949 | 1,395 | £145 £235 |
| 1950 | 1,405 | £150 £240 |
| 1951 | 1,468 | £150 £240 |
| 1952 | 1,012 | £160 £250 |

## ELIZABETH II (1952–   )

| DATE AND PLACE OF ISSUE | MINTAGE | UNC |
|---|---|---|
| 1953 St. Paul's Cathedral | 1,025 | — £850 |
| 1953 Proof in gold | unrecorded | Ex. rare |
| 1953 Proof Matt | | Very rare |
| 1954 Westminster Abbey | 1,020 | — £165 |
| 1955 Southwark Cathedral | 1,036 | — £180 |
| 1955 Proof Matt | | — £2500 |
| 1956 Westminster Abbey | 1,088 | — £180 |
| 1957 St. Albans Cathedral | 1,094 | — £180 |
| 1958 Westminster Abbey | 1,100 | — £180 |
| 1959 St. George's Chapel, Windsor | 1,106 | — £180 |
| 1960 Westminster Abbey | 1,112 | — £180 |
| 1961 Rochester Cathedral | 1,118 | — £180 |
| 1962 Westminster Abbey | 1,125 | — £180 |
| 1963 Chelmsford Cathedral | 1,131 | — £180 |
| 1964 Westminster Abbey | 1,137 | — £180 |
| 1965 Canterbury Cathedral | 1,143 | — £180 |
| 1966 Westminster Abbey | 1,206 | — £180 |
| 1967 Durham Cathedral | 986 | — £190 |
| 1968 Westminster Abbey | 964 | — £190 |
| 1969 Selby Cathedral | 1,002 | — £185 |
| 1970 Westminster Abbey | 980 | — £185 |
| 1971 Tewkesbury Abbey | 1,018 | £185 |
| 1972 York Minster | 1,026 | £185 |
| 1973 Westminster Abbey | 1,004 | £185 |
| 1974 Salisbury Cathedral | 1,042 | £185 |
| 1975 Peterborough Cathedral | 1,050 | £185 |
| 1976 Hereford Cathedral | 1,158 | £185 |
| 1977 Westminster Abbey | 1,138 | £195 |
| 1978 Carlisle Cathedral | 1,178 | £185 |
| 1979 Winchester Cathedral | 1,188 | £185 |
| 1980 Worcester Cathedral | 1,198 | £185 |

| DATE AND PLACE OF ISSUE | MINTAGE | UNC |
|---|---|---|
| 1981 Westminster Abbey | 1,178 | £190 |
| 1982 St David's Cathedral | 1,218 | £190 |
| 1983 Exeter Cathedral | 1,228 | £190 |
| 1984 Southwell Minster | 1,238 | £190 |
| 1985 Ripon Cathedral | 1,248 | £190 |
| 1986 Chichester Cathedral | 1,378 | £190 |
| 1987 Ely Cathedral | 1,390 | £195 |
| 1988 Lichfield Cathedral | 1,402 | £195 |
| 1989 Birmingham Cathedral | 1,353 | £195 |
| 1990 Newcastle Cathedral | 1,523 | £195 |
| 1991 Westminster Abbey | 1,384 | £195 |
| 1992 Chester Cathedral | 1,424 | £195 |
| 1993 Wells Cathedral | 1,440 | £195 |
| 1994 Truro Cathedral | 1,433 | £195 |
| 1995 Coventry Cathedral | 1,466 | £195 |
| 1996 Norwich Cathedral | 1,629 | £195 |
| 1997 Birmingham Cathedral | 1,786 | £195 |
| 1998 Portsmouth Cathedral | 1,654 | £195 |
| 1999 Bristol Cathedral | 1,676 | £195 |
| 2000 Lincoln Cathedral | 1,686 | £195 |
| 2000 Silver Proof | 13,180 | £185 |
| 2001 Westminster Abbey | 1,132 | £200 |
| 2002 Canterbury Cathedral | 1,681 | £200 |
| 2002 Gold Proof | 2,002 | £2200 |
| 2003 Gloucester Cathedral | 1,608 | £200 |
| 2004 Liverpool Cathedral | 1,613 | £200 |
| 2005 Wakefield Cathedral | 1,685 | £205 |
| 2006 Guildford Cathedral | 1,937 | £205 |
| 2006 Silver Proof | 8,000 | £190 |
| 2007 Manchester Cathedral | 1,822 | £210 |
| 2008 St Patrick's Cathedral (Armagh) | 1,833 | £650 |
| 2009 St. Edmundsbury Cathedral | 1,602 | £650 |
| 2010 Derby Cathedral | 1,617 | £550 |
| 2011 Westminster Abbey | 1,734 | £550 |
| 2012 York Minster | | £450 |

*Despite the decimalisation of the coinage in 1971, in keeping with ancient tradition the Royal Maundy sets are still made up of four silver coins (4p, 3p, 2p and 1p). The designs for the reverse of the coins are a crowned numeral in a wreath of oak leaves—basically the same design that has been used for Maundy coins since Charles II.*

# MAUNDY ODDMENTS
# SINGLE COINS

| DATE | F | VF | EF |
|---|---|---|---|

## FOUR PENCE

*It is nowadays considered that the early small denomination silver coins 4d–1d were originally struck for the Maundy ceremony although undoubtedly many subsequently circulated as small change—therefore they are listed here under "Maundy silver single coins".*

### CHARLES II (1660–85)

| DATE | F | VF | EF |
|---|---|---|---|
| Undated | £60 | £90 | £165 |
| 1670 | £55 | £100 | £175 |
| 1671 | £50 | £80 | £155 |
| 1672/1 | £50 | £95 | £155 |
| 1673 | £55 | £85 | £155 |
| 1674 | £50 | £80 | £150 |
| 1674 7 over 6 | £60 | £95 | £175 |
| 1675 | £50 | £85 | £150 |
| 1675/4 | £55 | £95 | £175 |
| 1676 | £50 | £80 | £170 |
| 1676 7 over 6 | £60 | £95 | £180 |
| 1677 | £45 | £80 | £145 |
| 1678 | £45 | £75 | £140 |
| 1678 8 over 7 | £50 | £95 | £160 |
| 1679 | £45 | £70 | £135 |
| 1680 | £50 | £75 | £150 |
| 1681 | £45 | £85 | £160 |
| 1682 | £45 | £75 | £165 |
| 1682/1 | £55 | £80 | £170 |
| 1683 | £50 | £75 | £160 |
| 1684 | £50 | £80 | £165 |
| 1684 4 over 3 | £60 | £85 | £170 |

*Charles II*

### JAMES II (1685–88)

| DATE | F | VF | EF |
|---|---|---|---|
| 1686 | £50 | £90 | £175 |
| 1686 Date over crown | £60 | £95 | £185 |
| 1687 | £50 | £85 | £160 |
| 1687 7 over 6 | £60 | £90 | £170 |
| 1688 | £50 | £90 | £170 |
| 1688 1 over 8 | £60 | £95 | £175 |

### WILLIAM & MARY (1688–94)

| DATE | F | VF | EF |
|---|---|---|---|
| 1689 | £50 | £90 | £160 |
| 1689 GV below bust | £60 | £95 | £170 |
| 1689 GVLEELMVS | £110 | £195 | £300 |
| 1690 | £60 | £95 | £190 |
| 1690 6 over 5 | £75 | £110 | £200 |
| 1691 | £65 | £105 | £200 |
| 1691 1 over 0 | £75 | £115 | £210 |
| 1692 | £90 | £135 | £230 |
| 1692 Maria | £175 | £225 | £325 |
| 1692 2 over 1 | £110 | £135 | £235 |
| 1693 | £90 | £135 | £230 |
| 1693 3 over 2 | £75 | £130 | £230 |
| 1694 | £70 | £120 | £200 |

*William & Mary*

### WILLIAM III (1694–1702)

| DATE | F | VF | EF |
|---|---|---|---|
| 1698 | £65 | £115 | £195 |
| 1699 | £55 | £100 | £180 |
| 1700 | £60 | £110 | £190 |
| 1701 | £65 | £100 | £190 |
| 1702 | £70 | £120 | £190 |

### ANNE (1702–14)

| DATE | F | VF | EF |
|---|---|---|---|
| 1703 | £55 | £100 | £175 |
| 1704 | £50 | £90 | £160 |
| 1705 | £70 | £135 | £205 |

*Queen Anne*

| DATE | F | VF | EF | UNC |
|------|-----|-----|-----|-----|
| 1706 | £55 | £95 | £160 | — |
| 1708 | £60 | £105 | £185 | — |
| 1709 | £55 | £100 | £155 | — |
| 1710 | £50 | £85 | £145 | — |
| 1713 | £55 | £100 | £165 | — |

## GEORGE I (1714–27)

| | | | | |
|------|-----|-----|-----|-----|
| 1717 | £55 | £95 | £160 | — |
| 1721 | £55 | £100 | £170 | — |
| 1723 | £60 | £100 | £175 | — |
| 1727 | £60 | £95 | £170 | — |

## GEORGE II (1727–60)

| | | | | |
|------|-----|-----|-----|-----|
| 1729 | £50 | £85 | £140 | — |
| 1731 | £50 | £85 | £140 | — |
| 1732 | £45 | £85 | £135 | — |
| 1735 | £45 | £80 | £135 | — |
| 1737 | £50 | £80 | £135 | — |
| 1739 | £50 | £85 | £135 | — |
| 1740 | £45 | £75 | £120 | — |
| 1743 | £110 | £160 | £255 | — |
| 1743 3 over 0 | £120 | £180 | £260 | |
| 1746 | £50 | £70 | £120 | — |
| 1760 | £55 | £85 | £130 | — |

*George II*

## GEORGE III (1760–1820)

| | | | | |
|------|-----|-----|-----|-----|
| 1763 Young head | £45 | £80 | £120 | — |
| 1763 Proof | — | — | Extremely rare | |
| 1765 | £400 | £650 | £1050 | — |
| 1766 | £50 | £85 | £125 | — |
| 1770 | £120 | £195 | £300 | — |
| 1772 | £65 | £115 | £160 | — |
| 1776 | £55 | £105 | £155 | — |
| 1780 | £40 | £85 | £120 | — |
| 1784 | £40 | £80 | £115 | — |
| 1786 | £50 | £95 | £140 | — |
| 1792 Older head, Thin 4 | £70 | £115 | £185 | £280 |
| 1795 | — | £45 | £80 | £115 |
| 1800 | — | £40 | £75 | £110 |
| 1817 New coinage | — | £40 | £65 | £105 |
| 1818 | — | £40 | £65 | £100 |
| 1820 | — | £40 | £70 | £110 |

*George III*

## GEORGE IV (1820–30)

| | | | | |
|------|-----|-----|-----|-----|
| 1822 | — | — | £55 | £110 |
| 1823 | — | — | £50 | £100 |
| 1824 | — | — | £50 | £105 |
| 1826 | — | — | £50 | £100 |
| 1827 | — | — | £50 | £100 |
| 1828 | — | — | £50 | £95 |
| 1829 | — | — | £50 | £100 |
| 1830 | — | — | £50 | £100 |

## WILLIAM IV (1830–37)

| | | | | |
|------|-----|-----|-----|-----|
| 1831–37 | — | — | £60 | £125 |
| 1831 Proof | — | — | £225 | £335 |

## VICTORIA (1837–1901)

| | | | | |
|------|-----|-----|-----|-----|
| 1838 Proof | — | — | — | £400 |
| 1839 Proof | — | — | — | £325 |
| 1853 Proof | — | — | — | £345 |
| 1838–87 (Young Head) | — | — | £30 | £50 |
| 1841 | — | — | £40 | £60 |
| 1888–92 (Jubilee Head) | — | — | £30 | £45 |
| 1893–1901 (Old Head) | — | — | £25 | £40 |

| DATE | F | VF | EF | UNC |
|---|---|---|---|---|

### EDWARD VII (1901–10)

| | F | VF | EF | UNC |
|---|---|---|---|---|
| 1902–08 | — | — | £30 | £40 |
| 1909 & 1910 | — | — | £40 | £65 |
| 1902 Proof | — | — | £30 | £45 |

### GEORGE V (1910–36)

| | F | VF | EF | UNC |
|---|---|---|---|---|
| 1911–36 | — | — | £40 | £50 |
| 1911 Proof | — | — | £45 | £55 |

### GEORGE VI (1936–52)

| | F | VF | EF | UNC |
|---|---|---|---|---|
| 1937–52 | — | — | £40 | £60 |
| 1937 Proof | — | — | £30 | £50 |

### ELIZABETH II (1952– )

| | F | VF | EF | UNC |
|---|---|---|---|---|
| 1953 | — | — | £140 | £210 |
| 1954–85 | — | — | £40 | £65 |
| 1986–2007 | — | — | £50 | £75 |
| 2002 in Gold Proof | — | — | £480 | £725 |
| 2008 | — | — | £65 | £125 |
| 2009 | — | — | £65 | £125 |
| 2010 | — | — | £60 | £115 |
| 2011 | — | — | £60 | £115 |
| 2012 | — | — | £60 | £120 |

# THREEPENCE

### CHARLES II (1660–85)

| | F | VF | EF | UNC |
|---|---|---|---|---|
| Undated | £55 | £90 | £180 | — |
| 1670 | £50 | £85 | £145 | — |
| 1671 | £50 | £80 | £145 | — |
| 1671 GRVTIA | £65 | £100 | £215 | — |
| 1672 | £50 | £80 | £145 | — |
| 1673 | £50 | £80 | £145 | — |
| 1674 | £50 | £80 | £150 | — |
| 1675 | £55 | £90 | £150 | — |
| 1676 | £60 | £105 | £190 | — |
| 1676 ERA for FRA | £70 | £115 | £210 | — |
| 1677 | £50 | £75 | £145 | — |
| 1678 | £45 | £70 | £120 | — |
| 1679 | £40 | £70 | £120 | — |
| 1679 O/A in CAROLVS | £90 | £115 | £220 | — |
| 1680 | £50 | £85 | £155 | — |
| 1681 | £50 | £85 | £155 | — |
| 1682 | £50 | £85 | £155 | — |
| 1683 | £50 | £85 | £155 | — |
| 1684 | £50 | £90 | £160 | — |
| 1684/3 | £60 | £90 | £160 | — |

### JAMES II (1685–88)

| | F | VF | EF | UNC |
|---|---|---|---|---|
| 1685 | £55 | £90 | £175 | — |
| 1685 Struck on fourpence flan | £105 | £140 | £260 | — |
| 1686 | £50 | £80 | £155 | — |
| 1687 | £45 | £80 | £150 | — |
| 1687 7 over 6 | £50 | £80 | £150 | — |
| 1688 | £55 | £105 | £185 | — |
| 1688 8 over 7 | £60 | £110 | £195 | — |

### WILLIAM & MARY (1688–94)

| | F | VF | EF | UNC |
|---|---|---|---|---|
| 1689 | £45 | £85 | £170 | — |
| 1689 No stop on reverse | £55 | £95 | £180 | — |
| 1689 LMV over MVS (obverse) | £80 | £120 | £215 | — |
| 1690 | £65 | £100 | £175 | — |
| 1690 6 over 5 | £70 | £115 | £190 | — |
| 1691 First bust | £360 | £560 | £785 | — |
| 1691 Second bust | £260 | £415 | £550 | — |
| 1692 | £70 | £115 | £205 | — |

*William & Mary*

| DATE | F | VF | EF | UNC |
|---|---|---|---|---|
| 1692 G below bust................ | £75 | £125 | £210 | — |
| 1692 GV below bust.............. | £75 | £125 | £195 | — |
| 1692 GVL below bust........... | £70 | £115 | £210 | — |
| 1693................................. | £105 | £170 | £240 | — |
| 1693 3 over 2....................... | £110 | £180 | £250 | — |
| 1694................................. | £65 | £100 | £185 | — |
| 1694 MARIΛ ........................ | £105 | £140 | £245 | — |

## WILLIAM III (1694–1702)

| | | | | |
|---|---|---|---|---|
| 1698................................. | £60 | £105 | £175 | — |
| 1699................................. | £50 | £95 | £160 | — |
| 1700................................. | £60 | £115 | £180 | — |
| 1701................................. | £50 | £90 | £155 | — |
| 1701 GBA instead of GRA...... | £60 | £110 | £175 | — |

## ANNE (1702–14)

| | | | | |
|---|---|---|---|---|
| 1703................................. | £55 | £85 | £170 | — |
| 1703 7 of date above crown... | £65 | £110 | £180 | — |
| 1704................................. | £50 | £80 | £140 | — |
| 1705................................. | £65 | £105 | £175 | — |
| 1706................................. | £55 | £85 | £145 | — |
| 1707................................. | £45 | £85 | £135 | — |
| 1708................................. | £45 | £90 | £150 | — |
| 1709................................. | £45 | £95 | £155 | — |
| 1710................................. | £40 | £75 | £120 | — |
| 1713................................. | £50 | £100 | £150 | — |

*Queen Anne*

## GEORGE I (1714–27)

| | | | | |
|---|---|---|---|---|
| 1717................................. | £55 | £85 | £145 | — |
| 1721................................. | £55 | £85 | £155 | — |
| 1723................................. | £60 | £95 | £160 | — |
| 1727................................. | £60 | £95 | £160 | — |

## GEORGE II (1727–60)

| | | | | |
|---|---|---|---|---|
| 1729................................. | £50 | £80 | £130 | — |
| 1731................................. | £50 | £80 | £130 | — |
| 1731 Small lettering.............. | £55 | £100 | £145 | — |
| 1732................................. | £50 | £80 | £130 | — |
| 1731 Stop over head............. | £50 | £85 | £135 | — |
| 1735................................. | £45 | £80 | £130 | — |
| 1737................................. | £50 | £80 | £140 | — |
| 1739................................. | £50 | £75 | £145 | — |
| 1740................................. | £50 | £75 | £130 | — |
| 1743 Small and large lettering | £50 | £70 | £135 | — |
| 1743 Stop over head............. | £50 | £80 | £140 | — |
| 1746................................. | £35 | £65 | £120 | — |
| 1746 6 over 3....................... | £50 | £65 | £130 | — |
| 1760................................. | £55 | £75 | £140 | — |

*George II*

## GEORGE III (1760–1820)

| | | | | |
|---|---|---|---|---|
| 1762................................. | £25 | £40 | £60 | — |
| 1763................................. | £25 | £40 | £65 | — |
| 1763 Proof............................ | — | — | Extremely rare | |
| 1765................................. | £315 | £460 | £750 | — |
| 1766................................. | £45 | £80 | £135 | — |
| 1770................................. | £45 | £90 | £140 | — |
| 1772................................. | £40 | £70 | £105 | — |
| 1780................................. | £45 | £70 | £105 | — |
| 1784................................. | £65 | £90 | £160 | — |
| 1786................................. | £65 | £90 | £155 | — |
| 1792................................. | £65 | £105 | £190 | £285 |
| 1795................................. | — | £35 | £65 | £105 |
| 1800................................. | — | £40 | £65 | £110 |
| 1817................................. | — | £35 | £70 | £130 |
| 1818................................. | — | £35 | £70 | £130 |
| 1820................................. | — | £40 | £75 | £140 |

| DATE | F | VF | EF | UNC |
|------|---|----|----|-----|
| **GEORGE IV (1820–30)** | | | | |
| 1822 | – | – | £65 | £140 |
| 1823 | – | – | £60 | £130 |
| 1824 | – | – | £60 | £135 |
| 1825–30 | – | – | £60 | £130 |
| **WILLIAM IV (1830–37)** | | | | |
| 1831 Proof | – | – | £180 | £360 |
| 1831–1836 | – | – | £65 | £145 |
| 1837 | – | – | £80 | £160 |
| **VICTORIA (1837–1901)** | | | | |
| 1838 | – | – | £90 | £175 |
| 1839 | – | – | £95 | £200 |
| 1840 | – | – | £115 | £230 |
| 1841 | – | – | £165 | £310 |
| 1842 | – | – | £160 | £290 |
| 1843 | – | – | £105 | £190 |
| 1844 | – | – | £140 | £260 |
| 1845 | – | – | £70 | £140 |
| 1846 | – | – | £350 | £625 |
| 1847 | – | – | £325 | £600 |
| 1848 | – | – | £325 | £600 |
| 1849 | – | – | £180 | £310 |
| 1850 | – | – | £100 | £195 |
| 1851 | – | – | £105 | £205 |
| 1852 | – | – | £400 | £650 |
| 1853 | – | – | £400 | £650 |
| 1854 | – | – | £130 | £235 |
| 1855 | – | – | £135 | £235 |
| 1856 | – | – | £80 | £200 |
| 1857 | – | – | £120 | £230 |
| 1858 | – | – | £100 | £195 |
| 1859 | – | – | £85 | £165 |
| 1860 | – | – | £115 | £210 |
| 1861 | – | – | £100 | £200 |
| 1862 | – | – | £100 | £200 |
| 1863 | – | – | £130 | £250 |
| 1864 | – | – | £100 | £210 |
| 1865 | – | – | £105 | £215 |
| 1866 | – | – | £100 | £205 |
| 1867 | – | – | £100 | £200 |
| 1868 | – | – | £95 | £180 |
| 1869 | – | – | £120 | £235 |
| 1870 | – | – | £90 | £165 |
| 1871 | – | – | £85 | £170 |
| 1872 | – | – | £85 | £160 |
| 1873 | – | – | £80 | £150 |
| 1874 | – | – | £80 | £150 |
| 1875 | – | – | £70 | £135 |
| 1876 | – | – | £70 | £140 |
| 1877 | – | – | £70 | £130 |
| 1878 | – | – | £70 | £135 |
| 1879 | – | – | £75 | £145 |
| 1880 | – | – | £70 | £135 |
| 1881 | – | – | £70 | £135 |
| 1882 | – | – | £110 | £200 |
| 1883 | – | – | £70 | £130 |
| 1884 | – | – | £65 | £125 |
| 1885 | – | – | £60 | £110 |
| 1886 | – | – | £55 | £100 |
| 1887 | – | – | £65 | £145 |
| 1888–1892 (Jubilee Head) | – | – | £45 | £95 |
| 1893–1901 (Old Head) | – | – | £35 | £60 |

*Victoria Jubilee Head*

| DATE | F | VF | EF | UNC |
|------|---|----|----|----|

## EDWARD VII (1901–10)

| | F | VF | EF | UNC |
|------|---|----|----|----|
| 1902 | — | — | £25 | £45 |
| 1902 Proof | — | — | — | £50 |
| 1903 | — | — | £40 | £75 |
| 1904 | — | — | £50 | £90 |
| 1905 | — | — | £50 | £90 |
| 1906 | — | — | £45 | £85 |
| 1907 | — | — | £40 | £75 |
| 1908 | — | — | £35 | £65 |
| 1909 | — | — | £55 | £105 |
| 1910 | — | — | £60 | £120 |

## GEORGE V (1910–36)

| | F | VF | EF | UNC |
|------|---|----|----|----|
| 1911–34 | — | — | £40 | £70 |
| 1911 Proof | — | — | — | £65 |
| 1935 | — | — | £45 | £80 |
| 1936 | — | — | £60 | £100 |

## GEORGE VI (1936–52)

| | F | VF | EF | UNC |
|------|---|----|----|----|
| 1937–52 | — | — | £45 | £80 |
| 1937 Proof | — | — | — | £65 |

## ELIZABETH II (1952–  )

| | F | VF | EF | UNC |
|------|---|----|----|----|
| 1953 | — | — | £135 | £225 |
| 1954–85 | — | — | £40 | £65 |
| 1986–2007 | — | — | £45 | £70 |
| 2002 In gold (proof) | — | — | — | £550 |
| 2008 | — | — | — | £140 |
| 2009 | — | — | — | £140 |
| 2010 | — | — | — | £120 |
| 2011 | — | — | — | £120 |
| 2012 | — | — | — | £120 |

# TWOPENCE

## CHARLES II (1660–85)

| | F | VF | EF | UNC |
|------|---|----|----|----|
| Undated | £45 | £75 | £140 | — |
| 1668 | £55 | £75 | £150 | — |
| 1670 | £45 | £75 | £130 | — |
| 1671 | £40 | £70 | £130 | — |
| 1672 | £45 | £70 | £130 | — |
| 1672/1 | £50 | £80 | £140 | — |
| 1673 | £45 | £70 | £135 | — |
| 1674 | £45 | £75 | £135 | — |
| 1675 | £45 | £75 | £125 | — |
| 1676 | £50 | £80 | £140 | — |
| 1677 | £40 | £70 | £120 | — |
| 1678 | £35 | £60 | £115 | — |
| 1679 | £35 | £55 | £105 | — |
| 1680 | £45 | £70 | £120 | — |
| 1681 | £45 | £65 | £120 | — |
| 1682 | £40 | £65 | £130 | — |
| 1682/1 ERA for FRA | £55 | £80 | £180 | — |
| 1683 | £45 | £75 | £135 | — |
| 1684 | £45 | £75 | £140 | — |

Charles II

## JAMES II (1685–88)

| | F | VF | EF | UNC |
|------|---|----|----|----|
| 1686 | £50 | £75 | £145 | — |
| 1686 reads IACOBVS | £55 | £95 | £185 | — |
| 1687 | £50 | £80 | £145 | — |
| 1687 ERA for FRA | £60 | £100 | £190 | — |
| 1688 | £45 | £70 | £135 | — |
| 1688/7 | £50 | £75 | £145 | — |

James II

## WILLIAM & MARY (1688–94)

| | F | VF | EF | UNC |
|------|---|----|----|----|
| 1689 | £45 | £80 | £155 | — |
| 1691 | £40 | £70 | £120 | — |

| DATE | F | VF | EF | UNC |
|------|------|------|------|------|
| 1692 | £65 | £115 | £170 | — |
| 1693 | £45 | £85 | £145 | — |
| 1693 GV below bust | £60 | £90 | £150 | — |
| 1693/2 | £55 | £85 | £150 | — |
| 1694 | £40 | £70 | £125 | — |
| 1694 MARLA error | £60 | £105 | £230 | — |
| 1694 HI for HIB | £55 | £100 | £185 | — |
| 1694 GVLI under bust | £45 | £80 | £160 | — |
| 1694 GVL under bust | £45 | £80 | £160 | — |

## WILLIAM III (1694–1702)

| | | | | |
|------|------|------|------|------|
| 1698 | £50 | £90 | £150 | — |
| 1699 | £45 | £75 | £120 | — |
| 1700 | £50 | £85 | £145 | — |
| 1701 | £50 | £85 | £140 | — |

## ANNE (1702–14)

| | | | | |
|------|------|------|------|------|
| 1703 | £50 | £80 | £150 | — |
| 1704 | £40 | £65 | £120 | — |
| 1704 No stops on obverse | £50 | £75 | £145 | — |
| 1705 | £50 | £80 | £145 | — |
| 1706 | £45 | £80 | £140 | — |
| 1707 | £40 | £70 | £130 | — |
| 1708 | £45 | £70 | £130 | — |
| 1709 | £65 | £100 | £180 | — |
| 1710 | £40 | £65 | £105 | — |
| 1713 | £55 | £90 | £160 | — |

*Queen Anne*

## GEORGE I (1714–27)

| | | | | |
|------|------|------|------|------|
| 1717 | £40 | £70 | £110 | — |
| 1721 | £45 | £70 | £105 | — |
| 1723 | £50 | £75 | £140 | — |
| 1726 | £45 | £65 | £120 | — |
| 1727 | £45 | £70 | £130 | — |

## GEORGE II (1727–60)

| | | | | |
|------|------|------|------|------|
| 1729 | £35 | £60 | £100 | — |
| 1731 | £35 | £60 | £95 | — |
| 1732 | £40 | £65 | £100 | — |
| 1735 | £40 | £60 | £95 | — |
| 1737 | £35 | £65 | £95 | — |
| 1739 | £45 | £65 | £95 | — |
| 1740 | £40 | £60 | £95 | — |
| 1743 | £35 | £55 | £90 | · |
| 1743/0 | £40 | £70 | £105 | · |
| 1746 | £35 | £55 | £80 | · |
| 1756 | £35 | £55 | £80 | · |
| 1759 | £35 | £60 | £80 | · |
| 1760 | £35 | £60 | £85 | · |

*George II*

## GEORGE III (1760–1820)

| | | | | |
|------|------|------|------|------|
| 1763 | £30 | £55 | £80 | · |
| 1763 Proof | | | Extremely rar | |
| 1765 | £315 | £485 | £715 | · |
| 1766 | £35 | £60 | £85 | · |
| 1772 | £30 | £55 | £75 | — |
| 1780 | £30 | £55 | £75 | — |
| 1784 | £30 | £55 | £75 | — |
| 1786 | £40 | £60 | £75 | — |
| 1792 | — | £65 | £100 | £160 |
| 1795 | — | £25 | £55 | £75 |
| 1800 | — | £25 | £50 | £65 |
| 1817 | — | £30 | £55 | £75 |
| 1818 | — | £25 | £55 | £75 |
| 1820 | — | £25 | £55 | £75 |

| DATE | F | VF | EF | UNC |
|------|---|----|----|----|

### GEORGE IV (1820–30)

| | | | | |
|------|---|----|----|----|
| 1822–30 | — | — | £40 | £55 |
| 1825 TRITANNIAR | — | — | £60 | £95 |

### WILLIAM IV (1830–37)

| | | | | |
|------|---|----|----|----|
| 1831–37 | — | — | £40 | £60 |
| 1831 Proof | — | — | £70 | £180 |

### VICTORIA (1837–1901)

| | | | | |
|------|---|----|----|----|
| 1838–87 (Young Head) | — | — | £30 | £50 |
| 1859 BEITANNIAR | — | — | £65 | £115 |
| 1861 6 over 1 | — | — | £35 | £65 |
| 1888–92 (Jubilee Head) | — | — | £30 | £45 |
| 1893–1901 (Old Head | — | — | £25 | £45 |
| 1838 Proof | — | — | — | £195 |
| 1839 Proof | — | — | — | £190 |
| 1853 Proof | — | — | — | £220 |

### EDWARD VII (1901–10)

| | | | | |
|------|---|----|----|----|
| 1902–08 | — | — | £18 | £30 |
| 1909 | — | — | £35 | £65 |
| 1910 | — | — | £35 | £65 |
| 1902 Proof | — | — | £22 | £40 |

### GEORGE V (1910–36)

| | | | | |
|------|---|----|----|----|
| 1911–34 | — | — | £30 | £45 |
| 1935 | — | — | £32 | £50 |
| 1936 | — | — | £40 | £60 |
| 1911 Proof | — | — | £30 | £55 |

### GEORGE VI (1936–52)

| | | | | |
|------|---|----|----|----|
| 1937–47 | — | — | £30 | £45 |
| 1948–52 | — | — | £35 | £55 |
| 1937 Proof | — | — | £25 | £45 |

### ELIZABETH II (1952–  )

| | | | | |
|------|---|----|----|----|
| 1953 | — | — | £100 | £160 |
| 1954–85 | — | — | £35 | £50 |
| 1986–2007 | — | — | £35 | £50 |
| 2002 Gold Proof | — | — | — | £425 |
| 2008 | — | — | — | £95 |
| 2009 | — | — | — | £95 |
| 2010 | — | — | — | £75 |
| 2011 | — | — | — | £75 |
| 2012 | — | — | — | £70 |

# PENNY

### CHARLES II (1660–85)

| | | | | |
|------|---|----|----|----|
| Undated | £65 | £95 | £175 | — |
| 1670 | £60 | £95 | £155 | — |
| 1671 | £60 | £95 | £150 | — |
| 1672/1 | £60 | £95 | £150 | — |
| 1673 | £55 | £90 | £145 | — |
| 1674 | £55 | £90 | £145 | — |
| 1674 Gratia (error) | £75 | £130 | £230 | — |
| 1675 | £55 | £100 | £145 | — |
| 1675 Gratia (error) | £75 | £130 | £230 | — |
| 1676 | £65 | £100 | £160 | — |
| 1676 Gratia (error) | £80 | £140 | £245 | — |
| 1677 | £55 | £85 | £145 | — |
| 1677 Gratia (error) | £70 | £120 | £210 | — |
| 1678 | £135 | £245 | £350 | — |
| 1678 Gratia (error) | £165 | £250 | £380 | — |
| 1679 | £70 | £105 | £180 | — |
| 1680 | £55 | £85 | £155 | — |
| 1681 | £80 | £125 | £200 | — |
| 1682 | £60 | £90 | £170 | — |

*Charles II*

| DATE | F | VF | EF | UNC |
|------|---|----|----|-----|
| 1682 ERA for FRA | £65 | £130 | £225 | — |
| 1683 | £60 | £90 | £170 | — |
| 1683/1 | £65 | £120 | £200 | — |
| 1684 | £170 | £245 | £330 | — |
| 1684/3 | £180 | £250 | £340 | — |

## JAMES II (1685–88)

*James II*

| | F | VF | EF | UNC |
|---|---|----|----|-----|
| 1685 | £55 | £85 | £140 | — |
| 1686 | £55 | £85 | £145 | — |
| 1687 | £65 | £100 | £160 | — |
| 1687/8 | £65 | £105 | £165 | — |
| 1688 | £55 | £80 | £145 | — |
| 1688/7 | £60 | £90 | £160 | — |

## WILLIAM & MARY (1688–94)

| | F | VF | EF | UNC |
|---|---|----|----|-----|
| 1689 | £450 | £600 | £875 | — |
| 1689 MARIA | £400 | £600 | £875 | |
| 1689 GVIELMVS (Error) | £415 | £615 | £850 | — |
| 1690 | £60 | £125 | £200 | — |
| 1691 | £60 | £125 | £200 | — |
| 1692 | £200 | £300 | £500 | — |
| 1692/1 | £205 | £315 | £525 | — |
| 1693 | £75 | £130 | £215 | — |
| 1694 | £65 | £105 | £200 | — |
| 1694 HI for HIB | £80 | £140 | £235 | — |
| 1694 No stops on obverse | £75 | £135 | £225 | — |

## WILLIAM III (1694–1702)

| | F | VF | EF | UNC |
|---|---|----|----|-----|
| 1698 | £70 | £115 | £175 | — |
| 1698 HI. BREX (Error) | £85 | £145 | £235 | — |
| 1699 | £255 | £370 | £575 | — |
| 1700 | £75 | £115 | £180 | — |
| 1701 | £70 | £115 | £175 | — |

## ANNE (1702–14)

| | F | VF | EF | UNC |
|---|---|----|----|-----|
| 1703 | £60 | £100 | £160 | — |
| 1705 | £55 | £90 | £150 | — |
| 1706 | £50 | £75 | £135 | — |
| 1708 | £375 | £475 | £695 | — |
| 1709 | £50 | £80 | £135 | — |
| 1710 | £115 | £180 | £280 | — |
| 1713/0 | £65 | £100 | £150 | — |

## GEORGE I (1714–27)

| | F | VF | EF | UNC |
|---|---|----|----|-----|
| 1716 | £45 | £75 | £100 | — |
| 1718 | £45 | £75 | £100 | — |
| 1720 | £50 | £80 | £110 | — |
| 1720 HIPEX (Error) | £65 | £95 | £185 | — |
| 1723 | £55 | £95 | £145 | — |
| 1725 | £45 | £75 | £115 | — |
| 1726 | £45 | £75 | £115 | — |
| 1727 | £50 | £95 | £145 | — |

## GEORGE II (1727–60)

*George II*

| | F | VF | EF | UNC |
|---|---|----|----|-----|
| 1729 | £40 | £75 | £110 | — |
| 1731 | £40 | £70 | £110 | — |
| 1732 | £35 | £55 | £85 | — |
| 1735 | £35 | £55 | £85 | — |
| 1737 | £35 | £55 | £90 | — |
| 1739 | £40 | £55 | £85 | — |
| 1740 | £40 | £60 | £90 | — |
| 1743 | £35 | £65 | £90 | — |
| 1746 | £40 | £70 | £100 | — |
| 1746/3 | £45 | £75 | £100 | — |
| 1750 | £30 | £50 | £75 | — |
| 1752 | £30 | £50 | £75 | — |
| 1753 | £30 | £50 | £75 | — |
| 1754 | £30 | £50 | £75 | — |
| 1755 | £30 | £50 | £75 | — |
| 1756 | £30 | £55 | £70 | — |

| DATE | F | VF | EF | UNC |
|---|---|---|---|---|
| 1757 | £30 | £55 | £70 | — |
| 1757 No colon after Gratia | £40 | £65 | £85 | — |
| 1758 | £30 | £50 | £70 | — |
| 1759 | £30 | £45 | £70 | — |
| 1760 | £35 | £60 | £80 | — |

## GEORGE III (1760–1820)

| | F | VF | EF | UNC |
|---|---|---|---|---|
| 1763 | £40 | £55 | £85 | — |
| 1763 Proof | — | — | Extremely rare | |
| 1766 | £35 | £60 | £75 | — |
| 1772 | £40 | £60 | £70 | — |
| 1780 | £60 | £85 | £145 | — |
| 1781 | £30 | £45 | £70 | — |
| 1784 | £35 | £55 | £80 | — |
| 1786 | £30 | £50 | £75 | — |
| 1792 | £30 | £60 | £80 | £115 |
| 1795 | — | £20 | £40 | £55 |
| 1800 | — | £20 | £35 | £55 |
| 1817 | — | £20 | £35 | £45 |
| 1818 | — | £20 | £35 | £50 |
| 1820 | — | £20 | £40 | £50 |

*George III*

## GEORGE IV (1820–30)

| | F | VF | EF | UNC |
|---|---|---|---|---|
| 1822–30 | — | — | £35 | £50 |

## WILLIAM IV (1830–37)

| | F | VF | EF | UNC |
|---|---|---|---|---|
| 1831–37 | — | — | £35 | £55 |
| 1831 Proof | — | — | — | £165 |

## VICTORIA (1837–1901)

| | F | VF | EF | UNC |
|---|---|---|---|---|
| 1838–87 (Young Head) | — | — | £30 | £45 |
| 1888–92 (Jubilee Head) | — | — | £30 | £40 |
| 1893–1901 (Old Head) | — | — | £20 | £30 |
| 1838 Proof | — | — | — | £190 |
| 1839 Proof | — | — | — | £145 |
| 1853 Proof | — | — | — | £180 |

## EDWARD VII (1901–10)

| | F | VF | EF | UNC |
|---|---|---|---|---|
| 1902–08 | — | — | £20 | £30 |
| 1909 | — | — | £35 | £60 |
| 1910 | — | — | £40 | £75 |
| 1902 Proof | — | — | £20 | £35 |

## GEORGE V (1910–36)

| | F | VF | EF | UNC |
|---|---|---|---|---|
| 1911–14 | — | — | £35 | £60 |
| 1915 | — | — | £35 | £60 |
| 1916–19 | — | — | £35 | £60 |
| 1920 | — | — | £35 | £70 |
| 1921–28 | — | — | £35 | £60 |
| 1929 | — | — | £35 | £65 |
| 1930–34 | — | — | £35 | £60 |
| 1935 | — | — | £35 | £65 |
| 1936 | — | — | £40 | £70 |
| 1911 Proof | — | — | £35 | £65 |

## GEORGE VI (1936–52)

| | F | VF | EF | UNC |
|---|---|---|---|---|
| 1937–40 | — | — | £40 | £65 |
| 1941 | — | — | £45 | £75 |
| 1942–47 | — | — | £40 | £70 |
| 1948–52 | — | — | £45 | £80 |
| 1937 Proof | — | — | £40 | £65 |

## ELIZABETH II (1952– )

| | F | VF | EF | UNC |
|---|---|---|---|---|
| 1953 | — | — | £250 | £350 |
| 1965–85 | — | — | £40 | £65 |
| 1986–2007 | — | — | £40 | £70 |
| 2002 Proof in gold | — | — | — | £450 |
| 2008 | — | — | £70 | £120 |
| 2009 | — | — | £70 | £120 |
| 2010 | — | — | £65 | £100 |
| 2011 | — | — | £65 | £100 |
| 2012 | — | — | £65 | £100 |

# DECIMAL COINAGE

Since the introduction of the Decimal system in the UK, many coins have been issued for circulation purposes in vast quantities. In addition, from 1982 sets of coins to non-proof standard, and including examples of each denomination found in circulation, have been issued each year. For 1982 and 1983 they were to "circulation" standard and described as "Uncirculated". Individual coins from these sets are annotated "Unc" on the lists that follow. From 1984 to the present day they were described as "Brilliant Uncirculated" (BU on the lists), and from around 1986 these coins are generally distinguishable from coins intended for circulation. They were from then produced by the Proof Coin Division of the Royal Mint (rather than by the Coin Production Room which produces circulation-standard coins). For completeness however, we have included the annotations Unc and BU back to 1982, the start year for these sets.

It is emphasised that the abbreviations Unc and BU in the left-hand columns adjacent to the date refer to an advertising description or to an engineering production standard, not the preservation condition or grade of the coin concerned. Where no such annotation appears adjacent to the date, the coin is circulation-standard for issue as such.

We have included the "mintage" figures for circulation coins down to Half Penny. The figure given for the 1997 Two Pounds, is considerably less than the actual quantity struck, because many were scrapped before issue due to failing an electrical conductivity test. Where a coin is available in uncirculated grade at, or just above, face value or no price has been quoted.

Base metal Proof issues of circulation coinage (£2 or £1 to one or half penny) of the decimal series were only issued, as with Unc or BU, as part of Year Sets, but many of these sets have been broken down into individual coins, hence the appearance of the latter on the market.

The lists do not attempt to give details of die varieties, except where there was an obvious intention to change the appearance of a coin, e.g. 1992 20p.

2008 saw new reverses and modified obverses for all circulation denominations from the One Pound to the One Penny. All seven denominations were put into circulation dated 2008, all with both the old and the new reverses.

The circulation standard mintage figures have, in general been kindly supplied by courtesy of the Head of Historical Services and the Department of UK Circulation Coin Sales, both at the Royal Mint.

# KILO COINS
## (gold and silver)

The UK's first-ever Kilo coins were struck to commemorate the 2012 Olympic Games in 0.999 fine gold and 0.999 fine silver. They were followed by similar standard coins for the Queen's Diamond Jubilee. All were struck to proof standard:

| DATE | FACE VALUE | AUTH ISSUE QTY. | PRICE |
|---|---|---|---|
| 2012 Olympic Gold;<br>obverse: 1998 Rank-Broadley Royal Portrait,<br>reverse: Caro's individual Endeavour ............................. £1,000 | | 60 | £100,000 |
| 2012 Diamond Jubilee Gold;<br>obverse: Queen in Garter Robes (Rank-Broadley),<br>reverse: Royal Arms (Buckingham Palace Gates) ......... £1,000 | | 60 | £60,000 |
| 2012 Olympic Silver;<br>obverse: 1998 Rank-Broadley Royal Portrait,<br>reverse: Phillip's Team Endeavour.................................... £500 | | 2012 | £3,000 |
| 2012 Diamond Jubilee Silver;<br>obverse: Queen in Garter Robes (Rank-Broadley),<br>reverse: Royal Arms (Buckingham Palace Gates) ............ £500 | | 1250 | £2,600 |

# FIVE-OUNCE COINS
# (gold and silver)

Also appearing for the first time were Five -Ounce coins, minted in the same metals and standards as the Kilo Coins:

| DATE | FACE VALUE | AUTH ISSUE QTY. | PRICE |
|---|---|---|---|
| 2012 Olympic Gold;<br>obverse: 1998 Rank-Broadley Royal Portrait,<br>reverse: Pegasus (C Le Brun) ............................................... £10 | | 500 | £11,500 |
| 2012 Diamond Jubilee Gold;<br>obverse: Queen in Garter Robes (Rank-Broadley),<br>reverse: Queen seated (facing) ............................................ £10 | | 250 | £9,500 |
| 2012 Olympic Silver;<br>obverse: 1998 Rank-Broadley Royal Portrait,<br>reverse: Pegasus (C Le Brun) ............................................... £10 | | 7500 | £525 |
| 2012 Diamond Jubilee Silver;<br>obverse: Queen in Garter Robes (Rank-Broadley),<br>reverse: Queen seated (facing) ............................................ £10 | | 1952 | £450 |

# HUNDRED POUNDS AND BELOW
## (Britannia and Olympic Gold series)

In 1987 the gold £100 coin was introduced, known as the Britannia. It contained one Troy ounce of fine gold, alloyed to 22 carat, and this has continued to the present day. At the same time, and also continuing, coins of face value £50, £25 and £10 appeared, containing a half ounce, quarter ounce and one tenth of an ounce of fine gold respectively. From 1987 to 1989 the alloy was of copper (Red Gold), whereas from 1990 to the present day the alloy has been of silver and copper (yellow gold).

Proof sets of these coins are listed in the "Proof and Specimen Sets" section. In addition, non-proof coins have been minted, it is believed for each of the four coins for every year. The one ounce £100 Britannia is primarily issued as a bullion coin in the non-proof standard, originally in competition with the South African Krugerrand. Its price is quoted daily on the financial pages of some newspapers.

There were five reverse designs by Philip Nathan:- 1987-1996 Standing Britannia, 1997 Chariot, 1998-2000 Standing Britannia, 2001 Una and the Lion, 2002 Standing Britannia, 2003 Britannia's Helmeted Head, 2004 Standing Britannia, 2005 Britannia seated, 2006 Standing Britannia. For 2007 the design is a Seated Britannia with lion at her feet, by Christopher Le Brun. The 2008 design is of Britannia standing and facing left, by John Bergdahl. The 2009 reverse is similar to that of 1997, Britannia on a chariot, while 2010 has Suzie Zamit's Britannia potrait with a Corinthian style helmet. The 2011 design is by David Mach, and portrays a seated Britannia with trident and shield, replicating the design on a 1937 penny, superimposed on a Union Flag. The rotation of the coin from left to right, or vice-versa, creates an illusion of Britannia moving with the ripple of the flag.

In general the proof coins have reverse features frosted, The proofs with Standing Britannia and Una and the Lion reverses include P NATHAN on the reverse, whereas the equivalent bullion coins include NATHAN. The other three reverses have PN on both proofs and bullion coins.

The issue of the second series of three coins in the Olympic Games gold proof coin was in 2011, with the completion of the 9-coin series in 2012. The obverses all have the 1998 Ian Rank-Broadley portrait of the Queen, but a few 2011 £100 coins were issued without his initials IRB under her portrait. Reverses are summarised below:

| DATE | FACE VALUE | FINE GOLD WEIGHT | FEATURED GOD | FEATURED PART OF OLYMPIC MOTTO |
|------|-----------|------------------|--------------|--------------------------------|
| 2010 | £100<br>£25<br>£25 | 1 Troy oz<br>1/4 Troy oz<br>1/4 Troy oz | Neptune<br>Diana<br>Mercury | CITIUS |
| 2011 | £100<br>£25<br>£25 | 1 Troy oz<br>1/4 Troy oz<br>1/4 Troy oz | Jupiter<br>Juno<br>Apollo | ALTIUS |
| 2012 | £100<br>£25<br>£25 | 1 Troy oz<br>1/4 Troy oz<br>1/4 Troy oz | Mars<br>Vulcan<br>Minerva | FORTIUS |

2012 was also the 25th anniversary of the Gold Britannia coin series, and the reverse design chosen was that of the 1987 coins, standing Britannia, by Philip Nathan.

# HUNDRED POUNDS AND BELOW
## (Britannia Platinum series)

2007 saw the issue of four-coin proof sets in platinum, 0.9995 fine. The denomination and designs are similar to those of the Gold series of the same year. The issue was repeated in 2008, and again in 2009, above rule applies. It is understood that no bullion coins have been issued.

# FIVE POUNDS (Sovereign series)

*This series is all minted in gold, and, except where stated, have the Pistrucci St George and Dragon reverse. BU coins up to 2001 bear a U in a circle.*

| DATE | Mintage | UNC |
|---|---|---|
| 1980 Proof | 10,000 | £950 |
| 1981 Proof | 5,400 | £950 |
| 1982 Proof | 2,500 | £975 |
| 1984 BU | 15,104 | £950 |
| 1984 Proof | 8,000 | £975 |
| 1985 New portrait BU | 13,626 | £950 |
| 1985 — Proof | 6,130 | £900 |
| 1986 BU | 7,723 | £950 |
| 1987 Uncouped portrait BU | 5,694 | £950 |
| 1988 BU | 3,315 | £950 |
| 1989 500th Anniversary of the Sovereign. Enthroned portrayal obverse and Crowned shield reverse BU | 2,937 | £1000 |
| 1989 — Proof | 5,000 | £1150 |
| 1990 Reverts to couped portrait BU | 1,226 | £900 |
| 1990 Proof | 1,721 | £950 |
| 1991 BU | 976 | £900 |
| 1991 Proof | 1,336 | £950 |
| 1992 BU | 797 | £900 |
| 1992 Proof | 1,165 | £950 |
| 1993 BU | 906 | £900 |
| 1993 Proof | 1,078 | £950 |
| 1994 BU | 1,000 | £900 |
| 1994 Proof | 918 | £950 |
| 1995 BU | 1,000 | £900 |
| 1995 Proof | 1,250 | £950 |
| 1996 BU | 901 | £900 |
| 1996 Proof | 742 | £950 |
| 1997 BU | 802 | £950 |
| 1997 Proof | 860 | £1000 |
| 1998 New portrait BU | 825 | £975 |
| 1998 Proof | 789 | £1000 |
| 1999 BU | 991 | £975 |
| 1999 Proof | 1,000 | £1000 |
| 2000 ("Bullion") | 10,000 | £900 |
| 2000 BU | 994 | £950 |
| 2000 Proof | 3,000 | £950 |
| 2001 BU | 1,000 | £900 |
| 2001 Proof | 3,500 | £950 |
| 2002 Shield rev. ("Bullion") | — | £900 |
| 2002 BU | — | £900 |
| 2002 Proof | 3,000 | £975 |
| 2003 BU | — | £950 |
| 2003 Proof | — | £1000 |
| 2004 BU | — | £950 |
| 2004 Proof | — | £975 |
| 2005 Noad's heraldic St George and Dragon BU | — | £1000 |
| 2005 — Proof | — | £1250 |
| 2006 BU | — | £900 |
| 2006 Proof | — | £950 |
| 2007 BU | — | £900 |
| 2007 Proof | — | £950 |
| 2008 BU | — | £120 |
| 2008 Proof | — | £900 |
| 2009 BU | — | £950 |
| 2009 Proof | — | £1250 |
| 2010 BU | — | £900 |
| 2010 Proof | — | £1000 |
| 2011 BU | — | £950 |
| 2011 Proof | — | £1200 |
| 2012 Day St George and Dragon BU | 1,250 | — |
| 2012 — Proof | — | — |

NOTE: The prices quoted in this guide are set at August 2012 with the price of gold at £920 per ounce and silver £16 per ounce— market fluctuations will have a marked effect on the values of modern precious metal coins.

*Pistrucci's famous rendering of St George and the Dragon.*

*The obverse of the 1989 gold coins portray HM the Queen enthroned.*

# FIVE POUNDS (Crown series)

*This series commenced in 1990 when the "Crown" was declared legal tender at £5, instead of 25p as all previous issues continued to be. Mintage is in cupro-nickel unless otherwise stated. BU includes those in individual presentation folders, and those in sets sold with stamp covers and/or banknotes.*

| DATE | Mintage | UNC |
|---|---|---|
| 1990 Queen Mother's 90th Birthday. | 2,761,431 | £8 |
| 1990 — BU | 48,477 | £10 |
| 1990 — Silver Proof | 56,800 | £40 |
| 1990 — Gold Proof | 2,500 | £1200 |
| 1993 Coronation 40th Anniversary | 1,834,655 | £8 |
| 1993 — BU | — | £10 |
| 1993 — Proof | — | £15 |
| 1993 — Silver Proof | 100,000 | £45 |
| 1993 — Gold Proof | 2,500 | £1200 |
| 1996 HM the Queen's 70th Birthday | 2,396,100 | £8 |
| 1996 — BU | — | £10 |
| 1996 — Proof | — | £15 |
| 1996 — Silver Proof | 70,000 | £45 |
| 1996 — Gold Proof | 2,127 | £1200 |
| 1997 Royal Golden Wedding | 1,733,000 | £10 |
| 1997 — BU | — | £12 |
| 1997 — — with £5 note | 5,000 | £75 |
| 1997 — Proof | — | £20 |
| 1997 — Silver Proof | 75,000 | £45 |
| 1997 — Gold Proof | 2,750 | £1200 |
| 1998 Prince of Wales 50th birthday | 1,407,300 | £8 |
| 1998 — BU | — | £12 |
| 1998 — Proof | — | £20 |
| 1998 — Silver Proof | — | £50 |
| 1998 — Gold Proof | — | £1200 |
| 1999 Princess of Wales Memorial. | 1,600,000 | £10 |
| 1999 — BU | — | £12 |
| 1999 — Proof | — | £20 |
| 1999 — Silver Proof | 350,000 | £50 |
| 1999 — Gold Proof | 7,500 | £1200 |
| 1999 Millennium | 3,796,300 | £8 |
| 1999 — BU | — | £15 |
| 1999 — Proof | — | £22 |
| 1999 — Silver Proof | 100,000 | £45 |
| 1999 — Gold Proof | 2,500 | £1200 |
| 2000 — | 3,147,092* | £8 |
| 2000 — BU | — | £15 |
| 2000 — — with special Millennium Dome mintmark | — | £20 |
| 2000 — Proof | — | £22 |
| 2000 — Silver Proof with gold highlight | 50,000 | £50 |
| 2000 — Gold Proof | 2,500 | £1200 |
| 2000 Queen Mother's 100th Birthday | incl. above* | £7 |
| 2000 — BU | — | £12 |
| 2000 — Silver Proof | 100,000 | £55 |
| 2000 — — — Piedfort | 14,850 | £150 |
| 2000 — Gold Proof | 3,000 | £1200 |
| 2001 Victorian Era. | 851,491 | £7 |
| 2001 — BU | — | £12 |
| 2001 — Proof | — | £20 |
| 2001 — Silver Proof | 100,000 | £45 |
| 2001 — — with frosted relief | — | £150 |
| 2001 — Gold Proof | 3,000 | £1200 |
| 2001 — — with frosted relief | 750 | £1400 |
| 2002 Golden Jubilee | 3,687,882* | £7 |
| 2002 — BU | — | £12 |
| 2002 — Proof | — | £20 |
| 2002 — Silver Proof | 75,000 | £45 |
| 2002 — Gold Proof | 5,502 | £1200 |

| DATE | Mintage | UNC |
|---|---|---|
| 2002 Queen Mother Memorial............................................ incl. above* | | £7 |
| 2002 — BU.......................................................................... | — | £12 |
| 2002 — Silver Proof ........................................................ | 25,000 | £45 |
| 2002 — Gold Proof............................................................ | 3,000 | £1200 |
| 2003 Coronation Jubilee ................................................. | 1,307,147 | £7 |
| 2003 — BU.......................................................................... | — | £10 |
| 2003 — Proof ................................................................... | — | £20 |
| 2003 — Silver Proof ........................................................ | — | £45 |
| 2003 — Gold Proof............................................................ | — | £1200 |
| 2004 Entente Cordiale Centenary ...............................1,205,594 | | £6 |
| 2004 — Proof Reverse Frosting ..................................... | — | £15 |
| 2004 — Silver Proof ........................................................ | — | £35 |
| 2004 — — Piedfort........................................................ | — | £150 |
| 2004 — Gold Proof............................................................ | — | £1200 |
| 2004 — Platinum Proof Piedfort...................................... | 501 | £3750 |
| 2005 Trafalgar Bicentenary................................ | 1,075 516 | £12 |
| 2005 — BU.......................................................................... | — | £14 |
| 2005 — Proof ................................................................... | — | £20 |
| 2005 — Silver Proof ........................................................ | — | £45 |
| 2005 — — Piedfort........................................................ | — | £100 |
| 2005 — Gold Proof............................................................ | — | £1100 |
| 2005 Bicentenary of the Death of Nelson ................................incl. above* | | £12 |
| 2005 — BU.......................................................................... | — | £14 |
| 2005 — Proof ................................................................... | — | £22 |
| 2005 — Silver Proof ........................................................ | — | £50 |
| 2005 — — Piedfort........................................................ | — | £100 |
| 2005 — Gold Proof............................................................ | — | £110 |
| 2005 — Platinum Proof Piedfort...................................... | 200 | £4000 |
| 2006 Queen's 80th birthday ........................................... | — | £10 |
| 2006 — BU.......................................................................... | — | £12 |
| 2006 — Proof ................................................................... | — | £20 |
| 2006 — Silver Proof ........................................................ | — | £45 |
| 2006 — — Piedfort, selective gold plating on reverse ........ | — | £120 |
| 2006 — Gold Proof............................................................ | — | £120 |
| 2006 — Platinum Proof Piedfort...................................... | 250 | £4000 |
| 2007 Queen's Diamond Wedding ................................... | — | £10 |
| 2007 BU .............................................................................. | — | £12 |
| 2007 — Proof ................................................................... | — | £20 |
| 2007 — Silver Proof ........................................................ | — | £45 |
| 2007 — — Piedfort........................................................ | — | £100 |
| 2007 — Gold Proof............................................................ | — | £950 |
| 2007 — Platinum Proof Piedfort...................................... | — | £4000 |
| 2008 Prince of Wales 60th Birthday .............................. | — | £10 |
| 2008 — BU.......................................................................... | — | £12 |
| 2008 — Proof ................................................................... | — | £15 |
| 2008 — Silver Proof ........................................................ | — | £45 |
| 2008 — — Piedfort........................................................ | — | £100 |
| 2008 — Gold Proof............................................................ | — | £1100 |
| 2008 Elizabeth I 450th Anniversary of Accession ..................... | — | £12 |
| 2008 — BU.......................................................................... | — | £15 |
| 2008 — Proof ................................................................... | — | £20 |
| 2008 — Silver Proof ........................................................ | — | £45 |
| 2008 — — Piedfort........................................................ | — | £100 |
| 2008 — Gold Proof............................................................ | — | £1100 |
| 2008 — Platinum Proof Piedfort...................................... | — | £4000 |
| 2009 500th Anniversary of Henry VIII accession...................... | 30,000 | £10 |
| 2009 — BU.......................................................................... | — | £15 |
| 2009 — Proof ................................................................... | — | £25 |
| 2009 — Silver Proof ........................................................ | — | £45 |
| 2009 — — Piedfort........................................................ | — | £120 |
| 2009 — Gold Proof............................................................ | 1,509 | £1350 |
| 2009 — Platinum Proof Piedfort...................................... | 100 | £4500 |
| 2009 Olympic Countdown (3 years) BU ........................ | — | £12 |
| 2009 — Silver Proof ........................................................ | — | £75 |
| 2009 — — Piedfort........................................................ | — | £120 |
| 2009 Olympic Celebration of Britain "The Mind" series (incl. green logo): | | |
| Stonehenge Silver Proof ......................................... | — | £65 |
| Palace of Westminster/Big Ben Silver Proof................. | — | £65 |
| — Cu Ni Proof........................................................ | — | £25 |

233

| DATE | Mintage | UNC |
|---|---|---|
| Angel of the North Silver Proof .................................... | — | £65 |
| Flying Scotsman Silver Proof...................................... | — | £65 |
| Globe Theatre Silver Proof......................................... | — | £65 |
| Sir Isaac Newton Silver Proof .................................... | — | £65 |
| 2010 350th Anniversary of the Restoration of the Monarchy ... | 15,000 | — |
| 2010 — BU.................................................................... | — | — |
| 2010 — Proof ............................................................... | — | — |
| 2010 — Silver Proof ..................................................... | — | £50 |
| 2010 — — — Piedfort.................................................... | — | £100 |
| 2010 — Gold Proof........................................................ | — | £1350 |
| 2010 Olympic Countdown (2 years) BU ....................... | — | — |
| 2010 — Silver Proof ..................................................... | — | — |
| 2010 — — — Piedfort .................................................... | — | — |
| 2010 — Gold Proof........................................................ | — | — |
| 2010 Olympic Celebration of Britain, "The Body" series (incl. red logo): | | |
| Coastline of Britain (Rhossili Bay) Silver Proof.............. | — | £65 |
| Giants Causeway Silver Proof.................................... | — | £65 |
| River Thames Silver Proof.......................................... | — | £65 |
| British Fauna (Barn Owl) Silver Proof.......................... | — | £65 |
| British Flora (Oak Leaves and Acorn) Silver Proof ......... | — | £65 |
| Weather Vane Silver Proof.......................................... | — | £65 |
| 2010 Olympic Celebration of Britain "The Spirit" series (incl. blue logo): | | |
| Spirit of London (Kind Hearts etc.) Silver Proof ............. | — | £65 |
| — CuNi Proof............................................................... | — | £20 |
| Humour Silver Proof.................................................... | — | £65 |
| Unity (Floral emblems of Britain) Silver Proof................ | — | £65 |
| Music Silver Proof....................................................... | — | £65 |
| Anti-slavery Silver Proof............................................. | — | £65 |
| 2011 90th Birthday of the Duke of Edinburgh BU.................... | — | £10 |
| 2011 — Silver Proof ..................................................... | — | £65 |
| 2011 — — — Piedfort..................................................... | — | £115 |
| 2011 — Gold Proof ....................................................... | — | £1650 |
| 2011 — Platinum Proof Piedfort..................................... | — | £6350 |
| 2011 Royal Wedding of Prince William and Catherine Middleton BU................................................................... | — | £10 |
| 2011 — Silver Proof ..................................................... | — | £56 |
| 2011 — Gold-plated Silver Proof .................................. | — | £85 |
| 2011 — Silver Proof Piedfort........................................ | — | £90 |
| 2011 — Gold Proof........................................................ | — | £1550 |
| 2011 — Platinum Proof Piedfort..................................... | — | £5450 |
| 2011 Olympic Countdown (1 year) BU ......................... | — | £10 |
| 2011 — Silver Proof ..................................................... | — | £66 |
| 2011 — — — Piedfort .................................................... | — | £125 |
| 2011 — Gold Proof........................................................ | — | £1600 |
| 2012 Diamond Jubilee BU................................................ | — | £13 |
| 2012 — Proof ............................................................... | — | — |
| 2012 — Silver Proof ..................................................... | — | £83 |
| 2012 — Gold-plated silver proof .................................. | — | £100 |
| 2012 — Silver Piedfort Proof........................................ | — | £145 |
| 2012 — Gold proof........................................................ | — | £2400 |
| 2012 — Platinum Piedford Proof.................................... | — | £6400 |
| 2012 Olympic Countdown (Games Time) BU ................ | — | £13 |
| 2012 — Silver Proof ..................................................... | — | £100 |
| 2012 — Silver Piedfort Proof........................................ | — | £175 |
| 2012 — Gold proof........................................................ | — | £2880 |
| 2012 Official Olympic BU ............................................... | — | £15 |
| 2012 — Silver Proof ..................................................... | — | £100 |
| 2012 — Silver Piedfort Proof........................................ | — | £175 |
| 2012 — Gold proof........................................................ | — | £2880 |
| 2012 Official Paralympic BU ........................................... | — | £15 |
| 2012 — Silver Proof ..................................................... | — | £100 |
| 2012 — Silver Piedfort Proof........................................ | — | £175 |
| 2012 — Gold proof........................................................ | — | £2880 |

# DOUBLE SOVEREIGN

*As with the Sovereign series Five Pound coins, those listed under this heading bear the Pistrucci St George and Dragon reverse, except where otherwise stated, and are minted in gold. They are, and always have been, legal tender at £2, and have a diameter indentical to that of the base metal Two Pound coins listed further below under a different heading. The denomination does not appear on Double Sovereigns.*

| DATE | Mintage | UNC |
|---|---|---|
| 1980 Proof | 10,000 | £550 |
| 1982 Proof | 2,500 | £550 |
| 1983 Proof | 12,500 | £500 |
| 1985 New Portrait Proof | 5,849 | £600 |
| 1987 Proof | 14,301 | £500 |
| 1988 Proof | 12,743 | £500 |
| 1989 500th Anniversary of the Sovereign. Enthroned portrayal obverse and Crowned shield reverse Proof | 14,936 | £600 |
| 1990 Proof | 4,374 | £600 |
| 1991 Proof | 3,108 | £600 |
| 1992 Proof | 2,608 | £600 |
| 1993 Proof | 2,155 | £600 |
| 1996 Proof | 3,167 | £600 |
| 1998 New Portrait Proof | 4,500 | £525 |
| 2000 Proof | 2,250 | £600 |
| 2002 Shield reverse Proof | 8,000 | £550 |
| 2003 Proof | 2,250 | £600 |
| 2004 Proof | — | £600 |
| 2005 Noad heraldic St George and Dragon Proof | — | £650 |
| 2006 Proof | — | £575 |
| 2007 Proof | — | £600 |
| 2008 Proof | — | £600 |
| 2009 Proof | — | £600 |
| 2010 Proof | — | £600 |
| 2011 Proof | — | — |
| 2012 Day St George and Dragon BU | — | — |
| 2012 — Proof | — | — |

# TWO POUNDS AND BELOW
# (Britannia Silver Series)

*This series commenced in 1997, and, as with the Gold Britannia series, sets of the coins are listed in the "Proof and Specimen Sets" section. Coins contain one Troy ounce of fine silver (£2) alloyed to Britannia standard, i.e. 95.8 per cent fine silver, or fractions of one ounce as follows: half ounce (£1), quarter ounce (50 pence) and one tenth of an ounce (20 pence). Reverses change anually, all four coins of any particular date being of the same design. The reverses by Philip Nathan appear as follows:*

*1997 Chariot, 1998 Standing Britannia, 1999 Chariot, 2000 Standing Britannia, 2001 Una and the Lion, 2002 Standing Britannia, 2003 Britannia's Helmeted Head, 2004 Standing Britannia, 2005 Britannia Seated, 2006 Standing Britannia, 2009 Chariot.*

*The 2007 design is by Christopher Le Brun, and features a seated Britannia with Lion at her feet. The 2008 is by John Bergdahl, and features a standing Britannia facing left.*

*Two pounds Britannia coins to BU or "bullion" standard have been issued as individual coins for each year from 1998 onwards. 2010 features Suzie Zamit's Britannia with a portrait with a Corinthian style helmet.*

*The 2011 coins feature a seated Britannia and Union Flag, as described in the Britannia gold series above.*

*2012 saw the 15th anniversary of the Silver Series, but the reverse chosen was that of the Standing Britannia by Philip Nathan, which also marked the 25th Gold series. In addition, there is a 9-coin proof set of Half-Ounce silver coins dated 2012 featuring each of the Reverses used in the past, a 25th Anniversary collection.*

*Not shown to actual size*

# TWO POUNDS

This series commenced in 1986 with nickel-brass commemorative coins, with their associated base metal and precious metal BU and proof coins. From 1997 (actually issued in 1998) a thinner bi-metal version commenced with a reverse theme of the advance of technology, and from this date the coin was specifically intended to circulate. This is true also for the parallel issues of anniversary and commemorative Two Pound issues in 1999 and onwards. All have their BU and proof versions, as listed below.

In the case of Gold Proofs, a few have Certificates of Authenticity and/or green boxes of issue describing the coin as a Double Sovereign. All Gold Proofs since 1997 are of bi-metallic gold except for 2001 (red gold with the inner circle coated in yellow gold) and 2002 (Technology issue, uncoated red gold).

| DATE | Mintage | UNC |
|---|---|---|
| 1986 Commonwealth Games | 8,212,184 | £6 |
| 1986 — BU | — | £8 |
| 1986 — Proof | — | £12 |
| 1986 — Silver BU | — | £20 |
| 1986 — — Proof | — | £25 |
| 1986 — Gold Proof | — | £595 |
| 1989 Tercentenary of Bill of Rights. | 4,392,825 | £10 |
| 1989 — BU (issued in folder with Claim of Right) | — | £25 |
| 1989 — Proof | — | £15 |
| 1989 — Silver Proof (Pair as above) | — | £50 |
| 1989 — — — Piedfort (Pair as above) | — | £85 |
| 1989 Tercentenary of Claim of Right (issued in Scotland) | 381,400 | £15 |
| 1989 — BU (see above) | — | £25 |
| 1989 — Proof | — | £15 |
| 1989 — Silver Proof (see above) | — | £50 |
| 1989 — — — Piedfort (see above) | — | £85 |
| 1994 Tercentenary of the Bank of England | 1,443,116 | £5 |
| 1994 — BU | — | £8 |
| 1994 — Proof | — | £12 |
| 1994 — Silver Proof | — | £35 |
| 1994 — — Piedfort | — | £60 |
| 1994 — Gold Proof | — | £600 |
| 1994 — — — with Double Sovereign obverse (no denomination) | — | £675 |
| 1995 50th Anniversary of End of WWII. | 4,394,566 | £5 |
| 1995 — BU | — | £8 |
| 1995 — Proof | — | £12 |
| 1995 — Silver Proof | — | £35 |
| 1995 — — Piedfort | — | £60 |
| 1995 — Gold Proof | — | £650 |
| 1995 50th Anniversary of The United Nations | 1,668,575 | £5 |
| 1995 — BU | — | £6 |
| 1995 — Proof | — | £10 |
| 1995 — Silver Proof | — | £35 |
| 1995 — — Piedfort | — | £60 |
| 1995 — Gold Proof | — | £650 |
| 1996 European Football Championships. | 5,195,350 | £6 |
| 1996 — BU | — | £8 |
| 1996 — Proof | — | £10 |
| 1996 — Silver Proof | — | £35 |
| 1996 — — Piedfort | — | £60 |
| 1996 — Gold Proof | — | £650 |
| 1997 | 13,734,625 | £4 |
| 1997 BU | — | £8 |
| 1997 Proof | — | £12 |
| 1997 Silver Proof | — | £35 |
| 1997 — — Piedfort | — | £60 |
| 1997 Gold Proof (red (outer) and yellow (inner) 22ct) | — | £600 |
| 1998 **New Portrait** | — | £3 |
| 1998 BU | 91,110,375 | £8 |
| 1998 Proof | — | £12 |
| 1998 Silver Proof | — | £35 |
| 1998 — — Piedfort | — | £60 |

| DATE | Mintage | UNC |
|---|---|---|
| 1999 | 33,719,000 | £3 |
| 1999 Rugby World Cup | 4,933,000 | £5 |
| 1999 — BU | — | £6 |
| 1999 — Silver Proof (gold plated ring) | — | £40 |
| 1999 — — Piedfort (Hologram) | — | £95 |
| 1999 — Gold Proof | — | £650 |
| 2000 | 25,770,000 | £3 |
| 2000 BU | — | £5 |
| 2000 Proof | — | £10 |
| 2000 Silver Proof | — | £40 |
| 2000 Gold Proof | — | £595 |
| 2001 | 34,984,750 | £3 |
| 2001 BU | — | £4 |
| 2001 Proof | — | £10 |
| 2001 Marconi | 4,558,000 | £3 |
| 2001 — BU | — | £4 |
| 2001 — Proof | — | £10 |
| 2001 — Silver Proof (gold plated ring) | — | £40 |
| 2001 — — — Reverse Frosting (issued in set with Canada $5) | — | — |
| 2001 — — — Piedfort | — | £60 |
| 2001 — Gold Proof | — | £600 |
| 2002 | 13,024,750 | £3 |
| 2002 BU | — | £4 |
| 2002 Proof | — | £10 |
| 2002 Gold Proof (red 22ct) | — | £650 |
| 2002 Commonwealth Games, Scotland | 771,750 | £3 |
| 2002 — Wales | 558,500 | £3 |
| 2002 — Northern Ireland | 485,500 | £3 |
| 2002 — England | 650,500 | £3 |
| 2002 — BU (issued in set of 4) | — | £20 |
| 2002 — Proof (issued in set of 4) | — | £25 |
| 2002 — Silver Proof (issued in set of 4) | — | £120 |
| 2002 — — — Piedfort (painted) (issued in set of 4) | — | £240 |
| 2002 — Gold Proof (issued in set of 4) | — | £650 |
| 2003 | 17,531,250 | £3 |
| 2003 BU | — | £4 |
| 2003 Proof | — | £12 |
| 2003 DNA Double Helix | 4,299,000 | £3 |
| 2003 — BU | — | £4 |
| 2003 — Proof | — | £10 |
| 2003 — Silver Proof (Gold-plated ring) | — | £40 |
| 2003 — — — Piedfort | — | £65 |
| 2003 — Gold Proof | — | £600 |
| 2004 | 11,981,500 | £3 |
| 2004 BU | — | £4 |
| 2004 Proof | — | £12 |
| 2004 Trevithick Steam Locomotive | 5,004,500 | £4 |
| 2004 — BU | — | £5 |
| 2004 — Proof | — | £12 |
| 2004 — Silver BU | — | £25 |
| 2004 — — Proof (Gold-plated ring) | — | £45 |
| 2004 — — — Piedfort | — | £65 |
| 2004 — Gold Proof | — | £600 |
| 2005 | 3,837,250 | £3 |
| 2005 BU | — | £5 |
| 2005 Proof | — | £7 |
| 2005 Gunpowder Plot | 5,140,500 | £4 |
| 2005 — BU | — | £5 |
| 2005 — Proof | — | £6 |
| 2005 — Silver Proof | — | £35 |
| 2005 — — — Piedfort | — | £75 |
| 2005 — Gold Proof | — | £600 |
| 2005 End of World War II | 10,191,000 | £3 |
| 2005 — BU | — | £4 |
| 2005 — Silver Proof | — | £35 |

| DATE | Mintage | UNC |
|---|---|---|
| 2005 — — — Piedfort | — | £70 |
| 2005 — Gold Proof | — | £650 |
| 2006 | 16,715,000 | £3 |
| 2006 Proof | — | £6 |
| 2006 Brunel, The Man (Portrait) | 7,928,250 | £3 |
| 2006 — BU | — | £4 |
| 2006 — Proof | — | £6 |
| 2006 — Silver Proof | — | £35 |
| 2006 — — — Piedfort | — | £70 |
| 2006 — Gold Proof | — | £600 |
| 2006 Brunel, His Achievements (Paddington Station) | 7,452,250 | £3 |
| 2006 — BU | — | £4 |
| 2006 — Proof | — | £7 |
| 2006 — Silver Proof | — | £35 |
| 2006 — — — Piedfort | — | £70 |
| 2006 — Gold Proof | — | £600 |
| 2007 | 10,270,000 | £3 |
| 2007 Proof | — | £8 |
| 2007 Tercentenary of the Act of Union | 7,545,000 | £3 |
| 2007 BU | — | £4 |
| 2007 — Proof | — | £8 |
| 2007 — Silver Proof | — | £35 |
| 2007 — — — Piedfort | — | £70 |
| 2007 — Gold Proof | — | £600 |
| 2007 Bicentenary of the Abolition of the Slave Trade | 8,445,000 | £3 |
| 2007 — BU | — | £4 |
| 2007 — Proof | — | £7 |
| 2007 — Silver Proof | — | £35 |
| 2007 — — — Piedfort | — | £70 |
| 2007 — Gold Proof | — | £600 |
| 2008 | 15,346,000 | £3 |
| 2008 BU | — | £4 |
| 2008 Proof | — | £12 |
| 2008 Centenary of 4th Olympiad, London | 910,000 | £3 |
| 2008 — BU | — | £4 |
| 2008 — Proof | — | £12 |
| 2008 — Silver Proof | — | £40 |
| 2008 — — — Piedfort | — | £85 |
| 2008 — Gold proof | — | £600 |
| 2008 Olympic Games Handover Ceremony | 853,000 | £3 |
| 2008 — BU | — | £7 |
| 2008 — Silver Proof | — | £45 |
| 2008 — — — Piedfort | — | £75 |
| 2008 — Gold Proof | — | £600 |
| 2009 | 8,775,000 | £3 |
| 2009 BU | — | £4 |
| 2009 Proof | — | £10 |
| 2009 Silver Proof | — | £40 |
| 2009 250th Anniversary of birth of Robert Burns | 3,253,000 | £3 |
| 2009 — BU | — | £8 |
| 2009 — Proof | — | £12 |
| 2009 — Silver Proof | — | £35 |
| 2009 — — — Piedfort | — | £75 |
| 2009 — Gold Proof | — | £600 |
| 2009 200th Anniversary of birth of Charles Darwin | 3,903,000 | £3 |
| 2009 — BU | — | £8 |
| 2009 — Proof | — | £12 |
| 2009 — Silver Proof | — | £35 |
| 2009 — — — Piedfort | — | £70 |
| 2009 Gold Proof | — | £600 |
| 2010 | 2,015,000 | £3 |
| 2010 BU | — | £8 |
| 2010 Proof | — | £12 |
| 2010 Silver Proof | — | £40 |
| 2010 Florence Nightingale 150 Years of Nursing | 4,810,000 | £4 |
| 2010 — BU | — | £10 |

| DATE | Mintage | UNC |
|---|---|---|
| 2010 — Proof | — | £12 |
| 2010 — Silver Proof | — | £40 |
| 2010 – — – Piedfort | — | £75 |
| 2010 — Gold Proof | — | £650 |
| 2011 | 3,185,000 | £4 |
| 2011 BU | — | £5 |
| 2011 Proof | — | £12 |
| 2011 Silver Proof | — | £35 |
| 2011 500th Anniversary of the Mary Rose | 1,040,000 | £4 |
| 2011 — BU | — | £9 |
| 2011 — Proof | — | £12 |
| 2011 — Silver Proof | — | £40 |
| 2011 — — — Piedfort | — | £75 |
| 2011 — Gold Proof | — | £800 |
| 2011 400th Anniversary of the King James Bible | 975,000 | £4 |
| 2011 — BU | — | £9 |
| 2011 — Proof | — | £15 |
| 2011 — Silver Proof | — | £45 |
| 2011 — — — Piedfort | — | £75 |
| 2011 — Gold Proof | — | £800 |
| 2012 | — | — |
| 2012 BU | — | — |
| 2012 Proof | — | — |
| 2012 Silver Proof | — | — |
| 2012 200th Anniversary of birth of Charles Dickens | — | — |
| 2012 — BU | — | £9 |
| 2012 — Proof | — | — |
| 2012 — Silver Proof | — | £50 |
| 2012 – — – Piedfort | — | £88 |
| 2012 — Gold Proof | — | £995 |
| 2012 handover to Rio de Janeiro | — | — |
| 2012 — BU | — | £10 |
| 2012 Silver Proof | — | 75 |
| 2012 – — – Piedfort | — | £105 |
| 2012 — Gold Proof | — | £1195 |

# SOVEREIGN

*All are minted in gold, bear the Pistrucci St George and Dragon reverse except where stated, and are legal tender at one pound.*

| | | |
|---|---|---|
| 1974 | 5,002,566 | £300 |
| 1976 | 4,150,000 | £300 |
| 1978 | 6,550,000 | £300 |
| 1979 | 9,100,000 | £300 |
| 1979 Proof | 50,000 | £350 |
| 1980 | 5,100,000 | £300 |
| 1980 Proof | 91,200 | £350 |
| 1981 | 5,000,000 | £350 |
| 1981 Proof | 32,960 | £350 |
| 1982 | 2,950,000 | £300 |
| 1982 Proof | 22,500 | £350 |
| 1983 Proof | 21,250 | £350 |
| 1984 Proof | 19,975 | £350 |
| 1985 New portrait Proof | 17,242 | £350 |
| 1986 Proof | 17,579 | £350 |
| 1987 Proof | 22,479 | £350 |
| 1988 Proof | 18,862 | £350 |
| 1989 500th Anniversary of the Sovereign—details as Five Pounds (Sov. Series). Proof | 23,471 | £650 |
| 1990 Proof | 8,425 | £350 |
| 1991 Proof | 7,201 | £350 |
| 1992 Proof | 6,854 | £350 |
| 1993 Proof | 6,090 | £350 |

**NOTE:** The prices quoted in this guide are set at August 2012 with the price of gold at £920 per ounce and silver £16 per ounce—market fluctuations will have a marked effect on the values of modern precious metal coins.

| DATE | Mintage | UNC |
|---|---|---|
| 1994 Proof | 7,165 | £350 |
| 1995 Proof | 9,500 | £350 |
| 1996 Proof | 9,110 | £350 |
| 1997 Proof | 9,177 | £350 |
| 1998 New Portrait Proof | 11,349 | £350 |
| 1999 Proof | 11,903 | £375 |
| 2000 (first Unc issue since 1982) | 129,069 | £300 |
| 2000 Proof | 12,159 | £350 |
| 2001 | 49,462 | £300 |
| 2001 Proof | 10,000 | £350 |
| 2002 Shield Rev. ("bullion") | 74,263 | £300 |
| 2002 Proof | 20,500 | £350 |
| 2003 ("bullion") | 43,208 | £300 |
| 2003 Proof | — | £350 |
| 2004 ("bullion") | 28,821 | £300 |
| 2004 Proof | — | £350 |
| 2005 Noad heraldic St George and Dragon | — | £325 |
| 2005 — Proof | — | £450 |
| 2006 ("bullion") | — | £280 |
| 2006 Proof | — | £400 |
| 2007 ("bullion") | — | £300 |
| 2007 Proof | — | £350 |
| 2008 ("bullion") | — | £300 |
| 2008 Proof | — | £350 |
| 2009 ("bullion") | — | £300 |
| 2009 Proof | — | £350 |
| 2010 ("bullion") | — | £300 |
| 2010 Proof | — | £350 |
| 2011 ("bullion") | — | £350 |
| 2011 Proof | — | £400 |
| 2012 Day St George and Dragon "bullion" | — | £350 |
| 2012 — BU | — | £350 |

(the above two coins are probably identical, but are separately
advertised by The Royal Mint, both under code UKB12 RN)

| 2012 — Proof | | £495 |

| ABBREVIATIONS COMMONLY USED TO DENOTE METALLIC COMPOSITION | |
|---|---|
| Cu | Copper |
| Cu/Steel | Copper plated Steel |
| Ag/Cu | Silver plated copper |
| Ae | Bronze |
| Cu-Ni | Cupro-Nickel |
| Ni-Ag | Nickel Silver (note-does not contain silver) |
| Brass/Cu-Ni | Brass outer, Cupro-Nickel inner |
| Ni-Brass | Nickel-Brass |
| Ag | Silver |
| Au/Ag | Gold plated silver |
| Au | Gold |
| Pl | Platinum |

# HALF SOVEREIGN

*Legal Tender at 50 pence, otherwise the notes for the Sovereign apply.*

| DATE | Mintage | UNC |
|---|---|---|
| 1980 Proof only | 86,700 | £160 |
| 1982 | 2,500,000 | £160 |
| 1982 Proof | 21,590 | £175 |
| 1983 Proof | 19,710 | £175 |
| 1984 Proof | 19,505 | £175 |
| 1985 New portrait Proof | 15,800 | £175 |
| 1986 Proof | 17,075 | £175 |
| 1987 Proof | 20,687 | £175 |
| 1988 Proof | 18,266 | £175 |
| 1989 500th Anniversary of the Sovereign—details as | | |
| Five Pounds (Sov. Series) Proof | 21,824 | £480 |
| 1990 Proof | 7,889 | £175 |
| 1991 Proof | 6,076 | £175 |
| 1992 Proof | 5,915 | £175 |
| 1993 Proof | 4,651 | £175 |
| 1994 Proof | 7,167 | £175 |
| 1995 Proof | 7,500 | £175 |
| 1996 New Portrait Proof | 7,340 | £180 |
| 1997 Proof | 9,177 | £175 |
| 1998 Proof | 7,496 | £175 |
| 1999 Proof | 9,403 | £175 |
| 2000 | 146,822 | £145 |
| 2000 Proof | 9,708 | £175 |
| 2001 | 98,763 | £145 |
| 2001 Proof | 7,500 | £175 |
| 2002 Shield reverse ("bullion") | 61,347 | £145 |
| 2002 Proof | — | £175 |
| 2003 ("bullion") | 47,805 | £145 |
| 2003 Proof | — | £175 |
| 2004 ("bullion") | 32,479 | £145 |
| 2004 Proof | — | £175 |
| 2005 Noad heraldic St George and Dragon | — | £185 |
| 2005 — Proof | — | £200 |
| 2006 ("bullion") | — | £145 |
| 2006 Proof | — | £180 |
| 2006 ("bullion") | — | £145 |
| 2007 Proof | — | £180 |
| 2008 ("bullion") | — | £150 |
| 2008 Proof | — | £180 |
| 2009 ("bullion") | — | £150 |
| 2009 Proof | — | £180 |
| 2010 ("bullion") | — | £170 |
| 2010 Proof | — | £190 |
| 2011 ("bullion") | — | £175 |
| 2011 Proof | — | £200 |
| 2012 Day St. George and Dragon "bullion" or BU | — | £195 |
| (see remarks in the Sovereign section, code UKBH12 RN) | — | £195 |
| 2012 — Proof | — | £250 |

# QUARTER SOVEREIGN

Minted in 22ct Gold, this new denomination was introduced in 2009, and follows on from two different patterns of 1853.

| DATE | Mintage | UNC |
|---|---|---|
| 2009 ("bullion") | — | £85 |
| 2009 Proof | — | £100 |
| 2010 ("bullion") | — | £85 |
| 2010 Proof | — | £100 |
| 2011 ("bullion") | — | £95 |
| 2011 Proof | — | £100 |
| 2012 Day St George and Dragon "bullion" or BU | | |
| (see remarks in the Sovereign section, code UKBH12 RN) | | £99 |
| 2012 — Proof | — | £130 |

# ONE POUND

Introduced into circulation in 1983 to replace the £1 note, all are minted in nickel-brass unless otherwise stated. The reverse changed yearly until 2008, and until 2008 the Royal Arms was the "definitive" version. 2008 also saw the introduction of the Matthew Dent Uncrowned Shield of the Royal Arms, a new "definitive", and this reverse appeared in 2008 and every year since then. 2010 and 2011 also saw the new Capital Cities series of four coins, although none of these has yet appeared in circulation. Collectors and others should be aware of the many different counterfeit £1 coin versions in circulation, a high proportion of which do not have matching obverses and reverses although many do.

| DATE | Mintage | UNC |
|---|---|---|
| 1983 Royal Arms | 443,053,510 | £5 |
| 1983 — Unc | 1,134,000 | £5 |
| 1983 — Proof | 107,800 | £7 |
| 1983 — Silver Proof | 50,000 | £32 |
| 1983 — — Piedfort | 10,000 | £125 |
| 1984 Scottish Thistle | 146,256,501 | £5 |
| 1984 — BU | 199,430 | £6 |
| 1984 — Proof | 106,520 | £7 |
| 1984 — Silver Proof | 44,855 | £30 |
| 1984 — — Piedfort | 15,000 | £50 |
| 1985 **New portrait.** Welsh Leek | 228,430,749 | £4 |
| 1985 — BU | 213,679 | £5 |
| 1985 — Proof | 102,015 | £6 |
| 1985 — Silver Proof | 50,000 | £30 |
| 1985 — — Piedfort | 15,000 | £50 |
| 1986 Northern Ireland Flax | 10,409,501 | £3 |
| 1986 — BU | — | £6 |
| 1986 — Proof | — | £7 |
| 1986 — Silver Proof | — | £30 |
| 1986 — — Piedfort | — | £55 |
| 1987 English Oak | 39,298,502 | £3 |
| 1987 — BU | — | £5 |
| 1987 — Proof | — | £6 |
| 1987 — Silver Proof | — | £30 |
| 1987 — — Piedfort | — | £65 |
| 1988 Crowned Shield Of The Royal Arms | 7,118,825 | £3 |
| 1988 — BU | — | £5 |
| 1988 — Proof | — | £5 |
| 1988 — Silver Proof | — | £35 |
| 1988 — — Piedfort | — | £65 |
| 1989 Scottish Thistle | 70,580,501 | £2 |
| 1989 — BU | — | £6 |
| 1989 — Proof | — | £9 |
| 1989 — Silver Proof | — | £30 |
| 1989 — — Piedfort | — | £55 |
| 1990 Welsh Leek | — | £2 |
| 1990 — BU | 97,269,302 | £5 |
| 1990 — Proof | — | £7 |
| 1990 — Silver Proof | — | £30 |
| 1991 Northern Ireland Flax | 38,443,575 | £2 |

*1983, 1993, 1998, 2003*
**DECUS ET TUTAMEN**

*1984, 1989*
**NEMO ME IMPUNE LACESSIT**

*1985, 1990*
**PLEIDIOL WYF I'M GWLAD**

*1986, 1991*
**DECUS ET TUTAMEN**

| DATE | Mintage | UNC |
|---|---|---|
| 1991 — BU | — | £6 |
| 1991 — Proof | — | £7 |
| 1991 — Silver Proof | — | £32 |
| 1992 English Oak | 36,320,487 | £2 |
| 1992 — BU | — | £6 |
| 1992 — Proof | — | £7 |
| 1992 — Silver Proof | — | £32 |
| 1993 Royal Arms | 114,744,500 | £3 |
| 1993 — BU | — | £6 |
| 1993 — Proof | — | £7 |
| 1993 — Silver Proof | — | £34 |
| 1993 — — Piedfort | — | £55 |
| 1994 Scottish Lion | 29,752,525 | £4 |
| 1994 — BU | — | £6 |
| 1994 — Proof | — | £7 |
| 1994 — Silver Proof | — | £34 |
| 1994 — — Piedfort | — | £55 |
| 1995 Welsh Dragon | 34,503,501 | £3 |
| 1995 — BU | — | £6 |
| 1995 — — (Welsh) | — | £6 |
| 1995 — Proof | — | £10 |
| 1995 — Silver Proof | — | £34 |
| 1995 — — Piedfort | — | £60 |
| 1996 Northern Ireland Celtic Cross | 89,886,000 | £4 |
| 1996 — BU | — | £6 |
| 1996 — Proof | — | £7 |
| 1996 — Silver Proof | — | £35 |
| 1996 — — Piedfort | — | £60 |
| 1997 English Lions | 57,117,450 | £4 |
| 1997 — BU | — | £6 |
| 1997 — Proof | — | £7 |
| 1997 — Silver Proof | — | £35 |
| 1997 — — Piedfort | — | £60 |
| 1998 **New portrait.** Royal Arms. BU | — | £8 |
| 1998 — Proof | — | £10 |
| 1998 — Silver Proof | — | £32 |
| 1998 — — Piedfort | — | £50 |
| 1999 Scottish Lion. BU | — | £6 |
| 1999 — Proof | — | £13 |
| 1999 — Silver Proof | — | £35 |
| 1999 — — Reverse Frosting | — | £45 |
| 1999 — — Piedfort | — | £55 |
| 2000 Welsh Dragon | 109,496,500 | £3 |
| 2000 — BU | — | £5 |
| 2000 — Proof | — | £7 |
| 2000 — Silver Proof | — | £35 |
| 2000 — — Reverse Frosting | — | £45 |
| 2000 — — Piedfort | — | £55 |
| 2001 Northern Ireland Celtic Cross | 63,968,065 | £3 |
| 2001 — BU | 58,093,731 | £5 |
| 2001 — Proof | — | £6 |
| 2001 — Silver Proof | — | £35 |
| 2001 — — Reverse Frosting | — | £45 |
| 2001 — — Piedfort | — | £50 |
| 2002 English Lions | 77,818,000 | £3 |
| 2002 — BU | — | £5 |
| 2002 — Proof | — | £8 |
| 2002 — Silver Proof | — | £35 |
| 2002 — — Reverse Frosting | — | £45 |
| 2002 — — Piedfort | — | £50 |
| 2002 — Gold Proof | — | £350 |
| 2003 Royal Arms | 61,596,500 | £4 |
| 2003 — BU | — | £6 |
| 2003 — Proof | — | £10 |
| 2003 — Silver Proof | — | £35 |
| 2003 — — Piedfort | — | £50 |
| 2004 Forth Railway Bridge | 39,162,000 | £4 |
| 2004 — BU | — | £6 |
| 2004 — Proof | — | £10 |

*1987, 1992*
*DECUS ET TUTAMEN*

*1988*
*DECUS ET TUTAMEN*

*1994, 1999*
*NEMO ME IMPUNE LACESSIT*

*1995, 2000*
*PLEIDIOL WYF I'M GWLAD*

*1996, 2001*
*DECUS ET TUTAMEN*

*1997, 2002*
*DECUS ET TUTAMEN*

| DATE | Mintage | UNC |
|---|---|---|
| 2004 — Silver Proof ............................................... | — | £35 |
| 2004 — — — Piedfort .............................................. | — | £50 |
| 2004 — Gold Proof................................................. | — | £350 |
| 2005 Menai Bridge.................................................. | 99,429,500 | £4 |
| 2005 — BU ............................................................. | — | £6 |
| 2005 — Proof ......................................................... | — | £10 |
| 2005 — Silver Proof ............................................... | — | £35 |
| 2005 — — — Piedfort .............................................. | — | £50 |
| 2005 — Gold Proof................................................. | — | £350 |
| 2006 Egyptian Arch ................................................ | 38,938,000 | £4 |
| 2006 — BU ............................................................. | — | £6 |
| 2006 — Proof ......................................................... | — | £10 |
| 2006 — Silver Proof ............................................... | — | £35 |
| 2006 — — — Piedfort .............................................. | — | £55 |
| 2006 — Gold Proof................................................. | — | £350 |
| 2007 Gateshead Millennium Bridge .......................... | 26,180,160 | £4 |
| 2007 — BU ............................................................. | — | £6 |
| 2007 — Proof ......................................................... | — | £10 |
| 2007 — Silver Proof ............................................... | — | £40 |
| 2007 — — — Piedfort .............................................. | — | £55 |
| 2007 — Gold Proof................................................. | — | £350 |
| 2008 Royal Arms .................................................... | 3,910,000 | £4 |
| 2008 — BU ............................................................. | — | £6 |
| 2008 — Proof ......................................................... | — | £8 |
| 2008 — Silver Proof ............................................... | — | £35 |
| 2008 — Gold Proof................................................. | — | £350 |
| 2008 — Platinum Proof ........................................... | — | £475 |
| 2008 A series of 14 different reverses, the 25th Anniversary of the modern £1 coin, Silver Proof with selected gold highlighting on the reverses. the latter being all those used since 1983, the coins being with appropriate edge lettering ................................. | — | £420 |
| 2008 The same as above, Gold Proof ( the 2008 Royal Arms being already listed above)...................................................... | — | — |
| 2008 **New Rev.,** Shield of the Royal Arms, no border beads on Obv......................................................... | 29,518,000 | £4 |
| 2008 BU ................................................................. | — | £5 |
| 2008 Proof.............................................................. | — | £6 |
| 2008 Silver Proof ................................................... | — | £35 |
| 2008 Silver Proof Piedfort ...................................... | — | £50 |
| 2008 Gold Proof ..................................................... | — | — |
| 2008 Platinum Proof............................................... | — | £575 |
| 2009....................................................................... | 7,820,000 | £4 |
| 2009 BU ................................................................. | — | £5 |
| 2009 Proof.............................................................. | — | £6 |
| 2009 Silver Proof ................................................... | — | £35 |
| 2009 Gold Proof ..................................................... | — | £595 |
| 2010....................................................................... | 38,505,000 | £4 |
| 2010 BU ................................................................. | — | £5 |
| 2010 Proof.............................................................. | — | £6 |
| 2010 Silver BU....................................................... | — | £30 |
| 2010 — Proof ......................................................... | — | £40 |
| 2010 City Series (London) ....................................... | 2,635,000 | £4 |
| 2010 — BU ............................................................. | — | £5 |
| 2010 — Proof ......................................................... | — | £6 |
| 2010 — Silver Proof ............................................... | — | £33 |
| 2010 — — — Piedfort .............................................. | — | £55 |
| 2010 — Gold Proof................................................. | — | £620 |
| 2010 City Series (Belfast) ....................................... | 6,205,000 | £3 |
| 2010 — BU ............................................................. | — | £4 |
| 2010 — Proof ......................................................... | — | £6 |
| 2010 — Silver Proof ............................................... | — | £35 |
| 2010 — — — Piedfort .............................................. | — | £55 |
| 2010 — Gold Proof................................................. | — | £600 |
| 2011....................................................................... | 39,550,000 | £2 |
| 2011 BU ................................................................. | — | £3 |
| 2011 Proof.............................................................. | — | £8 |
| 2011 Silver BU (in 21st and 18th Birthday cards) ....... | — | £45 |
| 2011 — Proof ......................................................... | — | £55 |
| 2011 City Series (Cardiff)........................................ | 1,615,000 | £4 |
| 2011 — BU ............................................................. | — | £5 |

*2004*
**PATTERNED EDGE**

*2005*
**PATTERNED EDGE**

*2006*
**PATTERNED EDGE**

*2007*
**PATTERNED EDGE**

*2008 (proof sets—silver and gold)*
**DECUS ET TUTAMEN**

*2008, 2009, 2010, 2011*
**DECUS ET TUTAMEN**

*2011*
**Y DDRAIG GOCH
DDYRY CYCHWYN**

| | | |
|---|---|---|
| 2011 — Proof | — | £7 |
| 2011 — Silver Proof | — | £40 |
| 2011 — — — Piedfort | — | £75 |
| 2011 — Gold Proof | — | £800 |
| 2011 City Series (Edinburgh) | — | £4 |
| 2011 — BU | — | £5 |
| 2011 — Proof | — | £8 |
| 2011 — Silver Proof | — | £45 |
| 2011 — — — Piedfort | — | £75 |
| 2011 — Gold Proof | — | £800 |
| 2012 | — | — |
| 2012 BU | — | — |
| 2012 Proof | — | — |
| 2012 Silver BU (in Silver Baby Gift) | — | £50 |
| 2012 Silver Proof | — | £150 |
| 2012 -- with selective gold plating | — | — |
| 2012 Gold Proof | — | — |

*2011*
**NISI DOMINUS FRUSTRA**

# FIFTY PENCE

*Introduced as legal tender for 10 shillings to replace the banknote of that value prior to decimalisation, coins of the original size are no longer legal tender. Unless otherwise stated, i.e. for commemoratives, the reverse design is of Britannia. The reverse legend of NEW PENCE became FIFTY PENCE from 1982.*

*The description of "Unc" has been used against some 50 pence pieces dated 2009 and 2011 (for Olympic and Paralympic sports) to distinguish them from coins minted to circulation standard and BU standard, being a standard between the latter two. The uncirculated standard coins have a more even rim than the circulation standard examples, particularly observable on the obverse.*

*All 29 sports coins dated 2011 have now been issued to circulation, a million or more of each (below). There is no limit to each of the uncirculated versions, while there is a 30,000 limit to each silver BU version.*

| DATE | Mintage | UNC |
|---|---|---|
| 1969 | 188,400,000 | £5 |
| 1970 | 19,461,500 | £5 |
| 1971 Proof | — | £8 |
| 1972 Proof | — | £7 |
| 1973 Accession to EEC | 89,775,000 | £5 |
| 1973 — Proof | — | £10 |
| 1973 — Silver Proof Piedfort | — | £2500 |
| 1974 Proof | — | £7 |
| 1975 Proof | — | £8 |
| 1976 | 43,746,500 | £5 |
| 1976 Proof | — | £7 |
| 1977 | 49,536,000 | £5 |
| 1977 Proof | — | £6 |
| 1978 | 72,005,000 | £5 |
| 1978 Proof | — | £6 |
| 1979 | 58,680,000 | £5 |
| 1979 Proof | — | £6 |
| 1980 | 89,086,000 | £5 |
| 1980 Proof | — | £6 |
| 1981 | 74,002,000 | £6 |
| 1981 Proof | — | £8 |
| 1982 | 51,312,000 | £5 |
| 1982 Unc | — | £6 |
| 1982 Proof | — | £8 |
| 1983 | 62,824,000 | £5 |
| 1983 Unc | — | £6 |

| DATE | Mintage | UNC |
|---|---|---|
| 1983 Proof ................................................. | — | £8 |
| 1984 BU ..................................................... | — | £6 |
| 1984 Proof ................................................. | — | £8 |
| 1985 **New portrait** ........................ estimated approx | 3,400,000 | £1 |
| 1985 BU ..................................................... | — | £5 |
| 1985 Proof ................................................. | — | £6 |
| 1986 BU ..................................................... | — | £5 |
| 1986 Proof ................................................. | — | £11 |
| 1987 BU ..................................................... | — | £4 |
| 1987 Proof ................................................. | — | £11 |
| 1988 BU ..................................................... | — | £4 |
| 1988 Proof ................................................. | — | £11 |
| 1989 BU ..................................................... | — | £4 |
| 1989 Proof ................................................. | — | £11 |
| 1990 BU ..................................................... | — | £4 |
| 1990 Proof ................................................. | — | £11 |
| 1991 BU ..................................................... | — | £5 |
| 1991 Proof ................................................. | — | £10 |
| 1992 BU ..................................................... | — | £7 |
| 1992 Proof ................................................. | — | £12 |
| 1992 Presidency of EC Council and EC accession 20th anniversary (includes 1993 date) ................................................. | 109,000 | £15 |
| 1992 — BU .................................................. | — | £10 |
| 1992 — Proof ............................................. | — | £12 |
| 1992 — Silver Proof .................................... | — | £30 |
| 1992 — — Piedfort ..................................... | — | £65 |
| 1992 — Gold Proof...................................... | — | £500 |
| 1993 BU ..................................................... | — | £5 |
| 1993 Proof ................................................. | — | £12 |
| 1994 50th Anniversary of the Normandy Landings ..... | 6,705,520 | £5 |
| 1994 — BU (also in presentation folder) ................... | — | £8 |
| 1994 — Proof ............................................. | — | £12 |
| 1994 — Silver Proof .................................... | — | £35 |
| 1994 — — Piedfort ..................................... | — | £55 |
| 1994 — Gold Proof...................................... | — | £500 |
| 1995 BU ..................................................... | — | £8 |
| 1995 Proof ................................................. | — | £12 |
| 1996 BU ..................................................... | — | £8 |
| 1996 Proof ................................................. | — | £12 |
| 1996 Silver Proof ....................................... | — | £25 |
| 1997 BU ..................................................... | — | £7 |
| 1997 Proof ................................................. | — | £9 |
| 1997 Silver Proof ....................................... | — | £25 |
| 1997 **New reduced size** ........................................ | 456,364,100 | £4 |
| 1997 BU ..................................................... | — | £5 |
| 1997 Proof ................................................. | — | £6 |
| 1997 Silver Proof ....................................... | — | £25 |
| 1997 — — Piedfort ..................................... | — | £35 |
| 1998 **New portrait** ................................................. | 64,306,500 | £2 |
| 1998 BU ..................................................... | — | £5 |
| 1998 Proof ................................................. | — | £7 |
| 1998 Presidency and 25th anniversary of EU entry ... | 5,043,000 | £3 |
| 1998 — BU .................................................. | — | £5 |
| 1998 — Proof ............................................. | — | £7 |
| 1998 — Silver Proof .................................... | — | £30 |
| 1998 — — Piedfort ..................................... | — | £45 |
| 1998 — Gold Proof...................................... | — | £400 |
| 1998 50th Anniversary of the National Health Service | 5,001,000 | £3 |
| 1998 — BU .................................................. | — | £5 |
| 1998 — Silver Proof (believed not issued as Cu-Ni proof) | — | £30 |
| 1998 — — Piedfort ..................................... | — | £45 |
| 1998 — Gold Proof...................................... | — | £400 |
| 1999............................................................ | 24,905,000 | £2 |
| 1999 BU ..................................................... | — | £5 |
| 1999 Proof ................................................. | — | £10 |
| 2000............................................................ | 27,915,500 | £1 |
| 2000 BU ..................................................... | — | £5 |
| 2000 Proof ................................................. | — | £7 |
| 2000 150th Anniversary of Public Libraries ............... | 11,263,000 | £5 |

| DATE | Mintage | UNC |
|---|---|---|
| 2000 — BU | — | £6 |
| 2000 — Proof | — | £9 |
| 2000 — Silver Proof | — | £30 |
| 2000 — — Piedfort | — | £45 |
| 2000 — Gold proof | — | £350 |
| 2001 | 84,998,500 | £1 |
| 2001 BU | — | £5 |
| 2001 Proof | — | £7 |
| 2002 | 23,907,500 | — |
| 2002 BU | — | £5 |
| 2002 Proof | — | £7 |
| 2002 Gold Proof | — | £300 |
| 2003 | 23,583,000 | — |
| 2003 BU | — | £5 |
| 2003 Proof | — | £6 |
| 2003 Suffragette | 3,124,030 | — |
| 2003 — BU | — | £6 |
| 2003 — Proof | — | £7 |
| 2003 — Silver Proof | — | £30 |
| 2003 — — Piedfort | — | £45 |
| 2003 — Gold Proof | — | £300 |
| 2004 | 35,315,500 | — |
| 2004 BU | — | £5 |
| 2004 Proof | — | £8 |
| 2004 Roger Bannister | 9,032,500 | £5 |
| 2004 — BU | — | £6 |
| 2004 — Proof | — | £8 |
| 2004 — Silver Proof | — | £30 |
| 2004 — — Piedfort | — | £45 |
| 2004 — Gold Proof | — | £300 |
| 2005 | 25,363,500 | £3 |
| 2005 BU | — | £6 |
| 2005 Proof | — | £8 |
| 2005 Samuel Johnson | 17,649,000 | £3 |
| 2005 — BU | — | £5 |
| 2005 — Proof | — | £8 |
| 2005 — Silver Proof | — | £30 |
| 2005 — — Piedfort | — | £45 |
| 2005 — Gold Proof | — | £300 |
| 2006 | 24,567,000 | — |
| 2006 Proof | — | £8 |
| 2006 Silver Proof | — | £30 |
| 2006 Victoria Cross, The Award | 12,087,000 | £3 |
| 2006 — BU | — | £5 |
| 2006 — Proof | — | £8 |
| 2006 — Silver Proof | — | £30 |
| 2006 — — — Piedfort | — | £45 |
| 2006 — Gold Proof | — | £300 |
| 2006 Victoria Cross, Heroic Acts | 10,000,500 | — |
| 2006 — BU | — | £5 |
| 2006 — Proof | — | £8 |
| 2006 — Silver Proof | — | £30 |
| 2006 — — — Piedfort | — | £45 |
| 2006 — Gold Proof | — | £350 |
| 2007 | 5,300,000 | — |
| 2007 BU | — | £6 |
| 2007 Proof | — | £8 |
| 2007 Centenary of Scout Movement | 7,710,750 | £5 |
| 2007 — BU | — | £6 |
| 2007 — Proof | — | £12 |
| 2007 — Silver Proof | — | £30 |
| 2007 — — Piedfort | — | £55 |
| 2007 — Gold Proof | — | £400 |
| 2008 | 700,000 | — |
| 2008 — BU | — | £5 |
| 2008 — Proof | — | £6 |
| 2008 — Silver Proof | — | £25 |
| 2008 — Gold Proof | — | £400 |
| 2008 — Platinum Proof | — | £1500 |

| DATE | Mintage | UNC |
|---|---|---|
| 2008 **New Shield Rev.** Obv. rotated by approx. | | |
|   26 degrees | 12,320,000 | £5 |
| 2008 BU | — | £6 |
| 2008 Proof | — | £8 |
| 2008 Silver Proof | — | £25 |
| 2008 Silver Proof Piedfort | — | £45 |
| 2008 Gold Proof | — | £400 |
| 2008 Platinum Proof | — | £1500 |
| 2009 BU | — | £4 |
| 2009 Proof | — | £6 |
| 2009 Silver Proof | — | £20 |
| 2009 250th Anniversary of Kew Gardens | 210,000 | £4 |
| 2009 — BU | — | £6 |
| 2009 — Proof | — | £25 |
| 2009 — Silver Proof | — | £35 |
| 2009 — — Piedfort | — | £55 |
| 2009 — Gold Proof | — | £400 |
| 2009 Olympic and Paralympic Sports | | |
|   (Track & Field Athletics) Unc | 100,000 | £2 |
| 2009 16 different reverses from the past marking the | | |
|   40th Anniversary of the 50p coin. Proof | — | £225 |
| 2009 — Silver Proof | — | £475 |
| 2009 — Gold Proof | 125 | £7950 |
| 2009 — — Piedfort | 40 | £19,950 |
| 2010 BU | — | £4 |
| 2010 Proof | — | £25 |
| 2010 Silver Proof | — | £35 |
| 2010 100 years of Girl Guiding UK | 7,410,090 | — |
| 2010 — BU | — | £7 |
| 2010 — Proof | — | £20 |
| 2010 — Silver Proof | — | £35 |
| 2010 — — Piedfort | — | £55 |
| 2010 — Gold Proof | — | £575 |
| 2011 BU | — | — |
| 2011 Proof | — | — |
| 2011 Silver Proof | — | £45 |
| 2011 50th Anniversary of the WWF | 3,200,000 | — |
| 2011 — BU | — | £5 |
| 2011 — Proof | — | £25 |
| 2011 — Silver Proof | — | £45 |
| 2011 — — Piedfort | — | £65 |
| 2011 — Gold Proof | — | £675 |
| 2011 Olympic & Paralympic Sports Issues: | | |
|   Aquatics circ, head clear of lines | 1,312,000 | — |
|   — Head with lines Unc (as illustrated above) | — | £200 |
|   — Head clear of lines. Unc | — | £3 |
|   — Silver BU | 30,000 | £35 |
|   Archery Circ | 1,310,000 | — |
|   — Unc | — | £3 |
|   — Silver BU | 30,000 | £35 |
|   Track & Field Athletics circ | 1,310,000 | — |
|   — Unc | — | £3 |
|   — Silver BU | 30,000 | £35 |
|   Badminton circ | 1,305,000 | — |
|   — Unc | — | £3 |
|   — Silver BU | 30,000 | £35 |
|   Boccia circ | 1,305,000 | — |
|   — Unc | — | £3 |
|   — Silver BU | 30,000 | £35 |
|   Boxing circ | 1,305,000 | — |
|   — Unc | — | £3 |
|   — Silver BU | 30,000 | £35 |
|   Volleyball circ | 1,005,000 | — |
|   — Unc | — | £3 |
|   — Silver BU | 30,000 | £35 |
|   Canoeing | 1,010,000 | — |
|   — Unc | — | £3 |
|   — Silver BU | 30,000 | £35 |
|   Cycling circ | 1,000,000 | — |

| DATE | Mintage | UNC |
|---|---|---|
| — Unc ........................................................... | — | £3 |
| — Silver BU.................................................... | 30,000 | £35 |
| Equestrian circ ............................................... | 1,005,000 | — |
| — Unc ........................................................... | — | £3 |
| — Silver BU.................................................... | 30,000 | £35 |
| Fencing circ.................................................... | 1,005,000 | — |
| — Unc ........................................................... | — | £3 |
| — Silver BU.................................................... | 30,000 | £35 |
| Football circ................................................... | 1,000,000 | — |
| — Unc ........................................................... | — | £3 |
| — Silver Bu .................................................... | 30,000 | £35 |
| Goalball circ .................................................. | 1,005,000 | — |
| — Unc ........................................................... | — | £3 |
| — Silver BU.................................................... | 30,000 | £35 |
| Gymnastics circ.............................................. | 1,008,313 | — |
| — Unc ........................................................... | — | £3 |
| — Silver BU.................................................... | 30,000 | £35 |
| Handball circ ................................................. | 1,005,000 | — |
| — Unc ........................................................... | — | £3 |
| — Silver BU.................................................... | 30,000 | £35 |
| Hockey circ ................................................... | 1,001,000 | — |
| — Unc ........................................................... | — | £3 |
| — Silver BU.................................................... | 30,000 | £35 |
| Judo circ ....................................................... | 1,005,000 | — |
| — Unc ........................................................... | — | £3 |
| — Silver BU.................................................... | 30,000 | £35 |
| Modern Pentathlon circ................................... | 1,005,000 | — |
| — Unc ........................................................... | — | £3 |
| — Silver BU.................................................... | 30,000 | £35 |
| Rowing circ ................................................... | 1,005,000 | — |
| — Unc ........................................................... | — | £3 |
| — Silver BU.................................................... | 30,000 | £35 |
| Sailing circ .................................................... | 1,005,000 | — |
| — Unc ........................................................... | — | £3 |
| — Silver BU.................................................... | 30,000 | £35 |
| Shooting circ ................................................. | 1,005,000 | — |
| — Unc ........................................................... | — | £3 |
| — Silver BU.................................................... | 30,000 | £35 |
| Taekwondo circ ............................................. | 1,005,000 | — |
| — Unc ........................................................... | — | £3 |
| — Silver BU.................................................... | 30,000 | £35 |
| Table Tennis circ............................................ | 1,010,000 | — |
| — Unc ........................................................... | — | £3 |
| — Silver BU.................................................... | 30,000 | £35 |
| Tennis circ .................................................... | 1,006,000 | — |
| — Unc ........................................................... | — | £3 |
| — Silver BU.................................................... | 30,000 | £35 |
| Triathlon circ................................................. | 1,011,000 | — |
| — Unc ........................................................... | — | £3 |
| — Silver BU.................................................... | 30,000 | £35 |
| Basketball circ............................................... | 1,100,000 | — |
| — Unc ........................................................... | — | £3 |
| — Silver BU.................................................... | 30,000 | £35 |
| Weightlifting circ............................................ | 1,000,000 | — |
| — Unc ........................................................... | — | £3 |
| — Silver BU.................................................... | 30,000 | £35 |
| Wheelchair Rugby circ ................................... | 1,005,000 | — |
| — Unc ........................................................... | — | £3 |
| — Silver BU.................................................... | 30,000 | £35 |
| Wrestling circ................................................. | 1,005,000 | — |
| — Unc ........................................................... | — | £3 |
| — Silver BU.................................................... | 30,000 | £35 |
| 2012 BU ........................................................ | — | — |
| 2012 Proof..................................................... | — | — |
| 2012 Silver Proof with selective gold plating ............. | — | — |
| 2012 Gold Proof............................................. | — | — |

# TWENTY-FIVE PENCE (CROWN)

*This series is a continuation of the pre-decimal series, there having been four crowns to the pound. The coins below have a legal tender face value of 25p to this day, and are minted in cupro-nickel except where stated otherwise.*

| DATE | Mintage | UNC |
|---|---|---|
| 1972 Royal Silver Wedding | 7,452,100 | £2 |
| 1972 — Proof | 150,000 | £8 |
| 1972 — Silver Proof | 100,000 | £25 |
| 1977 Silver Jubilee | 37,061,160 | £2 |
| 1977 — in Presentation folder | Incl. above | £3 |
| 1977 — Proof | 193,000 | £8 |
| 1977 — Silver Proof | 377,000 | £20 |
| 1980 Queen Mother 80th Birthday | 9,306,000 | £2 |
| 1980 — in Presentation folder | Incl. above | £3 |
| 1980 — Silver Proof | 83,670 | £30 |
| 1981 Royal Wedding | 26,773,600 | £2 |
| 1981 — in Presentation folder | Incl. above | £3 |
| 1981 — Silver Proof | 218,140 | £30 |

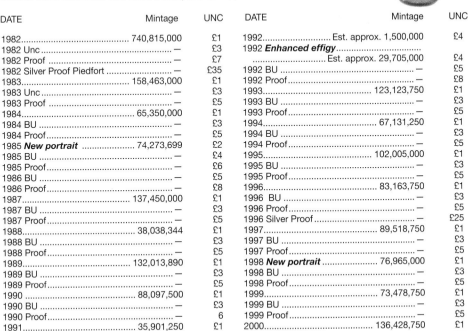

# TWENTY PENCE

*The series commenced in 1982, some 11 years after the introduction of decimal coinage. Its presence from introduction date meant that there was no requirement for ten pence circulation—standard coins until the latter's size was reduced in 1992. Unlike the circulation coins on either side of it in face value, it's alloy is 84% copper and 16% nickel.*

| DATE | Mintage | UNC | DATE | Mintage | UNC |
|---|---|---|---|---|---|
| 1982 | 740,815,000 | £1 | 1992 | Est. approx. 1,500,000 | £4 |
| 1982 Unc | — | £3 | 1992 *Enhanced effigy* | | |
| 1982 Proof | — | £7 | | Est. approx. 29,705,000 | £4 |
| 1982 Silver Proof Piedfort | — | £35 | 1992 BU | — | £5 |
| 1983 | 158,463,000 | £1 | 1992 Proof | — | £8 |
| 1983 Unc | — | £3 | 1993 | 123,123,750 | £1 |
| 1983 Proof | — | £5 | 1993 BU | — | £3 |
| 1984 | 65,350,000 | £1 | 1993 Proof | — | £5 |
| 1984 BU | — | £3 | 1994 | 67,131,250 | £1 |
| 1984 Proof | — | £5 | 1994 BU | — | £3 |
| 1985 *New portrait* | 74,273,699 | £2 | 1994 Proof | — | £5 |
| 1985 BU | — | £4 | 1995 | 102,005,000 | £1 |
| 1985 Proof | — | £6 | 1995 BU | — | £3 |
| 1986 BU | — | £5 | 1995 Proof | — | £5 |
| 1986 Proof | — | £8 | 1996 | 83,163,750 | £1 |
| 1987 | 137,450,000 | £1 | 1996 BU | — | £3 |
| 1987 BU | — | £3 | 1996 Proof | — | £5 |
| 1987 Proof | — | £5 | 1996 Silver Proof | — | £25 |
| 1988 | 38,038,344 | £1 | 1997 | 89,518,750 | £1 |
| 1988 BU | — | £3 | 1997 BU | — | £3 |
| 1988 Proof | — | £5 | 1997 Proof | — | £5 |
| 1989 | 132,013,890 | £1 | 1998 *New portrait* | 76,965,000 | £1 |
| 1989 BU | — | £3 | 1998 BU | — | £3 |
| 1989 Proof | — | £5 | 1998 Proof | — | £5 |
| 1990 | 88,097,500 | £1 | 1999 | 73,478,750 | £1 |
| 1990 BU | — | £3 | 1999 BU | — | £3 |
| 1990 Proof | — | 6 | 1999 Proof | — | £5 |
| 1991 | 35,901,250 | £1 | 2000 | 136,428,750 | £1 |
| 1991 BU | — | £3 | 2000 BU | — | £3 |
| 1991 Proof | — | £6 | 2000 Proof | — | £5 |

| DATE | Mintage | UNC | DATE | Mintage | UNC |
|---|---|---|---|---|---|
| 2000 Silver Proof | — | £25 | 2008 Platinum Proof | — | £750 |
| 2001 | 148,122,500 | £1 | 2008 New Rev., date on Obv. | 81,920,000 | — |
| 2001 BU | — | £3 | 2008 — paired with old Obv. (thus no date).. | | |
| 2001 Proof | — | £5 | Est. approx. 120,000 (?) . | | £100 |
| 2002 | 93,360,000 | £1 | 2008 BU | — | £3 |
| 2002 BU | — | £3 | 2008 Proof | — | £6 |
| 2002 Proof | — | £5 | 2008 Silver Proof | — | £15 |
| 2002 Gold Proof | — | £225 | 2008 — — Piedfort | — | £30 |
| 2003 | 153,383,750 | £1 | 2008 Gold Proof | — | £275 |
| 2003 BU | — | £4 | 2008 Platinum Proof | — | £750 |
| 2003 Proof | — | £6 | 2009 | 94,500,300 | — |
| 2004 | 120,212,500 | £1 | 2009 BU | — | £5 |
| 2004 BU | — | £4 | 2009 Proof | — | £7 |
| 2004 Proof | — | £6 | 2009 Silver Proof | — | £15 |
| 2005 | 124,488,750 | — | 2010 | 91,700,500 | — |
| 2005 BU | — | £4 | 2010 BU | — | £5 |
| 2005 Proof | — | £6 | 2010 Proof | — | £7 |
| 2006 | 114,800,000 | — | 2010 Silver Proof | — | £15 |
| 2006 BU | — | £6 | 2011 | 39,550,000 | — |
| 2006 Proof | — | £7 | 2011 BU | — | — |
| 2006 Silver Proof | — | £15 | 2011 Proof | — | — |
| 2007 | 117,075,000 | — | 2011 Silver Proof | — | — |
| 2007 BU | — | £4 | 2012 | — | — |
| 2007 Proof | — | £6 | 2012 BU | — | — |
| 2008 | 11,900,000 | — | 2012 Proof | — | — |
| 2008 BU | — | £4 | 2012 Silver Proof (issued in set with Victorian | | |
| 2008 Proof | — | £7 | 4 Shilling piece) | — | — |
| 2008 Silver Proof | — | £15 | 2012- - with selective gold plating | — | — |
| 2008 Gold Proof | — | £275 | 2012 — Gold Proof | — | — |

# TEN PENCE

The series commenced before decimalisation with the legend NEW PENCE, this changed to TEN PENCE from 1982. These "florin-sized" coins up to 1992 are no longer legal tender. Cupro-nickel was replaced by nickel-plated steel from 2011.

| DATE | Mintage | UNC | DATE | Mintage | UNC |
|---|---|---|---|---|---|
| 1968 | 336,143,250 | £3 | 1981 Proof | — | £5 |
| 1969 | 314,008,000 | £4 | 1982 BU | — | £4 |
| 1970 | 133,571,000 | £3 | 1982 Proof | — | £6 |
| 1971 | 63,205,000 | £3 | 1983 BU | — | £3 |
| 1971 Proof | — | £4 | 1983 Proof | — | £4 |
| 1972 Proof only | — | £5 | 1984 BU | — | £4 |
| 1973 | 152,174,000 | £3 | 1984 Proof | — | £6 |
| 1973 Proof | — | £4 | 1985 New portrait BU | — | £5 |
| 1974 | 92,741,000 | £3 | 1985 Proof | — | £7 |
| 1974 Proof | — | £4 | 1986 BU | — | £4 |
| 1975 | 181,559,000 | £3 | 1986 Proof | — | £6 |
| 1975 Proof | — | £4 | 1987 BU | — | £4 |
| 1976 | 228,220,000 | £3 | 1987 Proof | — | £7 |
| 1976 Proof | — | £4 | 1988 BU | — | £5 |
| 1977 | 59,323,000 | £4 | 1988 Proof | — | £7 |
| 1977 Proof | — | £4 | 1989 BU | — | £6 |
| 1978 Proof | — | £6 | 1989 Proof | — | £9 |
| 1979 | 115,457,000 | £2 | 1990 BU | — | £6 |
| 1979 Proof | — | £4 | 1990 Proof | — | £9 |
| 1980 | 88,650,000 | £3 | 1991 BU | — | £6 |
| 1980 Proof | — | £4 | 1991 Proof | — | £9 |
| 1981 | 3,487,000 | £3 | 1992 BU | — | £5 |

| DATE | Mintage | UNC | DATE | Mintage | UNC |
|---|---|---|---|---|---|
| 1992 Proof | — | £7 | 2005 | 69,604,000 | — |
| 1992 Silver Proof | — | £12 | 2005 BU | — | £2 |
| 1992 *Size reduced (24.5mm)* | 1,413,455,170 | £3 | 2005 Proof | — | £4 |
| 1992 BU | — | £4 | 2006 | 118,803,000 | — |
| 1992 Proof | — | £5 | 2006 BU | — | £3 |
| 1992 Silver Proof | — | £12 | 2006 Proof | — | £7 |
| 1992 — — Piedfort | — | £25 | 2006 Silver Proof | — | £22 |
| 1993 BU | — | £2 | 2007 | 72,720,000 | — |
| 1993 Proof | — | £7 | 2007 BU | — | £4 |
| 1994 BU | — | £2 | 2007 Proof | — | £7 |
| 1994 Proof | — | £7 | 2008 | 9,720,000 | — |
| 1995 | 43,259,000 | £1 | 2008 BU | — | £4 |
| 1995 BU | — | £5 | 2008 Proof | — | £5 |
| 1995 Proof | — | £7 | 2008 Silver Proof | — | £25 |
| 1996 | 118,738,000 | £2 | 2008 Gold Proof | — | £250 |
| 1996 BU | — | £4 | 2008 Platinum Proof | — | £350 |
| 1996 Proof | — | £7 | 2008 *New Rev.*, no border beads | | |
| 1996 Silver Proof | — | £25 | on Obv. | 53,900,000 | — |
| 1997 | 99,196,000 | £2 | 2008 BU | — | £4 |
| 1997 BU | — | £4 | 2008 Proof | — | £5 |
| 1997 Proof | — | £4 | 2008 Silver Proof | — | £25 |
| 1998 *New portrait* BU | — | £6 | 2008 — — Piedfort | — | £35 |
| 1998 Proof | — | £10 | 2008 Gold Proof | — | £250 |
| 1999 BU | — | £4 | 2008 Platinum Proof | — | £350 |
| 1999 Proof | — | £11 | 2009 | 60,000,000 | — |
| 2000 | 134,733,000 | £1 | 2009 BU | — | £3 |
| 2000 BU | — | £4 | 2009 Proof | — | £5 |
| 2000 Proof | — | £7 | 2009 Silver Proof | — | £25 |
| 2000 Silver Proof | — | £15 | 2010 | 25,320,500 | — |
| 2001 | 129,281,000 | £1 | 2010 BU | — | £5 |
| 2001 BU | — | £3 | 2010 Proof | — | £7 |
| 2001 Proof | — | £4 | 2010 Silver Proof | — | £25 |
| 2002 | 80,934,000 | £2 | 2011 Nickel-plated steel | 40,601,850 | — |
| 2002 BU | — | £3 | 2011 — BU | — | — |
| 2002 Proof | — | £5 | 2011 — Proof | — | — |
| 2002 Gold Proof | — | £250 | 2011 Silver Proof | — | — |
| 2003 | 88,118,000 | — | 2012 | — | — |
| 2003 BU | — | £3 | 2012 BU | — | — |
| 2003 Proof | — | £5 | 2012 Proof | — | — |
| 2004 | 99,602,000 | — | 2012 Silver proof with selective gold plating | — | — |
| 2004 BU | — | £3 | 2012 Gold Proof | — | — |
| 2004 Proof | — | £5 | | | |

# FIVE PENCE

*This series commenced simultaneously with the Ten Pence (qv). They were the same size and weight as their predecessor, the shilling, and such coins up to 1990 are no longer legal tender.*

| DATE | Mintage | UNC | DATE | Mintage | UNC |
|---|---|---|---|---|---|
| 1968 | 98,868,250 | £3 | 1977 Proof | — | £9 |
| 1969 | 120,270,000 | £3 | 1978 | 61,094,000 | £4 |
| 1970 | 225,948,525 | £3 | 1978 Proof | — | £4 |
| 1971 | 81,783,475 | £3 | 1979 | 155,456,000 | £4 |
| 1971 Proof | — | £3 | 1979 Proof | — | £4 |
| 1972 Proof | — | £7 | 1980 | 220,566,000 | £3 |
| 1973 Proof | — | £8 | 1980 Proof | — | £4 |
| 1974 Proof | — | £8 | 1981 Proof | — | £7 |
| 1975 | 141,539,000 | £3 | 1982 BU | — | £7 |
| 1975 Proof | — | £6 | 1982 Proof | — | £9 |
| 1976 Proof | — | £7 | 1983 BU | — | £5 |
| 1977 | 24,308,000 | £8 | 1983 Proof | — | £6 |

| DATE | Mintage | UNC |
|---|---|---|
| 1984 BU | — | £4 |
| 1984 Proof | — | £6 |
| 1985 **New Portrait**. BU | — | £2 |
| 1985 Proof | — | £7 |
| 1986 BU | — | £2 |
| 1986 Proof | — | £7 |
| 1987 | 48,220,000 | — |
| 1987 BU | — | £3 |
| 1987 Proof | — | £5 |
| 1988 | 120,744,610 | — |
| 1988 BU | — | £3 |
| 1988 Proof | — | £5 |
| 1989 | 101,406,000 | — |
| 1989 BU | — | £4 |
| 1989 Proof | — | £5 |
| 1990 BU | — | £2 |
| 1990 Proof | — | £5 |
| 1990 Silver Proof | — | £10 |
| 1990 **Size reduced (18mm)** | 1,634,976,005 | £2 |
| 1990 BU | — | £3 |
| 1990 Proof | — | £4 |
| 1990 Silver Proof | — | £12 |
| 1990 — — Piedfort | — | £15 |
| 1991 | 724,979000 | — |
| 1991 BU | — | £3 |
| 1991 Proof | — | £5 |
| 1992 | 453,173,500 | — |
| 1992 BU | — | £3 |
| 1992 Proof | — | £7 |
| 1993 BU | — | £3 |
| 1993 Proof | — | £5 |
| 1994 | 93,602,000 | — |
| 1994 BU | — | £5 |
| 1994 Proof | — | £7 |
| 1995 | 183,384,000 | — |
| 1995 BU | — | £5 |
| 1995 Proof | — | £7 |
| 1996 | 302,902,000 | — |
| 1996 BU | — | £4 |
| 1996 Proof | — | £7 |
| 1996 Silver proof | — | £25 |
| 1997 | 236,596,000 | — |
| 1997 BU | — | £4 |
| 1997 Proof | — | £7 |
| 1998 **New portrait** | 217,376,000 | — |
| 1998 BU | — | £4 |
| 1998 Proof | — | £7 |
| 1999 | 195,490,000 | — |
| 1999 BU | — | £4 |
| 1999 Proof | — | £7 |
| 2000 | 388,512,000 | — |
| 2000 BU | — | £4 |
| 2000 Proof | — | £7 |
| 2000 Silver Proof | — | £25 |
| 2001 | 337,930,000 | — |
| 2001 BU | — | £3 |
| 2001 Proof | — | £5 |
| 2002 | 219,258,000 | — |
| 2002 BU | — | £3 |
| 2002 Proof | — | £5 |
| 2002 Gold Proof | — | £120 |
| 2003 | 333,230,000 | — |
| 2003 BU | — | £3 |
| 2003 Proof | — | £5 |
| 2004 | 271,810,000 | — |
| 2004 BU | — | £3 |
| 2004 Proof | — | £5 |
| 2005 | 236,212,000 | — |
| 2005 BU | — | £3 |
| 2005 Proof | — | £5 |
| 2006 | 317,697,000 | — |
| 2006 BU | — | £3 |
| 2006 Proof | — | £7 |
| 2006 Silver Proof | — | £15 |
| 2007 | 246,720,000 | — |
| 2007 BU | — | £5 |
| 2007 Proof | — | £7 |
| 2008 | 86,400,000 | — |
| 2008 BU | — | £3 |
| 2008 Proof | — | £4 |
| 2008 Silver Proof | — | £15 |
| 2008 Gold Proof | — | £125 |
| 2008 Platinum Proof | — | £200 |
| 2008 **New Rev.,** no border beads on Obv | 109,460,000 | — |
| 2008 BU | — | £4 |
| 2008 Proof | — | £5 |
| 2008 Silver Proof | — | £15 |
| 2008 — — Piedfort | — | £35 |
| 2008 Gold Proof | — | £125 |
| 2008 Platinum Proof | — | £220 |
| 2009 | 125,520,300 | — |
| 2009 BU | — | £6 |
| 2009 Proof | — | £7 |
| 2009 Silver Proof | — | £15 |
| 2010 | 180,250,500 | — |
| 2010 BU | — | £4 |
| 2010 Proof | — | £5 |
| 2010 Silver Proof | — | £15 |
| 2011 Nickel-plated steel | 50,400,000 | — |
| 2011 — BU | — | — |
| 2011 — Proof | — | — |
| 2011 Silver Proof | — | — |
| 2012 | — | — |
| 2012 BU | — | — |
| 2012 Proof | — | — |
| 2012 Silver Proof with selective gold plating | — | — |
| 2012 Gold Proof | — | — |

# TWO PENCE

*Dated from 1971, and legal tender from Decimal Day that year, early examples are found in the blue Specimen decimal set wallets of 1968. They were minted in bronze up to 1991, and mainly in copper-plated steel from 1992. However details of where this rule does not totally apply (1992, 1996, 1998–2000 and 2002, 2006, 2008 and 2009) are given below. As with other denominations, "NEW" was replaced by the quantity of pence in word from 1982.*

| DATE | Mintage | UNC |
|---|---|---|
| 1971 | 1,454,856,250 | £2 |
| 1971 Proof | — | £3 |
| 1972 Proof | — | £5 |
| 1973 Proof | — | £6 |
| 1974 Proof | — | £6 |
| 1975 | Est. approx. 273,145,000 | £2 |
| 1975 Proof | — | £2 |
| 1976 | Est. approx. 53,779,000 | £2 |
| 1976 Proof | — | £2 |
| 1977 | 109,281,000 | £2 |
| 1977 Proof | — | £2 |
| 1978 | 189,658,000 | £3 |
| 1978 Proof | — | £2 |
| 1979 | 260,200,000 | £2 |
| 1979 Proof | 408,527,000 | £2 |
| 1980 | — | £1 |
| 1980 Proof | — | £2 |
| 1981 | 353,191,000 | £4 |
| 1981 Proof | — | £4 |
| 1982 Legend changed to TWO PENCE | — | £4 |
| 1982 Proof | — | £5 |
| 1983 | — | £2 |
| 1983 Error NEW instead of TWO | — | £500 |
| 1983 Proof | — | £4 |
| 1984 | — | £2 |
| 1984 Proof | | £4 |
| 1985 **New portrait** | 107,113,000 | £1 |
| 1985 | — | £2 |
| 1985 Proof | — | £4 |
| 1986 | 168,967,500 | 50p |
| 1986 BU | — | £2 |
| 1986 Proof | — | £4 |
| 1987 | 218,100,750 | 50p |
| 1987 BU | — | £2 |
| 1987 Proof | — | £4 |
| 1988 | 419,889,000 | 50p |
| 1988 BU | — | £2 |
| 1988 Proof | — | £4 |
| 1989 | 359,226,000 | 50p |
| 1989 BU | — | £2 |
| 1989 Proof | — | £4 |
| 1990 | 204,499,700 | 50p |
| 1990 BU | — | £2 |
| 1990 Proof | — | £3 |
| 1991 | 86,625,250 | 50p |
| 1991 BU | — | £2 |
| 1991 Proof | — | £5 |
| 1992 Copper plated steel | 102,247,000 | £1 |
| 1992 Bronze BU | — | £2 |
| 1992 — Proof | — | £5 |
| 1993 | 235,674,000 | 50p |
| 1993 BU | — | £2 |
| 1993 Proof | — | £3 |
| 1994 | 531,628,000 | 50p |
| 1994 BU | — | £1 |

| DATE | Mintage | UNC |
|---|---|---|
| 1994 Proof | — | £5 |
| 1995 | 124,482,000 | — |
| 1995 BU | — | £2 |
| 1995 Proof | — | £5 |
| 1996 | 296,278,000 | — |
| 1996 BU | — | £2 |
| 1996 Proof | — | £5 |
| 1996 Silver Proof | — | £25 |
| 1997 | 496,116,000 | — |
| 1997 BU | — | £2 |
| 1997 Proof | — | £5 |
| 1998 **New portrait** | Est. approx. 120,243,000 | — |
| 1998 BU | — | £2 |
| 1998 Proof | — | £4 |
| 1998 Bronze | Est. approx. 93,587,000 | £1 |
| 1999 | 353,816,000 | £1 |
| 1999 Bronze BU | — | £2 |
| 1999 — Proof | — | £4 |
| 2000 | 536,659,000 | — |
| 2000 BU | — | £3 |
| 2000 Proof | — | £5 |
| 2000 Silver Proof | — | £22 |
| 2001 | 551,880,000 | — |
| 2001 BU | — | £2 |
| 2001 Proof | — | £4 |
| 2002 | 168,556,000 | — |
| 2002 BU | — | £3 |
| 2002 Proof | — | £4 |
| 2002 Gold Proof | — | £120 |
| 2003 | 260,225,000 | — |
| 2003 BU | — | £2 |
| 2003 Proof | — | £4 |
| 2004 | 356,396,000 | — |
| 2004 BU | — | £2 |
| 2004 Proof | — | £4 |
| 2005 | 280,396,000 | — |
| 2005 BU | — | £1 |
| 2005 Proof | — | £2 |
| 2006 | 170,637,000 | — |
| 2006 BU | — | £3 |
| 2006 Proof | — | £4 |
| 2006 Silver Proof | — | £15 |
| 2007 | 254,500,000 | — |
| 2007 BU | — | £3 |
| 2007 Proof | — | £5 |
| 2008 | 10,600,000 | — |
| 2008 BU | — | £3 |
| 2008 Proof | — | £5 |
| 2008 Silver Proof | — | £20 |
| 2008 Gold Proof | — | £125 |
| 2008 Platinum Proof | — | — |
| 2008 New Rev., no border beads on Obv | 129,530,000 | — |
| 2008 — BU | — | £2 |
| 2008 — Proof | — | £4 |

| DATE | Mintage | UNC | DATE | Mintage | UNC |
|------|---------|-----|------|---------|-----|
| 2008 — Silver Proof | — | £20 | 2010 Silver Proof | — | £45 |
| 2008 — Silver Proof Piedfort | — | £45 | 2011 | 93,900,000 | — |
| 2008 — Gold Proof | — | £400 | 2011 BU | — | — |
| 2008 — Platinum Proof | — | £800 | 2011 Proof | — | — |
| 2009 | 65,200,000 | — | 2011 Silver Proof | — | — |
| 2009 BU | — | £3 | 2012 | — | — |
| 2009 Proof | — | £5 | 2012 BU | — | — |
| 2009 Silver Proof | — | £45 | 2012 Proof | — | — |
| 2010 | 38,000,000 | — | 2012 Silver Proof with selective gold plating | — | — |
| 2010 BU | — | £3 | 2012 Gold Proof | — | — |
| 2010 Proof | — | £6 | | | |

# ONE PENNY

*The history of this coin is very similar to that of the Two Pence coin (qv) except that all 1998 examples were of copper-plated steel.*

| DATE | Mintage | UNC | DATE | Mintage | UNC |
|------|---------|-----|------|---------|-----|
| 1971 | 1,521,666,250 | £1 | 1988 | 793,492,000 | — |
| 1971 Proof | — | £2 | 1988 BU | — | £2 |
| 1972 Proof | — | £5 | 1988 Proof | — | £3 |
| 1973 | 280,196,000 | £2 | 1989 | 658,142,000 | — |
| 1973 Proof | — | £5 | 1989 BU | — | £2 |
| 1974 | 330,892,000 | £2 | 1989 Proof | — | £3 |
| 1974 Proof | — | £3 | 1990 | 529,047,500 | £2 |
| 1975 | 221,604,000 | £2 | 1990 BU | — | £3 |
| 1975 Proof | — | £4 | 1990 Proof | — | £4 |
| 1976 | 300,160,000 | £2 | 1991 | 206,457,000 | — |
| 1976 Proof | — | £3 | 1991 BU | — | £2 |
| 1977 | 285,430,000 | £2 | 1991 Proof | — | £4 |
| 1977 Proof | — | £3 | 1992 Copper-plated steel | 253,867,000 | £3 |
| 1978 | 292,770,000 | £3 | 1992 Bronze BU | — | £6 |
| 1978 Proof | — | £3 | 1992 — Proof | — | £4 |
| 1979 | 459,000,000 | £3 | 1993 | 602,590,000 | — |
| 1979 Proof | — | £3 | 1993 BU | — | £2 |
| 1980 | 416,304,000 | £2 | 1993 Proof | — | £5 |
| 1980 Proof | — | £3 | 1994 | 843,834,000 | £1 |
| 1981 | 301,800,000 | £2 | 1994 BU | — | £2 |
| 1981 Proof | — | £3 | 1994 Proof | — | £5 |
| 1982 Legend changed to ONE PENNY | 100,292,000 | — | 1995 | 303,314,000 | £1 |
| | | | 1995 BU | — | £3 |
| 1982 Unc | — | £1 | 1995 Proof | — | £5 |
| 1982 Proof | — | £2 | 1996 | 723,840,060 | — |
| 1983 | 243,002,000 | £1 | 1996 BU | — | £2 |
| 1983 Unc | — | £2 | 1996 Proof | — | £5 |
| 1983 Proof | — | £4 | 1996 Silver Proof | — | £28 |
| 1984 | 154,759,625 | — | 1997 | 396,874,000 | — |
| 1984 BU | — | £2 | 1997 BU | — | £2 |
| 1984 Proof | — | £3 | 1997 Proof | — | £4 |
| 1985 New portrait | 200,605,245 | — | 1998 New portrait | 739,770,000 | — |
| 1985 BU | — | £2 | 1998 — BU | — | £3 |
| 1985 Proof | — | £3 | 1998 — Proof | — | £4 |
| 1986 | 369,989,130 | — | 1999 | 891,392,000 | £2 |
| 1986 BU | — | £2 | 1999 Bronze BU | — | £4 |
| 1986 Proof | — | £3 | 1999 Bronze Proof | — | £8 |
| 1987 | 4999,946,000 | — | 2000 | 1,060,420,000 | — |
| 1987 BU | — | £2 | 2000 BU | — | £2 |
| 1987 Proof | — | £3 | 2000 Proof | — | £4 |

| DATE | Mintage | UNC |
|---|---|---|
| 2000 Silver Proof | — | £25 |
| 2001 | 928,698,000 | — |
| 2001 BU | — | £2 |
| 2001 Proof | — | £4 |
| 2002 | 601,446,000 | — |
| 2002 BU | — | £2 |
| 2002 Proof | — | £4 |
| 2002 Gold Proof | — | £120 |
| 2003 | 539,436,000 | — |
| 2003 BU | — | £2 |
| 2003 Proof | — | £3 |
| 2004 | 739,764,000 | — |
| 2004 BU | — | £2 |
| 2004 Proof | — | £4 |
| 2005 | 536,318,000 | — |
| 2005 BU | — | £2 |
| 2005 Proof | — | £3 |
| 2006 | 524,605,000 | — |
| 2006 BU | — | £2 |
| 2006 Proof | — | £4 |
| 2006 Silver Proof | — | £15 |
| 2007 | 548,002,000 | — |
| 2007 BU | — | £4 |
| 2007 Proof | — | £7 |
| 2008 | 180,600,000 | — |
| 2008 BU | — | £3 |
| 2008 Proof | — | £5 |
| 2008 Silver Proof | — | £15 |
| 2008 Gold Proof | — | £100 |
| 2008 Platinum Proof | — | £185 |
| 2008 New Rev, no border beads on Obv | 386,830,000 | — |
| 2008 — BU | — | £2 |
| 2008 — Proof | — | £3 |
| 2008 — Silver Proof | — | £15 |
| 2008 — Silver Proof Piedfort | — | £25 |
| 2008 — Gold Proof | — | £100 |
| 2008 — Platinum Proof | — | £185 |
| 2009 | 469,207,800 | — |
| 2009 BU | — | £3 |
| 2009 Proof | — | £4 |
| 2009 Silver BU, in "Lucky Baby Gift Pack" | — | £15 |
| 2009 — Proof | — | £15 |
| 2010 | 402,602,000 | — |
| 2010 BU | — | £3 |
| 2010 Proof | — | £4 |
| 2010 Silver BU, in "Lucky Baby Gift Card" | — | £15 |
| 2010 — Proof | — | £15 |
| 2011 | 210,404,000 | — |
| 2011 BU | — | £2 |
| 2011 Proof | — | £3 |
| 2011 Silver BU in "Lucky Baby Pack" | — | £18 |
| 2011 – Proof | — | £15 |
| 2012 | — | — |
| 2012 BU | — | — |
| 2012 Proof | — | — |
| 2012 Silver BU (three different packagings) | — | — |
| 2012 Silver Proof with selective gold plating | — | — |
| 2012 Gold Proof | — | — |

# HALF PENNY

*No longer legal tender, its history tracks that of the Two Pence and One Penny.*

| DATE | Mintage | UNC |
|---|---|---|
| 1971 | 1,394,188,250 | £2 |
| 1971 Proof | — | £3 |
| 1972 Proof | — | £5 |
| 1973 | 365,680,000 | £2 |
| 1973 Proof | — | £3 |
| 1974 | 365,448,000 | £2 |
| 1974 Proof | — | £3 |
| 1975 | 197,600,000 | £2 |
| 1975 Proof | — | £3 |
| 1976 | 412,172,000 | £2 |
| 1976 Proof | — | £3 |
| 1977 | 66,368,000 | £1 |
| 1977 Proof | — | £3 |
| 1978 | 59,532,000 | £1 |
| 1978 Proof | — | £4 |
| 1979 | 219,1322,000 | £2 |
| 1979 Proof | — | £4 |
| 1980 | 202,788,000 | £2 |
| 1980 Proof | — | £3 |
| 1981 | 46,748,000 | £2 |
| 1981 Proof | — | £4 |
| 1982 Legend changed to HALF PENNY | 190,752,000 | 50p |
| 1982 Unc | — | £2 |
| 1982 Proof | — | £3 |
| 1983 | 7,600,000 | 50p |
| 1983 Unc | — | £1 |
| 1983 Proof | — | £4 |
| 1984 | 40,000 | £4 |
| 1984 BU | — | £5 |
| 1984 Proof | — | £6 |

# PROOF AND SPECIMEN SETS

NOTE: The prices quoted in this guide are set at August 2012 with the price of gold at £920 per ounce and silver £16 per ounce—market fluctuations will have a marked effect on the values of modern precious metal coins.

*The following listings are an attempt to include all officially marketed products from the Royal Mint of two coins or more, but excluding those which included non-UK coins. It is appreciated that not all have been advertised as new to the public, but it is assumed that at some time they have been, or will be, available. In a few cases, therefore, the prices may be conjectural but are, nevertheless, attempts at listing realistic value, in some instances based on an original retail price. In the case of Elizabeth II sets, if no metal is stated in the listing, the coins in the sets are of the same metal as the circulation coin equivalent. In addition to the above we have excluded historical gold coin sets, such as sets of sovereigns from different mints, where the dates of the coins vary from one set to another.*

DATE                    FDC

**GEORGE IV**
1826 £5–farthing (11 coins) ................................................................................................................£30,000

**WILLIAM IV**
1831 Coronation £2–farthing (14 coins) .............................................................................................£28,000

**VICTORIA**
1839 "Una and the Lion" £5–farthing (15 coins)................................................................................£65,000
1853 Sovereign–quarter farthing, including "Gothic"crown (16 coins) ............................................£40,000
1887 Golden Jubilee £5–3d (11 coins) ..............................................................................................£15,000
1887 Golden Jubilee Crown–3d (7 coins)............................................................................................£3,000
1893 £5–3d (10 coins)........................................................................................................................£15,000
1893 Crown–3d (6 coins)......................................................................................................................£5000

**EDWARD VII**
1902 Coronation £5–Maundy penny, matt proofs (13 coins) ..............................................................£5500
1902 Coronation Sovereign–Maundy penny, matt proofs (11 coins) ..................................................£3,500

**GEORGE V**
1911 Coronation £5–Maundy penny (12 coins)....................................................................................£6700
1911 Sovereign–Maundy penny (10 coins) .........................................................................................£3500
1911 Coronation Halfcrown–Maundy penny (8 coins) .........................................................................£1100
1927 New types Crown–3d (6 coins)......................................................................................................£850
**GEORGE VI**
1937 Coronation £5–half sovereign (4 coins) ......................................................................................£5700
1937 Coronation Crown–farthing including Maundy money (15 coins) ...................................................£400
1950 Mid-century Halfcrown–farthing (9 coins) .....................................................................................£175
1951 Festival of Britain, Crown–farthing (10 coins) ..............................................................................£200

**ELIZABETH II**
1953 Proof Coronation Crown–farthing (10 coins) ................................................................................£120
1953 Currency (plastic) set halfcrown–farthing (9 coins) ........................................................................£15
1968 Specimen decimal set 10p, 5p and 1971-dated bronze in blue wallet (5 coins)..............................£3
1970 Proof Last £sd coins (issued from 1972) Halfcrown–halfpenny (8 coins).......................................£20
1971 Proof (issued 1973) 50p–half penny (6 coins).................................................................................£18
1972 Proof (issued 1976) 50p–half penny (7 coins including Silver Wedding crown) ..............................£24
1973 Proof (issued 1976) 50p–half penny (6 coins).................................................................................£16
1974 Proof (issued 1976) 50p–half penny (6 coins).................................................................................£18
1975 Proof (issued 1976) 50p–half penny (6 coins).................................................................................£18
1976 Proof 50p–half penny (6 coins)........................................................................................................£18
1977 Proof 50p–half penny (7 coins including Silver Jubilee crown) .......................................................£22
1978 Proof 50p–half penny (6 coins)........................................................................................................£16
1979 Proof 50p–half penny (6 coins)........................................................................................................£18

| DATE | FDC |
|---|---|
| 1980 Proof gold sovereign series (4 coins) | £2500 |
| 1980 — 50p–half penny (6 coins) | £16 |
| 1981 Proof £5, sovereign, Royal Wedding Silver crown, 50p–half penny (9 coins) | £800 |
| 1981 — 50p–half penny (6 coins) | £18 |
| 1982 Proof gold sovereign series (4 coins) | £2500 |
| 1982 — 50p–half penny (7 coins) | £20 |
| 1982 Uncirculated 50p–half penny (7 coins) | £15 |
| 1983 Proof gold double-sovereign to half sovereign (3 coins) | £1000 |
| 1983 — £1–half penny (8 coins) (includes H. J. Heinz sets) | £25 |
| 1983 Uncirculated £1–half penny (8 coins) (includes Benson & Hedges and Martini sets) | £30 |
| 1983 — — (8 coins) (only Benson & Hedges and Martini sets) with "2 NEW PENCE" legend | £1000 |
| 1983 — 50p–half penny (7 coins) (H. J. Heinz sets) | £16 |
| 1984 Proof gold five pounds, sovereign and half-sovereigns (3 coins) | £1000 |
| 1984 — £1 (Scottish rev.)–half penny (8 coins) | £20 |
| 1984 BU £1 (Scottish rev.)–half penny (8 coins) | £16 |
| 1985 New portrait proof gold sovereign series (4 coins) | £1250 |
| 1985 Proof £1–1p in de luxe case (7 coins) | £25 |
| 1985 — in standard case | £20 |
| 1985 BU £1–1p (7 coins) in folder | £15 |
| 1986 Proof gold Commonwealth Games £2, sovereign and half sovereign (3 coins) | £1000 |
| 1986 — Commonwealth Games £2–1p, de luxe case (8 coins) | £30 |
| 1986 — — in standard case (8 coins) | £25 |
| 1986 BU £2–1p in folder (8 coins) | £20 |
| 1987 Proof gold Britannia set (4 coins) | £2000 |
| 1987 — — £25 and £10 (2 coins) | £450 |
| 1987 — double- to half sovereign (3 coins) | £1000 |
| 1987 — £1–1p in de luxe case (7 coins) | £35 |
| 1987 — £1–1p in standard case (7 coins) | £25 |
| 1987 BU £1–1p in folder (7 coins) | £20 |
| 1988 Proof gold Britannia set (4 coins) | £2000 |
| 1988 — — £25 and £10 (2 coins) | £450 |
| 1988 — double- to half sovereign (3 coins) | £1000 |
| 1988 — £1–1p in de luxe case (7 coins) | £35 |
| 1988 — £1–1p in standard case (7 coins) | £30 |
| 1988 BU £1–1p in folder (7 coins) (includes Bradford & Bingley sets) | £18 |
| 1989 Proof gold Britannia set (4 coins) | £2000 |
| 1989 — — £25 and £10 (2 coins) | £450 |
| 1989 — 500th anniversary of the sovereign series set (4 coins) | £2000 |
| 1989 — — double- to half sovereign (3 coins) | £1000 |
| 1989 — Silver Bill of Rights £2, Claim of Right £2 (2 coins) | £65 |
| 1989 — — Piedfort as above (2 coins) | £100 |
| 1989 BU £2 in folder (2 coins) | £25 |
| 1989 Proof £2 (both)–1p in de luxe case (9 coins) | £35 |
| 1989 — in standard case (9 coins) | £30 |
| 1989 BU £1–1p in folder (7 coins) | £25 |
| 1990 Proof gold Britannia set (4 coins) | £2000 |
| 1990 — — sovereign series set (4 coins) | £2000 |
| 1990 — — double- to half sovereign (3 coins) | £1000 |
| 1990 — silver 5p, 2 sizes (2 coins) | £28 |
| 1990 — £1–1p in de luxe case (8 coins) | £35 |
| 1990 — £1–1p standard case (8 coins) | £30 |
| 1990 BU £1–1p in folder (8 coins) | £20 |
| 1991 Proof gold Britannia set (4 coins) | £2000 |
| 1991 — — sovereign series set (4 coins) | £2000 |
| 1991 — — double- to half sovereign (3 coins) | £1000 |
| 1991 — £1–1p in de luxe case (7 coins) | £35 |
| 1991 — £1–1p in standard case (7 coins) | £28 |
| 1991 BU £1–1p in folder (7 coins) | £18 |
| 1992 Proof gold Britannia set (4 coins) | £2000 |
| 1992 — — sovereign series set (4 coins) | £2000 |
| 1992 — — double- to half sovereign (3 coins) | £1000 |
| 1992 — £1–1p including two each 50p and 10p in de luxe case (9 coins) | £38 |
| 1992 — £1–1p as above in standard case (9 coins) | £32 |
| 1992 BU £1–1p as above in folder (9 coins) | £16 |
| 1992 Proof silver 10p, two sizes (2 coins) | £25 |
| 1993 Proof gold Britannia set 1 (4 coins) | £2000 |
| 1993 — — sovereign series set (4 coins plus silver Pistrucci medal) | £2000 |

| DATE | FDC |
|---|---|
| 1993 — — double- to half sovereign (3 coins) | £1000 |
| 1993 — Coronation anniversary £5–1p in de luxe case (8 coins) | £38 |
| 1993 — — in standard case (8 coins) | £35 |
| 1993 BU £1–1p including 1992 EU 50p (8 coins) | £15 |
| 1994 Proof gold Britannia set (4 coins) | £2000 |
| 1994 — — sovereign series set (4 coins) | £2000 |
| 1994 — — £2 to half sovereign (3 coins) | £1000 |
| 1994 — Bank of England Tercentenary £2–1p in de luxe case (8 coins) | £38 |
| 1994 — — in standard case (8 coins) | £35 |
| 1994 BU £1–1p in folder (7 coins) | £18 |
| 1994 Proof gold 1992 and 1994 50p (2 coins) | £350 |
| 1994 — "Family silver" set £2–50p (3 coins) | £65 |
| 1995 Proof gold Britannia set (4 coins) | £2000 |
| 1995 — — sovereign series  (4 coins) | £2000 |
| 1995 — — £2 to half sovereign (3 coins) | £850 |
| 1995 — 50th Anniversary of WWII £2–1p in de luxe case (8 coins) | £40 |
| 1995 — — as above in standard case (8 coins) | £35 |
| 1995 BU as above in folder (8 coins) | £16 |
| 1995 Proof "Family Silver" set £2 (two) and £1 (3 coins) | £90 |
| 1996 Proof gold Britannia set (4 coins) | £2000 |
| 1996 — — sovereign series set (4 coins) | £2000 |
| 1996 — — double- to half sovereign (3 coins) | £1000 |
| 1996 — Royal 70th Birthday  £5–1p in de luxe case (9 coins) | £50 |
| 1996 — — as above in standard case (9 coins) | £45 |
| 1996 BU Football £2–1p in folder (8 coins) | £20 |
| 1996 Proof gold Britannia £10 and half-sovereign (2 coins) | £550 |
| 1996 — — sovereign and silver £1 (2 coins) | £250 |
| 1996 — — "Family silver" set £5–£1 (3 coins) | £85 |
| 1996 — silver 25th Anniversary of Decimal currency £1–1p (7 coins) | £150 |
| 1996 Circulation and BU 25th Anniversary of Decimalisation 2s 6d–halfpenny (misc.) and £1–1p in folder (14 coins) | £25 |
| 1997 Proof gold Britannia set (4 coins) | £2000 |
| 1997 — — sovereign series set (4 coins) | £2000 |
| 1997 — — £2 to half sovereign (3 coins) | £1000 |
| 1997 — — Silver Britannia set (4 coins) | £150 |
| 1997 — Golden Wedding £5–1p in red leather case | £45 |
| 1997 — — as above in standard case (10 coins) | £35 |
| 1997 BU £2 to 1p in folder (9 coins) | £25 |
| 1997 Proof silver 50p set, two sizes (2 coins) | £45 |
| 1997/1998 Proof silver £2 set, both dates (2 coins) | £70 |
| 1998 Proof gold Britannia set (4 coins) | £2000 |
| 1998 — — sovereign series set (4 coins) | £2000 |
| 1998 — — — double- to half sovereign (3 coins) | £1000 |
| 1998 Proof silver Britannia set (4 coins) | £185 |
| 1998 — Prince of Wales  £5–1p (10 coins) in red leather case | £45 |
| 1998 — — as above in standard case (10 coins) | £38 |
| 1998 BU £2–1p in folder (9 coins) | £16 |
| 1998 Proof silver European/NHS 50p set (2 coins) | £60 |
| 1998 BU Britannia/EU 50p set (2 coins) | £8 |
| 1999 Proof gold Britannia set (4 coins) | £2000 |
| 1999 — — Sovereign series set (4 coins) | £2000 |
| 1999 — — — £2 to half sovereign (3 coins) | £1000 |
| 1999 — Princess Diana £5–1p in red leather case (9 coins) | £65 |
| 1999 — — as above in standard case (9 coins) | £45 |
| 1999 BU £2–1p (8 coins) in folder | £20 |
| 1999 Proof "Family Silver" set. Both £5, £2 and £1 (4 coins) | £150 |
| 1999 Britannia Millennium set. Bullion £2 and BU £5 (2 coins) | £30 |
| 1999/2000 Reverse frosted proof set, two x £1 (2 coins) | £75 |
| 2000 Proof gold Britannia set (4 coins) | £2000 |
| 2000 — — Sovereign series set (4 coins) | £2000 |
| 2000 — — double- to half sovereign (3 coins) | £1000 |
| 2000 Millennium £5–1p in de luxe case (10 coins) | £50 |
| 2000 — — as above in standard case (10 coins) | £45 |
| 2000 — Silver set Millennium £5 to 1p plus Maundy (13 coins) | £225 |
| 2000 BU £2–1p set in folder (9 coins) | £20 |
| 2000 Millennium "Time Capsule" BU £5 to 1p (9 coins) | £30 |
| 2001 Proof gold Britannia set (4 coins) | £2000 |

| DATE | FDC |
|---|---|
| 2001 — — Sovereign series set (4 coins) | £2000 |
| 2001 — — — £2–half sovereign (3 coins) | £1000 |
| 2001 — — Silver Britannia set (4 coins) | £150 |
| 2001 — Victoria £5–1p in Executive case (10 coins) | £100 |
| 2001 — — as above in red leather case (10 coins) | £75 |
| 2001 — — as above in "Gift" case (10 coins) | £48 |
| 2001 — — as above in standard case (10 coins) | £40 |
| 2001 BU £2–1p in folder (9 coins) | £18 |
| 2002 Proof gold Britannia set (4 coins) | £2000 |
| 2002 — — Sovereign series set, all Shield rev. (4 coins) | £2000 |
| 2002 — — — double- to half sovereign (3 coins) | £1000 |
| 2002 — — Golden Jubilee set £5–1p plus Maundy (13 coins) | £4500 |
| 2002 — Golden Jubilee £5–1p in Executive case (9 coins) | £75 |
| 2002 — — as above in red leather de luxe case (9 coins) | £50 |
| 2002 — — as above in "Gift" case (9 coins) | £42 |
| 2002 — — as above in standard case (9 coins) | £40 |
| 2002 BU £2–1p (8 coins) in folder | £16 |
| 2002 Proof Gold Commonwealth Games £2 set (4 coins) | £2000 |
| 2002 — Silver Piedfort Commonwealth Games £2 set (4 coins) | £250 |
| 2002 — — Commonwealth Games £2 set (4 coins) | £125 |
| 2002 — Commonwealth Games £2 set (4 coins) | £30 |
| 2002 BU Commonwealth Games £2 set (4 coins) in folder | £25 |
| 2003 Proof gold Britannia set (4 coins) | £2000 |
| 2003 — — — £50–£10 (3 coins) | £1000 |
| 2003 — — — type set, one of each £100 reverse (4 coins) | £2500 |
| 2003 — — Sovereign series set (4 coins) | £2000 |
| 2003 — — — series £2–half sovereign (3 coins) | £1000 |
| 2003 — — Silver Britannia set (4 coins) | £45 |
| 2003 — — — type set (one of each £2 reverse) (4 coins) | £85 |
| 2003 — £5 to 1p, two of each £2 and 50p in Executive case (11 coins) | £80 |
| 2003 — — as above in red leather case (11 coins) | £55 |
| 2003 — — as above in standard case (11 coins) | £48 |
| 2003 BU £2 (two)–1p in folder (10 coins) | £22 |
| 2003 Proof silver Piedfort set. DNA £2, £1 and Suffragette 50p (3 coins) | £150 |
| 2003 Proof "Family Silver" set £5, Britannia and DNA £2, £1 and Suffragette 50p (5 coins) | £175 |
| 2003 Circ & BU "God Save the Queen" Coronation anniversary set 5s/0d to farthing (1953) and £5 to 1p (2003) in folder (19 coins) | £55 |
| 2003 Circulation or bullion "Royal Sovereign" collection, example of each Elizabeth II date (21 coins) | £3500 |
| 2004 Proof gold Britannia set (4 coins) | £2000 |
| 2004 — — — £50 to £10 (3 coins) | £1000 |
| 2004 — — Sovereign series set (4 coins) | £2000 |
| 2004 — — — Series £2–half sovereign (3 coins) | £1000 |
| 2004 (Issue date) Royal Portrait gold sovereign set, all proof except the first: Gillick, Machin, Maklouf and Rank-Broadley sovereigns, and the 2nd, 3rd and 4th of above half-sovereigns, various dates (7 coins) | £1500 |
| 2004 Proof silver Britannia set (4 coins) | £150 |
| 2004 — "Family Silver" set £5, Britannia and Trevithick £2, £1 and Bannister 50p (5 coins) | £165 |
| 2004 — Silver Piedfort set, Trevithick £2, £1 and Bannister 50p (3 coins) | £175 |
| 2004 — £2 to 1p, two each of £2 and 50p in Executive case (10 coins) | £75 |
| 2004 — — as above in red leather case (10 coins) | £45 |
| 2004 — — as above in standard case (10 coins) | £38 |
| 2004 BU £2 to 1p in folder (10 coins) | £22 |
| 2004 — "New Coinage" set, Trevithick £2, £1 and Bannister 50p (3 coins) | £10 |
| 2004 BU "Season's Greetings" £2 to 1p and Royal Mint Christmas medal in folder (8 coins) | £17 |
| 2005 Proof Gold Britannia set (4 coins) | £2000 |
| 2005 — — — £50 to £10 (3 coins) | £1000 |
| 2005 — — Sovereign series set (4 coins) | £2000 |
| 2005 — — — series, double to half sovereign (3 coins) | £1000 |
| 2005 — Silver Britannia (4 coins) | £135 |
| 2005 — Gold Trafalgar and Nelson £5 crowns (2 coins) | £2000 |
| 2005 — Silver, as above (2 coins) | £85 |
| 2005 — Piedfort, as above (2 coins) | £135 |
| 2005 — Silver Piedfort set, Gunpowder Plot and World War II £2, £1 and Johnson 50p (4 coins) | £200 |
| 2005 — £5 to 1p, two of each of £5, £2 and 50p in Executive case (12 coins) | £80 |
| 2005 — — as above in red leather case (12 coins) | £58 |
| 2005 — — as above in standard case (12 coins) | £45 |

| DATE | FDC |
|---|---|
| 2005 BU Trafalgar and Nelson £5 crowns in pack (2 coins) | £25 |
| 2005 — £2 (two) to 1p in folder (10 coins) | £25 |
| 2005 — "New Coinage" set, Gunpowder Plot £2, £1 and Johnson 50p (3 coins) | £10 |
| 2005 — "Merry Xmas" £2 to 1p and Royal Mint Christmas medal in folder (8 coins) | £20 |
| 2006 Proof Gold Britannia set (4 coins) | £2000 |
| 2006 — — Sovereign Series set (4 coins) | £2000 |
| 2006 — — — series, double to half sovereign (3 coins) | £1000 |
| 2006 — Silver Britannia (4 coins) | £145 |
| 2006 — Silver Brunel £2 coin set (2 coins) | £75 |
| 2006 — — Piedfort Brunel £2 coin set (2 coins) | £125 |
| 2006 — Gold Brunel £2 coin set (2 coins) | £950 |
| 2006 — Silver VC 50p coin set (2 coins) | £58 |
| 2006 — Silver Piedfort VC 50p coin set ( 2 coins) | £115 |
| 2006 — Gold VC 50p coin set (2 coins) | £675 |
| 2006 — Silver proof set, £5 to 1p plus Maundy coins (13 coins) | £325 |
| 2006 — — Piedfort collection £5, with trumpets enhanced with 23 carat gold, both Brunel £2, £1, both VC 50p (6 coins) | £350 |
| 2006 — — Britannia £2 "Golden Silhouette" collection, five different reverses, all dated 2006 (5 coins) | £350 |
| 2006 — £5 to 1p, three of each £2 and 50p in Executive case (13 coins) | £80 |
| 2006 — as above in red leather case (13 coins) | £55 |
| 2006 — as above in standard case (13 coins) | £45 |
| 2006 BU £2 (two), £1, 50p (two) and to 1p in folder (10 coins) | £18 |
| 2006 Proof Brunel £2 in folder (2 coins) | £15 |
| 2006 — VC 50p in folder (2 coins) | £15 |
| 2006 — Gold Half-Sovereign set dated 2005 Noad and 2006 Pistrucci St George and the Dragon (2 coins) | £250 |
| 2007 — Gold Britannia set (4 coins) | £2000 |
| 2007 — — Sovereign Series set (4 coins) | £2000 |
| 2007 — — — series, double to half sovereign (3 coins) | £1000 |
| 2007 — — Sovereign and half-sovereign (2 coins) | £375 |
| 2007 — "Family Silver" set, Britannia, £5 crown, Union and Slavery £2, Gateshead £1 and Scouting 50p (6 coins) | £225 |
| 2007 Proof Silver Piedfort Collection, as "Family Silver" above but excluding a Britannia (5 coins) | £300 |
| 2007 — Silver £1 Bridge series coins, dated 2004 to 2007 (4 coins) | £135 |
| 2007 — Silver Proof Piedfort £1 Bridge Series, dated 2004 to 2007 (4 coins) | £275 |
| 2007 — Gold £1 Bridge series coins, dated as above (4 coins) | £1950 |
| 2007 — £5 to 1p, three £2 and two 50p in Executive case (12 coins) | £85 |
| 2007 — as above, Deluxe in red leather case (12 coins) | £65 |
| 2007 — as above, in standard case (12 coins) | £50 |
| 2007 BU £2 (two) to 1p (9 coins) | £18 |
| 2007 Proof Silver Britannia (four coins) | £145 |
| 2007 Proof Platinum Britannia (4 coins) | £5000 |
| 2007 Satin Proof Silver Britannia, 20th Anniversary Collection, six different reverses, all dated 2007 (6 coins) | £300 |
| 2007 50th Anniversary Sovereign set, 1957 circulation standard and 2007 Proof (2 coins) | £450 |
| 2008 Proof Gold Britannia set (4 coins) | £2000 |
| 2008 — Platinum Britannia set (4 coins) | £5000 |
| 2008 — Silver Britannia set (4 coins) | £150 |
| 2008 Gold Sovereign series set (4 coins) | £2000 |
| 2008 — — — double to half-sovereign (3 coins) | £1000 |
| 2008 — — Sovereign and half-sovereign (2 coins) | £500 |
| 2008 — "Family silver" set, 2x £5, Britannia £2, Olympiad £2 and Royal Arms £1 (5 coins) | £200 |
| 2008 — Silver Piedfort Collection, 2x £5, Olympiad £2 and Shield of Royal Arms £1 (4 coins) | £285 |
| 2008 — 2 x £5, 2 x £2, £1 to 1p in Executive case (11 coins) | £85 |
| 2008 — as above, Deluxe in black leather case (11 coins) | £55 |
| 2008 - as above, in standard back case (11 coins) | £60 |
| 2008 BU 2 x £2, Royal Arms £1 tp 1p (9 coins) | £18 |
| 2008 — "Emblems of Britain" ("old" Revs) Royal Arms £1 to 1p (7 coins) | £12 |
| 2008 — "Royal Shield of Arms" ("new" Revs) Shield of Royal Arms £1 to 1p (7 coins) | £12 |
| 2008 — Above two sets housed in one sleeve | £22 |
| 2008 Proof Base Metal "Royal Shield of Arms" set, £1 to 1p (7 coins) | £38 |
| 2008 — Silver Emblems of Britain" set, £1 to 1p (7 coins) | £160 |
| 2008 — — "Royal Shield of Arms" set, £1 to 1p (7 coins) | £160 |
| 2008 — — Above two sets in one black case | £325 |
| 2008 — Gold "Emblems of Britain" set, £1 to 1p (7 coins) | £3500 |
| 2008 — — "Royal Shield of Arms" set, £1 to 1p (7 coins) | £3500 |
| 2008 — — Above two sets in one oak-veneer case | £6750 |
| 2008 — Platinum "Emblems of Britain" set, £1 to 1p (7 coins) | £8500 |

DATE      FDC

2008 — — "Royal Shield of Arms" set, £1 to 1p (7 coins) .......................... £8500
2008 — — Above two sets in one walnut veneer case .......................... £15750
2008 — Silver Piedfort "Royal Shield of Arms" set, £1 to 1p (7 coins) .......... £325
2008 — Gold set of 14 £1 coins, one of each Rev used since 1983,
   all dated 2008 (25th anniversary)   (14 coins) .......................... £9500
2008 — Silver with gold Rev highlighting as above (14 coins) .................. £500
2008 — 2 x £2, Royal Arms £1 to 1p (9 coins) Christmas Coin Sets,
   two different outer sleeves, Father Christmas or Three Wise men .......... £20
2009 Proof Gold Britannia set (4 coins) .......................................... £2200
2009 — Platinum Britannia set (4 coins) ........................................ £4000
2009 — Silver Britannia set (4 coins) ............................................ £150
2009 — Gold Sovereign series set (5 coins) ...................................... £2700
2009 — — double to half-sovereign (3 coins) .................................... £1000
2009 — — sovereign and half-sovereign (2 coins) ................................ £450
2009 — "Family Silver" set, Henry VIII £5, Britannia £2, Darwin and Burns £2,
   £1 and Kew 50p (6 coins) .................................................... £225
2009 — Silver Piedfort collection, Henry VIII £5, Darwin and Burns £2
   and Kew Gardens 50p (4 coins) .............................................. £275
2009 — Silver Set, £5 to 1p (12 coins) .......................................... £275
2009 — Base metal Executive set, £5 to 1p (12 coins) ............................ £80
2009 — — Deluxe set, £5 to 1p (12 coins) ........................................ £55
2009 — — Standard set, £5 to 1p (12 coins) ...................................... £45
2009 BU Base metal set, £2 to 1p (11 coins) ...................................... £22
2009 — — —, £1 to 1p "Royal Shield of Arms" set (7 coins) ...................... £12
2009 — — —, £2 to 1p (8 coins) .................................................. £15
2009 Proof set of 50p coins as detailed in FIFTY PENCE section, CuNi (16 coins) .. £195
2009 — Silver (16 coins) ......................................................... £425
2009 — Gold (16 coins) .......................................................... £8200
2009 — Gold Piedfort (16 coins) ................................................. £19950
2009 "Mind" set of £5 coins, silver (6 coins) .................................... £350
2010 Gold Britannia set (4 coins) ............................................... £2750
2010 — —, (£50 to £10 (3 coins) ................................................. £1500
2010 — Silver Britannia set (4 coins) ............................................ £140
2010 — Gold Olympic Series "Faster", £100 and £25 (2), (3 coins) ................ £2000
2010 — — Sovereign series set (5 coins) ......................................... £2750
2010 — — double to half (3 coins) ............................................... £1250
2010 — — — sovereign to quarter (3 coins) ....................................... £550
2010 — "Silver Celebration" set, Restoration £5, Nightingale £2, London and Belfast £1
   and Girlguiding 50p (5 coins) ............................................... £185
2010 Silver Piedfort set, coins as in "Silver Celebration" set (5 coins) .......... £300
2010 — Silver Collection, £5 to 1p (13 coins) ................................... £300
2010 — Base Metal Executive Set, £5 to 1p (13 coins) ............................ £80
2010 — — Deluxe set ............................................................. £50
2010 — — Standard set ........................................................... £40
2010 BU — Capital Cities £1 (2 coins) ........................................... £15
2010 — — Set, £2 to 1p (12 coins) ............................................... £35
2010 — — Definitive pack, £2 to 1p (8 coins) .................................... £20
2010 Proof "Body" Collection of £5 coins, silver (6 coins) ...................... £300
2010 Proof "Spirit" Collection of £5 coins, silver (6 coins) .................... —
2011 Proof Gold Britannia set (4 coins) ......................................... £2750
2011 — — Premium set (3 coins) .................................................. £1500
2011 — Sovereign set (5 coins) .................................................. £3000
2011 — — double to half (3 coins) ............................................... £1200
2011 — — sovereign to quarter (3 coins) ......................................... £650
2011 — Silver Britannia set (4 coins) ........................................... £180
2011 — Olympic gold "Higher" set (3 coins) ...................................... £2650
2011 — — — "Faster" (2010) and "Higher" set (6 coins) in 9-coin case .......... £5300
2011 — Silver Collection, £5 to 1p (14 coins) ................................... £400
2011 — — Celebration set, Duke of Edinburgh £5, Mary Rose and King James bible
   Cardiff and Edinburgh £1 and WWF 50p (6 coins) ............................. £250
2011 — — — Piedfort, as above (6 coins) ......................................... £395
2011 Executive Proof Base metal set (14 coins) .................................. £85
2011 De-luxe Proof Base metal set (14 coins) .................................... £50
2011 Standard Proof Base metal set (14 coins) ................................... £40
2011 BU set including £2, £1 and 50p commemoratives (13 coins) .................. £26
2011 BU set of Definitives (8 coins) ............................................ £25

| DATE | FDC |
|---|---|
| 2011 Proof gold Britannia set (4 coins`) | £2750 |
| 2011 — — — Premium set (3 coins) | £1500 |
| 2011 — Sovereign set (5 coins) | £3000 |
| 2011 — — Double to half (3 coins) | £1200 |
| 2011 — — Sovereign to Quarter (3 coins) | £650 |
| 2011 — Silver Britannia set (4 coins | £180 |
| 2011 Olympic gold "Higher" set (3 coins) | £2650 |
| 2011 — — "Faster" (2010) and "Higher" set (6 coins) in 9-coin case | £5300 |
| 2011 — Silver collection, £5 to 1p (14 coins) | £400 |
| 2011 — — Celebration set, Duke of Edinburgh £5, Mary Rose and King James Bible £2, Cardiff and Edinburgh £1 and WWF 50p (6 coins) | £250 |
| 2011 — — — Piedfort, as above (6 coins) | £395 |
| 2011 Exexutive Proof Base metal set (14 coins) | £82 |
| 2011 De-luxe Proof Base metal set (14 coins) | £50 |
| 2011 Standard Proof Base metal set (14 coins) | £45 |
| 2011 BU set including £2, £1 and 50p commemoratives (13 coins) | £26 |
| 2011 BU set of Definitives (8 coins) | £20 |
| 2011 Celebration set. King James bible | £2 |
| 2012 Proof Gold Britannia Set (4 coins) | £3600 |
| 2012 — — — £50 down (3 coins) | £1900 |
| 2012 — Sovereign set (5 coins) | £4000 |
| 2012 — — Double to Half (3 coins) | £1650 |
| 2012 — — Sovereign to Quarter (3 coins) | £825 |
| 2012 — Silver Britannia set (4 coins) | £195 |
| 2012 — Silver Britannia Half-Ounce Anniversary (9 coins) | £500 |
| 2012 BU Sovereign set Double to Half (3 coins) | £1550 |
| 2012 Proof Olympic gold Stronger set (3 coins) | £3500 |
| 2012 — — — 2x £25 (2 coins) | £1200 |
| 2010, 2011, 2012 Proof Olympic gold complete set (9 coins) | £10,500 |
| 2009, 2010, 2011, 2012 Complete Countdown sets: | |
| Gold Proof (4 coins) | £11,500 |
| Silver Proof Piedport (4 coins) | — |
| Silver Proof (4 coins) | £348 |
| CuNi BU (4 coins) | £45 |
| 2012 Proof Gold set, Diamond Jubilee £5, Dickens & Technology £2 £1 to 1p (10 coins) | £8500 |
| 2012 Proof Silver set, as above with Selective Gold plating on £1 to 1p coins (10 coins) | £490 |
| 2012 Proof set (Premium) (10 coins) | £99 |
| 2012 Proof set (Collector) (10 coins) | £55 |
| 2012 BU set, include Diamond Jubilee £5 (10 coins) | £39 |
| 2012 BU set, Technology £2 to 1p (8 coins) | £21 |
| 2012 Proof Gold, Diamond Jubilee £5 and Double Sovereign (2 coins) | £3200 |
| 2012 — Olympic and Paralympic £5 (2 coins) | £5500 |

*In addition to the above the Royal Mint produce the BU sets detailed above in Wedding and in Baby gift packs each year. Also the following patterns have been made available:*

| | |
|---|---|
| 1999 (dated 1994) Bi-metal £2, plus three unprocessed or part-processed elements | — |
| 2003 Set of patterns of £1 coins with bridges designs, in gold, hall-marked on edges (4 coins) | — |
| 2003 — silver £1 as above (4 coins) | £150 |
| 2004 — gold £1 featuring heraldic animal heads, hall-marked on edge (4 coins) | £1000 |
| 2004 — silver £1 featuring heraldic animal heads, hall-marked on edge (4 coins) | £350 |

*We have included above the incomplete Olympic proof gold set of 2010 and 2011, six coins out of nine. There are other series of Olympic coins which will form sets in the future, and for which appropriate cases or packaging have, or will become available:*

| | |
|---|---|
| 2011 BU Silver 50p of Sports (29 coins) | — |
| 2011 Unc CuNi 50p of Sports (29 coins) | £85 |
| 2009–2012 Olympic Countdown 4-coin £5 Proof sets in gold, silver, silver Piedfort, also BU in CuNi | — |

*The following sets were, or will be, completed in batches, to be assembled by the recipients in packaging supplied by the Royal Mints :*

| | |
|---|---|
| 2011 BU Silver 50p, Olympic and Paralympic Sports (29 coins) | £1350 |
| 2011 Unc CuNi 50p, Sports (29 coins) | £90 |

*The prices shown for the two sets are the latest for the supply of complete sets from the Royal Mint.*

# SCOTLAND

*The coins illustrated are pennies representative of the reign, unless otherwise stated.*

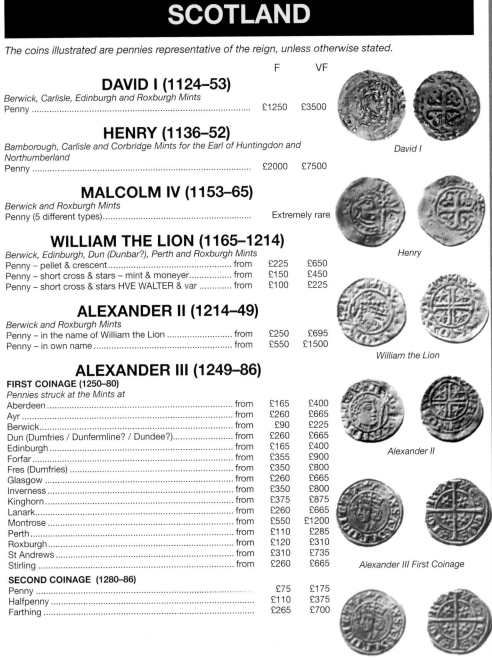

| | F | VF |
|---|---|---|

## DAVID I (1124–53)
*Berwick, Carlisle, Edinburgh and Roxburgh Mints*
Penny ................................................................................... £1250 £3500

*David I*

## HENRY (1136–52)
*Bamborough, Carlisle and Corbridge Mints for the Earl of Huntingdon and Northumberland*
Penny ................................................................................... £2000 £7500

## MALCOLM IV (1153–65)
*Berwick and Roxburgh Mints*
Penny (5 different types)......................................................... Extremely rare

*Henry*

## WILLIAM THE LION (1165–1214)
*Berwick, Edinburgh, Dun (Dunbar?), Perth and Roxburgh Mints*
Penny – pellet & crescent.............................................. from £225 £650
Penny – short cross & stars – mint & moneyer................. from £150 £450
Penny – short cross & stars HVE WALTER & var ............ from £100 £225

## ALEXANDER II (1214–49)
*Berwick and Roxburgh Mints*
Penny – in the name of William the Lion ......................... from £250 £695
Penny – in own name ..................................................... from £550 £1500

*William the Lion*

## ALEXANDER III (1249–86)
**FIRST COINAGE (1250–80)**
*Pennies struck at the Mints at*
Aberdeen ......................................................................... from £165 £400
Ayr .................................................................................. from £260 £665
Berwick............................................................................ from £90 £225
Dun (Dumfries / Dunfermline? / Dundee?)...................... from £260 £665
Edinburgh ........................................................................ from £165 £400
Forfar .............................................................................. from £355 £900
Fres (Dumfries) ............................................................... from £350 £800
Glasgow .......................................................................... from £260 £665
Inverness ......................................................................... from £350 £800
Kinghorn .......................................................................... from £375 £875
Lanark.............................................................................. from £260 £665
Montrose ......................................................................... from £550 £1200
Perth................................................................................ from £110 £285
Roxburgh ......................................................................... from £120 £310
St Andrews ...................................................................... from £310 £735
Stirling ............................................................................. from £260 £665

*Alexander II*

*Alexander III First Coinage*

**SECOND COINAGE (1280–86)**
Penny .............................................................................. £75 £175
Halfpenny ........................................................................ £110 £375
Farthing ........................................................................... £265 £700

*Alexander III Second Coinage*

F    VF

## JOHN BALIOL (1292–1306)

**FIRST COINAGE** *(Rough Surface issue)*

| | | |
|---|---|---|
| Penny .................................................................................. from | £125 | £275 |
| Halfpenny ........................................................................... from | £650 | Ex. rare |
| Penny – St. Andrews ......................................................... from | £175 | £475 |
| Halfpenny – St. Andrews .................................................. from | £800 | Ex. rare |

**SECOND COINAGE** *(Smooth Surface issue)*

| | | |
|---|---|---|
| Penny .................................................................................. from | £200 | £475 |
| Halfpenny ........................................................................... from | £200 | £525 |
| Farthing .............................................................................. | Extremely rare | |
| Penny – St. Andrews ......................................................... from | £350 | £950 |
| Halfpenny – St. Andrews.................................................... | Extremely rare | |

*John Baliol*

## ROBERT BRUCE (1306–29)

*Berwick Mint*

| | | |
|---|---|---|
| Penny .................................................................................. from | £550 | £1500 |
| Halfpenny ........................................................................... from | £850 | £2175 |
| Farthing .............................................................................. from | £1750 | £4375 |

*Robert Bruce*

## DAVID II (1329–71)

*Aberdeen and Edinburgh Mints*

| | | |
|---|---|---|
| Noble.................................................................................. | Extremely Rare | |
| Groat (Edinburgh) .............................................................. from | £115 | £300 |
| Groat (Aberdeen) ............................................................... from | £375 | £1000 |
| Halfgroat (Edinburgh)......................................................... from | £125 | £325 |
| Halfgroat (Aberdeen) ......................................................... from | £525 | £1250 |
| Penny (Edinburgh) ............................................................. from | £85 | £180 |
| Penny (Aberdeen) .............................................................. from | £275 | £750 |
| Halfpenny ........................................................................... from | £225 | £800 |
| Farthing .............................................................................. from | £550 | £1250 |

*David II*

## ROBERT II (1371–90)

*Dundee, Edinburgh and Perth Mints*

| | | |
|---|---|---|
| Groat.................................................................................. from | £95 | £250 |
| Halfgroat ............................................................................ from | £100 | £350 |
| Penny ................................................................................. from | £95 | £250 |
| Halfpenny ........................................................................... from | £80 | £200 |

*Robert II*

## ROBERT III (1390–1406)

*Aberdeen, Dumbarton, Edinburgh, Perth Mints*

| | | |
|---|---|---|
| Lion or crown..................................................................... from | £1250 | £3750 |
| Demy lion or halfcrown...................................................... from | £675 | £2000 |
| Groat.................................................................................. from | £90 | £225 |
| Halfgroat ............................................................................ from | £175 | £350 |
| Penny ................................................................................. from | £225 | £600 |
| Halfpenny ........................................................................... from | £300 | £850 |

## JAMES I (1406–37)

*Aberdeen, Edinburgh, Inverness, Linlithgow, Perth, Stirling Mints*

| | | |
|---|---|---|
| Demy .................................................................................. rom | £950 | £2500 |
| Half demy ........................................................................... from | £750 | £2250 |
| Groat.................................................................................. from | £125 | £350 |
| Penny ................................................................................. from | £250 | £650 |
| Halfpenny ........................................................................... | Extremely rare | |

## JAMES II (1437–60)

*Aberdeen, Edinburgh, Linlithgow, Perth, Roxburgh, Stirling Mints*

| | | |
|---|---|---|
| Demy .................................................................................. from | £950 | £2500 |
| Lion.................................................................................... from | £1250 | £4500 |

*Robert III Lion*

| | F | VF |
|---|---|---|
| Half lion | Extremely rare | |
| Early groats (fleur-de-lis) ........ from | £195 | £550 |
| Later groats (crown) ........ from | £225 | £650 |
| Halfgroat ........ from | £500 | £1200 |
| Penny (billon) ........ from | £250 | £650 |

# JAMES III (1460–88)

*Aberdeen, Berwick and Edinburgh Mints*

| | F | VF |
|---|---|---|
| Rider | £1750 | £4500 |
| Half rider | £1750 | £4500 |
| Quarter rider | £2500 | £7000 |
| Unicorn | £1250 | £3500 |
| Groat ........ from | £130 | £375 |
| Halfgroat ........ from | £225 | £625 |
| Penny (silver) ........ from | £500 | Ex. rare |
| Plack (billon) ........ from | £175 | £450 |
| Half plack) ........ from | £195 | £525 |
| Penny (billon) ........ from | £95 | £500 |
| Farthing (copper) | Extremely rare | |
| Penny – ecclesiastical issue ........ from | £75 | £200 |
| Farthing – ecclesiastical issue ........ from | £125 | £350 |

*James III Groat, Berwick Mint*

# JAMES IV (1488–1513)

*Edinburgh Mint*

| | F | VF |
|---|---|---|
| Unicorn | £1500 | £4250 |
| Half unicorn | £1250 | £3500 |
| Lion or crown | Extremely rare | |
| Half lion | Extremely rare | |
| Groat ........ from | £400 | £1375 |
| Halfgroat ........ from | £650 | £1750 |
| Penny (silver) ........ from | £150 | £400 |
| Plack ........ from | £50 | £125 |
| Half plack | Extremely rare | |
| Penny (billon) ........ from | £55 | £125 |

# JAMES V (1513–42)

*Edinburgh Mint*

| | F | VF |
|---|---|---|
| Unicorn | £2050 | £5125 |
| Half Unicorn | Extremely rare | |
| Crown | £1100 | £3500 |
| Ducat or Bonnet piece ........ from | £1250 | £5000 |
| Two-thirds ducat | £2500 | £6500 |
| One-third ducat | £3500 | £9500 |
| Groat ........ from | £175 | £500 |
| One-third groat ........ from | £275 | £775 |
| Plack ........ from | £60 | £175 |
| Bawbee ........ from | £75 | £195 |
| Half bawbee ........ from | £140 | £325 |
| Quarter bawbee | Extremely rare | |

*James IV Unicorn*

# MARY (1542–67)

*Edinburgh and Stirling Mints*
**FIRST PERIOD (1542–58)**

| | F | VF |
|---|---|---|
| Crown | £1325 | £3500 |
| Twenty shillings | Extremely rare | |
| Lion (Forty-four shillings) | £1250 | £3500 |
| Half lion (Twenty-two shillings) | £1000 | £2750 |
| Ryals (Three pounds | £3500 | £9500 |
| Half ryal | £4500 | £12500 |
| Portrait testoon | £3500 | £10000 |

*James V Ducat or Bonnet Piece*

| | F | VF |
|---|---|---|
| Non-portrait testoon........................................ from | £225 | £550 |
| Half testoon ................................................ from | £250 | £750 |
| Bawbee ...................................................... from | £75 | £195 |
| Half bawbee ................................................ from | £125 | £325 |
| Bawbee - Stirling.......................................... | £175 | £495 |
| Penny (facing bust)........................................ from | £250 | £725 |
| Penny (no bust) ........................................... from | £175 | £500 |
| Lion........................................................... from | £65 | £175 |
| Plack......................................................... from | £80 | £225 |

### SECOND PERIOD (Francis and Mary, 1558–60)

| | F | VF |
|---|---|---|
| Ducat (Sixty shillings) ................................... | Extremely rare | |
| Non-portrait testoon...................................... from | £350 | £1000 |
| Half testoon ............................................... from | £400 | £1150 |
| 12 penny groat ............................................ from | £80 | £225 |
| Lion.......................................................... from | £45 | £125 |

### THIRD PERIOD (Widowhood, 1560–65)

| | F | VF |
|---|---|---|
| Portrait testoon............................................ | £3250 | £9500 |
| Half testoon. .............................................. | £3000 | £8500 |

*Mary Lion or Forty-Four Shillings*

### FOURTH PERIOD (Henry and Mary, 1565–67)

| | F | VF |
|---|---|---|
| Portrait ryal. .............................................. | £45000 | £125000 |
| Non-portrait ryal .......................................... from | £450 | £1100 |
| Two-third ryal.............................................. from | £750 | £1950 |
| One-third ryal.............................................. from | £850 | £2250 |

### FIFTH PERIOD (Second widowhood, 1567)

| | F | VF |
|---|---|---|
| Non-portrait ryal .......................................... from | £850 | £2250 |
| Two thirds ryal ............................................ from | £425 | £1050 |
| One-third ryal.............................................. from | £650 | £1550 |

# JAMES VI (1567–1603)
## (Before accession to the English throne)
### FIRST COINAGE (1567–71)

| | F | VF |
|---|---|---|
| Ryal........................................................... from | £450 | £1300 |
| Two-thirds ryal ............................................ from | £350 | £950 |
| One-third ryal.............................................. from | £375 | £1050 |

### SECOND COINAGE (1571–80)

| | F | VF |
|---|---|---|
| Twenty pounds ............................................ | £22500 | £65000 |
| Noble (or half merk)....................................... from | £200 | £550 |
| Half noble (or quarter merk)............................. from | £150 | £375 |
| Two merks or Thistle dollar.............................. from | £1500 | £3750 |
| Merk ........................................................ from | £2500 | £7250 |

### THIRD COINAGE (1580–81)

| | F | VF |
|---|---|---|
| Ducat........................................................ | £5000 | £14500 |
| Sixteen shillings........................................... | £2500 | £7250 |
| Eight shillings.............................................. | £1950 | £5750 |
| Four shillings .............................................. | £4000 | £9500 |
| Two shillings ............................................... | Extremely rare | |

### FOURTH COINAGE (1582–88)

| | F | VF |
|---|---|---|
| Lion noble.................................................. | £5500 | £15000 |
| Two-third lion noble....................................... | £4750 | £13500 |
| One-third lion noble ...................................... | Extremely rare | |
| Forty shillings ............................................. | £5000 | £14500 |
| Thirty shillings............................................. | £450 | £1300 |
| Twenty shillings ........................................... | £425 | £1250 |
| Ten shillings ............................................... | £425 | £1250 |

*James VI Fourth coinage*
*Ten Shillings*

|  | F | VF |
|---|---|---|

**FIFTH COINAGE (1588)**
Thistle noble ................................................ £1700 £5250

**SIXTH COINAGE (1591–93)**
"Hat" piece ................................................... £3500 £10000
"Balance" half merk................................ from £275 £850
"Balance" quarter merk........................... from £725 £2000

**SEVENTH COINAGE (1594–1601)**
Rider........................................................... £850 £2250
Half rider.................................................... £1200 £3500
Ten shillings......................................... from £200 £550
Five shillings........................................ from £175 £450
Thirty pence......................................... from £225 £625
Twelve pence....................................... from £130 £375

**EIGHTH COINAGE (1601–04)**
Sword and sceptre piece ..................... from £575 £1500
Half sword and sceptre piece............... from £425 £1250
Thistle-merk......................................... from £120 £275
Half thistle-merk .................................. from £85 £225
Quarter thistle-merk ............................ from £75 £210
Eighth thistle-merk .............................. from £70 £200

**BILLON AND COPPER ISSUES**
Eightpenny groat .................................. from £50 £125
Fourpenny groat ................................... from £350 £1000
Twopenny plack.................................... from £130 £375
Hardhead.............................................. from £45 £125
Twopence ............................................. from £80 £230
Penny plack.......................................... from £160 £750
Penny .................................................... from £500 £1250

*James VI Seventh Coinage Rider*

# JAMES VI (1603–25)
## (After accession to the English throne)

Unit....................................................... from £850 £2150
Double crown ...................................... from £1100 £3250
British crown........................................ from £550 £1550
Halfcrown............................................. from £750 £2150
Thistle crown ...................................... from £650 £2050
Sixty shillings...................................... from £350 £1050
Thirty shillings..................................... from £175 £500
Twelve shillings................................... from £175 £575
Six shillings......................................... from £500 Ex. rare
Two shillings........................................ from £50 £140
One shilling.......................................... from £125 £350
Copper twopence................................. from £30 £80
Copper penny....................................... from £85 £250

*James VI Seventh Coinage 10 Shillings*

# CHARLES I (1625–49)
**FIRST COINAGE (1625–36)**

Unit........................................................... £1050 £3250
Double crown ........................................... £1000 £3150
British crown................................ Extremely rare
Sixty shillings........................................... £600 £1750
Thirty shillings.......................................... £125 £350
Twelve shillings........................................ £150 £425
Six shillings...................................... from £325 £950
Two shillings ............................................ £45 £110
One shilling............................................... £150 £495

*James VI after accession thirty shillings*

|  | F | VF |
|---|---|---|

### SECOND COINAGE (1636)
| | F | VF |
|---|---|---|
| Half merk | £90 | £260 |
| Forty penny piece | £75 | £210 |
| Twenty penny piece | £70 | £200 |

### THIRD COINAGE (1637–42)
| | | F | VF |
|---|---|---|---|
| Unit | from | £825 | £2500 |
| Half unit | from | £950 | £2950 |
| British crown | from | £600 | £1750 |
| British half crown | from | £525 | £1500 |
| Sixty shillings | | £575 | £1500 |
| Thirty shillings | from | £110 | £350 |
| Twelve shillings | from | £125 | £350 |
| Six shillings | from | £80 | £225 |
| Half merk | from | £95 | £275 |
| Forty pence | from | £45 | £110 |
| Twenty pence | from | £25 | £60 |

*Charles I Third Coinage
Sixty Shillings*

### FOURTH COINAGE (1642)
| | F | VF |
|---|---|---|
| Three shillings thistle | £60 | £150 |
| Two shillings large II | £40 | £110 |
| Two shillings small II | £60 | £155 |
| Two shillings no value | £80 | £225 |

### COPPER ISSUES
(1629 Issue)
| | F | VF |
|---|---|---|
| Twopence (triple thistle | £30 | £85 |
| Penny | £175 | £500 |

(1632-39 Issue)
| | | F | VF |
|---|---|---|---|
| Twopence (Stirling turner | from | £30 | £75 |

(1642-50 ISSUE)
| | F | VF |
|---|---|---|
| Twopence (CR crowned | £25 | £70 |

*Charles I Fourth Coinage
Two Shillings*

# CHARLES II (1660–85)

### FIRST COINAGE
**Four merks**
| | | F | VF |
|---|---|---|---|
| 1664 Thistle above bust | | £800 | £2250 |
| 1664 Thistle below bust | | £1250 | £3500 |
| 1665 | | Extremely rare | |
| 1670 | varieties from | £950 | £2700 |
| 1673 | | £950 | £2700 |
| 1674 F below bust | varieties from | £800 | £2250 |
| 1675 | | £800 | £2250 |

**Two merks**
| | F | VF |
|---|---|---|
| 1664 Thistle above bust | £650 | £1750 |
| 1664 Thistle below bust | £850 | £2250 |
| 1670 | £850 | £2250 |
| 1673 | £650 | £1750 |
| 1673 F below bust | £750 | £1950 |
| 1674 | £850 | £2250 |
| 1674 F below bust | £850 | £2250 |
| 1675 | £550 | £1550 |

**Merk**
| | | F | VF |
|---|---|---|---|
| 1664 | varieties from | £250 | £715 |
| 1665 | | £275 | £780 |
| 1666 | | £295 | £850 |
| 1668 | | £185 | £520 |

*Charles II two merks*

|  | | F | VF |
|---|---|---|---|
| 1669 | varieties from | £100 | £275 |
| 1670 | | £145 | £410 |
| 1671 | | £125 | £350 |
| 1672 | varieties from | £110 | £325 |
| 1673 | varieties from | £140 | £390 |
| 1674 | | £230 | £650 |
| 1674 F below bust | | £210 | £585 |
| 1675 F below bust | | £175 | £475 |
| 1675 | | £210 | £585 |

**Half merk**

|  | | F | VF |
|---|---|---|---|
| 1664 | | £250 | £650 |
| 1665 | varieties from | £200 | £520 |
| 1666 | varieties from | £225 | £585 |
| 1667 | | £200 | £520 |
| 1668 | | £125 | £325 |
| 1669 | varieties from | £100 | £295 |
| 1670 | varieties from | £125 | £350 |
| 1671 | varieties from | £100 | £295 |
| 1672 | | £175 | £455 |
| 1673 | | £150 | £425 |
| 1675 F below bust | | £150 | £390 |
| 1675 | | £175 | £455 |

**SECOND COINAGE**
**Dollar**

|  | F | VF |
|---|---|---|
| 1676 | £550 | £1350 |
| 1679 | £650 | £1500 |
| 1680 | £650 | £1500 |
| 1681 | £550 | £1350 |
| 1682 | £450 | £1200 |

**Half Dollar**

|  | F | VF |
|---|---|---|
| 1675 | £330 | £950 |
| 1676 | £530 | £1525 |
| 1681 | £400 | £1140 |

**Quarter Dollar**

|  | | F | VF |
|---|---|---|---|
| 1675 | | £195 | £550 |
| 1676 | varieties from | £110 | £295 |
| 1677 | varieties from | £110 | £295 |
| 1678 | | £165 | £450 |
| 1679 | | £185 | £500 |
| 1680 | | £135 | £295 |
| 1681 | | £135 | £295 |
| 1682 | varieties from | £135 | £295 |

**Eighth Dollar**

|  | | F | VF |
|---|---|---|---|
| 1676 | varieties from | £85 | £195 |
| 1677 | | £125 | £300 |
| 1678/7 | | £195 | £495 |
| 1679 | | Extremely rare | |
| 1680 | varieties from | £150 | £345 |
| 1682 | varieties from | £225 | £495 |

**Sixteenth Dollar**

|  | | F | VF |
|---|---|---|---|
| 1677 | | £75 | £200 |
| 1678/7 | varieties from | £120 | £320 |
| 1679/7 | | £135 | £360 |
| 1680 | varieties from | £135 | £360 |
| 1681 | | £75 | £200 |

*Charles II Dollar*

*Charles II Sixteenth Dollar*

*Charles II Bawbee*

273

| | F | VF |
|---|---|---|

**Copper Issues**

| | | F | VF |
|---|---|---|---|
| Twopence CR crowned .................................... varieties from | | £25 | £70 |
| Bawbees 1677-79 ............................................. varieties from | | £75 | £250 |
| Turners 1677-79 ............................................... varieties from | | £60 | £150 |

## JAMES VII (1685–89)

**Sixty shillings**

| | | F | VF |
|---|---|---|---|
| 1688 proof only .................................................. varieties from | | — | £2300 |

**Forty shillings**

| | F | VF |
|---|---|---|
| 1687................................................................. varieties from | £400 | £950 |
| 1688................................................................. varieties from | £450 | £1150 |

**Ten shillings**

| | F | VF |
|---|---|---|
| 1687................................................................................. | £150 | £425 |
| 1688................................................................. varieties from | £250 | £700 |

## WILLIAM & MARY (1689–94)

*James VII ten shillings*

**Sixty shillings**

| | F | VF |
|---|---|---|
| 1691................................................................................. | £295 | £1100 |
| 1692................................................................................. | £350 | £1100 |

**Forty shillings**

| | F | VF |
|---|---|---|
| 1689................................................................. varieties from | £295 | £850 |
| 1690................................................................. varieties from | £185 | £525 |
| 1691................................................................. varieties from | £195 | £550 |
| 1692................................................................. varieties from | £195 | £550 |
| 1693................................................................. varieties from | £195 | £550 |
| 1694................................................................. varieties from | £225 | £775 |

**Twenty shillings**

| | F | VF |
|---|---|---|
| 1693................................................................................. | £450 | £1300 |
| 1694................................................................................. | Extremely rare | |

**Ten shillings**

| | F | VF |
|---|---|---|
| 1689................................................................................. | Extremely rare | |
| 1690................................................................. varieties from | £295 | £750 |
| 1691................................................................. varieties from | £125 | £350 |
| 1692................................................................. varieties from | £140 | £400 |
| 1694................................................................. varieties from | £250 | £700 |

**Five shillings**

| | F | VF |
|---|---|---|
| 1691................................................................................. | £200 | £575 |
| 1694................................................................. varieties from | £120 | £350 |

**Copper Issues**

| | F | VF |
|---|---|---|
| Bawbees 1691–94............................................. varieties from | £100 | £275 |
| Bodle (Turners) 1691–94.................................. varieties from | £55 | £180 |

*William & Mary ten shillings*

## WILLIAM II (1694–1702)

| | F | VF |
|---|---|---|
| Pistole ............................................................................. | £3000 | £7500 |
| Half pistole ...................................................................... | £3750 | £8500 |

**Forty shillings**

| | F | VF |
|---|---|---|
| 1695................................................................. varieties from | £175 | £450 |
| 1696................................................................................. | £200 | £495 |
| 1697................................................................................. | £250 | £550 |
| 1698................................................................................. | £200 | £495 |
| 1699................................................................................. | £325 | £650 |
| 1700................................................................................. | Extremely rare | |

|  | F | VF |
|---|---|---|
| **Twenty shillings** | | |
| 1695 | £200 | £550 |
| 1696 | £200 | £550 |
| 1697 .......................... varieties from | £250 | £700 |
| 1698 .......................... varieties from | £175 | £650 |
| 1699 | £225 | £625 |
| **Ten shillings** | | |
| 1695 | £150 | £375 |
| 1696 | £150 | £375 |
| 1697 .......................... varieties from | £150 | £375 |
| 1698 .......................... varieties from | £150 | £375 |
| 1699 | £295 | £750 |
| **Five shillings** | | |
| 1695 | £95 | £275 |
| 1696 | £85 | £250 |
| 1697 .......................... varieties from | £95 | £275 |
| 1699 | £95 | £275 |
| 1700 | £95 | £275 |
| 1701 | £125 | £350 |
| 1702 | £150 | £425 |
| **Copper Issues** | | |
| Bawbee 1695–97 .......................... varieties from | £85 | £325 |
| Bodle (Turners) 1695–97 .......................... varieties from | £50 | £150 |

*William II ten shillings*

# ANNE (1702–14)

**Pre -Union 1702-7**

| **Ten shillings** | F | VF |
|---|---|---|
| 1705 | £175 | £450 |
| 1706 .......................... varieties from | £225 | £650 |
| **Five shillings** | | |
| 1705 .......................... varieties from | £85 | £225 |
| 1706 | £85 | £225 |

*Anne five shillings*

**POST-UNION 1707-14**
See listing in English section.

# JAMES VIII (The Old Pretender) (1688–1766)

A number of Guineas and Crowns in various metals were struck in 1828 using original dies prepared by Norbert Roettiers, all bearing the date 1716. These coins are extremely rare and are keenly sought after.

**Our grateful thanks go to David Stuart of ABC Coins & Tokens who has spent many hours updating the Scottish section for 2013**

# ISLE OF MAN

| DATE | F | VF | EF | UNC |
|------|---|----|----|-----|

## PENNY

| DATE | F | VF | EF | UNC |
|------|---|----|----|-----|
| 1709 Cast | £45 | £125 | £275 | — |
| 1709 Silver cast Proof | — | — | — | £2000 |
| 1709 Brass | £45 | £110 | £265 | — |
| 1733 "Quocunque" | £40 | £55 | £245 | £360 |
| 1733 "Ouocunoue" | £40 | £65 | £260 | £650 |
| 1733 Bath metal "Quocunque" | £30 | £50 | £220 | — |
| 1733 Silver Proof | — | — | — | £785 |
| 1733 Bronze Proof | — | — | — | £475 |
| 1733 Proof | — | — | — | £675 |
| 1733 Cap frosted | £30 | £50 | £250 | £400 |
| 1733 Brass, cap frosted | £40 | £60 | £275 | £550 |
| 1733 Silver Proof cap frosted | — | — | — | £600 |
| 1733 Bronze annulets instead of pellets | £50 | £95 | £350 | £275 |
| 1758 | £30 | £45 | £200 | £450 |
| 1758 Proof | — | — | — | £650 |
| 1758 Silver Proof | — | — | — | £1000 |
| 1786 Engrailed edge | £35 | £50 | £250 | £450 |
| 1786 Engrailed edge Proof | — | — | — | £500 |
| 1786 Plain edge Proof | — | — | — | £1000 |
| 1786 Pellet below bust | £35 | £60 | £275 | £550 |
| 1798 | £35 | £60 | £200 | £450 |
| 1798 Proof | — | — | — | £390 |
| 1798 Bronze Proof | — | — | — | £390 |
| 1798 Copper-gilt Proof | — | — | — | £1770 |
| 1798 Silver Proof | — | — | — | £2500 |
| 1813 | £40 | £60 | £185 | £400 |
| 1813 Proof | — | — | — | £450 |
| 1813 Bronze Proof | — | — | — | £450 |
| 1813 Copper-gilt Proof | — | — | — | £2500 |
| 1839 | £35 | £50 | £155 | £350 |
| 1839 Proof | — | — | — | £475 |

## HALF PENCE

| DATE | F | VF | EF | UNC |
|------|---|----|----|-----|
| 1709 Cast | £50 | £125 | £250 | — |
| 1709 Brass | £55 | £185 | £490 | — |
| 1723 Silver | £695 | £1250 | £3100 | — |
| 1723 Copper | £300 | £600 | £1750 | £2500 |
| 1733 Copper | £35 | £55 | £225 | £425 |
| 1733 Bronze | £35 | £55 | £225 | £425 |
| 1733 Silver Proof plain cap | — | — | — | £650 |
| 1733 Silver Proof frosted cap | — | — | — | — |
| 1733 Bronze Proof | — | — | — | £470 |
| 1733 Bath metal plain cap | £40 | £50 | £215 | — |
| 1733 Bath metal frosted cap | £40 | £50 | £215 | — |
| 1758 | £40 | £50 | £215 | £400 |
| 1758 Proof | — | — | — | £770 |
| 1786 Engrailed edge | £30 | £45 | £120 | £350 |
| 1786 Proof engrailed edge | — | — | — | £450 |
| 1786 Plain edge | £40 | £65 | £250 | £350 |
| 1786 Proof plain edge | — | — | — | £650 |
| 1786 Bronze Proof | — | — | — | £450 |
| 1798 | £35 | £45 | £150 | £350 |
| 1798 Proof | — | — | — | £450 |
| 1798 Bronze Proof | — | — | — | £400 |

| DATE | F | VF | EF | UNC |
|---|---|---|---|---|
| 1798 Copper-gilt Proof | — | — | — | £1500 |
| 1798 Silver Proof | — | — | — | £1500 |
| 1813 | £30 | £45 | £125 | £275 |
| 1813 Proof | — | — | — | £375 |
| 1813 Bronze Proof | — | — | — | £350 |
| 1813 Copper-gilt Proof | — | — | — | £1250 |
| 1839 | £30 | £45 | £100 | £250 |
| 1839 Bronze Proof | — | — | — | £450 |

## FARTHING

| DATE | F | VF | EF | UNC |
|---|---|---|---|---|
| 1839 Copper | £30 | £45 | £100 | £250 |
| 1839 Bronze Proof | — | — | — | £400 |
| 1839 Copper-gilt Proof | — | — | — | £2500 |

The last issue of coins made in the Isle of Man had been in 1839 but in 1970 Spink & Son Ltd was commissioned to produce a modern coinage for the Isle of Man Government which was struck at the Royal Mint. From 1973 onwards the Pobjoy Mint took over the contract and has been a very prolific producer of definitive and commemorative issues. It is not proposed to give a complete listing of all these coins but the Crown and 25p, which from the collector's point of view are the most interesting in the series, have been selected. Additionally a special 50p coin is issued to celebrate Christmas each year.

**The listings that follow are of the ordinary uncirculated cupro-nickel crown-size coins.** The Island has also issued most of the coins listed in other metals, including silver, gold and platinum in non proof and proof form and in 1984 some were also issued in silver clad cupro-nickel in proof form.

| DATE | UNC |
|---|---|
| 1970 Manx Cat | £15 |
| 1972 Royal Silver Wedding | £15 |
| 1974 Centenary of Churchill's birth | £15 |
| 1975 Manx Cat | £15 |
| 1976 Bi-Centenary of American Independence | £15 |
| 1976 Centenary of the Horse Drawn Tram | £10 |
| 1977 Silver Jubilee | £10 |
| 1977 Silver Jubilee Appeal | £10 |
| 1978 25th Anniversary of the Coronation | £10 |
| 1979 300th Anniversary of Manx Coinage | £10 |
| 1979 Millennium of Tynwald (5 coins) | £20 |
| 1980 Winter Olympics | £15 |
| 1980 Derby Bicentennial | £15 |
| 1980 22nd Olympics (3 coins) | £20 |
| 1980 80th Birthday of Queen Mother | £10 |
| 1981 Duke of Edinburgh Award Scheme (4 coins) | £15 |
| 1981 Year of Disabled (4 coins) | £15 |
| 1981 Prince of Wales' Wedding (2 coins) | £15 |
| 1982 12th World Cup—Spain (4 coins) | £20 |
| 1982 Maritime Heritage (4 coins) | £20 |
| 1983 Manned Flight (4 coins) | £20 |
| 1984 23rd Olympics (4 coins) | £20 |
| 1984 Quincentenary of College of Arms (4 coins) | £20 |
| 1984 Commonwealth Parliamentary Conference (4 coins) | £20 |
| 1985 Queen Mother (6 coins) | £20 |
| 1986 13th World Cup—Mexico (6 coins) | £15 |
| 1986 Prince Andrew Wedding (2 coins) | £15 |
| 1987 200th Anniversary of the United States Constitution | £15 |

| DATE | UNC |
|---|---|
| 1987 America's Cup Races (5 coins)................................................ | £25 |
| 1988 Bicentenary of Steam Navigation (6 coins) ............................... | £30 |
| 1988 Australia Bicentennial (6 coins) .............................................. | £30 |
| 1988 Manx Cat ........................................................................... | £15 |
| 1989 Royal Visit .......................................................................... | £10 |
| 1989 Bicentenary of the Mutiny on the Bounty (4 coins) .................... | £20 |
| 1989 Persian Cat......................................................................... | £15 |
| 1989 Bicentenary of Washington's Inauguration (4 coins) ................. | £20 |
| 1990 150th Anniversary of the Penny Black ...................................... | £15 |
| 1990 World Cup—Italy (4 coins) .................................................... | £20 |
| 1990 25th Anniversary of Churchill's Death (2 coins)........................ | £15 |
| 1990 Alley Cat ............................................................................. | £15 |
| 1990 Queen Mother's 90th Birthday ................................................ | £10 |
| 1991 Norwegian Forest Cat .......................................................... | £10 |
| 1991 Centenary of the American Numismatic Association.................. | £10 |
| 1991 1992 America's Cup .............................................................. | £15 |
| 1991 10th Anniversary of Prince of Wales' Wedding (2 coins)............ | £15 |
| 1992 Discovery of America (4 coins)................................................ | £20 |
| 1992 Siamese Cat ....................................................................... | £15 |
| 1992 1992 America's Cup .............................................................. | £10 |
| 1993 Maine Coon Cat .................................................................. | £10 |
| 1993 Preserve Planet Earth—Dinosaurs (2 coins)............................ | £15 |
| 1994 Preserve Planet Earth—Mammoth........................................... | £15 |
| 1994 Year of the Dog.................................................................... | £15 |
| 1994 World Football Cup (6 coins) ................................................. | £30 |
| 1994 Japanese Bobtail Cat ........................................................... | £10 |
| 1994 Normandy Landings (8 coins)................................................. | £40 |
| 1994 Preserve Planet Earth—Endangered Animals (3 coins)............. | £20 |
| 1995 Man in Flight—Series i (8 coins) ............................................ | £60 |
| 1995 Man in Flight—Series ii (8 coins) ........................................... | £60 |
| 1995 Queen Mother's 95th Birthday ............................................... | £15 |
| 1995 Year of the Pig .................................................................... | £15 |
| 1995 Turkish Cat .......................................................................... | £15 |
| 1995 Preserve Planet Earth—Egret and Otter................................... | £15 |
| 1995 America's Cup ..................................................................... | £15 |
| 1995 Aircraft of World War II (19 coins) ........................................... | £130 |
| 1995 Famous World Inventions—Series i (12 coins).......................... | £120 |
| 1996 Year of the Rat .................................................................... | £15 |
| 1996 70th Birthday of HM the Queen .............................................. | £20 |
| 1996 The Flower Fairies—Series i (4 coins) ..................................... | £40 |
| 1996 Famous World Inventions—Series ii (6 coins) .......................... | £40 |
| 1996 Olympic Games (6 coins) ...................................................... | £35 |
| 1996 Preserve Planet Earth—Killer Whale and Razorbill ................... | £15 |
| 1996 Burmese Cat ....................................................................... | £15 |
| 1996 Robert Burns (4 coins).......................................................... | £30 |
| 1996 King Arthur & the Knights of the Round Table (5 coins) ............. | £35 |
| 1996 European Football Championships (8 coins).............................. | £50 |
| 1996 Football Championships Winner ............................................. | £15 |
| 1996 Explorers (2 coins)................................................................ | £20 |
| 1997 Year of the Ox ..................................................................... | £20 |
| 1997 The Flower Fairies—Series ii (4 coins) .................................... | £25 |
| 1997 Royal Golden Wedding (2 coins) ............................................ | £20 |
| 1997 Explorers—Eriksson and Nansen (2 coins) .............................. | £15 |
| 1997 Long-haired Smoke Cat ........................................................ | £15 |
| 1997 10th Anniversary of the "Cats on Coins" series (silver only) ...... | £45 |
| 1997 90th Anniversary of the TT Races (4 coins).............................. | £35 |
| 1998 The Millennium (16 coins issued over 3 years).......................... | £96 |
| 1998 Year of the Tiger .................................................................. | £20 |
| 1998 FIFA World Cup (4 coins)....................................................... | £35 |
| 1998 Birman Cat .......................................................................... | £20 |
| 1998 The Flower Fairies—Series iii (4 coins) ................................... | £30 |
| 1998 18th Winter Olympics, Nagano (4 coins)................................... | £30 |
| 1998 Explorers—Vasco da Gama and Marco Polo (2 coins) ............. | £25 |
| 1998 125th Anniversary of Steam Railway (8 coins) ......................... | £65 |
| 1998 International Year of the Oceans (4 coins)................................ | £33 |
| 1999 50th Birthday of HRH the Prince of Wales ............................... | £15 |
| 1999 Year of the Rabbit................................................................. | £15 |

| DATE | UNC |
|---|---|
| 1999 27th Olympics in Sydney (5 coins) | £40 |
| 1999 Rugby World Cup (6 coins) | £40 |
| 1999 Wedding of HRH Prince Edward and Sophie Rhys-Jones | £15 |
| 1999 Queen Mother's 100th Birthday (4 coins) | £35 |
| 1999 The Millennium (4 coins) | £35 |
| 1999 Titanium Millennium crown | £15 |
| 2000 Year of the Dragon | £15 |
| 2000 Scottish Fold cat | £15 |
| 2000 Millennium—own a piece of time | £15 |
| 2000 Explorers, Francisco Piarro and Wilem Brents (2 coins) | £15 |
| 2000 Life and times of the Queen Mother (4 coins) | £30 |
| 2000 Queen Mother's 100th Birthday | £15 |
| 2000 60th Anniversary of the Battle of Britain | £15 |
| 2000 BT Global Challenge | £15 |
| 2000 18th Birthday of HRH Prince William | £15 |
| 2001 Year of the Snake | £15 |
| 2001 The Somali cat | £15 |
| 2001 Life and times of the Queen Mother (2 coins) | £15 |
| 2001 Explorers, Martin Frobisher and Roald Amundsen (2 coins) | £15 |
| 2001 75th Birthday of HM the Queen | £15 |
| 2001 Joey Dunlop | £15 |
| 2001 Harry Potter (6 coins) | £80 |
| 2002 Year of the Horse | £15 |
| 2002 The XIX Winter Olympiad, Salt Lake City (2 coins) | £20 |
| 2002 World Cup 2002 in Japan/Korea (4 coins) | £35 |
| 2002 The Bengal Cat | £15 |
| 2002 The Queen's Golden Jubilee—i (1 coin) | £15 |
| 2002 Introduction of the Euro | £15 |
| 2002 The Queen's Golden Jubilee—ii (4 coins) | £60 |
| 2002 A Tribute to Diana Princess of Wales—5 years on | £30 |
| 2003 Year of the Goat | £15 |
| 2003 The Balinese Cat | £15 |
| 2003 Anniversary of the "Star of India" | £15 |
| 2003 Lord of the Rings (5 coins) | £60 |
| 2004 Olympics (4 coins) | £50 |
| 2004 100 Years of Powered Flight (2 coins) | £30 |
| 2005 Lord of the Rings: The Return of the King | £30 |
| 2005 Manx Hero Lt. John Quilliam and the Battle of Trafalgar (2 coins) | £30 |
| 2005 The Himalayan Cat with kittens | £20 |
| 2005 Bicentenary of the Battle of Trafalgar (6 coins) | £55 |
| 2005 60th Anniversary of D-Day (6 coins) | £65 |
| 2005 60th Anniversary of Victory in Europe | £30 |
| 2005 200th Anniversary of the Battle of Trafalgar | £30 |
| 2005 400th Anniversary of the Gun Powder Plot (2 coins) | £30 |
| 2005 Bicentenary of the Battle of Trafalgar and Death of Nelson | £30 |
| 2005 Italy and the Isle of Man TT races (2 coins) | £30 |
| 2005 Harry Potter and the Goblet of Fire (4 coins) | £35 |
| 2006 100 Years of Norwegian Independence | £25 |
| 2006 80th Birthday of Her Majesty the Queen (4 coins) | £35 |
| 2006 The Battles that Changed the World—Part II (6 coins) | £55 |
| 2006 150th Anniversary of the Victoria Cross (2 coins) | £30 |
| 2006 30th Anniversary of the first Translantic Flight | £25 |
| 2007 The Ragdoll Cat | £15 |
| 2007 Fairy Tales—Sleeping Beauty, The Three Little Pigs (2 coins) | £25 |
| 2007 The Graceful Swan | £15 |
| 2007 The Royal Diamond Wedding Anniversary | £15 |
| 2007 The Centenary of the TT races | £15 |
| 2007 The Centenary of the Scouting | £15 |
| 2008 50th Anniversary of Paddington Bear | £15 |
| 2008 Prince Charles 60th Birthday | £15 |
| 2008 Centenary of the Olympics | £15 |
| 2008 Burmilla Cat | £15 |
| 2008 Year of Planet Earth | £15 |
| 2008 The Adorable Snowman | £15 |
| 2008 UEFA European Football Championships | £15 |
| 2008 The Return of Tutankhamun | £30 |

279

| DATE | UNC |
|---|---|
| 2008 The Olympic Collection—The Olympics coming to London ...... | £15 |
| 2009 Winter Olympics (2 coins)............................................................ | £30 |
| 2009 The Chinchilla Cat .................................................................... | £15 |
| 2009 40th Anniversary of the 1st Concorde Test Flight ..................... | £15 |
| 2009 50 Years of Championship Racing ............................................. | £15 |
| 2009 Fifa World Cup South Africa 2010.............................................. | £15 |
| 2010 2012 Olympics ......................................................................... | £60 |
| 2010 50 Years of racing by the Suzuki Racing Team ......................... | £15 |
| 2010 Abyssinian Cat and her Kitten................................................... | £15 |
| 2010 Celebrating 15 Years of the Gold Noble.................................... | £25 |
| 2010 25th Anniversary of the Gold Angel coin................................... | £15 |
| 2011 Year of the Rabbit coloured coin............................................... | £25 |
| 2011 Engagement of HRH Prince William to Catherine Middleton..... | £12 |
| 2011 Royal Wedding of HRH Prince William and Catherine Middleton | £12 |
| 2011 Buckingham Palace.................................................................... | £12 |
| 2011 A Lifetime of Service—Queen Elizabeth II and Prince Philip...... | £12 |
| 2011 The Turkish Angora Cat ............................................................ | £12 |
| 2011 Donatello's famous Chellini Madonna........................................ | £12 |
| 2011 TT Races .................................................................................. | £12 |
| 2012 European Football Championships (4 coins)............................... | £12 |
| 2012 Manx Cat Coin........................................................................... | £12 |
| 2012 Centenary of RMS *Titanic* ....................................................... | £12 |
| 2012 Juno Moneta Coin...................................................................... | £12 |
| 2012 Petra Coin ................................................................................ | £15 |
| 2012 River Thames Diamond Jubilee Pageant ................................... | £15 |

# GUERNSEY

| DATE | F | VF | EF | UNC |
|---|---|---|---|---|
| **TEN SHILLINGS** | | | | |
| 1966 | — | £5 | £9 | £12 |
| 1966 Proof | — | — | — | £20 |
| **THREEPENCE** | | | | |
| 1956 | £1 | £4 | £8 | £10 |
| 1956 Proof | — | — | — | £15 |
| 1959 | £1 | £4 | £8 | £12 |
| 1966 Proof | — | — | — | £15 |
| **EIGHT DOUBLES** | | | | |
| 1834 | £10 | £15 | £50 | £175 |
| 1858 5 berries | £6 | £10 | £50 | £150 |
| 1858 4 berries | £6 | £10 | £50 | £160 |
| 1864 1 stalk | £6 | £10 | £40 | £70 |
| 1864 3 stalks | £6 | £10 | £30 | £65 |
| 1868 | £6 | £10 | £30 | £65 |
| 1874 | £4 | £6 | £15 | £50 |
| 1885H | £4 | £6 | £15 | £45 |
| 1889H | £3 | £4 | £15 | £40 |
| 1893H small date | £3 | £4 | £15 | £40 |
| 1893H large date | £3 | £4 | £15 | £40 |
| 1902H | £3 | £4 | £15 | £40 |
| 1903H | £3 | £4 | £15 | £40 |
| 1910 | £3 | £4 | £15 | £40 |
| 1911H | £3 | £4 | £15 | £45 |
| 1914H | £1 | £3 | £10 | £30 |
| 1918H | £1 | £3 | £8 | £25 |
| 1920H | £1 | £3 | £8 | £25 |
| 1934H | £1 | £3 | £10 | £35 |
| 1934H Proof | — | — | — | £150 |
| 1938H | £1 | £3 | £10 | £25 |
| 1945H | — | £2 | £8 | £15 |
| 1947H | — | £2 | £8 | £15 |
| 1949H | — | £2 | £9 | £15 |
| 1956 | — | £1 | £7 | £15 |
| 1956 | — | £1 | £5 | £15 |
| 1959 | — | £1 | £5 | £15 |
| 1966 Proof | — | — | — | £30 |
| **FOUR DOUBLES** | | | | |
| 1830 | £4 | £9 | £50 | £125 |
| 1830 Mule with obv. St Helena 1/2d | — | £850 | — | — |
| 1858 | £6 | £12 | £50 | £125 |
| 1864 Single stalk | £2 | £6 | £20 | £60 |
| 1864 3 stalks | £2 | £6 | £20 | £65 |
| 1868 | £3 | £7 | £22 | £70 |
| 1874 | £2 | £6 | £22 | £70 |
| 1885H | £2 | £6 | £20 | £45 |
| 1889H | £2 | £3 | £15 | £35 |
| 1893H | £2 | £3 | £15 | £35 |
| 1902H | £2 | £3 | £10 | £30 |
| 1903H | £2 | £3 | £13 | £30 |
| 1906H | £2 | £3 | £10 | £26 |
| 1908H | £2 | £3 | £10 | £26 |
| 1910H | £2 | £3 | £10 | £26 |
| 1911H | £2 | £3 | £8 | £25 |
| 1914H | £2 | £3 | £13 | £40 |
| 1918H | £2 | £3 | £12 | £35 |
| 1920H | £2 | £3 | £10 | £35 |
| 1945H | £2 | £3 | £10 | £35 |
| 1949H | £2 | £3 | £12 | £35 |
| 1956 | £1 | £2 | £8 | £15 |
| 1966 Proof | — | — | — | £15 |

| DATE | F | VF | EF | UNC |
|------|---|----|----|----|
| **TWO DOUBLES** | | | | |
| 1858...................................................... | £6 | £9 | £50 | £200 |
| 1868 Single stick ................................. | £6 | £11 | £55 | £200 |
| 868 3 stalks .......................................... | £7 | £13 | £80 | £205 |
| 1874...................................................... | £4 | £9 | £50 | £150 |
| 1885H.................................................... | £3 | £6 | £17 | £35 |
| 1889H.................................................... | £3 | £4 | £17 | £35 |
| 1899H.................................................... | £3 | £5 | £21 | £42 |
| 1902H.................................................... | £3 | £4 | £19 | £35 |
| 1902H.................................................... | £3 | £4 | £19 | £35 |
| 1906H.................................................... | £3 | £4 | £19 | £35 |
| 1908H.................................................... | £3 | £5 | £19 | £35 |
| 1911H.................................................... | £3 | £5 | £22 | £42 |
| 1914H.................................................... | £3 | £5 | £22 | £42 |
| 1917H.................................................... | £7 | £18 | £80 | £210 |
| 1918H.................................................... | £3 | £4 | £13 | £30 |
| 1920H.................................................... | £3 | £4 | £13 | £30 |
| 1929H.................................................... | £2 | £3 | £11 | £18 |
| | | | | |
| **ONE DOUBLE** | | | | |
| 1830...................................................... | £3 | £4 | £22 | £45 |
| 1868...................................................... | £4 | £10 | £35 | £100 |
| 1868/30 ................................................. | £5 | £7 | £27 | £85 |
| 1885H.................................................... | £2 | £3 | £8 | £20 |
| 1889H.................................................... | £1 | £2 | £6 | £20 |
| 1893H.................................................... | £1 | £2 | £6 | £20 |
| 1899H.................................................... | £1 | £2 | £6 | £20 |
| 1902...................................................... | £1 | £2 | £6 | £20 |
| 1903H.................................................... | £1 | £2 | £6 | £20 |
| 1911H.................................................... | £1 | £2 | £8 | £20 |
| 1911 (new shield) ................................. | £1 | £2 | £6 | £20 |
| 1914H.................................................... | £1 | £2 | £8 | £20 |
| 1929H.................................................... | £1 | £2 | £6 | £20 |
| 1933H.................................................... | £1 | £2 | £6 | £20 |
| 1938H.................................................... | £1 | £2 | £6 | £20 |

# DECIMAL COINAGE

**Ordinary circulating coinage from 1986 onwards is usually available in uncirculated condition at a small premium above face value thus it is not listed here. The coins listed are cupro-nickel unless otherwise stated.**

| | UNC |
|---|---|
| **ONE HUNDRED POUNDS—Gold** | |
| 1994 50th Anniversary of Normandy Landings. Proof ........................... | £1600 |
| 1995 Anniversary of the Liberation. Proof.............................................. | £1600 |
| | |
| **FIFTY POUNDS—Gold** | |
| 1994 50th Anniversary of Normandy Landings. Proof ........................... | £950 |
| 1995 Anniversary of the Liberation. Proof............................................. | £950 |
| 1998 Queen Elizabeth and Queen Mother Gold Proof........................... | £1000 |
| 1999 Queen Elizabeth and Queen Mother Gold .................................... | £900 |
| 2004 Anniversary of D-Day.................................................................... | £1100 |
| | |
| **TWENTY-FIVE POUNDS—Gold** | |
| 1994 50th Anniversary of Normandy Landings....................................... | £400 |
| 1994 — Proof......................................................................................... | £400 |
| 1995 Anniversary of the Liberation. Proof............................................. | £400 |
| 1995 Queen Mothers 95th Birthday ...................................................... | £400 |
| 1996 European Football Championships. Proof ..................................... | £400 |
| 1997 Royal Golden Wedding. Proof....................................................... | £400 |
| 1998 Royal Air Force. Proof .................................................................. | £400 |
| 2000 Queen Mother 100th Birthday. Proof............................................ | £400 |
| 2001 Queen Victoria centennial Proof................................................... | £400 |
| 2001 Queen Victoria gold proof ............................................................ | £400 |
| 2001 HM the Queen's 75th Birthday. Proof........................................... | £400 |
| 2002 Princess Diana memorial. Proof ................................................... | £400 |
| 2002 Duke of Wellington. Proof............................................................. | £400 |
| 2002 Golden Jubilee. Proof................................................................... | £400 |

| DATE | UNC |
|------|-----|
| 2002 Queen Mother. Proof ............................................................ | £400 |
| 2003 Golden Jubilee. Proof .......................................................... | £400 |
| 2004 Anniversary of D-Day. Proof ............................................... | £400 |
| 2006 FIFA World Cup. Proof ......................................................... | £400 |

**TEN POUNDS**

| | |
|------|-----|
| 1994 50th Anniversary of Normandy Landings. Gold proof .................... | £200 |
| 1995 Anniversary of the Liberation. Gold proof .................................. | £200 |
| 2000 Century of Monarchy. Silver proof......................................... | £160 |
| 2000 Guernsey Gold Proof 'Nugget' .............................................. | £200 |
| 2001 19th Century Monarchy. Silver proof...................................... | £160 |
| 2002 18th Century Monarchy. Silver proof...................................... | £160 |
| 2004 Anniversary of D-Day. Silver proof ....................................... | £195 |
| 2012 Diamond Jubilee. 5 oz Silver proof ....................................... | — |

**FIVE POUNDS**

| | |
|------|-----|
| 1995 Queen Mother's 95th birthday.............................................. | £25 |
| 1995 — Silver proof.................................................................. | £55 |
| 1995 — Small size gold............................................................. | £250 |
| 1996 HM the Queen's 70th birthday ............................................. | £18 |
| 1996 — Silver proof.................................................................. | £55 |
| 1996 European Football Championships ........................................ | £35 |
| 1996 — Silver proof.................................................................. | £55 |
| 1997 Royal Golden Wedding....................................................... | £25 |
| 1997 — Silver proof.................................................................. | £55 |
| 1997 — Small size gold. BU........................................................ | £180 |
| 1997 Castles of the British Isles—Castle Cornet, Guernsey............ | £18 |
| 1997 — Silver proof.................................................................. | £65 |
| 1997 Castles of the British Isles—Caernarfon Castle. Silver proof........ | £75 |
| 1997 Castles of the British Isles—Leeds Castle. Silver proof ............. | £75 |
| 1998 Royal Air Force. .............................................................. | £15 |
| 1998 Royal Air Force. Silver proof................................................ | £70 |
| 1999 Millennium. Brass ............................................................. | £25 |
| 1999 — Silver proof.................................................................. | £55 |
| 1999 Wedding of HRH Prince Edward and Sophie Rhys-Jones............ | £25 |
| 1999 — Silver proof.................................................................. | £55 |
| 1999 Queen Mother .................................................................. | £25 |
| 1999 — Silver proof.................................................................. | £80 |
| 1999 Winston Churchill ............................................................. | £15 |
| 1999 — Gold ........................................................................... | £1200 |
| 2000 Queen Mother's 100th Birthday ........................................... | £10 |
| 2000 — Silver proof.................................................................. | £85 |
| 2000 — Small size gold. Proof ................................................... | £170 |
| 2000 Centuries of the British Monarchy........................................ | £45 |
| 2000 — Silver proof.................................................................. | £85 |
| 2000 — Small size gold. Proof ................................................... | £180 |
| 2001 The Reign of Queen Victoria............................................... | £20 |
| 2001 — Gold proof ................................................................... | £360 |
| 2001 — Proof .......................................................................... | £60 |
| 2001 — Silver proof.................................................................. | £60 |
| 2001 HM the Queen's 75th Birthday ............................................ | £15 |
| 2001 — Silver proof.................................................................. | £60 |
| 2001 — Small size gold. Proof ................................................... | £180 |
| 2001 19th Century Monarchy...................................................... | £20 |
| 2001 — Silver proof.................................................................. | £60 |
| 2001 — Small size gold. Proof ................................................... | £180 |
| 2002 Golden Jubilee (two types)................................................. | £15 |
| 2002 — Silver proof.................................................................. | £65 |
| 2002 Princess Diana Memorial.................................................... | £15 |
| 2002 — Proof .......................................................................... | £60 |
| 2002 — Gold proof ................................................................... | £1200 |
| 2002 Century of Monarchy......................................................... | £15 |
| 2002 — Silver proof.................................................................. | £60 |
| 2002 — Small size gold. Proof ................................................... | £180 |
| 2002 Queen Mother Memoriam .................................................. | £20 |
| 2002 — Proof .......................................................................... | £25 |
| 2002 — Silver proof.................................................................. | £65 |
| 2002 — Small size gold proof .................................................... | £180 |

| DATE | UNC |
|---|---|
| 2002 — Large size gold proof ......................................... | £1200 |
| 2003 Duke of Wellington .............................................. | £15 |
| 2003 — Silver proof.................................................... | £50 |
| 2003 — Small size gold proof....................................... | £160 |
| 2003 — Large size gold proof....................................... | £1200 |
| 2003 Prince William.................................................... | £20 |
| 2003 — Silver proof.................................................... | £60 |
| 2003 — Gold proof..................................................... | £1150 |
| 2003 Golden Hind....................................................... | £20 |
| 2003 17th Century Monarchy....................................... | £22 |
| 2003 History of the Royal Navy, Nelson......................... | £20 |
| 2003 — Nelson with coloured flag. Proof....................... | £30 |
| 2004 — Invincible. Silver proof.................................... | £50 |
| 2004 16th Century monarchs....................................... | £15 |
| 2004 History of the Railways, Mallard........................... | £12 |
| 2004 — City of Truro ................................................. | £15 |
| 2004 — The Boat Train............................................... | £12 |
| 2004 — The Train Spotter .......................................... | £15 |
| 2004 History of the Royal Navy, Henry VIII.................... | £15 |
| 2004 — Invincible...................................................... | £15 |
| 2004 Anniversary of D-Day ........................................ | £12 |
| 2004 — Silver proof................................................... | £50 |
| 2004 — Gold proof..................................................... | £1150 |
| 2004 Anniversary of the Crimean War. Plain ................. | £12 |
| 2004 — with colour ................................................... | £15 |
| 2004 — Silver proof................................................... | £55 |
| 2004 — Gold proof with colour .................................... | £1200 |
| 2005 200th Anniversary of the Battle of Trafalgar .......... | £25 |
| 2005 60th Anniversary of the Liberation of the Channel Islands............ | £25 |
| 2005 End of World War II. Silver proof .......................... | £55 |
| 2005 — Gold proof..................................................... | £1200 |
| 2005 Anniversary of Liberation. Gold proof ................... | £1250 |
| 2006 Royal 80th Birthday. Silver proof.......................... | £55 |
| 2006 FIFA World Cup. Silver proof ............................... | £55 |
| 2006 Great Britons—Sir Winston Churchill Silver. Issued as part of set. | £60 |
| 2006 80th Birthday of Her Majesty the Queen................ | £25 |
| 2007 History of the Royal Navy—Henry VIII, The Golden Hind (2 coins)...... | £65 |
| 2007 Royal Diamond Wedding...................................... | £25 |
| 2011 350th Anniversary of the Crown Jewels. Silver proof. | £95 |
| 2011 90th Anniversary of the British Legion (gold-plated copper)............. | £40 |
| 2011 — Silver proof.................................................... | £95 |
| 2011 40th Anniversary of decimalisation, proof.............. | £20 |
| 2011 Anniversary of the sinking of the *Titanic* ............. | £20 |
| 2011 — Silver proof.................................................... | £55 |
| 2011 30th Birthday of Duke of Cambridge...................... | £20 |
| 2011 — Silver proof.................................................... | £55 |
| 2011 Wedding of Prince William and Kate Middleton....... | £25 |
| 2011 — Silver proof.................................................... | £55 |
| 2011 400th Anniversary of the King James Bible ............ | £25 |
| 2012 Diamond Jubilee £5............................................ | — |
| 2012 — Gold proof..................................................... | — |

**TWO POUNDS**

| | |
|---|---|
| 1985 40th anniversary of Liberation.............................. | £10 |
| 1985 — Proof ........................................................... | £27 |
| 1985 — Silver proof................................................... | £55 |
| 1986 Commonwealth Games, in plastic case................. | £12 |
| 1986 — in special folder............................................ | £12 |
| 1986 — .500 Silver .................................................... | £45 |
| 1986 — .925 Silver proof............................................ | £55 |
| 1987 900th Anniv. of death of William the Conqueror, in folder.............. | £14 |
| 1987 — Silver proof................................................... | £55 |
| 1987 — Gold proof..................................................... | £1300 |
| 1988 William II, in presentation folder .......................... | £14 |
| 1988 — Silver proof................................................... | £55 |
| 1989 Henry I, in presentation folder ............................ | £14 |
| 1989 — Silver proof................................................... | £55 |
| 1989 Royal Visit........................................................ | £14 |
| 1989 — Silver proof................................................... | £55 |
| 1990 Queen Mother's 90th birthday.............................. | £14 |

| DATE | F | VF | EF | UNC |
|------|---|----|----|----|
| 1990 — Silver proof | | | | £55 |
| 1991 Henry II, in presentation folder | | | | £14 |
| 1991 — Silver proof | | | | £55 |
| 1993 40th Anniversary of the Coronation | | | | £14 |
| 1993 — Silver proof | | | | £60 |
| 1994 Anniversary of the Normandy Landings | | | | £14 |
| 1994 — Silver proof | | | | £55 |
| 1995 50th Anniversary of Liberation | | | | £14 |
| 1995 — Silver proof | | | | £55 |
| 1995 — Silver Piedfort proof | | | | £100 |
| 1997 Conserving Nature i | | | | £10 |
| 1997 — Silver proof | | | | £55 |
| 1997 Bimetallic Latent image | | | | £5 |
| 1997 — Proof | | | | £8 |
| 1998 Conserving Nature ii | | | | £10 |
| 1998 Bimetallic Latent image | | | | £5 |
| 2003 — | | | | £6 |
| 2006 — | | | | £8 |
| 2011 Prince Philip's 90th Birthday (conjoined portraits) | | | | — |
| 2011 — Silver proof | | | | — |

**ONE POUND**

| DATE | F | VF | EF | UNC |
|------|---|----|----|----|
| 1981 | | | | £10 |
| 1981 Gold proof | | | | £145 |
| 1981 Gold piedfort | | | | £345 |
| 1983 New specification, new reverse | | | | £9 |
| 1985 New design (in folder) | | | | £9 |
| 1995 Queen Mother's 95th Birthday. Silver proof | | | | £50 |
| 1996 Queen's 70th Birthday. Silver proof | | | | £55 |
| 1997 Royal Golden Wedding. Silver BU | | | | £18 |
| 1997 — Silver proof | | | | £55 |
| 1997 Castles of the British Isles—Tower of London. Silver proof only | | | | £27 |
| 1998 Royal Air Force. Silver proof | | | | £42 |
| 1999 Wedding of Prince Edward. Silver proof | | | | £55 |
| 1999 Queen Mother. Silver proof | | | | £55 |
| 1999 Winston Churchill. Silver proof | | | | £55 |
| 2000 Millennium. Silver proof (gold plated) | | | | £65 |
| 2000 Queen Mother's 100th Birthday. Silver proof | | | | £42 |
| 2001 | | | | £2 |
| 2001 HM the Queen's 75th Birthday. Silver proof | | | | £42 |
| 2002 William of Normandy. Silver | | | | £20 |
| 2003 | | | | £2 |
| 2006 | | | | £2 |

**FIFTY PENCE**

| DATE | F | VF | EF | UNC |
|------|---|----|----|----|
| 1969 | | | | £4 |
| 1970 | | | | £6 |
| 1971 Proof | | | | £9 |
| 1981 | | | | £4 |
| 1982 | | | | £4 |
| 1985 New design | | | | £4 |
| 2000 60th Anniversary of the Battle of Britain. | | | | £4 |
| 2000 — Silver proof | | | | £55 |
| 2000 — Silver piedfort | | | | £55 |
| 2000 — Gold proof | | | | £365 |
| 2003 | | | | £2 |
| 2006 | | | | £2 |
| 2008 | | | | £2 |
| 2012 The Diamond Jubilee (coloured portrait) | | | | — |

**TWENTY-FIVE PENCE**

| DATE | F | VF | EF | UNC |
|------|---|----|----|----|
| 1972 Royal Silver Wedding | | | | £12 |
| 1972 — Silver proof | | | | £42 |
| 1977 Royal Silver Jubilee | | | | £9 |
| 1977 — Silver proof | | | | £42 |
| 1978 Royal Visit | | | | £9 |
| 1978 — Silver proof | | | | £42 |
| 1980 Queen Mother's 80th birthday | | | | £9 |
| 1980 — Silver proof | | | | £42 |
| 1981 Royal Wedding | | | | £9 |
| 1981 — Silver proof | | | | £42 |

# JERSEY

| DATE | F | VF | EF | UNC |
|---|---|---|---|---|
| **FIVE SHILLINGS** | | | | |
| 1966 | — | £3 | £7 | £15 |
| 1966 Proof | — | £3 | £9 | £25 |
| | | | | |
| **ONE QUARTER OF A SHILLING** | | | | |
| 1957 | — | £2 | £5 | £10 |
| 1960 Proof | — | — | £5 | £14 |
| 1964 | — | — | £4 | £10 |
| 1966 | — | — | £4 | £10 |

| | F | VF | EF | UNC |
|---|---|---|---|---|
| **ONE TWELFTH OF A SHILLING** | | | | |
| 1877H | £2 | £3 | £18 | £55 |
| 1877H Proof in nickel | — | — | — | £1275 |
| 1877 Proof only | — | — | — | £475 |
| 1877 Proof in nickel | — | — | — | £1265 |
| 1881 | £3 | £3 | £14 | £60 |
| 1888 | £2 | £3 | £14 | £48 |
| 1894 | £2 | £3 | £17 | £48 |
| 1909 | £2 | £3 | £14 | £35 |
| 1911 | £2 | £3 | £7 | £30 |
| 1913 | £2 | £3 | £7 | £30 |
| 1923 Spade shield | £2 | £3 | £7 | £30 |
| 1923 Square shield | £2 | £3 | £7 | £30 |
| 1926 | £2 | £3 | £8 | £42 |
| 1931 | £2 | £3 | £5 | £12 |
| 1933 | £2 | £3 | £7 | £12 |
| 1935 | £2 | £3 | £7 | £12 |
| 1937 | £2 | £3 | £7 | £12 |
| 1946 | £2 | £3 | £7 | £12 |
| 1947 | — | £3 | £7 | £12 |
| "1945" GVI | — | — | £1 | £9 |
| "1945" QE2 | — | — | £1 | £7 |
| 1957 | — | — | £1 | £7 |
| 1960 1660–1960 300th anniversary | — | — | £1 | £7 |
| 1960 Mule | — | — | — | £150 |
| 1966 "1066–1966" | — | — | £1 | £7 |

| | F | VF | EF | UNC |
|---|---|---|---|---|
| **ONE THIRTEENTH OF A SHILLING** | | | | |
| 1841 | £4 | £8 | £40 | £195 |
| 1844 | £4 | £9 | £40 | £195 |
| 1851 | £5 | £12 | £60 | £200 |
| 1858 | £4 | £9 | £45 | £195 |
| 1861 | £5 | £13 | £60 | £175 |
| 1865 Proof only | — | — | — | £700 |
| 1866 with LCW | £2 | £5 | £95 | £145 |
| 1866 without LCW Proof only | — | — | — | £390 |
| 1870 | £4 | £8 | £40 | £110 |
| 1871 | £4 | £8 | £42 | £110 |

| | F | VF | EF | UNC |
|---|---|---|---|---|
| **ONE TWENTY-FOURTH OF A SHILLING** | | | | |
| 1877H | £3 | £4 | £11 | £55 |
| 1877 Proof only | — | — | — | £300 |
| 1888 | £3 | £4 | £11 | £42 |
| 1894 | £3 | £4 | £11 | £42 |
| 1909 | £3 | £4 | £11 | £42 |
| 1911 | £2 | £3 | £8 | £42 |
| 1913 | £2 | £3 | £8 | £42 |

| DATE | F | VF | EF | UNC |
|---|---|---|---|---|
| 1923 Spade shield | £2 | £3 | £9 | £33 |
| 1923 Square shield | £2 | £3 | £8 | £35 |
| 1926 | £2 | £3 | £8 | £22 |
| 1931 | £2 | £3 | £8 | £22 |
| 1933 | £2 | £3 | £8 | £22 |
| 1935 | £2 | £3 | £8 | £22 |
| 1937 | £1 | £2 | £6 | £16 |
| 1946 | £1 | £2 | £6 | £19 |
| 1947 | £1 | £2 | £6 | £16 |

### ONE TWENTY-SIXTH OF A SHILLING
| | | | | |
|---|---|---|---|---|
| 1841 | £4 | £7 | £30 | £90 |
| 1844 | £4 | £7 | £25 | £90 |
| 1851 | £3 | £6 | £25 | £90 |
| 1858 | £4 | £11 | £48 | £180 |
| 1861 | £3 | £6 | £25 | £65 |
| 1866 | £3 | £6 | £27 | £77 |
| 1870 | £3 | £6 | £20 | £55 |
| 1871 | £3 | £6 | £20 | £55 |

### ONE FORTY-EIGHTH OF A SHILLING
| | | | | |
|---|---|---|---|---|
| 1877H | £6 | £12 | £57 | £130 |
| 1877 Proof only | — | — | — | £400 |

### ONE FIFTY-SECOND OF A SHILLING
| | | | | |
|---|---|---|---|---|
| 1841 | £9 | £25 | £60 | £195 |
| 1861 Proof only | — | — | — | £650 |

## DECIMAL COINAGE
**Ordinary circulating coinage from 1986 onwards is usually available in uncirculated condition at a small premium above face value thus it is not listed here.**

### ONE HUNDRED POUNDS
| | |
|---|---|
| 1990 50th Anniversary of the Battle of Britain. Gold Proof. | £1000 |
| 1995 50th Anniversary of Liberation. Gold proof | £1000 |

### FIFTY POUNDS
| | |
|---|---|
| 1972 Silver Wedding. Gold proof | £850 |
| 1990 50th Anniversary of the Battle of Britain. Gold proof | £850 |
| 1995 50th Anniversary of Liberation. Gold proof | £820 |
| 2003 Golden Jubilee. Silver Proof (100mm) | £650 |

### TWENTY-FIVE POUNDS
| | |
|---|---|
| 1972 25th Royal Wedding anniversary. Gold | £300 |
| 1972 — Gold proof | £380 |
| 1990 50th Anniversary of Battle of Britain. Gold proof | £350 |
| 1995 50th Anniversary of Liberation. Gold proof | £350 |
| 2002 Princess Diana memorial. Gold proof | £350 |
| 2002 Queen Mother. Gold proof | £350 |
| 2002 Golden Jubilee. Gold proof | £350 |
| 2002 Duke of Wellington. Gold proof | £350 |
| 2003 Golden Jubilee. Gold proof | £350 |
| 2003 History of the Royal Navy. Naval Commanders | £350 |
| 2003 — Francis Drake | £350 |
| 2003 Sovereign of the Seas | £350 |
| 2004 60th Anniversary of D-Day. Gold proof | £350 |
| 2004 Charge of the Light Brigade. Gold proof | £350 |
| 2004 HMS Victory. Gold proof | £350 |
| 2004 John Fisher 1841–1920 Gold proof | £350 |
| 2004 The Coronation Scot. Gold proof | £350 |
| 2004 The Flying Scotsman. Gold proof | £350 |
| 2004 Golden Arrow. Gold proof | £350 |
| 2004 Rocket and Evening Star. Gold proof | £350 |

| DATE | UNC |
|---|---|
| 2005 Andrew Cunningham. Gold proof | £350 |
| 2005 HMS Conqueror. Gold Proof | £350 |
| 2005 200th Anniversary of Nelson. Gold proof | £350 |
| 2009 500th Anniversary of Accession. Gold proof | £350 |

## TWENTY POUNDS
| | |
|---|---|
| 1972 Royal Wedding. The Ormer. Gold | £300 |
| 1972 — Gold proof | £300 |

## TEN POUNDS
| | |
|---|---|
| 1972 25th Royal Wedding anniversary. Gold | £75 |
| 1972 — Gold proof | £180 |
| 1990 50th Anniversary of the Battle of Britain. Gold proof | £180 |
| 1995 50th Anniversary of Liberation. Gold proof | £140 |
| 2003 Coronation Anniversary. Gold/silver proof | £50 |
| 2004 Crimea. Silver proof | £20 |
| 2205 Trafalgar. Silver proof | £20 |
| 2005 — Silver/gold proof | £110 |
| 2005 End of World War II. Silver proof | £25 |
| 2007 Diamond Wedding. Platinum proof | £280 |
| 2008 History of RAF. Silver proof | £25 |
| 2008 — Silver/Gold proof | £110 |
| 2011 Royal Wedding of HRH Prince William & Catherine Middleton, silver (65mm) | £395 |

(Enlarged)

(Reduced)

(Enlarged)

## FIVE POUNDS
| | |
|---|---|
| 1972 Gold proof | £65 |
| 1990 50th Anniversary of the Battle of Britain. Silver Proof (5 ounces) | £180 |
| 1997 Royal Golden Wedding | £10 |
| 1997 — Silver proof | £25 |
| 2000 Millennium. Silver proof | £35 |
| 2002 Princess Diana memorial | £12 |
| 2002 — Silver proof | £30 |
| 2002 — Gold proof | £820 |
| 2002 Royal Golden Jubilee | £25 |
| 2003 Golden Jubilee | £20 |
| 2003 — Silver proof | £55 |
| 2003 — Gold proof | £1100 |
| 2003 Prince William 21st Birthday | £15 |
| 2003 — Silver Proof | £55 |
| 2003 —Gold proof | £1200 |
| 2003 Naval Commanders | £15 |
| 2003 — Silver proof | £55 |
| 2003 — Gold proof | £1200 |
| 2003 Francis Drake | £15 |
| 2003 — Silver proof | £55 |
| 2003 — Gold proof | £1200 |
| 2003 Sovereign of the Seas | £15 |
| 2003 — Silver proof | £55 |
| 2003 — Gold proof | £1200 |
| 2004 60th Anniversary of 'D' Day | £15 |
| 2004 — Silver proof | £55 |
| 2004 — Gold proof | £1200 |
| 2004 Charge of the Light Brigade | £15 |
| 2004 — Silver proof | £50 |
| 2004 — Gold proof | £1200 |
| 2004 HMS Victory | £15 |
| 2004 — Silver proof | £55 |
| 2004 — Gold proof | £1200 |
| 2004 John Fisher 1841–1920 | £15 |
| 2004 — Silver proof | £55 |
| 2004 —Gold proof | £1200 |
| 2004 The Coronation Scot | £15 |
| 2004 — Silver proof | £55 |

| DATE | UNC |
|------|-----|
| 2004 — Gold proof | £1200 |
| 2004 The Flying Scotsman | £15 |
| 2004 — Silver proof | £55 |
| 2004 — Silver/Gold proof | £500 |
| 2004 — Gold proof | £1200 |
| 2004 Golden Arrow | £15 |
| 2004 — Silver proof | £55 |
| 2004 — Gold proof | £1200 |
| 2005 Driver and Fireman | £15 |
| 2005 — Silver proof | £45 |
| 2005 — Gold proof | £1100 |
| 2005 Box Tunnel and King Loco | £15 |
| 2005 — Silver Proof | £45 |
| 2005 — Gold Proof | £1100 |
| 2005 Rocket and Evening Star | £15 |
| 2005 — Silver proof | £45 |
| 2005 — Silver/Gold proof | £500 |
| 2005 — Gold proof | £1200 |
| 2005 200th Anniversary of the Battle of Trafalgar | £30 |
| 2005 Andrew Cunningham | £20 |
| 2005 — Silver proof | £60 |
| 2005 — Gold proof | £1200 |
| 2005 HMS Conqueror | £15 |
| 2005 — Silver proof | £20 |
| 2005 — Gold proof | £1200 |
| 2005 Battle of Trafalgar | £15 |
| 2005 — Silver proof | £45 |
| 2005 — Gold proof (9mm) | £500 |
| 2005 — Gold proof (38.6mm) | £1200 |
| 2005 Returning Evacuees | £15 |
| 2005 — Silver proof | £45 |
| 2005 — Gold proof | £1200 |
| 2005 Searchlights and Big Ben | £15 |
| 2005 — Silver proof | £45 |
| 2005 — Gold proof | £1200 |
| 2006 60th Anniversary of the Liberation of the Channel Islands | £30 |
| 2006 80th Birthday of Her Majesty the Queen (3-coin set) | — |
| 2006 Sir Winston Churchill | £15 |
| 2006 — Silver proof | £45 |
| 2006 — Gold proof | £1200 |
| 2006 Charles Darwin | £15 |
| 2006 — Silver proof | £45 |
| 2006 — Gold proof | £1200 |
| 2006 Bobby Moore | £20 |
| 2006 — Silver Proof | £55 |
| 2006 — Gold Proof | £1250 |
| 2006 Florence Nightingale | £20 |
| 2006 — Silver proof | £55 |
| 2006 — Gold proof | £1200 |
| 2006 Queen Mother | £20 |
| 2006 — Silver proof | £55 |
| 2006 — Gold proof | £1200 |
| 2006 Henry VIII | £15 |
| 2006 — Silver proof | £55 |
| 2006 — Gold proof | £1200 |
| 2006 Princess Diana | £20 |
| 2006 — Silver Proof | £60 |
| 2006 — Gold Proof | £1350 |
| 2006 Sir Christopher Wren | £15 |
| 2006 — Silver proof | £55 |
| 2006 — Gold proof | £1200 |
| 2006 HM the Queen's 80th Birthday — Streamers | £15 |
| 2006 — Silver proof | £55 |
| 2006 — Gold proof | £1200 |
| 2006 HM the Queen's 80th Birthday — Trooping colour | £20 |
| 2006 — Proof | £60 |

| DATE | UNC |
|------|-----|
| 2006 — Silver proof............................................................ | £1100 |
| 2006 — Silver/Gold proof................................................. | £650 |
| 2006 — Gold proof............................................................ | £1200 |
| 2006 HM the Queen's 80th Birthday—Wembley Stadium ...... | £20 |
| 2006 — Silver proof........................................................... | £55 |
| 2006 — Gold proof............................................................ | £1200 |
| 2006 Guy Gibson .............................................................. | £15 |
| 2006 — Silver proof........................................................... | £55 |
| 2006 — Gold proof............................................................ | £1200 |
| 2006 Eric James Nicholson................................................ | £15 |
| 2006 — Silver proof........................................................... | £55 |
| 2006 — Gold proof............................................................ | £1200 |
| 2006 Hook, Chard and Bromhead ...................................... | £15 |
| 2006 — Silver proof........................................................... | £55 |
| 2006 — Gold proof............................................................ | £1200 |
| 2006 1st Lancs Fusiliers .................................................... | £15 |
| 2006 — Silver proof........................................................... | £55 |
| 2006 — Gold proof............................................................ | £1200 |
| 2006 Noel Chavasse ......................................................... | £15 |
| 2006 — Silver proof........................................................... | £55 |
| 2006 — Gold proof............................................................ | £1200 |
| 2006 David Mackay............................................................ | £15 |
| 2006 — Silver proof........................................................... | £55 |
| 2006 — Gold proof............................................................ | £1200 |
| 2006 Coronation Scot. Silver proof ................................... | £60 |
| 2006 Flying Scotsman. Silver proof ................................... | £60 |
| 2006 Fireman and Driver. Silver proof ............................... | £60 |
| 2006 Box Tunnel. Silver proof ........................................... | £60 |
| 2007 Diamond Wedding balcony scene waving ................... | £15 |
| 2007 — Silver proof........................................................... | £60 |
| 2007 Diamond Wedding cake ............................................ | £15 |
| 2007 — Silver proof........................................................... | £60 |
| 2007 Diamond Wedding balcony scene waving ................... | £15 |
| 2007 —Silver proof............................................................ | £60 |
| 2007 Diamond Wedding HM the Queen and Prince Philip ..... | £20 |
| 2007 — Silver proof........................................................... | £60 |
| 2007 Diamond Wedding arrival at Abbey............................ | £20 |
| 2007 — Silver proof........................................................... | £55 |
| 2007 — Gold proof............................................................ | £1200 |
| 2008 George & Dragon....................................................... | £20 |
| 2008 Dambusters, Wallis, Chadwick, Gibson ..................... | £15 |
| 2008 — Silver/Copper proof ............................................. | £30 |
| 2008 — Silver proof........................................................... | £55 |
| 2008 Frank Whittle ............................................................ | £15 |
| 2008 — Silver proof........................................................... | £55 |
| 2008 — Gold proof............................................................ | £1200 |
| 2008 R. J. Mitchell............................................................. | £15 |
| 2008 — Silver proof........................................................... | £55 |
| 2008 — Gold proof............................................................ | £1200 |
| 2008 Maj. Gen. Sir Hugh Trenchard .................................. | £15 |
| 2008 — Silver proof........................................................... | £55 |
| 2008 — Gold proof............................................................ | £1200 |
| 2008 Bomber Command...................................................... | £15 |
| 2008 — Silver proof........................................................... | £55 |
| 2008 — Gold proof............................................................ | £1200 |
| 2008 Coastal Command ..................................................... | £20 |
| 2008 — Silver proof........................................................... | £60 |
| 2008 — Gold proof............................................................ | £1300 |
| 2008 Fighter Command ...................................................... | £20 |
| 2008 — Silver proof........................................................... | £60 |
| 2008 — Gold proof............................................................ | £1300 |
| 2008 Battle of Britain......................................................... | £20 |
| 2008 — Silver proof........................................................... | £60 |
| 2008 — Gold proof............................................................ | £1300 |
| 2008 RBL Poppy ............................................................... | £20 |
| 2008 — Silver proof........................................................... | £60 |
| 2008 — Gold proof............................................................ | £1300 |

| DATE | UNC |
|---|---|
| 2008 Flying Legends | £15 |
| 2008 — Silver proof | £55 |
| 2008 — Gold proof | £1200 |
| 2009 George & Dragon. Silver proof | £500 |
| 2009 Battle of Agincourt. Silver proof | £55 |
| 2009 Battle of the Somme. Silver proof | £55 |
| 2009 Capt. Cook and *Endeavour*. Silver proof | £55 |
| 2009 500th Anniversary of Accession of Henry VIII. Silver proof | £55 |
| 2011 Landmark birthdays of HM the Queen & Prince Philip | £15 |
| 2011 90th Anniversary of the British Legion (poppy-shaped) | £40 |
| 2011 — Silver proof | £95 |
| 2011 — 5oz silver | £500 |
| 2011 — Gold proof | £2500 |
| 2011 30th Birthday of the Duke of Cambridge. Silver proof | £50 |
| 2011 Wedding of Prince William and Kate Middleton. Silver proof | £50 |
| 2011 Spirit of the Nation (4 coins). Silver proof, each | £50 |
| 2012 HM the Queen's Diamond Jubilee. Gold proof | £2000 |

## TWO POUNDS FIFTY PENCE

| | |
|---|---|
| 1972 Royal Silver Wedding | £22 |
| 1972 — Silver proof | £33 |

## TWO POUNDS

(note all modern Proof coins have frosted relief)

| | |
|---|---|
| 1972 Royal Silver Wedding. Silver | £22 |
| 1972 — Silver proof | £35 |
| 1981 Royal Wedding, nickel silver (crown size) | £4 |
| 1981 — in presentation pack | £7 |
| 1981 — Silver proof | £20 |
| 1981 — Gold proof | £450 |
| 1985 40th Anniversary of Liberation (crown size) | £5 |
| 1985 — in presentation pack | £12 |
| 1985 — Silver proof | £20 |
| 1985 — Gold proof | £1365 |
| 1986 Commonwealth Games | £6 |
| 1986 — in presentation case | £8 |
| 1986 — .500 silver | £12 |
| 1986 — .925 silver proof | £20 |
| 1987 World Wildlife Fund 25th Anniversary | £80 |
| 1987 — Silver proof | £25 |
| 1989 Royal Visit | £14 |
| 1989 — Silver proof | £25 |
| 1990 Queen Mother's 90th Birthday | £14 |
| 1990 — Silver proof | £25 |
| 1990 — Gold proof | £600 |
| 1990 50th Anniversary of the Battle of Britain, silver proof | £30 |
| 1993 40th Anniversary of the Coronation | £14 |
| 1993 — Silver proof | £20 |
| 1993— Gold proof | £600 |
| 1995 50th Anniversary of Liberation | £14 |
| 1995 — Silver Proof | £25 |
| 1995 — — Piedfort | £75 |
| 1996 HM the Queen's 70th Birthday | £14 |
| 1996 — Silver proof | £25 |
| 1997 Bi-metal | £5 |
| 1997 — Silver proof | £50 |
| 1997 — new portrait | £5 |
| 1998 — | £5 |
| 2003 — | £5 |
| 2005 — | £5 |
| 2006 — | £5 |
| 2007 — | £5 |
| 2011 Prince Philip's 90th Birthday | £12 |
| 2012 HM the Queen's Diamond Jubilee. Gold proof | £1000 |

DATE | UNC

**ONE POUND**

1972 Royal Silver Wedding ........................................................................ £15
1972 — Silver proof............................................................................ £20
1981.................................................................................................. £15
1981 Silver proof ............................................................................... £15
1981 Gold proof ................................................................................. £320
1983 New designs and specifications on presentation card (St Helier)..... £4
1983 — Silver proof............................................................................ £18
1983 — Gold  proof............................................................................ £395
1984 Presentation wallet (St Saviour)................................................... £21
1984 — Silver proof............................................................................ £45
1984 — Gold  proof............................................................................ £450
1984 Presentation wallet (St Brelade) .................................................. £20
1984 — Silver proof............................................................................ £45
1984 — Gold  proof............................................................................ £490
1985 Presentation wallet (St Clement) .................................................. £25
1985 — Silver proof............................................................................ £45
1985 — Gold  proof............................................................................ £490
1985 Presentation wallet (St Lawrence) ................................................ £25
1985 — Silver proof............................................................................ £40
1985 — Gold  proof............................................................................ £490
1986 Presentation wallet (St Peter) ...................................................... £16
1986 — Silver proof............................................................................ £35
1986 — Gold  proof............................................................................ £490
1986 Presentation wallet (Grouville) ..................................................... £18
1986 — Silver proof............................................................................ £40
1986 — Gold  proof............................................................................ £490
1987 Presentation wallet (St Martin)..................................................... £18
1987 — Silver proof............................................................................ £40
1987 — Gold  proof............................................................................ £490
1987 Presentation wallet (St Ouen) ...................................................... £12
1987 — Silver proof............................................................................ £40
1987 — Gold  proof............................................................................ £490
1988 Presentation wallet (Trinity)......................................................... £13
1988 — Silver proof............................................................................ £40
1988 — Gold  proof............................................................................ £490
1988 Presentation wallet (St John)....................................................... £14
1988 — Silver proof............................................................................ £40
1988 — Gold  proof............................................................................ £490
1989 Presentation wallet (St Mary)....................................................... £14
1989 — Silver proof............................................................................ £40
1989 — Gold  proof............................................................................ £490

**1991 Ship Building in Jersey Series**

1991 "Tickler". Nickel-brass ................................................................ £5
1991 "Tickler". Silver proof................................................................. £25
1991 — Gold proof Piedfort ................................................................ £490
1991 "Percy Douglas". Nickel-brass .................................................... £5
1991 "Percy Douglas". Silver proof ..................................................... £25
1991 — Gold proof Piedfort ................................................................ £450
1992 "The Hebe". Nickel-brass............................................................ £5
1992 "The Hebe". Silver proof............................................................. £25
1992 — Gold proof Piedfort ................................................................ £490
1992 "Coat of Arms". Nickel-brass ...................................................... £5
1992 "Coat of Arms". Silver proof ....................................................... £25
1992 — Gold proof Piedfort ................................................................ £450
1993 "The Gemini". Nickel-brass ......................................................... £5
1993 "The Gemini". Silver proof .......................................................... £25
1993 — Gold proof Piedfort ................................................................ £490
1993 "The Century". Nickel-brass........................................................ £5
1993 "The Century". Silver proof ......................................................... £25
1993 — Gold proof Piedfort ................................................................ £490
1994 "Resolute". Nickel-brass ............................................................. £5

| DATE | UNC |
|---|---|
| 1994 "Resolute". Silver proof | £25 |
| 1994 — Gold proof Piedfort | £490 |
| 1997 — Nickel-brass | £5 |
| 1998 — — Nickel-brass | £5 |
| 2003 — — Nickel-brass | £5 |
| 2005 — — Nickel-brass | £5 |
| 2006 — — Nickel-brass | £5 |
| 2007 Diana Commem. Gold proof | £280 |
| 2012 Diamond Jubilee. Gold Proof £1 | — |
| 2012 Anniversary of the *Titanic* | — |

**FIFTY PENCE**

| | |
|---|---|
| 1969 | £10 |
| 1972 Royal Silver Wedding. Silver | £11 |
| 1972 — Silver proof | £11 |
| 1980 — | £1 |
| 1980 Arms | £2 |
| 1980 — Proof | £5 |
| 1981 — | £1 |
| 1981 — | £5 |
| 1981 — Proof | £5 |
| 1983 Grosnez Castle | £10 |
| 1983 — Silver proof | £12 |
| 1984 — | £2 |
| 1985 40th Anniversary of Liberation | £3 |
| 1986 | £5 |
| 1986 | £5 |
| 1987 | £5 |
| 1988 | £5 |
| 1989 | £5 |
| 1990 | £5 |
| 1992 | £5 |
| 1994 | £5 |
| 1997 | £5 |
| 1997 Smaller size | £4 |
| 1998 — | £3 |
| 2003 | £3 |
| 2003 Coronation Anniversary (4 types) | £4 |
| 2003 — 4 types. Silver proof | £15 |
| 2005 | £4 |
| 2006 | £4 |
| 2009 | £4 |
| 2011 Diamond Jubilee (full colour reverse, gold-plated) | £15 |

**TWENTY-FIVE PENCE**

| | |
|---|---|
| 1977 Royal Jubilee | £3 |
| 1977 — Silver proof | £20 |

**TWENTY PENCE**

| | |
|---|---|
| 1982 Corbiere Lighthouse (cased) | £8 |
| 1982 — Silver proof piedfort | £35 |
| 1983 — Obv. with date, rev. no date on rocks | £5 |
| 1983 — — Silver proof | £15 |
| 1984 — | £1 |
| 1986 — | £1 |
| 1987 — | £1 |
| 1989 — | £1 |
| 1992 — | £1 |
| 1994 — | £1 |
| 1996 — | £1 |
| 1997 — | £1 |
| 1998 — | £1 |

| DATE | UNC |
|---|---|
| 2002 — | £1 |
| 2003 — | £1 |
| 2005 — | £1 |
| 2006 — | £1 |
| 2007 — | £1 |
| 2009 — | £1 |

### SOVEREIGN—Gold sovereign size
| | |
|---|---|
| 1999 The Millennium. King William on Throne | £250 |
| 1999 — Gold proof | £300 |

### TEN PENCE
| | |
|---|---|
| 1968 Arms | £1 |
| 1975 Arms | £1 |
| 1979 (dated 1975 on thick flan) | £2 |
| 1980 — | £1 |
| 1980 — Proof | £5 |
| 1981 - | £1 |
| 1981 — Proof | £5 |
| 1983 L'Hermitage | £1 |
| 1983 — Silver proof | £5 |
| 1984 — | £1 |
| 1985 — | £1 |
| 1986 — | £1 |
| 1987 — | £1 |
| 1988 — | £1 |
| 1989 — | £1 |
| 1990 — | £1 |
| 1992 — | £1 |
| 1997 — | £1 |
| 2002 — | £1 |
| 2003 — | £1 |
| 2005 — | £1 |
| 2006 — | £1 |
| 2007 — | £1 |

### FIVE PENCE
| | |
|---|---|
| 1968 Arms | £1 |
| 1980 — | £1 |
| 1981 — | £1 |
| 1981 — Proof | £2 |
| 1983 Seymour Towers | £1 |
| 1983 — Silver proof | £5 |
| 1984 — | £1 |
| 1985 — | £1 |
| 1986 — | £1 |
| 1987 — | £2 |
| 1988 — | £1 |
| 1990 — | £1 |
| 1991 — | £1 |
| 1992 — | £5 |
| 1993 — | £1 |
| 1997 — | £4 |
| 1998 — | £1 |
| 2002 — | £1 |
| 2003 — | £1 |
| 2005 — | £5 |
| 2006 — | £1 |
| 2008 — | £1 |

Other denominations are generally available at face value or a small premium above.

DATE UNC

## ONE THOUSAND POUNDS
2003 Concorde. Gold proof....................................................... —
2004 D-Day Anniversary. Gold proof......................................... —
2011 Royal Wedding of Prince William and Catherine Middleton............. —

## ONE HUNDRED POUNDS
1994 50th Anniversary of D-Day Landings. Gold proof ........................... £280
2003 Prince Wiliam. Gold proof (100mm) .................................. —
2005 Trafalgar Anniversary. Gold proof (100mm)...................................... —

## FIFTY POUNDS
1994 50th Anniversary of D-Day Landing. Gold proof............................ £500
2003 Anniversay of Coronation (4 types). Silver proof ea. (100mm) ......... £500
2003 Prince William. Silver proof (100mm)............................... £500
2004 Anniversary of D-Day. Silver proof (100mm) .................................... £500
2005 200th Anniversary of the Battle of Trafalgar. Silver proof (100mm)... £500

## TWENTY FIVE POUNDS
1993 40th Anniversary of Coronation. Gold proof.............................. £200
1994 50th Anniversary of D-Day Landings. Gold proof ........................... £200
1997 Royal Golden Wedding. Gold proof ................................ £295
1997 — Silver proof......................................................... £40
1999 Winston Churchill. Gold proof ..................................... £350
2000 Queen Mother. Gold proof........................................... £325
2000 60th Anniversary of the Battle of Britain. Gold proof ..................... £275
2001 Royal Birthday. Gold proof ........................................ £300
2002 Golden Jubilee. Gold proof ........................................ £295
2002 Princess Diana. Gold proof ........................................ £295
2002 Duke of Wellington. Gold proof .................................... £300
2003 Prince William. Gold proof......................................... £300
2003 HMS Mary Rose. Gold proof....................................... £300
2004 D-Day Anniversary. Gold proof..................................... £395
2004 The Rocket. Gold proof............................................. £295
2004 Merchant Navy Class Locomotive. Gold proof ....................... £295
2005 Battle of SAints Passage. Gold proof................................ £295
2006 World Cup 2006 (4 Coins). Gold ea................................. £350

## TEN POUNDS
1994 50th Anniversary of D-Day Landing. Gold proof............................ £150
2003 Concorde. Silver proof (65mm) ..................................... £280
2005 60th Anniversary of the Liberation of the Channel Islands (65mm)... £250
2007 80th Birthday of Her Majesty the Queen (65mm)............................ £180
2008 Concorde. Silver proof ............................................ £180
2008 90th Anniversary of the end of WWI. Silver Proof ........................... £180
2009 50th Anniversary of the Mini—Silver with colour................... £180
2012 Prince William's 30th Birthday ..................................... —

## FIVE POUNDS
1995 Queen Mother ..................................................... £15
1995 — Silver proof........................................................ £50
1995 — Silver piedfort.................................................... £155
1995 — Gold proof........................................................ £900
1996 HM the Queen's 70th Birthday ..................................... £18
1996 — Silver proof....................................................... £60
1996 — Silver piedfort.................................................... £150
1996 — Gold proof...................................................... £1000
1999 Eclipse of the Sun ................................................ £25
1999 — Silver proof with colour centre................................... £55
1999 Winston Churchill. Gold proof .................................... £1000
2000 60th Anniversary of the Battle of Britain........................... £22
2000 — Silver proof...................................................... £55
2000 Queen Mother. 100th Birthday. Silver proof ...................... £50
2000 Millennium. Silver proof........................................... £35

| DATE | UNC |
|------|-----|
| 2001 HM Queen's 75th Birthday. | £15 |
| 2001 — Silver proof | £45 |
| 2002 Golden Jubilee. Silver proof | £50 |
| 2002 50 Years of Reign. | £15 |
| 2002 —Silver proof | £50 |
| 2002 Diana memorial | £15 |
| 2002 — Silver proof | £45 |
| 2002 — Gold proof | £900 |
| 2002 Duke of Wellington | £20 |
| 2002 — Silver proof | £50 |
| 2002 — Gold proof | £900 |
| 2003 Prince William | £20 |
| 2003 — Silver proof | £50 |
| 2003 — Gold proof | £900 |
| 2003 Mary Rose | £18 |
| 2003 — Silver proof | £120 |
| 2003 Alfred the Great. Silver proof | £150 |
| 2003 —Gold proof | £300 |
| 2003 Last Flight of Concorde | £25 |
| 2003 — Silver proof | £150 |
| 2003 — Gold proof | £395 |
| 2004 Anniversary of D-Day | £20 |
| 2004 — Silver proof | £75 |
| 2004 — Gold proof | £40 |
| 2004 Florence Nightingale | 318 |
| 2004 — Silver proof | £45 |
| 2004 150th Anniversary of the Crimean War | £20 |
| 2004 — Silver proof | £45 |
| 2004 — Gold proof | £395 |
| 2004 The Rocket | £20 |
| 2004 — Silver proof | £45 |
| 2004 — Gold proof | £875 |
| 2004 Royal Scot | £20 |
| 2004 — Silver proof | £45 |
| 2004 Merchant Navy Class Locomotive | £20 |
| 2004 — Silver proof | £45 |
| 2005 End of WWII. Silver proof | £45 |
| 2005 — Gold proof | £875 |
| 2005 200th Anniversary of the Battle of Trafalgar | £16 |
| 2005 — Silver proof | £50 |
| 2005 History of the Royal Navy. John Woodward. Silver proof | £30 |
| 2005 Anniversary of Liberation. Gold proof | £780 |
| 2005 Anniversary of the Battle of Saints Passage | £15 |
| 2005 — Silver proof | £45 |
| 2005 HMS Revenge 1591 | £15 |
| 2005 — Silver proof | £45 |
| 2006 80th Birthday of Her Majesty the Queen (3-coin set) ea | £20 |
| 2006 Gold plated portraits of Her Majesty the Queen | — |
| 2006 80th Birthday of Her Majesty the Queen (3-coin set) ea | £16 |
| 2007 History of the Royal Navy—*Mary Rose* (2 coins) ea | £16 |
| 2007 150th Anniversary of the Victoria Cross (18 coin set). Silver proof | — |
| 2007 Monarchs of England (12 coin set). Gold plated | — |
| 2008 90th Anniversary of the end of WWI (3 coins). Gold proof | — |
| 2008 Classic British Motorcars (18 coin set). Silver proof. | — |
| 2008 Concorde. Gold proof. | £300 |
| 2009 50th Anniversary of the Mini (4 coins). Silver proof ea. | £25 |
| 2011 Royal Engagement gold proof | £300 |
| 2011 — Gold plated silver proof | £150 |
| 2011 — Silver proof | £55 |
| 2011 — Curpro Nickel | £15 |
| 2011 John Lennon Silver proof | £55 |
| 2011 Battle of Britain 70th Anniversary silver proof | £55 |
| 2012 RMS *Titanic* | — |

DATE                                                                UNC

## TWO POUNDS
| | |
|---|---|
| 1989 Royal Visit | £12 |
| 1989 — Silver proof | £25 |
| 1989 — Silver piedfort | £45 |
| 1989 — Gold proof | £1200 |
| 1990 Queen Mother's 90th Birthday | £12 |
| 1990 — Silver proof | £25 |
| 1990 — Silver piedfort | £45 |
| 1990 — Gold proof | £1200 |
| 1992 40th Anniversary of Accession | £15 |
| 1992 — Silver proof | £35 |
| 1992 — Silver piedfort | £50 |
| 1992 — Gold proof | £1200 |
| 1993 40th Anniversary of Coronation | £15 |
| 1993 — Silver proof | £35 |
| 1993 — Silver piedfort | £50 |
| 1994 50th Anniversary of D-Day Landings | £15 |
| 1994 — Silver proof | £35 |
| 1994 — Silver piedfort | £50 |
| 1995 50th Anniversary of Return of Islanders | £15 |
| 1995 — Silver proof | £35 |
| 1995 — Silver piedfort | £50 |
| 1995 — Gold proof | £1200 |
| 1997 WWF Puffin | £18 |
| 1997 — Silver proof | £35 |
| 1997 Royal Golden Wedding | £20 |
| 1997 — Silver proof | £50 |
| 1999 Eclipse of the Sun. Silver | £20 |
| 1999 — Silver proof | £50 |
| 1999 — Gold proof | £1250 |
| 2000 Millennium. Silver proof | £50 |

## ONE POUND
| | |
|---|---|
| 1993 40th Anniversary of Coronation Silver proof | £50 |
| 1995 50th Anniversary of VE Day Silver proof | £45 |
| 1995 — Gold proof | £500 |
| 2008 Concorde. Gold proof | £275 |
| 2009 50th Anniversary of the Mini. Gold proof | £375 |

*Alderney's coinage is often issued as part of a set incorporating coins from other countries. Illustrated is the special set issued to mark the 90th Anniversary of the end of World War I which also included coins from the Cayman and Solomon Islands as well as Alderney.*

# IRELAND

As in the English hammered section (q.v.) the prices given here are for the most common coins in the series. For a more specialised listing the reader is referred to Coincraft's Standard Catalogue of Scotland, Ireland, Channel Islands & Isle of Man, or other specialised publications. Collectors should be aware that with most of the coins of the Irish series there are many varieties struck at different mints. The coins listed are all silver unless mentioned otherwise. Another important factor to consider when collecting early Irish coins is that few examples exist in high grades.

|  | F | VF |
|---|---|---|

## HIBERNO-NORSE ISSUES (995–1155)
Penny, imitating English silver pennies,
many various types .............................. £210 £500

*Hiberno-Norse phase II example.*

## JOHN, Lord of Ireland (1185–99)
| | F | VF |
|---|---|---|
| Halfpenny, profile ................................. | | Extremely rare |
| Halfpenny, facing ................................. | £95 | £300 |
| Farthing ............................................... | £360 | £1000 |

## JOHN de COURCY, Lord of Ulster (1177–1205)
| | F | VF |
|---|---|---|
| Halfpenny ............................................. | | Extremely rare |
| Farthing ............................................... | £675 | £2750 |

*John Lord of Ireland penny.*

## JOHN as King of England and Lord of Ireland (c. 1199–1216)
| | F | VF |
|---|---|---|
| Penny ................................................... | £65 | £275 |
| Halfpenny ............................................. | £150 | £400 |
| Farthing ............................................... | £650 | £2200 |

## HENRY III (1216–72)
| | F | VF |
|---|---|---|
| Penny ................................................... | £65 | £300 |

## EDWARD I (1272–1307)
| | F | VF |
|---|---|---|
| Penny ................................................... | £65 | £300 |
| Halfpenny ............................................. | £65 | £300 |
| Farthing ............................................... | £140 | £400 |

*Henry III penny.*

*No Irish coins were struck for Edward II (1307–27).*

## EDWARD III (1327–77)
Halfpenny .............................................. Extremely rare

*No Irish coins were struck for Richard II (1377–99), Henry IV (1399–1413) or Henry V (1413–22).*

## HENRY VI (1422–61)
Penny ................................................... Extremely rare

*Edward I penny.*

| | F | VF |
|---|---|---|

# EDWARD IV (1461–83)

| | F | VF |
|---|---|---|
| "Anonymous crown" groat | £650 | £13000 |
| — penny | £1100 | — |
| "Titled crown" groat | £1600 | — |
| — halfgroat | | Extremely rare |
| — penny | | Extremely rare |
| Cross on rose/Sun groat | £1750 | — |
| Bust/Rose on sun double groat | £2250 | £6850 |
| — groat | £2250 | — |
| — halfgroat | | Extremely rare |
| — penny | | Extremely rare |
| Bust/Cross & pellets groat—First issue | £125 | £500 |
| — halfgroat | £600 | £1500 |
| — penny | £75 | £350 |
| — halfpenny | | Extremely rare |
| — Second (light) issue | £100 | £450 |
| — halfgroat | £650 | £1600 |
| — penny | £90 | £235 |
| — halfpenny | | Extremely rare |
| Bust/Rose on cross groat | £550 | £1400 |
| — penny | £65 | £195 |

Edward IV groat. "Anonymous crown" issue.

**Billon/Copper issues**

| | F | VF |
|---|---|---|
| Small crown/Cross farthing (1460–61) | £1700 | — |
| — half farthing ("Patrick") | £1050 | — |
| Large crown/Cross farthing (1462) | | Extremely rare |
| Patricius/Salvator farthing (1463–65) | £350 | £2000 |
| — half farthing | | Extremely rare |
| Shield/Rose on sun farthing | £175 | £850 |

Edward IV penny struck in Dublin.

# RICHARD III (1483–85)

| | F | VF |
|---|---|---|
| Bust/Rose on cross groat | £1100 | £3850 |
| — halfgroat | | Unique |
| — penny | | Unique |
| Bust/Cross and pellets penny | £100 | £3000 |
| Shield/Three-crowns groat | £650 | £2750 |

# HENRY VII (1485–1509)

*Early issues (1483–90)*

| | F | VF |
|---|---|---|
| Shield/Three crowns groat | £150 | £475 |
| — halfgroat | £260 | £585 |
| — penny | £625 | £2200 |
| — halfpenny | | Extremely rare |

*Later issues (1488–90)*

| | F | VF |
|---|---|---|
| Shield/Three crowns groat | £100 | £350 |
| — halfgroat | £200 | £600 |
| — penny | £500 | £1300 |
| Facing bust groat (1496–1505) | £125 | £350 |
| — halfgroat | £1100 | — |
| — penny | £950 | — |

Richard III bust/rose on cross groat.

# LAMBERT SIMNEL
## (as EDWARD VI, Pretender, 1487)

| | F | VF |
|---|---|---|
| Shield/Three crowns groat | £1250 | £4000 |

Henry VII groat.

| | F | VF |
|---|---|---|

# HENRY VIII (1509–47)

| | F | VF |
|---|---|---|
| "Harp" groat ................................ | £90 | £300 |
| — halfgroat.......................................... | £500 | £2300 |

*The "Harp" coins have crowned initials either side of the reverse harp,*
*e.g. HR (Henricus Rex), HA (Henry and Anne Boleyn), HI (Henry and Jane*
*Seymour), HK (Henry and Katherine Howard).*

Posthumous (Portrait) issues

| | F | VF |
|---|---|---|
| Sixpence ................................ | £140 | £475 |
| Threepence ........................................ | £150 | £525 |
| Threehalfpence.................................... | £510 | £1750 |
| Threefarthings .................................... | £650 | £2000 |

*Henry VIII Posthumous portrait issues threepence.*

# EDWARD VI (1547–53)

| | F | VF |
|---|---|---|
| Shilling (base silver) 1552 (MDLII).......... | £1000 | £3500 |
| Brass contemporary copy.................... | £90 | £365 |

# MARY (1553–54)

| | F | VF |
|---|---|---|
| Shilling 1553 (MDLIII)........................... | £850 | £3300 |
| Shilling 1554 (MDLIIII).......................... | | Extremely rare |
| Groat................................................ | | Extremely rare |
| Halfgroat............................................ | | Extremely rare |
| Penny ............................................... | | Extremely rare |

# PHILIP & MARY (1554–58)

| | F | VF |
|---|---|---|
| Shilling.............................................. | £350 | £1400 |
| Groat................................................ | £100 | £350 |
| Penny ............................................... | | Extremely rare |

# ELIZABETH I (1558–1603)

*Philip & Mary shilling*

*Base silver portrait coinage*

| | F | VF |
|---|---|---|
| Shilling.............................................. | £350 | £1400 |
| Groat................................................ | £180 | £685 |

*Fine silver, portrait coinage (1561)*

| | F | VF |
|---|---|---|
| Shilling.............................................. | £270 | £900 |
| Groat................................................ | £325 | £1100 |

*Third (base silver) shield coinage*

| | F | VF |
|---|---|---|
| Shilling ............................................. | £200 | £675 |
| Sixpence............................................ | £150 | £475 |

*Copper*

| | F | VF |
|---|---|---|
| Threepence........................................ | £200 | £675 |
| Penny ............................................... | £60 | £195 |
| Halfpenny .......................................... | £100 | £300 |

# JAMES I (1603–25)

| | F | VF |
|---|---|---|
| Shilling.............................................. | £100 | £395 |
| Sixpence............................................ | £75 | £235 |

## Coins struck under Royal Licence
## from 1613

| | F | VF |
|---|---|---|
| "Harrington" farthing (small size)........... | £55 | £195 |
| "Harrington" farthing (large size) ........... | £50 | £175 |
| "Lennox" farthing ............................... | £50 | £175 |

*Elizabeth I "fine" shilling of 1561.*

# CHARLES I (1625–49)

During the reign of Charles I and the Great Rebellion many coins were struck under unusual circumstances, making the series a difficult but fascinating area for study. Many of the "coins" were simply made from odd-shaped pieces of plate struck with the weight or value.

|  | F | VF |
|---|---|---|
| ## Coins struck under Royal Licence from 1625 | | |
| "Richmond" farthing | £45 | £150 |
| "Maltravers" farthing | £55 | £195 |
| "Rose" farthing | £45 | £175 |
| ## Siege money of the Irish Rebellion, 1642–49 | | |
| *"Inchiquin" Money (1642)* | | |
| Crown | £2200 | £5750 |
| Halfcrown | £1900 | £5000 |
| Shilling | | Extremely rare |
| Ninepence | | Extremely rare |
| Sixpence | | Extremely rare |
| Groat | | Extremely rare |
| | | |
| *"Dublin" Money (1643)* | | |
| Crown | £900 | £3300 |
| Halfcrown | £600 | £2500 |
| | | |
| *"Ormonde" Money (1643–44)* | | |
| Crown | £500 | £1300 |
| Halfcrown | £325 | £975 |
| Shilling | £130 | £450 |
| Sixpence | £130 | £450 |
| Groat | £120 | £350 |
| Threepence | £110 | £300 |
| Twopence | £475 | £1275 |
| *"Ormonde" gold coinage (1646)* | | |
| Double pistole. 2 known (both in museums) | | Extremely rare |
| Pistole. 10 known (only 1 in private ownership | | Extremely rare |
| | | |
| *"Ormonde" Money (1649)* | | |
| Crown | | Extremely rare |
| Halfcrown | £1200 | £3750 |
| | | |
| *Dublin Money 1649* | | |
| Crown | £2800 | £7750 |
| Halfcrown | £2200 | £4650 |

*Charles I "Ormonde" crown.*

### Issues of the Confederated Catholics

| *Kilkenny issues (1642–43)* | | |
|---|---|---|
| Halfpenny | £265 | £825 |
| Farthing | £390 | £1100 |
| | | |
| *Rebel Money (1643–44)* | | |
| Crown | £2500 | £5500 |
| Halfcrown | £2950 | £5500 |
| *"Blacksmith's" Money (16??)* | | |
| Imitation of English Tower halfcrown | £675 | £3000 |

*A rare Charles I "Rebel" halfcrown.*

|  | F | VF |
|---|---|---|

### Local Town issues of "Cities of Refuge"

*Bandon*
Farthing (copper) .................................. | | Extremely rare

*Cork*
| | F | VF |
|---|---|---|
| Shilling ................................................ | | Extremely rare |
| Sixpence.............................................. | £750 | £1200 |
| Halfpenny (copper) ............................... | | Extremely rare |
| Farthing (copper) ................................. | £560 | — |

*Kinsale*
| Farthing (copper) ................................. | £400 | — |
|---|---|---|

*Youghal*
| Farthing (copper) ................................. | £490 | £1850 |
|---|---|---|

*Halfpenny of Charles I.*

# CHARLES II (1660–85)

| | Fair | F | VF | EF |
|---|---|---|---|---|
| *"Armstrong" coinage* | | | | |
| Farthing (1660–61)................................ | £65 | £235 | — | — |
| | | | | |
| *"St Patrick's" coinage* | | | | |
| Halfpenny ............................................ | £225 | £465 | — | — |
| Farthing ............................................... | £65 | £165 | £500 | £1500 |
| | | | | |
| *Legg's Regal coinage* | | | | |
| Halfpennies | | | | |
| 1680 large lettering.............................. | £35 | £90 | £275 | — |
| 1681 large lettering.............................. | — | £195 | £675 | — |
| 1681 small lettering ............................. | | | Extremely rare | |
| 1682 small lettering ............................. | — | £195 | £625 | — |
| 1683 small lettering ............................. | £30 | £40 | £395 | — |
| 1684 small lettering ............................. | £40 | £110 | £650 | — |

# JAMES II (1685–88)

## REGAL COINAGE

**Halfpennies**
| | Fair | F | VF | EF |
|---|---|---|---|---|
| 1685..................................................... | £22 | £75 | £300 | £700 |
| 1686..................................................... | £22 | £60 | £200 | £600 |
| 1687..................................................... | | | Extremely rare | |
| 1688..................................................... | £22 | £85 | £300 | £1300 |

*"St Patrick" farthing of Charles II.*

|  | Fair | F | VF | EF |
|---|---|---|---|---|
| **EMERGENCY COINAGE** | | | | |

### GUN MONEY
*Most of these coins were struck in gun metal but a few rare specimens are also known struck in gold and in silver*

| | Fair | F | VF | EF |
|---|---|---|---|---|
| **Crowns** | | | | |
| 1690 (many varieties).....................from | £45 | £60 | £520 | — |
| **Large halfcrowns** | | | | |
| Dated July 1689–May 1690 | | | | |
| Prices from ........................................... | £35 | £60 | £200 | — |
| **Small halfcrowns** | | | | |
| Dated April–October1690 | | | | |
| Prices from ........................................... | £35 | £60 | £200 | — |
| **Large shillings** | | | | |
| Dated from July 1689–April 1690 | | | | |
| Prices from ........................................... | £35 | £55 | £120 | £450 |
| **Small shillings** | | | | |
| Dated from April–September 1690 | | | | |
| Prices from ........................................... | £25 | £35 | £120 | £400 |

"Gun Money" crown.

| | Fair | F | VF | EF |
|---|---|---|---|---|
| **Sixpences** | | | | |
| Dated from June 1689–October 1690 | | | | |
| Prices from ........................................... | £35 | £60 | £250 | — |
| ***PEWTER MONEY*** (1689–90) | | | | |
| Crown.................................................... | £700 | £1100 | £2950 | — |
| Groat.................................................... | | Extremely rare | | |
| Penny large bust.................................. | £230 | £650 | — | — |
| — small bust ....................................... | £165 | £485 | £1350 | — |
| Halfpenny large bust ........................... | £130 | £325 | £750 | — |
| — small bust ....................................... | £110 | £225 | £675 | — |
| ***LIMERICK MONEY*** (1690–91) | | | | |
| Halfpenny, reversed N in HIBERNIA...... | £35 | £75 | £245 | — |
| Farthing, reversed N in HIBERNIA........ | £35 | £75 | £245 | — |
| — normal N ......................................... | £45 | £100 | £275 | — |

# WILLIAM & MARY (1688–94)

| **Halfpennies** | Fair | F | VF | EF |
|---|---|---|---|---|
| 1692...................................................... | £12 | £40 | £100 | £600 |
| 1693...................................................... | £12 | £40 | £85 | £600 |
| 1694...................................................... | £20 | £45 | £110 | £645 |

# WILLIAM III (1694–1702)

| | Fair | F | VF | EF |
|---|---|---|---|---|
| 1696 Halfpenny draped bust................. | £35 | £65 | £220 | — |
| 1696 — crude undraped bust .............. | £45 | £265 | £850 | — |

William & Mary half-penny of 1693.

*No Irish coins were struck during the reign of Queen Anne (1706–11).*

| DATE | F | VF | EF | UNC |
|------|---|----|----|-----|

# GEORGE I (1714–27)

**Farthings**

| | | | | |
|--|--|--|--|--|
| 1722 D.G. REX Harp to left (Pattern) | £650 | £1550 | £2300 | — |
| 1723 D.G. REX Harp to right | £120 | £225 | £500 | — |
| 1723 DEI GRATIA REX Harp to right | £35 | £65 | £200 | £575 |
| 1723 — Silver Proof | — | — | — | £2100 |
| 1724 DEI GRATIA REX Harp to right | £60 | £130 | £350 | £850 |

**Halfpennies**

| | | | | |
|--|--|--|--|--|
| 1722 Holding Harp left | £55 | £130 | £385 | £950 |
| 1722 Holding Harp right | £45 | £110 | £350 | £795 |
| 1723/2 Harp right | £50 | £120 | £350 | £795 |
| 1723 Harp right | £25 | £65 | £200 | £500 |
| 1723 Silver Proof | — | — | — | £3500 |
| 1723 Obv. Rs altered from Bs | £35 | £100 | £265 | — |
| 1723 No stop after date | £25 | £80 | £265 | £475 |
| 1724 Rev. legend divided | £40 | £100 | £300 | — |
| 1724 Rev. legend continuous | £40 | £110 | £375 | — |

# GEORGE II (1727–60)

**Farthings**

| | | | | |
|--|--|--|--|--|
| 1737 | £35 | £60 | £175 | £425 |
| 1737 Proof | — | — | — | £450 |
| 1737 Silver Proof | — | — | — | £900 |
| 1738 | £35 | £65 | £165 | £420 |
| 1744 | £35 | £65 | £165 | £420 |
| 1760 | £30 | £45 | £100 | £325 |

*Halfpenny of George II*

**Halfpennies**

| | | | | |
|--|--|--|--|--|
| 1736 | £25 | £60 | £200 | £450 |
| 1736 Proof | — | — | — | £625 |
| 1736 Silver Proof | — | — | — | £1300 |
| 1737 | £25 | £45 | £175 | — |
| 1738 | £30 | £60 | £200 | — |
| 1741 | £30 | £60 | £200 | — |
| 1742 | £30 | £60 | £200 | — |
| 1743 | £30 | £60 | £180 | — |
| 1744/3 | £30 | £60 | £185 | — |
| 1744 | £30 | £60 | £300 | — |
| 1746 | £30 | £60 | £235 | — |
| 1747 | £30 | £60 | £225 | — |
| 1748 | £30 | £60 | £225 | — |
| 1749 | £30 | £60 | £225 | — |
| 1750 | £30 | £60 | £225 | — |
| 1751 | £30 | £60 | £225 | — |
| 1752 | £30 | £60 | £225 | — |
| 1753 | £30 | £60 | £225 | — |
| 1755 | £30 | £100 | £315 | — |
| *1760 | £30 | £55 | £200 | — |

# GEORGE III (1760–1820)

*All copper unless otherwise stated*

**Pennies**

| | | | | |
|--|--|--|--|--|
| 1805 | £17 | £40 | £180 | £400 |
| 1805 Proof | — | — | — | £545 |
| 1805 in Bronze Proof | — | — | — | £550 |
| 1805 in Copper Gilt Proof | — | — | — | £550 |
| 1805 in Silver Proof (restrike) | — | — | — | £3200 |
| 1822 | £17 | £40 | £180 | £395 |

*George III proof penny 1805*

| DATE | F | VF | EF | UNC |
|------|-----|-----|------|------|
| 1822 Proof | — | — | — | £565 |
| 1823 | £12 | £25 | £150 | £375 |
| 1823 Proof | — | — | — | £565 |

**Halfpennies**

| | F | VF | EF | UNC |
|------|-----|-----|------|------|
| 1766 | £30 | £55 | £165 | — |
| 1769 | £30 | £55 | £165 | — |
| 1769 Longer bust | £40 | £75 | £200 | £595 |
| 1774 Pattern only Proof | — | — | — | £1950 |
| 1775 | £30 | £55 | £200 | £425 |
| 1775 Proof | — | — | — | £630 |
| 1776 | £55 | £140 | £400 | — |
| 1781 | £45 | £60 | £165 | £400 |
| 1782 | £45 | £60 | £165 | £400 |
| 1805 | £18 | £45 | £120 | £400 |
| 1805 Copper Proof | — | — | — | £400 |
| 1805 in Bronze | — | — | — | £275 |
| 1805 in Gilt Copper | — | — | — | £430 |
| 1805 in Silver (restrike) | — | — | — | £1775 |
| 1822 | £18 | £40 | £120 | £400 |
| 1822 Proof | — | — | — | £595 |
| 1823 | £18 | £40 | £120 | £400 |
| 1823 Proof | — | — | — | £645 |

*One of the scarcer dates, a
1776 George III halfpenny.*

*NB Prooflike Uncirculated Pennies and Halfpennies of 1822/23 are often misdescribed
as Proofs. The true Proofs are rare. Some are on heavier, thicker flans.*

**Farthings**

| | F | VF | EF | UNC |
|------|-----|-----|------|------|
| 1806 | £18 | £35 | £85 | £175 |
| 1806 Copper Proof | — | — | — | £350 |
| 1806 Bronzed Copper Proof | — | — | — | £250 |
| 1806 Copper Gilt Proof | — | — | — | £350 |
| 1806 Silver Proof (restrike) | — | — | — | £1100 |
| 1822 George IV (Pattern) Proof | — | — | — | £1750 |

## TOKEN ISSUES BY THE BANK OF IRELAND

**Five Pence in Silver**

| | F | VF | EF | UNC |
|------|-----|-----|------|------|
| 1805 | £30 | £45 | £75 | £330 |
| 1806 | £30 | £65 | £150 | £350 |
| 1806/5 | £55 | £140 | £450 | £1350 |

**Ten Pence in Silver**

| | F | VF | EF | UNC |
|------|-----|-----|------|------|
| 1805 | £17 | £35 | £95 | £225 |
| 1806 | £17 | £60 | £150 | £265 |
| 1813 | £17 | £35 | £90 | £250 |
| 1813 Proof | — | — | — | £425 |

**Thirty Pence in Silver**

| | F | VF | EF | UNC |
|------|-----|-----|------|------|
| 1808 | £40 | £95 | £230 | £575 |

**Six Shillings**

| | F | VF | EF | UNC |
|------|-----|-----|------|------|
| 1804 in Silver | £95 | £200 | £400 | £1700 |
| 1804 Proof | — | — | — | £1750 |
| 1804 in Copper (restrike) | — | — | — | £750 |
| 1804 Copper Gilt | — | — | — | £1700 |
| 1804 in Gilt Silver | — | — | — | £2950 |

*1804 six shillings.*

*In this series fully struck specimens, with sharp hair curls, etc., are worth appreciably
more than the prices quoted.*

**Our grateful thanks go to Del Parker, specialist in Irish rarities, for supplying the images
for this section. An impressive and extensive range of Irish coins can be viewed and
purchased at his website at www.irishcoins.com.**

# IRISH FREE STATE/EIRE

| DATE | F | VF | EF | UNC |
|---|---|---|---|---|

## TEN SHILLINGS

| | F | VF | EF | UNC |
|---|---|---|---|---|
| 1966 Easter Rising | — | £12 | £17 | £35 |
| 1966 Cased Proof | — | — | — | £40 |
| 1966 special double case | — | — | — | £70 |

## HALF CROWNS

| | F | VF | EF | UNC |
|---|---|---|---|---|
| 1928 | £7 | £12 | £40 | £80 |
| 1928 Proof | — | — | — | £85 |
| 1930 | £12 | £35 | £130 | £495 |
| 1931 | £12 | £35 | £165 | £530 |
| 1933 | £12 | £25 | £165 | £430 |
| 1934 | £12 | £12 | £55 | £250 |
| 1937 | £60 | £150 | £600 | £1600 |
| 1938 | | | | Unique |
| 1939 | £7 | £17 | £30 | £95 |
| 1939 Proof | — | — | — | £635 |
| 1940 | £8 | £13 | £35 | £85 |
| 1941 | £7 | £17 | £35 | £85 |
| 1942 | £7 | £130 | £35 | £80 |
| 1943 | £85 | £200 | £925 | £3300 |
| 1951 | £2 | £3 | £17 | £50 |
| 1951 Proof | — | — | — | £500 |
| 1954 | £2 | £3 | £9 | £75 |
| 1954 Proof | — | — | — | £500 |
| 1955 | £2 | £3 | £9 | £45 |
| 1955 | — | — | — | £590 |
| 1959 | £2 | £3 | £12 | £45 |
| 1961 | £2 | £3 | £25 | £55 |
| 1961 Obv as 1928, rev. as 1951 | £30 | £60 | £300 | — |
| 1962 | £2 | £3 | £6 | £32 |
| 1963 | £2 | £3 | £6 | £25 |
| 1964 | £2 | £3 | £6 | £25 |
| 1966 | £2 | £3 | £6 | £25 |
| 1967 | £2 | £3 | £6 | £25 |

## FLORINS

| | F | VF | EF | UNC |
|---|---|---|---|---|
| 1928 | £3 | £6 | £25 | £55 |
| 1928 Proof | — | — | — | £70 |
| 1930 | £4 | £12 | £140 | £445 |
| 1930 Proof | | | | Unique |
| 1931 | £5 | £19 | £170 | £445 |
| 1933 | £4 | £17 | £140 | £445 |
| 1934 | £6 | £110 | £240 | £695 |
| 1934 Proof | — | — | — | £3000 |
| 1935 | £3 | £12 | £65 | £190 |
| 1937 | £6 | £25 | £140 | £400 |
| 1939 | £2 | £6 | £35 | £75 |
| 1939 Proof | — | — | — | £650 |
| 1940 | £3 | £6 | £30 | £75 |
| 1941 | £3 | £6 | £35 | £70 |
| 1941 Proof | — | — | — | £800 |
| 1942 | £6 | £12 | £30 | £75 |
| 1943 | £2675 | £5250 | £9500 | £22200 |
| 1951 | 60p | £2 | £12 | £45 |
| 1951 Proof | — | — | — | £475 |
| 1954 | 60p | £2 | £9 | £40 |
| 1954 Proof | — | — | — | £375 |

| DATE | F | VF | EF | UNC |
|---|---|---|---|---|
| 1955........................................ | — | £2 | £6 | £40 |
| 1955 Proof............................... | — | — | — | £545 |
| 1959........................................ | 40p | £2 | £6 | £35 |
| 1961........................................ | 60p | £3 | £13 | £50 |
| 1962........................................ | 40p | £2 | £6 | £25 |
| 1963........................................ | 30p | £2 | £6 | £20 |
| 1964........................................ | 30p | £2 | £6 | £20 |
| 1965........................................ | 30p | £2 | £6 | £20 |
| 1966........................................ | 30p | £2 | £6 | £20 |
| 1968........................................ | 30p | £2 | £6 | £20 |

## SHILLINGS

| | F | VF | EF | UNC |
|---|---|---|---|---|
| 1928........................................ | £2 | £6 | £17 | £45 |
| 1928 Proof............................... | — | — | — | £70 |
| 1930........................................ | £6 | £25 | £95 | £450 |
| 1930 Proof............................... | — | — | — | £850 |
| 1931........................................ | £3 | £17 | £95 | £450 |
| 1933........................................ | £3 | £17 | £95 | £450 |
| 1935........................................ | £3 | £13 | £50 | £150 |
| 1937........................................ | £6 | £60 | £220 | £1200 |
| 1939........................................ | £2 | £6 | £25 | £60 |
| 1939 Proof............................... | — | — | — | £700 |
| 1940........................................ | £2 | £6 | £17 | £55 |
| 1941........................................ | £2 | £5 | £17 | £55 |
| 1942........................................ | £2 | £5 | £12 | £45 |
| 1951........................................ | 60p | £2 | £6 | £25 |
| 1951 Proof............................... | — | — | — | £450 |
| 1954........................................ | 60p | £2 | £6 | £25 |
| 1954 Proof............................... | — | — | — | £500 |
| 1955........................................ | 60p | £2 | £6 | £25 |
| 1959........................................ | 60p | £2 | £6 | £35 |
| 1962........................................ | 30p | £2 | £3 | £20 |
| 1963........................................ | 30p | £2 | £3 | £12 |
| 1964........................................ | 30p | £2 | £3 | £12 |
| 1966........................................ | 30p | £2 | £3 | £12 |
| 1968........................................ | 30p | £2 | £3 | £12 |

## SIXPENCES

| | F | VF | EF | UNC |
|---|---|---|---|---|
| 1928........................................ | 60p | £2 | £11 | £40 |
| 1928 Proof............................... | — | — | — | £50 |
| 1934........................................ | 60p | £3 | £17 | £90 |
| 1935........................................ | 85p | £3 | £25 | £125 |
| 1939........................................ | 60p | £2 | £6 | £50 |
| 1939 Proof............................... | — | — | — | £635 |
| 1940........................................ | 60p | £2 | £6 | £50 |
| 1942........................................ | 60p | £2 | £9 | £60 |
| 1945 ....................................... | £3 | £11 | £35 | £95 |
| 1946........................................ | £3 | £6 | £65 | £400 |
| 1947........................................ | £2 | £2 | £22 | £75 |
| 1948........................................ | 60p | £3 | £13 | £65 |
| 1949........................................ | 60p | £2 | £8 | £45 |
| 1950........................................ | £2 | £3 | £25 | £95 |
| 1952........................................ | 60p | £2 | £4 | £20 |
| 1953........................................ | 60p | £2 | £4 | £20 |
| 1953 Proof............................... | — | — | — | £115 |
| 1955........................................ | 60p | £2 | £4 | £22 |
| 1956........................................ | 60p | £2 | £3 | £22 |
| 1956 Proof............................... | — | — | — | £165 |
| 1958........................................ | £2 | £3 | £11 | £65 |
| 1958 Proof............................... | — | — | — | £375 |
| 1959........................................ | 30p | 60p | £3 | £15 |
| 1960........................................ | 30p | 60p | £2 | £15 |

| DATE | F | VF | EF | UNC |
|---|---|---|---|---|
| 1961 | — | £2 | £3 | £20 |
| 1962 | £2 | £6 | £30 | £70 |
| 1963 | 60p | £3 | £6 | £15 |
| 1964 | 60p | £2 | £4 | £10 |
| 1966 | 60p | £2 | £4 | £10 |
| 1967 | 60p | £2 | £2 | £8 |
| 1968 | 60p | £2 | £2 | £8 |
| 1969 | £2 | £3 | £6 | £15 |

## THREEPENCES

| | F | VF | EF | UNC |
|---|---|---|---|---|
| 1928 | £2 | £3 | £9 | £30 |
| 1928 Proof | — | — | — | £40 |
| 1933 | £3 | £13 | £70 | £365 |
| 1934 | 70p | £3 | £10 | £75 |
| 1935 | £2 | £4 | £30 | £225 |
| 1939 | £3 | £7 | £60 | £365 |
| 1939 Proof | — | — | — | £1150 |
| 1940 | £2 | £3 | £13 | £60 |
| 1942 | — | £2 | £6 | £45 |
| 1943 | £2 | £3 | £13 | £75 |
| 1946 | — | £1 | £6 | £40 |
| 1946 Proof | — | — | — | £270 |
| 1948 | £2 | £3 | £25 | £75 |
| 1949 | — | £2 | £6 | £35 |
| 1949 Proof | — | — | — | £235 |
| 1950 | — | £2 | £6 | £20 |
| 1950 Proof | — | — | — | £225 |
| 1953 | — | £2 | £4 | £15 |
| 1956 | — | £2 | £3 | £8 |
| 1961 | — | 60p | £2 | £5 |
| 1962 | — | 60p | £2 | £8 |
| 1963 | — | 60p | £2 | £8 |
| 1964 | — | 60p | £2 | £5 |
| 1965 | — | 60p | £2 | £5 |
| 1966 | — | 60p | £2 | £5 |
| 1967 | — | 60p | £2 | £5 |
| 1968 | — | — | £2 | £5 |

## PENNIES

| | F | VF | EF | UNC |
|---|---|---|---|---|
| 1928 | £2 | £3 | £11 | £45 |
| 1928 Proof | — | — | — | £55 |
| 1931 | £2 | £4 | £35 | £115 |
| 1931 Proof | — | — | — | £950 |
| 1933 | £2 | £5 | £50 | £225 |
| 1935 | 60p | £2 | £25 | £70 |
| 1937 | 90p | £2 | £35 | £120 |
| 1937 Proof | — | — | — | £950 |
| 1938 | | | | 2 known |
| 1940 | £6 | £30 | £140 | — |
| 1941 | 60p | £2 | £9 | £30 |
| 1942 | — | 60p | £4 | £15 |
| 1943 | — | £2 | £6 | £30 |
| 1946 | — | £2 | £4 | £15 |
| 1948 | — | £2 | £4 | £15 |
| 1949 | — | £2 | £4 | £15 |
| 1949 Proof | — | — | — | £395 |
| 1950 | — | £2 | £6 | £30 |
| 1952 | — | £2 | £4 | £10 |
| 1962 | — | £2 | £4 | £12 |
| 1962 Proof | — | — | — | £165 |
| 1963 | — | — | £2 | £10 |
| 1963 Proof | — | — | — | £100 |

| DATE | F | VF | EF | UNC |
|------|---|----|----|----|
| 1964 | — | — | £2 | £8 |
| 1965 | — | — | 60p | £5 |
| 1966 | — | — | 60p | £4 |
| 1967 | — | — | 60p | £4 |
| 1968 | — | — | 60p | £4 |
| 1968 Proof | — | — | — | £245 |

## HALFPENNIES

| | | | | |
|------|---|----|----|----|
| 1928 | £2 | £3 | £12 | £32 |
| 1928 Proof | — | — | — | £40 |
| 1933 | £6 | £17 | £65 | £500 |
| 1935 | £3 | £6 | £30 | £160 |
| 1937 | £2 | £4 | £12 | £50 |
| 1939 | £3 | £6 | £35 | £175 |
| 1939 Proof | — | — | — | £850 |
| 1940 | £2 | £4 | £50 | £180 |
| 1941 | 60p | £2 | £6 | £25 |
| 1942 | 60p | £2 | £6 | £25 |
| 1943 | 60p | £2 | £7 | £30 |
| 1946 | £2 | £3 | £17 | £70 |
| 1949 | 60p | £2 | £6 | £25 |
| 1953 | — | £2 | £3 | £10 |
| 1953 Proof | — | — | — | £495 |
| 1964 | — | — | 60p | £3 |
| 1965 | — | — | 90p | £4 |
| 1966 | — | — | 60p | £3 |
| 1967 | — | — | 60p | £3 |

## FARTHINGS

| | | | | |
|------|---|----|----|----|
| 1928 | £3 | £4 | £9 | £15 |
| 1928 Proof | — | — | — | £45 |
| 1930 | £3 | £4 | £9 | £30 |
| 1931 | £4 | £6 | £14 | £35 |
| 1931 Proof | — | — | — | £845 |
| 1932 | £4 | £6 | £17 | £45 |
| 1933 | £3 | £4 | £12 | £30 |
| 1935 | £4 | £6 | £17 | £35 |
| 1936 | £4 | £6 | £17 | £35 |
| 1937 | £3 | £4 | £12 | £30 |
| 1939 | £3 | £4 | £6 | £15 |
| 1939 Proof | — | — | — | £595 |
| 1940 | £4 | £5 | £8 | £20 |
| 1941 | £3 | £4 | £6 | £12 |
| 1943 | £3 | £4 | £6 | £12 |
| 1944 | £3 | £4 | £6 | £12 |
| 1946 | £3 | £4 | £6 | £12 |
| 1949 | £4 | £6 | £8 | £25 |
| 1949 Proof | — | — | — | £450 |
| 1953 | £3 | £4 | £5 | £8 |
| 1953 Proof | — | — | — | £315 |
| 1959 | £3 | £4 | £5 | £10 |
| 1966 | £3 | £4 | £5 | £10 |

*For the 1928–50 copper issues it is worth noting that UNC means UNC with some lustre. BU examples with full lustre are extremely elusive and are worth much more than the quoted prices.*

# IRISH DECIMAL COINAGE

| DATE | MINTAGE | BU |
|---|---|---|

**HALF PENCE**

| | | |
|---|---|---|
| 1971 | 100,500,000 | £5 |
| 1975 | 10,500,000 | £6 |
| 1976 | 5,500,000 | £6 |
| 1978 | 20,300,000 | £5 |
| 1980 | 20,600,000 | £4 |
| 1982 | 9,700,000 | £4 |
| 1985 | 2,800,000 | Rare |
| 1986. Only issued in the 1986 set | 19,750,000 | £325 |

**ONE PENNY**

| | | |
|---|---|---|
| 1971 | 100,500,000 | £3 |
| 1974 | 10,000,000 | £10 |
| 1975 | 10,000,000 | £15 |
| 1976 | 38,200,000 | £5 |
| 1978 | 25,700,000 | £8 |
| 1979 | 21,800,000 | £10 |
| 1980 | 86,700,000 | £3 |
| 1982 | 54,200,000 | £5 |
| 1985 | 19,200,000 | £8 |
| 1986 | 36,600,000 | £5 |
| 1988 | 56,800,000 | £5 |
| 1990 | 65,100,000 | £5 |
| 1992 | 25,600,000 | £6 |
| 1993 | 10,000,000 | £6 |
| 1994 | 45,800,000 | £5 |
| 1995 | 70,800,000 | £3 |
| 1996 | 190,100,000 | 95p |
| 1998 | 40,700,000 | 95p |
| 2000 | Unknown | 95p |

**TWO PENCE**

| | | |
|---|---|---|
| 1971 | 75,500,000 | £3 |
| 1975 | 20,000,000 | £8 |
| 1976 | 5400,000 | £10 |
| 1978 | 12,000,000 | £10 |
| 1979 | 32,400,000 | £8 |
| 1980 | 59,800,000 | £6 |
| 1982 | 30,400,000 | £5 |
| 1985 | 14,500,000 | £6 |
| 1986 | 23,900,000 | £6 |
| 1988 | 35,900,000 | £5 |
| 1990 | 34,300,000 | £5 |
| 1992 | 10,200,000 | £8 |
| 1995 | 55,500,000 | £5 |
| 1996 | 69,300,000 | £2 |
| 1998 | 33,700,000 | £2 |
| 2000 | Unknown | 95p |

**FIVE PENCE**

| | | |
|---|---|---|
| 1969 Toned | 5,000,000 | £5 |
| 1970 | 10,000,000 | £5 |
| 1971 | 8,000,000 | £6 |
| 1974 | 7,000,000 | £8 |
| 1975 | 10,000,000 | £8 |
| 1976 | 20,600,000 | £5 |
| 1978 | 28,500,000 | £5 |
| 1980 | 22,200,000 | £5 |
| 1982 | 24,400,000 | £4 |
| 1985 | 4,200,000 | £8 |
| 1986 | 15,300,000 | £5 |
| 1990 | 7,500,000 | £5 |

| DATE | MINTAGE | BU |
|---|---|---|
| Size reduced to 18.4mm | | |
| 1992 | 74,500,000 | £5 |
| 1993 | 89,100,000 | £5 |
| 1994 | 31,100,000 | £5 |
| 1995 | 12,000,000 | £5 |
| 1996 | 14,700,000 | £2 |
| 1998 | 158,500,000 | 75p |
| 2000 | Unknown | 75p |

**TEN PENCE**

| | | |
|---|---|---|
| 1969 | 27,000,000 | £8 |
| 1971 | 4,000,000 | £10 |
| 1973 | 2,500,000 | £16 |
| 1974 | 7,500,000 | £12 |
| 1975 | 15,000,000 | £12 |
| 1976 | 9,400,000 | £12 |
| 1978 | 30,900,000 | £10 |
| 1980 | 44,600,000 | £7 |
| 1982 | 7,400,000 | £7 |
| 1985 | 4,100,000 | £8 |
| 1986. Only issued in the 1986 set | 11,280 | £265 |

| Size reduced to 22mm | | |
|---|---|---|
| 1993 | 80,100,000 | £5 |
| 1994 | 58,500,000 | £5 |
| 1995 | 16,100,000 | £5 |
| 1996 | 18,400,000 | £3 |
| 1997 | 10,000,000 | £3 |
| 1998 | 10,000,000 | £3 |
| 1999 | 24,500,000 | £2 |
| 2000 | Unknown | £1.50 |

## TWENTY PENCE

1985. Only 600 minted and 556 melted down, only 3 known   Extremely rare
1986............................................................. 50,400,000   £6
1988............................................................. 20,700,000   £6
1992............................................................. 14,800,000   £5
1994............................................................. 11,100,000   £5
1995............................................................. 18,200,000   £5
1996............................................................. 29,300,000   £5
1998............................................................. 25,000,000   £3
1999............................................................. 11,000,000   £3
2000................................................................. Unknown   £2

## FIFTY PENCE

1970................................................................ 9,000,000   £7
1971.................................................................. 650,000   £6
1974................................................................ 1,000,000   £55
1975................................................................ 2,000,000   £55
1976................................................................ 3,000,000   £45
1977................................................................ 4,800,000   £55
1978................................................................ 4,500,000   £45
1979................................................................ 4,000,000   £45
1981................................................................ 6,000,000   £25
1982................................................................ 2,000,000   £25
1983................................................................ 7,000,000   £25
1986. Only issued in the 1986 set...................... 10,000   £295
1988................................................................ 7,000,000   £5
1988 Dublin Millennium................................... 5,000,000   £5
1988 — Proof ................................................... 50,000   £25
1996................................................................ 6,000,000   £7
1997................................................................ 6,000,000   £7
1998.............................................................. 13,800,000   £5
1999................................................................ 7,000,000   £4
2000................................................................. Unknown   £4

## ONE POUND

1990.............................................................. 42,300,000   £5
1990 Proof ....................................................... 50,000   £25
1994.............................................................. 14,900,000   £5
1995................................................................ 9,200,000   £5
1995 UN silver proof in case of issue................................ 2,850   £175
1996................................................................ 9,200,000   £5
1998.............................................................. 22,960,000   £4
1999.............................................................. 10,000,000   £5
2000................................................................ 4,000,000   £5
2000 Millennium ............................................. 5,000,000   £5
2000 – Silver Proof Piedfort.............................. 90,000   £35

## OFFICIAL COIN SETS ISSUED BY THE CENTRAL BANK

1971 Specimen set in green wallet. 6 coins............................£16
1975 6 coin set..........................................................................£55
1978 6 coin set..........................................................................£55
1978 6 coin set. Black cover, scarce......................................£75
1982 6 coin set. Black cover....................................................£75
1986 Specimen set in card folder 1/2p to 50p, 7 coins. Very scarce. Most
sets have glue problems ......................................................£600
1996 7 coin set..........................................................................£55
1998 7 coin set..........................................................................£50
2000 Millennium set. Last decimal set ...............................£125
2000 — With 1999 instead of the 2000 £1 coin .....................£245

# OFFICIAL AND SEMI-OFFICIAL COMMEMORATIVE MEDALS

It is probably a strong love of history, rather than the strict disciplines of coin collecting that make collectors turn to commemorative medals. The link between the two is intertwined, and it is to be hoped that collectors will be encouraged to venture into the wider world of medallions, encouraged by this brief guide, originally supplied by Daniel Fearon (author of the *Catalogue of British Commemorative Medals)* and kindly updated again this year by Charles Riley.

| DATE | VF | EF |
|---|---|---|
| **JAMES I** | | |
| 1603 Coronation (possibly by | | |
| C. Anthony), 29mm, Silver | £1200 | £1170 |
| | | |
| **QUEEN ANNE** | | |
| 1603 Coronation, 29mm, AR | £650 | £1100 |
| | | |
| **CHARLES I** | | |
| 1626 Coronation (by N. Briot), 30mm, Silver | £750 | £1000 |
| 1633 Scottish Coronation (by N. Briot), 28mm, | | |
| Silver | £450 | £750 |
| 1649 Memorial (by J. Roettier). Struck after the | | |
| Restoration, 50mm, Bronze | £120 | £275 |
| | | |
| **CHARLES II** | | |
| 1651 Scottish Coronation, in exile (from design | | |
| by Sir J. Balfour), 32mm, Silver | £800 | £1500 |
| | | |
| **CROMWELL** | | |
| 1651 Lord Protector (by T. Simon), 38mm, | | |
| Silver | £400 | £900 |
| — Cast examples | £120 | £275 |
| | | |
| **CHARLES II** | | |
| 1661 Coronation (by T. Simon), 29mm | | |
| — Gold | £1800 | £3200 |
| — Silver | £350 | £550 |
| 1685 Death (by N. Roettier), 39mm, Bronze | £150 | £325 |

*James I Coronation, 1603*

*Charles II Coronation, 1661*

| DATE | VF | EF |
|---|---|---|

**JAMES II**
1685 Coronation (by J. Roettier), 34mm
— Gold .................................................. £1900 £3600
— Silver ................................................. £375 £800

**MARY**
1685 Coronation (by J. Roettier), 34mm
— Gold .................................................. £1500 £3000
— Silver ................................................. £300 £600

**WILLIAM & MARY**
1689 Coronation (by J. Roettier), 32mm
— Gold .................................................. £1750 £3000
— Silver ................................................. £350 £495
1689 Coronation, "Perseus" (by G. Bower),
   38mm, Gold ....................................... £1750 £3000

**MARY**
1694 Death (by N. Roettier), 39mm, Bronze........ £95 £230

**WILLIAM III**
1697 "The State of Britain" (by J. Croker), 69mm,
   Silver .............................................. £850 £1400

**ANNE**
1702 Accession, "Entirely English" (by J. Croker), 34mm
— Gold .................................................. £1300 £2600
— Silver ................................................. £95 £180
1702 Coronation (by J. Croker), 36mm
— Gold .................................................. £1500 £2600
— Silver ................................................. £200 £300
1707 Union with Scotland (by J. Croker, rev. by S. Bull), 34mm
— Gold .................................................. £1500 £2800
— Silver ................................................. £150 £250
1713 Peace of Utrecht (by J. Croker—issued in gold to Members
of Parliament), 34mm
— Gold .................................................. £2500 £5000
— Silver ................................................. £130 £300

*Queen Anne, 1702–1713.*

**GEORGE I**
1714 Coronation (by J. Croker), 34mm
— Gold .................................................. £1500 £3000
— Silver ................................................. £195 £295
1727 Death (by J. Dassier), 31mm, Silver ........... £120 £300

**GEORGE II**
1727 Coronation (by J. Croker), 34mm
— Gold .................................................. £1500 £3000
— Silver ................................................. £175 £350

**QUEEN CAROLINE**
1727 Coronation (by J. Croker), 34mm
— Gold .................................................. £1750 £3000
— Silver ................................................. £190 £400
1732 The Royal Family (by J. Croker), 70mm
— Silver ................................................. £1500 £3000
— Bronze................................................. £400 £700

*George I Coronation, 1714.*

| DATE | VF | EF |
|---|---|---|

### GEORGE III
1761 Coronation (by L. Natter), 34mm
— Gold ......................................................... £2250 £3500
— Silver ....................................................... £350 £550
— Bronze...................................................... £150 £250

### QUEEN CHARLOTTE
1761 Coronation (by L. Natter), 34mm
— Gold ......................................................... £1750 £3500
— Silver ....................................................... £375 £600
— Bronze...................................................... £150 £295
1810 Golden Jubilee, "Frogmore", 48mm, Silver £150 £300
— Bronze...................................................... £95 £195

### GEORGE IV
1821 Coronation (by B. Pistrucci), 35mm
— Gold ......................................................... £1500 £3000
— Silver ....................................................... £175 £395
— Bronze...................................................... £60 £110

### WILLIAM IV
1831 Coronation (by W. Wyon; rev.shows
   Queen Adelaide), 33mm
— Gold ......................................................... £1500 £2600
— Silver ....................................................... £175 £325
— Bronze...................................................... £65 £100

### QUEEN VICTORIA
1838 Coronation (by B. Pistrucci), 37mm
— Gold ......................................................... £1500 £3000
— Silver ....................................................... £150 £300
— Bronze...................................................... £45 £95

*George III, Coronation, 1761*

*Queen Victoria Coronation, 1838*

*Queen Victoria Diamond Jubilee 1897*

| DATE | VF | EF |
|------|----|----|

**1887 Golden Jubilee (by J. E. Boehm, rev. by Lord Leighton)**
— Gold, 58mm ..................................................... £2800 £3500
— Silver, 78mm .................................................... £250 £500
— Bronze, 78mm .................................................. £95 £180
**1897 Diamond Jubilee (by T. Brock),**
— Gold, 56mm ..................................................... £3000 £4000
— Silver, 56mm .................................................... £95 £125
— Bronze, 56mm .................................................. £45 £75
— Gold, 25mm ..................................................... £350 £450
— Silver, 25mm .................................................... £35 £55

## EDWARD VII
**1902 Coronation (August 9) (by G. W. de Saulles)**
— Gold, 56mm ..................................................... £3000 £3600
— Silver, 56mm .................................................... £95 £125
— Bronze, 56mm .................................................. £35 £60
— Gold, 31mm ..................................................... £450 £600
— Silver, 31mm .................................................... £25 £45
*\*Some rare examples of the official medal show the date as June 26, the original date set for the Coronation which was postponed because the King developed appendicitis.*

## GEORGE V
**1911 Coronation (by B. Mackennal)**
— Gold, 51mm ..................................................... £3000 £3600
— Silver, 51mm .................................................... £95 £250
— Bronze, 51mm .................................................. £30 £60
— Gold, 31mm ..................................................... £450 £600
— Silver, 31mm .................................................... £25 £35

*George V Silver Jubilee, 1935*

**1935 Silver Jubilee (by P. Metcalfe)**
— Gold, 58mm ..................................................... £3500 £4100
— Silver, 58mm .................................................... £100 £150
— Gold, 32mm ..................................................... £600 £795
— Silver, 32mm .................................................... £25 £40

## PRINCE EDWARD
**1911 Investiture as Prince of Wales (by W. Goscombe John)**
— Gold, 31mm ..................................................... £1000 £1950
— Silver, 31mm .................................................... £45 £95

## EDWARD VIII
**1936 Abdication (by L. E. Pinches), 35mm**
— Gold.................................................................. £750 £1600
— Silver................................................................ £45 £65
— Bronze.............................................................. £20 £40

## GEORGE VI
**1937 Coronation (by P. Metcalfe)**
— Gold, 58mm ..................................................... £3500 £4000
— Silver, 58mm .................................................... £60 £95
— Gold, 32mm ..................................................... £600 £795
— Silver, 32mm .................................................... £35 £75
— Bronze, 32mm .................................................. £10 £15

*Edward, Prince of Wales, 1911*

| DATE | VF | EF |
|------|-----|-----|

## ELIZABETH II
1953 Coronation (by Spink & Son)
| | | |
|---|---|---|
| — Gold, 57mm ................................................. | £3500 | £4000 |
| — Silver, 57mm ................................................ | £75 | £140 |
| — Bronze, 57mm ............................................. | £45 | £95 |
| — Gold, 32mm ................................................. | £350 | £575 |
| — Silver, 32mm ............................................... | £40 | £65 |
| — Bronze, 32mm ............................................. | £10 | £20 |

1977 Silver Jubilee (by A. Machin)
| | | |
|---|---|---|
| — Silver, 57mm ................................................ | — | £100 |
| — Silver, 44mm ................................................ | — | £50 |

*\*The gold medals are priced for 18ct—they can also be found as 22ct and 9ct, and prices should be adjusted accordingly.*

## PRINCE CHARLES
1969 Investiture as Prince of Wales (by M. Rizello)
| | | |
|---|---|---|
| — Silver, 57mm ................................................ | — | £75 |
| — Bronze gilt, 57mm.......................................... | — | £40 |
| — Silver, 45mm ................................................ | — | £65 |
| — Gold, 32mm .................................................. | — | £450 |
| — Silver, 32mm ................................................ | — | £45 |
| — Bronze, 32mm .............................................. | — | £5 |

*Prince Charles, Prince of Wales 1969.*

## QUEEN ELIZABETH THE QUEEN MOTHER
1980 80th Birthday (by L. Durbin)
| | | |
|---|---|---|
| — Silver, 57mm ................................................ | — | £90 |
| — Silver, 38mm ................................................ | — | £50 |
| — Bronze, 38mm .............................................. | — | £20 |

*N.B.—Official Medals usually command a premium when still in their original case of issue.*

# DIRECTORY *section*

O N the following pages will be found the most useful names and addresses needed by the coin collector.

At the time of going to press with this edition of the YEARBOOK the information is correct, as far as we have been able to ascertain. However, people move and establishments change, so it is always advisable to make contact with the person or organisation listed before travelling any distance, to ensure that the journey is not wasted.

Should any of the information in this section not be correct we would very much appreciate being advised in good time for the preparation of the next edition of the COIN YEARBOOK.

# Dealers who display this symbol are Members of the

# British Numismatic Trade Association

*The primary purpose of the Association is to promote and safeguard the highest standards of professionalism in dealings between its Members and the public. In official consultations it is the recognised representative of commercial numismatics in Britain.*

*For a free Membership Directory please send a stamped addressed envelope to:*

**General Secretary, BNTA, PO Box 2, Rye, East Sussex TN31 7WE
Tel/Fax: 01797 229988 Email: secretary@bnta.net**

*The BNTA will be organising the following events:*

**COINEX 2013—27 & 28 September, COINEX 2014—26 & 27 September
at The Ballroom, Millennium Hotel, London Mayfair,
44 Grosvenor Square, London W1K 2HP**

## BNTA MEMBERS IN COUNTY ORDER

### LONDON AREA

\*A.H. Baldwin & Sons Ltd
  www.baldwin.co.uk
ATS Bullion Ltd
  www.atsbullion.com
Beaver Coin Room
  www.beaverhotel.co.uk
Bonhams incorporating Glendining's
  www.bonhams.com
Keith Chapman
  www.anglosaxoncoins.com
\*Classical Numismatic Group Inc /
Seaby Coins
  www.cngcoins.com
\*Philip Cohen Numismatics
  www.coinheritage.co.uk
Coin Invest Direct.com
  www.coininvestdirect.com

Andre de Clermont
  www.declermont.com
\*Dix Noonan Webb
  www.dnw.co.uk
Christopher Eimer
  www.christophereimer.co.uk
GK Coins Ltd
  www.gkcoins.co.uk
Harrow Coin & Stamp Centre
\*Knightsbridge Coins
C. J. Martin (Coins) Ltd
  www.antiquities.co.uk
Nigel Mills
  www.nigelmills.net
Morton & Eden Ltd
  www.mortonandeden.com
Moruzzi Ltd
  www.moruzzi.co.uk

\*Colin Narbeth & Son Ltd
  www.colin-narbeth.com
Numismatica Ars Classica
  www.arsclassicacoins.com
\*Pavlos S Pavlou
Physical Gold Ltd
  www.physicalgold.co.uk
Predecimal.com incorporating
Rotographic Publications
  www.predecimal.com
Roma Numismatics Ltd
  www.romanumismatics.com
Simmons Gallery
  www.simmonsgallery.co.uk
\*Spink & Son Ltd
  www.spink.com
Surena Ancient Art & Numismatic
The London Coin Company Ltd
  www.thelondoncoincompany.com

*(Those members with a retail premises are indicated with an*

# The BNTA is a member of the International Numismatic Commission.

## AVON

Saltford Coins
www.saltfordcoins.com

## BEDFORDSHIRE

*Cambridge Coins and Jewellery
www.cambridgecoins.co.uk
Simon Monks
www.simonmonks.co.uk

## BERKSHIRE

Frank Milward
*Douglas Saville Numismatic Books
www.douglassaville.com

## BUCKINGHAMSHIRE

Charles Riley
www.charlesriley.co.uk

## CAMBRIDGESHIRE

*Den of Antiquity International Ltd
www.denofantiquity.co.uk

## CHESHIRE

A F Brock & Co Ltd
www.afbrock.co.uk

## CORNWALL

Richard W Jeffery

## DEVON

Glenn S Ogden
www.glennogdencoins.com

## DORSET

*Dorset Coin Co. Ltd
www.dorsetcoincompany.co.uk

## ESSEX

Time Line Originals
www.time-lines.co.uk

## GLOUCESTERSHIRE

Silbury Coins Ltd
www.silburycoins.com

## HAMPSHIRE

*SPM Jewellers
www.spmjewellers.co.uk
Studio Coins
www.studiocoins.net
*Victory Coins
West Essex Coin Investments

## HERTFORDSHIRE

Michael Dickinson
DRG Coins and Antiquities
www.drgcoinsantiquities.com
K B Coins
David Miller
David Seaman
www.davidseamancoins.co.uk

## KENT

London Coins
www.londoncoins.co.uk
*Peter Morris
www.petermorris.co.uk

## LANCASHIRE

*Colin de Rouffignac
James Murphy

## MONMOUTHSHIRE

Anthony M. Halse
www.coinsandtokens.com

## NORFOLK

BucksCoins
www.westminsterauctions.com
*Roderick Richardson
www.roderickrichardson.com
Chris Rudd
www.celticcoins.com

## NORTHAMPTONSHIRE

*Giuseppe Miceli Coin & Medal
Centre

## NOTTINGHAMSHIRE

History in Coins
www.historyincoins.com

## OXFORDSHIRE

*Richard Gladdle
Gladdle@plumpudding.org

## SUFFOLK

*Lockdale Coins Ltd
www.lockdales.com
Mike R. Vosper Coins
www.vosper4coins.co.uk

## SURREY

Allgold Coins
www.allgoldcoins.co.uk
Daniel Fearon
www.danielfearon.com
M. J. Hughes
www.gbgoldcoins.co.uk

KMCC Ltd
Mark Rasmussen Numismatist
www.rascoins.com

## SUSSEX

John Newman Coins
www.johnnewmancoins.com
Tim Wilkes
www.wilkescoins.com

## TYNE AND WEAR

*Corbitts Ltd
www.corbitts.com

## WARWICKSHIRE

*Peter Viola
*Warwick & Warwick Ltd
www.warwickandwarwick.com

## WEST MIDLANDS

*Birmingham Coins
David Craddock
Paul Davis Birmingham Ltd
*Format of Birmingham Ltd
Mint Coins Ltd

## WORCESTERSHIRE

J. Whitmore

## YORKSHIRE

Airedale Coins
www.airedalecoins.co.uk
AMR Coins
www.amrcoins.com
Paul Clayton
Paul Davies Ltd
Weighton Coin Wonders*
www.weightoncoin.co.uk

## WALES

Lloyd Bennett
www.coinsofbritain.com
*Cardiff Coins & Medals
www.cardiffcoins.com
*Paul Dawson York Ltd
*North Wales Coins Ltd
Colin Rumney
Nigel Tooley Ltd
www.coincabinet.co.uk

## SCOTLAND

*Scotmint Ltd
www.scotmint.com

## IRELAND

Ormonde Coins
www.ormondecoins.com

# www.bnta.net

# MUSEUMS
*& libraries*

## Listed below are the Museums and Libraries in the UK which have coins or items of numismatic interest on display or available to the general public.

### A

• Anthropological Museum, University of Aberdeen, Broad Street, **Aberdeen**, AB9 1AS (01224 272014).

• Curtis Museum (1855), High Street, **Alton**, Hants (01420 2802). *General collection of British coins.*

• Ashburton Museum, 1 West Street, **Ashburton**, Devon. *Ancient British and Roman antiquities including local coin finds.*

• Ashwell Village Museum (1930), Swan Street, **Ashwell**, Baldock, Herts. *Roman coins from local finds, local trade tokens, Anglo-Gallic coins and jetons.*

• Buckinghamshire County Museum (1862), Church Street, **Aylesbury**, Bucks (01296 88849). *Roman and medieval English coins found locally, 17th/18th century Buckinghamshire tokens, commemorative medals.*

### B

• Public Library and Museum (1948), Marlborough Road, **Banbury**, Oxon (01295 259855). *Wrexlin Hoard of Roman coins.*

• Museum of North Devon (1931), The Square, **Barnstaple**, EX32 8LN (01271 46747). *General coin and medal collection, including local finds. Medals of the Royal Devonshire Yeomanry.*

• Roman Baths Museum, Pump Room, **Bath**, Avon (01225 461111 ext 2785). *Comprehensive collection of Roman coins from local finds.*

• Bagshaw Museum and Art Gallery (1911), Wilton Park, **Batley**, West Yorkshire (01924 472514). *Roman, Scottish, Irish, English hammered, British and foreign coins, local traders' tokens, political medalets, campaign medals and decorations.*

• Bedford Museum (1961), Castle Lane, **Bedford** (01234 353323). *Collections of the Bedford Library and Scientific Institute, the Beds Archaeological Society and Bedford Modern School (Pritchard Memorial) Museum.*

• Ulster Museum (1928), Botanic Gardens, **Belfast** BT9 5AB (01232 381251). *Irish, English and British coins and commemorative medals.*

• Berwick Borough Museum (1867), The Clock Block, Berwick Barracks, Ravensdowne, **Berwick**. TD15 1DQ (01289 330044). *Roman, Scottish and medievial coins.*

• Public Library, Art Gallery and Museum (1910), Champney Road, **Beverley**, Humberside (01482 882255). *Beverley trade tokens, Roman, English, British and foreign coins.*

• Bignor Roman Villa (1811), **Bignor**, nr Pulborough, West Sussex (017987 202). *Roman coins found locally.*

• City Museum and Art Gallery (1861), Chamberlain Square, **Birmingham** B3 3DH (0121 235 2834). *Coins, medals and tokens (special emphasis on the products of the Soho, Heaton, Birmingham and Watt mints.*

• Blackburn Museum, Museum Street, **Blackburn**, Lancs (01254 667130). *Incorporates the Hart (5,000 Greek, Roman and early English) and Hornby (500 English coins) collections, as well as the museum's own collection of British and Commonwealth coins.*

• Museum Collection, Town Hall, **Bognor Regis**, West Sussex. *Roman, English and British coins and trade tokens.*

• Museum and Art Gallery,(1893), Civic Centre, **Bolton**, Lancashire (01204 22311 ext 2191). *General collection of about 3000 British and foreign coins, and over 500 British medals. Numismatic library.*

• Art Gallery and Museum, Central Library, Oriel Road, **Bootle**, Lancs. *Greek, Roman, English, British and some foreign coins, local trade tokens.*

• Roman Town and Museum (1949) Main Street, **Boroughbridge**, N. Yorks. YO2 3PH (01423 322768). *Roman coins.*

• The Museum (1929), The Guildhall, **Boston**, Lincs (01205 365954). *Small collection of English coins.*

• Natural Science Society Museum (1903), 39 Christchurch Road, **Bournemouth,** Dorset (01202 553525). *Greek, Roman and English hammered coins (including the Hengistbury Hoard), local trade tokens.*

• Bolling Hall Museum (1915), Bolling Hall Road, **Bradford,** West Yorkshire BD4 7LP (01274 723057). *Some 2,000 coins and tokens, mostly 18th–20th centuries.*

• Cartwright Hall Museum and Art Gallery (1904), Lister Park, **Bradford,** West Yorkshire BD9 4NS (01274 493313). *Roman coins found locally.*

• Museum and Art Gallery (1932), South Street, **Bridport,** Dorset (01308 22116). *Roman coins, mainly from excavations at Claudian Fort.*

• The City Museum (1820), Queen's Road, **Bristol** BS8 1RL (0117 9 27256). *Ancient British, Roman (mainly from local hoards), English hammered coins, especially from the Bristol mint, and several hundred local trade tokens.*

• District Library and Museum (1891), Terrace Road, **Buxton,** Derbyshire SK17 6DU (01298 24658). *English and British coins, tokens and commemorative medals. Numismatic library.*

*C*

• Segontium Museum (1928), Beddgelert Road, **Caernarfon,** Gwynedd (01286 675625) *Roman coins and artifacts excavated from the fort.*

• Fitzwilliam Museum (1816), Department of Coins and Medals, Trumpington Street, **Cambridge** (01223 332900). *Ancient, English, medieval European, oriental coins, medals, plaques, seals and cameos.*

• National Museum & Galleries of Wales, Cathays Park, **Cardiff** (029 20397951). *Greek, Celtic, Roman and British coins and tokens with the emphasis on Welsh interest. Also military, civilian and comm. medals.*

• Guildhall Museum (1979), Greenmarket, **Carlisle,** Cumbria (01228 819925). *General collection of coins and medals.*

• Tullie House (1877), Castle Street, **Carlisle,** Cumbria (01228 34781). *Roman, medieval and later coins from local finds, including medieval counterfeiter's coin-moulds.*

• Gough's Caves Museum (1934), The Cliffs, **Cheddar,** Somerset (01934 343). *Roman coins.*

• Chelmsford and Essex Museum (1835), Oaklands Park, Moulsham Street, **Chelmsford,** Essex CM2 9AQ (01245 615100). *Ancient British, Roman, medieval and later coins mainly from local finds, local medals.*

• Town Gate Museum (1949), **Chepstow,** Gwent. *Local coins and trade tokens.*

• Grosvenor Museum (1886), Grosvenor Street, **Chester** (01244 21616). *Roman coins from the fortress site, Anglo-Saxon, English medieval and post-medieval coins of the Chester and Rhuddlan mints, trade tokens of Chester and Cheshire, English and British milled coins.*

• Public Library (1879), Corporation Street, **Chesterfield,** Derbyshire (01246 2047). *Roman coins from local finds, Derbyshire trade tokens, medals, seals and railway passes. Numismatic library and publications.*

• Red House Museum (1919), Quay Road, **Christchurch,** Dorset (01202 482860). *Coins of archaeological significance from Hampshire and Dorset, notably the South Hants Hoard, ancient British, Armorican, Gallo-Belgic, Celtic and Roman coins, local trade tokens and medals.*

• Corinium Museum (1856), Park Street, **Cirencester,** Glos (01285 655611). *Roman coins.*

• Colchester and Essex Museum (1860), The Castle, **Colchester,** Essex (01206 712931/2). *Ancient British and Roman coins from local finds, medieval coins (especially the Colchester Hoard), later English coins and Essex trade tokens, commemorative medals.*

*D*

• Public Library, Museum and Art Gallery (1921), Crown Street, **Darlington,** Co Durham (01325 463795). *Coins, medals and tokens.*

• Borough Museum (1908), Central Park, **Dartford,** Kent (01322 343555). *Roman, medieval and later English hammered coins, trade tokens and commemorative medals.*

• Dartmouth Museum (1953), The Butterknowle, **Dartmouth,** Devon (01803 832923). *Coins and medals of a historical and maritime nature.*

• Museum and Art Gallery (1878), The Strand, **Derby** (01332 255586). *Roman coins, English silver and copper regal coins, Derbyshire tradesmen's tokens, British campaign medals and decorations of the Derbyshire Yeomanry and the 9/12 Royal Lancers.*

• Museum and Art Gallery (1909), Chequer Road, **Doncaster,** South Yorkshire (01302 734293). *General collection of English and foreign silver and bronze coins. Representative collection of Roman imperial silver and bronze coins, including a number from local hoards. English trade tokens, principally of local issues, medals.*

• Dorset County Museum(1846), **Dorchester,** Dorset (01305 262735). *British, Roman, medieval and later coins of local interest.*

• Central Museum (1884), Central Library, St James's Road, **Dudley,** West Midlands (01384 453576). *Small general collection of coins, medals and tokens.*

• Burgh Museum (1835), The Observatory, Corberry Hill, **Dumfries** (01387 53374)**.** *Greek, Roman, Anglo-Saxon, medieval English and Scottish coins, especially from local hoards. Numismatic library.*

• Dundee Art Galleries and Museums (1873). Albert Square, **Dundee** DD1 1DA (01382 23141). *Coins and medals of local interest.*

• The Cathedral Treasury (995 AD), The College, **Durham** (0191-384 4854). *Greek and Roman coins bequeathed by Canon Sir George Wheeler (1724), Renaissance to modern medals, medieval English coins, especially those struck at the Durham ecclesiastical mint.*

• Durham Heritage Centre, St Mary le Bow, North Bailey, **Durham** (0191-384 2214). *Roman, medieval and later coins, mainly from local finds.*

*E*

• Royal Museum of Scotland (1781), Queen Street, **Edinburgh** EH1 (0131 225 7534). *Roman, Anglo-Saxon, English and Scottish coins, trade tokens, commemorative medals and communion tokens. Numismatic library. Publications.*

• Royal Albert Memorial Museum (1868), Queen St, **Exeter** EX4 3RX (01392 265858). *Roman and medieval. Coins of the Exeter Mint.*

*G*

• Hunterian Museum (1807), Glasgow University, University Avenue, **Glasgow** G12 8QQ (0141 339 8855). *Greek, Roman, Byzantine, Scottish, English and Irish coins, Papal and other European medals, Indian and Oriental coins, trade and communion tokens.*

• Art Gallery and Museum (1888), Kelvingrove, **Glasgow** G3 (0141 357 3929). *General collection of coins, trade tokens, communion tokens, commemorative and military medals.*

• Museum of Transport (1974), Kelvin Hall, Bunhouse Road, **Glasgow** G3 (0141 357 3929). *Transport tokens and passes, commemorative medals, badges and insignia of railway companies and shipping lines.*

• City Museum and Art Gallery (1859), Brunswick Road, **Gloucester** (01452 524131). *Ancient British, Roman, Anglo-Saxon (from local finds), early medieval (from local mints), Gloucestershire trade tokens.*

• Guernsey Museum and Art Gallery, St Peter Port, **Guernsey** (01481 726518). *Armorican, Roman, medieval and later coins, including the coins, medals, tokens and paper money of Guernsey.*

• Guildford Museum (1898), Castle Arch, **Guildford,** Surrey GU1 3SX (01483 444750). *Roman and medieval coins and later medals.*

*H*

• Gray Museum and Art Gallery, Clarence Road, **Hartlepool,** Cleveland (01429 268916). *General collection, including coins from local finds.*

• Public Museum and Art Gallery (1890), John's Place, Cambridge Road, **Hastings,** East Sussex (01424 721952). *General collection of English and British coins, collection of Anglo-Saxon coins from Sussex mints.*

• City Museum (1874), Broad Street, **Hereford** (01432 268121 ext 207). *Coins from the Hereford mint and local finds, Herefordshire trade tokens, general collection of later coins and medals.*

• Hertford Museum (1902), 18 Bull Plain, **Hertford** (01992 582686). *British, Roman, medieval and later English coins and medals.*

• Honiton and Allhallows Public Museum (1946), High Street, **Honiton,** Devon (01404 44966). *Small general collection, including coins from local finds.*

• Museum and Art Gallery (1891), 19 New Church Road, **Hove,** East Sussex (01273 779410). *English coins, Sussex trade tokens and hop tallies, campaign medals, orders and decorations, comm. medals.*

• Tolson Memorial Museum (1920), Ravensknowle Park, **Huddersfield,** West Yorkshire (01484 541455). *Representative collection of British coins and tokens, Roman and medieval coins, mainly from local finds.*

• Hull and East Riding Museum (1928), 36 High Street, **Hull** (01482 593902). *Celtic, Roman and medieval coins and artifacts from local finds. Some later coins including tradesmen's tokens.*

*I*

• The Manx Museum, Douglas, **Isle of Man** (01624 675522). *Roman, Celtic, Hiberno-Norse, Viking, medieval English and Scottish coins, mainly from local finds, Manx traders' tokens from the 17th to 19th centuries, Manx coins from 1709 to the present day.*

*J*

• Jersey Museum, Weighbridge, St Helier, **Jersey** (01534 30511). *Armorican, Gallo-Belgic, Roman, medieval English and French coins, coins, paper money and tokens of Jersey.*

*K*

• Dick Institute Museum and Art Gallery (1893), Elmbank Avenue, **Kilmarnock,** Ayrshire (01563 26401). *General collection of coins and medals, and the Hunter-Selkirk collection of communion tokens.*

*L*

• City Museum (1923), Old Town Hall, Market Square, **Lancaster** (01524 64637). *Roman, Anglo-Saxon, medieval English coins, provincial trade tokens, medals of the King's Own Royal Lancashire Regiment.*

• City Museum (1820), Municipal Buildings, The Headrow, **Leeds,** West Yorkshire (01532 478279). *Greek, Roman, Anglo-Saxon, English medieval, Scottish, Irish, British, Commonwealth and foreign coins. Several Roman and Saxon hoards. The Backhouse collection of Yorkshire banknotes, the Thornton collection of Yorkshire tokens, British and foreign commemorative medals.*

• Leicester Museum and Art Gallery (1849), New Walk, **Leicester** (01533 554100). *Roman, medieval and later coins, mainly from local finds, tokens, commemorative medals, campaign medals and decorations.*

• Pennington Hall Museum and Art Gallery, **Leigh,** Lancashire. *Roman and British coins and medals.*

• Museum and Art Gallery (1914), Broadway, **Letchworth,** Herts (01462 65647). *Ancient British coins minted at Camulodunum, Roman, medieval and English coins, Hertfordshire trade tokens, commemorative and campaign medals.*

• City Library, Art Gallery and Museum (1859), Bird Street, **Lichfield,** Staffs (01543 2177). *Roman, medieval and later English coins, Staffordshire trade tokens and commemorative medals.*

• Liverpool Museum(1851), William Brown Street, **Liverpool** L3 8EN (0151 207 0001). *General collection of Roman, medievaland later British coins, tokens.*

• Bank of England Museum, Threadneedle Street, **London** EC2 (020-7601 5545). *Exhibits relating to gold bullion, coins, tokens and medals, the design and manufacture of banknotes, and a comprehensive collection of bank notes dating from the 17th century to the present day.*

• British Museum(1752), HSBC Coin Gallery, Great Russell Street, **London** WC1 (020-7636 1555). *Almost a million coins, medals, tokens and badges of all period from Lydia, 7th century BC to the present time. Extensive library of books and periodicals.*

• British Numismatic Society (1903), Warburg Institute, Woburn Square, **London** WC1. *Library containing over 5,000 volumes, including sale catalogues, periodicals and pamphlets. Open to members only.*

• Cuming Museum (1906), Walworth Road, **London** SE17 (020-7703 3324/5529). *Some 8,000 items, including Greek, Roman, medieval English and modern British coins, English tokens and commemorative medals.*

• Gunnersbury Park Museum (1927), Acton, **London** W3. *Ancient British, Greek, Roman, medieval English, British and some foreign coins, tradesmen's tokens and commemorative medals, including local finds.*

• Horniman Museum and Library (1890), London Road, Forest Hill, **London** SE23 (020-7699 2339). *General collection, primitive currency, some tokens.*

• Imperial War Museum, Lambeth Road, **London** SE1 6HZ (020-7416 5000). *Emergency coinage of two world wars, occupation and invasion money, extensive collection of German Notgeld, commemorative, propaganda and military medals, badges and insignia.*

• Sir John Soane's Museum (1833), 13 Lincoln's Inn Fields, **London** WC2 (020-7405 2107). *Napoleonic medals and medallic series of the late 18th and early 19th centuries.*

• National Maritime Museum, Romney Road, Greenwich, **London** SE10 (020-8858 4422). *Commemorative medals with a nautical or maritime theme, naval medals and decorations.*

• Victoria and Albert Museum (1852), South Kensington, **London** SW7 (020-7938 8441). *Byzantine gold and medieval Hispano-Mauresque coins (Department of Metalwork), large collection of Renaissance and later medals (Department of Architecture and Sculpture). Numismatic books.*

• Ludlow Museum (1833). The Assembly Rooms. Castle Square, **Ludlow** (01584 873857). *Roman and medieval coins from local finds.*

• Luton Museum and Art Gallery (1927), Wardown Park, **Luton**, Beds (01582 36941). *Coins, tokens and medals.*

## M

• Museum and Art Gallery (1858), **Maidstone**, Kent (01622 754497). *Ancient British, Roman, Anglo-Saxon and medieval coins found in Kent, modern British coins, Kent trade tokens, banknotes, hop tallies and tokens, primitive currency, collections of Kent Numismatic Society.*

• The Manchester Museum (1868), The University, **Manchester** M13 (0161-275 2634). *Very fine collections of Greek and Roman coins, comprehensive collections of English, European and Oriental coins, over 30,000 in all.*

• Margate Museum (1923), The Old Town Hall, Market Place, **Margate**, Kent (01843 225511 ext 2520). *Small collection of coins, including Roman from local finds.*

• Montrose Museum and Art Gallery (1836). Panmure Place, **Montrose**, Angus DD10 8HE (01674 73232). *Scottish and British coins.*

## N

• Newark-on-Trent Museum (1912), Appleton Gate, **Newark**, Notts (01636 702358). *Siege pieces, trade tokens and coins from local finds and hoards.*

• Newbury District Museum, The Wharf, **Newbury**, Berkshire (01635 30511). *Ancient British, Roman and medieval coins and artifacts, later coins and tokens.*

• The Greek Museum, Percy Building, **Newcastle-upon-Tyne** (0191 2226000 ext 7966). *Ancient coins.*

## O

• Heberden Coin Room, Ashmolean Museum (1683), **Oxford** (01865 278000). *Extensive collections of all periods, notably Greek, Roman, English and Oriental coins, Renaissance portrait and later medals, tokens and paper money. Large library. Numerous publications.*

## P

• Peterborough Museum (1881), Priestgate, **Peterborough**, Cambs (01733 340 3329). *Roman (mainly from local hoards and finds), Anglo-Saxon, medieval English, British and modern European coins, English and British commemorative medals and tokens.*

• City Museum and Art Gallery (1897), Drake Circus, **Plymouth**, Devon (01752 264878). *General collections of British and Commonwealth coins and tokens, Devon trade tokens and Plymouth tradesmen's checks, Ancient British and Roman coins from local sites.*

• Waterfront Museum, 4 High Street, **Poole**, Dorset (01202 683138). *General collection of British and foreign coins, medals and tokens (view by appointment).*

• City Museum (1972), Museum Road, Old **Portsmouth** PO1 (023 80827261). *Roman, medieval and later coins mainly from local finds and archaeological excavation, British coins, trade tokens of Hampshire, commemorative medals.*

• Harris Museum and Art Gallery (1893), Market Square, **Preston**, Lancashire (01772 58248). *English and British coins, tokens and medals.*

## R

• The Museum of Reading (1883), Blagrave Street, **Reading**, Berks (0118 939 9800). *British, Roman and medieval English coins, many from local finds, tradesmen's tokens and commemorative medals.*

• Rochdale Museum (1905), Sparrow Hill, **Rochdale**, Lancs (01706 41085). *Roman and medieval coins from local finds, Rochdale trade tokens, miscellaneous British and foreign coins and medals.*

• Municipal Museum and Art Gallery (1893), Clifton Park, **Rotherham** (01709 382121). Collection includes *Roman coins from Templeborough Forts, medieval English coins from local hoards and a general collection of British coins.*

## S

• Saffron Walden Museum (1832) (1939), Museum Street, **Saffron** Walden, Essex (01799 522494). *Ancient British, Roman, medieval and later coins, mainly from local finds and archaeological excavation, trade tokens and commemorative medals.*

• Verulamium Museum, St Michael's, **St Albans**, Herts (01727 819339). *Coins and artifacts excavated from the Roman town.*

• Salisbury and South Wiltshire Museum (1861), The Cathedral Close, **Salisbury,** Wilts (01722 332151). *Collection of coins minted or found locally, including finds of Iron Age, Roman, Saxon and medieval coins, as well as 18th and 19th century tradesmen's tokens.*

• Richborough Castle Museum (1930), **Sandwich,** Kent (0304 612013). *Roman coins of 1st–5th centuries from excavations at the Richborough site.*

• Scarborough Museum (1829), The Rotunda, Vernon Road, **Scarborough**, North Yorkshire (01723 374839). *Collection of over 4,000 Roman coins, 1,500 English and 600 coins from local finds, siege pieces and trade tokens.*

• Shaftesbury and Dorset Local History Museum (1946), 1 Gold Hill, **Shaftesbury**, Dorset (01747 52157). *Hoard of Saxon coins.*

• City Museum (1875), Weston Park, **Sheffield** (0114 2 768588). *Over 5,000 coins of all periods, but mainly English and modern British. European coins, imperial Roman (including three hoards of about 500 coins each), Yorkshire trade tokens, British historical medals, campaign medals. Library.*

• Rowley's House Museum, Barker Street, **Shrewsbury**, Salop (01743 361196). *Coins minted at Shrewsbury 925-1180, Civil War coinage of 1642, Shropshire tradesmen's tokens, English coins and medals.*

• Museum of Archaeology (1951), God's House Tower, Town Quay, **Southampton**, Hants (023 8022 0007). *Main emphasis lies in Ancient British, Roman and medieval English coins from local archaeological excavations. General collection of later coins and medals.*

• Atkinson Art Gallery (1878), Lord Street, **Southport,** Lancs (01704 533133). *Roman coins.*

• Botanic Gardens Museum, Churchtown, **Southport,** Lancs (01704 87547). *English and British coins and medals, military medals and decorations.*

• Southwold Museum (1933), St Bartholomew's Green, **Southwold**, Suffolk (01502 722375). *General collection of coins, specialised Suffolk trade tokens.*

• Stamford Museum (1961), Broad Street, **Stamford**, Lincs (01780 66317). *General collection of coins, medals and tokens, including a selection from the Stamford mint.*

• Municipal Museum (1860), Vernon Park, Turncroft Lane, **Stockport**, Cheshire (0161 474 4460) *Miscellaneous collection of coins, tokens and medals.*

• Stroud Museum (1899), Lansdown, **Stroud**, Glos (01453 376394). *Ancient British, Roman, Saxon, Norman, later medieval English, British coins and Gloucestershire trade tokens.*

• Museum and Art Gallery (1846), Borough Road, **Sunderland**, Tyne & Wear (0191 514 1235). *Roman imperial, medieval and later English, including examples of the pennies minted at Durham, modern British and foreign coins, 17th-19th century tradesmen's tokens, local medallions and campaign medals.*

• Swansea Museum (1835), Victoria Road, **Swansea**, W. Glamorgan, SA1 1SN (0792 653765). *Coins and medals of local interest.*

## T

• Tamworth Castle and Museum (1899), The Holloway, **Tamworth**, Staffs (01827 63563). *Anglo-Saxon coins, medieval English including coins of the Tamworth mint, later English and British coins, tokens, commemorative medallions and medals.*

• Somerset County Museum, Taunton Castle, **Taunton**, Somerset (01823 255510/320200). *Celtic, Roman, Anglo-Saxon, early Medieval, tokens, medallions and banknotes. Strong emphasis on locally-found items.*

• Thurrock Local History Museum (1956), Civic Square, **Tilbury**, Essex (01375 390000 ext 2414). *Roman coins.*

• Royal Cornwall Museum (1818), River Street, **Truro,** Cornwall (01872 72205). *Coins, tokens and medals pertaining principally to the county of Cornwall.*

## W

• Wakefield Museum (1919), Wood Street, **Wakefield,** West Yorkshire (01924 295351). *Roman and medieval English silver and copper coins.*

• Epping Forest District Museum, 39/41 Sun Street, **Waltham Abbey**, Essex EN 9. *Ancient British, Roman and medieval coins, Essex tradesmen's tokens of local interest.*

• Warrington Museum and Art Gallery (1848). Bold Street, **Warrington**, Cheshire, WA1 1JG (01925 30550). *Coins, medals and tokens.*

• Worcester City Museum (1833), Foregate Street, **Worcester** (01905 25371). *Roman, medieval and later coins and tokens. Coins of the Worcester mint.*

• Wells Museum (18903), 8 Cathedral Green, **Wells**, Somerset (01749 3477). *Ancient and modern British and world coins, local trade tokens and medals.*

• Municipal Museum and Art Gallery (1878), Station Road, **Wigan**, Lancashire. *British, Commonwealth and foreign coins from about 1660 to the present. Roman coins from local sites, commemorative medals.*

• City Museum (1851), The Square, **Winchester**, Hants (01962 848269). *Roman and medieval coins chiefly from local hoards and finds. Hampshire tradesmen's tokens and commemorative medals. Small reference library.*

• Wisbech and Fenland Museum (1835), Museum Square, **Wisbech**, Cambridgeshire (01945 583817), *British Roman, medieval and later coins, medals and tokens.*

## Y

• The Museum of South Somerset (1928), Hendford, **Yeovil**, Somerset (01935 24774). *Roman coins from local sites, medieval English, modern British coins and medals and a fine collection of tokens (particularly 17th century Somerset).*

• Castle Museum (1938), **York** (01904 653611). *English and British coins, campaign medals, orders and decorations, comemorative medals.*

• Jorvik Viking Centre (1984), Coppergate, **York** (01904 643211). *Coins and artefacts pertaining to the Viking occupation of York.*

• The Yorkshire Museum (1823), **York** (01904 629745). *Roman imperial, medieval English and later coins, about 12,000 in all.*

# CLUB *directory*

Details given here are the names of Numismatic Clubs and Societies, their date of foundation, and their usual venues, days and times of meetings. Meetings are monthly unless otherwise stated. Finally, the telephone number of the club secretary is given; the names and addresses of club secretaries are withheld for security reasons, but full details may be obtained by writing to the Secretary of the British Association of Numismatic Societies, Keith Sugden, Honorary Curatorial Assistant, Department of Numismatics, Manchester Museum, Oxford Road, Manchester M13 9PL or visiting the website at www.coinclubs.freeserve.co.uk.

**Banbury & District NS** (1967). St John's Social Club, St John's Church, Oxford Road, Banbury 2nd Mon (exc Jul & Aug), 19.45. (01295 275128).

**Bath & Bristol Numismatic Society** (1950). Fry's Club, Keynsham, Bristol. 2nd Thu, 19.30. (0117 968 7259).

**Bedfordshire Numismatic Society** (1966). 2nd Thu. Dave Allen, Secretary (01234 870645).

**Bexley Coin Club** (1968). St Martin's Church Hall, Erith Road, Barnehurst, Bexleyheath, Kent. 1st Mon (exc Jan & Aug), 19.30. (020 8303 0510).

**Birmingham Numismatic Society** (1964). Friend's Meeting House, Bull Street. (0121 308 1616).

**Matthew Boulton Society** (1994). PO Box 395, Bir-mingham B31 2TB (0121 781 6558 fax 0121 781 6574).

**Bradford & District Numismatic Society** (1967). East Bowling Unity Club, Leicester Street, Bradford, West Yorkshire. 3rd Mon, 19.00. (01532 677151).

**British Cheque Collectors' Society** (1980). John Purser, 71 Mile Lane, Cheylesmore, Coventry, West Midlands CV3 5GB.

**British Numismatic Society** (1903). Warburg Institute, Woburn Square, London WC1H 0AB. Monthly meetings (exc Aug & Dec), 18.00. (020 7323 8585)

**Cambridgeshire Numismatic Society** (1946). Friends' Meeting House, 12 Jesus Lane (entrance in Park Street), Cambridge, CB5 8BA. 3rd Mon, Sept–June, 19.30. (01480 210992).

**Chester & North Wales Coin & Banknote Society** (1996). Liver Hotel, 110 Brook Street, Chester. 4th Tue, 20.00. (0151 478 4293)

**Crew & District NS.** Memorial Hall, Church Lane, Wistaston, Crewe. 2nd Tue, 19.30 (exc Jan & July). (01270 569836)

**Derbyshire NS** The Friends Meeting House, St Helen's Street, Derby. (01283 223893)

**Devon & Exeter NS,** Courtenay Room, The St James Centre, Stadium Way, Exeter. 3rd Wed. (01395 568830)

**Essex Numismatic Society** (1966). Chelmsford Museum, Moulsham Street, Chelmsford, Essex. 4th Fri (exc Dec), 20.00. (01277 656627).

**Glasgow & West of Scotland NS** (1947). Woodside Halls, 26 Glenfarg Street, Glasgow, G3. 2nd Thu, Oct-May, 19.30. (0141 9424776).

**Harrow Coin Club** (1968). The Scout Building, off Walton Road, Wealdstone, Harrow. 2nd and 4th Mon, 19.30. (01923 826392).

**Havering Numismatic Society** (1967). Fairkytes Arts Centre, Billet Lane, Hornchurch, Essex. 1st Tue, 19.30. (07910 124549).

**Horncastle & District Coin Club** (1963). Bull Hotel, Bull Ring, Horncastle, Lincs. 2nd Thu (exc Aug), 19.30. (01754 2706).

**Huddersfield Numismatic Society** (1947). The Albert Hotel, Victoria Lane, Huddersfield. 1st Mon (exc Jul & Aug), 19.30. (01484 866814).

**Hull & District Numismatic Society** (1967). The Young People's Institute, George Street, Hull. Monthly (exc Aug & Dec), 19.30. (01482 441933).

**International Bank Note Society** (1961). Victory Services Club, 63–79 Seymour Street, London W1. Website: www.ibns.org.uk. Last Thu (exc Dec), 18.00. (www.ibnslondon.org.uk).

**Ipswich NS**, Citizens Advice Bureau, 19 Tower Street, Ipswich. (01473 728653)

**International Bank Note Society (East Midlands Branch)**, Wollaton Park Community Association, Wollaton Park, Nottingham. (0115 928 9720).

**International Bank Note Society, Scottish Chapter** (1995). West End Hotel, Palmerston Place, Edinburgh. Last Sat (exc Dec), 14.30.

**Ireland, Numismatic Society of (Northern Branch).**Denman International, Clandeboye Road, Bangor or Shaws Bridge Sports Assoc.123 Milltown Road, Belfast. 1st Fri 19.30. (028 9146 6743)

**Ireland, Numismatic Society of. (Southern Branch).** Ely House, 8 Ely Place, Dublin. Third Fri, 20.00. (0035 3 283 2027).

**Ipswich Numismatic Society** (1966). Ipswich Citizens Advice Bureau, 19 Tower Street, Ipswich, Suffolk. Monthly meetings, 19.30. (01473 728653).

**Kent Towns Numismatic Society** (1913). (Mr. R. Josland, 01634 721187).

**Kingston Numismatic Society** (1966). St Paul's Parish Hall, 280 Hook Road, Chessington, Surrey. Meetings 3rd Thu (exc Dec & Jan), 19.30. (020-8397 6944).

**Lancashire & Cheshire Numismatic Society** (1933). Reception Room, 2nd Floor, Manchester Central Library, St Peter's Square, Manchester. Monthly, Sep-June, Sat (14.00). Manchester Museum (May & Dec only). (0161 275 2661).

**Lincolnshire Numismatic Society** (1932). Grimsby Bridge Club, Bargate, Grimsby, South Humberside. 4th Wed (exc Aug), 19.30.

**London Numismatic Club** (1947). Warburg Institute, Woburn Square, London WC1H 0AB. First Tuesday of month (except January and August), 1830. (01223 332918).

**Loughborough Coin & Search Society** (1964). Wallace Humphry Room, Shelthorpe Community Centre, Loughborough, Leics. 1st Thu, 19.30. (01509 261352).

**Mid Lanark Coin Circle** (1969). Hospitality Room, The Civic Centre, Motherwell, Lanarkshire. 4th Thu, Sep–Apr (exc Dec), 19.30. (0141-552 2083).

**Morecambe & Lancaster Numismatic Society.** Monthly, 19.30. (01524 411036).

**Newbury Coin & Medal Club** (1971). Monthly, 20.00. (01635 41233).

**Northampton Numismatic Society** (1969). Old Scouts RFC, Rushmere Road, Northampton.

**Norwich Coin & Medal Society,** The White Horse, Trowse, Norwich. (01603 408393).

**Norwich Numismatic Society** (1967). Assembly House, Theatre Street, Norwich, Norfolk. 3rd Mon, 19.30. (01603 408393).

**NS of Nottinghamshire** (1948). Highfields Fire Station, Hassocks Lane, Beeston, Nottingham. 2nd Tue (Sep-Apr), 18.45. (0115 9257674).

**Nuneaton & District Coin Club** (1968). United Reformed Church Room, Coton Road, opposite Council House, Nuneaton, Warwickshire. 2nd Tue, 19.30. (01203 371556).

**Orders & Medals Research Society** (1942). National Army Museum, Royal Hospital Road, Chelsea, London SW3. Monthly, 14.30 (020-8680 2701).

**Ormskirk & West Lancashire Numismatic Society** (1970). The Eagle & Child, Maltkiln Lane, Bispham Green L40 1SN. 1st Thu, 20.15. (01704 531266).

**Peterborough & District Numismatic Society** (1967). Belsize Community Centre, Celta Road Peter-borough, Cambs. 4th Tue (exc July & Aug), 19.30. (01733 562768 or 567763).

**Plymouth Numismatics Society** (1970). Mutley Conservative Club, Mutley Plain, Plymouth, Devon. Meetings on second Wed (exc Dec), 19.30. (01752 490 394).

**Preston & District Numismatic Society** (1965). Eldon Hotel, Eldon Street, Preston, Lancs. 1st and 3rd Tue, 20.00. (012572 66869).

**Reading Coin Club** (1964). Abbey Baptist Church, Abbey Square, Reading. 1st Mon, 20.00. (01753 516390).

**Romsey Numismatic Society** (1969). Romsey WM Conservative Club, Market Place, Romsey, Hants SO5 8NA. 4th Fri (exc Dec), 19.30. (01703 253921).

**Rotherham & District Coin Club** (1982). Rotherham Art Centre, Rotherham, South Yorkshire. 1st Wed, 19.00. (01709 528179).

**Royal Mint Coin Club,** PO Box 500, Cardiff CF1 1HA (01443 222111).

**Royal Numismatic Society** (1836). Warburg Institute, Woburn Square, London, WC1H 0AB. (some meetings held at British Museum). Third Thursday of monthly (Oct-June), 18.00. Joe Cribb, Coins and Medals, British Museum, London WC1B 3DG (020-7323 8175).

**Rye Coin Club** (1955). Rye Further Education Centre, Lion Street, Rye, East Sussex. 2nd Thu (Oct-Dec, Feb-May), 19.30. (01424 422974).

**St Albans & Hertfordshire Numismatic Society** (1948). St Michael's Parish Centre, Museum Entrance, Verulamium Park, St Albans, Herts AL3 4SL. 2nd Tue (exc Aug), 19.30. (01727 824434).

**South East Hants Numismatic Society.** The Langstone Conservative Club, Havant. Second Fri. Contact: Tony Matthews, (01292 389419)

**South Manchester Numismatic Society** (1967). Nursery Inn, Green Lane, Heaton Mersey, Stockport. 1st & 3rd Mondays of each month (excl. Public hols), 20.15. (0161-476 3184).

**South Wales & Monmouthshire Numismatic Society** (1958). 1st Mon (except Bank Holidays when 2nd Mon, 19.30. (For location tel: 029 20561564).

**Thurrock Numismatic Society** (1970). Stanley Lazell Hall, Dell Road, Grays, Essex. 3rd Wed, 19.00.

**Tyneside Numismatic Society** (1954). RAFA Club, Eric Nelson House, 16 Berwick Road, Gateshead, Tyne & Wear. Meetings on second Wed, 19.30. (01661 825824).

**Wessex NS** (1948). Edward Wright Room, Beaufort Community Centre, Southbourne, Bournemouth, Dorset. 2nd Thurs (exc Aug), 20.00. (020 7731 1702).

**Wiltshire Numismatic Society** (1965). The Raven Inn, Poulshot, Nr. Devizes, Wiltshire. 3rd Mon, March -Dec, 20.00. (01380 828453).

**Worthing & District Numismatic Society** (1967). The Beechwood Hall Hotel, Wykeham Road, Worthing, BN11 4JD. 3rd Thu, 20.00. (01634 260114).

**Yorkshire Numismatic Society** (1909). Swarthmore Institute, Woodhouse Square, Leeds. 1st Sat (exc Jan, Aug & Dec) (0113 3910848).

## Important Notice to Club Secretaries:

If your details as listed are incorrect please let us know in time for the next edition of the **COIN YEARBOOK.** Amendments can be sent via post or email to: abbey@tokenpublishing.com

# IMPORTANT ORGANISATIONS

**ADA**
**The Antiquities**
**Dealers Association**
*Secretary: Susan Hadida, Duke's Court, 32 Duke Street, London SW1Y 6DU*

**IBNS**
**International**
**Bank Note Society**
*Membership Secretary: Clive Rice, 25 Copse Side, Binscombe, Godalming, Surrey, GU7 3RU*

**ANA**
**The American**
**Numismatic Association**
*818 North Cascade Avenue, Colorado Springs, CO 80903-3279, USA*

**RNS**
**Royal Numismatic Society**
*Dept of Coins & Medals, British Museum, London WC1B 3DG.*

**BNTA**
**The British Numismatic**
**Trade Association**
*Secretary: Mrs R. Cooke, General Secretary, BNTA, PO Box 2, Rye, East Sussex TN31 7WE*

**BAMS**
**British Art Medal Society**
*Philip Attwood, Dept of Coins & Medals, British Museum, London WC1B 3DG.*

**IAPN**
**International Association of**
**Professional Numismatists**
*Secretary: Jean-Luc Van der Schueren, 14 Rue de la Bourse, B–1000, Brussels.*

**BNS**
**British Numismatic Society**
*Dr K. Clancy, The Royal Mint, Llantrisant, Pontyclun, Mid Glamorgan CF72 8YT*

**Society activities are featured every month in the "Diary Section" of COIN NEWS— available from all good newsagents or on subscription. Telephone 01404 44166 for more details or log onto www.tokenpublishing.com**

# DIRECTORY
*of auctioneers*

Listed here are the major auction houses which handle coins, medals, banknotes and other items of numismatic interest. Many of them hold regular public auctions, whilst others handle numismatic material infrequently. A number of coin companies also hold regular Postal Auctions—these are marked with a **P**

**Art Coins Roma**
Via Del Babuino 89, 00187 Rome, Italy.
(+39 0632609795, wwwartcoinsroma.it)

**Baldwin's Auctions Ltd**
11 Adelphi Terrace, London WC2N 6BJ.
(020 7930 6879 fax 020 7930 9450,
auctions@baldwin.sh, www.baldwin.sh).

**Banking Memorabilia**
PO Box 14, Carlisle CA3 8DZ. (016974 76465).

**Blyth & Co**
7/9 Market Square, Ely, Cambs, CB7 4NP.
(01353 668320, auctions@fenlord.com).

**Bonhams (incorporating Glendinings)**
Montpelier Street, Knightsbridge, London
SW7 1HH. (020 7393 3914, www.bonhams.com).

**A. F. Brock & Company**
269 London Road, Hazel Grove, Stockport,
Cheshire SK7 4PL. (0161 456 5050
fax 0161 456 5112, info@afbrock.
co.uk, www.afbrock.co.uk).

**BSA Auctions**
Units 17-18, Station Yard South, Worcester Road,
Leominster, Herefordshire, HR6 8TW. (01885
488871, bids@birmauctions.co.uk,
www.birmauctions.co.uk).

**Bushey Auctions**
(020 8386 2552, enquiries@busheyauctions.
com, www.busheyauctions.com).

**Christie, Manson & Wood Ltd**
8 King Street, St James's, London SW1Y 6QT.
(020 7839 9060).

**Classical Numismatic Group Inc (Seaby Coins)**
14 Old Bond Street, London W1X 4JL.
(020 7495 1888 fax 020 7499 5916,
cng@historicalcoins.com, **P**
www.historicalcoins.com). **P**

**Coins4u.net**
38 Livingstone Place, Galashiels, Scotland
TD1 1ED. Online coin auction.

**Corbitts**
5 Moseley Sreet, Newcastle upon Tyne NE11YE.
(0191-232 7268, fax 0191-261 4130).

**Croydon Coin Auctions**
PO Box 201, Croydon, CR9 7AQ. (020 8656 4583,
www.croydoncoinauctions.co.uk).

**Dix Noonan Webb** (IAPN)
16 Bolton Street, Piccadilly, London.
(020 7016 1700, auctions@dnw.co.uk,
www.dnw.co.uk).

**Dublin Coin Auction**
5 St. Assam's Park, Raheny, Dublin 5.
(00 353 868 714 880).

**Edinburgh Coin Shop**
11 West Crosscauseway, Edinburgh EH8 9JW.
(0131 668 2928 fax 0131 668 2926). **P**

**Jean Elsen & ses Fils s.a.**
Avenue de Tervueren 65, B–1040, Brussels.
(0032 2 7346356, www.elsen.eu).

**Fellows & Sons**
Augusta House, 19 Augusta Street, Hockley,
Birmingham B18 6JA. (0121-212 2131,
www.fellows.co.uk).

**B. Frank & Son**
3 South Avenue, Ryton, Tyne & Wear NE40 3LD.
(0191 413 8749 fax 0191 413 2957,
bfrankandson@aol.com).

**T. Gillingham**
42 Highbury Park, Warminster, Wilts BA12 9JF.
(01985 216486).

**Goldberg Coins & Collectibles**
350 South Beverly Drive, Ste. 350, Beverly
Hills CA 90212. (001 310.432.6688, fax: 001
310.551.2626, www.goldbergcoins.com).

**Graves, Son & Pilcher Fine Arts**
71 Church Road, Hove, East Sussex BN3 2GL.
(01273 735266, fax 01273 723813).

**Helios Numismatik**
Ottostrasse 5, D–80333, München, Germany
(+49 089 5527949 0, www.helios-numismatik.
de).

**Heritage World Coin Auctions**
3500 Maple Avenue, 17th Floor, Dallas, Texas
75219–3941, USA. (001 214 528 3500,
fax 001 214 443 8425,
www.heritagecoins.com).

**International Coin Exchange**
Charter House, 5 Pembroke Row, Dublin 2.
(+353 (0) 868493353, email: auctionice@gmail.
com).

**Kleeford Coin Auctions**
1Parkhall House, 42b Shop Lane, Nether Heage,
Belper, Derbyshire DE56 2AR. (01773 856900).
🅿

**Fritz Rudolf Künker**
Gutenbergstrasse 23, 49076, Osnabrück,
Germany. (0049 541 962020, fax: 0049 541 96
20222, www.kuenker.com).

**Lakeland Coin Auctions**
The Riverside Hotel, Penrith,
Cumbria (venue). (01946 832693,
www.lakelandcoinauctions.co.uk).

**W. H. Lane & Son**
65 Morrab Road, Penzance, Cornwall TR18 2QT.
(01736 61447 fax 01736 50097).

**Lawrence Fine Art Auctioneers**
South Street, Crewkerne, Somerset TA18 8AB.
(01460 73041).

**Lockdale Coins**
52 Barrack Square, Martlesham Heath, Ipswich,
Suffolk, IP5 3RF37. (01473 218588,
www.lockdales.com).

**London Coins**
4–6 Upper Street South, New Ash Green, Kent
DA3 8JJ. (01474 871464, email:
info@londoncoins.co.uk, www.londoncoins.co.uk).

**Morton & Eden Ltd**
45 Maddox Street, London W1S 2PE.
(020 7493 5344 fax 020 7495 6325,
info@mortonandeden.com,
www.mortonandeden.com).

**Mowbray Collectables**
Private Bag 63000, Wellington New Zealand.
(+64 6 364 8270,
www.mowbraycollectables.co.nz).

**Neales**
192–194 Mansfield Road, Nottingham NG1 3HU.
(0115 9624141, fax 0115 9856890).

**Noble Numismatics**
169 Macquire Street, Sydney, Australia. (+61 2
9223 4578, www.noble.com.au).

**Numismatica Ars Classica NAC AG**
3rd Floor, Genavco House, 17 Waterloo Place,
London SW1Y 4AR (020 783 97270,
email: info@arsclassicacoins.com).

**Pacific Rim Online Auction**
111 Princes Highway, Kogarah, NSW, Australia.
(+61 2 9588 7111,
www.pacificrimonlineauctions.com )
Online coin auction.

**Penrith, Farmers' & Kids PLC**
Skirsgill Saleroom, Penrith, Cumbria, CA11 0DN.
(01768 890781, www.pfkauctions.co.uk)

**R & W Coin Auctions**
307 Bretch Hill, Banbury, Oxon OX16 0JD
(01295 275128).

**Regency Auctions**
Unit 1, The Capricorn Centre, Cranes Farm
Road, Essex SS14 3JA. (0871 423 8871,
wwwregencyauctions.co.uk).

**Simmons Gallery**
PO Box 104, Leytonstone, London. (Tel: 0207
8989 8097. info@simmonsgallery.co.uk,
www.simmonsgallery.co.uk). 🅿

**Sovereign Auctions**
Golden Cross House, 6–8 Duncannon Street,
Charing Cross, London WC2N 4JF. (07890
764452/07854 547351, info@sovereignauctions.
co.uk).

**Spink & Son Ltd**
69 Southampton Row, Bloomsbury, London
WC1B 4ET. (020 7563 4000, fax 020 7563 4066,
info@spink.com, www.spink.com).

**Spink Coins & Medals**
47 The Shambles, York, YO1 7XL.
(01904 654769, info@spink.com,
www.spink.com

**Stacks, Bowers and Ponterio**
118061 Fitch, Irvine, California 92614, USA.
(001 949 253 0916, www.stacksbowers.com

**St James's Auctions**
43 Duke Street, St James's, London SW1Y 6DD.
(020 7930 7597/7888/8215, www.sixbid.com).

**Tennants Auctioneers**
The Auction Centre, Leyburn, North Yorkshire
DL8 5SG. (01969 623780, www.tennants.co.uk).

**The-saleroom.com**
115 Shaftesbury Avenue, London WC2H 8AF.
Live bidding in real-time auctions from around
the world. (www.the-saleroom.com).

**Thomson Roddick & Metcalf**
Coleridge House, Shaddongate, Carlisle
CA2 5TU. (01228 528939,
www.thomsonroddick.com).

**Timeline Auctions**
PO Box 193, Upminster RM14 3WH. (01708
222824, www.timelineauctions.com).

**Mavin International**
20 Kramat Lane, #01-04/05 United House,
Singapore 228773. (+65 6238 7177)
mail@mavininternational.com).

**Warwick & Warwick**
Chalon House, Scarbank, Millers Road, Warwick
CV34 5DB. (01926 499031 fax 01926 491906,
richard.beale@warwickandwarwick.com,
www.warwickandwarwick.com).

**Westminster Auctions**
PO Box 199, Dereham, Norfolk, NR19 9BU.
(01362 638045, info@westminsterauctions.com,
www.westminsterauctions.com).

**Whyte's Auctions**
38 Molesworth Street, Dublin2, Ireland.
(+00 3531 676 2888, www.whytes.com).

# DIRECTORY *of fair*

Listed below are the names of the fair organisers, their venue details where known along with contact telephone numbers. Please call the organisers direct for information on dates etc.

**Aberdeen**
Jarvis Amatola Hotel, 'Great Western Road, also venues in **Glenrothes** and **Glasgow.** *Cornucopia Collectors Fairs (01382 224946).*

**Birmingham**
National Motor Cycle Museum, Bickenhill, Birmingham. *Midland Stamp & Coin Fair (01694 731781, www.midlandfair.co.uk).*

**Birmingham**
Collingwood Centre, Collingwood Drive, Great Barr, Birmingham. *Dave Burnett Fairs (0776 5792998).*

**Bristol**
Patchway Community College, Hempton Lane, Almondsbury, Bristol. *Minster Stamps (01522 857343, minsterstamps@ntlworld. com).*

**Britannia Medal Fair**
Carisbrooke Hall, The Victory Services Club, 63/79 Seymour Street, London W2 2HF. *Token Publishing Ltd (01404 46972).*

**Colchester**
Stanway Football Club, New Farm Road, Colchester. *ClickCollect Fairs (01485 578117).*

**Cardiff**
City Hall, Cardiff. *M. J. Promotions. (01792 415293).*

**Dublin**
Serpentine Hall, RDS, Ballsbridge, Dublin 4. *Mike Kelly (00353 86 87 14 880).*

**Eastleigh**
The Pavilion, Southampton University, Wide Lane Sports GroundEastleigh, Hants. *South Coast Coin Fair (07890 764452).*

**East Grinstead**
Sackville School, Bourg-De-Peague Avenue, East Grinstead, RH19 3TY. *John Terry Fairs (01342 326317).*

**Ely**
The Maltings, Ship Lane, Ely. *ClickCollect (01485 578117).*

**Exeter**
The America Hall, De La Rue Way, Pinhoe, Exeter. *Michael Hale Collectors Fairs (01761 414304).*

**Harrogate**
Old Swan Hotel, Swan Road, Harrogate HG1 2SR. *Simon Monks (01234 270260).*

**Lichfield**
Civic Hall, Castle Dyke, City Centre. *C. S. Fairs (01562 710424).*

**London**
Holiday Inn, Coram St., Bloomsbury, London WC1. *London Coin Fair. (01694 731781).*

**London**
Jury's Hotel, 16-22 Great Russell Street, London WC1 3NN. *Bloomsbury Fairs (01694 731781).*

**Plymouth**
Lower Guildhall. *Bruce Stamps (01749 813324).*

**Stowmarket**
Stowmarket Football Club, Bury Road, Stowmarket. *ClickCollect (01485 578117).*

**Suttton Coldfield**
Fellowship Hall, South Parade. *C. S. Fairs (01562 710424).*

**Newcastle upon Tyne**
The Park Hotel, Tynemouth, Newcastle upon Tyne. *B. Frank & Son (0191 413 8749).*

**Wakefield**
Cedar Court Hotel, Denby Dale Road, Calder Grove, Wakefield *Eddie Smith (01552 684681).*

**West Bromwich**
Town Hall, High Street. *C. S. Fairs (01562 710424).*

**York**
The Grandstand, York Race Course. *York Coin Fair (01793 513431, 020 8946 4489 or 01425 656459).*

Information correct at time of going to press

**Important annual events** — The B.N.T.A. (Coinex), Tel: 01797 229 988 for details
The I.B.N.S. (World Paper Money Fair), Email: enquiries@wpmf.info for details

# COIN, MEDAL & BANKNOTE FAIRS

## THE LONDON COIN FAIR

### HOLIDAY INN

London, Bloomsbury, Coram Street, WC1N 1HT

2012 dates: 3rd November

2013 dates: 2nd February, 1st June,
7th September, 2nd November

## THE MIDLAND COIN FAIR

### NATIONAL MOTORCYCLE MUSEUM

Bickenhill, Birmingham, B92 0EJ

*(Opposite the NEC on the M42/A45 junction)*

2012 dates: 14th October, 11th November, 9th December

2013 dates: 13th January, 10th February, 10th March, 14th April,
12th May, 9th June, 14th July, 11th August, 8th September,
13th October, 10th November, 8th December

## BLOOMSBURY COIN FAIR

### BLOOMSBURY HOTEL

16-22 Great Russell Street
London WC1 3NN

2012 dates: 1st December

2013 dates: 5th January, 2nd March, 6th April, 4th May,
6th July, 3rd August, 5th October, 7th December

For more information please contact:
Lu Veissid, Hobsley House, Frodesley, Shrewsbury SY5 7HD
Tel: 01694 731781

# www.coinfairs.co.uk

# DEALERS *directory*

The dealers listed below have comprehensive stocks of coins and medals, unless otherwise stated. Specialities, where known, are noted. Many of those listed are postal dealers only, so to avoid disappointment always make contact by telephone or mail in the first instance, particularly before travelling any distance.

Abbreviations:
ADA —— Antiquities Dealers Association
ANA  — American Numismatic Association
BADA — British Antique Dealers Association
BNTA — British Numismatic Trade Association
IAPN — International Association of Professional Numismatists
IBNS — International Bank Note Society
**P** —— Postal only
**L** —— Publishes regular lists

## ABC Coins & Tokens
PO Box 52, Alnwick, Northumberland NE66 1YE. (01665 603851, email: d–stuart@d–stuart.demon. co.uk, www.abccoinsandtokens.com).

## A. Ackroyd (IBNS)
62 Albert Road, Parkstone, Poole, Dorset BH12 2DB. (Tel/fax 01202 739039, www.AAnotes.com).
**P L** *Banknotes and cheques*

## Airedale Coins (ANA, BNTA)
PO Box 7, Bingley, West Yorkshire, BD16 1XU. (01535 272754 fax 01535 275727, email: info@airedalecoins.com, www.airedalecoins. co.uk). **P L** *British and modern coins of the world.*

## Joan Allen Electronics Ltd
190 Main Road, Biggin Hill, Kent TN16 3BB. (01959 571255). Mon–Sat 09.00–17.00.
**Metal detectors.**

## Allgold of Sevenoaks
P.O Box 260, Wallington, SM5 4H. (0844 5447952, email: sales@allgoldcoins.co.uk, www.allgoldcoins. co.uk). *Quality Sovereigns.*

## A. J. W. Coins
Taunton, Somerset. (0845 680 7087, email: andrewwide@ajw-coins.co.uk, www.ajw-coins. co.uk). **P** *Sovereigns and CGS-UK specialist.*

## AMR COINS
(07527 569308, www.amrcoins.com). *Quality English coins specialising in rare hammered and milled coins.*

## Ancient & Gothic
PO Box 5390, Bournemouth, BH7 6XR. (01202 431721).**P L***Greek, Roman, Celtic and Biblical coins. English hammered coins & antiquities.*

## Otavio Anze
Avenida Oaula Ferreira, 2159 Vila Bonilha. Pirtuba. Sao Paulo. SP. Brazil.
*Coins, Antiques and collectables.*

## Argentum Coins
Row Foot, SowerbyRow, Carlisle, Cumbria CA4 0QG. (01697 476990, www.argentumandcoins. co.uk).
*British milled coins from 1662 to date.*

## Arghans
Unit 9, Callington Business Park, Tinners Way Moss side, Callington PL17 7SH. (01579 382405, email: keithp44@waitrose.com). *British banknotes.*

## ARL Collectables
(www.litherlandcollectables.com).
*Coins, banknotes, medallions and paper emphemera.*

## S P Asimi
Cabinet at The Emporium, 112 High Street, Hungerford, Berkshire RG17 0NB. (01488 686959) *British milled coins.*

## ATS Bullion (BNTA)
2, Savoy Court, Strand. London WC2R 0EZ. (020 7240 4040, email: bullion@atslimited.fsnet. co.uk). *Bullion and modern coins.*

## Keith Austin (IBNS)
10A-12-2 Pearl View Condo, Jalan Bunga Pudak, 1200, Tanjang Bunga, Penang, Malaysia. (0060 84890 7830).
**L** *Banknotes.*

## Mark Bailey
120 Sterte Court, Sterte Close, Poole, Dorset BH15 2AY. (01202 674936). **P L***Ancient, modern, world coins and antiquities.*

## A. H. Baldwin & Sons Ltd (ANA, BADA, BNTA, IAPN)
11 Adelphi Terrace, London WC2N 6BJ. 09.00–17.00 weekdays.
(email: coins@baldwin.sh) *Coins, tokens, commemorative medals, war medals and decorations, numismatic books.*

## Banking Memorabilia (IBNS)
(016974 76465).
09.00–18.00 (not Sun). *Cheques, banknotes, related ephemera.*

**G. Barrington Smith**
Cross Street, Oadby, Leicestershire LE2 4DD.
(01533 712114). 08.30–17.15 weekdays. *Albums, catalogues and accessories.*

**Bath Stamp and Coin Shop**
Pulteney Bridge, Bath, Avon BA2 4AY.
(01225 463073). Mon–Sat 09.30–17.30. *British.*

**Michael Beaumont**
PO Box 8, Carlton, Notts NG4 4QZ. (0115 9878361). Ⓟ *Gold & Silver English/Foreign Coins.*

**Beaver Coin Room** (BNTA)
57 Philbeach Gardens, London SW5 9ED.
(020 7373 4553). Ⓟ *European coins and medals.*

**R. P. & P. J. Beckett**
Maesyderw, Capel Dewi, Llandyssul, Dyfed
SA44 4PJ. (Fax only 01559 395631, email:
becket@xin.co.uk). Ⓟ *Coin sets and banknotes.*

**Lloyd Bennett** (BNTA)
PO Box 2, Monmouth, Gwent NP5 3YE. (01600
890634). Abergavenny Market (Tue), Monmouth
Market (Fri–Sat) 09.00–16.00. *English hammered, milled and coins of the world.*

**Berkshire Coin Centre**
35 Castle Street, Reading, Berkshire RG1 7SB.
(0118 957 5593). 0630–15.00 W, Th, Fri & Sat.
Sat. *British British and world coins and militaria.*

**Beron Coins**
64 Rosewood Close, Glascote, Tamworth, Staffs
B77 3PD. (01827 54541). Ⓟ Ⓛ *British & world coins.*

**Stephen J. Betts**
4 Victoria Street, Narborough, Leics LE9 5DP.
(0116 2864434). Ⓟ Ⓛ *Medieval and modern coins, counters, jetons and tokens, countermarks and medals.*

**Bigbury Mint**
River Park, Ermington Mill, Ivybridge, Devon
PL21 9NT. (01548 830717. *Specialists in reproduction hammered coins*

**Birchin Lane Gold Coin Company**
6 Castle Court, St Michael's Alley (off Cornhill),
London EC3V 9DS. (020 7621 0370/020 7263 3981).
Mon–Fri 10.00–16.30. *Gold and bullion coins.*

**Barry Boswell and Kate Bouvier**
24 Townsend Lane, Upper Boddington, Daventry,
Northants NN11 6DR. (01327 261877, fax 01327
261391, email: Barry.Boswell@btinternet.com).
Ⓟ Ⓛ *British and world banknotes.*

**James & C. Brett**
17 Dale Road, Lewes, East Sussex BN7 1LH.
Ⓟ Ⓛ *British and world coins.*

**J. Bridgeman Coins**
129a Blackburn Road, Accrington, Lancs
(01254 384757). 09.30–17.00 (closed Wednesday).
*British & World coins.*

**Brighton Coin Company** (ANA, BNTA)
The Hove Coin Shop, Church Road, Hove, (01273
737537) Mon–Fri 9.45–17.30, Sat 9.45–15.30
(closed alternate Wednesdays and Saturdays).
*World coins.*

**Britco**
23 Orkney Close, Stenson Fields, Derby DE24
3LW. (Tel: 01332 760189. http://stores.ebay.
co.uk/britcoins). *18th to 20th Century British coins.*

**BRM Coins**
3 Minshull Street, Knutsford, Cheshire WA16 6HG.
(01565 651480 and 0606 74522). Mon–Fri 11.00–
15.00, Sat 11.00–1.00 or by appt. *British coins.*

**A. F. Brock & Company**
269 London Road, Hazel Grove, Stockport,
Cheshire SK7 4PL. (0161 456 5050/5112, email
info@afbrock.co.uk, www.afbrock.co.uk).
*Auctioneers and valuers.*

**Bucks Coins**
Jordan House, Jordan Lane, Whitwell, Norfolk
NR10 4RQ. (07825 440085). *English milled coins.*

**Iain Burn**
2 Compton Gardens, 53 Park Road, Camberley,
Surrey GU15 2SP. (01276 23304).
*Bank of England & Treasury notes.*

**BBM Coins**
8–9 Lion Street, Kidderminster, Hereford &
Worcester, DY10 1PT. (01562 515007). Wed, Th, Fri.
10.00–14.00 or by appointment.
*World coins.*

**Cambridge Coins**
52 High Street, Biggleswade SG18 0LJ. 01767
6003000/07787 358689. Email: shop@cambridge
coins.co.uk, www.cambridgecoins.co.uk). *Coins, medals, banknotes, bullion and jewellery.*

**Cambridgeshire Coins**
355 Newmarket Road, Cambridge CB5 8JG.
(01223 503073, info@cambridgeshirecoins.com,
www.cambridgeshirecoins.com).
*Coins, banknotes and accessories.*

**Cambridge Stamp Centre Ltd**
9 Sussex Street, Cambridge CB4 4HU.
(01223 63980). Mon–Sat 09.00–17.30.
*British coins.*

**Castle Galleries**
81 Castle Street, Salisbury, Wiltshire SP1 3SP.
(01722 333734). Tue, Thu Fri 09.00–17.00,
Sat 09.30–16.00. *British coins, medals and tokens.*

**Cathedral Coins**
23 Kirkgate, Ripon, North Yorkshire HG4 1PB.
(01765 701400). Mon–Sat 10.00–17.00.

**Cathedral Court Medals**
First Floor Office, 30A Market Place, West Ripon,
North Yorks HG4 1BN. (01765 601400). *Coin and medal sales. Medal mounting and framing.*

**David L. Cavanagh**
49 Cockburn Street, Edinburgh EH1 1BS.
(0131 226 3391). Mon–Sat 11.00–17.00. *British coins.*

**Central Bank of Ireland**
Currency Centre, Sandyford Road, Dublin 16,
Ireland. Issuer of *new coin and banknote issues of Ireland.*

**Certified Coin Investment**
PO Box 83, Longfield DA3 9AX.
(01474 874895). *English milled coins.*

## C. G. S.
4-6 Upper Street South, New Ash Green, Longfield, Kent DA3 8JJ. (01474 874895, email: info@cgs-uk. biz). *Coin grading service.*

## Lance Chaplin
17 Wanstead Lane, Ilford, Essex IG1 3SB. (020 8554 7154. www.shaftesburycoins.com). **P L***Roman, Greek, Celtic, hammered coins and antiquities.*

## Chard (BNTA)
521 Lytham Road, Blackpool, Lancs FY4 1RJ. (01253 343081. www.chards.co.uk). Mon–Sat 09.00–17.00. *British, and world coins.*

## Nigel A. Clark
28 Ulundi Road, Blackheath, London SE3 7UG. (020 8858 4020, email: nigel.a.clark@btinternet.com). **P L** *Tokens (Mainly 17th century) and British Farthings.*

## Classical Numismatic Group (IAPN)
14 Old Bond Street, London W1X 4JL. (020 7495 1888 Fax 020 7499 5916, email cng@cngcoins.com, www.cngcoins.com). **P** *Ancient and world coins. Publishers of the Classical Numismatic Review.*

## Paul Clayton (BNTA)
PO Box 21, Wetherby, West Yorkshire LS22 5JY. (01937 72441). *Modern gold coins.*

## André de Clermont (BNTA)
PO Box 3615, London, SW10 0YD. (020 7351 5727, Fax 020 7352 8127). *World coins, especially Islamic & Oriental coins, Latin America.*

## M. Coeshaw
PO Box 115, Leicester LE3 8JJ. (0116 287 3808). **P** *Coins, banknotes, coin albums and cases.*

## Philip Cohen Numismatics (ANA, BNTA)
20 Cecil Court, Charing Cross Road, London WC2N 4HE. (020 7379 0615). Mon–Sat 11.00–17.30.

## Coin & Collectors Centre
PO Box 22, Pontefract, West Yorkshire WF8 1YT. (01977 704112, email sales@coincentre.co.uk, www.coincentre.co.uk). **P** *British coins.*

## Coinage of England
51 Arnhem Wharf, 2 Arnhem Place, Canary Wharf, London, E1 3RU. (020 7538 5686, www.coinageofengland.co.uk ). *Fine and rare English Coins.*

## Coincraft (ANA, IBNS)
44/45 Great Russell Street, London, WC1B 3JL. (020 7636 1188 and 020 7637 8785 fax 020 7323 2860, email: info@coincraft.com). Mon–Fri 09.30–17.00, Sat 10.00–14.30. **L** *(newspaper format). Coins and banknotes.*

## Coinote Services Ltd
74–74a Elwick Road, Hartlepool TS26 9AP. (01429 890894). **P L** *Coins & banknotes 1615 to date. Accessories, & books. Also at Scorton indoor market, Sundays. Stockton on Tees market, Wednesdays.*

## Coinswap.co.uk
*Swap, sell or trade coins.*

## Coins Historic
PO Box 5043, Lower Quinton, Stratford Upon Avon, Warks CV37 8WH. (01789 721117). *Celtic, Roman, Greek and English hammered coins.*

## Coins of Beeston
PO Box 19, Beeston, Notts BG9 2NE. **P L** *Tokens, medals and paranumismatics.*

## Coins of Canterbury
PO Box 47, Faversham, Kent ME13 7HX. (01795 531980). **P** *English coins.*

## Collectors' World (Mark Ray)
188 Wollaton Road, Wollaton, Nottingham NG8 1HJ. (01159 280347). *Coins, Banknotes, Accessories.*

## Constantia CB
15 Church Road, Northwood, Middlesex HA6 1AR. **P** *Roman and medieval hammered coins.*

## Colin Cooke
P.O. Box 602, Altrincham, WA14 5UN. (0161 927 9524 fax 0161 927 9540, email coins@colin cooke.com, www.colincooke.com). **L** *British coins.*

## Colonial Coins & Medals
218 Adelaide Street, Brisbane, QLD 4001. (Email:coinshop@bigpond.net.au). *Auctions of World coins*

## Corbitts (BNTA)
5 Mosley Street, Newcastle Upon Tyne NE1 1YE. (0191 232 7268 fax: 0191 261 4130). *Dealers and auctioneers of all coins and medals.*

## David Craddock
PO Box 3785, Camp Hill, Birmingham B11 2NF. (0121 733 2259) **L** *Crown to farthings. Copper and bronze specialist. Some foreign.*

## Roy Cudworth
8 Park Avenue, Clayton West, Huddersfield HD8 9PT. *British and world coins.*

## Mark Davidson
PO Box 197, South Croydon, Surrey, CR3 0ZD. (020 8651 3890). *Ancient, hammered coinage.*

## Paul Davis
PO Box 418, Birmingham, B17 0RZ. (0121 427 7179). *British and World Coins.*

## R. Davis
(01332 862755 days/740828 evenings). *Maker of traditional coin cabinets.*

## Paul Davies Ltd (ANA, BNTA, IAPN)
PO Box 17, Ilkley, West Yorkshire LS29 8TZ. (01943 603116 fax 01943 816326). **P** *World coins.*

## Ian Davison
PO Box 256, Durham DH1 2GW (0191 3750808). **L** *English hammered and milled coins 1066–1910.*

## Dei Gratia
PO Box 3568, Buckingham MK18 4ZS (01280 848000). **P L** *Pre–Roman to modern coins, antiquities, banknotes.*

## Den of Antiquity
(01223 863002, www.denof antiquity.co.uk.) *Ancient and medieval coins.*

## Clive Dennett (BNTA)
66 St Benedicts Street, Norwich, Norfolk NR2 4AR. (01603 624315). Mon–Fri 09.00–17.30, Sat 09.00–16.00 (closed 1.00–2.00 & Thu). **L** *Specialising in paper money.*

**C. J. Denton** (ANA, BNTA, FRNS)
PO Box 25, Orpington, Kent BR6 8PU (01689 873690). **P** *Irish coins.*

**Detecnicks**
3 Orchard Crescent, Arundel Road, Fontwell. West Sussex BN18 0SA. (01243 545060 fax 01243 545922) *Retail shop.*
*Wide range of detectors.*

**Michael Dickinson** (ANA, BNTA)
Ramsay House, 825 High Road Finchley, London N12 8UB. (0181 441 7175). **P**
*British and world coins.*

**Dorset Coin Co Ltd** (BNTA)
193 Ashley Road, Parkstone, Poole, Dorset BH14 9DL. (01202 739606, fax 01202 739230. www.dorsetcoincompany.co.uk). **P L**
*Separate coin and banknote lists.*

**Douglassaville.com**
(0118 918 7628). *Out of print, second-hand and rare coin and medal books.*

**Dyas Coins & Medals**
30 Shaftmoor Lane, Acocks Green, Birmingham B27 7RS. (0121 707 2808). Fri 10.30–18.30, Sun 10.30–13.00. *World coins and medals.*

**Eagle Coins**
Winterhaven, Mourneabbey, Mallow, Co. Cork, Ireland. (010 35322 29385). **P L** *Irish coins.*

**Early World Coins**
7–9 Clifford Street, York, YO1 9RA. (08454 900724).

**Eden Coins**
PO Box 77, Brierley Hill, West Midlands DY5 2GS. (01384 834648). **P**
*English coins, tokens and medals.*

**Edinburgh Coin Shop** (ANA)
11 West Crosscauseway, Edinburgh EH8 9JW. (0131 668 2928 fax 0131 668 2926). Mon–Sat 10.00–17.30. **L**
*World coins and medals. Postal auctions.*

**Educational Coin Company**
Box 892, Highland, New York 12528, USA. (+ 845 691 6100.) *World banknotes.*

**Christopher Eimer** (ANA, BNTA, IAPN)
PO Box 352 London NW11 7RF. (020 8458 9933 fax 020 8455 3535, email: art@christophereimer. co.uk). **P** *Commemorative medals.*

**Malcolm Ellis Coins**
Petworth Road, Witley, Surrey, GU8 5LX. (01428 685566, email: malcolm.ellis@wizardvideo.co.uk, www.malcolmelliscoins.co.uk). *Collectors ⌐ ⌐alers of British and foreign coins and*

NR3 1HN. (01603 ⌐⌐es–Wed. 09.00– ⌐⌐ 00. *Mainly*

11 1QL.

⌐h Street, ⌐41631).

**Michael E. Ewins**
Meyrick Heights, 20 Meyrick Park Crescent, Bournemouth, Dorset BH3 7AQ. (01202 290674). **P**
*World coins.*

**I. Fine & Son Ltd**
Victoria House, 93 Manor Farm Road, Wembley, Middlesex HA10 1XB. (020 8997 5055). **P** *British & World coins.*

**Robin Finnegan Stamp Shop**
83 Skinnergate, Darlington, Co Durham DL3 7LX. (01325 489820/357674). Mon–Sat 10.00–17.30 (closed Wed). *World coins.*

**Richard N. Flashman**
54 Ebbsfleet Walk, Gravesend, Kent, DA11 9EW. **L** **P** *British banknotes.*

**David Fletcher (Mint Coins)** (ANA, BNTA)
PO Box 64, Coventry, Warwickshire CV1 5YR. (024 7671 5425, Fax 024 7601 0300). **P**
*World new issues.*

**Format of Birmingham Ltd** (ANA, BNTA, IAPN, IBNS)
2nd Floor, Burlington Court, Lower Temple Street, Birmingham, B2 4JD. (0121 643 2058 fax 0121 643 2210). Mon–Fri 09.30–7.00. **L** *Coins, tokens and medals.*

**B. Frank & Son** (ANA, IBNS)
3 South Avenue, Ryton, Tyne & Wear NE40 3LD. (0191 413 8749. www.b–frank–and–son. co.uk). **P L** *Banknotes and cheques, coins of the world. Organiser of the North of England fair.*

**Galata Coins Ltd** (ANA)
The Old White Lion, Market Street, Llanfylin, Powys SY22 5BX. (01691 648 765). **P** *British and world coins.*

**G. B. Gold Coins**
PO Box 1515, Kingston Upon Thames KT1 9UE. (07917 160308, www.gbgoldcoins.co.uk). *British and World coins specialising in sovereigns and krugerands.*

**G. Gant**
Glazenwood, 37 Augustus Way, Witham, Essex CM8 1HH. **P** *British and Commonwealth coins.*

**A. & S. Gillis**
59 Roykilner Way, Wombwell, Barnsley, South Yorkshire S73 8DY. (01226 750371, email: catalogues@gilliscoins.com. www.gilliscoins. com). **P L** *Ancient coins and antiquities.*

**G. K. Coins**
17 Hanover Square, London W1S 1HU (020 7518 0383, fax: 020 7518 0302, email: george@gkcoins. com, www.gkcoins.com). *Rare and common sovereigns. British and world coins.*

**Richard Gladdle – Northamptonshire**
(01327 858511, email: gladdle@plumpudding.org). *Tokens.* **P L**

**Glance Back Books**
17 Upper Street, Chepstow, Gwent NP6 5EX. (01291 626562). 10.30–17.30. *Coins, banknotes.*

**Glendining's (Bonhams)** (ANA, BNTA)
101 New Bond Street, London W1Y 9LG (020 7493 2445). Mon–Fri 08.30–17.00, Sat 08.30–13.00. *Auctioneers.*

**Glenely Coins**
73 Ladymead, Cricklade, Swindon, Wiltshire SN6 6EP. (01793 750307, email: chris_kellow@hotmail. com). *British coins.*

**GM Coins**
(01242 701144, email: gmcoins@blueyonder.co.uk, www.gmonlinecoins.co.uk/gmcoins). *Hammered and milled coins.*

**Goulborn**
4 Sussex Street, Rhyl LL18 1SG. (Tel: 01745 338112). *Coins and banknotes.*

**Ian Gradon**
PO Box 359, Durham DH7 6WZ. (0191 3719 700, email: igradon960@aol.com, www.worldnotes. co.uk). **L** *World banknotes.*

**Grantham Coins** (BNTA)
PO Box 60, Grantham, Lincs. (01476 870565).**P L** *English coins and banknotes.*

**Eric Green—Agent in UK for Ronald J. Gillio Inc**
1013 State Street, Santa Barbara, California, USA 93101. (020 8907 0015, Mobile 0468 454948). *Gold coins, medals and paper money of the world.*

**Philip Green**
Suite 207, 792 Wilmslow Road, Didsbury, Manchester M20 6UG. (0161 440 0685). *Gold coins.*

**R. I. Groves**
8 Catherine Street, Dumfries DG1 1JA. (01387 266617, email: richard@l-groves.demon.co.uk, www.worldcoins.biz). **P** *British & world coins.*

**Ian Haines**
PO Box 45, Hereford, HR2 7YP. (01432 268178). **P L** *British and foreign coins and banknotes.*

**Anthony Halse**
PO Box 1856, Newport, Gwent NP6 2JN. (01633 413238).**P L** *English and foreign coins and tokens.*

**A. D. Hamilton & Co** (ANA)
7 St Vincent Place, Glasgow G1 5JA. (0141 221 5423, email jeffineman@hotmail.com, www.adhamilton.co.uk). Mon–Sat 10.00–17.00. *British and World coins.*

**Peter Hancock**
40–41 West Street, Chichester, West Sussex PO19 1RP. (01243 786173). Tues–Sat. *World coins, medals and banknotes.*

**Munthandel G. Henzen**
PO Box 42, NL – 3958ZT, Amerogngen, Netherlands. (0031 343 430564 fax 0031 343 430542, email: info@henzen.org, www.henzen.org). **L** *Ancients, Dutch and foreign coins.*

**History In Coins.com**
(01949 836988, www.historyincoins.com). *World coins.*

**Craig Holmes**
6 Marlborough Drive, Bangor, Co Down BT19 1HB. **P L** *Low cost banknotes of the world.*

**R. G. Holmes**
11 Cross Park, Ilfracombe, Devon EX34 8BJ. (01271 864474). **P L**
*Coins, world crowns and banknotes.*

**John L. Homan**
Oxford Grange, Marsh Lane, Barrow Haven, Barrow–on–Humber, South Humberside DN19 7ER. (01469 32109). **P** *Greek, Roman and Byzantine.*

**Homeland Holding Ltd** (IBNS)
Homeland, St John, Jersey, Channel Islands JE3 4AB. (01534 65339). Mon–Fri 09.00–2.00. *World coins.*

**HTSM Coins**
26 Dosk Avenue, Glasgow G13 4LQ.**P L**
*British and foreign coins and banknotes.*

**T. A. Hull**
15 Tangmere Crescent, Hornchurch, Essex RM12 5PL.**P L** *British coins, farthings to crowns, tokens.*

**J. Hume**
107 Halsbury Road East, Northolt, Middlesex UB5 4PY. (020 8864 1731).**P L** *Chinese coins.*

**D. A. Hunter**
(Email: coins@dahunter.co.uk, www.dahunter.co.uk/ coins).**P L**
*UK and World Coins.*

**D. D. & A. Ingle**
380 Carlton Hill, Nottingham. (0115 9873325). Mon–Sat 09.30–17.00. *World coins.*

**R. Ingram Coins**
206 Honeysuckle Road, Bassett, Southampton, Hants SO16 3BU. (023 8032 4258, email: info@ ringramcoins.com, www.ringramcoins.com).**P L**
*Dealers in UK coins.*

**Intercol London** (ANA, IBNS)
43 Templars Cresent, London N3 3QR. (020 8349 2207) **P** *Paper money of the World.*

**Isle of Wight Mint**
PO Box 195, Cowes, Isle of Wight, PO30 9DP. (www.iowmint.org). *Producer of Isle of Wight bullion.*

**J. B. J. Coins**
(www.jbjcoins.dk). *World coins and banknotes.*

**F. J. Jeffery & Son Ltd**
Haines Croft, Corsham Road, Whitley, Melksham, Wilts SN12 8QF. (01225 703143).**P**
*British, Commonwealth and foreign coins.*

**Richard W. Jeffery**
Trebehor, Porthcurno, Penzance, Cornwall TR19 6LS. (01736 871263). **P** *British and world coins. Banknotes.*

**Jersey Coin Co Ltd**
26 Halkett Street, St Helier, Jersey, Channel Islands. (01534 25743). Mon–Sat 09.00–17.00. *World coins.*

**J. G. Coins**
PO Box 206, Southshore, Blackpool FY1 6GZ. (01253 349138).**P L** *British Coins.*

**Jumbo Coins**
22 Woodend Lane, Stalybridge, Cheshire SK (0161 338 5741). Fri–Sat 14.00–19.00. *Wo medals and tokens.*

**Kates Paper Money**
Kate Gibson, PO Box 819, Camberle GU16 6ZU. (01276 64181, www.katespapermoney.co.uk). *Banknotes.*